IF MAHAN
RAN
THE GREAT
PACIFIC
WAR

IF MAHAN RAN THE GREAT PACIFIC WAR

An Analysis of World War II Naval Strategy

John A. Adams

INDIANA UNIVERSITY PRESS
Bloomington · Indianapolis

This book is a publication of

Indiana University Press
601 North Morton Street
Bloomington, IN 47404-3797 USA

http://iupress.indiana.edu

Telephone orders	800-842-6796
Fax orders	812-855-7931
Orders by e-mail	iuporder@indiana.edu

The paper used in this publication meets the minimum requirements
of American National Standard for Information Sciences—Permanence
of Paper for Printed Library Materials, ANSI Z39.48-1984.

Manufactured in the United States of America

Library of Congress Cataloging-in-Publication Data

Adams, John A., date-
  If Mahan ran the Great Pacific War : an analysis of World War II naval strategy /
John A. Adams.
      p. cm.
  Includes bibliographical references and index.
  ISBN 978-0-253-35105-0 (cloth : alk. paper) 1. Naval strategy—Case studies.
2. Mahan, A. T. (Alfred Thayer), 1840–1914—Influence. 3. Naval strategy—
History—20th century. 4. World War, 1939–1945—Naval operations. 5. World
War, 1939–1945—Pacific Ocean. I. Title.
  V163.A43 2008
  940.54'5—dc22
                              2008000604

1 2 3 4 5 13 12 11 10 09 08

CONTENTS

Maps by Bill Nelson

ACKNOWLEDGMENTS

As a graduate student in the early 1970s, I had the privilege of studying economic history under the tutelage of Dr. Stanley Engerman. He taught his students that history should be more than a compilation from the records of an extended "he said, she said." Many historical events occur because more or less rational decision makers attempt to solve very pressing problems by using their experience and what they call common sense to come to a solution. Dr. Engerman taught us to carefully collect data and analyze it within a framework derived from standard economic theory. Using this approach to assess the business viability of the very distasteful practice of slavery, Dr. Engerman produced convincing evidence, which appears in his book *Time on the Cross,* co-written with Robert William Fogel, that slavery was the growth industry in the United States just before the Civil War. Without the war, slavery was likely to continue indefinitely.

Over a long business career, I have called on this approach, collecting data and using economics to reach usable conclusions, to clear the smoke from heated arguments about many specific business problems. Using economics to organize and interpret seemingly contradictory and incomplete information makes sense in business. Similarly, using a framework grounded in military science to sort out hazy and incomplete information about events in military history, instead of relying on the statements from the point of view of the most articulate (or verbose) of the participants, should show similar promise. This notion is the initial motivation for *If Mahan Ran the Great Pacific War*. I am deeply indebted to Dr. Engerman for so firmly planting the seed. I also wish to remember another noted historian, the late Dr. Stephen Ambrose, who admonished his students to remember that history is a story that needs to be told in a manner that invites readers along on the journey.

The history faculty at Virginia Military Institute has been very supportive of my efforts. I wish to thank Dean Casey Brower and Dr. Eric Osborne for their encouragement and helpful comments. I especially wish to thank Dr. Kip Muir, himself a noted naval historian, for his enthusiastic support and the many hours he put in editing and proofreading the words I slapped together to tell this story. I especially appreciated his very tactful approach at improving my efforts to communicate my ideas. I also wish to thank Bob Sloan at Indiana University Press for his patient effort in leading me through the editing process.

I hope my less than perfect effort inspires others to extend this approach as a more objective and fruitful method of dissecting the record of military events to find the lessons it contains. Of course, I claim sole responsibility for any errors that remain in this volume.

John A. Adams
Conifer Mountain, Colorado

**IF MAHAN
RAN
THE GREAT
PACIFIC
WAR**

1

SINK TEN SHIPS
AND WE WIN
THE WAR!

Hindsight is notably cleverer
than foresight.
—*Nimitz*

Who Is This Guy Mahan?

Ironically, Alfred Thayer Mahan was born at West Point in 1840. His father was on the faculty of the United States Military Academy. From an early age, Alfred was exposed to martial thinking, but he eschewed the army for a career at sea. After attending Columbia he received appointment to the U.S. Naval Academy, graduating second in a class of twenty.

His career as a naval line officer drew little attention. While his competence was acknowledged, some said he wasn't the best of ship handlers. However, he believed there was more to being a naval officer than being just a good seaman. Naval officers were first of all warriors concerned with the best way of exercising the power entrusted to them to achieve national objectives. Seas are vast and navies occupy only a minuscule portion of their surface. In Mahan's view, a naval officer had to understand where his ships needed to be and when their presence became decisive in order to win the war.

Mahan lobbied hard for creation of a naval war college, where naval officers could become war leaders as well as sailors. Near the end of a forty-year active career, he accepted a position at the newly formed Naval War College at Newport, Rhode Island. The retired captain lectured on naval history and strategy. Later the retired naval professor was raised to rank of rear admiral. However, his active-duty rank will be used throughout this study.

The nineteenth century witnessed several major revolutions in naval technology. Since the dawn of oceangoing navies, squadrons of sailing ships had gained advantage from their relative position to both the enemy and the prevailing wind at time of battle. For centuries, naval tactics revolved around gaining the "weather gage." The fleet that had the wind in its sails had the speed to literally sail around an opponent that was not in a position to gather the energy of moving wind. Steam power changed all this. Now both fleets had equal maneuvering energy regardless of wind. Soon steam-powered ships gained armor plate: the *Monitor* and the *Merrimac*. These contestants made virtually all the wooden ships of 1862 obsolete. The *Monitor* featured large cannon in a revolving turret instead of a row of smaller weapons fired broadside. These powerful naval rifles in rotating turrets were the only way to counter armor plate. These three technological revolutions—steam power, armor plating, and the mounting of weapons in revolving turrets—combined to almost completely transform naval warfare. By 1890, armored, turreted, steam-powered battleships were just reaching the dawn of their day in the sun. After the turn of the century a fourth innovation, wireless telegraphy, reduced the isolation of captain and admiral alike, radically altering naval command and control.

Mahan and many others recognized that tactics are heavily influenced by the technology of the age. In the realm of strategy, Mahan posited that many principles vary little with technological change. He looked back to the age of sail, to history, in order to answer the questions of where to place his ships and when. His best-known work, *The Influence of Sea Power upon History (1660–1783),* was published in 1890.

World War II was truly global. In that aspect it was not unique. Its antecedent was not just the First World War but the naval war from 1778 to 1782, with England on one side and France and Spain on the other. That conflict involved three major theaters. The most critical lay between the English coast along the Channel and the principal fleet bases of England's opponents: Brest, Cádiz, and Toulon. A misstep here could cause the loss of a decisive fleet engagement, which would place one's homeland in mortal danger. The second theater, the West Indies, contained some of the combatants' most valuable overseas properties, among them the sugar islands and Jamaica. Large fleet actions were fought in the Caribbean and along the North American coastline to secure their possession. The third theater was India. The English and French fleets repeatedly dueled for control of trade with the subcontinent.

In appreciating Mahan's ideas, it is critical to recognize that he applied them to global warfare. Mahan was not simply looking at battles in isolation. That view is properly the realm of tactics. Instead he concentrated on broad factors that would decide the outcome of wars. By analyzing many battles from the age of sail, Mahan distilled his principles of naval strategy. He was a prolific writer. Yet Captain Mahan never laid out a concise list of principles, the way J. F. C. Fuller codified his nine principles of land war. Many of his conclusions are contained in richly detailed critiques of battles in the age of sail. With apology to the rich detail of his observations, several principles may be extracted from that commentary. Two Mahanian grand postulates about sea power and five subordinate propositions about naval strategy summarize his most important conclusions. They form the crux of the remainder of this analysis of the "Great Pacific War."

Postulate A.

No nation can become a great world power without a great navy. Overseas colonies are required to support naval bases on which to project a globe-girdling navy.

This notion captivated naval leaders, heads of state, and political thinkers alike. At the level of national strategy, Mahan extolled the virtues of international trade, a strong navy to retain command of the seas, and overseas or colonial bases to support the fleet. His arguments gave legitimacy to the colonial aspirations that enthralled much of aristocratic Europe. This propelled him to celebrity. "Mahan's classic brew of imperialism and saltwater" intoxicated many a statesman bent on world hegemony.[1] Mahan received much recognition during his later years. Teddy Roosevelt frequently consulted him. The British Admiralty presented him to the queen. Oxford, Cambridge, Harvard, Yale, Columbia, and Dartmouth all conferred honorary degrees. Franklin D. Roosevelt was given a copy of Influence as a teenager and read it avidly. One biographer dubbed FDR "the leading civilian exponent of Mahan's Doctrines."[2]

Postulate B.

Naval warfare is characterized by a rapid stream of events presenting incomplete and conflicting information about the true state of affairs. The sine qua non of the naval officer is to employ his judgment to separate the critical from the peripheral and to make rapid decisions that shape and dominate the action before conditions change yet again.

Arleigh "31-Knot" Burke, an American hero of the Pacific war in World War II who went on to become chief of naval operations (CNO), expressed a closely related notion: "What is the difference between an incompetent naval officer and a great naval officer?—About 10 seconds."[3] The most important asset a navy can have is a roster of officers who can dominate events in this ever-changing rapid-fire environment that is constantly enshrouded in incomplete and contradictory information.

From his extensive study of naval history, Mahan distilled basic propositions about naval strategy that he believed changed little over time or with the advent of technology. These principles rose above technical considerations that governed the tactical execution of strategy. Again, Mahan never wrote a simple concise list. Had he done so, he undoubtedly would have included these points:

1. The objective of your fleet is to destroy the enemy fleet.

The fleet exists to gain command of the sea. If the enemy retains a viable fleet— often referred to as a "fleet in being"—he can maneuver it into some position that will disrupt a segment of your shipping. Therefore the first *and only* priority is to destroy the enemy fleet. If an admiral leaves an enemy a fleet in being, he will have to constantly guard against an enemy challenge to friendly sea control at a time and place not to the admiral's liking.

In his analysis of the period from the Anglo-Dutch wars in the 1660s to the global naval war of 1778–82, Mahan constantly underscores this principle and generally praises English understanding of it. He maintains an uncompromising position in the face of two alternative strategies.

One alternative is the "*guerre de course,*" the war against commercial shipping advocated by the French. Mahan acknowledged that commerce raiding can achieve valuable results. However, only defeat of the enemy's battle fleet is decisive. If the enemy destroys your main battle fleet, your unprotected commerce raiders will soon be run down and driven from the seas. "It is not the taking of individual ships or convoys, be they few or many, that strikes the money power of a nation; it is possession of that overbearing power on the sea which drives the enemy's flag from it."[4]

Another alternative strategy would be to roll up the enemy's bases as opposed to directly challenging the enemy's fleet. After all, men live on land. The ultimate political objectives are likely to be changes in possession of a key point (such as

Gibraltar) or landmass (such as North America). Mahan's rejoinder was simple logic. One could attack the enemy's bases one by one while risking the creation of a decisive fleet transaction by the enemy at the time and place of his choosing. An alternative would be to first defeat the enemy fleet and then pick off unsupported enemy bases at one's leisure. In his observations of the Anglo-French clash in Indian waters, he noted "first, the disabling of the hostile fleet, next, the capture of certain strategic ports."[5]

Notice that one doesn't simply attack the enemy—say, his base structure. One must attack and dominate the enemy's *battle fleet*. This seemingly simple distinction becomes all-important. Winning the decisive naval battle against the enemy's battle line is tantamount to winning the naval war. Closing or capturing some bases but leaving an enemy battle fleet free to roam the seas is not.

With great discomfort, Mahan recognized a corollary. He quoted a recognized authority, the eighteenth-century French admiral Grivel: "If two maritime powers are at strife, the one that has the fewest ships must always avoid doubtful engagements."[6]

This corollary could grate against Mahan's second principle of fleet handling. So Mahan added: ". . . but such a course cannot be consistently followed for years without affecting the spirit and tone of the officers charged with it."[7]

2. Never divide the fleet.

In war many demands will be made for naval protection. Everyone screams for ships to defend his locality against the enemy. Government leaders see competing priorities and objectives everywhere.

Decisive defeat of the enemy's battle fleet requires supreme effort. Each belligerent strains to his utmost to prevail, somewhat like two wrestlers in a clinch for a takedown. An extra few ounces of strength may spell the difference between catastrophic loss and total victory. Nothing, *absolutely nothing*, should distract from this supreme effort. After destroying the enemy battle fleet, the victor can attend to secondary considerations, or the ultimate political goals of the war, without being molested. Mahan underscores this point in war after war: "The lesson is the same in all ages."[8]

The lesson, however, does not come easily to most civilian leaders. Politics is the art of compromise. But compromise is the bane of strategy. Strategic thinking must pare a problem down to its most critical facet, and then make a hard, uncompromising choice to concentrate all to win at that facet. To hedge one's bet is to risk not being strong enough at the decisive point. That is not very *politique*.

Never, NEVER divide the fleet.

Napoleon understood a parallel principle in land warfare. Mahan's principle takes concentration to its final degree. The emperor was the master at bringing independently marching army corps together, *at concentrating them,* at the right time and place to decisively defeat an enemy army in the field. He attempted to replicate this principle at sea. Napoleon's strategic maneuvers at sea in 1805 attempted to amalgamate the French fleets from the West Indies, Rochefort, and Toulon with the Spanish fleet. He anticipated meeting in the Channel an English fleet that had been reduced by its many diversions to interests around the globe, and crushing it. Then the Grand Armée, debarking from transports, would march on London. What the emperor did not count on was an admiral by the name of Nelson intercepting the French and Spanish squadron near the Cape of Trafalgar.

3. "The nation that would rule the sea must always attack."
—Admiral George Monck

Mahan quotes this famous seventeenth-century English general and admiral, who became the first Duke of Albemarle, to underscore his third central principle.[9] The sea is vast and even the largest fleet is small by comparison. If the initiative is ceded to the enemy, eventually his squadrons will appear where they will do you the most damage. You must attack him. Force him to fear your thrust rather than allow him to create a thrust of his own. Furthermore, sailors left too long without action lose their edge.

A corollary to the primary point: "An enemy beaten and in flight should be pursued with ardor."[10] Once you have him at a disadvantage, finish him. Don't let him recoup his strength and create another opportunity for you to lose.

The cumulative effect of sea power on distant battlefields can be decisive even when the ships themselves don't engage in combat. "The noiseless, steady, exhausting pressure with which sea power acts, cutting off the resources of the enemy while maintaining its own, supporting the war in scenes where it does not appear itself. . . . the overwhelming sea power of England was the determining factor [in a century and a half] of European history."[11] This benefit inures to the power that attains naval superiority and retains the initiative.

4. Well-trained crews and officers who understand war are decisive fleet attributes. Over time, the better leadership will prevail.[12]

Mahan did not equivocate: "Quantity will disappear before quality."[13] The protagonist who invests in well-trained seamen will do far better than the one who acquires good ships but pays scant attention to the quality of their crew. Officers have to know about war as well as the sea. "The military men [are] superior to the mere seamen."[14]

5. "To interfere thus with the commander in the field . . . is generally disaster."[15]

Acquire and educate first-rate naval officers. Critical to their performance is almost split-second judgment of what to do in the face of the enemy. Command from seniors by remote control negates the reason for having such officers in the first place and leaves one vulnerable to an opponent who refrains from this temptation. Choose and train well, then have faith in what you have created.

In addition to these bedrock principles, Captain Mahan made some very acute observations about future developments in naval warfare:

- "The torpedo cruiser, pure and simple, is a type of weapon destined to survive in fleets."[16] It is likely to evolve into a class of larger ships with better sea-keeping qualities. One could not have better described Japanese cruisers armed with "long lance" torpedoes.

- The navy needs refueling and repair bases but not too many.[17] Many bases create a chain of targets the enemy can exploit. Admirals will have the tendency to divide the fleet to defend them. One or two well-defended bases are superior to a string of vulnerable ones. The Japanese would learn about this problem firsthand. Americans would be a little slow to pick up on this vulnerability. When they did, they thought they had invented "island hopping."

- "extreme rapidity of encounters."[18] Almost a hundred years before "information warfare" came into vogue, real-time information and the ability of empowered commanders on the scene to instantly process it and adjust to the new situation was key to success. Mahan cited the tremendous edge information gave a combatant. This was especially true about intelligence of the enemy.[19]

- Avoid melee battles where ships of both sides intermix while they pound away at friend as well as foe.[20] Since the beginning of armed human combat, warriors have desired weapons with the reach to hit the enemy from a place that the enemy can't hit back. A man with a spear has an advantage over an opponent with a short sword until the swordsman gets in close in a melee. In 1942, the airplane's range was ten times that of 16-inch naval guns. If you have the advantage in the air, there is no reason to close to "melee" gunnery range—despite the romantic notions of your naval officers.

- "Popular governments are not generally favorable to military expenditures."[21] This notion must be modified to exclude times of clear, nation-threatening danger. In a period of an ethereal, evolving threat like Japan in the 1930s, the imperial dictatorship did have an advantage over a potentially stronger America. The relative change of the ratio of forces over time as the threat became more perceptible became a prime driver of Japanese strategy.

On the eve of World War II, Mahan was required reading at naval war colleges in Japan and Great Britain as well as in the United States. Rear Admiral Shinshi Akiyama, a longtime professor at the Japanese Naval War College as well as an experienced seaman, wrote *Essential Instructions on Naval Battles,* which became something of a bible for Japanese line officers.[22] Mahan's influence in the work is unmistakable. Akiyama spent 1897–1900 in the United States studying naval matters, and for a time received private tutoring from Captain Mahan himself.

Rank-and-file naval officers carefully studied Mahan's writings. While still an ensign, Richmond Kelly "Terrible" Turner, who first served as operations officer to Admiral Ernest King, the chief of naval operations, and then commanded amphibious landings from Guadalcanal to Okinawa, recorded in his fitness reports that he had read all of Mahan's main works.[23] In 1937, then commander Turner delivered an address at the Naval War College in which he said, "The chief strategic function of the fleet is the creation of situations that will bring about decisive battle."[24] Pure Mahan.

Mahanian thought permeated the U.S. Navy. Secretary of War Henry Stimson once caustically remarked that the navy "frequently seemed to retire from the realm of logic into a dim religious world in which Neptune was God, Mahan his prophet and The United States Navy the only true Church."[25]

Unlike Churchill, President Roosevelt was keen to stick to the essential strategic matter at hand and not be diverted by side issues. In a memorandum for the president dated March 5, 1942, Admiral King wrote: "2. You have expressed the view—concurred in by all of your chief military advisors—that we should determine on a *very few* lines of military and concentrate our efforts on these lines."[26] Perhaps reading Mahan had left an impression on the commander in chief besides "navies are great."

More of Mahan's works were translated into Japanese than any other language. Japanese naval officers of 1941 were very familiar with his works and embraced his central idea. Samuel Eliot Morison, the semi-official Navy historian, admiral, and Harvard professor, observed that senior Japanese naval officers were "oriental disciples of Mahan."[27] As we examine the basic strategic questions of the great naval war in the Pacific, we will allow Captain Mahan, whose theories had been embraced by both antagonists, to jump back and forth between the sides.

One can hear Mahan's echo in the Imperial Japanese Navy's operation manual. "Battle is the sole means of victory. So everything should satisfy what the battle demands."[28] Akiyama Sato Tetsutaro, a leading naval strategist at the beginning of the twentieth century, became known as "the Japanese Mahan."

After the war Commander Masataka Chihaya, Japanese Naval College Class of 1944, stated that the idea of "decisive battle" had dominated Japanese war planning and strategic thinking.[29] This is classic Mahan.

Admirals often opine that generals know next to nothing about the deployment of fleets. Of course the "green suiters" reciprocate by questioning the admirals' acumen regarding land campaigns. Carl von Clausewitz was one of the greatest military theoreticians. Along with several other military authors, notably Baron Antoine-Henri de Jomini, he attempted to extract from the campaigns of Napoleon the most essential truths about the strategy of land warfare.

In the main body of their writings, the musings of Mahan and Clausewitz read quite differently. But Clausewitz also had an overriding directive on how to select an objective: Study your enemy. Select that one element or aspect of the enemy that is essential for him to prosecute the war. Clausewitz called this the enemy's "center of gravity." Concentrate all of your efforts on dislocating or destroying the center of gravity and you win the war. As this will require an enormous effort, you cannot expend any energy on anything else. Choose your objective carefully. Choose one that is of decisive importance, and focus all of your effort on attaining it.

"Center of gravity" was an unfortunate choice of phrase by Clausewitz to communicate his most essential idea. It can easily be confused with "center of mass" or interpreted to mean going after the enemy's strongest military units. The strongest units *might* be the right center of gravity. It might be something else entirely. In 1812, the Russians correctly concluded that Napoleon's "center of gravity" was stamina. How long could he hold out in a scorched Moscow in the middle of winter? History's judgment of Russian strategy in this case was absolute even though Napoleon's Old Guard was never defeated.

The essential element of Mahan's thesis is a subset of Clausewitz's center of gravity. Both strategists advise concentrating everything on the single most important objective. Only Mahan specifies that in naval warfare, the enemy's fleet in being is *the* center of gravity. This would not have bothered Clausewitz in the least. In most cases, the Prussian general believed the center of gravity would be the enemy's armed forces.[30]* Given this similarity, one might expect great similarity between the American army's and the navy's approach to Pacific strategy in World War II. However, that expectation will not be realized—far from it.

Purpose of This Study

The codification of Mahan's principal concepts above provides a calculus of naval strategy. In Mahan's name, we will use that calculus to evaluate the major strategic and operational decisions made by both sides in the Pacific theater of 1941–45. Prior to World War II, the precepts of Captain Mahan were well studied by naval officers and diplomats, Japanese and American. In many instances, we will observe planners and decision makers drawing on these concepts. Occasionally, they will even invoke Mahan's name. Where Mahanian calculus points to a clear alternative among the options, we will explore that alternative, restricting ourselves to the resources and information in hand at the time the decision was made.

At first reading, Mahan's concepts are not difficult to grasp. Some readers might find them somewhat simplistic. But Mahan demands some very painful behavior of the decision maker. Correct strategy against a peer opponent inevitably forces severe choices that exclude allocating resources to legitimate alternative and secondary requirements. If an admiral is to have overwhelming strength at the critical point, he must accept vulnerability at other less critical but still important locations. This can be risky and is not for the faint of heart. The decision maker often must deny many legitimate requests for resources from some very good people in order to achieve the required concentration. Mahan's approach requires iron discipline. It is not easy.

Very powerful forces constantly act to pull decision makers away from an otherwise strategically correct course of action. The first group leads in the direction of "suboptimization." Suboptimization occurs when a subordinate leader, individual or, most frequently, subunit of the larger whole follows a course of action that maximizes the subunit's goal or perceived goal for the whole in a manner that causes effort and energy to be diverted from the overall strategic effort.

---

*In fact, Mahan does not appear to have been very familiar with Clausewitz's writings. However, Jomini makes a very similar point: "to throw by strategic movements the mass of an army, successively, upon the decisive points of a theater of war."[31]

If the front line of a football team decides the team needs to pass and executes its blocking assignments, the backfield, attempting to execute the running play the quarterback called for, is not likely to gain much yardage. A single basketball player trying to maximize the number of hoops he makes isn't likely to set up shots to be made by other players even if that would give the team its best score. Imagine the problem of the admiral who is attempting to concentrate his fleet Mahanian style when his superiors demand he detach ships to protect Port A and Port B, whose citizens are screaming for attention.

Suboptimization is a leech that burrows into virtually all large organizations. The more clear the overall objective and the methods of obtaining it are, the less suboptimization there is likely to be. That is why consensus in organizations is important. The greater the discipline, the greater the control top leaders have of their subordinates, the less independent the identity of a subunit is from the whole, the less suboptimization hamstrings correct execution of strategy. Our analysis will reveal enormous cases of suboptimization. During the Pacific war of 1941–45, suboptimization by both the Japanese and the Americans repeatedly blocked the path toward adopting a correct strategy. Suboptimization repeatedly changed the course of the war.

One American navy official remarked about a specific decision: "It was good for the Nation but it wasn't good for the Navy." Such notions, though often re-peated, have no legitimacy. Independent of the nation, the navy has no intrinsic value. When many subordinate decision makers begin doing what is best for the army or this theater of war or some other unit, they generate huge problems for the strategist. It's even worse when these notions gain voice in the room where strategy is being drafted.

A second source of problems emanates from a very valuable analytical tool. Economists teach managers the concept of incremental analysis. Consider the case where a manufacturing plant's overall production is a function of the amount of labor, the amount of machinery, and the available floor space. Rather than use all available funds to expand one of the three inputs, economics teaches managers to find the increase in a dollar's worth of spending on each of the three inputs. Carefully measure each change and continue to reallocate production dollars until the combination is reached that maximizes total production.

Incremental analysis is a proper and extremely powerful tool. The vast major-ity of problems in managing business and government are correctly solved using incremental analysis. But the strategist is not attempting to move an opposing force a small amount. He is seeking catastrophic change: to *dislocate* or *destroy* the opponent. If he misses by a little, he may fail totally. He is not in an arena where incremental changes can win. He needs *overwhelming* force. He wants to completely overmatch his opponent and cause him to collapse or run away. There is a business analogy for those so disposed. When introducing a new product to the market, one doesn't shortchange the marketing effort. Instead the largest effort possible that makes the biggest splash possible is preferred. Either the new product cuts through the competing clutter or it fails. Instead of the nice smooth differentiable (in terms of calculus) curve on which marginal analysis is based, one is faced with two stark outcomes: success or failure. No sensible manager withholds a little effort when that little bit might make all the difference. But some very smart managers-turned-strategists have come up with the horrible notion of graduated escalation. Mahanian concentration is its antithesis.

If leadership is accustomed to incremental analysis and—as is always the case—the path forward is shrouded and fraught with uncertainty, that leadership may fall back on incrementalism and come up with notions like graduated response. Splitting the fleet into penny packets and using just enough to get the job done feels like a familiar response. Besides, it leaves more packets to meet the many competing needs. Like suboptimization, incrementalism can become another impediment to the execution of strategy.

Three other definitions will sharpen the analysis.

"Tactics" is the employment of military units in contact with the enemy. In naval warfare, it is the ship-to-ship fighting and the movement of ships in the presence of the enemy in order to gain battle advantage. Almost everything that occurs within a naval battle is tactical. "Crossing the T" and "hammer and anvil" torpedo plane attacks are tactical.

"Strategy" is the designation of the ultimate objective, the military end state, that friendly armed forces will strive to achieve in order to win the war and the general approach used to achieve that objective. In order to reach that final end state, a strategy often identifies critical intermediate objectives that must be achieved and sometimes the directions of approach to those objectives. War Plan Orange, described below, is a strategic plan.

Since the time of Napoleon, a single land battle by itself seldom determines the outcome of a war. To achieve one of the intermediate strategic objectives, battles have to be stitched together into a campaign. Generals have to think of the end state required at the conclusion of one battle in order to set up favorable conditions for the next one. Mahan writes of *the* decisive battle. By the time of World War II, admirals had to combine several subsidiary operations to create either one or several battles that would determine which fleet would prevail.

At the "operational level of war," military officers stitch together a series of battles or large-scale movements to achieve either an intermediate or the final

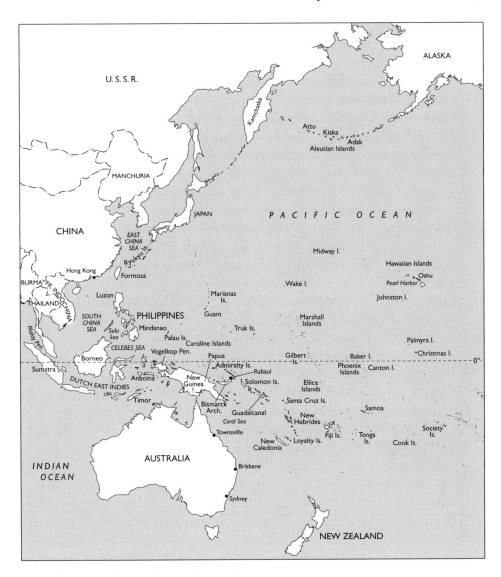

Map 1a. Pacific Ocean. Map by Bill Nelson.

strategic objective. Think of this as campaign planning. Armies and fleets shouldn't just blunder into each other and fight. The operational art determines when, where, and for what reason forces should seek battle. A skilled practitioner of the operational art seeks battle only to advance progress toward the motivating strategic objective.

For example, in early 1942 many senior American officers believed capture of the Japanese base at Rabaul to be a critical intermediate strategic objective. The Allies couldn't take it in a single battle. Instead a series of battles around Guadalcanal and then an approach via intermediate landings in the Solomons and New Guinea would be required. Assembling all of these moves to achieve victory at Rabaul involved the operational level of war. Tasks One, Two, and Three of General George C. Marshall's "Proposed Joint Directive for Offensive Operations in the Southwest Pacific Area" (see chapter 5) are components of an operational plan. Often senior commanders in a theater spend most of their time creating operational-level plans to plot a series of battles that achieve the objectives identified by the strategy that came from the joint or combined chiefs. Each battle or move is aimed at achieving an end state that allows a subsequent battle or move toward achieving the objective. Recognizing the desired end state changes the focus of the battle. The "winner" at Coral Sea wasn't the fleet that sank the greatest tonnage. From an operational perspective, the winner was the Allied side because it prevented the Japanese from achieving their objective: an air base at Port Moresby that would threaten the sea lanes to Australia.

Most of Mahan's writings involve naval strategy. However, a strategy that cannot be successfully executed at the tactical level by the forces available is doomed to failure. On the other hand, the strategist who underestimates the tactical capability he commands often selects an underperforming strategy. The Pacific theaters of World War II provide several examples of both. In order to evaluate the strategic decisions that were made, the tactical record, "the facts," for many critical battles are summarized and used to examine the strategic analysis that was performed.

The relative combat power or capability, often referred to as the "correlation of forces," is critical to understanding both strategic and tactical decision making. We will look at that data. Strategy involves moving forces through time and space to create advantage and achieve objectives. "Combat power" is more than a simple bean count of opposing weapons and their capability. It is better thought of as bean count of weapons x troop/sailor training to use them x officers' ability to employ both of the preceding x the ability to supply, move, and communicate with the entire mass. Notice that the relationship is multiplicative. A zero in any one of the variables sets the entire equation to zero.

While our focus is on the strategic and operational levels, occasionally we will need to move down to the tactical level to establish specific facts and conditions or to gain tactical information critical to strategic or operational calculations. Because the six carrier versus carrier fights of the war were so critical, they will be followed in some detail. This analysis of World War II in the Pacific will be carried out according to Mahan, or at least according to the principles gleaned from his writings.

Sink Ten Ships and Win the Naval War

Mahan's overarching strategic advice: Don't try to defend far-flung ports and installations. Don't "penny packet" the fleet by sending squadrons against many seemingly vulnerable enemy targets. Instead, concentrate everything you have on devastating the enemy's main battle fleet. Accomplish this and you will be able to sail where you please while your enemy lacks all ability to move naval squadrons of significant size.

This is the most critical lesson from Mahan. In 1941, each side possessed, at most, ten capital ships of the line in the Pacific. Destroy them and the back of the enemy's fleet would be broken. Your battle fleet could then annihilate anything the enemy set afloat to oppose you. Without a battle fleet to constrain the movement of yours, the enemy is helpless to prevent your fleet from doing as it pleases in the ocean. Your fleet can drive enemy merchantmen from the sea while ensuring the safety of friendly ones. It can isolate and take any intermediate bases. It can convoy an invasion force to any land objective the army is capable of taking. And it can destroy any invasion convoy the enemy is stupid enough to set in motion.

But which ten ships were the critical ones?

If America's principal Pacific base had been attacked on December 7, 1931, the proper target would have been battleships and their support facilities, not carriers. At that time, battleships alone were the final arbitrators of naval power. To demonstrate the growing influence of airpower, General Billy Mitchell sank a non-maneuvering, undefended, obsolete target battleship with huge bombs delivered via biplane. Mitchell's demonstration involved a stationary battleship; aircraft of that time did not have the carrying power, performance, or endurance to prosecute effective attacks on heavily armored, maneuvering targets that shot back. Despite their potential, carrier-based aircraft had not sufficiently developed the lifting power to strike decisively. Carriers of 1931 launched valuable aerial scouts. But they were not anti-battleship weapons.

Most naval analysts recognized the vulnerability of carrier decks to damage. Carriers resembled seagoing eggshells carrying hammers. Their strike aircraft could dish out a lot of punishment, but carrier landing decks and hangar spaces were large, flat, and vulnerable. Prewar experiments both on land and at sea identified the difficulty of intercepting inbound air strikes. Analysts thought each fleet's carriers might succumb early in a fleet engagement to enemy strike aircraft, leaving the decision to a battle of the dreadnoughts. Maybe the gun club proponents weren't so wrong after all. In a world without radar, many of their prognostications would have been much closer to the mark.

In 1939, few people in the world had any idea how directed radio waves were going to shift the balance of air power decidedly toward the defenders. Radar solved the problem of identifying incoming strikes in time to launch interceptors. By allowing effective active defense by carrier fighters before the strikers came within bomb range, radar substantially improved carrier survivability. Soon carrier commanders clamored for larger onboard fighter complements. British carriers sacrificed larger plane complements—i.e., more fighters—for the added weight of armored decks, a questionable tradeoff once radar was factored in. Admiral Yamamoto had no inkling of radar.

In a 1934 presentation at the Naval War College, the only rated aviator on the faculty lectured that aircraft alone could not win the naval battle.[32] They simply did not have sufficient payload and performance to deliver the knockout blow. However, airpower must first concentrate on knocking out the enemy fleet before attacking shore installations.[33]

The 1930s were a period of rapid aircraft development. For example, in 1937, a young Mitsubishi engineer, Jiro Horikoshii, designed the A6M "Zero." He innovated with long ailerons (which permitted a great roll rate) combined with low wing loading (enabling a tight turn) which made the design remarkably maneuverable, especially when compared with the heavier (but sturdier) machines emerging from the Grumman "ironworks." Although outclassed by 1943, at the time of Pearl Harbor it terrorized American aircraft. The Zero had its faults. With a power plant rated at 1130 hp, the Zero couldn't match the 2000 hp engines installed in American fighters from 1943 onward. The Zero had neither pilot protective armor nor self-sealing gas tanks. It came apart quickly when hit with hot American metal.

Similarly, naval attack aircraft development leaped ahead. Underpowered biplanes gave way to sleek all metal monoplanes powered by 1000 hp engines and capable of carrying 1000 lb torpedoes or armor piercing bombs. Initially, airstrike tacticians focused on delivering torpedoes by air. All naval authorities recognized their ship-killing capability. But torpedo bombers needed to approach their quarry low and slow, making them easy targets and giving ships time to maneuver evasively. Dive-bombers capable of *accurately* delivering heavy armor piercing bombs onto a maneuvering warship became the real ship-killer. The initial Japanese Vals and American Devastators performed the task but weren't ideal. By 1942, the Douglas Dauntless and Aichi Judy admirably fit the bill.

Naval aircraft capable of delivering battleship killing weapons, augmented by improved carrier defensive measures, crowned the fleet carrier as the new capital ship. The transition from a battleship battle line to the carrier task group as the principal naval arbitrator changed much at the tactical and operational levels. Battles would be fought from far over the horizon instead of between lines of big gunships at 20,000 yards. Campaign planners had to take into account the effective aircraft range from various fleet and base locations.

More importantly, whether naval tactics were dominated by battleships or by carriers, Mahan's observations on strategy remained relevant. Both the naval flight officers, and the gunnery experts agreed: destroy the striking power of the enemy battle fleet, and you win the naval war.

To a sailor, there is something romantic about the majestic big ships and their enormous artillery. Naval officers tend to be traditionalists, slow to accept innovation that has yet to prove itself operationally. Even today many naval enthusiasts are diehard members of the "Weren't battleships great!" club. Imagine the pull of these majestic behemoths on men who had dedicated their lives to them. The "big gun club" in both the Japanese and the American navies fought vigorously to maintain dominance. One Japanese air officer remarked that when he advocated attack by air strikes only, "not only was my idea attacked, but even my mental soundness was doubted!"[34] Battleship tonnage dominated prewar building plans. The gun club had many powerful members in the navy of each antagonist. Minoru Genda, the Japanese aviation expert and architect of the Pearl Harbor air strike, is very clear on this point: "Only because of a strong, unyielding demand by Admiral Isoroku Yamamoto . . . was the idea [for an air strike on Pearl Harbor] finally materialized."[35]

The gun club valued carrier-based aviation for its scouting capability. Oceans are big places. The enemy fleet might slip away from a decisive engagement if not properly spotted and tracked. Airplanes put eyes on the enemy far more quickly than any cruiser.

Surprisingly, both the American and the Japanese navies gave strong support to the potential combat power of the carriers. The British navy did not.[36]

During the twenties, American Naval War College studies determined the effectiveness of massive first strikes by carrier-based aircraft. The number of aircraft in the air was critical.[37] How many attackers can you get off and how many defenders can you support simultaneously? This relationship would come to dominate naval warfare in the Pacific. Mahan would have readily recognized this as an extension of the measurement of a battle line's broadside throw weight in the days of the gun-armed ship. Admirals are often accused of readying to fight the last war. Supposedly only a catastrophic defeat brings to bear enough pressure to overcome the inertia of tradition in a conservative organization. The Naval War College air studies stand out as a shining counterexample. Had the American navy remained battleship-bound in the 1930s, it wouldn't have had the initial carriers that blunted the Japanese offensive. There wouldn't have been enough experience to create the second group of carriers, the Essex class (and the aircraft designs that armed them), which were critical in the American advance across the Pacific.

From the beginning of naval airpower, Japan had been in the forefront. Throughout the twenties, advisers from Britain's Royal Navy regularly visited Japan, cross-fertilizing new ideas between the two naval powers.

The official doctrine of the U.S. Navy in the late thirties was the "balanced fleet."[38] It did not sanction the independent aircraft carrier task forces that some air-minded officers preached. But it said that the aircraft carrier, the battleship, and the cruiser or destroyer each had a critical role to play. As late as 1939 the Naval War College taught that naval aviation, while a useful recon adjunct, could not bring about a decision between battle fleets.[39]

Even around 1940 most naval airpower enthusiasts viewed carriers as only the opening salvo against battleships. Air strikes would slow up the enemy's capital ships and degrade their firepower especially by disabling sensitive fire control equipment. Undamaged friendly battleships would then catch up to the crippled enemy ships and use their heavy broadsides to send them beneath the waves. Early naval fights in World War II, the British against the *Bismarck* in the North Atlantic and the gun battles between the British and Italian fleets in the Mediterranean, reinforced this view.

Beginning in 1938 Japanese naval doctrine denoted the aircraft carrier as the new "ship of the line" with the responsibility of making long-range crippling strikes against the enemy's fleet.[40] This was the same year that Admiral King had "attacked" Pearl Harbor from the north. During fleet exercises, he finagled to get the very latest fighters on board the Saratoga for the strike: a squadron of Marine *biplanes*. Even before the technologies matured, future U.S. naval leaders recognized that flight decks, not large ordnance, would become the fleet's primary weapon. Yamamoto heeded Mahan's admonition to concentrate. Under his direction, First Air Fleet, containing six big carriers and no battleships, formed in 1941. It was the first of its kind in the world. First Air Fleet would carry out the Pearl Harbor raid.

By December 7, thinking officers on both sides of the Pacific knew another revolution in naval warfare had become reality. Rear Admiral John H. Towers, chief of aeronautics, declared, "It's the aircraft carrier that will spearhead the next war." His prognostication put Towers on the cover of *Time* in June 1941. By that date, the fleet carrier was *the* ship to kill.

Why pursue and destroy the carriers to the exclusion of all else?

By 1941, perceptive admirals like Yamamoto, King, and Chester A. Nimitz, the admiral who would command the U.S. Pacific Fleet in World War II, knew surface fleets could not operate against an enemy carrier fleet in the open ocean without air cover of their own. Eliminate Japan's carrier aviation and there was nothing the Imperial Japanese Navy could do to prevent U.S. naval air from driving Japanese battleships from the seas and transiting the Pacific Ocean at will. What could naval artillery with a 20-mile range do against carriers whose ship-killing aircraft could easily outrange them by a hundred miles?

The Pacific covers a third of the globe. Most of it is a great empty. Within an open rectangle bounded by the Aleutians, the Philippines, Indonesia (which in 1941 was the Dutch East Indies), and North America there are no world-class resources, no great industrial plants, no prize worthy of a world war. Unlike Europe, the Pacific offers no expanses that are war objectives because of their intrinsic value.

The military and economic value of the Pacific lies in the ability of one nation to transit it at will while denying similar access to the enemy. Thus, the strategic naval objective of the Pacific war was control of transit over the ocean.

Oceans are controlled by fleets of ships and aircraft. Fleets are far smaller in relation to oceans than mass armies are to continents. As World War I demonstrated, it is possible to dig a trench from one side of a continent to the other and fill it with enough soldiers to contain one's enemy. Even if enough ships were gathered to form an ocean-spanning picket line, they would do little except provide easy targets for a concentrated enemy fleet. There is no nautical equivalent of trench works. Fleets don't occupy oceans the way armies occupy countries. Fleets dominate oceans through their ability to move at will to destroy anything they choose.

If an enemy has an effective fleet in being that can sail on the open ocean, then you will have great difficulty preventing him from interdicting the transit of your ocean-borne commerce. An ocean is too big for any fleet to police or defend. The better your intelligence, the more successful you can be. However, at some point the enemy will appear and cause damage before you can move to prevent the attack. Mahan understood this critical truth about naval warfare. The only way to control the sea is to destroy the enemy fleet itself. Destroy his fleet and your enemy loses his ability to interfere with your oceanic movement and to sail the trade routes for his own benefit.

For at least three hundred years prior to 1941, the decisive force in naval warfare was a line of heavy gunships that could crush the enemy fleet. Now the aircraft carrier and her main battery, her air wing, assumed the mantle of arbiter of
the sea. In the early forties, planes outranged battleship guns by a factor of ten.
In the open ocean, a battleship squadron would succumb to a repeated hail of
aerial bombs and torpedoes without ever coming within gunnery range of an
enemy carrier battle group.

Table 1.1 on p. 21 details Japan's carrier roster. It is much shorter than most
interested students of naval history realize.

This was Japan's entire carrier strength on December 7, 1941. Ten ships. A
more precise cut might have included only the first six on the list. They were
Japan's first-line fleet carriers, the ones that made up First Air Fleet as it weighed
anchor for Pearl Harbor. Of the others, *Ryujo* was tonnage limited and, like
America's *Ranger,* too small to be a first-line carrier for Pacific operation. *Hosho*
was the first purpose-built carrier. Surprisingly it survived the war and was not
scrapped until 1947. *Zuiho* and *Shoho* were light carriers better suited to provide
scouts in support of battleship squadrons.

At first glance, the Imperial Japanese Navy's reciprocal objective appeared
even easier. The American carrier fleet as of December 7, 1941, is shown in Table
1.2 on p. 21.

Ranger could make only 27 knots compared to 30+ for the others. It carried
only 3,675 tons of oil; the others carried 6,000–9,000 tons or more. Therefore
she was ill suited for the Pacific. She remained in the Atlantic so we will exclude
it from our count. *Ranger's* design limitations derived from prewar Naval Limitation Treaty restrictions on cumulative tonnage for all aircraft carriers, to "pay
for" the large size of *Saratoga* and *Lexington.* Similarly *Wasp's* limited tonnage
offset *Enterprise* and *Yorktown. Wasp* was truly a light carrier (CVL), like the last
four on the Japanese list. America's first experimental aircraft-carrying ship,
Langley, had become an aircraft ferry. She was sunk off Java in early 1942.

Saratoga and *Lexington* started their lives as battle cruisers. They were re-
designed as carriers because the U.S. had reached its treaty-limited big gunship
allocation and also because forward-looking naval officers had come to realize
the importance of carriers. *Yorktown* and *Enterprise* performed yeoman duties.
In December 1941, *Wasp* and *Hornet* were also in the Atlantic.

Perhaps the war could be won by sinking fewer than ten ships. Early in the
war each side had only six truly Pacific-capable fleet carriers. Without them, neither navy would have been capable of any appreciable offensive action when
faced by the carriers of its opponent. Quite a short target list indeed. Perhaps this
section should have been titled "Sink Six Ships . . ."?

Table 1.1: Japanese Carriers as of December 7, 1941
(compiled from Jentschura et al.)

SHIP	COMPLETED	TONNAGE	SPEED	AIRCRAFT
*Kaga**	1928	38,200	28	90
*Akagi**	1927	36,500	31	91
Soryu	1937	15,900	34	64
Hiryu	1939	17,300	34	64
Shokaku	1941	25,675	34	72
Zuikaku	1941	25,675	34	72
Hosho	1922	7,470	25	26
*Ryujo**	1933	10,600	29	48
Zuiho	1940	11,262	28	30
Shoho	1942	11,262	28	30

* Data after modernization in 1930s.

Table 1.2: U.S. Carriers as of December 7, 1941

SHIP	COMPLETED	STANDARD TONNAGE	AIRCRAFT
Saratoga	1928	33,000	80
Lexington	1927	33,000	80
Ranger	1934	14,500	60
Yorktown	1937	19,800	78
Enterprise	1938	19,800	80
Wasp	1940	14,500	70
Hornet	1941	20,000	80

Japanese planes were superior to their American counterparts on carrier decks. With many more cockpit hours and combat in China under their belts, Japanese pilots were the clear superiors. The American navy of 1941 was undergoing expansion; it was full of recruits and young officers new to their jobs. At the outset, Japan had both the sharper blades and the better trained swordsmen.

Battle squadron speed still mattered a great deal. Air strikes had a range of 150–250 miles. The acme of good carrier admiralship was to dart just within range of the enemy fleet, launch, and then dart just outside of the range of the enemy's counterstrike. The fleet with longer-range aircraft had a built-in advantage in this endeavor. Japanese retained an aircraft range advantage throughout the war. However, they paid for this with less survivable aircraft that carried smaller weapon loads.

Throughout our analysis, we will continue to calculate the two navies' relative advantage in aircraft and fleet carriers. During the war, many escort (CVE) or "jeep" carriers joined both navies. However, they could only make 18 knots compared to the 30 or more knots of the "fast carriers" (CVs and CVLs). Therefore, they were not suitable for battle-fleet duty. Instead they served as convoy exports, as support ships for amphibious invasions, and as aircraft ferries. While they performed admirably as anti-submarine warfare (ASW) ships, convoy escorts, and providers of close air support for slow invasion fleets of 14-knot transports, CVEs are excluded from our carrier counts. They could not begin to bring enemy fast carriers to heel or to counter-maneuver against them as they darted just in and out of range during fast-carrier duels.

The shorter list of American carriers active in December 1941 makes Japan's tasks appear easier. But Japan's strategic questions were far more complicated. The Roosevelt administration had employed many measures to convince the Japanese to curb their aggression in China and Southeast Asia. In order to underscore this point, Roosevelt had published the navy's extensive building plan of 1940. Including previous authorizations, 12 battleships, 11 fleet carriers, 19 cruisers, 207 destroyers, and 88 submarines were to be constructed. Virtually every Japanese admiral believed America could do this and more. American shipyards could gear up for mass production because the country's industries could deliver the mountains of raw materials that were needed. Steel mills could cast huge amounts of ship's plate. Engine builders could crank out engines en masse. Legions of machine shops could fabricate thousands of parts and assemblies in wholesale lots.

Japan's ability to cast and cut metal was tiny in comparison. Each ship was essentially handcrafted by skilled tradesmen with limited infrastructure to support them. The Japanese navy well understood the time constraint they were up against. If it didn't force the Americans to quit the war by the end of 1942, the emperor's valiant sailors would be overwhelmed by a wave of new American ships that Japanese industry could not hope to match.

Relative carrier strength was the single best indicator of naval power of the two protagonists. A comparison of Table 1.3 to Table 1.4 demonstrates the overwhelming problem the announced American building plan posed for the Japanese navy. By mid-1943 the emperor's fleet would be overwhelmed. By early 1944, the situation would be absolutely hopeless, almost regardless of the victories Japan might have won before that date. As Yamamoto repeatedly said, victory for Japan had to come swiftly. Japanese soldiers would never march into San Fran-

Table 1.3: Japanese Wartime Carrier Construction

SHIP	COMPLETED	TONNAGE	SPEED	AIRCRAFT
		Ships that reached the fleet		
Hiyo	7/42	24,100	23–26*	53
Junyo	5/42	24,100	23–26*	53
Ryuho	10/42	13,360	27	31
Taiho	3/44	30,300	33	53
		Ships that did not reach the fleet		
Unru	8/44	17,150	32	65
Katsuragi	10/44	17,150	32	65
Amagi	8/44	17,150	32	65
Shinano	11/44	64,800	32	47
		Partial conversions		
Sea plane tenders				
Chiyoda	10/43	11,190	29	30
Chitose	1/44	11,190	29	30
Battleships				
Ise	1943	22 sea planes. Could not land aboard ship.		
Hyuga	1943	22 sea planes. Could not land aboard ship.		

cisco, let alone Washington. A Japanese victory would have to be sealed with a negotiated peace.

In addition Japan produced six 20-knot escort carriers (*Taiyo, Onuyo, Unyo, Kaiyo, Shinyo,* and *Chuyo*) and a handful of aircraft ferries. The United States produced over a hundred escort carriers.

This paltry list of reinforcements is even less impressive than it appears. *Hiyo* and *Junyo* were converted from merchant ships while still on the ways. Plagued with chronic engine trouble, they seldom made more than 23 knots and had trouble operating with other fleet carriers. *Taiho* was Japan's answer to the *Essex.* However, the single example completed made only a brief appearance in the Philippine Sea before human error blew it apart. Purists might view these four plus the first six Japanese fleet carriers as the critical ten that needed to be sunk.

The *Unru* class of carriers might have been of some help. However, by August 1944, Japan had run out of carrier pilots. This was a critical weakness that will be referred to time after time. Three more *Unrus* weren't completed. There was no

Table 1.4: U.S. Wartime Fleet Carrier Construction

CLASS	COMPLETED	TYPE	TONNAGE	AIRCRAFT
Essex		CV	27,100	90
Essex	12/42			
Lexington	2/43			
Yorktown	4/43			
Intrepid	4/43			
Bunker Hill	5/43			
Wasp	11/43			
Hornet	11/43			
Franklin	1/44			
Hancock	4/44			
Ticonderoga	5/44			
Randolph	6/44			
Bennington	8/44			
Shangri-La	9/44			
Bon Homme Richard	11/44			
Antietam	1/45			
Boxer	4/45			
Lake Champlain	6/45			
Independence		CVL	11,000	33
Princeton	10/42			
Independence	1/43			
Belleau Wood	3/43			
Cowpens	5/43			
Monterey	6/43			
Cabot	7/43			
Langley	8/43			
Bataan	8/43			
San Jacinto	12/43			
Midway		CVB	45,000	120
Midway	3/45			
Roosevelt	4/45			
Coral Sea	(delayed)			

reason to do so. By the time the sea plane tenders and battleships were given flight decks, it was the same story: no pilots. In other words, we can forget about all but the first four ships that reached the fleet. It wasn't much of a reinforcement.

Table 1.4 lists the impressive American wartime carrier construction. Final authorization to build the first of the new fleet carriers, *Essex,* was dated 3 July 1940. Her keel was laid on 28 April 1942. The dates above are commissionings.

Normally a carrier is available for fleet use several months later, after adjustments to correct deficiencies identified in her shakedown cruise.

Compare Table 1.4 with Table 1.3. The salient fact was the overwhelming advantage America's industrial potential would generate in the shipyard. From the outset, everyone knew Japan would suffer overwhelming disadvantage by 1943. The first seven *Essex*-class carriers delivered in 1943 alone carry more naval striking power than the entire Japanese First Air Fleet. The light carriers were meant to be stopgaps. Using embarked aircraft as a relative measure, light carriers are equal to about half their larger sisters. This says nothing of improved American airplane types (Hellcat, Dauntless, Avenger) and technological advances (radar fighter direction) that were unmatched by Japan. The quality of American pilots would continuously improve as they gained combat experience and added training, while Japanese pilot quality would drop with each loss as experienced pilots were replaced by fledglings who still needed coaching in basic airmanship.

The swing in the relative carrier airpower between Japan and the U.S. generated a huge change in American strategic choices as the war progressed. This was an effect that staff planners on both sides could easily calculate and project. The admirals of both navies had access to this critical data if they only chose to acknowledge it. Often this is overlooked as details of the naval conflict are recounted.

Yamamoto pointed to the obvious. In a long war or a war of attrition Japan could not prevail. Still he wanted to hit Pearl Harbor rather than to let the undisciplined "faceless" Yankee Giant hesitate in its own passivity. What might have happened had the Japanese rampaged through Southeast Asia and then stopped? Would America have acted against this fait accompli? Would this have been the better strategy for Japan? Japan's admirals might then have returned to the earlier strategy of ambushing American ships in midocean, whittling them down to a level where they could be defeated in a decisive battle with the Imperial Fleet. However, time was against the Japanese. A war of attrition might take so long that American shipbuilders would deliver the truly decisive blow.

One can commit a great mistake by viewing an island airstrip as an "unsinkable aircraft carrier." A key attribute of the carrier is its ability to maneuver, to change the position from which airpower is projected. Unfortunately, islands don't possess this capability. Tactically, an airfield within the battle area can be superior to the more fragile carrier. If land-based and sea-based air strikes of equal power are launched at each other, an equal level of bombing is likely to leave the carrier too damaged to continue air operations while the heavily damaged field can launch repeat strikes. Subsequent rounds become one-sided engagements as land-based aircraft pound carriers until they sink while the carriers can launch neither defending fighters nor retaliatory strikes.

However, an opponent need only skirt an island by a couple of hundred miles and its airstrip becomes impotent. Between Honolulu and Tokyo there are no choke points, such as Gibraltar, that are "must-have" locations. If one or two intermediate bases are required, they can be selected from among many atolls and islands. A three-hundred-mile swerve to avoid a Japanese-fortified island is a small price to pay to avoid any major fight with land-based aviation *that does not lead to the destruction of one of Japan's ten key ships.*

Aircraft substantially reduced the desirability of bringing friendly surface ships within gun range of the enemy vessels. Once air superiority is established friendly aircraft can pummel an enemy fleet with little risk to friendly ships. Entering the gun range of major enemy surface ships that are not already crippled by air strikes promises to return casualty for casualty. Many modern-day "gun club" enthusiasts fail to recognize that a desirable trait in American admirals after the winter of 1943 was the ability to avoid gunfights with major Japanese surface units.

Land-based heavy bombers also had a major effect on strategic war planning. Mahan's admonition was designed to destroy the principal naval asset that could defend whatever the enemy wanted defended. Elimination of the enemy's fleet was the prerequisite for invasion or blockade. Now 1,500-mile-range heavy bombers added a third end state that had to be considered. Capture of large airfields within bomber range of the enemy's homeland might become a decisive objective that wins the war. However, try as they might, high-altitude bombers never had much success against maneuvering ships. Air-delivered mines were another, far more effective matter.

America's War Plan Orange*

American interwar plans assigned a code color to each potential adversary. As Great Britain was associated with the redcoats (and in 1941 used red map symbols to denote friendly units) it became Red. Black was Germany. Japan was Orange. For two decades, American naval planners refined plans to defeat the Japanese. By 1941, most career American naval officers were familiar with the

---

*The latest revision of the plan, assuming a major war with Black (Germany) and Orange (Japan), was labeled Rainbow 5. Many continued to refer to the Japan portion as "Orange" although Rainbow 5 was a more correct reference.

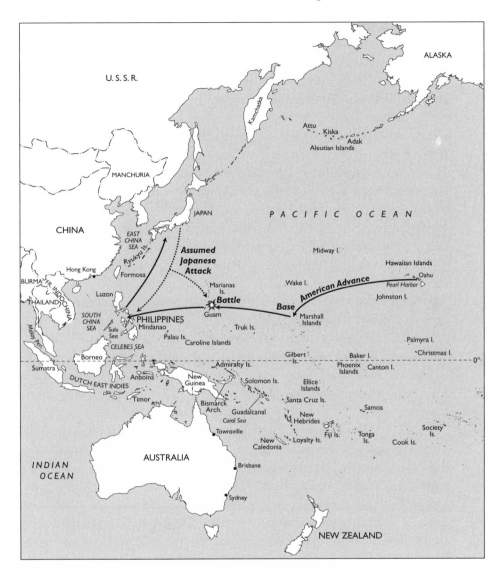

Map 1b. Stylized War Plan Orange. Map by Bill Nelson.

outline of War Plan Orange. Naval campaigns across the central Pacific had been war-gamed at the Naval War College 127 times.

The plan envisioned that the American/Filipino army would defend a bastion on the Bataan Peninsula at the mouth of Manila harbor against a Japanese invasion. The navy, using the time gained from the army's defense, would concentrate the fleet and sally forth to Philippine waters. Americans assumed the Japanese would land in the Philippines and lay siege to the Bataan redoubt. By resisting the American advance across the central Pacific, the Japanese might precipitate a decisive battle in midocean. The American battle line would defeat the Japanese fleet in waters near the Philippines. If necessary, an invasion of Japan would be mounted from the Philippines.

The primary War Plan Orange objective was to kill Japan's battle fleet. Once it was defeated, the relief of the Philippines would become a routine operation. A seaward approach to Japan itself would lie open to the army assembled around Manila Bay. Orange couldn't have been more Mahanian.

This was the plan in the 1920s, when combat would have been between battleships. It was the plan in the late thirties when carriers came to the fore. Tactics changed dramatically. But the overall strategic plan did not change even in the face of a radical change in the technology. This is what Mahan predicted.

Kill those ten ships, the carriers, and the rest of Japan's trans-Pacific war machine falls apart. Without the mobile air umbrella provided by carrier air groups, battleships cannot hope to survive a sea voyage of any length. Invasion transports can't sail more than two hundred miles from friendly shore (i.e., the radius of land-based air cover). Ships transporting raw materials from the South Seas have no way to get to Japan. Supply ships to outlying bases are helpless.

Sink the carriers and forget about everything else. You have won the naval war. This is the most concentrated form of what Clausewitz called the center of gravity.

Japanese planners envisioned roughly the same opening scenario. They planned to use light units (destroyers, torpedo boats, etc.) and submarines based in Japan's central Pacific possessions in the Marshalls and Carolines to attrite the American fleet as it transited the Pacific. At a point of the Imperial Navy's choosing, probably somewhere in the Mandated Islands in the central Pacific,* the Japanese battle fleet would ambush the Americans. Far from their Pearl Harbor base and probably in need of maintenance and resupply, the Americans would be crushed. Mahan's impact on the thinking of both countries is unmistakable. There was one major asymmetry. The Japanese never thought of invading the vast American continent.

If Honolulu had been a thousand miles from Tokyo, all America would have needed was the biggest possible carrier fleet and sufficient anti-aircraft and anti-

---

*Islands, principally in the Marshalls and the Carolines, made Japanese trust territories by the League of Nations after World War I. Most were former German possessions. The mandate was viewed as a reward for Japan's participation in World War I against Germany.

submarine escorts to protect the carriers in the 600- or 700-mile "center" of the sea lane. At its peak, the U.S. "Big Blue Fleet" (sailor jargon for the main U.S. battle fleet) had no more than nine heavy and five light fast carriers. Perhaps four times that number of destroyers and anti-aircraft cruisers would have sufficed. But Tokyo was 4,000 miles from Pearl Harbor—more if one adds the "zigzag" to intermediate bases among the central Pacific islands.

Fuel oil was the fleet's largest need—but there were others. Ships are very large complicated machines. Fixing one on the open ocean was an incredibly difficult task. Simply transferring large-caliber ammunition among the swells required great skill and wasn't attempted until near the end of the war. A large number of supply and service ships, often called "the sea train," would have to accompany the combatants to provide support.

Initial versions of War Plan Orange envisioned the fleet sailing directly from Honolulu to the Philippines. This was dubbed the "through ticket." After working out the numbers, most logisticians felt that a fleet could not operate more than 2,000 miles from a major naval base. The question of an intermediate base surfaced in the early twenties. By 1935 an intermediate hop to create a base, probably in the Marshalls, was formally incorporated into War Plan Orange.

The demise of the "through ticket" part of the plan led the marines to develop the ability to conduct an amphibious landing in the face of determined opposition. Some forward-thinking officers started early on the problem. In 1921, Captain (later Major) Earl Hancock "Pete" Ellis authored a document titled "Advanced Base Force Operations in Micronesia." It anticipated the need for forward fleet bases in order for the U.S. Navy to meet the Imperial Japanese Navy in a major fleet engagement somewhere in the central Pacific. Japan would deny the U.S. the ability to land on islands and create bases. Therefore the U.S. needed forced-entry capability. This created a new role for the U.S. Marine Corps, one that has become synonymous with the Marines. Prior to this Plan Orange requirement, the Marines were more a seagoing military police force than an amphibious army. The pioneering work of Ellis and others gave the Corps twenty years to develop the doctrine and equipment required to execute landings in the face of opposition. This Marine Corps capability would also enhance the invasion of Japan should it be required.

In developing their concepts, Marines at Quantico concentrated on the islands and atolls of the central Pacific. This was the route War Plan Orange assumed the fleet would take toward its decisive battle with the ships of the Rising Sun. In an era almost devoid of American military intelligence capability, marine and navy officers assembled valuable information on future central Pacific battlefields. Many of the prewar generation of Marine officers faced the "Guam

Problem"—an exercise defending and retaking an island—as an exercise in amphibious assault and defense in the Pacific.

Virtually all military commanders eschew frontal assault of a heavily defended position. They can be taken only with enormous loss of blood. Unfortunately, it is not always possible to find a weakness or a method of outmaneuvering a well-prepared defense. This is particularly true with the kind of small islands and atolls found in the central Pacific. Sometimes there is no alternative but gory assault on a position one simply *must* have. While it should have been viewed as a tool of last resort, the Marine Corps had to develop the capability to land in the face of heavy opposition if War Plan Orange was not to have serious impediments placed in its trans-Pacific path.

"Amphibious operation" is not synonymous with "opposed landing." In many instances, the campaign planner can pick a select a relatively undefended point of entry to a landmass. Both the Japanese army and navy had worked out doctrine for unopposed landings. Despite their plans for conquest, the Japanese never created a capability for, or carried out, an invasion of a large, heavily defended enemy beach.[41] Most Japanese landings during World War II were ship-to-shore movements to undefended beaches. Wake was an exception—and an initial bloody loss. Japan had no ability to attack Singapore, or Oahu, from the sea. Considering their plans and the possibility of more organized Allied defenses, this is a shocking shortcoming in Japanese capability.

Even more shipping was now needed to supply the Marines and their base. The old battleships, too slow to maneuver with the fast carriers, might come in useful to support the Marine landings. The demand for escorts to cover this geometrically growing fleet ballooned.

The Bureau of Ships, the organization within the Department of the Navy that designs and supervises the construction of ships, had figured out how to build 28-knot battleships and stay within Naval Limitation Treaty limits on ship size. In case the carriers proved unable to handle their entire task, a few of them were ordered to supplement the roster. They would be able to defend U.S. carriers against night-time ambush by enemy battleships; they could send crippled enemy ships to the bottom and provide large anti-aircraft platforms while waiting on their primary assignment. (The secondary nature of fast battleship missions is the reason *Iowa*s 5 and 6, as well as the even more impressive four *Montana*s were first downgraded then dropped from the building program and lowly destroyers and escort carriers added.)

All these hundreds of ships were added because the single naval objective, those ten carriers, was so far away. Anything that added to the distance exacerbated the problem. Kill those ten ships and it would be all over. Anything that detracted from that goal, or lengthened the path to that goal, would be prolonging the war.

Before they formulated plans for the strike at Pearl Harbor, the Japanese wanted to entice the American fleet into the western Pacific and sink it there. The Philippines appeared to interdict the sea lane from Japan to Jakarta. But some force must physically do it. A handful of B-17s from Clark Field in the Philippines could have caused some damage but could not have interdicted the sea lanes between Japan and the oil to the south. "Level" bombing (as opposed to dive-bombing) just wasn't that accurate. A concentrated U.S. battle fleet protected by three carriers would have not been a match for Yamamoto's six fleet carriers. Given the tremendous qualitative advantage the Imperial Navy gained in training, this might have been a far less risky strategy.

Before the war, U.S. Army Air Corps planners envisioned attacking surface ships with nine aircraft formations consisting of high-altitude bombers dropping their weapons in a precise pattern. Their calculations of weapons effectiveness were based on what happened when each bomber independently aimed at a stationary target. They then used a rule of thumb to extrapolate the bombers' effects on moving targets. Furthermore, planners did not take the effects of weather, variable winds, enemy anti-aircraft fire, and ship countermaneuvers into account.[42] As one veteran observed: "When I'm bending over that bombsight trying to get lined up on one of those Jap ships and the bullets start coming through the windows in front of me, they take my mind off my work."[43] The assumed effectiveness would have required guided "smart" bombs—technology that was fifty years in the future.

General Marshall, for one, was taken in by the advice of his air advisers. At a "not for attribution" press briefing, he displayed a map of the Philippines and the Pacific showing the lethal radii of B-17s operating against ships from various bases. By 1941, combat experience had repeatedly demonstrated that horizontal bombers with "dumb" bombs could not hit maneuvering ships from high altitudes. As the semi-official U.S. Air Force history of World War II states, Army Air Forces "estimates of the capabilities of the B17 and the B24 under war conditions were unsupported by practical experience."[44] This was common knowledge among Japanese naval officers.

In 1941, the IJN was probably the most experienced and the best-trained navy on the planet. "The Japanese naval air force was in operation almost constantly from August 1937 and by the end of that year its carrier pilots were the most experienced in the world."[45] Japanese carrier aviators averaged 700 hours in the cockpit. The average for their American counterparts was less than half that.[46]

The role of Japanese cruisers in the "decisive engagement" was to attack the American fleet with torpedoes the night before the clash of the opposing battleships. Japanese cruiser and destroyer men trained arduously in the dark and in bad weather to fulfill their role. On the other hand, American gunnery practice often was conducted on calm seas in bright daylight so each ship had an equal chance of obtaining a high score. The difference in training standards would decide many a night cruiser fight in the Solomons from mid-1942 until mid-1943.

Japanese cruiser squadrons were potent weapons, but their range was limited. The ideal American strategy would have been to avoid giving them a way to close in and strike at American forces. Caught in the open ocean during the day, they were even more vulnerable than battleships to air attack. The close-in naval fighting along the Solomon chain in 1942–43 demonstrated their lethality when they could approach their quarry in restricted waters under the cover of night.

In 1938, Japanese naval doctrine recognized that the carrier had become the central "ship of the line," instead of the battleship. IJN's air arm was roughly twice the size of its army counterpart. Naval aviation had been heavily engaged in China for the previous four years. Had a major fleet clash erupted in the mid-Pacific during late 1941 or early 1942, the Japanese would have held most of the advantages.

A Competing Strategy

A Mahanian approach concentrates all effort possible on defeating the enemy's battle line—in this case his carriers. Mahan warned against an anti-commerce strategy, which was what the Germans pursued with their U-boats.

In the Pacific, the major competing strategy became the domination of large ocean areas via amphibious invasion. War Plan Orange envisioned a relatively small amphibious capability to seize one or two mid-Pacific bases so the fleet could continue to chase the enemy battle fleet. Only a handful of ships landed the Marines at Guadalcanal. Japanese amphibious efforts were of similar size. By the end of 1943, American amphibians mustered hundreds of ships that generated a need for additional hundreds to support and supply the "gators" and the troops they landed ashore.

As we shall see, some commanders felt the dominant weapon, the real arbiter of command of the Pacific, was the large amphibious fleet. Many of these commanders were members of the "black shoe" gun club—the admirals who looked to the battleship rather than the carrier as the deciding source of firepower. The amphibians were to land enough troops ashore to construct an ever-larger land-based air umbrella. Operating under that umbrella, attack aviation could sanitize the area of all enemy action save a handful of starving guerrilla-like refugees hiding in the jungle. As in a land campaign, the constantly expanding umbrella would drive the enemy from the area being contested and ultimately hunt down enemy remnants in their own homeland. Such a strategy is the antithesis of what Mahan taught.

2

INITIAL JAPANESE STRATEGIC CHOICES

Japan's War Aims

The underlying causes of, as well as the buildup to, the summer of 1941 are beyond the scope of this work. Only a few salient points that emotionally and culturally frame the strategic thinking of the period will be touched on. Needless to say, the antagonists didn't like each other. Both participants generated enough racial slurs to sicken their descendants. Westerners viewed Japanese as sneaky, untrustworthy, conniving, demons that wore Coke bottle glasses and slinked around on spindly legs. They had no regard for human life and couldn't be perceived as civilized humans. Westerners might be forgiven for believing that these scrawny creatures were inferior soldiers—after all, many Asians thought Asian troops couldn't stand up against the professional troops of their European colonial masters. When Japanese airpower devastated General Douglas MacArthur's aircraft in a single day, he could not believe the meatball-decorated aircraft had been piloted by Japanese. He mused that German airmen must have been brought in for the job.

Similarly, most Japanese of the time held much of western civilization in contempt. Yankee "big noses" stuck them into everyone else's business. Western notions of democracy, capitalism, and free trade appeared to threaten traditional Japanese values of honor and respect for authority. Even Japanese authors noted that "the Japanese have had an incurable liking all along for totalitarianism . . . The Japanese once liked, and may in the future like, to bask in a blissful sense of national one-ness."[1]

While they marveled at western technological innovation, many Japanese thought the decadent Americans, addicted to their soft way of life, could not stand up to warriors properly inculcated in the code of Bushido. It was the warrior, not the weapon, that would prevail. For this reason many senior Japanese leaders discounted the sober technical analyses by staff officers that showed the material discrepancies between Japan and the West.

Few contemporary westerners understand just how ambitious the Japanese leadership of 1940 was. Everyone recognizes the megalomania of an Alexander the Great, a Napoleon, or a Hitler. They wanted to rule the world. But in 660 AD, the Japanese emperor Jimmu decreed that the rule of his house should be extended to all points of the compass. The eight corners of the world should be gathered under the imperial roof. The Japanese term for this notion is *hakko ichiu*. Throughout their history Japanese held *hakko ichiu* as a central belief so fundamental that it was never questioned. Just as Americans in the nineteenth century believed that Manifest Destiny was their God-given fate, so did the Japanese believe it was their fate to control Asia. The superiority of the Japanese race above others was so obvious to them that it was beyond mention.

In a letter, Jimmu, "Emperor of the Rising Sun," addressed the emperor of China as "Emperor of the Setting Sun." It is hard for a non-Japanese to overestimate how fundamental this belief is and how much it girded the decision makers formulating Japanese foreign policy in pre–World War II Japan.

During the last quarter of the nineteenth century, Japan made enormous industrial, technological, and military strides. By 1890 Japanese elites felt they were at least the equals of the best in Europe. However, they were sure that westerners could never match Japanese spirit. The Japanese watched as European powers colonized the world. Japan, too, needed foreign resources and additional living space. In Japan before the Second World War, 80 million people lived on four major islands with a total land area less than California's, much of it mountainous. Government corruption was pandemic. Rural poverty produced starvation and hardship for many. Peasants as well as the ruling elite saw expansion to the Asian mainland as the answer to their economic woes. Why shouldn't Japan seize underdeveloped and poorly managed lands in Manchuria? Japanese anger boiled at "being told by the Europeans that the right of colonial aggression belonged only to white faces."[2]

Strong emotions congealed into *Kodo Ha,* or "Way of the Emperor." This movement among tradition-oriented officers and members of the middle class combined hatred of the very rich Japanese merchant class with populist hatred of white men and their industrial civilization.[3] Many Japanese longed for a return of traditional Japanese values that revolved around the perceived military virtues of the samurai, personal discipline, and Japanese international supremacy.

In 1928, the year of Hirohito's rise to the Chrysanthemum Throne, Prince Konoe Fumimaro advised the emperor: "As a result of our one million annual increase in population, our national life is heavily burdened. We cannot wait for a rationalizing adjustment of the world system."[4] In other words, Japan must expand overseas by force of arms.

The first Japanese army units had entered Manchuria during the Russo-Japanese War in 1904. By the 1930s most Japanese viewed Manchuria as a natural extension of their own country. The following year Prince Konoe, Japan's prime minister, announced a "New Order in East Asia." China must recognize the "independence" of—meaning the Japanese subjugation of—Manchuria. Nippon's manifest destiny transcended the Sea of Japan. It was only natural to protect that which was Japanese. After all, the United States was an inferior culture. Americans shouldn't be allowed to challenge or block rightful Japanese access to territory on the mainland of Asia.[5] During the war a major publication, *Asahi Shimbun,* reported: "That the Americans are morally inferior is common knowledge among those who know America."[6]

Competing Risks

For decades Japanese expansionists had backed advances into China. However, a major deterrent, the Soviet Union, lurked to the north. Russia's traditional role as enemy had been underscored in Tsushima Strait at the beginning of the century. Border clashes of 1939 demonstrated Soviet firepower and Japanese weakness in mobile land combat against a continental power.

A modern economy had vulnerabilities of its own. The Japanese are a remarkably resourceful people, but their home islands are resource-poor. Many senior Japanese officers felt that Germany's 1918 defeat was due to a lack of raw

Table 2.1: Japan's Estimated Annual Need for Oil

Annual consumption

Army	5.7 million barrels
Navy	17.6
Civilian economy	12.6
Total	35.6

Annual production

Home	1.6
Synthetic	1.6
Total	3.2

materials.[7] Of all Japan's needs crude oil was most critical. Manchuria, which had been renamed Manchukuo by the Japanese, had none.

Japan had to have oil. The numbers were inescapable.

In the year ending March 31, 1941, Japan imported 22.85 million barrels of crude and 15.11 million barrels of refined petroleum. (By the end of the twentieth century, America was consuming 18 million barrels of crude *a day.*) About 80 percent of Japan's imported oil originated in the United States.

In 1941, Japan had about 42.7 million barrels in storage. The fields of the East Indies produced 65.1 million barrels a year, more than enough to meet Japan's needs.[8] The navy consumed half of Japan's oil imports. In 1941, the problem at hand—as the navy saw it—was to secure East Asian oil without disrupting its flow for more than a year. Earlier, the Japanese had pressured the Dutch to agree to, in effect, Japanese control of the oil fields. The Hague had rebuffed Japanese commercial proposals. Most Japanese foreign exchange was deposited in America. In an effort to restrain Japanese aggression in China, Roosevelt issued an executive order freezing all Japanese funds. Now Japan didn't have cash in the Dutch East Indies to pay for cargos. From Japan's perspective, the choice was either war or submission to American economic diplomacy. Given the history of Japanese-American relationships, the second alternative was intolerable.

The Netherlands and France lay prostrate under Nazi jackboots. Britain was fighting desperately for its life. None of them could seriously challenge an expedition into the South Seas led by the Imperial Japanese Navy. But would the Imperial Navy have to fight the British for the possession of the riches of the South Seas?

There was also the meddlesome United States. Used aggressively, the American fleet could block access to the South Seas. From an advanced wartime base at

Manila harbor, the American battle line could block sea-borne commerce from Japan to Java—unless it was eliminated.

The traditionalist Japanese army looked west to solve Japan's problems and feared intervention from the North. The "modern" navy looked south for a solution but feared an attack from the East.

What was Japan's best move?

Japanese Decision Making

Strategy is a most deceptive discipline. At first glance, it appears so easy. Survey the big picture and write down a platitude. But the difference in outcome between two similar-sounding proposals can be dramatic. It takes a practiced ear to hear the true difference between a disastrous proposal and an achievable one. To perceive the difference, one must understand the rudimentary calculus that underlies most of strategy.

Strategy is about choices. War fought between two opponents in the same class is exhausting. Each will exert its utmost to dislodge or unbalance the other. Neither side can afford to commit energy except to the single most important objective. Otherwise its better-focused opponent will prevail at the point of decision.

The most critical decision strategy must make is to select the single correct focal point. A mistake here can send a mighty war machine off in a useless direction and allow a smaller adversary with a better strategy to prevail. God is not always "on the side of the bigger battalions." A very smart adversary can best a larger but duller opponent. The Japanese were very much of this opinion.

In order to succeed, a strategy must be tightly focused. Secondary and competing operations and objectives can sap just enough resources to cause the main effort to fail. Mahan strongly advocated this position. The best way to integrate all available power toward the most critical task is to entrust a single decision maker with responsibility for the entire effort. This notion is antithetical to a system of competing interest groups trading off their agendas and desires within a political process. Military theoreticians and commanders alike so highly value the ability to completely focus effort that the notion has been encapsulated in one of the most important principles of war: "unity of command." Unity of command means one boss for one task. It means supreme team effort on the part of everyone to achieve the team objective—despite differences of opinion within the team. At senior levels unity of command is extremely difficult to achieve. Napoleon said, "Nothing is more important than unity of command" and "One bad general is better than two good ones." During World War II failure to achieve unity of command frequently led to faulty strategic decision making on both sides.

Normally the strategist looks to the national leader to define the overall national goals and to rank them if there are more than one. Only there was no single national leader in prewar Imperial Japan except the emperor himself. The civil government was almost totally separate from the military. The prime minister had no authority to form a single policy. The constitution of 1889 had been dictated by Emperor Meiji. It was designed to set up competing sets of advisers to the emperor. These included the Privy Council, the Imperial Household, and a weak legislature, the Diet. But only the emperor could force a final decision among competing factions and overrule everybody by fiat, or imperial rescript. Under the Japanese system, the army minister had to be a senior serving general and the navy minister an admiral. Either branch's general staff could effectively block any proposed government by refusing to nominate one of its own as its respective minister. All the players understood this tacit ability of both the army and navy to veto any proposed government.

Government machinery was geared to advise the emperor. But to incorrectly advise the emperor was dangerous to one's health. Custom required a failed adviser to commit ritual suicide. Therefore a great premium was placed on building consensus before presenting a problem to the emperor. Without the ability to form consensus, the government quickly deadlocked itself into inactivity. Alternatively, each segment of the government went on its own uncoordinated way. Such lack of coordination afflicted the Japanese throughout the war.

We have already seen that civilian authority had crumbled before the power of the army and navy. A peace-oriented prime minister attempted to find compromise but he was replaced before the fall was out: "For the diehards in Japan, 'compromise' meant humiliation."[9] An erratic foreign minister, who did favor attacking the Soviet Union in Hitler's wake, would also be replaced. Instead, real power rested with the army and navy. Each had a different worldview and the attitude that the core beliefs of its parent service were even more important than Japan itself. The army viewed expansion into China as its crusade and the Soviet Union as its greatest threat. Naval leaders knew that ships without oil came to "all stop" as fast as did a modern economy. Neither Japan nor China had oil. If America cut off the supply, the only other alternative was to seize a new supply from the Dutch East Indies in the area referred to as the South Seas.

Hideki Tojo ultimately became the prime minister, war minister, and army chief of staff, giving him incredible power. It was as if he were president of the United States, secretary of war, and army chief of staff simultaneously. He embodied many of the worst traits of Japan's 1941 elite. Born in 1884, son of a former low-level samurai, he was less a master of tactics and strategy than of bureaucracy and paperwork. As commander of the military police of the Kwantung Army in China, he acquired the nickname "Razor" and the reputation of bully. Tojo had attended the War College. As an American author normally sympathetic to the concerns of East Asians, Edwin Hoyt, describes him: "General Tojo, no matter his military skills, was essentially stupid, very badly educated and worse read. He was the prime example of what happened to Japan since 1853 [the date Commodore Dewey 'opened' Japan to western influence]."[10] He was a man of few words but uncompromising discipline. To his credit he had a reputation for selecting the best candidate, instead of a crony, for a position. This and his iron discipline won Tojo the admiration and loyalty of most army officers.

An excerpt of his moral code for the fighting man reveals Tojo's traditionalist bent: "a sublime sense of self sacrifice must guide you throughout life and death. Think not of death, as you push through, with every ounce of your effort, in fulfilling your duties. Make it your joy to do everything with all your spiritual and physical strength. Fear not to die for the cause of everlasting justice."[11]

Like most Kwantung officers he was an ardent advocate of expansionism. He viewed the Soviets as the biggest potential threat and remained focused on them. He connived to create the Soviet border incident of 1939 and was startled at the pummeling Japanese soldiers took from Soviet firepower. Ultimately, he felt, Japan must destroy Soviet power in the Far East.

The noted naval historian Admiral Morison observed: "Tojo believed the prestige of the Army to be more important than the fate of the Japanese nation."[12] John Bradley, formerly chairman of the department of history at West Point, noted that for Tojo "diplomacy alone could bring dishonor, he was convinced that Japan could win."[13] This kind of loyalty to some cause other than the nation's supreme interest is almost always fatal among strategists.

Tojo had little understanding of the Americans. Throughout the war, he minimized America's industrial might, tenacity, and the fighting ability of her servicemen. He viewed Americans as soft, addicted to their luxuries, and morally spineless. Japanese society was geared for war. An estimated 28.5 percent of Japan's GNP went to succor its war machine. Prior to the buildup for World War II, the United States spent a puny 1.5 percent of its GNP on defense.[14]

By the summer of 1941, the Japanese foreign minister, Yosuke Matsuoka, favored a move on the Soviet Union. Given Tojo's consolidated power and the acquiescence of Navy Minister Shigetaro Shimada, one might conclude that unity on this matter was easily achieved. It was not.

The top of the navy hierarchy, if not a vacuum, was an area of very low pressure. No one accused the navy minister, Admiral Shimada, of being brilliant, energetic, or forceful. Most felt he was appointed navy minister because he was very sympathetic to Tojo's views. Many senior naval officers saw Shimada as little more than Tojo's lackey and not as the navy's true standard-bearer.

Supposedly new naval plans emanated from the chief of naval staff, Admiral Osami Nagano. Nagano was more an administrator and naval diplomat than a sea dog.[15] His sole seagoing command had been a light cruiser in 1919. He was a timid sort who was on the verge of retirement in 1941. One officer on his staff described him a master of "band wagon riding," presumably with Tojo holding the reins.[16]

Nagano left much to his chief of operations, Rear Admiral Sigeru Fukudome. Until 1941, he had been chief of staff to Isoruku Yamamoto, commander of the Imperial Fleet. Service with his air-minded boss had had an influence on him. After returning from a carrier air strike exercise in May 1940, Fukudome remarked: "It is beginning to look as if there is no way a surface fleet can elude aerial torpedoes."[17] While Yamamoto was careful not to use Fukudome as his mouthpiece on the naval general staff, there was a good deal of common ground between them. Yamamoto's demand to strike Pearl Harbor came as no surprise to the naval general staff. An able officer, Fukudome penned most of the fleet's operation orders based on the vaguest of guidance. Fukudome tended toward the conservative and the conventional.[18]

Unintentionally, this condition allowed Yamamoto's strong ideas to carry unusual weight. By the late thirties he was "the man [to] whom, above all others, the navy looked for leadership."[19] He was subordinate to Nagano roughly in the same manner that Nimitz would be subordinate to King. But Yamamoto and his staff were far more energetic than Nagano. Some felt he had as much influence on naval strategy as either the navy minister or the naval chief of staff.[20] Yamamoto often found little value in the work product of the navy section of the general staff.[21] The strength of his confidence matched against Nagano's indecisiveness allowed Yamamoto to ultimately prevail. An intelligent, articulate proponent of naval air power, he also had quite a reputation as a gambler.

Yamamoto was a brilliant leader and a naval thinker of the first rank. In 1936, a Japanese Naval War College paper had discussed an attack on Pearl Harbor. One of Yamamoto's operations officers had been in attendance.[22] The admiral began toying with the concept of a Pearl Harbor raid in 1940.[23] That was when Roosevelt shifted the main base of the Pacific Fleet from California to Hawaii.

Yamamoto had studied English at Harvard and hitchhiked extensively through the U.S. He understood America's vast economic strength and her immense resources. His firsthand knowledge convinced him that American economic might would be a crushing advantage if it were harnessed for war. He thought an extended war with America was unwinnable. On the national strategic level he was right: it was best to avoid the war with the Americans altogether.

Likewise, the navy was not enthusiastic about China. Japan was a maritime nation. The resources it really needed were the oil of Java, the rice and rubber of Southeast Asia, and the mineral resources deposited along the periphery of the South Seas. Captain Mahan would have enthusiastically echoed this refrain.

Oddly, neither the army nor the navy thought it could defeat its chosen foreign enemy in open, extended war. While the Imperial Army blustered about Bushido and the superiority of its warrior code, the clashes with the Soviets along the Siberian border had engendered a healthy respect for Russian firepower and skill at mobile warfare. No general had much desire for another direct clash with Soviet might.

Yamamoto's opinion that Japan could not win a lengthy war against the United States was actually conventional Japanese wisdom in 1941. The carrier data from the last chapter underscores the point for anyone who can add. All the players understood that Japan could not hope to match U.S. industrial might in an extended war.

Whatever direction Japan chose, Japanese leadership understood victory had to come quickly. War would be fought for limited ends. No one was going to march to Washington or Moscow. For that matter, they weren't going to march to Lake Baikal or San Francisco either.

Japanese strategists did not have to read tea leaves to discern the relative importance Americans assigned to the German and Japanese threats. In the spring of 1941, the U.S. Navy transferred a carrier, three battleships, four light cruisers, and two destroyer squadrons from the Pacific to the Atlantic. Despite objection from his Pacific Fleet commander, Roosevelt ordered the remaining fleet to move from San Diego to Pearl Harbor. FDR knew the Japanese respected MacArthur, who had retired from the U.S. Army in December 1937. To further demonstrate American resolve to remain ensconced in the Pacific, the president recalled that old warhorse to the colors with three-star rank.

The Summer of '41

On the other hand, Japan faced a plethora of enemy weaknesses. On 22 June, Hitler's panzers tore into the Soviet Union. Swirling battles left tens of thousands of Soviet soldiers as prisoners. Should Japan attack the Soviets before Hitler finished them in order to partake of the spoils? The Japanese army had a plan to attack north if the Nazis entered Moscow by August. To hell with what the navy or the civilian government thought. This would be too great an opportunity to miss.

Prior to his assault on the Communists, Hitler had tried to entice the Japanese to attack Singapore—to tear at the moth-eaten British lion. This enticed a navy that had held the British service as its standard. The navy argued there was nothing to profit from up north. Let Hitler tie down the Russian bear. Go for the riches of the South Seas and secure oil for the fleet.

The colonial powers all lay prostrate. The French in Indochina now had German masters in Paris. So did the Dutch. The British, fighting for their life as a nation, had few resources to spare defending distant Pacific colonies.

Instead of acting on a well-thought-out plan to capitalize on one opportunity or another, Japan now blundered into world war while seeking only a minor advantage in the Chinese theater. Cascading events rather than rational strategic choice set Japan on a collision course with both the Russian Bear and the American Eagle.

By the summer of 1941, the Japanese army could move at will within much of China. It dutifully marched up China's major rail lines, defeating any force unlucky enough to oppose the emperor's warriors. But when the Japanese left the immediate area, the peasants went back to their own ways, ignoring imperial edicts.

This could not continue. The Japanese army was convinced that outside help seeping through China's southern border was sustaining passive resistance. In May 1941 Roosevelt made Chiang Kai-shek's China eligible for Lend-Lease supplies and equipment. Aid trickled by road and railroad through India and Burma. The army opined that the last vestiges of support and supply leaking through French Indochina was the last succor that supported such insolent behavior. If only the support arriving via Burma and French Indochina (modern Vietnam and Laos) could be staunched, Japanese generals thought the Chinese behemoth would finally collapse from its own weight.

Hitler's onslaught drained all of Britain's strength. Nationalist unrest in India led to violence. The British had few resources available to maintain control. In order to appease the Japanese and avert yet another hot war, the British acquiesced to Japanese demands in Burma. The border with China was closed.

"We will endeavor to the last to occupy French Indo China peacefully but if resistance is offered we will crush it by force, occupy the country and set up martial law." Japan would use Indochina "to launch from there a rapid attack when the international situation is suitable."[24] Most of France had been occupied by the Germans. The Japanese expected that strong-arming the Vichy government would be a comparatively easy task. On 19 July Japan issued it an ultimatum: close China-bound supply channels and allow Japanese forces unrestricted movement through French Indochina or face the consequences.

In a belated attempt to restrain Japanese entry into Indochina, FDR offered some major concessions. On 24 July, Roosevelt offered to guarantee Japan equal access to the food and raw materials of Indochina in exchange for Japanese recognition of the neutrality of this French possession. This might have become a major diplomatic opening. If the same concept could have been extended to South Seas oil, the Japanese navy's major concern would have been alleviated. Japan's strategic dilemma could have been much simplified. Realpolitik states-men might have seized on this possibility and crafted a phased solution to Japan's situation. After all, no Japanese in a responsible position thought an all-out war against America could be won. With access to oil and other resources, Japan could turn north against the Soviets and seek a solution to the Chinese question.

France was occupied. Who were they to object? At the time Admiral Darlan told U.S. Ambassador William Leahy that the Japanese would agree to leave French colonial administration in place if France agreed to Japanese occupation of its colony. Better to have something colonial to come back to.[25] The captive Vichy government announced it would allow Japan a joint protectorate over In-dochina. The Japanese army entered Indochina as an "invitee." There was no at-tempt to capitalize on the opportunity FDR had belatedly offered.

Japanese decision makers could scarcely believe America's rejoinder.[26] On the 26th, Roosevelt embargoed all petroleum shipments to Japan. That covered 80 percent of Japan's imports. How could the money-worshipping Americans turn down all this business? The Depression was fresh in everyone's mind. Given Roosevelt's modest response to earlier provocation, many Japanese leaders never thought he would act this decisively and accept this much economic pain. But the American president went even further: he froze all Japanese assets in the United States, effectively denying Japan the ability to purchase oil on the world market. Both the British government and the Dutch government in exile, to which the government of the Dutch East Indies remained loyal, supported America's action and also froze Japanese assets.[27]

Admiral Harold R. Stark, then chief of naval operations (CNO), advised Pres-ident Roosevelt that an oil embargo would precipitate a Japanese attack on the Dutch East Indies. Stark wanted to avoid a fight until the Pacific Fleet was better prepared.[28] For the previous twenty years the American navy had been anticipat-ing war with the Japanese. But it was Admiral Stark who had concluded in his "Plan Dog" that Germany was the more dangerous of the two potential enemies and the one that had to be defeated first. By the summer of 1941, his destroyers were skirmishing with German U-boats. He did not need another major naval war at this time and was opposed to the embargo.[29]

Instead it was the traditionally more isolationist American army that favored aggressive action against the Japanese. The army's objective was less direct. Its planners had concluded that defeating the Nazi hordes without hundreds of Soviet divisions tying down the bulk of the Wehrmacht was almost impossible. Keeping the Soviets in the war was critical. In the summer of 1941 they were losing badly. Tying up the Japanese and preventing them from attacking the hard-pressed Soviets was one of the few proactive steps America could take.[30] Aggressive action dovetailed with Roosevelt's desire to do as much as he could to relieve pressure against the last democratic bulwark actively resisting the Nazi horde, the British. Japan may have miscalculated American resolve because they did not recognize the critical interlocking objectives motivating U.S. calculus. Still, America wanted to avoid direct conflict. In a forlorn effort to keep American boys from dying in foreign wars most Americans clung to the slogan of "Arms, not armies." Roosevelt's ever-sensitive political antennae warned him not to move too precipitously.

The Japanese weren't looking for war with the pesky Americans at this stage. If only the Americans would mind their own business and allow Japan to proceed. As in World War I, Japan thought it would be far better to remain at peace and build its economic and financial strength through trade with the warring western countries. While the Europeans tore themselves, and Russia, to shreds, Japan could quietly subjugate China. Had Mahan been of counsel to the Japanese army and navy, he certainly would have agreed on this course of action. Here was a golden opportunity for Japan to become preeminent in the Pacific, the ocean of the future.

Throughout the summer diplomatic efforts to resolve the impasses emanated from both sides. But Japan's military was not about to back down. Neither was FDR. Both sides knew war was approaching. Japan's military did not want for aggressive action. On July 30, the Japanese bombed the American civilian oil tanker *Tutuila* in Chungking. The Americans did not react. Many Japanese leaders felt the Americans would back down when confronted with firm resolve.

Alternative Japanese National Strategies

The embargo had forced Japan's hand. One of Japan's greatest fears had become a reality that demanded immediate action. With the embargo in effect, the oil would soon run out. General Teiichi Suzuki, president of the Japanese Planning Board, stated, "If the present condition is left unchecked, Japan will find herself totally exhausted and unable to rise in the future." He believed America's actions would bring about Japan's collapse within two years. Suzuki pressed for immediate decision on war or peace. Admiral Nagano had only enough oil for a year and a half, which was insufficient time for "sweeping victory against US; he felt every effort should be used to find a peaceful solution with US."[31] Admiral Soemu Toyoda, a senior officer who would ultimately command the Imperial Fleet, also favored a peaceful solution. "Japanese military leaders chose to believe that Germany's 1918 defeat was overwhelmingly caused by lack of raw materials."[32] Regardless of what American diplomacy did or did not do, Japan was going to make a grab for the riches of the South Seas.

A planning organ of the cabinet came up with a mundane military solution. Go directly for the oil in the Dutch East Indies in November. Then initiate "surprise attacks on Britain and the U.S." in December. Expect the Soviet Union to enter the war in the second or third quarter of 1942.[33] One might label this the blundering worst of all scenarios. However, it must have given any decision maker pause to consider the tremendous risks of any military action. Mahan would have shaken his head in disappointment.

While the ministers argued during the summer of 1941, Japanese planners refined four alternative strategies for the military conquest of Southeast Asia (see Map 2).

A. Drive straight into the East Indies without taking any intermediate objectives. Malaya and the Philippines may be taken in a subsequent operation.

B. Advance sequentially via the stepping-stones of the Philippines to Borneo then on to Java, Sumatra, and Malaya.

C. Advance similar to B but in reverse: Malaya, Sumatra, Borneo, Java, Philippines.

D. Advance simultaneously via Malaya and the Philippines into the East Indies.[34]

These alternatives were formulated before anyone advocated the attack on Pearl Harbor. Most saw the first option as too risky. The army liked the advance via Malaya (C). It was in their realm and avoided immediate conflict with the U.S. Without the Americans, the British would be hard-pressed to reinforce Singapore. The navy did not like the Malaya route. Transit via sea from Japan was exposed to sorties from Manila Bay or the airfields around it. The navy advocated option B and immediate elimination of a forward base for the American threat. The army responded that this would much delay capture of the ultimate objective, East Indies oil, and gave the Allies too much time to prepare its defense.

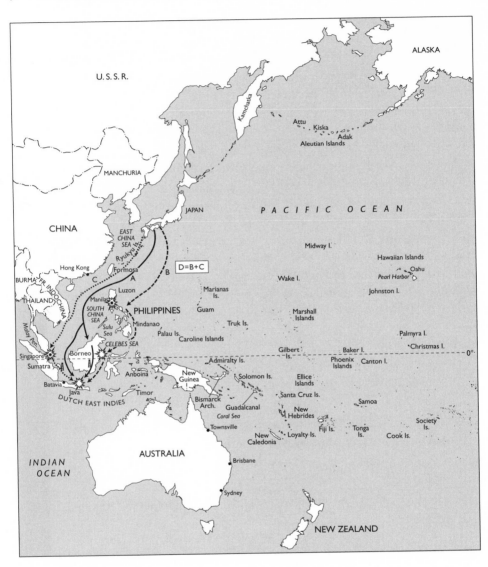

Map 2. Four Routes to the South Seas. Map by Bill Nelson.

Throughout the events that led to war, most Japanese leaders hoped for a limited conflict. It was natural that Japan run Asia and keep the resources of the South Pacific for Asians. Once the insolent white men had been given a sound thrashing and taught a strict lesson, they would acquiesce in Japan's Greater East Asia Co-prosperity Sphere the way continental Europe accepted the British Empire. As long as the U.S. left the Japanese sphere alone, the Americans could pursue their decadent ways with no fear from Asia. There was no reason for the cultures to fight to the death. Admiral Nagano promulgated a national strategy that achieved Japan's national goals with the most limited use of military force.

Like the American War Plan Orange described in the previous chapter, Imperial Navy planners had war-gamed a "Great Pacific War" many times over the years. IJN admirals expected the American fleet to charge across the central Pacific to the rescue of the Philippines. During the American crossing, Japanese light units, subs, aircraft, and torpedo-armed surface vessels, making sorties from the Japanese Mandated Islands, would whittle Uncle Sam's sailors down to size. Like many planners the Japanese longed to repeat their most recent decisive victory: Admiral Togo's thorough trouncing of the Imperial Russian fleet in the Tsushima Strait in 1905.

The Japanese battle fleet had been designed to emphasize offensive firepower rather than endurance at sea. Somewhere between the Marianas and the Home Islands, the IJN would engage and destroy the meddling Americans.[35] The entire naval structure was designed to prevail in a great decisive battle somewhere in the islands of the central Pacific. This scenario was classic Mahan. Japanese officers also had inhaled deeply the heady, if somewhat musty, aroma of "Mahan's classic brew of imperialism and saltwater."

The central idea contained within War Plan Orange—America's version of the "Great Pacific War"—was a rapid advance to the Philippines. Japanese assumptions about the likely American response were right on the money: this is exactly what they thought the Yankees would do. As Japanese strength grew, their thinking was to move the decisive battle forward to the Marshalls. This brought American and Japanese planning assumptions directly into line: a decisive clash in the middle of the Pacific.

Captain Mahan would have been stern with Japan's naval war planners. Eliminate an enemy intermediate base—the Philippines? No. If you destroy the enemy fleet, the base becomes meaningless. To Mahan, option B would have been strategic nonsense. But it reads as sensibly as the others. The difference between good strategy and nonsense can be a few seemingly innocuous words.

Admiral Nagano had studied Mahan. He believed in the dominance of sea power and the need to use the navy as a single overwhelming force. He favored employing the fleet, en masse, to invade and secure the South Seas.[36] Essentially, he wanted to avoid the Americans altogether and go directly for the final prize. If the U.S. Navy sortied, it would be destroyed in a decisive naval battle somewhere around the Marianas. This approach followed the strategy of Togo: Grab something the enemy has that you want. Wait for him to sally forth far from his own base. Pick a point that maximizes Japan's advantages. Ambush your enemy there and destroy him in a decisive naval battle. Nagano might not have consistently advocated this position. However, it is clear the naval general staff continued to plan for a central Pacific ambush and decisive battle strategy even after the Pearl Harbor attack had been approved.[37]

More emphatically than Mahan, Clausewitz would have reminded the Japanese leaders that wars are fought to secure political aims. It appeared that the Imperial Armed Forces could seize the South Seas in a lightning strike. Germany occupied France so Indochina wasn't a problem. Take Malaya if need be—England was fighting for her life against Hitler. Present the Americans with a fait accompli and then open negotiations. Japan desired limited war for specific means. This was a rational military strategy to reach the stated objectives.

The "no Philippines invasion" alternative (A) is more Mahanian than it appears on the surface. The greatest potential risk to Japanese southward movement was the American fleet. However, it was not at all clear that Roosevelt would be free to employ it. After all, Europe, where most Americans had roots, had been at war for two years. Yet American public opinion prevented the president from coming to the direct aid of the British. The Dutch were very unpopular colonial rulers of what is now Indonesia. In any case, most Americans didn't know where the Dutch East Indies were. Why would controlled statements from liberated South Seas natives move the indolent Americans when radio broadcasts from burning London had failed? Japanese diplomacy could have emphasized the wisdom of previously announced American policy to grant the Philippines independence and offered assurances that Japan would respect the new country's neutrality. In another parallel alternative, Japan could have opted to "take custody" of the Dutch East Indies without attacking America. Germans occupied the Netherlands. Some form of fig leaf could be conjured up. Take the oil and then see what happens.

If the Americans did react, perhaps they would be stupid enough to come charging across the Pacific and into a trap. There would be time to reposition the Imperial Fleet for its long-studied ambush tactics in the central Pacific. The decisive battle between the fleets would take place on Japanese terms. Captain Mahan would have understood Nagano's line of reasoning.

On Map 2, the Philippines appears to be a major threat to sea-borne communications between Japan and the Dutch East Indies. However, the threat from Americans based in the Philippines in 1941 was more apparent than real. The American Asiatic Fleet, the cruiser *Houston,* two light cruisers, and a handful of destroyers and submarines, could not seriously challenge the Imperial Fleet. While American airpower in the Philippines was the largest concentration of modern bombers outside the United States, only 35 B-17s and 39 twin-engine bombers were in the archipelago. They were protected by 107 P-40s and a dozen open-cockpit P-26s. By 1941 the Imperial Navy knew high-altitude bombers seldom could hit maneuvering ships. As the opening strikes of the war would prove, Taiwan-based Japanese airpower could neutralize Luzon-based bombers. Besides, Japan-bound convoys from the South Seas did not have to come within 500 miles of an American heavy-bomber base. Close analysis demonstrates that the Philippines could be avoided. This was critical as scarce resources need not be expended in the opening phase on an archipelago that contained nothing the Japanese needed.

A Philippine invasion had been part of the Japanese war plan for some time. Going against a long-entrenched assumption can be very difficult. Despite the lack of a strategic objective in the Philippines (oil, or the main American battle fleet), invasion of these islands remained an integral part of most officers' thinking. Japanese planners assumed that the operation would be completed before the American fleet, charging from Hawaii to rescue the Filipinos, arrived on the scene.[38] The Americans weren't likely to advance until they assembled a force equal to 150 percent of the firepower of the Japanese battle line.[39] That was the reason the Japanese needed time to attrit it in the Marshall Islands with attacks by land-based air and submarines before the Japanese battle line engaged in decisive combat.

Options B and D were very un-Mahanian. In December 1941, the United States had no Philippine-based military capability that could interfere with Japanese exploitation of the South Seas. Land-based airpower there was ineffective. If the United States would acquiesce to Japanese expansion, avoid the Philippines. A lengthy campaign to subjugate this colony creates only more to defend —more to dissipate the Japanese fleet. If war with the United States is inevitable, then Mahan would demand the Japanese destroy the American fleet at the outset.

In the actual discussion that followed, the army tended to favor option C— advance starting from Malaya and then seizing South Seas oil. One can understand the army's unease at leaving potentially hostile ground forces to its rear. Securing Malaya, Singapore, and French Indochina would eliminate that threat. Furthermore, the army was convinced that Anglo-American supplies were seeping into China through Southeast Asia and wanted to plug this route. The navy argued against any immediate offensive so it would have more time to prepare. If that line of reasoning failed, the navy favored option B, advance via the Philippines. For a group supposedly so steeped in Mahan and committed to the "Decisive Battle," that was very un-Mahanian. The army solution via Malaya can be viewed as a variation of option A, that protects the Japanese landward flank without directly confronting the Americans.

Popular history lionizes Yamamoto's decision to attack Pearl Harbor. Would Japanese history have been less painful if Admiral Nagano had prevailed? If the Americans had responded militarily, would the traditional Japanese strategy of mid-Pacific ambush have been more successful? Imponderables, but interesting ones some future strategist might want to pause on before choosing a course of action.

No War with America

The critical question that determined Japan's national strategy was whether the Japanese could successfully strike the British and the Dutch possessions in the South Seas without inducing an American counterstrike. America had nothing the Japanese wanted. Would America overtly prevent Japan from obtaining what was rightfully hers by sortieing the Pacific Fleet?

The United States could do virtually nothing to prevent Japan's lightning strike for East Indies oil. Again the map was deceiving. Facilities in Manila were nowhere near developed enough to support the American fleet with anything but the basics. The danger posed by the American fleet in Hawaii was more apparent than real. Many ships were not combat-ready. Most would have to return to the West Coast to bring their crews to wartime strength and to upload supplies. When Roosevelt ordered the Pacific Fleet out to Pearl Harbor in 1940, the Pacific Fleet commander, Admiral James O. Richardson, was so vociferously opposed, on grounds of operational readiness, that Roosevelt had him replaced. The Japanese were aware the Hawaii-based fleet was unable to sortie into the western Pacific to interdict a rapid Japanese advance. Spies in Hawaii had a good idea of the fleet's normal mode of operation.

Many elder Japanese admirals were less than anxious to initiate war with the United States. They remembered that the war against Russia in 1904–1905 had been a closer contest than revisionist propagandists wanted people to believe. Admiral Soemu Toyoda, who would become Combined Fleet commander during the end battles of 1944–45, was among them. Yamamoto, the Combined Fleet commander at the beginning of the war, was against starting war against America.[40]

Overall, Japan produced 3.8 percent of worldwide manufacturing in 1938. America produced 28.7 percent. An economic pygmy was contemplating attacking a giant. Despite America's 1940 shipbuilding program, the Japanese pointed to the limited allocation of U.S. treasure for ordnance to buttress their claim that overall economic capacity was unimportant. That delusion might well be marked as the basis of the most fundamental error in Japan's national strategy: picking a war with the Americans. Mahan understood the huge impact of financial strength and industrial organization on naval power.

Japan didn't want to conquer America. However, no one had developed a realistic exit strategy for a limited war with the United States. Then why start a war in the first place? Why not present the Americans with a fait accompli? Recognize the neutrality of the United States and its Philippine protectorate. After all, President Manuel Quezon of the Philippines was thinking of a unilateral declaration of neutrality regardless of what the Americans did. That would strengthen the hand of the American isolationist movement. In addition, a split between Manila and Washington would hand America a dilemma in democracy.

This approach was not completely without merit. In 1959, Admiral Stark wondered "whether we would have been in the war yet if Japan had not attacked us." American predilection for isolationism was intense. "To a large part of the American people, a war with Japan over Malaya or the Netherlands Indies would have appeared as an effort to pull British and Dutch chestnuts out of the fire."[41]

Japanese diplomats had heard senior American leaders warn against imperial belligerency. During the negotiations of late summer 1941, Admiral Stark, the chief of naval operations, told Japan's ambassador to the United States, Admiral Kichisaburo Nomura, "if you attack us we will break your empire before we are through with you. While you may have initial success due to timing and surprise, the time will come when you too will have your losses but there will be this great difference. You not only will be unable to make up your losses but you will grow weaker as time goes on; while on the other hand we not only will make up our losses but will grow stronger as time goes on. It is inevitable that we shall crush you before we are through with you." Nomura made no reply.[42]

By mid-October, Japanese planners had concluded:

a. Germany's invasion and rapid summer victories had neutralized the Soviet threat.

b. Great Britain would spend her entire strength defending her home island and could not undertake major operations in the Pacific.

c. The forces which America and Britain could immediately deploy were insufficient to prevent Japanese seizure of the South Seas and its defensive perimeter.

d. With the Burma Road severed, China would be forced to negotiate.

e. The United States would need eighteen months to mobilize for the offensive. The Japanese carrier fleet, based centrally in Truk, could parry thrusts on the outer defensive barrier.

f. Resources from the South Seas could be shipped to Japan within that time to stoke Japan's industrial production.

g. As a "soft democracy," the United States would be unable to sustain an offensive in the face of the casualties a fanatical Japanese defense of the Pacific would inflict. America would tire and negotiate.[43]

Even at this late date, points c, e, f, and g certainly did not preclude a strategy that avoided attacking America. Would America fight if neither the United States nor its possessions were attacked in a general Japanese South Seas offensive? As late as November FDR himself agonized over that question. At a cabinet meeting, he polled each secretary orally. Each responded the American people would support war but no one showed much conviction.[44] Everyone counseled as much delay as possible.

However, such dispassionate analysis was not central to the final decision. America had confronted Japan. Should Japan back down or answer this insult with war? The Japanese foreign minister voiced the opinion of many that American treachery was driving Japan to ruin. "[Japan] must take steps to break asunder this ever strengthening chain of encirclement which is being woven under the guidance of and with the participation of England and the United States, acting like a cunning dragon seemingly asleep."[45] From July to October, Prime Minister Prince Konoe sought to avoid war with America. A diplomatic solution must be found. But none was to be had. With the army and navy chiefs of staff pointing to dwindling oil supplies and requesting a "war or peace decision" by mid-October, a final meeting was held at the prime minister's residence.

Prime Minister Konoe continued to press for a diplomatic solution. The navy minister vacillated. Tojo, the war minister, did not. He opined that concessions to the Americans would require Japanese withdrawal from Indochina and from China itself. This was unthinkable. The army would withhold its support from any government that would advocate such a course of action. Without army support, Konoe had little choice but to resign. The army insinuated that any navy hesitation was indecision and cowardice.[46]

Earlier accounts of Japanese decision making were obscured by the myth that Hirohito was a figurehead who floated above the debate over war and peace. More recent scholarship[47] has clarified our view. Although the army initiated the "Manchurian Incident" without orders from Tokyo, Hirohito acquiesced in its aggression. He agreed with the idea of Japanese supremacy in Manchuria. In a long series of meetings, Hirohito actively created Japanese national reaction to world events and the formulation of Japanese war strategy. As early as 1940, he sanctioned plans to incorporate the Dutch East Indies and British Malaya into Japan's New Order.[48] At that time many Japanese leaders thought direct military confrontation with America could be avoided. However, five days before the United States embargoed Japan, the ever-wavering Admiral Nagano advocated an attack on America. Nagano felt time was against the Japanese. An initial onslaught should be pursued to take advantage of the large difference in readiness between the opposing fleets. He suggested an assault on the Philippines to support the navy's defense of the South Seas.[49] Hirohito took note of Nagano's change in position and was distressed. He criticized his admiral for the change in plans and admonished him for proposing it without a long-term plan for defeating America. At the same time, Hirohito also blocked the army's desire to take on its traditional adversary, the Soviet Union.

But since the spring of 1941, the consensus among the admirals had been that war with the Americans was inevitable.[50] How could it be otherwise? Since 1923 imperial defense policy had identified the United States as the probable enemy. America, "the bitter adversary with whom war was inevitable."[51]

After the oil embargo was instituted, the army came around to the navy's thinking about finishing with America sooner rather than later. This would free imperial forces to face the eventual conflict with the Soviet Union, perhaps in the spring of 1942. Most Japanese thought Germany would prevail. They wanted to be aligned with the winners.

Attempts to open direct negotiations between FDR and Prime Minister Konoe failed. Japan's oil reserves began declining. The peacetime navy used 1.5 million barrels per month. A great battle required 3 million barrels. Japan was not ready to cease its aggression in China, which had precipitated the oil embargo. Neither could it continue on its current course of slow oil starvation. The government split into a "peace" faction centered on the prime minister and a war faction centered in the army and navy ministries.

Japan's leadership plodded on through August without resolving the impasse. However, many players, laboring under the Americans' unwillingness to negotiate some relief to the oil embargo, came to view an attack on the United States as inevitable if war did break out. At a September 6 meeting with the emperor, the war faction pushed for a deadline to commit to war if diplomacy failed. Hirohito was concerned that the army and navy were not well coordinated to embark on a war with the western powers. Rarely did the emperor speak during an audience. He recited a famous poem written by Emperor Meiji on the eve of the Russo-Japanese War when he was concerned about the possible outcome.

All the seas in every quarter
are brothers to one another.
Why, then, do the winds and waves of strife
Rage so turbulently throughout the world?

Both the army and navy chiefs of staff felt they had been rebuked.[52] The emperor would not speak again at such a meeting until 1945. The army and navy ministers promised to give diplomacy more emphasis and to correct deficiencies in Japan's incomplete readiness for war. The emperor expected progress in the talks with the Americans by early October.

In a dispassionate world, Japan's logical choice would have been not to challenge the United States. All of the war games and many of the decision makers were sure that America's industrial might would be decisive in a long war. But pressure for war from the army and navy ministries remained relentless. The Americans remained intransigent. Tojo in particular felt that backing down before the Americans would make them even more difficult to deal with in the future. Konoe could see that the emperor was swayed by the arguments of the army and the navy. On 16 October he resigned as prime minister.

The Japanese navy had mobilized in mid-1940. A new Fourth Fleet, based in the Carolines, readied itself to take objectives in the South Seas. Having trained to a fever pitch, the navy would become a wasting asset. With a weapon in hand it was almost impossible not to wield it before the Americans made good their announced preparations.

Konoe and Tojo, the war minister, recommended that Prince Higashikuni form a government. Hirohito disagreed. Involvement of the prince might jeopardize the future of the Imperial House. Instead he substituted his personal choice—Tojo.[53]

Tojo and his army cronies couldn't stand leaving the insolent Americans untouched. The reader must recognize how deeply embedded this feeling was among many Japanese. Otherwise it is impossible to understand why Admiral Nagano's proposal was rejected after cursory consideration. As a member of the Japanese Naval General Staff of 1941 reflected, "The Japanese people are romantic and illogical."[54]

When Tojo was named prime minister, Admiral Stark warned all U.S. commanders in the Pacific that war was imminent. The period from 18 October to 5 November was extraordinarily tense for everyone involved. Tojo's elevation sealed Japan's national strategy. Without analysis of how to win against the Americans, Japan committed to war with the U.S. A seventeen-hour "liaison meeting" nailed down the final arguments on November 1. Tojo briefed the emperor and received his approval on November 2. On the 5th the Japanese leadership set a deadline. If there was no resolution of the crisis with the United States (later extended to 29 November), Japan would attack. On November 8, Hirohito received a detailed briefing on the Pearl Harbor attack plan.

Japan's National Strategy

Few knowledgeable Japanese thought their home country could win an extended war against America. A group of dispassionate players sitting in a war game might have been able to conclude that the only way of winning against America was not to fight her but to come up with an alternative national strategy. However, it is hard to imagine a prideful Japanese government coming to any conclusion that did not include war with America. In the late thirties, the majority of officers attending the Japanese Naval War College thought war with the United States was inevitable.[55]

So the national strategy—war to eliminate the American threat to Japanese seizure of their South Seas prize—came to be. Now it was up to the naval men to generate a military strategy to achieve the national aim. Like any learned man, Mahan would have shuddered at the odds against achieving this national goal. The Japanese historian Hiroyuke Agawa observed, "The Imperial Army and Navy, unfortunately, were wedded to the idea that fighting spirit was everything, and material resources were nothing."[56] Japan's warriors would prevail against the soft, unprincipled, undisciplined Americans despite the disparity in material means. Every true Japanese knew this.

The naval general staff insisted on the maximum concentration of force.[57] Thus they gave lip service to Mahan's overarching principle. Admiral Nagano's initial plan had been to concentrate the fleet and strike directly for the prize, South Seas oil. Yamamoto disagreed vehemently. "If we have war with the United States, we will have no hope of winning unless the United States Fleet in Hawaiian waters can be destroyed," he said.[58] He worried that the American fleet, already concentrated at Pearl Harbor, might attain a superior tactical position before the Japanese fleet could recover from South Seas operation. Deal with the enemy fleet first. Mahan, who might have listened intently if uncomfortably to Nagano, would now be smiling broadly.

Game theorists call it the "minimax" solution. Assume your opponent does the worst thing he can do to you. Then select the strategy that minimizes your loss. In this case, the conclusion had to be to crush the American fleet in the opening move. Mahan would have understood this.

Since early 1941, Yamamoto had been studying how best to attack the American fleet at Pearl Harbor. He did not like current planning which assigned the bulk of the navy to invading the South Seas while a smaller contingent awaited an American counterattack from Hawaii.[59] His planners came back with a design that employed four of Japan's six large fleet carriers. Yamamoto said to throw in all six. If one was to gamble, weight the odds in one's favor. Yamamoto insisted that only the best air commanders be assigned to lead the strike. Mahan would have underscored the importance of having highly trained and competent leaders.

Nagano didn't like Yamamoto's plan. Admiral Fukudome, his chief of operations, gave it only a 40 percent chance of success. He thought little of the almost unproved ability of aircraft to sink heavily defended battleships. Later he wrote, "I expected that more damage would be inflicted by submarine attacks, which would be continued over a longer period, than by the air attacks."[60] The Pearl Harbor strike force required several at-sea refuelings, procedures for which were still under development. Japanese carriers needed to arrive undetected, always a chancy endeavor. However, the spy had obtained information that the Americans rarely if ever searched to the north of the islands. This was the direction from which the strike force would approach Pearl Harbor.

Admiral Ugaki, chief of staff to Yamamoto, recorded in his diary that Japan could not establish a Greater East Asia Co-prosperity Sphere without first destroying the fleets of England and the United States.[61] Mahan would have given Ugaki an "A" for his analysis. Many officials of the Japanese government believed destruction of American fleet would result in an early negotiated peace, thereby securing the Co-prosperity Sphere.[62]

If the navy's top leadership did not agree to this strategy, Yamamoto declared he would resign. In Japan's highly charged political climate in 1941, this threat carried much weight. On 3 November, only thirty-five days before the actual attack, Nagano approved Yamamoto's plan.

The final Japanese plan was called the "Centrifugal Offensive." While it would be fantastically successful, the plan dispersed rather than concentrated effort. All six big carriers and a modest escort force departed for Pearl Harbor. Most of the battleships and two of the three remaining light carriers remained in home waters as a general reserve. The southern fleet was split almost fifty-fifty to support attacks in Malaya and the Philippines.

The Japanese knew they were biting off a lot. Their estimated calculations of enemy strength are listed in Table 2.2 on p. 59.

Only eleven divisions, nine tank regiments, and two air groups were assigned to the Centrifugal Offensive.[63] This wasn't much of a force to secure such a vast

Table 2.2: Japanese Estimates of Allied Strength

	TROOPS	AIRCRAFT
Malaya	70,000	320
Burma	35,000	60
Philippines	42,000	170
East Indies	85,000	300[64]

Table 2.3: Allocation of Japanese Combat Aircraft

	Aircraft	
	ARMY	NAVY
Malayan Campaign	550	150
Philippines Campaign	175	300
China	150	
Manchuria (reserve)	450	
Japan	50	275
Marshalls	50	
Pearl Harbor attack force	400	
Combined Fleet	75[65]	

objective. Compare this with the twenty-eight Japanese divisions in China proper and the thirteen guarding the "neutral" Manchurian border with the Soviets. At the same time hundreds of German and Soviet divisions were clashing on the plains of the Soviet Union.

The Twenty-fifth Army, the Malaya attack force, was assigned only three divisions. Burma, the East Indies, and the Philippines each received two. Another pair remained in reserve.[66]

Japanese first-line air strength was modest and similarly dispersed.

According to the Centrifugal Offensive plan, the Japanese army would occupy Thailand while the navy knocked out the American fleet at Pearl Harbor. The Philippines, Malaya, Borneo, and Sumatra would be invaded. Finally Java would be taken. The riches of the Dutch East Indies and Southeast Asia would provide the raw materials Japan craved. *Hakko ichiu* would be attained. A distant defensive perimeter would be extended out into the Pacific wastes to protect these rich prizes. Japan could fend off American attacks against the Pacific empty until the big noses lost interest and returned to their jazz and soft living. As Samuel Eliot Morison stated: "No such vast plan of conquest had ever been formulated in modern history. Apparently it never occurred to the average Japanese that there was anything wrong with it."[67]

The Japanese plan envisioned three stages.[68] The Centrifugal Offensive would conquer the Greater East Asia Co-prosperity Sphere, including all that oil, rice, metal ores, and rubber. Quick results were expected. The Philippines would fall within fifty days and Malaya in one hundred. All of the Netherlands East Indies would be secured within five months.

This would be followed by a period of consolidation. Many in Asia were tired of centuries of exploitation by the whites. At first millions readily subscribed to the Japanese plan of Asia for Asians. A defensive cordon would be erected among the vast Pacific Ocean waste. Using the resources gained from expansion, Japan would fiercely defend against an attempted American advance. If necessary, some of the Pacific could be traded for time. There was nothing of value east of the Philippines. Soon the Americans would tire of the casualties and agree to a negotiated settlement that let Japan retain the Greater East Asia Co-prosperity Sphere.

Mahan would have been dazzled by Japanese ambition. Japanese calculus had exactly the right dimensions. Mahan viewed the world as a series of locations containing sites of economic value, such as raw materials connected by sea-lanes. Stake out what your nation needs. Dominate the sea-lanes that tie them together. Strike hard offensively at the enemy fleet that can challenge your domination. Defeat it decisively. With your rival unable to interfere, grow economically strong with the riches you have secured (or stolen, depending on the point of view). But Mahan would have been appalled at the lack of concentration on the primary impediment to Japanese success.

To a stunned and silent nation Tojo read Japan's declaration of war. The broadcast closed with the song "Umi Kukaba":

> Across the sea, corpses in the water;
> Across the mountain, corpses in the field;
> I shall die for the Emperor,
> I shall never look back."[69]

3

PEARL HARBOR

In 1948, Admiral Morison summed up the impact of the Japanese raid on Pearl Harbor: "One can search military history in vain for an operation more fatal to the aggressor. On the tactical level, the Pearl Harbor attack wrongly concentrated on ships rather than on permanent installations and oil tanks. On the strategic level it was idiotic. On the high political level it was disastrous."[1]

Sixty years later, nothing needs to be added. Yamamoto's plan, while tactically audacious, was a strategic disaster. At the operational level, it was not bold enough to achieve the objective of crippling the American fleet. Mahan would have agreed that Yamamoto identified the most critical objective, the American battle fleet. But the admiral neither concentrated sufficient combat power nor created a plan that, successfully executed, would have achieved the objective.

The inveterate gambler plunked down a large bet. He should have placed even more chips on the opening throw.

At the time of the Pearl Harbor attack, Admiral Husband E. Kimmel commanded the U.S. Pacific Fleet. One of his prewar plans officers stated, "I thought it would be utterly stupid for the Japanese to attack the United States at Pearl Harbor. . . . I did not believe we could move the United States Fleet to the Western Pacific until such time as the material condition of the ships was improved."[2] The surprise of the Pearl Harbor attack was one of its main attributes. Never again would the Japanese find the Americans as stunned as they were on December 7, 1941. But a knockout blow was needed. Yamamoto planned only a sharp slap.

Japan's national strategy contained two objectives. First, seize the riches of the South Seas, especially oil. Second, eliminate the only force that could threaten this new prize—the U.S. Pacific Fleet. Captain Mahan's advice would have been uncompromising: Focus everything on the enemy fleet. Once it is destroyed, all else will be there for the taking. This was the essence of Mahan on war-fighting strategy. Despite all their study, the Japanese naval leadership had not learned Mahan's lesson.

Japanese naval strategists placed far more emphasis on the South Seas operation. An even greater error squandered resources on secondary objectives like the Philippines. Had those resources been focused on Mahan's prime objective, the enemy's fleet, Japanese success in the initial period of the war would have lasted far longer. That was Japan's best bet for a negotiated peace.

Command Problems and Strike Planning
against the American Fleet

At the turn of the century, during the Russo-Japanese War, Admiral Togo slaughtered the Russian Baltic fleet as it steamed to relieve what remained of the Russian Pacific squadron, which had already suffered a Japanese sneak attack. He patiently waited while the Russians sailed halfway around the globe and then ambushed them in the Tsushima Strait. Ensign Yamamoto lost two fingers during this battle.

While American naval officers gathered each year at the Naval War College to war-game Plan Orange, their Japanese counterparts were also preparing for their own Great Pacific War. Japanese planners understood the logic that underpinned Plan Orange without ever seeing a copy. They assumed the Americans would assemble a great fleet and sail to relieve the Philippines if Japan invaded or threatened it. In the tradition of Tsushima, they planned to ambush the advancing

American fleet as it traversed the Japanese Mandated Islands. Initially, torpedo boats, submarines, and destroyers would attrit the advancing Americans. At a point chosen by the emperor's admirals, the Imperial Fleet could crush the Americans in a decisive fleet engagement. To this end, Japan might first invade or threaten the Philippines to draw the American fleet west to its doom.

By 1940, it was apparent that an attack on the Philippines would not immediately lure the American fleet into another Tsushima. The American advance would be no rush. Instead the Americans would assemble sufficient strength from both its Atlantic and Pacific fleets to crush the smaller Japanese fleet. Prewar naval tacticians had estimated that a 1.5:1 superiority in combat power would assure victory in a fleet engagement.[3] This much power provided the edge first to suppress enemy firepower and then to concentrate your own hitting power against enemy ships one at a time until they sink. Each enemy ship sunk or put out of action makes the odds even more favorable for you. Note the 5:5:3 ratio of tonnage in the prewar Naval Limitation Treaty gave both Britain and the U.S. each a 1.67:1 superiority over Japan. The Americans could amass the 1.5:1 ratio that promised victory given both fleets were handled competently. The Imperial Navy's oil stockpile would last less than a year and a half. Once the huge American shipbuilding program began launching bottoms in wholesale lots, victory would move out of Japan's reach. For these reasons, Yamamoto wanted to strike the American fleet first. Long before formal planning began on the Pearl Harbor operation, he had confided to a former classmate and fellow admiral that "Japan must deal the U.S. Navy a fatal blow at the outset of the war."[4] So the Tsushima model was superseded. Long-nurtured plans to patiently wait until the American fleet sallied to regain the Philippines and then ensnare it in a carefully laid ambush in the central Pacific were scrapped. Instead a surprise attack on the American fleet while it slept at anchor in its home port could meet the Mahanian objective. Cripple the Pacific fleet, especially its carriers, and the United States would have no tool with which to interfere in subsequent Japanese operations. But to accomplish this, Pearl Harbor had to be more than a raid. It had to be a decisive battle.

Rudimentary plans for an attack at Pearl Harbor had been drawn up at the Japanese Naval War College as early as 1936. Several of Yamamoto's staff had participated.[5] Now the staff envisioned one or two carrier divisions (four carriers) making the strike. This would be an adjunct to the South Seas strategy. Damage the American fleet sufficiently so that it could not interfere with expansion from the Philippines to the oil fields of the Dutch East Indies. If the fleet wasn't at Pearl, Yamamoto was prepared to hunt it on the open ocean. He thought the proposed strike carried insufficient weight. So he threw all six big fleet carriers into the Pearl Harbor attack.[6] Yamamoto was willing to lose two or three of them at Pearl in order to get a decisive result.[7] Captain Mahan would have held him to this critical point. If you are going to take the risk, finish the job.

The Japanese admiral entrusted with tactical command at Pearl was Chuichi Nagumo. Although he had commanded the First Air Fleet since April, he had little save seniority to recommend him. A battleship admiral, he did not know a lot about airpower. Nor did he have a reputation for aggressive action. At first, he expressed opposition to the Pearl Harbor strike plan.[8] The plan to attack Pearl Harbor also worried Admiral Nagano, chief of the naval general staff and Yamamoto's boss. He was the one who picked Nagumo for the assignment.

Admiral Nagumo reminded his fellow admirals that a few bomb hits could cripple a carrier. This could have been a pretext to move him to an alternate senior position, perhaps back with the more durable battleships that he knew best. Captain Mahan would have severely checked Nagano for not providing a more enthusiastic leader like Vice Admiral Jisaburo Ozawa, a carrier expert and right after Nagumo in seniority. Mahan repeatedly underscored that the quality of combat leaders makes more difference than virtually any other factor.

Nagumo was not a favorite of Yamamoto. In his diary, Yamamoto's chief of staff, Ugaki, denigrated Nagumo.[9] Ugaki proposed Vice Admiral Ozawa, who was to show his skill at handling carriers off the Marianas, as recounted in chapter 8. Yamamoto agreed. But Ozawa had just been posted to command the South Seas fleet, the main instrument to capture the riches in that area. Yamamoto remained on good terms with Nagumo.[10] Switching the assignments of Nagumo and Ozawa might have changed the course of the war. After threatening to resign if the Pearl Harbor raid was not carried out, Yamamoto was hardly in a position to argue with his boss's selection. He did volunteer to lead the carrier force if Nagumo wasn't confident with the planned strike.[11] Nagumo did not relent in his opposition to the Pearl Harbor strike until 3 November.

Nagumo would have much preferred command of the South Seas fleet. A simple switch of Ozawa and Nagumo might have resulted in a far different Great Pacific War.

Rear Admiral Yamaguchi, commander of Second Carrier Division, First Air Fleet, enthusiastically supported the Pearl Harbor strike. He strongly felt that the American fleet was the key to the Pacific. Destroy it and Japan could move at will. If it remained intact, Japan would not be able to exploit any victory in the South Seas.[12] Obviously, Mahan would have found him a promising admiral.

Being unversed in aerial tactics, Nagumo left most of the detailed planning for Pearl Harbor to his principal air staff officer, Commander Minoru Genda. Genda's squadron, "the Flying Circus," had won its laurels in the air over China.

Many in the fleet air arm called his successful aerial tactics "Gendaisms."[13] Genda had been a naval attaché in London when British carrier aircraft sank Italian battleships in Taranto harbor. Many thought "mad Genda"[14] exerted so much influence that the First Air Fleet was sometimes referred to as "Genda's Fleet." Both a strategic and operational thinker, Genda's views became well-known at the headquarters of both Yamamoto and Nagano. It would have been hard to find a more influential non-flag officer in any nation's service.

Genda understood that America's ability to project a fleet into the far Pacific was the strategic target, not battleship row. In February 1941, after learning of Yamamoto's desire to hit the American fleet at Pearl Harbor, Genda drafted his own version of an attack plan. At the operational level, he made these observations:

- The main objective of the attack should be U.S. carriers.
- Destroy land-based aviation on the ground, if possible. With their aircraft destroyed, the Americans won't be able to counterstrike the Japanese fleet.
- Every available carrier should participate in the operation.
- The American fleet should be left in a condition that prevents any advance into the western Pacific for six months.
- Follow up the air strike with an invasion of Hawaii.[15]

Genda wanted an all-out attack on the Americans as the primary objective of the opening phase of the war. "If Hawaii is occupied, America will lose her largest and best advanced base, and furthermore, our command of future operations will be very good."[16] The U.S. Navy would be pushed back to the mainland. Mahan would have instantly recognized the star quality of this officer. He had come closer to defining the correct objective than Yamamoto. But he needed to be more precise.

Genda submitted his paper to Admiral Onishi, operations officer of the naval staff in Tokyo. The admiral was one of the navy's foremost flyers. His opinion was much respected among the flying community. Onishi's primary observation: "With our present strength, we are not able to take the offensive in both the eastern and southern areas. First we must destroy the larger part of the American Fleet."[17] Exactly so! Captain Mahan would have stood up and saluted Admiral Onishi. What is the essence of strategy? Despite Genda's clear formulation, Yamamoto was more than a little vague as to the end state he wanted after the Pearl Harbor attack. Mahan would have underscored the supreme importance of eliminating the American fleet. If necessary, add resources to the main effort *to the exclusion of all other operations.* There would be time for the emperor's fleet to sail into the East Indies after the American ability to intervene has been eliminated. A great strategist must have the moral and intellectual courage to champion the right plan even in the face of determined disagreement from the senior most leadership. The bridge of a warship under attack is not the only venue at which courage is measured.

Genda's design placed supreme emphasis exactly where Mahan would have put it: on the enemy fleet. Onishi's remark underscored the flaw in Yamamoto's strategic thinking. Many of his suggestions were incorporated into the final operations order. But the most fundamental flaw was not corrected. To really cripple the fleet, the attack must have high assurance of both killing the carriers and denying the Americans their Pearl Harbor base for the longest possible time. Instead, the planning focused on killing battleships. Yamamoto was confused in his choice of capital ship. No follow-on objectives were listed.

Genda wanted to throw a knockout blow. While not exactly saying so, his superiors, in effect, wanted a successful raid. The distinction is the reason for the difference in Yamamoto's failing grade from both Mahan and Morison and Genda's A.

Initially Genda advocated an amphibious invasion of Oahu. But American strength on that island was simply too great. Two coast artillery regiments armed with mobile 155mm to 240mm howitzers and coastal guns as large as 16 inches dominated every approach to the island. Two infantry divisions defended the guns. Carrier aviation could not possibly take out this much power. Mahan agreed with the conventional wisdom that battleships should not duel with effective coastal artillery given all the latter's advantages in stability and fire control. To do so might destroy the Japanese battle line. Tackling a two-division force was far beyond the capability of any amphibious assault the Japanese could mount. Remember, Japanese capability was limited to unopposed landings. Besides, troop transports could not hope to approach a beach defended by such intact artillery. So the attack on Pearl Harbor would have to be made from beyond the range of 16-inch coastal guns.

The First Air Fleet steamed across the stormy North Pacific in order to avoid detection. Nagumo attacked Pearl Harbor from the north, just the way Admiral King had in Fleet Problem XIX in the spring of 1938. Future American carrier admirals John "Slew" McCain and Leigh Noyes commanded carriers under King during that maneuver. Despite Admiral Stark's "imminent war warning" of 27 November instructing all commanders to make preparations to defend against attack, Admiral Kimmel, commander of the U.S. Pacific Fleet, had not provided PBYs for distant ocean surveillance. A spy in Hawaii, Takeo Yoshikawa, discovered the Americans didn't patrol north of Oahu. A Signal Corps subaltern ignored the reports of a semi-trained radar crew that a large group of aircraft was inbound. Had the Japanese been discovered, Nagumo was prepared to fight his way in.

Actually there had been plenty of generalized war warning to America's Pacific commanders. On October 16, when the "peace" government resigned and Konoe was replaced by Tojo as prime minister, Stark instructed the Pacific and Asiatic fleet commanders to prepare for the "strong possibility that the Japanese would attack." Admiral Stark correctly assessed the possibility of an air strike. This warning was also relayed to General MacArthur in the Philippines and General Walter Short in Hawaii.[18]

Admiral Kimmel's letter of instruction to the fleet dated October 14 indicated that a surprise air attack on the fleet anchorage at Pearl Harbor prior to a declaration of war was a possibility. The fleet had to be prepared for any eventuality.[19] Air attack was rated as more likely than sabotage attempts. Given this instruction, the lack of better air defense preparation is surprising.

In Japanese war games of the raid, complete surprise resulted in devastating results for the Americans. If the Japanese raiders were detected in time for the Americans to launch preemptive strikes as many as two of the six big carriers might be lost but the American fleet would be severely crippled.[20] Yamamoto was more than prepared to accept this risk.

If land-based air power was destroyed and American carriers weren't within striking distance, what did a Japanese striking fleet have to fear? It would not be easy to find. It could sit 250–300 miles away from the islands. U.S. submarines sortieing from West Loch of Pearl Harbor would have taken days to first find the fleet and then get into position. In 1941, limitations in submarine speed and cruising range meant that submarine commanders had to guess where the surface warships would go, then take up their own positions and lie in wait. Nagumo's carriers had no choke point or other area they had to transit. Surface ships had to first find the Japanese and then transit to their predicted position. A squadron of cruisers or destroyers could have done little against the two fast battleships and other escorts screening the six fleet carriers.

The first task for the raid was undoubtedly the attainment of air supremacy. Mahan would have understood this instantly. It was just an airborne version of the precepts he distilled from the age of sail. If air superiority could not be achieved, then continuing carrier operations within air range of the islands carried significant risk.

Before anything else, the large air contingent on Hawaii's airfields had to be destroyed. Contemporary naval doctrine held that gaining superiority over land-based aviation was a tougher job than fighting carriers.

The Actual Raid

Nagumo's six carriers carried 81 fighters, 135 dive-bombers, 104 "horizontal" bombers carrying modified battleship armor piercing shells, and 40 torpedo bombers for a total of 279 "strikers." In December 1941 Japanese carrier pilots were the best trained in the world. American ranks were filled with many trainees new to the colors. Furthermore, the Americans were not prepared for immediate combat. Japan's pilots and planes were at the peak of readiness. American P-40s and Wildcats could not hold their own against Nagumo's Zeros.

Carrier Striking Force Operations Order No. 3, dated 23 November 1941, scheduled only two strikes. Targets were described in detail in paragraph 3:

> 3. Targets
> A. The First Attack Units
> The targets of the first group will be limited to about 4 battleships and four aircraft carriers; the order of the targets will be battleships and the aircraft carriers. The second group will attack the enemy based air strength.
> [Ford Island & Wheeler Field]
>
> B. The Second Attack Units
> The first group will attack enemy airbases
> [Kaneohe, Ford Island, Barber's Point, Hickam Field]
> The targets for the second group will be limited to four or five enemy aircraft carriers. If the number of targets is insufficient, they will select targets in the order of cruisers and battleships.

In paragraph 4, detailed instructions are listed flight by flight. Nowhere is there mention of targeting port facilities.

Carrier Striking Task Force Operations Order No. 1, also dated 23 November, states in part:

> 1. Upon completion of the air attacks, The Task Force will immediately withdraw and return to Japan . . ."

> "In the event that, during this operation an enemy fleet attempts to intercept our force or a powerful enemy force is encountered and there is danger of attack, the Task Force will launch a counter attack."[21]

Both of these documents were signed by Nagumo. Undoubtedly Yamamoto was aware of their content. There are no instructions to go hunting American carriers. The instructions were to counterattack only.

The Japanese raid achieved complete tactical surprise. The first strike approached from the north, circled to the west, and began its attack runs at 0749, 7 December 1941. The force contained 140 strike aircraft escorted by 43 fighters. Raiders split between attacking airfields and battleship row. Within ten minutes most American aircraft had been hit on the ground. All battleships received hits. Four of them either sank or capsized. If *Enterprise,* one of only four U.S. carriers in the Pacific, had been on schedule, she would have been dockside in Pearl on the 7th. Army anti-aircraft guns and ammunition were locked down and were of little help in resisting the strike. Shipboard anti-aircraft gunners did better.

A second strike of 135 strikers and 46 fighters circled to the east and committed to their attack runs at 0855. This time, anti-aircraft fire was more effective and some interceptors were in the air. A few ships were under way in the harbor. By the time the second strike pulled off, forty-five minutes later, eight battleships, three light cruisers, three destroyers, and four auxiliaries were sunk, heavily damaged, or lying in the mud of Pearl Harbor. A total of 2,403 American servicemen lost their lives. Another 1,178 were wounded. All of this happened between breakfast and lunch. The Japanese lost 29 aircraft and a handful of midget submarines.

American battleships were moored in two parallel lines snug against Ford Island. One problem Japanese airmen faced was how to attack the "inward" battleships that were moored where torpedoes couldn't reach them. Sixteen-inch armor-piercing shells were modified so they could be dropped by air. It was a modified 16-inch battleship shell, delivered by airplane, that caused the magazine explosion on the battleship *Arizona* that split it asunder. Even in their twilight, the behemoths tore at each other, even if via proxy aircraft.

On the morning of the raid, American land-based airpower on Oahu was not all that impressive:

Nagumo started the engagement with 340 first-line aircraft. He lost 29 over Oahu and probably a few more that made it back to their carriers but were no longer airworthy. Obviously he now possessed dominant air superiority. His six carriers retained more than enough combat power to deal with all three American carriers that might be in the area, especially given that the latter weren't on full combat footing.

Before the raid, a dozen B-17s and a dozen twin-engine army A-20s constituted the long-range threat. They were backed up by some obsolete B-18s and a pair of A-12s. The Marines had 32 obsolescent Vindicator dive-bombers but their crews were not far into their training cycle. The bombers were defended by 99 P-40s and 11 Wildcats; both models were inferior to the Zero. The army also

Table 3.1: Status of U.S. Army Aircraft

	AVAILABLE	NOT AVAIL	DESTROYED	DAMAGED
Fighters (30 obsolete)	108	59	56	88
Bombers (21 obsolete)	35	27	18	34
Observation	11	2	3	6

Table 3.2: Status of U.S. Navy Aircraft

	AVAILABLE	DESTROYED	DAMAGED
Patrol	61	8	46
Scout bombers	36	1	21
Misc	45	8	20[22]

fielded 39 obsolete P-36s and 14 open cockpit P-26s which had no chance of sharing the air with Mitsubishi Zeros.

Virtually none of these aircraft posed any threat to fast, maneuvering carriers. As demonstrated at Midway six months later, repeated strikes by attacks of up to B-17s hit nothing. Four B-26 crews, supposedly trained for anti-shipping duty, also came up empty; two of them were shot down. Marine Vindicator pilots were not trained for steep attacks and were not very effective. Twelve were lost at Midway. Not a ship was hit. Even first-line aircraft, shiny new TBF torpedo bombers, with poorly trained crews did no better. Again no hits were made while five of six were lost to enemy action. And these guys were alerted and had time to ready for combat. High-flying army bombers could hit ships only by chance. It is hard to find any real land-based threat that could do much damage.

The Japanese plan scheduled only two strikes. Nagumo faithfully executed both. Orders contained no provisions for additional optional strikes. Nevertheless, crews began hanging ordnance on aircraft as they returned from the second strike. But armorers were loading anti-ship weapons in case the American carriers were spotted. The majority of pilots wanted to continue the attacks: "our keenest desire . . . was to find and destroy the enemy carriers."[23]

Back on the flagship, *Akagi*, Genda was trying to assess the damage done to the Americans. He had tasked some pilots in the second strike to do visual reconnaissance and report back. Their reports were colorful but lacked detail. Fuchida, the officer in command of the air strikes, later stated that lack of decent poststrike information was a major detriment. Everyone reported much heavier anti-aircraft fire. Eight aircraft had been lost on the first strike. Twenty from the second wave went down. Genda made one decision: the vulnerable torpedo bombers would not participate in a third strike.[24]

Fuchida had circled the harbor in his shot-up plane for two hours until all the stragglers turned north toward the carriers. Rising smoke obscured his view. But the damage he personally saw was enormous. Fuchida landed back on *Akagi* about noon. Sea and weather conditions were worsening. After checking reports of other pilots, he ascended to the bridge where Nagumo, Genda, and several other staff officers awaited.

Fuchida reported to Nagumo that American airpower "appeared to have been decisively smashed."[25] He recounted his personal observation of four battleships sunk and four badly damaged. The air commander wanted to return for a third strike to rip up the oil farms and repair facilities. He guessed that American carriers lay to the south and wanted to initiate an air search for them. However, Nagumo relied on a report from his chief of staff, Rear Admiral Kusaka, that perhaps between 40 and 50 multi-engine American bombers remained operational. Radio intelligence had supplied this information. In light of this potential threat, Kusaka was ready to turn toward Japan. Actually a six-carrier fleet should have easily handled a 50-bomber formation especially one that didn't contain "precision strike" dive-bombers. Nagumo's fighter strength was between about 60 and 70 (depending on the distribution of damage to returning aircraft). Surprisingly, Genda also advised against a third strike and was ready to withdraw.

Nagumo signaled Yamamoto that no American carriers had been caught in the harbor. Yamamoto's operation officer, Rear Admiral Kamahito Kuroshima, prepared a response ordering Nagumo to seek out the American "flattops." Yamamoto said, "Don't send it. Nagumo is thousands of miles away. He may have information we do not have."[26] Mahan emphasized that commanders on the spot should not receive interference from above. But here, the reasoning is circular. Yamamoto had erred in not properly defining the end state or the objective that Nagumo's fleet should have achieved. Now the actual result was better than any Japanese had expected. What a great time to extend Nagumo's orders and exploit success. Yamamoto failed again. Don't fault Nagumo.

Nagumo was concerned about the location of the American carriers. He asked Fuchida directly if the U.S. Navy, after the morning's damage, could sortie west within the next six months. Fuchida responded that it could not. Nagumo dismissed Fuchida with well-earned words of praise. Commander Genda picked up the conversation. If the Americans attacked the fleet, they could be easily handled. He recommended staying in the area for several days to take down the American carriers as they came to assist Pearl Harbor.

Nagumo thought it better to bring his six carriers home than to risk loss by staying in the area and searching for the American carriers.[27] He estimated the strike had already been 80 percent successful and had fulfilled his orders. Kusaka concurred. Nagumo broke radio silence to inform Yamamoto he was retiring. Some on Yamamoto's staff suggested Nagumo be given instructions to continue the attack. Yamamoto demurred. He did not want to override the commander on the scene.

In hindsight, it is easy to criticize Nagumo. No one can really comprehend the enormous burden of command in combat. Speaking of the British fleet commander at battle of Jutland in World War I, Winston Churchill remarked: "Jellicoe is the only man that can lose the war in a day." How does one remember to get dressed, let alone think creatively, with such an overbearing weight on his head? Decisive fleet battles come down to combat among a relatively small number of vessels—in this case ten, or six, fleet carriers. What happens if one suffers a fatal explosion from an aviation gas leak while another suffers failure of its rudder? A master stroke about to be launched at the enemy fizzles and the enemy finally stumbles on your fleet with his second-best blow. The most brilliant admiral is helpless.

Since the time of Napoleon, loss in a single land battle has seldom been decisive in itself. Land warfare among equals is composed of a series of battles woven together in a campaign. A field army can get hurt in a battle but seldom loses so much of its power that it cannot fight another day. Random breakdown of a few among thousands of tanks has nowhere the impact of perhaps two problems among six carriers. For example, the Germans in 1944 suffered a catastrophic loss in the pocket at Falaise, France. British and American armies chased the Germans to the Franco-German border. A supply-induced stall allowed the Germans the time to recover. With newfound strength they stalled the Allies for three months and then generated a massive counterattack. Despite these reverses, the Allied campaign yielded a decisive result.

The real fault lay in Yamamoto's deeply flawed Fleet Order No. 3. It did not even come close to describing the required end state. Later Yamamoto openly admitted the error: "Events have shown that it was a great mistake not to have launched another attack against Pearl Harbor."[28] Admiral Ugaki, chief of staff to Yamamoto, expressed a similar opinion. In his 9 December diary entry he penned, "If I were the commander in chief of the task force, I would be prepared to expand the war result to the extent of completely destroying Pearl Harbor."[29] That entry probably reflects Yamamoto's inner thoughts as well.

Yamamoto had known he had a weak commander—Nagumo—and that this commander would have to make one of the most critical decisions of the war. How hard should the Pearl Harbor attack be pressed? Yamamoto could have found reasons to have sailed with the attack force himself and been present to make the call. Failing this, it was absolutely his responsibility to clearly define the end state he desired and the amount of risk he was willing to accept.

What specific end condition was desired? Destruction of the American battle line? Elimination of land-based airpower on Oahu? Elimination of Pearl Harbor as a naval base?

Was there a follow-on assignment? Remain in the area until one or two or three enemy carriers were destroyed?

What was the maximum acceptable risk? Loss of two carriers? Loss of X percent of carrier-based aviation? What level of risk was acceptable to refuel the carriers and stay on station?

Sometimes this type of analysis sounds like so much pedantic hair-splitting. Here the lack of it undermined the most important operation Japan would mount in the entire war. After initiating an extremely high-risk operation, Yamamoto left the decision as to when and under what conditions of damage and degree of mission accomplishment to break off to a tactical commander he knew was weak-kneed. This is *not* the mark of a first-rank commander.

J. F. C. Fuller has likened combat to a fight between two desperate men in a completely blacked-out room. Each holds a knife in one hand as he furtively feels into the nothingness for some hint of his adversary's whereabouts. The person who first detects the other lives. Japan unquestionably won the first skirmish at Pearl Harbor. American land-based airpower as well as her battle fleet lay in ruin. Nagumo chose to quit before he suffered any damage. The effects Yamamoto wanted were not achieved because he had not specified what he wanted. Yamamoto could have been far more explicit in stating his intention of *what* was to be done without limiting his subordinate's freedom to determine *how* to do it. Given Nagumo's reluctance about the strike and his reputation for exercising caution when audacity was called for only underscores Yamamoto's failure.

The First Air Fleet moved north. Nagumo ordered a 360-degree air search for dawn the next morning. His thoughts were defensive, not offensive. Some on his staff still argued for another strike at Pearl. Instead the admiral ordered his attack aircraft readied for anti-ship duty. As he retreated, a Combined Fleet order was received, tasking the First Air Fleet to bomb Midway if the situation permitted. As is common in winter in the North Pacific, waves roiled the Japanese carriers. Even Genda didn't like the idea of an unsupported air strike at Midway. Why reveal the Japanese location to the Americans?

Fuchida had a far more constructive idea. Why not pull into Truk, pick up supplies and several regiments of ground troops, and invade Midway?[30] Japanese control of Midway's airfield would eliminate Hawaii's outer early-warning station. Genda heartily supported this idea. He wanted to take also Johnston Island,

Hawaii's outpost to the southeast. Nagumo began to listen. However Nagano's staff at Imperial Naval Headquarters thought little of the idea. Both they and Yamamoto's headquarters staff felt the war result at Pearl was sufficient. A return to Hawaii would absorb a lot of shipping. Follow-up wasn't needed. Any hope of corrective action died with the naval general staff in Tokyo. Captain Mahan would have been tapping the podium: It's the *carriers*. What is your plan to destroy the American carriers?

Captain Baron Sadatoshi Tomioka (who later became a rear admiral) was an intelligent, practical, but also cultivated member of Fukudome's staff. He and Fukudome worried that a return to Oahu would consume 500,000 tons of oil that the navy couldn't spare. No plans had been drafted for an Oahu invasion. Japanese planners knew the Hawaiian Islands weren't self-sufficient in food and a tremendous logistical operation would have to be mounted. Naval general staff (NGS) didn't relish makeshift plans that might lead to disaster. The NGS operations section was firmly against another foray to Hawaii.[31] Large operations are difficult to generate without meticulous study of intelligence and at least the outline of a decent operational and logistical plan. An off-the-cuff Japanese assault on Oahu would have been an unmitigated disaster.

Fixes to the Pearl Harbor Operation

The job of the operational commander is to create a campaign plan that achieves the strategic objective. One can almost see a scowling Mahan crinkling the paper as he read Nagumo's carrier task force orders. Mahan would have stated that the best, the *only* military strategy was to destroy the American fleet. It was the only serious threat to Japanese ambitions in the South Seas. Yamamoto's raid was breathtakingly bold, but it went nowhere near far enough. Japan's high-risk decision to make war on America demanded that the operational planners take on a high-risk operation to realize the potential for an early decisive victory. Never would the Americans be as unprepared as in the first days of the war. The operational tempo of the U.S. Navy up to December 7 indicated that a peace mentality had prevailed. Both Morison and Mahan would have given the Pearl Harbor plan a failing grade before the Imperial Japanese Navy ever weighed anchor. At the strategic level, Yamamoto's Pearl Harbor raid did not achieve the objective of crippling America's fleet. Two additional conditions were required: destruction of America's Pacific carriers and shutting down Pearl Harbor for an extended period. Killing the carriers was probably the easier of the two.

Commander Genda, Nagumo's air operations officer and author of the Pearl Harbor attack, recognized the need to focus on the American carriers. How to bring them to battle? After all, the Pacific is a big place. Genda mused that an invasion of Midway would be sufficient challenge to bring out American carriers. What if America lost Hawaii's sentinel? Pearl had just been bombed. Wouldn't all of America's efforts be consumed defending the last group of islands between the IJN and California?

Japanese intelligence believed four carriers, *Enterprise, Lexington, Yorktown,* and *Hornet,* were based with the battle fleet at Pearl Harbor. They were mistaken. Only the first three berthed there. *Hornet,* as well as *Wasp,* sailed the Atlantic. Intelligence correctly placed *Saratoga* on America's West Coast and surmised it would soon rejoin the fleet.

A spy report came in on the morning before launch: there were no carriers in Pearl Harbor.[32] Had all four Pacific-based carriers been present and offered battle, Nagumo would have had the 1.5:1 superiority that was the benchmark for a successful operation. Even if U.S. forces had been alerted, the Japanese would have had the edge in both training and naval aircraft capability. Everyone knew the Wildcat could not perform as well as the Zero. Kates and Vals outranged 1941 vintage American Vindicators and Devastators by as much as a hundred miles. This gave Nagumo the ability to find the Americans first and launch a strike outside of the American range for a counterstrike.

It was within the capability of the Japanese fleet to amass a decisive advantage over the American combat fleet even if the Americans had the good luck to assemble all of their carrier strength at one time in the waters near Hawaii. A feasible solution to Japan's tactical problem existed. Captain Mahan might have made the following review:

As a worst-case scenario, let's assume the Americans assembled all four carriers Japanese intelligence believed were in the Pacific just off Pearl Harbor before the First Air Fleet became aware of them. The count would be six Japanese carriers to America's four. Through heroic effort, the Americans manage to proportionally outfight the Japanese. Both sides lose two carriers. Now Japan is favored with a ratio of four carriers to two. With both sides on guard, the outcome is likely to be total destruction of the Americans with little Japanese loss. Even in a worst-case scenario, the Japanese achieve this portion of their primary objective.

Even if all first-line carrier strength of both navies was neutralized, Japan still wins a clear advantage. *There would be no force left in the Pacific capable of interfering with Japanese expansion into the South Seas.* With both sides' carriers and America's battle line out of the fight, the Japanese battle line would dominate. Perhaps covered by planes from a pair of second-line fleet carriers, it could reign supreme in 1930s style. Nothing west of San Francisco, save a twenty-mile ring around Oahu's coastal guns, could resist its power.

From a spy attached to their Honolulu legation, the Japanese knew the American navy came into port for the weekends. American admirals, concerned about sailor morale, created this regular schedule. However, Japan could not leave to chance the presence of American carriers at wharfside on Sunday morning. There had to be a contingency plan. It was reasonable to assume that Pearl's calls for help would draw American carriers to within striking distance of the American base. (In fact, that is what happened.) Most likely American carriers were exercising south of Hawaii. Fuchida thought repeated strikes on Pearl would lure them in.[33] Moving the First Air Fleet southwest of Pearl Harbor once American land-based airpower had been neutralized was a logical planning assumption.

Let's look at a more likely scenario. As was the case, American carriers were dispersed in the Pacific on training missions. Continuing strikes on Oahu for a second or third day undoubtedly would have drawn howls for help from Honolulu. Hawaii would have become an American carrier magnet. *Enterprise* was less than 200 miles from Pearl Harbor. Some of her aircraft flew to Ford Island at Pearl while the attack was in progress. One of the first orders from Pacific Fleet headquarters directed *Enterprise* and *Lexington* to rendezvous near Kauai to search for the Japanese fleet. As Morison stated, had these carriers come within reach of Nagumo's six carriers "the issue of so unequal a battle could hardly have been favorable to the weaker side."[34] While Vice Admiral William F. Halsey, commander of U.S. carriers, cursed his luck on not finding carriers in the rising sun, "we on the contrary may thank the Gods for this little favor."[35] *Saratoga* was also ordered to sortie from the West Coast to Pearl Harbor. As Admiral Ugaki observed before the strike fleet arrived in Hawaiian waters, "there will never again occur a better chance to push him [the American navy] down than this occasion."[36]

How long could the First Air Fleet have stayed in this ambush mode west-southwest of Oahu? Near the beginning of the war, the American carrier *Lexington* had been at sea for the better part of two months. The task force commander asked for permission to return to port for supplies. Admiral Nimitz, the navy commander in the Pacific, personally penned the response: "Carry on as long as you have hardtack, beans and salt willy. What the Hell are you worrying about?"[37] Yamamoto should have been similarly hard-nosed. A tag team of tankers could have been put together to support Nagumo's strike forces in Hawaiian waters for thirty days. Tanker capacity would have been the most limiting factor. The vice chief of the naval general staff, Vice Admiral Seiishi, had objected to the Pearl Harbor raid because all tankers were needed for the South Seas operation.[38] It was the other way around. During an extended fleet deployment, the small, less capable carriers *Hosho* and/or *Ryujo* could have been attached to the replenishment groups. In addition to providing limited protection, they could have flown off replacement aircraft to replace First Air Fleet battle losses.

In the early forties, both American and Japanese admirals expected carrier air strikes to damage heavy enemy units and slow them down. Friendly battleships, with their tremendous close-in destructive power, would finish off the enemy cripples. During the opening of the war, most of the Japanese battle line remained in Tokyo Bay. Those battleships would have been better used to support the First Air Fleet. They could have remained further west until air superiority had been achieved. As carrier strikes left behind cripples, especially among the cruisers escorting the carriers, the battleships could have moved in and finished the kills.

Much of this analysis begs the question of what level of risk Yamamoto and the Japanese High Command were willing to take. In the actual raid, Yamamoto dispatched his prize force, the First Air Fleet, on a trans-Pacific strike with virtually no advance reconnaissance of their path across the North Pacific. He chose a little traveled route and trusted to fate. What if the fleet had run across an American picket ship or his plan had been read by American code breakers? Yamamoto's answer was "We say sayonara, turn around, and sail for Japan." What an incredible risk he did take!

How about shutting down Pearl Harbor? This was an indirect way to curtail carrier group operations. An unwritten rule of thumb stated that a fleet couldn't operate more than 2,000 miles from its base. San Diego and Honolulu are separated by 2,500 empty ocean miles. Of course American warships operating from the West Coast had large enough fuel tanks to patrol out beyond Hawaii. But challenging Japan and her South Seas bastion would have been next to impossible.

Pearl Harbor's fuel tanks were the key. Four and one-half million barrels of fuel oil were stored in them. This was about two-thirds of the entire oil stock the Imperial Navy controlled. Burn the Pearl Harbor tank farms and the U.S. fleet would have to retreat to San Diego. All the military and commercial oil tankers available could transport 700,000 barrels, enough for the fleet to steam nine days.[39] It would have taken all tankers six round-trips (2,500 miles each way) to replace the oil, assuming quartermasters could find some place in the islands to store it. That would take months. Admiral Kimmel, commander of the Pacific Fleet during the Pearl Harbor attack, agreed. He testified that loss of the oil reserve at Pearl Harbor would have forced the fleet back to the West Coast.[40]

Destroy the machine shops and spare-parts bins along the "10–11 dock"—the repair dock—and the ships you drop into Pearl Harbor mud are likely to stay there for quite a while. Warships are very complicated machines. They need constant work. Without repair facilities at Pearl, fleet elements would have to make more and longer port visits on the West Coast. In 1941, ships could not transfer a significant amount of ammunition on the open ocean.

Mahan would have pointed out how destruction of the American battle fleet, especially its carriers, would have ensured the destruction of both the oil reserve and Pearl Harbor's repair capability. With the American fleet smashed, there would have been no impediment to isolating Oahu and reducing it by aerial bombardment. Again the ultimate Mahanian rule is pounded home: Concentrate everything on the destruction of the enemy fleet. Then all else is possible. But one must have the discipline to achieve that ultimate concentration. Despite all their reading of Mahan, the Japanese admirals failed to learn his most important lesson.

The Japanese should have been ready to subordinate everything to ensuring that the American fleet could not recover from the first blows. Mahan might have pointed out that a minor alteration to the Japanese war plan would have provided the resources required to underwrite an invasion of Kauai. With Pearl Harbor a combat zone, the Philippines would not pose a major threat. Land-based Japanese air, supported by a light carrier, did demolish the American air threat. Had the Japanese strike been less than successful, the B-17s at Clark Field in the Philippines would not have been a problem for long. The ground echelon of the Seventh Heavy Bombardment Group along with the air ordnance to support them was diverted to Australia when the war broke out.

Several days of aerial bombardment might have severely damaged Pearl's capabilities. But reconstruction would have begun almost immediately. How about a more permanent shutdown? As Commander Genda observed, "Whoever controls Pearl Harbor holds the central Pacific firm in his grasp. Unless Japan could take it and hold it, she could not defeat the U.S. Navy."[41]

But Oahu's stout defenses were simply too strong to be taken by direct assault. Even Mahan agreed that a fleet fight with fixed coast artillery batteries was suicidal. The two coastal artillery regiments on Oahu were armed with everything up to 16-inch guns. No amphibious invasion could be successful with this many guns ranging on the transports.

However, on December 7 the outer islands were virtually unguarded. Kauai was defended by only a battalion (minus a company) of the Hawaiian National Guard.* The Japanese legation in Honolulu could have verified this as easily as it

---

*On 6 December 1941, the following units were the only army units on Kauai: 3rd Bn 299th Infantry (less Co K, L) plus Co C First Platoon Signal Co Aircraft Warning. On Maui: 1st Bn 299th less Co C, Co K; on Molokai, Co C, K; big island of Hawaii, 2nd Bn 299th Inf (Pearl Harbor Investigation, p. 491).

verified vessel counts in Pearl Harbor. The island could have been quickly taken by an invading force of something substantially smaller than a division. Two Japanese regiments already had been positioned in the Marshalls. Kauai has more than enough level fields to welcome a large contingent of naval fighters and strike aircraft. Use the carriers to initially suppress Oahu's air power and the American fleet at anchor. Remain on station, destroying any naval vessels that threaten to sortie from Pearl and any reinforcements that might venture from the West Coast. Instead of holding the battle line in reserve, send it to escort the Kauai invasion force. If surviving American battleships sortie against the invasion, the battleship battle is joined on terms favoring Japan.

On the 8th the American Air Corps mustered 4 operational B-17s, 11 obsolete twin-engine B-18s, and about 75 fighters and recon aircraft on Oahu. The Marines could add about a dozen dive-bombers.[42] This was not a potent force with which to contest the air over Kauai.

The actual Japanese Pearl Harbor attack force had been accompanied by 8 train vessels. They left at 0900 on 26 November from Hitokappu Bay and moved eastward at 13 knots, not much above transport speed. In the early 1940s an invading force could traverse an ocean and head directly to a landing. If the 133 transports assigned to various Philippine invasion operations were reconfigured to carry a smaller invasion force, they would have been more than sufficient to carry this reduced force, ground personnel to service 150 aircraft, and a month's supplies. Under no circumstances, decreed Mahan, should a commander allocate *anything* to subordinate objectives until victory over the enemy fleet has been assured. This is Mahanian logic at its most basic. It's simple to say but very hard to enforce with so many competing interests at the campaign planning table. That is why the commander must be as tough in slicing away pet projects that detract from the primary objective as he is resolute in ordering his good men into harm's way.

As it would in the Midway operation, the invasion fleet would have sailed several hundred miles behind the carrier task force. Had the air strike been a failure, they could have turned away before coming within range of American land-based aircraft.

Use three of the smaller Japanese carriers to ferry additional aircraft to Kauai (or to replace losses among the First Air Fleet if required). Seaplane tenders and other air-capable ships can add to this effort and deliver all important ground equipment and fuel. Kauai's docks were on the primitive side but sufficed to move the island's crops. A hundred operational aircraft on Kauai would keep Pearl Harbor closed and prevent repair of the ships lying in the mud. Zeros would quickly establish air supremacy over Honolulu. Leave the battle fleet in

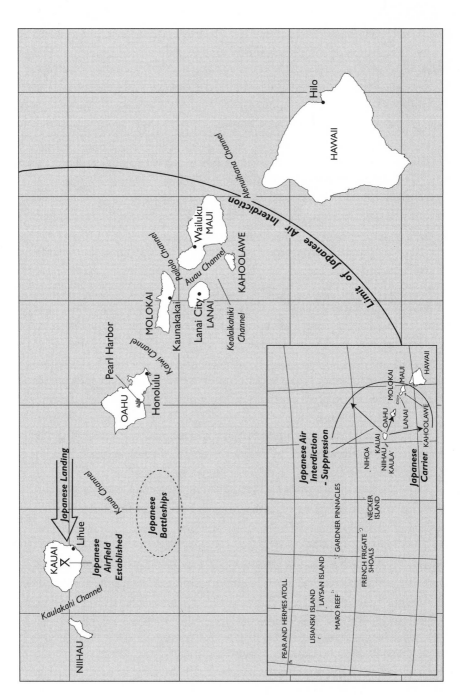

Map 3. The Kauai Alternative. Map by Bill Nelson.

place, protected by Kauai-based aviation, while the First Air Fleet rotated its carrier divisions home for necessary support. This prevents any reinforcements coming up from Oahu. The waters between the islands are notoriously rough and discourage the use of small craft.

If the American armed forces did not destroy themselves in enraged sorties against the strength of the Imperial Fleet standing off Kauai, they might attempt to reestablish themselves in the "Big Island" of Hawaii and attempt to lift the siege of Oahu. To prevent this, the Japanese could keep the Americans bottled on Oahu. The Big Island's garrison is but another National Guard battalion. Leapfrog from Kauai and invade the Big Island as soon as the Kauai-based air force is ready and the Japanese marines that led the Kauai assault have reembarked. Strong Japanese bases on both Kauai and the Big Island, backed by a viable imperial battle fleet and a functioning First Air Fleet would preclude any American operation west of Los Angeles in 1942. In this alternative scenario, Maui has a good fleet anchorage (Lahaina Roads) and is garrisoned by little more than a company. An outer island strategy also reduces concerns about feeding civilians because the main population center of the islands is Honolulu.

There are no stepping-stone islands between Hawaii and the West Coast. Nothing smaller than a B-17 could traverse the distance. Any attack would pit American carrier aviation against Japanese land-based aviation with the First Mobile Fleet lurking out there somewhere in ambush. Attempting a rescue of the islands before the *Essex*-class carriers arrived would be risky. Oahu is not self-sufficient in food. With no resupply, the inhabitants and large garrison would face starvation. All the Japanese would have had to do was to resist risking heavy Japanese ships on raids along America's coast.

Arriving Japanese warriors would not have met universal resistance. In the actual Pearl Harbor raid, a lone Japanese pilot crashed on the small and isolated island of Nihau. Two Japanese gardeners helped him to remove machine guns from his wreck and set them up. The island was "captured." Several days later an enraged Native Hawaiian charged the emplacement directly. Though he was hit several times, he reached the Japanese aviator and bashed his head in with a rock, ending the "occupation."[43]

Had the Japanese successfully pursued an outer-islands strategy, America would have been left with a major shock. Its fleet would have been crippled and a huge garrison would have been isolated on Oahu. Any relief from the West Coast would have had to face the Japanese battle line, which was covered by land-based air. Kauai bombers would have kept Oahu aviation nonoperational. Under constant bombardment, no one was going to try to lift wrecks from Pearl's mud or load fleet oilers from tank farms. Japanese subs could prowl the shipping lanes to the West Coast, adding to the hysteria and widening the time window the Japanese would have in which to return with an invasion force.

With Pearl Harbor neutralized, what use would American ground forces and a naval base in Manila Bay be? In the Japanese master plan, land-based air strikes were to destroy American airpower in the Philippines. If Pearl Harbor had been a smoking ruin and the islands under siege, how would reinforcements have been allocated—never mind conveyed—to the Philippines? There would have been no American fleet to counter the Japanese conquest of New Guinea. There would have been no "Miracle at Midway" because there would have been no ability to amass American carrier aviation against the First Mobile Fleet. An American southwest Pacific offensive in 1942 would have been an absolute impossibility. Australia and New Zealand would have been isolated.

With no support, Midway would have been easy picking. Japanese long-range aviation could have ferried on a route from Japan to Marcus, Midway, and finally Kauai. Several Japanese fighter types had the range to follow this route. There would have been no reason for the Imperial Fleet to enter the vast South Pacific wastes east or south of Java. With Hawaii and Singapore blocked, Australia and the Philippines would have been isolated. Japan could have harvested the riches of the South Seas at its leisure. A thrust into Burma would have left China isolated with only its own meager resources to resist Japan's plan. If Hitler could subdue the Soviets, Japan would achieve all of its aims.

Fanciful? Perhaps.

But General Henry "Hap" Arnold, commander of the Army Air Forces, observed, "I have always been of the opinion that, if the Japanese had had a well prepared plan; if they had had the troops and the ships; they could have continued their attack upon Hawaii with a landing operation, and taken over the islands."[44] On 9 December 1941, Admiral Stark, still the CNO, informed Admiral Kimmel, commander of the Pacific Fleet, that he expected the Japanese to invade Midway, Maui, and the big island of Hawaii.[45] He told Kimmel not to continue to base anything but submarines and small craft at Pearl. Stark told General George Marshall, chief of staff, U.S. Army, on the 11th that the Japanese had the ships and men to land on any of the outer islands and that they could blockade Oahu.[46]

In an "invade Kauai" alternative let's tabulate the reassignment of Japanese naval assets (see Table 3.3 on p. 83).

Before the carrier strike force departs Hawaiian waters for Japan, transfer two carrier wings to Kauai airstrips. In this manner, Japan retains air superiority. As part of the plan, two replacement carrier wings would have been worked up beginning in July 1941. This might have been the most valuable assemblage the

Table 3.3: Alternative Allocation of Japanese Ships

	HISTORICAL	INVADE KAUAI
Hawaii Strike		
CV	6	6
CVL		2
BB	2	8
CA	2	7
Transports		133
Philippines		
CV		
CVL	1	0
BB		
CA	5	0
Transports	133*	0

*85 of these were present during the Lingayen Gulf invasion of Luzon.

	HISTORICAL	INVADE KAUAI
Southeast Asia		
CV		
CVL	1	
BB	2	2
CA	7	7
Transports	x	x
Central Reserve		
CV		
CVL	2	
BB	6^{47}	

Japanese could have organized both in this alternative and in the actual course of the war.

Inspect the alternative columns. Which would have Mahan chosen? Start from a properly defined objective. Japan didn't want to just slap at the American fleet. The fleet's carriers and battle line had to be severely damaged and Hawaii suppressed as a base to have any chance of strategic victory. Assign sufficient forces to achieve the objective. If there are insufficient resources, then don't do it.

The United States armed forces were not sufficiently far along in their mobilization plans to dispatch immediate relief convoys. The first division to reinforce the Pacific, the 27th of the New York National Guard, didn't arrive until March 1942. Japanese submarines deployed between Hawaii and the continental U.S. would have prevented hasty ad hoc attempts to steam to the islands' rescue. This was part of Yamamoto's plan.

"Amateurs talk about strategy. Professionals speak in term of logistics." As we begin to analyze a potential Kauai operation, we can see how logistical constraints bind. Keeping the fleet investing Hawaii and the occupiers of Kauai supplied would have been the most difficult task of the Pearl operation. As impressive as the battleship *Yamato* appeared, Japan would have been better served if it could have been traded for an American service squadron of tankers and repair ships. One author estimated the turnaround time for Japanese merchantmen (*marus*) plying a Japan–Hawaii route at sixty days.[48] Add time to form convoys and discharge cargos and it might take ninety days. Assuming 25,000 occupying troops and 150 aircraft, something like 20 ships a month would have to unload. Almost half the invasion transport would be required to keep Kauai supplied.

The series of convoys transiting the North Pacific would have attracted every American raider above, on, or below the Pacific. The best buttress for the defense of this shipping would have been long-range patrol bombers based on Midway. Yamamoto's planners would have had to allow for that secondary objective.

The Japanese had plans to occupy Hawaii and even annex it into Japan.[49] A high percentage of the American population of the islands was of Japanese descent. By counting all other Asians, one could amass a majority. If American cringed from the blow on the islands, Japan would have won a rich prize. More likely a Japanese withdrawal from a demilitarized Hawaii would be an important negotiating chip in the diplomatic round Japanese leaders anticipated.

Remember, the Japanese thought (dreamed?) they could negotiate a peace with the Americans. Perhaps the offer of a withdrawal from Hawaii, return of American holdouts in Bataan, and free elections in a militarily neutralized Philippines might have appeased the Eagle. Old battleships sitting in the mud certainly didn't.

From Hong Kong to the South Seas

Let's return to the actual campaign. Conquest of Malaya, Singapore, the Philippines, and the East Indies was tasked to the Southern Army. This modest force, 11 divisions and 700 first-line aircraft, was to defeat the second-largest enemy (Britain) and capture all the fabled treasures of the South Seas.

In December 1941, the British remained the major colonial power in East Asia. Fabled Hong Kong represented her influence in China. Singapore was the Gibraltar of the Pacific, capstone of Malaya and the guardian of the Indian Ocean from the Pacific. To the west lay Burma and India. France was occupied by Germany; Japan's incursion into its Indochinese colonies was the move that precipitated the Great Pacific War. The Netherlands was completely subjugated by the

Nazis and her less-than-tight control of what is now Indonesia was already weakened. This archipelago contained the real prize: oil in Borneo and Sumatra.

Militarily, Hong Kong was extremely vulnerable to the huge Japanese military presence in mainland China. Tojo assigned the veteran 38th Division from the Japanese Army in China to pinch it off. The assault began on December 8. Eighteen days later the last Union Jack had been hauled down. To those not familiar with the correlation of forces around the colony, it was quite a shock. Regardless of the odds, white troops were supposed to hold out against Asian troops indefinitely.

"Malaya was perhaps the most humiliating campaign ever fought by the [British] Army, including Yorktown."[50] Unlike Hong Kong, Singapore had extensive coast artillery. For example the post office building along the harbor front had a secret floor in which large guns were casemented. Malaya was defended by about 40,000 British and Australian troops and a similar number of colonials. Most of the British navy had departed for the life-and-death struggles in European waters. However, the battleship *Prince of Wales* and the battle cruiser *Repulse* remained. They formed a powerful squadron that could devastate transports anchored off a landing beach. Japanese planners considered them a grave threat.[51]

However, many huge cracks ran through this impressive-looking shield. British rule was far less popular in the Far East than many in Whitehall wanted to admit. Colonial troops were ill-trained and unreliable. The Burmese were openly hostile. The British grip on India had been slipping since long before the opening salvos of World War II. Many indigenous people of that subcontinent were defying British rule.

As impressive as Singapore's seaward defenses were, the city was almost defenseless from landward. Careful Japanese intelligence work revealed this weakness. One of Japan's best generals, Tomoyuki Yamashita, who would be celebrated as the "Tiger of Malaya," planned to land several hundred miles up the Malay Peninsula at two small Thai airfields, at Singora and Pantani, and a larger one at Kota Bharu, Malaya. He would then move his troops rapidly southward through the heavily jungled peninsula to Singapore's back door. British commanders never really thought the Japanese would challenge them in Malaya.[52] Instead of concentrating their poorly trained troops along fixed positions to defend Singapore, they scattered them in penny packets to garrison the peninsula. British commanders always expected airpower would form their principal defense. However most of the Royal Air Force in Southeast Asia flew obsolescent Hurricanes or hopelessly obsolete Brewster Buffaloes. The Japanese inventory of first-line machines was not unlimited. In December 1941 only 300 operational

Zeros existed. Most of them flew from First Air Fleet carriers. Japanese airpower did begin the campaign with first-rate aerodromes around Saigon.

British gunners at Kota Bharu hit two of the three Japanese transports of-floading troops there. That was about the last success for the defenders of Malaya. Japanese army troops began moving south, often dislodging far larger British formations in the process. Japanese aircraft swept the Royal Air Force from the Malayan skies. *Prince of Wales* and *Repulse* sortied north to break up the Japanese landing forces. Admiral Sir Thomas Philips, commander of the squadron designated Force 2, neglected to call for any air cover at all, though some was available from Singapore. Like many others, "Tom Thumb" thought a well-handled capital ship could ward off air attackers.[53] "Poor Prince of Wales had always been known as a 'jinx ship'" to her crew.[54] A Royal Navy recon plane spotted the incoming Bettys but could not report because of mandated radio silence. Instead the Japanese bombers followed the hapless British plane back to the two capital ships. In one of the great shocks to the Admiralty, both were sunk by Japanese land-based aviation on 10 December. Unlike the ships at Pearl Harbor a few days before, the British capital ships were sunk in the open ocean while under full steam. This was a historic victory for Japanese naval aviation. It was the first time that maneuvering capital ships were sunk solely by airpower. Now the airplane stood as the supreme naval weapon. With the Royal Air Force shot up, Singapore suddenly seemed very vulnerable. British morale sank.

Yamashita's tank-led spearheads reached the muddy strait of Johore the night of 8 February. Lieutenant General Arthur Percival, the British commander of Singapore, had 80,000 defenders of Singapore Island with sufficient food and ammunition. However, defensive dispositions were atrocious. For example, trenches were not laid in one zone because the keepers of a golf course would not permit the fairway to be dug up!

It was all over in a week. Repeated bungling on the part of British commanders allowed Japanese troops to slip between defenders' positions. Yamashita, whose command had dwindled to 35,000 soldiers, demanded unconditional surrender. Percival complied on the evening of the 15th. He surrendered 70,000 officers and men.

Gathering of the South Seas riches had begun on January 6. A small invasion force covered by some cruisers landed in Brunie Bay. A few days later, small Japanese forces also landed on the island of Celebes to the east. Japanese paratroops and an amphibious landing took Tarakan Island off the east coast of Borneo. Japanese invaders, spearheaded by destroyers, landed further down the coast at the real prize, the huge oil complex at Balakpapan. Four old World War I American destroyers caught the transports off the coast at night and sank four of twelve. But this action only slowed the Japanese timetable by a single day. Bal-akpapan's oil was secured on 24 January.

The other great oil prize, Palembang on the southeast coast of Sumatra, was attacked on 14 February. This time the Dutch defenders had better luck. They mauled the Japanese troopers who had been dropped by air, and badly damaged the oil fields before they were taken. Again the Japanese were delayed a day. Conquest of the remainder of the Dutch East Indies was almost anticlimactic. The Dutch knew revolution was fermenting among the natives.[55] Several intense night surface engagements underscored the superiority of the Japanese navy and their "Long Lance" torpedoes at night.

In each advance, the Japanese would leapfrog about 400 miles. This was the radius of their land-based aircraft.[56] By 1941, the conventional wisdom on both sides regarded an advance beyond the range of existing land-based aviation as extremely risky.

What might have caught Mahan's eye was the tremendous gain made without commitment of significant Japanese heavy naval forces. Singapore and the two principal oil-producing areas were taken swiftly without the need for the First Mobile Air Fleet (as the First Air Fleet was renamed). Two light carriers and a pair of seaplane tenders provided sufficient air cover for operations around Borneo but were not critical to the operation. Subtract the rather large Philippine invasion force and redirect it to Kauai and the three critical objectives in the South Seas remain swift victories.

Granted, a pair of Japanese battleships (*Kongo* and *Haruna*) were placed in a supporting role. This was not a bad precaution given that *Repulse* and *Prince of Wales* were sortieing out of Singapore. But the battleships were not a primary cause of success. *Yamamato could have concentrated his big carriers, the battle line, and a large amphibious force against Hawaii for the entire first six months of the war without adversely impacting the conquest of the South Seas treasures.*

By the end of January Japan had much of Dutch East Indies in hand. The Dutch commander surrendered unconditionally on 8 March. Even before the war, the locals didn't want to obey their Dutch masters. This Japanese occupation was one of the most successful of the war. (The return of the Dutch after the war was met with a bloody insurrection. Indonesia gained its independence in 1949.)

The Philippines

At first glance, the Philippines appears to lie astride the shipping routes between Japan and the South Seas. Closer inspection of the map's scale demonstrates that there is a lot of open ocean out there. What would the United States use to interdict Japanese oil convoys? The U.S. Navy's Asiatic "Fleet" counted a single heavy cruiser, a couple of light cruisers, and a handful of destroyers. Airpower? As later developments proved, thirty-five B-17s wasn't much of a threat to Japanese shipping from the South Seas. These were America's largest operational grouping of Flying Fortresses at the time.[57] The first Japanese strike from Formosa hit all eighteen B-17s at Clark.

Apparently General MacArthur believed that despite the raid on Pearl Harbor the Philippines would remain neutral and not receive a Japanese attack.[58] President Quezon had mulled over just such a move.[59] Noted journalist Joseph Alsop relates an even more eye-opening tale. The day before Pearl Harbor, Alsop met with MacArthur in Manila. The general said that "the Japanese held the name of MacArthur in far too great respect to attack any area under his own protection, such as the Philippines."[60]

Open radio reports from Pearl Harbor were received in the Philippines in the early morning of the Pearl Harbor raid. Japanese aircraft did not appear over the Philippines until early afternoon. MacArthur's air commander, Major General Lewis Bereton, requested permission to launch B-17s against Taiwan or at least to move them south to Mindoro but was told by MacArthur's chief of staff, Major General Richard Sutherland, that his boss was too busy to see him.[61] Later Sutherland ordered Bereton not to engage in offensive raids without explicit authorization. MacArthur had received secret instructions from Washington to avoid the appearance of making a first strike. Bereton then requested permission to disperse his heavy bombers southward and scramble his fighters. Permission was denied. Despite repeated warnings from Bereton, MacArthur allowed his air force to be caught and destroyed on the ground by the first Japanese air strikes. Neither General Arnold nor General Marshall could understand how MacArthur got caught on the ground.

War Plan Orange directed the Philippine garrison to retreat into a prepared redoubt on the Bataan Peninsula. There it would prevent Japanese use of Manila harbor and await the American fleet's triumphant procession across the central Pacific. Army planners thought this might take six months and wanted MacArthur to stockpile accordingly. Navy planners thought rescue would take closer to two years, but they did not share their thoughts with their army counterparts. By 1941, every knowledgeable officer knew the Philippine garrison's chances of holding out until the fleet steamed west through a series of protracted struggles were slim at best.[62] When it came to the Philippines, War Plan Orange (or, more precisely, Rainbow 3 in this case) was unrealistically optimistic.

MacArthur's defense of the Philippines was marred by a series of horrible decisions. Before the Japanese assault, he viewed War Plan Orange with disdain.

On paper the Filipino army had ten divisions. About three months before Pearl Harbor, only one regiment from each had been called to service. Most of the remainder had barely performed small unit drill. In some companies neither the first sergeants nor their company clerks could read or write. Many languages are spoken in the Philippines. Often cadres could not communicate with recruits because of the language barrier. Few heavy weapons existed. The Filipino army's standard Enfield rifle predated the World War I Springfield. The official U.S. Army history states: "Discipline left much to be desired."[63] Discipline was purely a function for Filipino nationals, not U.S. cadre. Not a single court-martial was held before the war.

MacArthur's revised plans called for the Filipino army to resist landings anywhere in the archipelago. In November MacArthur persuaded the War Department that the "defeatist" war plan that called for a retreat into Bataan in favor of a forward defense at the beaches was too pessimistic. MacArthur anticipated a landing at Lingayen Gulf. Given the topography of Luzon, a Lingayen landing and an advance across the central plain to Manila was the best avenue of advance. The Sierra Madre mountains to the east and the Zambales Mountains to the west canalize movement and militate against large landings elsewhere. Both the Japanese in 1941 and the Americans in 1944 used this approach. MacArthur planned his deployments as if his raw, undisciplined recruits were seasoned troops. MacArthur mandated "no withdrawal from beach positions. The beaches were to be held at all costs."[64]

Forty-one thousand troops of the Japanese Fourteenth Army, along with tanks and other heavy weapons, came ashore along the eastern shore of Lingayen Gulf. Counting subsidiary landings, a total of 54,000 troops in two divisions carried in over a hundred transports invaded Luzon. Three Filipino infantry divisions and a cavalry regiment of Philippine Scouts were in the main invasion area.

Despite heavy surf and lack of specialized amphibious equipment, the invaders crossed the beach quickly. Filipino resistance was spotty at best. Given the Filipinos' almost total lack of training, this is understandable. Attempts to contain the Japanese advance proved disastrous. One defense line after another collapsed even before they could be properly manned. Due to the shock of the Japanese onslaught, one out of six Filipino conscripts, perhaps 12,000 in all, ran away to any place but Bataan. The last American horse-mounted cavalry regiment to see combat desperately attempted to cover the withdrawals and to prevent a rout. The Philippine Scouts, which had received decent training and were commanded by American officers, fought with great valor. Lieutenant Harold K. Johnson, who was present and who would later rise to become army chief of staff, said the beach defense plan was a "tragic error."[65]

Sometimes Americans forget the Filipino insurrection directed at the United States when it took over the reins from the Spanish in 1898. Commander John D. Bulkey, a PT boat squadron commander who regularly transported Mac-Arthur and other dignitaries, guessed "about 80% of Filipinos were against us or neutral only 20% were with us."[66] This is probably too pessimistic, as many ordinary Filipinos remained loyal to the country that had promised them independence long before war clouds threatened. Later the message of the Greater East Asia Co-prosperity Sphere fell on ears deafened by insults from Japanese conquerors. Filipino guerrillas made much of their islands unsafe for the Japanese to move about, except in armed convoys.

Behavior of some of the upper classes wasn't as sanguine. Seventy-five percent of Filipino senators and 30 percent of the Filipino House accepted positions in the puppet regime created under President Jose Laurel.[67]

Colonel Ernest B. Miller, an American tank battalion commander during the Luzon defensive campaign, commented, "Perhaps it was fortunate that, as we bivouacked amid the smoking ruins of Clark Field on that first day of the war, we could not see these things that were yet to come—food and materiel of war sabotaged by the same mismanagement and indecision that destroyed our airpower."[68]

Even through the Japanese invaders were not the Imperial Army's best, their veteran status and solid discipline soon routed the defenders. Imperial troops covered the 110 air miles from beach to Manila in eleven days. MacArthur cabled to Washington that he hadn't lost any men or supplies in his retreat.[69]

With no air or naval support and a disintegrating Filipino army, MacArthur's initial plan to resist Japanese invaders at the beachhead was sheer fantasy. American officers attached to the Filipino army were not surprised at the poor showing of the untrained new recruits. Brigadier General Clifford Bluemel of the pre–World War II Philippine Department described MacArthur's plan as "a terrible thing."[70] Earlier MacArthur's plans officer, Colonel James V. Collier, suggested the supplies be moved to Bataan as "a safety measure. Mac said, "Oh no!"[71] The next day the 71st Philippine Division guarding the highway to Manila collapsed after a brief fight. MacArthur ordered Major General Jonathan "Skinny" Wainwright to occupy a series of five delaying positions that MacArthur estimated would give him two weeks' time to prepare Bataan. As commander of the Philippine army, MacArthur knew, or should have known, the poor condition of his forces. He had had much time prior to December to see to their proper training as foot soldiers. By the afternoon of the first day of fighting, it was obvious to Wainwright that "such a ragtag force could not stop Himma"[72]—General Himma was the Japanese army invasion commander. That night MacArthur ordered the withdrawal into Bataan.

The general's disregard for War Plan Orange meant that no one had properly prepared the Bataan redoubt. Because of MacArthur's bungling lack of compliance to orders, 10 million bushels of wheat in a warehouse near Manila were abandoned to the enemy. President Quezon, enforcing a law prohibiting movement of foodstuffs from one province to another, blocked the movement of a large quantity of rice at the Filipino depot at Cabanatuan.[73] According to plan, this food, five months of rations, should have already been evacuated into Bataan. Instead the defenders went on half rations almost immediately. The deprivation of the Bataan defenders is one of the saddest pages in American military history.

Two days later, on 26 December, the Japanese Sixth Infantry, with 700 combat troops plus supporting troops, landed at Lamon Bay on Leyte's east coast, not far from Manila. Even an armchair general could see that the capital was doomed. MacArthur declared Manila an open city. His optimistic defense plans had entirely evaporated.

"At this point, McArthur might justifiably have been relieved."[74] "MacArthur had made disastrous mistakes in his handling of the Philippine crisis."[75] Dwight Eisenhower, then in the War Plans Division with responsibility for overseeing the Philippines, wrote in his diary, "I still think he might have made a better showing."[76]

Despite MacArthur's less-than-sterling performance, Roosevelt knew the country needed a hero more than it needed harsh truth. A Medal of Honor accompanied Roosevelt's personal order, as commander in chief, for MacArthur to leave the doomed Philippines for Australia. MacArthur's vow "I shall return" made heroic newspaper copy, and planted the seeds of future poor strategic decision making for the rest of the war. He resisted several attempts by his staff to begin the statement with "We." But the president understood what had happened. During a conversation with William Hassett of his inner staff on July 11, 1942, FDR remarked that the general "seems to have forgotten" the command laxity that permitted the destruction of MacArthur's air force on the ground despite abundant warning of Japanese attack. Given that he had had the additional warning of the Pearl Harbor attack, MacArthur's performance was far below that of the commanders in Hawaii.[77] However, only Kimmel and Short faced court-martial.

Nevertheless, the "Lion of Luzon" basked in the publicity created in the Philippines and echoed in Washington. His staff carefully focused the limelight on a single man. Of the 142 communiqués released between December 1941 and March 1942, 109 listed only one name: his.[78] In the words of Ronald Spector: "The troops on Luzon would have been defeated in any case, but without Mac-

Arthur they might have been defeated without being racked by disease and tortured by slow starvation."[79]

Toward the end of the siege, President Quezon wrote an impassioned communiqué to FDR via the War Department, recommending that the Philippines declare itself neutral and that all American forces withdraw. Quezon reasoned that the Japanese never would have landed in the Philippines if the Americans had not been there and that neutrality would spare his people further misery. He neglected the indications that Japan would have sought to annex the Philippines long before had the American army not garrisoned it.

Ike labeled the communication a "bombshell." Both he and Marshall forwarded it to the White House with great trepidation. Would Quezon make his thoughts public? How would Americans react if American soldiers were not withdrawn as they faced certain capture? Roosevelt's immediate response was "We can't do this at all." He labeled any such notion of declaring neutrality "ghastly in its responsibility and significance."[80]

America's First Pacific Countermoves

Ernest J. King, Naval Academy Class of 1901, chief of naval operations and commander in chief of the U.S. Fleet for almost all of World War II, was more responsible for the creation of American Pacific strategy than any other leader. While his personal habits left room for improvement (he was fond both of strong drink and of other men's wives), his mind was first-rate. His principal biographer, Thomas Buell, described him as "a disciple of Mahan."[81] Many of his classmates worked for the day they could captain their own ship. From the beginning, King wanted to command fleets.[82] While others saw promotion to rear admiral as the capstone of a career, King viewed it as a mere stepping-stone on the way to CNO. King read widely on military as well as naval matters. In an age that did not value joint operations, he was familiar with Napoleon and the clashes of the U.S. Civil War and fancied himself knowledgeable about war in many forms.

Gold wings of a naval aviator adorned his uniform. Many considered him the guardian of American carrier aviation. In the 1930s, he had headed the Bureau of Aeronautics and commanded Aircraft, Battle Force (commonly called Carrier Command). Many of the prominent aviation admirals served under him. Halsey was a division commander. J. H. Towers, John Hoover, and J. S. McCain all commanded carriers under King.

In a training operation that might have served as Nagumo's blueprint for December 1941, he had "successfully attacked" Pearl Harbor from the north with carrier aviation. In another fleet exercise, he moved his flag to the battleship

Idaho and the head of a battleship division and had the pleasure of "capping the T" of the enemy's battle fleet. Earlier in his career he had served aboard submarines, skippered destroyers, and commanded a replenishment ship. He first commanded a small fleet in 1931's Fleet Problem XII and commanded a major portion of the fleet in Problem XX in 1939. He was an all-around admiral and the first of his class to achieve flag rank. Prior to the war King "was the prime mover behind the development of US maritime airpower."[83] One of his daughters said her father was "one of the most even tempered men in the Navy. He was always in a rage." FDR once wrote King that he heard the CNO "shaves every morning with a blowtorch." Most felt he was the brightest of the service chiefs, and the most ornery. After the war, Admiral William Leahy, FDR's personal chief of staff, wrote, "The President had a high opinion of King's ability but also felt he was a very undiplomatic person, especially when the Admiral's low boiling point would be reached in some altercation with the British."[84] One must admire a leader like FDR who can obtain the best effort from a gifted person despite that person's significant faults.

King was very conversant with War Plan Orange. Yet his first strategic thoughts were of Australia. In a letter from the CNO to the president, King wrote:

> Australia—and New Zealand—are "white man's countries" which it is essential that we shall not allow to be overrun by Japanese because of the repercussions among the non-white races of the world.
>
> Our primary concern in the Pacific is to hold Hawaii and its approaches (via Midway) from the westward . . . Our next care in the Pacific is to preserve Australasia which requires that its communications be maintained via eastward of Samoa, Fiji and southward of New Caledonia.

In the last paragraph of the letter King reiterated:

> . . . useful lines of U.S. military endeavor in the Pacific, which may be summarized in an integrated, general plan of operations, namely:
> Hold Hawaii
> Support Australasia
> Drive northwestward from New Hebrides.[85]

King's innate aggressiveness caused him initially to give orders that scattered single-carrier task forces on dangerous raids that yielded meager results. American carriers left Pearl Harbor on January 5 and steamed southwest. They swatted at Rabaul, Kaving, and Lae but hit virtually nothing. Enemy airfields were empty. King had individual carrier groups committed to operations beyond the range of mutual support. Imagine what American dispositions against Nagumo's six-carrier fleet would have looked like in December 1941. Unsupported one-carrier task forces would have been swarmed by hundreds of planes painted with the Rising Sun and decimated.

Roosevelt had reached down the seniority list to appoint Chester A. Nimitz as commander of the Pacific Fleet after the Pearl Harbor disaster. At this stage of the war King felt Nimitz was untested.[86] However, Admiral Leahy wrote FDR that Nimitz was one of the three best admirals available. The others were Admiral Hart, the commander of the Asiatic Fleet, and King.[87]

Nimitz and his staff wanted to hold the carriers near Hawaii and look for a way to counter Japanese fleet movements. He was completely opposed to King's aggressive offensive[88] and quietly worked to curtail these high-risk/low-reward operations. Bases to the south of Honolulu weren't sufficiently developed. Because of the distances involved, two soldiers in South Pacific were the same logistic burden as three in Europe. King responded to Marshall on 2 March with a plan that initiated a step-by-step advance thru the New Hebrides, the Solomons, and the Bismarck Archipelago. This would divert the Japanese from Australia and India.

General George Marshall, the U.S. Army's chief of staff, was America's ultimate strategist. Churchill himself would later call him "the noblest Roman." That he was. His entire life is a shining example of a human placing service to country above any personal consideration. FDR elevated Marshall to chief of staff of the army in 1939 over several more senior generals. This proved the single most outstanding personnel selection of World War II.

Marshall would not be dissuaded from the strict priority given to the defeat of Germany over that of Japan and of invading western Europe as the best way of defeating Germany. Roosevelt agreed that Germany was to be defeated first. Marshall jealously guarded all military resources, lest some be diverted for secondary endeavors. For example, the army rejected a navy proposal to outpost Funafuti in the Ellice Islands to defend Samoa. Marshall didn't want even this modest endeavor to sap resources from Europe. As a strategist, Mahan would have agreed he was right. Concentrate only on the most important. Refuse any secondary priority that detracts from the main effort.

King wanted to fight the Japanese. The Pacific was the U.S. Navy's personal war. A constant tension existed between King's seeking resources for his war and Marshall's trying to maintain focus on a direct attack to defeat Germany. King's myopia on this score kept the navy from fully responding to the German submarine menace. It would take some diplomatic communication from Marshall before the severity of this threat was recognized among the highest-ranking blue jackets.

General Hap Arnold and the Army Air Forces were wedded to strategic bombing of the enemy's homeland. They saw no way of bombing Japan for many years. Summer of 1942 was time to begin concentrating four-engine bombers in England for the aerial assault on Germany. Diverting bombers to the Pacific was a misallocation of a precious resource to a secondary endeavor at the expense of the main effort.

Japan vs. Germany was a matter of national strategy that was beyond the purview of Mahan. He definitely would have approved of the approach to designate one specific objective and not divert assets to secondary objectives. We will take the split between the Pacific and the rest of the world as a given.

Looking at Pacific strategy, Mahan would have recognized the logic of Nimitz's positions. Defending Pearl Harbor and accumulating the resources required to defeat the enemy's battle fleet made sense. The downside was an eighteen-month wait until enough *Essex-* and *Independence*-class carriers joined the fleet to make a difference.

Mahan abhorred extended periods of defensive inaction. It gave the enemy too much time to cook up a decisive action at the worst possible point for the defender. The defender would have to shift his fleet reactively, ceding the initiative, exposing friendly fleet units to destruction, and forcing the survivors into a disadvantageous position for the next round.

Keeping Australia in the war was a useful national-level objective. But a passive patrol of the 5,000-mile sea lane from Honolulu to Sydney would invite a violent, concentrated Japanese strike that could generate a demoralizing American defeat. Mahan would have approved King's aggressive approach to this task. Yet he would have sought a more integrated strategy that focused on accelerating the time when the American fleet could win a decisive fight. Over the next two months, he would have observed significant movement in this direction attributed to inertia. Default instead of the crafting of a grand plan would generate results much more to Mahan's liking.

On April 16, Rear Admiral Richard Kelly Turner, then King's operation officer, presented a four-phase Pacific Ocean Campaign Plan:

1. Build up forces in South and SW Pacific to secure area and prepare for offensive.
2. Combined NZ Aus US offensive thru Solomons and New Guinea to capture Bismarck Archipelago.
3. Marshall & Carolines (ie CenPac)
4. Either Netherlands East Indies or Philippines.

Of course King approved.[89]

In the meantime, American carrier task forces carried out a series of small raids against Wake and against Japanese Mandated Islands in the central Pacific. They had little impact directly on the target islands, but the First Air Fleet left the waters around Rabaul in hot pursuit. Nagumo slowed his fleet only when U.S. news broadcasts made it apparent the raid had been completed and the American carriers were back in Hawaiian waters.

Nagumo's reaction underscores the difficulty of defending an area as enormous as the Pacific Ocean. If the enemy is willing to accept risk in order to seize the initiative, it is almost impossible to prevent him from striking some isolated base. This comes back to Mahan's notion of having very few well-guarded bases. In 1941, this meant that each should have sufficient airpower to fend off a carrier raid and enough coastal artillery to fend off night-raiding surface ships. The Marshalls raid pointed out the weakness of many Japanese central Pacific bases. The Imperial Navy reinforced their defenses. This would make many an American marine's job a lot tougher.

American newspapers, with little encouraging war news to report, understandably accepted the navy's overly optimistic reports of enemy damage. The most important result of these pinpricks was to give American carrier task forces and air crews shakedowns under real combat conditions. American training and experience levels began to move toward the high standard already attained by the Imperial Japanese Navy. The raids also increased Japanese radio traffic. American intercepts increased U.S. knowledge of Japanese encryption. In response to American raids in the Marshalls, the First Air Fleet dispatched carriers *Zuikaku* and *Shokaku* to patrol the ocean approaches to Japan. After all, the Americans might attempt the unthinkable.

Doolittle's Raid on Tokyo

With *Saratoga* rejoining the Pacific Fleet, America had five fleet carriers versus Japan's six fleet and four light carriers. In a head-to-head engagement, the Japanese retained more than a 1.5:1 superiority. Captain Mahan would have reminded the American naval leadership that the essence of the conflict was over naval airpower. Destroy the First Mobile Air Fleet and Japan's offensive capability would be at an end. The obvious strategy was to induce Japan to split its carrier fleet and then seek a decisive engagement with a single Japanese task force at favorable odds. Intelligence could provide a crucial advantage. If one combatant could identify a subsidiary operation that would require part of the enemy's fleet, he could concentrate all his forces on the subsidiary operation and gain a major strategic victory. He would do this not by defending or gaining some secondary geographic objective but by sinking enemy carriers. This process became the flywheel of American strategy for the remainder of 1942. See why Mahan was so adamant about not dividing the fleet?

FDR considered himself a navy man. Early in his career, he had been assistant secretary of the navy. During World War II he personally intervened in the selection of many flag officers. The president wanted immediate offensive action. He suggested a cruiser sweep of Japanese bases in the central Pacific.[90] Cruisers can hit anything except a battleship very hard. They are faster than and can run from battleships.

That might have done a little good—in 1925. If anyone needed proof that surface ships could not operate without air cover, he need only read the headlines about sinking of the battleship *Prince of Wales* and the battle cruiser *Repulse* on 10 December 1941. FDR, one of the most brilliant of presidents, was not a naval strategist. Admiral Ernest J. King was, and a good one at that. But America's next move belied that skill. In January 1942, King was looking for a spectacular way to swat at Japan. He knew the fleet was too weak to mete out real physical damage. The idea was to cause the Japanese military to lose face and to boost Allied morale. Tokyo was the obvious target, but Japanese defenses would not allow American carriers to get within 500 miles. Carrier-based aircraft of the day had trouble with a 200-mile round-trip strike. King's staff huddled with Arnold's staff. After some experimentation a way was found to fly modified large twin-engine B-25 bombers with a 500-mile range from American aircraft carriers. A squadron of the medium bombers under command of Lieutenant Colonel James Doolittle was assembled and began to train for carrier takeoffs. There was no way for a machine that big to land aboard a 1942 flattop.

FDR was informed at the last minute, but he heartily approved of the raid. Sixteen B-25s were hoisted aboard *Hornet*. By the middle of April, *Hornet*, escorted by *Enterprise*, four cruisers, and eight destroyers, was off the Japanese coast readying a launch. Doolittle's bombers waddled into the air while most of the task force sailors, including Halsey, held their breath. Thirteen B-25s, each carrying four 500-pound bombs, sprinkled their loads over Tokyo. Solo bombers hit Nagoya, Osaka, and Kobe. The bombs hit little of military value. Almost by accident the light carrier *Ryujo* was slightly damaged by a near miss.

The Tokyo raid was one of King's worst ideas. Instead of laying an ambush for Japanese carriers, he risked two of his four carriers in a publicity stunt. (Fletcher with *Yorktown* remained in reserve near the Phoenix Islands.) More than one authority has labeled the raid "suicidal."[91] If Mahan had been in control, he would have vehemently vetoed the operation.

When he heard of the possibility of a raid on Japan, Chiang Kai-shek attempted to dissuade FDR from authorizing it. He knew the Japanese would go crazy. Doolittle's crews were supposed to recover in China. After the B-25 raid, the Japanese in China went on a rampage, killing 250,000 Chinese.

Flying sixteen twin-engine bombers over Japan accomplished little of military value. Since Pearl Harbor and the disasters in the Far East, "many Americans began to regard the Japanese as endowed with fabulous fighting virtues and infinite military potentialities."[92] Perhaps a spectacular raid on Japan did more to deflate this myth than descendants of the victors can understand after the fact. Still, it was a great risk.

Japanese naval intelligence surmised the Americans might be planning an air strike on Japan.[93] The Japanese initiated Tactical Method No. 3 in response. As early as 8 February 1943 the Japanese were conducting countercarrier sweeps on the approach to Japan with units heavy enough to crush Halsey's task force.[94] The Fifth Carrier Division (*Shokaku* and *Zuikaku*) was dispatched to Truk to deal with the pesky Americans. For a while these ships patrolled east of Japan. A different roll of the dice and the Doolittle raid might have run into them.

What if the Japanese had caught the American raiding task force? The actual raid occurred on 18 April. Fifty percent of America's carrier force in the Pacific undertook a tremendous risk for a "feel-good" victory. If those two carriers had been lost near Japan, there could have been no American victory at Midway. How could anyone who had studied Mahan's works make such a grievous error? King's best-known biographer agrees with regard to the Doolittle raid: "King's strategy is susceptible to criticism."[95]

4
YAMAMOTO
DEFIES MAHAN

Nagumo's strike force steamed into Japanese waters from its Hawaii strike on 23 December. The Home Islands were awash in great news. On 10 December destruction of battlewagons *Prince of Wales* and *Repulse* had gutted British naval power in the Pacific. General Yamashita, "the Tiger of Malaya," was racing toward Singapore. That British bastion was doomed. Thailand had capitulated. Hong Kong would fall Christmas Day. The Japanese army had landed at several points in the Philippines and was on its way to conquering another land. Guam had been captured. After withstanding the first blow, Wake Island was now in Japanese hands. Troops landed in British Borneo.

A more knowledgeable observer would have focused on a glaring shortcoming. True, the American battleship line at Pearl had either capsized or settled into the harbor's mud. But Japan had not suppressed America's carrier task forces, her true battle fleet. The only instrument that could interfere with creation of the Greater East Asia Co-prosperity Sphere was battered, but by no means decked. Because of this failure, everything else would crumble to rust in less time than it took the paint on the new Japanese-language road signs to fade. It is exactly what Mahan would have predicted. Decisively defeat the enemy fleet and the ocean is yours. Leave him afloat and you doom yourself.

Upon its return from Pearl Harbor, the Japanese fleet acted as if it didn't know what to do next. Like a neophyte chess player, the Japanese squandered crucial moves because they could not recognize which attack to develop. The Japanese naval general staff was so ecstatic over the destruction of the American battleship line at Pearl Harbor that they were reluctant to back a return engagement to kill the carriers.[1] Mahan would have flagged this as a major and fundamental error.

Tojo himself rejected a major operation against China.[2] From personal experience, he knew assaulting this country of peasants was like hitting a sponge. Despite the force of the blow, the club left no impact when withdrawn. The navy reported that the results of Pearl Harbor would eliminate any U.S. Navy offensive capability until 1943.[3] Taking the navy at its word, the prime minister turned toward an advance on India.

Nagano remained passive. Under overall direction of Vice Admiral Shigeru Fukudome, chief of the First Bureau of the Naval General Staff, Captain Baron Sadatoshi Tomioka led the staff section working on plans. Captain Tomioka advocated invasion of Australia to eliminate the continent as a base for Allied counterattack. This became the naval general staff (NGS) contribution. For once, the army was more clear-sighted than the Imperial Japanese Navy. Their planners took one look at the troops required for this job and the logistics over a long line of communications and vetoed the idea. Instead, they felt that firm control of Papua, eastern New Guinea, would provide the air bases needed to cut the sea lanes between the United States and Australia. If that was to be the objective, officers of the naval general staff wanted to move against Noumea to the northeast. The Japanese war plan of 1938 anticipated expanding this far but not this quickly. The Australians were so sure the Japanese were coming, they withdrew their small force on Tulagi. That was exactly the intermediate island in the Solomons that the Japanese navy had targeted. Yamamoto did not have a follow-up to Pearl Harbor worked out. No chess master, or master strategist, would commit to an opening move without having subsequent attacks at the ready. This lack of follow-up operations reveals how limited Yamamoto's strategic vision was. In early January, he called his chief of staff, Rear Admiral Ugaki, and gave him the assignment of selecting what to do next. Ugaki enjoyed the reputation as an authority on strategy and a particularly effective staff officer. Many regarded him as assertive, aggressive, and very brainy. Retreating into his cabin for four days, he considered the alternatives. Should the fleet go west and invade India? Australia was a large potential base from which a counteroffensive could be mounted against Japan. Should it be invaded? Should the American fleet be pursued? No one seemed to have a cogent argument that ranked one objective over another. Captain Mahan might have wondered how so many non-strategists could have attained such high rank.

Ugaki finally reached his conclusion: "What would hurt the United States most is the loss of the fleet and of Hawaii. An attempted invasion of Hawaii and a decisive battle near there may seem a reckless plan, but its chance of success is not small. . . . The destruction of the U.S. Fleet would also mean that of the British fleet so we would be able to do anything we like. Thus it will be the shortest way to conclude the war."[4] Ugaki envisioned a multi-part operation. Three small island outposts to the northwest, west, and southwest of Hawaii would be taken. Midway, Johnston, and Palmyra islands would provide small advance airfields to support the invasion of Hawaii. More important, they should draw the American carrier fleet into decisive combat away from the resources on Oahu. From these advance bases an invasion of Hawaii would commence. With this conclusion, Ugaki handed the project over to the fleet operations officer, Captain Kameto Kuroshima. Kuroshima, brilliant but eccentric, shuddered at the thought of stranded garrisons on these distant islands. Although he had advocated another strike on Hawaii on 7 December, he was now afraid to approach the islands again. There would be no surprise attack the second time. Nor did he believe that the American fleet would sortie to defend Midway, Johnston, or Palmyra. Instead the decisive naval battle would have to be fought in Hawaiian waters. By the 27th, after gaming this alternative, he concluded that the fleet could not deal with ground-based air in Hawaii while defeating the American fleet.[5] Instead he advocated attacking what was left of the British fleet by advancing on Ceylon. That focused on a fleet, but not on the only fleet that could defeat the Japanese navy. The real threat was Halsey's carriers.

Submarine I-8 delivered an unanticipated benefit. It torpedoed *Saratoga* in the middle of January, sending that large carrier to Puget Sound for months of repairs. At least 20 percent of American carrier-based airpower was sidelined. Little concrete reinforcement arrived in Hawaii during January. Next to December 7, January was the weakest moment for the defenders of the Hawaiian Islands. This was the best time for the First Air Fleet to take on the American carriers. As of January, only 114 army and 94 navy aircraft were on hand in Hawaii.[6] It would take several months for the Americans to get anything useful organized. Although there would not be another "free kick" at Hawaii, a January or February attempt might have had a chance. Every day the Japanese fleet waited, American naval aviators got that much more experience and training, and American shipbuilders added that much more to the carriers taking shape on their ways. Time was Japan's biggest enemy. Major ground reinforcements, the 27th Infantry Division, would not arrive until March. With the arrival of that third division, the outer islands would be garrisoned. Then the "outer island option" would vanish forever. Mahan would have been curious why it took Ugaki four days to reach an obvious conclusion. Nevertheless, he did reach the right conclusion. Mahan would have been astounded that Yamamoto remained silent on the issue of the next objective for at least two months. Yamamoto and Ugaki should have known better. *Prince of Wales* and *Repulse* were sunk. Singapore's fall was imminent. The Rising Sun banner already flew over Hong Kong. British power in the Pacific was gone. Too bad (for the Japanese) that, back in July 1941, senior planners had not convinced senior leadership of the necessity of destroying U.S. fleet power.

Again staff planners concluded Japan could not defeat the American navy in Hawaiian waters. Ugaki was briefed on their conclusions on 27 January. Therefore, a two-stage operation was proposed. First, the American carrier fleet had to be destroyed. How to draw the U.S. fleet out? The fleet's solution, as Genda had concluded, was to threaten Hawaii by seizing Midway. Midway would become a valuable long-range reconnaissance base. While Japan prepared for a Hawaii invasion, patrol planes from both Midway and the Marshalls could detect any attempted American counterthrust. When the Hawaii invasion fleet was ready, those recon planes would provide critical intelligence while carriers were out of dive and torpedo bomber range of Oahu. Only unescorted B-17s could hit Midway from Oahu. Midway-based Japanese fighters could stop them. If the remnants of the American fleet sortied to deal with the problem, Japanese aircraft and fleet units could inflict further damage on the depleted Americans after losses in the decisive battle around Midway. Neither Fukudome nor Tomioka liked the idea of a Midway operation. Perhaps recognizing the difficulty in confronting Yamamoto, the vice admiral did not overtly voice his objections. Tomioka agreed with Kuroshima that Midway would become an impossible logistical problem. Nor would it be much of a base against Hawaii. Its two tiny islands were not big enough to handle the aircraft that would be needed for an invasion: Sand Island is but 850 acres and Eastern Island 328 acres. The Japanese army didn't like Midway either. Army officers suspected the operation would lead to a requirement for army forces to invade Hawaii, to the detriment of the China campaign. They feared the risks and saw little to gain if Midway was captured. At the same time, Naval General Staff (NGS) planners worried that once

Midway was in Japanese hands there would be insufficient shipping to maintain a significant number of planes there.

The naval general staff agreed that destruction of the U.S. fleet was the key to victory. But they thought the Americans would not risk carriers at Midway. The stakes weren't high enough. They could stand back and take on the Japanese fleet with the aid of land-based air from Oahu if the Japanese fleet attempted to move into Hawaiian waters. Every day of delay made that outcome more likely. Replacing the planes and aircrews of the First Air Fleet was a major problem. There were no reserves, no training pipeline. This in itself was reason enough to suspend use of naval air south and east of Rabaul. The NGS felt the constraint of logistics. There wasn't enough shipping to go around. Instead they wanted to go to New Caledonia. Expansion to a line between New Caledonia, Fiji, and Samoa had been part of the 1938 Japanese Basic War Plan.[7] Australia would scream for American naval support. This, in the opinion of the NGS, was more likely to draw out the American carriers. Adherents of Clausewitz would have understood the argument. The carriers were *the* center of gravity. Yamamoto sent his staff officers to argue with the naval general staff. Heated exchanges went on for quite some time. One of Yamamoto's representatives indicated that the fleet commander might resign if his views about Midway did not prevail. As with the planning for the Pearl Harbor raid, a Yamamoto threat became the deciding factor. Captain Mahan would have admired Yamamoto's moral courage, but not his delayed response.

Japanese leadership was well-informed about the American naval building plan. It was extensively covered in the American press that was routinely monitored by Japanese embassies in South America. A repatriated Japanese naval attaché, Commander Sanematsu, routinely lectured about his visit to American shipyards in 1940 and 1941. As Yamamoto stated, "The real battle is now a competition between Japanese discipline and American scientific technology."[8] Yet most Japanese decision makers either derided or disregarded this gathering threat. The common bias among many Japanese about their own racial superiority made handicapping this question a non-issue. Complacency settled in among the general staffs, a complacency that would prove deadly. Not so with Yamamoto. He retained his burning desire to bring the existing American carrier fleet to decisive battle and to crush it—a goal Mahan would obviously have approved.

Noted for his lack of punctuality, Kuroshima delayed, looking for an alternative. He focused on one of Ugaki's initial four options, the Indian Ocean.[9] That is how the Japanese navy began wasting precious months going off in the wrong direction. One might have thought an offensive into the Indian Ocean would have been quickly decided on. However, Ugaki resisted the idea. He wanted a precise definition of the operation's objective. Mahan would have agreed. Ultimately two were listed: destruction of the British fleet and capture of "strategic points." That might sound right. But what exactly were "strategic points"? Strategic for what end? Readers of strategic plans must be very wary of such high-sounding phrases that are devoid of any concrete meaning. Ugaki's request was an indirect method of underscoring the fact that there was no tangible reason for attacking into the Indian Ocean. The remaining British fleet was no threat to Japan or its ambitions in the South Seas. If the army couldn't handle Australia and its 9 million inhabitants, what would it do with hundreds of millions of Indians? India contained no oil, no food surplus. Why go off on a useless endeavor while leaving the prime business unfinished? Details of the Axis treaty between Germany and Japan were concluded on 19 January. Initially, it was thought a German-Japanese linkup across the Indian Ocean might be achieved. What real difference would that have made? Ugaki was very disappointed when he read the treaty's text. No joint operation was envisioned. There was no way the Japanese fleet could sail all the way to Suez on its own. Meanwhile, the navy wanted army troops to invade Ceylon. The army's answer was no. Nevertheless, the Indian operation was approved on or about 13 February. Tojo was convinced that Indians would revolt against their white masters if given encouragement. The Combined Fleet wanted to take the offensive, even though it couldn't correctly identify what to hit. It had taken more than a month to produce a defective follow-on plan. Nimitz had had time to take up his duties, strengthen his defenses, and increase the number of American ships and planes in the Pacific.

The Imperial Navy declined to force the American carriers into combat and instead embarked on a tour of the north Australian coast followed by an Indian Ocean cruise. It was a case of avoiding the difficult by engaging in the inconsequential. That must rank as one of the worst of strategic failures. Japan had embraced a high-risk strategy—war with America. For the Japanese navy to shy away from the only course that could vanquish America, while giving America additional undisturbed time to marshal her strength, was the height of folly. If Nagano and Yamamoto had been first-rank strategists, they would never have allowed such serious error. Yamamoto knew what the right answer was but did not press for its adoption. As a result, the Midway operation was delayed until June. Had it been undertaken in late January, the Americans, still in shock after Pearl Harbor, with less experienced crews and with King prone to undertake risky, small-scale attacks, would have put up a less effective defense. And all six of Nagumo's fleet carriers would have been available for the decisive fight. Instead, the First Air Fleet left Hiroshima Bay on 20 January headed for the South Seas. Despite the army's wishes, the navy decided to raid Australia anyway. During

February four of Nagumo's carriers made a militarily useless raid on Darwin, Australia. Fuchida observed that the fast carriers were not needed to complete the South Seas conquests. Nagumo's carriers were cast in "an unneeded and unworthy supporting role."[10] However, the political impact was huge. Fearing invasion, Australia recalled her troops from North Africa. None of these attacks accomplished anything of strategic significance for the Japanese cause.

After carrier planes bombed Darwin, the navy readied for the next task: send the six fleet carriers to sweep the Indian Ocean. Most of this operation was conducted during the first half of April. Tactically, it was a success. Japanese ships bombarded naval installations south of Calcutta on 6 April and raided Ceylon on the 9th. During the Indian Ocean operation the British carrier *Hermes,* two heavy cruisers, and a destroyer were sunk. Only seventeen Japanese aircraft were lost. But it was a strategic empty. With the loss of Singapore and the desperate fight against the Germans, Great Britain couldn't threaten Japanese hegemony in the South Seas. There was no reason to enter the Indian Ocean as long as the primary threat, the American carriers, remained at large. It was very clear that even a fleet-size raid had no chance of creating a significant linkup with Nazi forces pressing into Egypt. During the first quarter of 1942, Japan conquered more territory at less cost than any other nation-state in history. Elements of the First Area Army conquered Malaya and Borneo and backed the Americans into the Bataan Peninsula. Squadrons of Japanese cruisers and destroyers spearheaded the seaward advance. They brushed aside the combined American-British-Dutch-Australian (ABDA) task force that had been hastily assembled to defend the South Seas. The prized oil fields were seized before the end of February. There were many acts of heroism on both sides that cannot be touched on here. Disgustingly, there were also far too many acts of Japanese barbarism.

During those advances Japanese forces took territory in bites of 250–400 miles. Seldom did they advance beyond the range of available land-based air-power. "Leapfrogging" was an obvious solution to the vast expanses in the Pacific. MacArthur didn't invent it.

Strategic planning was supposedly the domain of the Japanese naval general staff. Now the NGS staffers looked to reassert themselves against Yamamoto and his crew. Only three months into the war, NGS thinking had turned defensive. Instead forcing the American fleet to fight on Japanese terms, they looked at three possible routes over which the Americans might advance. This drove Ugaki to distraction. He wanted the Japanese to stay on the offensive and retain the initiative.[11]

Although they were on the NGS list of possible routes of advance, the Aleutians really weren't a possibility. Anyone who has lived in that atrocious, foggy weather can tell you why. Second was the central Pacific via the Marshalls. This was the route of the secret American War Plan Orange. With Japan's battle fleet intact and its carrier fleet darting among Japanese-held islands, the central Pacific route was far too hard for the Americans to even contemplate. The third route began in Australia and came up the islands of the South Pacific. NGS thought this route was the most dangerous as it was most likely to see action.[12] To thwart an Allied advance from the South Pacific, Captain Tomioka wanted to conduct limited offensive operations against Fiji and Samoa in order to sever Australia from America. He thought a decisive fleet engagement could be forced there.

As a group NGS believed in the paramount importance of decisive naval combat. They closed their arguments with a statement that operations in the South Pacific would bring forth the American navy. Tomioka worried there were not sufficient aircraft to return the First Air Fleet to full strength. From the beginning of the war, Japanese leaders worried about this shortcoming, which would ultimately prove fatal. It was a primary reason why the NGS did not want to challenge the American navy around its home turf of Hawaii.

During this period of confusion over objectives Yamamoto said, "In the final analysis the success or failure of our entire strategy in the Pacific will be determined by whether or not we succeed in destroying the United States fleet, more particularly its carrier task forces."[13] Mahan could not have framed it better. The Japanese admiral continued: "By launching the proposed operation against Midway, we can succeed in drawing out the enemy's carrier strength and destroying it in decisive battle." Echo of the master. There was no confusion between geographical conquest and the true operational objective like at the naval general staff.

While the general staffs of the Japanese army and the Japanese navy were arguing Australia vs. South Pacific, Doolittle's B-25s embarrassed everyone by striking at Tokyo, the seat of the emperor! These impudent Americans needed to be put in their place. Even the army swung around to support Yamamoto's Midway operation. A reinforced army regiment was offered as the invasion force. However, the naval general staff still wanted to prosecute its South Pacific operation before Yamamoto struck at Midway. Yamamoto had to live within the constraints of the organization that contained him. The army general staff wanted carrier support for its offensive toward New Guinea and Fiji/Samoa.

Battle of the Coral Sea

In the Central Pacific, Truk was to be the defensive bastion (see Map 1a). Actually the Home Islands were almost as close to Hawaii as to this base in the Caroline Islands. But a fleet based in Truk was in a far better position to parry an American counterthrust regardless of which latitude the American fleet chose to sail on.

At first, Japanese plans did not include a major base at Rabaul. Vice Admiral Shigeyoshi Inoue pointed to the small but developable Australian base there. If the Americans built upon it, they would outflank Truk.[14] B-17s would be only 700 miles from the fleet bastion and thus able to pound it. Rabaul also added to the outer arc extending through Guam, Wake, and Makin in the Gilberts. Inoue especially wanted the larger airbase at Port Moresby because B-17s flying from there could, in turn, paste Rabaul. Ironically, Inoue, previously chief of the Naval Aeronautics Bureau, had been banished to the Fourth Fleet for his radical emphasis of naval air power over the gun club. He also wanted to take Tulagi, in the Solomons near Guadalcanal. The Japanese recognized before the war that the line—Port Moresby, Tulagi, Rabaul—was an alternative to the central Pacific approach to Japan. A Japanese invasion force kicked out the handful of Australian defenders holding Rabaul. As the official U.S. Army historian, Louis Morton, stated, "The fall of Rabaul alarmed the Australians as nothing else had."[15] This, along with the air strike on Darwin, convinced Canberra that invasion was imminent. American code breakers had intercepted and reported Japanese plans for the capture of Rabaul. This success significantly enhanced their credibility. Beginning in January, Halsey had Japanese-speaking radio-intercept specialists attached to his staff. He was the first task force commander to do so. Others quickly followed suit. Now that Rabaul was firmly in Japanese hands, it needed its own outpost to protect it. The Japanese army nominated Tulagi. Conceived in January, the initial operation to secure New Guinea had been scheduled to be completed in March. Vice Admiral Inoue's Fourth Fleet became the invasion force headed toward Port Moresby on the south coast of New Guinea. The light carrier *Hosho* with twenty-one embarked aircraft sailed as part of the invasion fleet's covering force. Admiral Inoue was considered one of the most unflappable admirals in the fleet. After Pearl Harbor, Nimitz, at King's urging, sent carrier groups to raid Japanese possessions in the Marshalls and Carolines. In early February, Vice Admiral Wilson Brown, with *Lexington,* was dispatched to hit Rabaul. Approaching New Britain, he ran into a lot of air opposition. While his combat air patrol (CAP, a defensive umbrella of fighters over the fleet) did a good job against unescorted bombers, he radioed Pearl Harbor that Rabaul had developed into something larger than a single carrier should take on. Nimitz dispatched Rear Admiral Frank "Jack" Fletcher in *Yorktown* to assist.

In the meantime the Japanese army began its conquest of Papua, eastern New Guinea, by landing at Lae and Huron. In response Admiral Brown sailed in *Lex-*

ington to intercept. Two days after the Japanese landing, American carrier aircraft hit the landing force. They sank two transports and two other craft and damaged nine vessels, including a light cruiser. The Japanese were shocked at the rapidity and lethality of the response. Admiral Inoue concluded he needed additional carrier support to complete his assignment. The naval general staff surmised that New Caledonia was far more important a target than Midway.[16]

Yamamoto was completely focused on Midway. However, he recognized he had to support the New Guinea operation in the meantime. Carrier Division 5, *Shokaku* and *Zuikaku,* was withdrawn from Midway preparations and directed to the South Seas. *Lexington* and *Yorktown* were still down in the Coral Sea. Yamamoto continued to look at Coral Sea developments as a diversion from his preparations for Midway.[17] By the first of May, Japanese naval intelligence estimated that four American carriers were available to fight in the decisive battle. All six Japanese fleet carriers would be required to achieve the desired 1.5:1 superiority. Yamamoto had to keep this simple relationship working for him. Before the *Essex* carriers arrived in strength he had to use his temporary superiority to destroy the American fleet in being and threaten the Americans sufficiently to bring them to the negotiating table. Yamamoto had the knockout instrument in his hands. This was no time to gamble on cheap shots. "Let's think for a minute," Mahan might have suggested to Yamamoto. Two American carriers had supported Doolittle's raid on Tokyo. Maybe the remaining carrier or two down in the Coral Sea could be isolated from their two raiding sisters! What an incredible opportunity! The real target is not Midway. It's the destruction of American carrier strength. Send all six big carriers and sink both of the American ones in the Coral Sea. The remaining two American flattops at Pearl Harbor had little chance, if any, in a second round at Midway. Yamamoto might have maneuvered his fleet into two engagements, first a big fight in the Coral Sea and then a second one at Midway. The odds in his favor would have been overwhelming. The American fleet wouldn't have stood a chance. In two decisive battles, not one, Yamamoto would have stood as the sole arbitrator of the Pacific. Unsupported New Caledonia would have fallen like an overripe coconut. Had he responded to the opportunity, Yamamoto could have achieved the objectives of the army and the NGS as well as his own, and forced the most forward American forces back to Hawaii. Most important, he could have sunk most or all of the American carriers in the Pacific by taking advantage of their separation into pairs. See how much the Doolittle raid might have cost?

Even with only *Shokaku* and *Zuikaku,* Coral Sea should have been a slaughter of American sea power, especially when Japanese carriers first rounded the Solomons and caught the Americans from an unexpected direction. Half the reason for the Midway operation might have been eliminated far from any American support. Subsequent operations should have been completely success-ful even if the Midway or other follow-on operation lagged a couple of weeks. Because of the American entrance into the Coral Sea, the correct response was to revert to the NGS solution: take Fiji and Samoa. Maybe the Americans would come out again. If not it would be on to Johnston Island and Hawaii.

Initial Japanese objectives for the Coral Sea operation were Port Moresby on the southern shore of New Guinea and Tulagi in the Solomons just north of Guadalcanal. Japanese air and sea units at Port Moresby could dominate north-ern and western Australia. Tulagi became an outpost for Rabaul and would pro-vide a stepping-stone to Fiji or Samoa. Bases there would cut the shipping lanes between Australia and the United States. With Australia isolated, Japanese lead-ers hoped America would punch itself out in battles along Japan's defensive perimeter and ultimately negotiate a peace. To achieve this, the Japanese devised a characteristically complex plan. Separate invasion forces were aimed at each objective. The New Guinea force would be covered by a force comprising the light carrier *Shoho*, four cruisers, and a destroyer. It would sail from Rabaul through the Coral Sea to Port Moresby. Carrier Division 5, detached from First Air Fleet and commanded by Vice Admiral Takeo Takagi, comprised two fleet carriers, two heavy cruisers, and six destroyers. It would swing east of the Sol-omons and enter the Coral Sea south of the Santa Cruz Islands. The two groups, including carriers, would not be in range to provide mutual support. As Admiral Morison stated: "This complex Japanese plan illustrates a fundamental defect in Japanese naval strategy. Whenever the Japanese planners disposed of sufficient strength, they divided forces and drafted an elaborate plan, the successful execu-tion of which required a tactical competence rare at any time in any Navy as well as the enemy's passive acceptance of the role he was expected to play."[18]

Time after time, we will see the Japanese repeat this mistake. We will observe Nimitz repeatedly taking advantage of the opportunities presented. Radio intel-ligence gave both sides the ability to obtain almost instantaneous tabs on the movement of enemy fleets. Traffic analysis and partial understanding of Ameri-can radio procedures allowed the Japanese to see faint shapes moving out in the fog of war. The breaking of Japanese codes allowed the Americans to read the hull numbers of Japanese ships at sea. This was a technical development that augmented some of Mahan's principles. Now a commander could be even less concerned with leaving his base of operations to go hunting with the majority of his force. There was even less reason to divide the fleet. Lieutenant Commander Joseph J. Rochefort headed the critical signals decryption shop under Admiral Nimitz at Pearl Harbor. He and his decoders provided ample warning of the

Japanese attack on Port Moresby. The Japanese presented Nimitz with the most inviting target of all. Despite what should have been a decisive edge in combat power, the IJN advanced a unit just large enough for the Americans to bite off. American intelligence knew that most of the Combined Fleet was in Japan after operations in Ceylon.[19] The Americans could move the two big fleet carriers, *Lexington* and *Yorktown,* to oppose *Shokaku* and *Zuikaku.* The plane counts (including the light carrier *Shoho*) gave the Japanese only a slight advantage. Yamamoto could exceed 1.5 to 1 any time he wanted to *if* he concentrated on one task. Therefore, 1 to 1 was an incredible opportunity for the Americans. Nimitz seized it without hesitation.

Coral Sea demonstrates both the decisive advantage undetected intelligence breakthroughs give and which fleet commander better understood Mahan. MacArthur felt that the Japanese occupation of Port Moresby would completely unhinge his contemplated southwest Pacific strategy. Nimitz considered the Port Moresby invasion a major threat—and an opportunity. He considered committing the battleship squadron that had assembled at San Francisco as the final line of naval defense for the West Coast to the upcoming fight. Battleships can track down enemy ships wounded by carrier strikes and send them to the bottom. Lack of tankers nixed the idea. By 1944, the American navy amassed a fleet train that was the logistical marvel of the Pacific. At the time of Pearl Harbor, the Pacific Fleet had but eleven tankers. Only four were rigged for refueling ships at sea.[20] This paltry refueling capability couldn't simultaneously support fast-carrier operations and the battleships.

Rochefort gave Nimitz ample time to position Fletcher's force where it could do most good. Nimitz's orders to Fletcher were to do as much damage as possible to the Japanese fleet. Halsey and his two carriers arrived back from the Tokyo raid about the time Fletcher departed. It would take *Enterprise* and *Hornet* at least five days to prepare to depart. *Hornet* would have to re-embark its carrier aircraft. Imagine the drubbing Carrier Division 5 would have taken if Halsey had been ready to go instead of fooling around transporting army B-25s! Sideshows frequently have great opportunity costs. Halsey's task force did depart for the Coral Sea but arrived too late to join the battle. They were approaching the Coral Sea when the carrier battle erupted.

Right after the Tulagi invasion force landed, American naval aircraft hit them. This confirmed to the Japanese that American carriers were present. Although American aim was poor, enough damage was done to cause the Japanese shipping around Tulagi to withdraw. Fletcher moved northeast to intercept the Japanese Port Moresby invasion force. As both planned and predicted, *Shokaku* and *Zuikaku* rounded the end of the Solomons and moved west into the Coral

Sea. They sailed southwest of Fletcher while the Americans looked for invaders from the north. Despite good American intelligence, the Japanese had emplaced their trap. Fletcher went for the vanguard warships of the invasion force. Fortunately a pilot spotted the light carrier *Shoho*. American strikers smothered the light ship, sending it to Davy Jones. This left *Shokaku* and *Zuikaku* primed to devastate the Americans with an unanswered first strike between large carriers. But an erroneous intelligence report caused Admiral Takagi to blunder. A recon plane misidentified an oiler and its attending destroyer as a carrier and cruiser. Takagi launched everything he had, sinking the tanker. Fletcher would have another chance. He readied a second strike but didn't know where *Zuikaku* and *Shokaku* were. Takagi did launch a second time. Instead of finding the American carriers, his strikers ran into American Wildcats vectored toward the Japanese by radar. Nine Japanese aircraft splashed into the sea. Additional aircraft were lost in the night landings that followed. Next morning *Lexington* and *Yorktown* faced *Shokaku* and *Zuikaku* in a straight carrier duel. The plane count was 122 to 121. Takagi's task force had the benefit of hiding in some squalls along a weak weather front. Fletcher had blue sky above him. In the first 1-to-1 carrier battle, the Americans came off second best. American Wildcat fighters and Devastator torpedo bombers were decidedly inferior to their Japanese counterparts. But that would be the same at Midway. Pilot for pilot, the Japanese were better trained. *Shokaku* was hit hard but survived the engagement. *Zuikaku* remained operational but had only half her aircraft complement remaining.

Fletcher's carriers got the worst of the exchange. *Lexington* sank and *Yorktown* took serious damage. Fletcher chose to withdraw. Nimitz agreed. Back at Rabaul, Admiral Inoue reached the same conclusion. Both *Shokaku* and *Zuikaku*, along with their escorts, also withdrew. The two big fleet carriers would be out of the war for many months. They would not be able to sail for Midway. With all friendly carriers leaving the area, the Port Moresby invasion force also returned toward base. Some might argue that the Japanese had scored a tactical victory because they inflicted greater damage. This measurement is irrelevant. At the operational level, the Americans achieved their objective while the Japanese did not. Port Moresby would never again be threatened with invasion.

At Coral Sea, it appeared to the Japanese that the American carriers were right where they wanted them. Both sides committed serious mistakes. Fletcher had a better reputation as a man than as an admiral.[21]

Takagi had not ordered a general search pattern for two days. At one time Carrier Division 5 sailed within sixty-five miles of Fletcher's carriers. The Americans were refueling in bright sunlight. A full-scale strike from *Shokaku* and *Zuikaku* easily might have sunk *Yorktown* as well as *Lexington*. Such is luck and the critical nature of tactical intelligence in naval engagements. A theater commander cannot correct the tactical mistakes of the units doing the fighting. The larger the margin of force he provides his tactical commanders, the greater the insurance he purchases against blunders. The seemingly innocuous decision to divert *Shokaku* and *Zuikaku* southward didn't seem like such a large price to pay. After all, they were scheduled to return before the Midway operation, the decisive battle, was to commence. The actual result: *Zuikaku* was too battered to depart for Midway. *Shokaku*'s pilot group was so depleted it didn't have enough strength to rejoin the fleet. Even if replacements had been available, only a week remained before it was to sail toward Midway. Five months into the conflict, the Japanese navy had suffered far fewer casualties than expected. But the Japanese navy was running out of pilots. Due to stringent training and selection regimens, the navy had been able to produce only 3,500 first-line pilots. Some officers felt 15,000 were needed.[22] At the beginning of the war Ugaki identified this as a major worry. Some officers recommended rotating some of the most experienced pilots into instructor billets. But the navy's "crack man" policy kept the best with the fleet.[23] Little was done to expand the pilot pool. From June 1942 onwards Japan would be running short of pilots. Slowly it would occur to the Americans that the pilot count rather than the carrier count might be Japan's greatest weakness. Shooting up the available pool of pilots might be easier than sinking ten ships.

Minor differences in tactical dispositions during the Coral Sea engagement could have yielded quite different results. Naval engagements are a risky and uncertain business. Nimitz was right at taking a crack at the Japanese. By eliminating unnecessary carrier operations elsewhere, either side might have committed additional forces that could have turned Coral Sea into a decisive engagement. If Coral Sea had resulted in both sides losing two fleet carriers before Midway, then the advantage would inure to the Japanese. The Japanese would have emerged with four carriers, the Americans with two, raising the Japanese advantage from 1.5:1 to 2:1. The addition of *Junyo* and *Hiyo* would have made the odds even more lopsided. Yamamoto thought two American carriers had been sunk or massively damaged at the battle of the Coral Sea. *Yorktown* limped into Pearl Harbor. Incredible effort by those machine shops and port facilities at Pearl that Nagumo had left virtually untouched transformed the damaged *Yorktown* into a ship capable of operating with Nimitz's other fleet carriers. Halsey's undamaged carriers needed five days at Pearl to prepare for further action. The yardsmen at Pearl repaired *Yorktown* and got her under way in forty-eight hours. Instead of 4:2 the ratio would be 4:3 at Midway. In terms of embarked aircraft, the odds were almost even.

What an incredible difference a single carrier makes. What if Carrier Division 5 had caught *Yorktown* in its first strike instead of a tanker? These reversals due to luck and uncontrollable events reduce even iron admirals to a puddle of slag. There are no words that can communicate the psychological burden admirals in the Great Pacific War faced. If we could experience that weight for only a few minutes, the actions of Nomura, Inoue, and Fletcher might make a lot more sense. One has to admire the steel courage in men like Halsey and Nimitz to unabashedly tear into situations where a small change in luck could have led to disaster.

After shuffling Carrier Division 5 around, the Combined Fleet decided to cancel further efforts to take Port Moresby. So why were *Shokaku* and *Zuikaku* placed at risk in the first place? Never, *never* divide the fleet.

Yamamoto's Midway Plan

Yamamoto's staff began serious preparations for the Midway campaign at the end of March. A month later their operational plan was complete. Much of it was the work of Captain Kuroshima. Before the war Kuroshima had authored a manual on how battleships would fight the decisive engagement. The Midway plan was submitted to Admiral Nagano. He promptly accepted his staff's work and secured an imperial rescript approving the operation.

Yamamoto still made no immediate provision for the invasion of Hawaii. After Midway his carriers would swing into Truk. Then a concentrated First Mobile Fleet would lead the attack on Fiji and Samoa. If all went well, Sydney and Melbourne on the Australian coast might be raided. The earliest an invasion of Hawaii could be scheduled was August.[24] Captain Mahan would have been appalled at this failure of forward planning. Again, it's the enemy fleet, not some geography, that is critical.

Yamamoto knew the clock was running out with every piece of steel riveted to complete the American building plan. He confided to his subordinates that he intended to ask the political authorities to open peace discussions with the Americans at the end of a successful Midway operation. Perhaps a real threat to Hawaii and the West Coast denuded of carriers would cause the Yankees to reassess their position. However, no advance from Midway to Hawaii was authorized.

The Japanese called it "Victory Disease." The South Seas conquest, Pearl Harbor, the Indian Ocean had all been too easy. Japan had expected to lose between 10 and 30 percent of its ships during the expansion phase.[25] Instead it had lost nothing larger than a destroyer. Perhaps Yamamoto's fever had risen a little as well.

Striving to achieve 1.5:1 superiority is one way is one way to approach the problem. Then again, life is full of rude awakenings. What if the enemy has a secret weapon—like Ultra code breaking? Or he comes up with strength uncounted by your intelligence—like medium bombers flying from carriers? Admiral Raymond Spruance, commander of TF1 at Midway and one of the best fleet commanders of the war, reminds us all: "I am more than ever impressed with the part that good or bad fortune sometimes plays in tactical engagements."[26] Yamamoto's upcoming battle was bet-your-country time. There was no reason not to amass as much strength as possible against the American battle fleet.

With the delivery of fleet carrier *Junyo* and the loss of light carrier *Shoho,* the Japanese fleet contained seven fleet and three light carriers. Before Coral Sea, the Americans had but three full-size carriers plus the *Hornet* in the Pacific. Carrier superiority led Yamamoto to conclude that he could take a swipe at Alaska as well as Midway. Perhaps he thought the combination of threats would make the Americans more likely to parley for a negotiated peace.

The grouping Yamamoto split off from his main fleet to attack the Aleutians was designated the Northern Area Force. Among its subgroupings, which included Carrier Division 2, were found carriers *Junyo* and *Ryujo* with 90 embarked aircraft, 3 heavy cruisers, a light cruiser, 14 destroyers, and several transports. It conducted an air strike against the main American Aleutian base at Dutch Harbor on 3 June, the day before the battle of Midway commenced. Yamamoto's intent was to draw off the U.S. Navy with this large diversionary force. With excellent intelligence from Rochefort's code breakers, the Americans were not fooled for a minute.

The Japanese Combined Fleet staff viewed the Alaskan operation as securing the "main effort" against attacks from the north. Some officers worried about bomber attacks from the Aleutians on the Home Islands. Who might have threatened the Combined Fleet from the north in the spring of 1942? Frosty the Snowman?

Despite his appreciation for carrier striking power, Yamamoto created a further subdivision of the fleet destined for Midway. Instead of moving the forces of the battle fleet assigned to the Midway operation en masse, he ordered Nagumo's lightly screened First Air Fleet to precede the main body of battleships by 300 miles. This put the two units out of range for mutual support. Aircraft couldn't make a round-trip between the two and the battleships would need 15 hours to close up on a circling carrier force in need of protective fire power. A better anti-aircraft screen for the carriers might have made a difference, even though battleship anti-air armament was a fraction of what it would be later in the war. Battleships were not as fast as the fleet carriers—a factor that can cause problems in task force maneuvers. But adding additional cruisers to Nagumo's screen would not have been a problem. One must repeat Morison's observation about Japanese organization for Coral Sea: the Japanese excessively subdivided their fleet and wrote overly complex plans. Yamamoto had available 8 carriers, 11 battleships, 22 cruisers, 65 destroyers, and 21 subs. The invasion force embarked in a dozen transports and contained 5,000 troops—half army, half navy. Two light carriers were assigned escort duty away from the First Air Fleet: little *Hosho*'s 8 aircraft patrolled over the main body of battleships, and *Zuiho*, with 24 aircraft, accompanied the invasion force, Second Fleet. Neither light carrier would have tipped the balance at Midway. Despite the unavailability of Carrier Division 5— *Shokaku* and *Zuikaku* had been badly damaged at Coral Sea—Combined Fleet officers remained confident of their plan.

Japanese intelligence raised its estimate of America's Pacific carrier strength. Assuming that two American carriers had been lost in the Coral Sea, the middle estimate was three fleet carriers and as many as three light carriers. Of course three fleet carriers actually opposed the Japanese at Midway. A thinking admiral carefully weighs the options whenever a 1:1 fight seems possible. If the two carriers headed for Alaska had instead joined the First Air Fleet, 90 aircraft would have been added to First Air Fleet's 198. The ratio of naval aircraft might improve to 1.4 to one. Six flight decks instead of four would have meant faster strike launches and more alternatives for returning aircraft. The difference might have been decisive. Good strategy forces one to eliminate the "would be nice" tasks from the most essential. One can hear Mahan arguing to leave Second Carrier Striking Force's parkas ashore and instead sending them the orders initially meant for Carrier Division 5. Japanese radio intelligence indicated that a two-carrier American task force might be operating east of the Solomons. A patrol plane confirmed that two carriers were out there. Intelligence officers guessed they might be *Enterprise* and *Hornet*. They were right: these were the ships from the Doolittle raid making their unsuccessful attempt to reach the Coral Sea fight. Yamamoto feared that the Americans might not come to the Midway party at all.[27] Then the naval general staff would be proven right. According to the plan, the First Air Fleet would strike Midway the day before the landings. A seaplane tender group would set up operations at a tiny island about 60 miles away. It operated 24 Zero float-planes and 8 float-scouts. Japanese planners expected to invade and secure Midway before the American fleet sortied in response. The main Japanese force was to remain 600 miles northwest of Midway so that if American aircraft flying over Midway provided early warning, the Japanese fleet remained out of striking range even of land-based bombers. Japanese long-range aircraft were to move to Midway from staging fields in the central Pacific. Even with only four carriers, a layered Japanese land-and-sea-based air defense would probably have prevented the American miracle that was about to happen. Nagumo's force was to position itself 300 miles east of the main body (First Fleet). Lesser task forces had assigned positions in the southward-facing formation. Submarines were to patrol along three cordon lines between Midway and Kauai to detect and report the movements of the American fleet. Yamamoto anticipated that his first strikes would be made by the carriers and submarines. The battleships of his main body would come up to finish the kill. If the entire American fleet sortied, Yamamoto had a contingency plan: to bring in the force currently in Alaskan waters for reinforcement. The Combined Fleet was to remain in position for up to a week awaiting the Americans.[28] At least this parameter was set beforehand, unlike the Pearl Harbor operation. During the trans-Pacific crossing, radio intelligence specialists aboard the flagship *Yamato* intercepted a transmission from an American submarine directly in front of the invasion group. Intelligence officers could not read the contents of American code but they recognized the marker for "Urgent." In addition, submarine I-168 reported increased activity on Midway. Yamamoto's staff surmised that the Japanese fleet had been spotted. This was five days before the Midway operation would commence—enough time for American vessels at Pearl Harbor to raise steam and transit the 1,100 miles to Midway ahead of the Japanese. But Yamamoto's staff officers showed little concern. They expected that the Americans had already guessed what the Combined Fleet was up to and had already sailed for Midway—a smug assumption, but it was correct. The American fleet had passed the Japanese patrol areas before the submarines were in place. Continued American radio traffic reinforced existing thinking aboard the Japanese flagship.

This change in assumed position of the American force altered the assumed timing of the American fleet's sortie. Instead of arriving after Midway had been secured, Yamamoto and his staff now estimated the Americans would enter the waters around the island before Nagumo. In an incredible leap of faith, they assumed Nagumo's carrier force had intercepted the same American transmission and similarly altered their operational assumptions. What an unbelievable mistake! Yamamoto's staff officers knew Nagumo's carrier fleet did not have good quality intercept electronics. It had been a staff discussion item before the fleet sailed. Yamamoto's chief of staff, aware of the weakness in radio equipment, had pleaded with Yamamoto's staff to rebroadcast intelligence that came in. This wasn't done. Even if Nagumo's intercept officers had picked up the American transmission, was it wise to assume that Nagumo's staff would interpret the transmission in the same way? Yamamoto assumed that the Americans had discovered the transport force, which contained transports and invasion ships. If the Americans already had that much information, why not break the radio silence of the battleship force and ensure that the carrier fleet and the main force both understood that there had been a change in assumption about the likely location of the American fleet? Yamamoto's approach toward Midway is an excellent example of the potential threat of electronic intelligence disorganizing an enemy that has been intimidated into not using his radios.

On the first of June, the Japanese main body had difficulty locating its refueling tankers. Curiously, radios were used to establish contact. Fleet staff officers surmised the Americans must now know the location of the main body if they hadn't figured it out before, so why not? Low-power radios were used instead of the high power needed to reach the more distant Nagumo. American electronic warriors did not pick up the broadcasts. The reasoning of Yamamoto's staff is curious, to say the least. Was refueling battleships more important than informing carriers that the risk of active enemy carriers had increased substantially? The number of American radio transmissions intercepted by the Japanese rose dramatically; 72 of 180 intercepts that day carried the "Urgent" marker.

Yamamoto knew he faced an alerted enemy. The Japanese armada contained many times the surface combat power of its American counterpart. What was left of the American battleship fleet was still based in San Francisco. However, American and Japanese naval aircraft strength was approximately equal. Yamamoto knew that this was the comparison that mattered. Despite these developments, he made no adjustments to his dispositions. His four carriers were screened by only two battleships, two cruisers, and a handful of destroyers. Yamamoto led with this fragile force. Nagumo's staff had pointed out this weakness before the operation commenced and recommended that battleship *Yamato* sail with the First Air Fleet and that Yamamoto assume tactical command.[29] That would have been a nice way of solving the command problem without upsetting the rest of the navy. This, too, had been pointed out to Yamamoto before the operation sailed.

Compare this Japanese inability to adapt to changing circumstances with Nimitz's response to the threat in the Coral Sea.

Nimitz's Countermoves

Today no sailors occupy the tiny islets of Midway. In the 1990s, after cleaning up aircraft fuel and oil spills, the U.S. Navy abandoned the now unimportant atoll to the gooney birds. But in May 1942 hardly another aircraft or gun could have been crammed into any of the 1,200 acres of dry ground at Midway.

Admiral Nimitz, commander, Pacific Ocean Area, was in a hole. Rochefort, his signals intercept officer, told him Yamamoto was sailing his 200-ship fleet to tiny Midway. Admiral King agreed with his staff that Yamamoto planned to trap and destroy a large portion of the American fleet.[30] King's intelligence staff thought Rochefort was being tricked by a ruse. Many on King's staff thought the Japanese would appear somewhere in the South Pacific. The prudent bet was to remain in Hawaiian waters and await the real enemy attack. One could not have faulted an American Pacific commander for deciding to fall back and hold Hawaii. He could have continued carrier raids around the Japanese periphery until enough *Essex* carriers arrived from the shipbuilders to counterattack from strength. Of course, he would have had a very aggressive King to contend with.

At this point in the war, Nimitz did not have King's unqualified support. King thought Rochefort had sold his Pacific commander a bill of goods. If Nimitz took a big gamble and lost, he might be out of a job. More important, the Pacific Ocean commander was about to bet America's last extant Pacific carrier strength on a risky fight the chief of naval operations disagreed with. All this because a lowly lieutenant commander was reading tea leaves in the basement of the radio intercept shack.

Yamamoto did not know how well informed his adversary was. Though the efforts of Joe Rochefort and his band of code breakers, Nimitz knew the broad outline of Yamamoto's plan. Rochefort reported the Combined Fleet's order of battle in correct detail. Convinced that his work product was accurate, the lieutenant commander told his four-star boss the Japanese would attack on the morning of 4 June from a bearing of 325 degrees, i.e., northwest of Midway. The Japanese would launch 175 miles from Midway at 0700. Rochefort didn't equivocate or hedge his bets. He displayed intellectual courage of the first rank. No commander could ask his intelligence people for a more precise picture of what the enemy was about to do. Intelligence production was so rapid Nimitz ordered "Fleet opposed Invasion-Midway" on 14 May, three weeks before the actual battle. After the battle Nimitz remarked that Rochefort was one degree and one hour off in his prediction.

If it hadn't been for the code breakers and an unflappable fleet commander, there would have been no battle of Midway. One of the frustrating challenges of oceanwide naval warfare is getting the two fleets to collide—on your terms. Recall that Halsey's two carriers had gone south to attempt to intercede in the Coral Sea. Without instant decisions based on timely intelligence, the American fleet would have been somewhere south of Hawaii. Yamamoto's invasion force would have rolled over Midway. Nimitz would have had to concentrate on Hawaii's defenses. The initiative would have remained with the Japanese. Nimitz could count. He recognized his three carriers could get about as many aircraft airborne as Nagumo's four fleet carriers. That was enough. His fleet would oppose Yamamoto's invasion fleet. Nimitz warned his subordinates that the Japanese would come gunning for American carriers. In response, his orders to task force commanders Spruance and Fletcher were to be aggressive: "Inflict maximum damage on enemy by employing strong attrition tactics."[31]

To this he added a letter:

> In carrying out the task assigned . . . you will be governed by the principle of calculated risk, which you will interpret to mean the avoidance of exposure of your force to attack by superior enemy forces without good prospect of inflicting, as a result of such exposure, greater damage on the enemy.[32]

Nimitz made his intent clear. In other words, don't be suicidal but take any decent shot you are presented. What if Nagumo had received similar instructions from Yamamoto in late November 1941 as he shoved off for Pearl Harbor—and had complied with their spirit?

Of all the American theater commanders during World War II, Admiral Chester Nimitz was the only one who, by himself, initiated offensive action when his adversary had the advantage in matériel. Behind the calm, even-tempered façade stood a fighter made of the toughest steel. He didn't have Halsey's trait of verbally chewing on his enemy, but he was every bit as aggressive. Moreover, his judgment was impeccable. He had resisted King's initial impulse to raid early with one-carrier task forces. That could have generated losses that would have prevented the American navy from opposing the Midway operation.

Nimitz did have some strong cards in the hole. Repairs had been completed on *Saratoga*. She would depart for Pearl Harbor during the battle. American battleships cruised the Pacific off the northern California coast. They could break up an invasion fleet approaching Hawaii under the cover of the hundreds of land-based planes that were now operating from those islands.

Captain Mahan constantly preached aggressive, offensive action. Seize and retain the initiative. Dictate the terms of battle to your enemy. Call the tune so he doesn't create mischief of his own by sailing to places you cannot defend. Yamamoto had demonstrated audacity. But Mahan truly would have been in awe of the bold decision of Admiral Chester A. Nimitz.

The Battle of Midway

With the carrier aircraft count about even, the fleet that struck first against the opposing carriers was likely to attain ascendancy. The battleships were not irrelevant. If the U.S. did not retain at least air superiority, the Japanese battle line would ensure that Midway was occupied by the Imperial Army. If the air battle ended in a draw or even with a slight American advantage, victory would go to the Japanese invaders shepherded by their battleships.

Yamamoto's initial plan assumed significant fleet action would occur only after Midway was taken.[33] One must evaluate Nagumo's action against this guidance. The incredible part of Midway was that Yamamoto had changed this assumption but failed to make sure that Nagumo knew it. Fear of American radio intelligence heavily contributed to the upcoming carrier kills. Nagumo knew nothing of the indications that the Americans were aware of his intentions.

The battle of Midway overflows with high drama and heroism, but we will only allude to the several aspects that reflect back on the strategy and operational design of the opposing admirals. Nagumo and his staff debated what they should do the morning of 4 June. The IJN's operational plan called for Japanese carrier aircraft to bomb Midway. After some hand-wringing, he decided go with a dawn air strike on Midway per Yamamoto's initial operations plan. That would destroy American land-based aviation so that the invasion force could approach unhindered. If American carriers exposed themselves, they would be another high-priority target. However, Yamamoto's failure to explicitly prioritize these competing objectives contributed to Nagumo's undoing.

On 3 June, a Midway-based patrol bomber (PBY) spotted the transports of the occupation force. At the battle's opening, on the 4th, Nagumo sent out a minimalist search pattern to look for American ships. The Japanese search pattern was flown by a mismatched force of slow float planes from the surface combatants and some untried long-range fighters from the carriers. Having the advantage of Rochefort's intelligence, Fletcher's opening move placed the American carriers at a point 200 miles northeast of Midway. From this position he would be in range to engage Japanese carriers launching raids against Midway. He reasoned that he did not want to get caught between Midway and the Japanese fleet. Nimitz had approved the maneuver. Early the next morning another search plane from Midway spotted the carriers. Midway-based aircraft, led by Marine Major Loften Henderson, whose name would be given to the field on Guadalcanal, rose to strike the enemy carriers. American marine and army flyers based at Midway were brave but only partially trained. Not a hit was made on a Japanese ship. Henderson lost his life. The only Midway-based aircraft that scored a hit during the entire battle was a torpedo-toting PBY against an oiler. Fletcher now had the vital information: location and strength of the Japanese fleet carriers. While over a hundred of Nagumo's aircraft swooped down on Midway in the morning light, Fletcher ordered Spruance to launch a massive strike from two of his carriers. Fletcher kept the third carrier's strike force in reserve. They were launched a couple of hours later and would show up over Nagumo's fleet at a very opportune moment.

Before the strike, each side had 230 carrier-borne aircraft available. Sixty-seven aircraft that raided Midway were either lost or so shot up that they were unavailable for further combat that day. After Nagumo's first swat at Midway, the operational plane count approached 1.5:1 in favor of the Americans! Returning Japanese aircraft reported that a second strike would be required. About a third of Nagumo's planes were on deck armed with anti-shipping ordnance in the event that American carriers were sighted. His fleet had already beaten off two attacks from Midway-based aircraft without loss. A mad scramble had ensued when the submarine *Nautilus* penetrated into the Japanese task force and fired a torpedo—which missed. Confident that he could beat off any further American attacks, Nagumo ordered the planes on deck rearmed for a second Midway strike. As high-explosive bombs were lifted onto Japanese carrier decks, the delayed float plane finally sighted American ships. First reports did not identify a carrier. Then the spotter reported at least one flattop.

For fifteen minutes, Nagumo vacillated. Finally he decided to go after the carrier—or maybe carriers. High-explosive bombs were shunted aside on flight decks so that torpedoes and armor-piercing bombs could be reattached to aircraft. That is when Spruance's 116 aircraft struck. First the brave crews of the American Devastator torpedo bombers approached on the deck. Their runs had to be straight and slow to properly deliver their torpedoes. The Devastators remained on their approaches despite being slashed into aluminum shreds by the machine guns of diving Zeros. Not a torpedo hit the enemy fleet. Of 41 attackers, only 6 torpedo bombers returned to American carrier decks. At about 1015, while the torpedo men were sacrificing themselves, Lieutenant Commander Wade McClusky led 37 Dauntlesses from *Enterprise* in a dive on the uncovered Japanese carriers. Due to navigational error, *Hornet*'s dive bombers did not locate the Japanese fleet. Within a minute, McClusky's airmen left *Akagi* and *Kaga* in flames. Fire detonated the high-explosive bombs that had just been removed from Japanese aircraft and remained unprotected on deck. It was 1030. The two big carriers were doomed. Within minutes, *Yorktown*'s dive bombers descended on *Soryu*. As they pulled off their target, the ship was engulfed in flames that led to her sinking. In the six minutes between McClusky's dive and the last Dauntless skimming away, Nagumo lost three carriers.

Much criticism directed against the admirals of both sides revolves around hesitation to take risk. How can anyone imagine the terror Nagumo must have endured thinking about those six minutes in which his fleet was eviscerated? Antiseptic words cannot begin to capture the overpowering paralysis such an image created in the leaders of both sides at Midway, who committed not only thousands of men but the survival of their home country to a single roll of the die.

Ground combat rarely generates such an incredible danger as the result of luck and a single tactical decision. It took a towering man, like a Nimitz or a Halsey, to overcome these horrible fears and to continue to attack. At Midway, Spruance also showed his mettle. That lesser admirals shrank away from this horror is not to denigrate their courage. Rather, it underscored the remarkable courage of those few admirals whose willpower overcame the impact of such debilitating risks.

Yamaguchi ached to avenge the Imperial Fleet's losses. A fifty-aircraft strike from the deck of undamaged *Hiryu* followed the Americans home. Despite good shooting by both anti-aircraft gunners and defending fighters, enough *Hiryu* attackers got through to hit *Yorktown* with three bombs and two torpedoes. The big aircraft carrier's wounds were likely mortal. It listed badly as seawater rushed into its breached hull. Meanwhile Dauntlesses, including some diverted from *Yorktown,* lifted off from *Enterprise* bound for *Hiryu.* Bombs from this second American carrier strike smothered the sole remaining Japanese fleet carrier at 1700. By 0100 it was clear she had to be abandoned. (Reports during the war mistakenly credited a carrier kill to *Nautilus.* This is not supported by Japanese accounts, which state that torpedoes hit the already doomed *Kaga* but did not explode.) A Japanese sub made further hits on *Yorktown,* ultimately sending her beneath the waves as well.

Right after McClusky's strike, Yamamoto heard that three of his carriers had been destroyed. Showing resolve, he ordered the two carriers supporting the Aleutian operation to sail south to join with the main body. Together, they would hunt down Fletcher's fleet. But calculations of sailing distance from Alaska indicated this could not be completed in time. *Hiryu* was now lost. Yamamoto no longer had a choice. Yamamoto's Midway invasion task forces numbered over 190 ships. By evening of the 4th, he had lost only four—his four fleet carriers. Seven battleships, their Rising Sun battle flags snapping in the wind, faced a battlewagon-less American fleet. Japanese troop transports remained untouched. Reluctantly, Yamamoto concluded the IJN did not have the strength to continue the operation and ordered a general retirement. No other decision better underscores the decisive effect of carrier losses and relative carrier strength had on the war in the Pacific. It really was about ten—or six—ships. And the Americans had just sunk four of them. Truly an incredible victory.

During the withdrawal, U.S. carrier-based planes hit several Japanese cruisers. Two of them collided. Additional bombs sent one of them down. Fletcher and Spruance, mindful both of Japanese battleships and Wake-based aircraft, did not pursue. Given the gun power of Yamamoto's battle line, no one should criticize this decision. What would have happened if the Americans had been trapped in the dark by the Japanese battle line?

Let's return to Nagumo's opening move. The objective of the Midway operation was to precipitate a major fleet action. Wasn't it likely the Americans were nearby? If intelligence had been shared, Nagumo would have been certain. In any event, wouldn't it have paid to hold off hitting Midway until noon in order to conduct a more thorough reconnaissance and to be ready to launch an overwhelming strike if American carriers were revealed? Midway wasn't going anywhere. And the invasion was scheduled for two days hence.

Had Nagumo completed his search before ordering the strike on Midway, the outcome of the battle would undoubtedly have been reversed. Had Yamamoto been more precise in his designation of objective, had available intelligence been shared, that search would have been made.

During the Japanese approach toward Midway, American radio traffic and the submarine contact and reports led Yamamoto to believe his forces had been spotted. Potentially battle-winning information lay on the flag bridge of Yamamoto's ship only a few hundred miles away from Nagumo. Because Yamamoto and his staff were intimidated by radio direction finders, this critical intelligence was not communicated. American electronic warriors made as large a contribution as the valor of McClusky's airmen. The prudent move was to radio Nagumo to ensure he had launched the widest possible search and readied a carrier counterstrike. Midway wasn't going anywhere. If the search had revealed nothing, then Midway could have been hit in the afternoon.

While Nagumo still might have lost several carriers, the odds were that the American fleet would have been devastated. The Japanese torpedo planes and their experienced crews were far more effective than the old American Devastators hauling faulty torpedoes.

In the actual battle, an incredible set of circumstances led to mortal hits on three Japanese carriers in six minutes. Had the Americans arrived sixty minutes later, a major Japanese strike would have been on its way toward the American fleet. Japanese carriers would have been less vulnerable to fire that, in the end, claimed all three. *Hiryu* fought on until a second American strike put her under. By that time three operational American carrier groups faced a single Japanese flattop. When the Americans got off the first strike, especially when a reciprocal strike was not airborne, the day had already gone against the Japanese. However, let's imagine that Nagumo had started with six carriers (add the two carriers in the Aleutians) instead of four. In this scenario, as in the actual event, the Americans leave three carriers burning. Now three Japanese carrier groups go after the Americans. In the actual battle a single carrier group severely damaged *Yorktown,* taking her out of the fight. It is reasonable to surmise that the group and a half (counting *Ryujo* as half) might have set a second American afire. In the next round, two Japanese fleet carriers and one light carrier face a single operational American carrier. The results become obvious. With cripples moving at reduced speed the untouched Japanese carriers can close the distance and finish their work over as many days as they need. As Yamamoto's plan envisioned, battleships could run down what is left of the damaged ships. Midway ultimately falls after battleships and carrier aircraft destroy everything above ground.

Six carriers and clarified instructions could have prevented large-scale Japanese losses. If the Japanese had lost three carriers while the Americans lost two (or three) plus Midway, it would have been a strategic victory for the Japanese. Nimitz would have been pinned to Hawaii until other carriers besides *Saratoga* reinforced the Pacific Fleet. Relative air combat power at Midway was roughly equal. However, Japan should have had a decisive advantage. Poor judgment in sending two fleet carriers to the Coral Sea and allocating scarce carrier assets to the Alaska operation set up an incredible American victory. Midway's outcome was not preordained. A lesser strategist than Mahan can recognize that an admiral who can achieve a decisive edge in fleet power but fails to do so is not a very good admiral. As at Pearl Harbor, Yamamoto could have achieved a decisive victory but did not. Zero for 2 is not much of a batting average.

Luck is in the draw. Every admiral has to play with a deck of cards that can deal catastrophe in a single hand. But there was much Yamamoto could have done to improve the odds. As at Coral Sea, Nimitz played his weak hand with magnificent skill. Yamamoto let opportunities to improve his position slip through his fingers. In both cases correct use of his command authority could have resulted in Japanese victory. One doesn't have to be Mahan to see the difference in the performance of the opposing admirals. Mahan always said the side with the superior war-fighting naval leader would ultimately prevail. May and June 1942 did not contradict him.

Deep gloom spread over the Imperial Fleet. For a time after the battle some naval officers feared the American carrier fleet would come to punish the Home Islands. It is hard to find fault with Professor Spector's conclusion: "For the Japanese, Midway was an ill-conceived, sloppily executed operation. Yet Yamamoto had the right idea."[34] Morison labeled Yamamoto's deployments "cockeyed."[35] Midway was *the* decisive battle. At the time most observers did not realize this. They looked for another round. Mahan would have applauded the objective of engaging the U.S. carriers, but he would have admonished Yamamoto: "Never, *never,* divide the fleet."

5
GUADALCANAL

Midway shocked Japan's naval leadership. Four carriers had been lost. This was a major reverse, but their job was to recover and again seek decisive battle. The disaster was concealed from the Japanese public—and from the army as well. Many senior naval officers saw it as the result of a cruel turn of fate rather than the prowess of the American navy.

The only way east from the Japanese-occupied central Pacific was through Hawaii. After Midway, both the naval general staff (NGS) and the Imperial Japanese Army placed that objective in the "too hard" category. Instead, they wanted to continue to expand into the South Pacific. Previously the NGS had concluded that because of the still weakened state of the U.S. Navy, an Allied counteroffensive must begin in Australia. Cutting the sea lanes to Australia or invading the island continent itself would prevent this from starting. After Midway, the assumptions underlying this conclusion seemed a lot less reliable.

Initially Rabaul had been an outpost for Truk. By May the army wanted two air bases as outposts for Rabaul. Port Moresby, on New Guinea, and Tulagi, across a narrow channel from Guadalcanal, would fill the requirement. The navy wanted to go one step further and cut the sea lanes between Australia and Hawaii altogether. French New Caledonia was an inviting target. Recall that only Yamamoto's threat to resign had deterred the NGS from making New Caledonia, instead of Midway, the primary thrust line.

Despite the losses at Midway, Yamamoto could still muster four fleet carriers —*Zuikaku, Shokaku, Hiyo,* and *Junyo. Hiyo* and *Junyo,* the two new carriers, were only two-thirds the size of those lost at Midway and they were several crucial knots slower. *Hiyo* experienced chronic engine problems. In addition, Japan had three operational light carriers. The surface combatants of the Imperial Fleet far outgunned anything the Americans could muster.

With the return of *Saratoga,* Nimitz again had three fleet carriers. When *Wasp* arrived from the Atlantic, he would have four. Several fast battleships had also joined the Pacific Fleet. Rehabilitated older battleships operated first from San Francisco and later from Pearl Harbor as a hedge against a renewed Japanese thrust from the mid-Pacific.

American assets were slowly accreting in the Pacific. It would be a lot tougher for the Imperial Fleet to achieve a 1.5:1 advantage against the Americans. U.S. reinforcements had made invasion of Hawaii impossible. The IJN general headquarters didn't expect any major U.S. offensive before 1943.[1] That was when the *Essex*-class carriers would make their numbers felt. Japan had perhaps a ten-month window in which to take decisive action or risk inevitable defeat. The only viable naval Japanese strategy was to force a major fleet engagement and destroy the American task forces before they became impossibly strong. Yamamoto had to precipitate a major fleet engagement as far away from American land-based airpower as possible and sink enough American carriers to eliminate their offensive capability. But he never came up with a plan to achieve this objective.

Mahan would have shaken his head. If Japan was to win, her navy must force the Americans to commit their carriers to a place that enhanced Japan's ability to win a confrontation as crucial as Midway but with the opposite results. The Japanese Mandated Islands in the central Pacific would allow Japanese land-based aviation to intervene while keeping far out of range of their American counterparts. Create an apparent weakness, a trap, for Nimitz. Draw him in and kill his fleet. That would have been the textbook strategy. This was a bad time for Yamamoto to come up short and in so doing cede the initiative to the Americans.

Midway had eliminated any significant Japanese capability for eastward expansion. Japanese planners began to recognize that they were overextended. This realization took time to sink in, however. A chain of American bases slowly began to crawl west. Instead of a springboard toward Australia's lifeline, New Guinea and Guadalcanal would become the outermost bulwark against America's westward movement.

Airfield construction began on Guadalcanal in July. Initially the Imperial Army had thought that it would be relatively simple to capture Port Moresby by sea. The battle of the Coral Sea laid any such notions to rest. Port Moresby would be protected by Australian army forces trekking over the Owen Stanley Mountains.

July passed without much original thought from either Yamamoto's or Nagano's staff. The best they could come up with was another proposal to invade India! The "provisional government" of the Indian nationalist Subhas Bose promised Japan's leaders that Bose could mobilize millions of Indians if Japanese arms could establish him on Indian soil. This fit well with Japanese bias. One way to induce an Indian uprising would be to capture Ceylon. This would take army troops. Once again, the army said no. The Japanese also canceled efforts to attack toward New Caledonia. On 4 August, Admiral Ugaki observed, "Nobody has supplied a good plan for the next stage operation for a long time."[2] Essentially, the imperial war machine had shifted to defense. The bastions of Japanese Pacific defense plans were the two major bases at Rabaul and Truk (see Map 1a). They were to be the bulwark against which the sortieing American fleet would dash itself. All positions to the east, including Guadalcanal and the lower Solomons, were simply outposts for the main defensive belt.

With carrier strength closer to balance, the side that had land-based aviation available at the place of battle might have just the winning edge. In the central Pacific during the summer of 1942, any U.S. move west of the Gilberts into the Japanese Mandated Islands would cede that advantage to the Japanese. The Midway victory secured Hawaii for the U.S., but the American fleet was not yet strong enough to advance across the central Pacific.[3] While badly hurt, the Imperial Japanese Navy, buttressed with land-based air, could still cripple the existing American fleet. Even after Midway, Allied planners feared an invasion of Australia. In this light, a Japanese air base at Guadalcanal continued southward movement with the intent to sever the sea lanes between America and Australia.

Admiral King first proposed a Guadalcanal landing to General Marshall in a letter dated 18 February 1942. He repeated the proposal in a memorandum to the president on 5 March.[4] This was before anyone could have anticipated the results of Coral Sea and Midway; it preceded the Japanese push to Tulagi. King wasn't clairvoyant. Perhaps he had a little luck. Since the beginning of the war, he had championed maintenance of the sea lanes to Australia, exactly the axis the Japanese naval general staff identified as the greatest potential threat. King never wavered from this view. Before the war, both belligerents had identified the central Pacific as the route to decisive battle. Now both had blundered into a far more circuitous path through the many islands of the South Pacific.

Guadalcanal was the end of the line for both, but neither side was about to cede it to the other. Out of sheer frustration, the outermost flank guard on each side continued to swing his extended spear at his counterpart. The ensuing struggles around Guadalcanal arose primarily from the stalemate in the central Pacific and the collision of two opponents seeking an alternative.

The American fleet was not ready to take on the Japanese fleet in a major open ocean fight. Admiral King recognized that the American fleet had nowhere near the strength to follow War Plan Orange across the central Pacific. Yet he itched to go on the offensive. In May King and his planners, led by Admiral Turner, developed a four-stage plan for an offensive:

1. Build bases in the South Pacific.
2. Seize Papua [Eastern New Guinea] and southern Solomons.
3. Capture Bismarck Archipelago, which included Rabaul on New Britain.
4. Invade either the East Indies or the Philippines.[5]

The huge Midway victory secured Hawaii, which in King's words meant that "enemy operations were confined to the South Pacific. It is to this area, therefore, that we gave our greatest attention."[6] King also recognized "in the first five months of the war, nearly every engagement with the enemy had demonstrated the importance of airpower in modern naval warfare."[7] An American offensive in the South Pacific will "draw Japanese forces to oppose it."[8] While Mahan would have preferred a precise plan aimed at drawing in and destroying Japanese carriers, the general outline of King's thinking is clear. Combat in the South Pacific was likely to draw significant elements of Japanese naval airpower to where they could be destroyed. King's emphasis on the South Pacific didn't start out as a campaign to chip away at Japanese carrier power a piece at a time, but that is what it evolved into.

On 28 May, Nimitz suggested to MacArthur that a Marine raider battalion could take Tulagi. Nimitz didn't want to occupy the island. He wanted to eliminate Japanese air reconnaissance capability based there. Recall Admiral Fletcher's strike on Tulagi before the battle of the Coral Sea. By that time American intelligence concluded there was "no tangible evidence of a Japanese expedition being

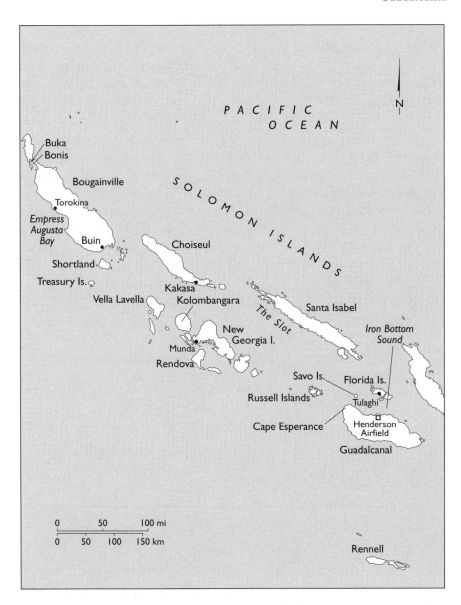

Map 5a. Guadalcanal and the Solomons. Map by Bill Nelson.

prepared against Australia."[9] However, Nimitz's objective placed a southwest Pacific tilt to American deployments. MacArthur, sitting in Brisbane and looking toward the Philippines, certainly agreed with this development.

Inertia from forces and bases already in the South Pacific combined with the realistic assessment that the American navy had yet to achieve dominance led both King and Nimitz separately to conclude that an offensive at Guadalcanal should be the next move. However, it was King who shepherded the concept from idea to operation. He instinctively recognized that the Japanese should be struck while they were still stunned by Midway. Guadalcanal was about the only ready opportunity. "Nimitz had no intention of committing his fleet until it had gained enough strength."[10] With four of Nagumo's carriers on the bottom, Nimitz was now ready.

General Marshall recognized how seemingly innocent first moves could come to dictate future direction.[11] Once placed, the logistical tail will tend to pull strategic direction to itself. Did the United States want to construct the support and facilities that far "down" in the Pacific? Marshall so cautioned King. At this juncture, Marshall did all he could to resist building South Pacific infrastructure to a level that it took on a life of its own. Events would demonstrate that his goal was a good one but that he was unsuccessful.

The Australians wanted to move from north of their country and into Timor to link up with the Dutch guerrillas who were fighting on that island. But this wish hardly registered in Washington or in MacArthur's HQ in Brisbane. Admiral Kelly Turner picked out a possible airfield site on Guadalcanal and targeted it as a landing site before knowledge of the Japanese construction there was available. Few decent airfield sites exist in the jungle-covered mountains and swamps of the Solomons. Creation of an airfield at Guadalcanal might just give the Americans the edge required to continue the carrier duels of 1942.

Japanese power in the South Pacific was centered at Rabaul, which is located at the northwestern end of the Solomons. It contains one of the best harbors in that part of the world. During peacetime, as much as 300,000 tons of freight, mostly coconuts and copra, were shipped through it. The land around Rabaul offered good sites for air bases. Japanese laborers constructed a cluster of four such bases plus some separate airstrips. Unlike Truk, Rabaul had not been under Japanese control before the war. At the time of the American invasion of Guadalcanal, the airfields held sixty Zeros, sixty Betty twin-engine bombers, and a gaggle of float planes and seaplanes used for recon. However, Rabaul was no Gibraltar. Allied descriptions vastly overrated its strength. There were no concrete coastal defenses or large-caliber coast defense guns. Only a few crude machine shops and warehouses were available for fleet support.

It appeared that Rabaul blocked MacArthur's way back to the Philippines. (As we shall see, it did not.) After Midway, MacArthur proposed Operation Tulsa, which would capture Rabaul in fourteen days. Rabaul's capture would roll the Japanese back to Truk, 700 miles away. All MacArthur claimed he needed was a two-carrier task force and a Marine division to add to his three army divisions.[12] Any naval planner could see this proposal was sophomoric. The main operating base at Truk would give the Japanese fleet more support than anywhere else away from the home islands. American operations against Rabaul would play to Japanese strengths. Only four-engine American bombers would be in supporting range. Performance of the Army Air Forces based in Australia at the time was horrendous. Japan could easily overwhelm any contemplated American fleet with a combination of land and naval airpower. King said it politely: "The balance of power at that moment was too delicate to make wise the attempted seizure of a position so exposed to enemy counterattack."[13] A far more modest beginning had to be selected.

A major squabble developed over who was to command operations aimed at Rabaul. Previously, the Joint Chiefs of Staff had agreed to split the Pacific between Nimitz in Honolulu and MacArthur in Australia. The boundary between them placed the Solomons in MacArthur's area. King was not about to allow his carriers to fall under command of a general. He cited Tulsa as an example of the inept commitments generals, untrained in naval warfare, would make.

Marshall insisted that operations in the Solomons remain under MacArthur's command. King angrily responded he was ready to attack Guadalcanal using only naval resources rather than place the fleet under a general. King and Marshall expended a lot of energy debating command relationships for upcoming operations. To many, this looked like a horrible case of interservice rivalry. What made it worse was the "personal loathing of MacArthur which permeated the U.S. naval high command from King on down."[14]

Thirty-five days before the Guadalcanal invasion was to be made, Marshall picked up his pen and wrote to King in cool-headed, logical prose.

PROPOSED JOINT DIRECTIVE FOR OFFENSIVE OPERATIONS IN THE SOUTH-WEST PACIFIC AREA

1. Objective. Offensive operations will be conducted with the ultimate objective of seizure and occupation of the New Britain–New Ireland–New Guinea area.
2. Purpose. To deny the area to Japan.
3. Tasks
   a. Task One. Seizure and occupation of Santa Cruz Islands, Tulagi and adjacent positions.
   b. Task Two. Seizure and occupation of the remainder of the Solomon Islands, Lae Salamaua and Northeast Coast of New Guinea.
   c. Task Three. Seizure and occupation of Rabaul and adjacent positions in the New Britain–New Ireland area.
      . . .
5. Forces
   . . .
   b. At least two carriers [will be assigned to Task One.][15]

The document went on to make a great compromise. Task One would be commanded by an admiral reporting to Nimitz. Tasks Two and Three would be commanded by MacArthur. It was a document of a methodical mind that calculates its way through problems. Marshall's plan envisioned a systematic, supported offensive that would not advance beyond the range of American land-based fighters after the initial landing at Guadalcanal.

The plan was straightforward. Unfortunately, its stated purpose was wrong!

Undoubtedly Captain Mahan would have tactfully picked his words in the presence of such a towering strategist as Marshall. Following part of King's earlier outline, General Marshall had penned a landlubber's strategy: "Purpose: To deny the area to Japan." If roads had connected the towns of Guadalcanal and Rabaul, then the order might have been appropriate. As long as the Japanese army could maneuver over the countryside, all of the connecting terrain would have to be cleared. But it was ocean, not land. The ocean area all the way to New Britain had no strategic value whatsoever. The strategic objective—the purpose—was to pull critical Japanese air and naval forces into engagements on terms unfavorable to them and to destroy them faster than they could be replaced. Once the American fleet gained dominance, it could move at will and the ocean area need not be conquered or occupied. If King had been more precise on this matter, his army counterpart might have learned more and learned it earlier. Often strategic statements are brief. However, a strategist must avoid tacit assumptions and implications that may not be understood or inferred by his entire audience.

At the Tehran Conference later in the war, Marshall admitted, "My military education and experience in the First World War has all been based on roads, rivers and railroads. During the last two years, however, I have been acquiring and education based on oceans and I have had to learn all over again."[16] King was more caustic. "It took me three months to educate Marshall about the importance of the Marianas but any educated naval officer would have understood it [immediately]."[17]

Mahan would have agreed that the highly capable General Marshall was in need of some naval education at the beginning of the war. As late as November 1941, General Marshall believed that land-based four-engine bombers would be the principal weapon used to defeat Japan should it choose war. As part of a deep background briefing for key journalists, he displayed a map of the Pacific marked with bomber operating ranges from several large air bases. Featured were Australia, the Philippines, and China. Rabaul, then in Australian hands, was also prominently displayed. Marshall told the journalists, "The Grand Strategy does not include the use of much naval force. . . . U.S. bombers can do the trick against Japanese naval strength and against Japanese cities without the use of our shipping."[18] Such erroneous thinking would lead a planner to conclude Clark Field in the Philippines was a major impediment to Japanese southward expansion in late 1941.

In fact, the ideal operation in late 1942 would result in pitting a pair of Japanese carriers against four American ones—or against a similarly deadly concentration of Allied land-based air. The worst scenario would place "at least two American carriers" (Map 5b) at risk within striking distance of concentrated Japanese land-based air, and without the opportunity to inflict critical damage on enemy naval air. Mahan would have reminded Marshall that occupying the geography was meaningless. Forces on the islands unsupported by a viable fleet were no threat to the Allies. This is a principal implication of Mahan's most basic element of naval strategy: dominate or destroy the enemy fleet and everything else falls into your lap.

MacArthur's plan called for a brace of supporting carriers the way a ground commander might call for additional reinforcing artillery from higher headquarters. Those guns have nowhere near the vulnerability—or critical status—of two of the only four carriers in the Pacific. Both naval and air force commanders realized the incredible speed of their forces and the importance of rapid concentration of all assets against enemy threats. They also recognized how fragile their forces were in comparison to their counterparts on solid ground. As Midway demonstrated, a campaign could be lost in a few unlucky minutes. Concentration is key in land as well as naval combat. However, ground commanders are not accustomed to leaving most contested area completely empty. On land the "line" normally extends to both sides of the "main effort." In naval combat, the carriers themselves are the strategic objectives. Places like Rabaul are important only when they influence the relative ability of one fleet to destroy the other. Otherwise, they are irrelevant.

That General Marshall could make such a fundamental error underscores why the upcoming fights around Guadalcanal had to be commanded by admirals. In fact, the battle of Guadalcanal was primarily a naval campaign that used the island as a fulcrum. Marines captured points on land that become critical to a naval fight. However, the principal objective was a naval one. This takes nothing away from the heroism of the marines and soldiers on that battered isle or the intense desperation of the land combat that went on for six months. Almost 4,000 sailors died in the waters around Guadalcanal. About 1,050 marines and soldiers died on shore.

By the summer of 1943 the accumulated delivery of carriers from American shipyards would create a "Big Blue Fleet" that could overpower the Japanese at any point in the Pacific. But that was a long way off and, as Mahan pointed out, a fleet left unused that long tends to go stale. American servicemen had a lot to learn. Mahan certainly would have applauded King's intent, which was to get his fleet into the fight in a manner that did not cause its destruction. One of Mahan's overarching precepts is that well-trained crews are a decisive advantage. But leaving the Japanese alone for a year, from Midway to the creation of the Big Blue Fleet, was not really an option.

Even so, King stuck his neck out a long way by committing to a major operation at Guadalcanal at this juncture. If it had been handled properly, the Japanese fleet could have inflicted a major loss on the Americans. However, King picked a point at the extreme end of the Japanese sphere of influence—a point that maximized American opportunity to achieve victory over an element of the Imperial Navy without facing Japan's concentrated wrath. He initiated a campaign that would grind down irreplaceable Japanese airpower while increasing the experience level of American combat forces. In the end he stressed a Japanese resource that was stretched even more: the supply of trained pilots.

King and Marshall decided to push Task One immediately. Marshall told MacArthur to continue planning for Tasks Two and Three, even if additional resources did not become available. As long as Guadalcanal was under Nimitz's tutelage, King figured he could tackle the rest of the command problem later.

Vice Admiral Robert Lee Ghormley, described by his peers as very bright but without the stomach for a knife fight, was designated commander of the South Pacific area under Nimitz. He would head an operation dubbed Watchtower. After looking at his troop and ship lists he said he could do the job but that it would be difficult. On 10 July, he received an order to attack Guadalcanal on 1 August. King's grizzled operations officer, Admiral Richmond Kelly "Terrible" (referring to his infamous temper) Turner, would command the amphibious task force. Fletcher described him as "tough, a brain and a son of a bitch."[19] Turner had developed a reputation for not working well with the army so his days as King's operations officer were probably numbered anyway. Like most other Washington-based admirals, Turner was overjoyed to get back to the fleet. Admiral Fletcher commanded the carrier task force and also reported to Ghormley.

Admiral Ghormley was down in Melbourne conferring with General MacArthur when word of General Marshall's three-task approach reached them. After looking at the resources and constantly accreting Japanese strength, Ghormley and MacArthur wired the Joint Chiefs: "The successful accomplishment of the operation is open to gravest doubts."[20] They did not like breaking the move against Rabaul into stages. They envisioned instead a single continuous operation. Until forces were accumulated to carry out all three phases, they argued the first should be postponed. Nimitz completely disagreed. He wanted to go imme-diately.[21] Given that the Japanese were consolidating their hold on the Solomons, an American operation required speed, not delay. Perform Task One and eject the enemy from Solomons before he tried to cut the sea lanes to Australia.

When he read the MacArthur–Ghormley cable, King blew his stack. He vented at Marshall: "Three weeks ago MacArthur stated that if he could be fur-nished amphibious forces and two carriers, he could push right through to Rabaul. He now feels that he not only cannot undertake this extended operation but not even the Tulagi operation."[22] King, who probably had been influenced by Admiral Hart's "unflattering" report on the defense of the Philippines, thought MacArthur "megalomaniacal." On 10 July, King and Marshall jointly issued the order to execute Watchtower. King's unwavering advocacy of a Guadalcanal op-eration makes him the unquestioned father of the battles that ensued. He did not anticipate such heavy and continuous Japanese reaction.[23] He had wanted to take a swipe at the enemy, not to cause a decisive fleet action. But that is what he was to get: at least two Japanese efforts to bring about decisive naval battle.

Ghormley did expect that the Guadalcanal landings would precipitate a major engagement with the Combined Fleet. Four days after Turner landed the mar-ines, Ghormley wrote to Nimitz that he expected an immediate Japanese attempt to "try to land an expedition against our positions in the Tulagi area and I want [American] carriers to hit their ships which carry the expedition toward their objective."[24] Whatever Ghormley's shortcomings, Mahan would have approved the vice admiral's understanding of Watchtower's objective. By itself Guadalcanal Island had no meaning. Making a small move a few hundred miles west was not all that important. Forcing the enemy fleet to commit carriers to an engagement on U.S. terms at a time and place of our choosing was everything. Next to this, the geographically oriented three tasks written by army planners receded into the distant background.

Rear Admiral Frank "Jack" Fletcher was in overall tactical command under Ghormley. On his dress uniform he wore the Medal of Honor, awarded for hero-ism rescuing refugees at Vera Cruz in 1914. Many found him personable, and he had a wide range of naval experience. While Fletcher had led at Coral Sea and Midway, many thought "Frank Fletcher surpassed Admiral Nagumo in timid-ity"[25] and that his leadership was neither creative nor inspired. Admiral "Terri-ble" Turner would command the amphibious force; his bite and tenacity gave credence to the amphibian's nickname— "alligator." General Alexander Vander-grift commanded the First Marine Division, "the Old Breed." Seldom has Amer-ica produced an officer with the intelligence, perception, courage, and concern of this great man.[26]

Admiral Fletcher perceived Guadalcanal as a carrier raid. On 26 July, only eleven days before the scheduled invasion, a critical conference convened on board Fletcher's flagship, *Saratoga*. Despite the importance of the meeting, Admiral Ghormley was unable to rearrange his schedule to attend. At the conference Admiral Fletcher expressed his lack of confidence in the upcoming operation and the planners without combat experience (i.e., Turner) who had developed it.[27] In a situation where fleet action is imminent, the navy does not like to be tethered to troops ashore. If American carriers and gunfire ships must remain within range of a beachhead, the enemy has a very good idea of where its quarry is. He is free to maneuver to a more advantageous position and is more likely to get off a battle-winning first strike. Vice Admiral Fletcher informed Rear Admiral Turner that his carriers would stand off Guadalcanal for no more than two days. No one at the meeting had the rank to modify that intent.

A change in Japanese codes had obscured Ultra's vision during the summer of 1942. However, traffic analysis, and the detailed communications from the Truk harbormaster in a code that could be read, gave American naval intelligence a reasonable picture of IJN dispositions. Many aircraft transfers to Rabaul—preparation for another Japanese effort at Port Moresby—had been recorded. Many cruisers and destroyers had moved south. Radio intelligence placed all of the Japanese carriers in home waters. Some were training new flyers. Fletcher had these reports.[28] If accurate, the likelihood of Japanese carriers conducting an ambush around Guadalcanal during the initial few days of landings was infinitesimal. Japanese carriers simply couldn't steam that fast.

Carrier deployment was critical to the success of the operation. Fletcher's carriers could operate south of Guadalcanal. The island and the marines would lie between them and any Japanese surface warships. Only twin-engine bombers from Rabaul had the range to reach the carriers and even that would be difficult. Japan had no airborne radar and would have no "eyes" on Fletcher's movement. However, submarines would pose a constant danger.

It would take at least a week for the Japanese carriers to assert themselves in strength. A week of local air dominance would allow uninterrupted discharge of all of the marines' supplies and equipment. Even a large night surface raid would be subject to air attack from American carriers either on the way in or on the way out. Given Ghormley's understanding of the likelihood of immediate Japanese reaction and the position of Japanese carriers, it was up to him to take firm control of the situation. One can imagine Mahan leaning forward to underscore this critical conclusion to a bright, if hesitant, vice admiral. Admiral Nimitz had directed Ghormley to "exercise strategic command in person."[29] Instead, Fletcher would be the senior officer in the waters off Guadalcanal during the operation.

King and his planners had developed almost every aspect of the Guadalcanal assault, and they had grossly underestimated the need for amphibious shipping. Japan's Philippine invasion, a secondary effort for them, had employed over 120 transports. Turner had 17. If army generals did not understand the critical nature of carriers, navy planners didn't understand the complexity of the logistics required to sustain land and air forces ashore. Eighty ships were lying idle in Noumea harbor (New Caledonia). No one knew what their holds contained. During an inspection trip, General Arnold judged navy logistics planning to be woefully inadequate.[30] For example, the army had to give the navy 20,000 pairs of shoes or the marines would have gone barefoot as their gear rapidly rotted in the heat and humidity.

Long before the First Marine Division had completed its preparations, the leathernecks recognized that the task ahead would be more difficult than originally thought. This was to be the first large American amphibious operation. Even the "Old Breed" was new to division-size landing operations. Soldiers and sailors fresh from basic training were new to their jobs. They were trying to assemble the pieces that had been shipped 8,000 miles from California to New Zealand. All kinds of items were lost or missing. And Ghormley's people had less than a month to sort it out and attack the Japanese. The marines had been working on amphibious doctrine since the 1920s. Sailors and leathernecks had tried to work out the kinks in the training ground at Chulebra. Now it was time for the graduation ceremony.

The landing on Guadalcanal faced little opposition. The American landings surprised the Japanese. Unarmed construction laborers disappeared into the jungle. The comparatively small number of armed troops followed them in. The first two marine battalions made shore without firing a shot. On Tulagi, the assault made by Marine raiders precipitated several sharp firefights. One of the last Japanese transmissions from Tulagi stated: "Enemy force overwhelming. We will defend our posts to the death."[31]

Japanese land-based air made its first strike on the day the marines landed. Despite combat air patrol (CAP) from American carriers, the raiders set fire to a transport. Fletcher's carriers lost 20 percent of their aircraft strength to accidents and Japanese raiders. Fletcher was greatly concerned.

Admiral Kinkaid, the carrier task force commander under Fletcher, was "certain" that enemy carriers were within striking distance the afternoon of August 8.[32] He ordered carrier-based scouts to search up to 280 miles out. That evening at a meeting on board Turner's flagship just off the invasion beach, Fletcher announced he was withdrawing his three-carrier task force even earlier than anticipated. Citing low fuel levels and diminution of his fighter strength, he said he would retire to Espiritu Santo. Many felt he feared airborne attacks either from Rabaul or from imagined Japanese carriers. Fletcher left even before Ghormley's concurrence to the maneuver had been transmitted.

Fletcher repeatedly used concerns about fuel levels to justify pulling ships out of range of enemy air. He initially anticipated fuel problems in late July as final preparations for the Guadalcanal invasion were made. When Fletcher withdrew, his destroyers had three days' fuel (less under active combat conditions), *Enterprise* had five days' worth, and her cruisers enough for seven to nine days.[33] There were tankers under Ghormley's control capable of replenishing Fletcher at sea.

Turner was shocked that Fletcher would leave the marines with their transports only half unloaded. He felt Fletcher's action was tantamount to desertion.[34] It was gruesome fact that the carriers were a more critical asset than the transports and the marines combined. It's quite another to order men onto the island and then not provide them enough support to unload their supplies and equipment so they would have a chance to defend themselves. There was no evidence that the carriers faced an overwhelming threat. However, Fletcher was convinced Japanese carriers were within striking distance of his fleet and said so at the time. Neither did he want his flattops exposed to land-based bombers the next morning.[35]

What happened also underscores the tremendous burden admirals face when making the decision to commit or not to commit to battle. Admirals on both sides were constantly haunted by Nagumo's debacle. He had lost three of his carriers in those "fatal six minutes" at Midway. It was a crushing weight no words can capture. On the evening of 8 August, that weight caused Fletcher's knees to buckle. It is far easier to criticize than to find the iron admiral who can continue to attack while under this almost unbearable pressure. Instead of denigrating Fletcher, one should gain even deeper admiration for men like Halsey, Spruance, Nimitz, Ozawa, and Yamamoto who could do so. Mahan repeatedly emphasized that the proper role of a naval officer is to develop the intuition to make these life-or-death calls rather than to concentrate on the ship technology at the time or the technical details required to keep ships at the peak of readiness. The commanders have to be at their peak as well as the hardware.

Turner's final defense was a task force of American and Australian surface ships guarding "the Slot" down the Solomons from Rabaul. A group of cruisers and destroyers commanded by British Rear Admiral Victor Crutchley, who had been seconded to the Australian navy, patrolled the night to either side of Savo Island. They were to prevent surface raiders from reaching the transports lying off the Guadalcanal beachhead.

The same night Fletcher pulled his carriers out, a group of Japanese cruisers and destroyers under Vice Admiral Gunichi Mikawa headed for Guadalcanal to punish the invaders. Turner was aware that Japanese cruisers had left Rabaul for a run down the Slot.

Mikawa planned a night attack with cruiser-launched torpedoes. Remember what Mahan predicted about this deadly weapon? Japanese night lookouts beat crude American radar and poorly executed communications and alerting procedures. There were two cruiser engagements between 0100 and 0230. Torpedoes detonated against the Allied victims before they knew where their assailants were. Japanese night gunnery also showed its superiority. When the action was over, an Australian and three American cruisers had begun the submerged steel carpet on the floor of "Iron Bottom Sound."

When he received the flash report of the cruiser battle, Forrest Sherman, then captain of *Wasp*, wanted to reverse course and engage. His carrier wing had received additional training in night operations. Three times he asked his task force commander to seek permission from Fletcher to do so. Rear Admiral Leigh Noyes, commander of the air support force under Fletcher, recognizing his boss's intentions, refused.

Fortunately for the Americans, Mikawa didn't enter the sound and destroy the fifteen or so transports lying just off shore. He feared daylight air strikes from American carriers would hit his task force and tarnish his victory. What if he had known that Fletcher had already withdrawn?

Yamamoto would have accepted the loss a couple of cruisers if he could have destroyed the transports in the wee hours of the 9th. The marines would have been stranded and little more than prisoners of war. The American incursion would have been crushed. Mikawa's thinking is a classic example of confusing tactical success with the attainment of the kind of major operational objective that can decide a campaign. Relative cruiser losses were unimportant when compared to the elimination of the American offensive. Then again, the specter of losing his force to whatever peril lay east of the burning Allied cruisers weighed as heavily on Mikawa as it did on Fletcher. Yamamoto roundly criticized Mikawa for this error and decreed he should never have another sea command.

The smashing tactical victory at Savo Island restored confidence to many Japanese sailors. Again they demonstrated the superiority of their training and fighting spirit.

To his credit Turner stayed another day to offload. The cruisers were on the bottom and the carriers had run, but "Terrible" was still passing the beans and bullets. Before he weighed anchor on the evening of the 9th, the marines had thirty-seven days' rations and four units of fire for their weapons (a unit of fire is the amount of ammunition each weapon will expend in a heavy day of combat).[36] Vandegrift and the First Marine Division were left to fend for themselves among the kunai grass and coconut palms.

So began six months of continuous displays of valor and courage by two adversaries determined to annihilate each other. Grizzled "China" marines, new "boots," and National Guardsmen from Nebraska and the Dakotas showed that American warriors did not lack for fighting spirit. Sons of Japanese farmers from Kyushu to Hokkaido demonstrated a perseverance to endure unbelievable hardship and to continue the fight that was not surpassed anywhere on the planet.

For the remainder of August, the marines withstood many assaults from a slow but steady drip of reinforcements brought in via "Tokyo Express"—ships that ran down the Slot from Rabaul at night to deliver supplies and reinforcements. Japanese grunts called it the "Rat Express."

After Savo, Fletcher's three carriers sailed in the eastern Coral Sea, outside of range to support the isolated marines. Marine fighters and dive-bombers were available in Hawaii, but no one had moved shipping early enough to bring them south to cover what was now an open gap of time in the reinforcement plan.

At first King tried to suppress the depressing news of Savo. He alone had been Watchtower's advocate. Now he felt the intense heat generated by the IJN as a result of his decision. Nimitz concluded that the primary cause for the disaster at Savo was that his sailors weren't "sufficiently battle minded." Inexperienced American blue jackets did not have the snap and the killer mindset of their more experienced Japanese counterparts. In North Africa in late 1942, before the debacle at Kasserine, the same was said of American soldiers. After the fighting in the waters around Guadalcanal, no one would ever make that statement about American sailors again.

King's attack at Guadalcanal solved Yamamoto's strategic problem. Now the IJN had a concentrated, stationary target that could influence the course of the war: not the miserable, isolated marines on Guadalcanal but rather the American fleet carriers that had to sail to their rescue.

The closest American operational airfield was 600 miles away at Espiritu Santo. Single-engine American combat aircraft had combat radii of 200–250 miles. Yamamoto needed to challenge the American carriers, kill them, and then dominate the waters southeast of Guadalcanal in order to starve out the marines and any aircraft they may have infiltrated into Guadalcanal. There was enough ocean to maintain a blockade out of range of aircraft based either at Espiritu Santo or at Guadalcanal. America would be forced to either surrender Guadalcanal or commit its carriers to break the blockade. Controlling the Slot, the approach to Guadalcanal down the length of the Solomon chain, or the discharge points for Japanese reinforcements on the island's north shore was not sufficient.

Yamamoto advocated the use of naval airpower. However, admirals on both sides still recognized the incredible hitting power of battleships. Dive-bombers threw 500- or 1,000-pound bombs at their adversaries, but a battleship's 14-inch shell weighs 1,400 pounds and a 16-inch shell 2,100 pounds. Battleships could fire far more times and with much greater accuracy than the attack planes of a carrier could bomb. The only problem was that they could shoot only 15 miles while aircraft could strike over 200 miles. Now the Americans had staked themselves to Guadalcanal. They could not maneuver away from battleships. The island became an opportunity for the Japanese to exploit their predominance in naval gun power.

The American navy had tethered itself to Guadalcanal. Now it was time for the Japanese superior carrier strength to defeat American carriers, the battleships to sink any damaged Americans still afloat, and the cruisers to cordon off Guadalcanal from the south by cutting the sea lanes to Espiritu Santo and all points south, east, or north. The result would be a resounding defeat that just might rock the Americans back to their senses.

Instead, the Japanese initially had little interest in Guadalcanal. In one of the twists of war, the Japanese misread the results of the night fight around Savo. Yamamoto's staff interpreted the withdrawal of naval units as a general withdrawal from Guadalcanal. Of course it was not. When elements of the Combined Fleet prepared to sail for Guadalcanal on 13 August, Ugaki remarked in his diary: "Some enemies still remained in the Tulagi and Guadalcanal area, but now they are supposed to have been left behind with small craft when the enemy withdrew."[37] He would not substantially change his assessment until Marine aircraft were spotted landing on the island.

The Japanese thought the American incursion was only a reconnaissance in force. "The recapture of Guadalcanal, the Japanese thought, would therefore not be too difficult and could be accomplished while the Port Moresby operation was in progress."[38] Ugaki recorded in his diary: ". . . send a troop there to mop up the enemy remnant, rescue the garrison and repair the airfield. The support force should simultaneously carry out operations as scheduled while the invasions of Moresby, Ocean [Island] and Nauru should be completed."[39]

On the 18th, the Tokyo Express landed 1,500 men of the Ichiki Detachment on Guadalcanal. This was the same unit that was to have secured Midway. Now it was given three days to defeat the marines on the island. Such was the incompetent state of Japanese intelligence that 1,500 men were sent to dislodge 10,000. When you know nothing, lead with your ego. Many brave Japanese died in futile charges into marine firepower. Disgraced, Colonel Ichiki Kiyono committed suicide.

Army Air Force observers did not tell the Imperial Navy the number of Americans they saw on Guadalcanal. Japanese commanders repeatedly sent small reinforcing detachments onto the island with unrealistic orders to crush the marines. Frequently the Japanese were outnumbered by the marines but continued to attack into the teeth of U.S. firepower. As historian Edward Hoyt lamented: "Imperial Headquarters did not pay much attention to the Guadalcanal problem, and instead of sending divisions, the Army sent battalions."[40]

As a measure of Ghormley's pessimism, he had his staff working on plans to withdraw from Guadalcanal right up until 20 August. On the 20th, a dozen Marine Dauntless dive-bombers and nineteen Wildcats flew off the escort carrier (CVE) *Long Island* and onto Henderson Field. From this date forward, land-based air had to be factored into the correlation of forces over the surrounding waters.

Ghormley worked hard to improve the aviation infrastructure at Guadalcanal. He had PBYs (patrol bombers) moved up and aviation supplies delivered by fast destroyer transports. King suggested moving the squadron of old battleships into the Solomons. Nimitz replied he didn't have the tanker capacity to handle them. Tankers again.

Reports of an operational American airfield finally galvanized thinking within senior Japanese naval staffs. Yamamoto had decided to move his flag to Truk to be nearer the decisive battle he sought. The main body, which began its southward cruise before marine aircraft landed at Guadalcanal, was instructed to skip the planned stop at Truk and head directly toward the American-infested island.

Japanese fleet carriers had done little since May except train in home waters. After the losses at Midway, the Japanese looked to form carrier task forces of two CVs and a CVL. The CVL carried a large percentage of fighters to defend the task force while the larger air groups on the CVs focused on attack.

Yamamoto assembled a huge armada including three carriers, three battleships (plus *Yamato,* which remained at Truk with Yamamoto aboard), and eight cruisers supported by a large number of destroyers and submarines. He planned to move all forces toward Guadalcanal in escort of a small transport force carrying another 1,500-man reinforcement detachment. Yamamoto intended this movement to precipitate a major fleet engagement.

The normally very perceptive Admiral Ugaki, Yamamoto's chief of staff, suffered from temporarily obscured mental vision. He wrote, "Landing on Guadalcanal by transports is hopeless unless the enemy planes are wiped out."[41] He became so focused on shutting down Henderson Field that he designated this as more important than sinking enemy carriers![42] Orders were issued to this effect. Imagine Mahan shuddering visibly. At the time the Cactus Air Force ("Cactus" was American code for Guadalcanal) operated fewer aircraft than a light carrier. The Japanese obsession with Guadalcanal had begun.

"My good admiral," Mahan might have said to Ugaki, "so much of your analysis has been correct. Unfortunately, you have allowed your pride to create an error of the first magnitude. Recall Truk is the main central Pacific operating base. Rabaul is its outpost. Guadalcanal is Rabaul's outpost. Guadalcanal's intrinsic value is a couple of coconuts. The Pacific is a vast empty. In the Japanese defensive scheme, the seas around the Solomons are a security zone. Combinations of time and space should be traded to set the American fleet up for the kill. Yes, Guadalcanal will be almost impossible to hold without eliminating American aviation at Henderson Field. That is a fine subordinate objective. But do not lose sight of the enemy's fleet. Destroy it and Guadalcanal is an afterthought."

Ugaki's error in strategic objective completely changed the character of the campaign. Guadalcanal was an expendable outpost that was best used to pin American task forces against. If Guadalcanal airpower was tipping the balance, then there were answers to this problem. A couple of batteries of medium field artillery firing regularly will shut down any airfield. The airfield and its installations couldn't maneuver. Field artillery could. Mount Austen, which rose above Henderson Field, and "Bed Check Charlie," the irritating biplane that observed the marines, could provide observation. Add bombers from Rabaul and 1,400-pound shells from battleships and the field would remain unusable regardless of who controlled the infantry front lines. Add a sea blockade and American carriers would have to fight on Japanese terms.

Let's assume the Japanese could not solve the problem posed by Henderson. In that case, they might have withdrawn up the Solomons to a defended Japanese airbase that allowed Japanese land-based airpower to prevail. The farther they retreated, the closer they would get to the big air bases on Rabaul. Pitting Japanese land-based air against American carriers would be the best conditions the emperor could pray for. Japan could kill American carriers without exposing their own.

But Yamamoto's plan, labeled KA, did not attempt to isolate Guadalcanal. Granted, carrier strength was about even. In the summer of 1942, nothing could stand up to Japanese battleships in a gunfight. Fourteen-hundred-pound 14-inch projectiles impacting against American 4-inch cruiser armor will do a lot more damage than 250-pound 8-inch projectiles against 10-inch battleship armor. In addition, Japanese cruiser men had demonstrated their superiority.

Americans would title the upcoming carrier clash "the battle of the Eastern Solomons." Radio intercepts gave the Americans a good picture of the workup of the Japanese fleet for its sortie toward Guadalcanal. Radio intelligence from CinCPac (Commander in Chief, Pacific Fleet—Nimitz's headquarters) informed Fletcher that he faced at least two fleet carriers and a light carrier.[43] On the 10th, CinCPac intelligence predicted a southward move led by carriers *Zuikaku*, *Shokaku*, and *Ryujo*—"a rough guess is that such a force could arrive in that area about August 24th."[44] Japanese attempts at radio deception were ineffective. By the 21st a clear picture of the ships concentrating at Truk for a run at Guadalcanal had emerged. Fletcher's own recon picked up the Japanese transports on the 23rd.

The Americans had at least ten days' warning of the upcoming fight. On the other hand, the Japanese had to feel their enemy out. Fletcher's three carrier groups were at sea, out of range of recon aircraft based at Rabaul. However, Yamamoto knew he would face three or four American fleet carriers. When the Combined Fleet left home waters, marine aircraft had not landed on Guadalcanal.

For the Japanese the battle of the Eastern Solomons was something akin to a meeting engagement on the high seas. Inspect the ship tracks of the engagement in Map 5b. The immediate reason for Japanese carriers to move south was to cover a large reinforcement for Guadalcanal. However, a major fleet action was expected. Nagumo understood that sinking U.S. carriers was far more important than escorting the troop convoy.[45] With American carriers out of the way, the transports should be able to make it on their own. Then Japanese battleships could pummel Henderson Field.

Moving south on the 22nd and 23rd, the Combined Fleet could not estimate the location of the American carriers.[46] It was decided that Rabaul-based bombers would attempt to destroy Henderson Field on the 24th. If an air search did not reveal American carriers, Japanese naval aviators would conduct a second strike on Henderson in the afternoon. Something appears to have been learned at Midway.

The Japanese pushed light carrier *Ryujo* and three destroyers out forward as bait to draw the wrath of American air strikes. This was a favorite Japanese tactic. Planes on the fleet carriers *Shokaku* and *Zuikaku* could then mount a full-blooded counterstrike.

The marines on Guadalcanal generated an air strike on the transports. So did *Saratoga*. Neither found the *marus* (literally "cows"—Japanese slang for merchantmen or transports). The Japanese transport commander, recognizing he had been spotted, had reversed course and sailed north.

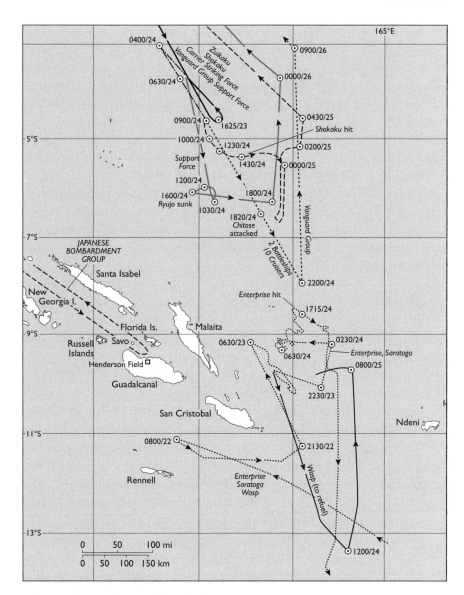

Map 5b. Battle of Eastern Solomons. Map by Bill Nelson.

Fletcher had a lot of warning and was anticipating a major fleet engagement. One might expect that he could have adjusted his fueling schedule so his carrier groups were concentrated and fully capable. Nevertheless, Fletcher felt the oil status of several of his destroyers was below what he wanted. Despite the impending major fleet action that American intelligence had amply outlined,

Fletcher detached the *Wasp* group, which moved 200 miles to the southeast to refuel. As at the beginning of the Guadalcanal campaign, Fletcher was worrying about his ships' fuel levels instead of creating tactical advantage. This retreat kept *Wasp* out of range during the carrier engagements of the 24th. It was the height of fleet mismanagement. In this case, inept refueling management effectively divided the fleet. Nimitz would later shake his head when he heard of it.[47]

Fletcher had three fleet carriers plus the equivalent of a light carrier in the Marine Air Group at Guadalcanal. Nagumo had two fleet carriers plus a light carrier. With *Wasp* Fletcher had at least 1.5:1 superiority—254 carrier-based plus 21 Guadalcanal-based aircraft vs. 177 IJN carrier combat aircraft. With *Wasp* out of position, the count was 177 to 176 in naval aircraft. With *Wasp* present, Fletcher could have gotten very aggressive. Pulling *Wasp* back was far more dangerous then either ordering the oilers forward or running the risk of stranding a couple of destroyers.

This potential American advantage shows how poor Yamamoto's intelligence was. No admiral would ever knowingly offer battle at such a disadvantage. Given the amount of uncertainty the Japanese operated under, Yamamoto must be roundly criticized for not amassing more carrier airpower before heading south.

By 0905 of the 24th, both fleets had sighted each other. The Americans had picked up Ugaki's "decoy" light carrier. But the PBY's report failed to give location information. Fletcher waited until midafternoon for better intelligence. If he delayed further, his aircraft would not return until after dark. Many of his pilots were not really night landing qualified.

As at Coral Sea, Fletcher sent a massive strike against the light carrier bait. But he held all of his fighters in a defensive Combat Air Patrol (CAP). Fifty Wildcats stacked up over the American task forces. Certainly, this was the decision of an admiral very concerned about his defenses.

Before the attackers reached *Ryujo*, recon planes found the two big Japanese carriers. Fletcher attempted to redirect the strike but communications failed. Perhaps that was a blessing in disguise. Remember the fate of unescorted American torpedo bombers at Midway? The fighters over *Ryujo* were far less numerous than those over the two fleet carriers. American bombs and a torpedo tore holes in *Ryujo,* sending her under.

A major Japanese strike force caught *Enterprise*. The CAP held Japanese torpedo bombers at bay. In a rare reversal of roles, some of the Dauntlesses and Avengers returning from the attack on *Ryujo* found themselves catching up with some of the Japanese attackers. Pilots accustomed to lining up large gray shapes in their bombsights became fighter jocks, firing machine guns into attacking

Japanese aircraft. Backseat gunners swiveled their mounts and fired broadside. Apparently it did some good. Three weapons-laden Japanese aircraft splashed. But twenty or thirty dive-bombers bore down on *Enterprise* and her consorts. They began their dives from 18,000 feet—one after another. Anti-aircraft gunners threw up clouds of flak; some of the Vals succumbed. In a five-minute period about 1640, three bombs hit the Big E, setting her brightly aflame. Outstanding damage control contained the fires. An hour later a well-manned *Enterprise* made 24 knots as she received her returning strikers.

Some of the Vals veered off and went after *North Carolina*. Several bombs splashed close to the battlewagon's armored hull but did little damage.

Enterprise was far from out of danger. Bomb-induced damage caused its rudder to jam at 10 degrees. While it could only run in a predictable circle, Nagumo's second strike went aloft to dispatch Big E. But luck intervened. The Japanese flight-plotting officer made a 40-degree error. The strike never sighted *Enterprise*. Almost certain destruction of the crippled carrier was averted. Naval combat is fraught with such unpredictable events.

Prior to the arrival of the Japanese strike, Fletcher had scraped together his remaining dive- and torpedo bombers and sent them off to hit *Shokaku* and *Zuikaku*. The torpedo bombers mistook surf breaking against a reef for enemy ships and scored nothing. While *Enterprise* was undergoing her ordeal, the American bombers from *Saratoga* found seaplane carrier *Chitose* instead. Near misses by the Dauntlesses stove in her unarmored sides, opening her engine spaces to the sea. Despite taking on a list that at one time measured 30 degrees, she made it back to port.

Admiral Kondo, commander of the Guadalcanal Supporting Forces (Second Fleet), recognized his vast superiority in surface combat power. He was eager to put it to use. Returning pilots had reported that two damaged American carriers lay to the south. As the sun came down, two battleships, ten cruisers, and a gaggle of destroyers headed toward the last reported location of the *Enterprise* at flank speed. The chase was to no avail. Fletcher had long since departed. There was no reason for the American navy to wait around for a pummeling by Japanese battleships.

Instead Kondo broke off pursuit at 2330 and turned north. He did not want to be greeted by American aircraft in the coming sunrise. When he turned north, Kondo was 200 miles northeast of Guadalcanal. Nagumo, commander of the Third Fleet, also decided to move his carriers north on the evening of first day. The lack of fire in that admiral's belly was obvious. Captain Aima of *Shokaku* wanted to remain in the area, pick up downed pilots, and resume combat in the morning.

The next day Guadalcanal-based aircraft, including navy planes from the carriers, caught up with the retreating transport convoy and sank several ships. Even a B-17 got a hit.

After Midway, Yamamoto failed either to take command of the fleet or to ensure that Nagumo aggressively pursued clearly expressed orders. Two objectives needed to be achieved. First, any American carriers placed at risk had to be destroyed. Second, sufficient naval power had to be moved *south* of the Solomons to isolate Guadalcanal. Yamamoto should have brought more airpower with him. *Hiyo, Junyo,* and *Zuiho* could have formed another carrier division, almost doubling Nagumo's airpower. These carriers had 134 aircraft. Had he had that power available, Eastern Solomons could have become a major strategic victory instead of one that merely granting the IJN an ephemeral tactical advantage.

Instead of thinking offensively, Yamamoto ordered his transports to withdraw and his fleet to cover the move. He intended to redispatch the supplies on smaller, more maneuverable ships. To say the least, Yamamoto's inability to retain perspective of the larger objective and the opportunity before him, in the words of a noted scholar of the Japanese navy, "is difficult to understand."[48] Ultimately this issue must be placed at Yamamoto's cabin door. Another question: When concentrating fleet strength is all-important, what sense did it make to keep Japan's mightiest battleship up at Truk serving as Yamamoto's abode?

The Imperial Navy had begun feeling the loss of skilled aviators. American pilots commented on the decline in the quality of their adversaries. The IJN needed to conserve its carrier-qualified pilots for carrier vs. carrier action. Instead, many Japanese carrier aircraft were flown off to join the fighting down in the Solomons. Critical irreplaceable resources were committed to an operation that could never have been decisive. What was that definition of strategy again?

The battle of the Eastern Solomons was characterized by caution and fleet mismanagement on both sides. It was as if two prizefighters had become punch-shy and avoided getting in too close. The impact was not symmetrical, however. Yamamoto had to win a decisive victory. A casualty-laced draw favored the Americans because time was on their side.

Mahan would have reminded us that one of the most important duties of senior admirals is to concentrate overwhelming force at the critical place and to ensure that the strategic objective is completely understood. Yamamoto would not have received a passing grade from the American Naval War College professor.

Fletcher had an opportunity to win a major victory. Instead he dispersed his forces in the face of the enemy. He gave the strikers no fighter escort. Nimitz had lost faith in the pessimistic Ghormley and the cautious Fletcher. Despite the outcome of the battle of the Eastern Solomons, he felt Ghormley had lost too many carriers. Earlier, when Nimitz met with King in San Francisco, the latter had wondered if Ghormley's pessimism and poor control of his operation made him a liability. Nimitz polled his senior staff. All agreed a change in leadership was required. Fletcher, who had received a minor wound during the battle, was detached for a stateside hospital. Later he was reassigned to the far less stressful post of commander, North Pacific. Ghormley would ultimately join Admiral Stark, another stress casualty, in London. He had been King's man.

With King's hearty concurrence, Nimitz brought in Vice Admiral William F. "Bull" Halsey as commander, South Pacific. Marines on Guadalcanal and sailors aboard ship cheered wildly at the news. Mahan would have agreed. Even more than the correct strategy, Mahan always underscored the preeminence of the best leadership.

On a personal level, the relief was "cordial" but "left both admirals ill at ease." Ghormley and Halsey had played football together at Annapolis. There are few events more distasteful than firing a friend.

Nimitz placed Rear Admiral Thomas Kinkaid in command of the carriers. Like Spruance he was a surface officer. Admiral Kinkaid had commanded Spruance's screen at Midway. During the battle of the Eastern Solomons he had commanded the *Enterprise* task force. Many of his peers cited his good sense, geniality, and self-confidence.

As they retired from the Guadalcanal area, *Zuikaku* and *Shokaku* transferred 30 Zeros to the airstrip on Buka. By the end of August, Rabaul was down to 88 aircraft, perhaps half of them operational. Recall that the Imperial Army had designated New Guinea, not Guadalcanal, as the main effort. After the battle of the Eastern Solomons, reinforcements were sent to Rabaul. By 20 September, 93 long-range Zeros, 38 short-range Zeros, 81 Bettys, 6 Vals, 4 recon, and 14 flying boats operated from Rabaul.[49]

At the end of August a sub-launched torpedo opened a large gash in "Sister Sara." *Saratoga* would be out for three months. This unlucky ship had caught a torpedo before, in early January off Oahu. *Enterprise* was also temporarily out of the war thanks to her pummeling during the Eastern Solomons fight. She would not emerge from Pearl until 16 October.

On 15 September, while supporting the movement of another marine regiment to Guadalcanal, *Wasp* was torpedoed by Japanese submarine I-19. Three warheads racked the carrier. Internal explosions ripped open fuel lines, making the fires impossible to control. She did not survive the ordeal. Japanese subs were proving fearsome. By neutralizing *Wasp* and *Saratoga*, Japanese submariners had won the equivalent of a major carrier engagement. Now the Americans were at a serious disadvantage and tied to a major commitment at Guadalcanal. Nimitz instituted an inquiry that revealed carriers had been cruising too slowly in the waters surrounding the Solomons.

After Midway, some senior Japanese officers wondered if the IJN had become overextended. After the battle of the Eastern Solomons, little question remained.[50] There would be no more talk about Fiji. In early September, the naval general staff decided that retaking Guadalcanal eclipsed New Guinea in importance. A division in Manchuria was ordered to the Solomons to accomplish this task. The army and the navy were finally on the same page.

With *Saratoga* and *Enterprise* sidelined and *Wasp* sunk, Yamamoto faced a tremendous opportunity. Of the U.S. carriers, only *Hornet* was operational. With a little work, he could have brought at least three fleet carriers against the single American defender. This was twice the 1.5:1 ratio that held promise of victory. If he drove the last American carrier from the sea, he could isolate Guadalcanal and, with the assistance of Rabaul-based bombers, destroy its airpower. Then the Old Breed would have to take to the hills and boil kunai grass for dinner.

This possibility remained for weeks after the battle of the Eastern Solomons. As Morison said, "if they had done so [pressed their attack on Guadalcanal] so in August or the first week in September, they could hardly have failed to clean up."[51] But Yamamoto generated no follow-up. He did nothing to capitalize on the evident opportunity. Mahan would have double-underlined the F the Japanese fleet commander had already earned.

For several months after the battle, American aviation, often from all three services, dominated the Slot by day. At night Japanese cruisers and destroyers held sway. Often American flyers would score on Tokyo Express shipping as it pulled off Guadalcanal in the early morning twilight. Each side reinforced and resupplied. However, the Japanese continued to underestimate American strength on the island.

By mid-October, the American navy had regained its moxie. Halsey was ready to challenge the Japanese to night combat. American cruisers and destroyers began interfering with the Tokyo Express. Rear Admiral Norman Scott led American blue jackets into a major surface engagement off Cape Esperance (the western tip of Guadalcanal) on the night of 11 October. Both sides made serious tactical errors. But American sailors were closing the experience gap with their Japanese counterparts. A Japanese cruiser and three destroyers were sunk (two by aircraft the next morning) in return for the loss of a single American tin can. The sand was running out of Yamamoto's hourglass.

But the Japanese were far from out of fighting spirit. Two nights later, a Japanese task force led by two battleships entered Iron Bottom Sound. That night

Henderson Field was the target of 900 rounds of 14-inch shells. Only 42 of 90 aircraft on Henderson remained operational. Most of the aviation gas blazed. For the rest of the campaign, marines referred to it as *the* bombardment. Cruisers repeated the event two nights later. During the next two nights Japanese cruisers fired 3,000 8-inch projectiles into marine positions. By the time that bombardment was over, most American aircraft on Guadalcanal were not airworthy. The sustained naval gunfire proved the best method of eliminating Henderson's usefulness short of outright capture.

Yamamoto had the stronger 16-inch-gun battleships *Mutu, Nagato,* and *Yamato,* which were far better protected and far more deadly, than the 14-inch-gun *Haruna* and *Kirishima* that had traversed the Slot. Why not bring them south after *Wasp* was sunk but before *Enterprise* returned? During this period, nothing could have stopped them. Put Henderson Field out of action and the Imperial Navy could seal off the sea route to Guadalcanal. Battleships were nowhere near as critical as aircraft carriers. Mahan would have roundly criticized any plan that did not concentrate all force at the decisive battle. To overlook a plan that could win the decisive engagement without risking the battle line (in 1942 the critical "battle line" was the *carriers*) was utter folly.

Instead of employing concentrated and sustained battleship power, the Japanese army and navy commanders decided to reverse the normal phasing of the attack. Normally the fleet would attack an enemy fortress. Then the army would come in and occupy the prize. Japanese commanders decided to reverse the process. First the army was to take Henderson Field. Then the fleet would move south to crush the American fleet.

Courageous Japanese soldiers had already proved the code of Bushido did not provide immunity against unsuppressed U.S. Marine machine guns. On 11 October, the Japanese did land a pair of 155mm howitzers and tractors to move them.[52] Due to poor deployment and lack of ammunition, however, they were more a nuisance than a decisive weapon. Mud Marines dubbed them "Pistol Pete." American destroyers firing from off shore silenced them. Had the Japanese pair of guns been a pair of batteries, they might have sunk the tin cans. Yet another opportunity was missed.

Both sides were losing perspective on Guadalcanal. For the Japanese, it should have been an expendable outpost used to bait the American fleet. For the Americans, it was a way to pin down the Japanese fleet in order to keep it from doing mischief in more important areas and to chew on it while American shipyards built an overpowering carrier fleet.

By October the Japanese army saw Guadalcanal's recapture a "matter of national pride." The Japanese were not the only ones who had begun to see Guadalcanal as a symbol of resolve. In Washington Roosevelt sensed: "The invasion of Guadalcanal had brought a subtle, unannounced change to the Japanese war that was felt by the people long before official announcements gave any indications. All autumn it had become growingly apparent that the euphoric days of constant victory had ended."[53] From FDR to the Joint Chiefs of Staff: "My anxiety about the Southwest Pacific is to make sure that every possible weapon gets into that area to hold Guadalcanal."[54] This from the president who had insisted Germany was the absolute priority.

On 23 October American cryptanalysts had penetrated deeply enough into the new Japanese code to discern that preparations for a massive Japanese offensive were under way. American intelligence analysts extracted most of the key elements of Yamamoto's design.

Yamamoto realized he needed to finish off Guadalcanal once and for all. The Japanese battle plan required the army to capture Henderson Field before he committed his fleet. The army (wrongly) said this was an objective well within reach. He planned to fly naval aircraft directly onto the "former" American airfield. The Japanese were sure this would precipitate major American naval reaction. Finally the decisive sea battle would be joined! Superiority in both aircraft carriers and battleships assured success. Win the crucial carrier battle and unleash the battleships to finish off what remained. Mahan might have muttered, "Slow learner but he *is* getting there."

Yamamoto began thinking in terms of a naval blockade. If his carriers knocked out their American counterparts, he was ready to commit his battleships to destroy the remainder of the American fleet. He had finally concentrated massively. Four carriers, five battleships, ten cruisers, and twenty-nine destroyers had been assembled at Truk and then sent south. They were to engage American naval forces as soon as the army signaled that Henderson Field had fallen.

Yamamoto divided his fleet into many task forces, thus limiting tactical concentration. For example, his five battleships were detailed to three different supporting forces of Admiral Kondo's Second Fleet. If battle lines did clash, Japan would not benefit from the entire weight of her available gun power. A number of Japanese officers had painful memories of split operations at Midway. Nevertheless, *Junyo,* with fifty-five aircraft, was detached to the advance group instead of being kept with the striking fleet. Rather than concentrating carrier strength to smash Halsey's two-carrier force, the Japanese had dissipated their striking power. What did Mahan say about dividing the fleet?

Nagumo's Third Fleet contained the carriers *Shokaku, Zuikaku,* and *Hiyo.* Sailing south, *Hiyo* suffered engine trouble—again. Her cantankerous power plant caught fire, sending her back to Truk. Loss of a carrier was serious. Yamamoto's air groups still contained 212 aircraft; Kinkaid had 169 aboard *Hornet* and the hurriedly repaired *Enterprise*. Japanese superiority was 1.25:1. The 48 naval and marine aircraft on Guadalcanal, if brought to bear, would even up the ratio. Relative plane count provides one rough measure of combat power. Despite pilot losses, Japanese aviators still averaged more cockpit time than their counterparts. The Zero retained its qualitative edge over the stubby Wildcat. While the fleet movement would cover a small Guadalcanal-bound reinforcement convoy, the Combined Fleet's primary mission was to destroy American carriers.[55]

Good intelligence gave Vice Admiral Halsey time to react. He had made a careful study of the fight off Midway and concluded that the primary cause for the decisive success was the tactical surprise of positioning the American fleet in an unsuspected location, to the northeast of Midway rather than in the southeast toward Hawaii. At the earliest chance, he was determined to replicate these conditions. News of Yamamoto's southward movement gave him his cue. Halsey had only been theater commander for a few days. Without hesitation, he maneuvered to generate a major fleet action.

Despite being at a disadvantage, "Halsey did not seriously consider evading battle."[56] In private Captain Mahan might have cautioned the American admiral. The correlation of forces was against the Americans. A Midway in reverse would doom Guadalcanal and halt any further offensive until new carriers joined the fleet in the summer of 1943. Then again, Mahan always preferred offensive action.

The Japanese army was having a much tougher time attempting to take Guadalcanal than it wanted to admit to the navy. Twice, Yamamoto had to reschedule the fleet's departure for the Solomons. The delay allowed enough time for the recently repaired *Enterprise* to rejoin the U.S. fleet.

With the removal of Admiral Fletcher, Rear Admiral Thomas C. Kinkaid, commander of the *Enterprise* task group at Eastern Solomons, was also designated the officer in tactical command over both carrier groups for the upcoming battle. *Enterprise* had just steamed down from Honolulu. Instead of operating adjacent to or south of Guadalcanal, Halsey ordered Kinkaid to move Big E, along with *Hornet*'s task force, to the northeast of the Santa Cruz Islands. Apparently Halsey, inspired by what had happened at Midway, was looking to ambush the Japanese fleet from the northeast, a direction they wouldn't expect. It was a bold play considering Halsey's weak hand. If positioned to the north of the Santa Cruz Islands, the Japanese fleet would be out of range of Guadalcanal's aircraft. Halsey's move was dangerous, even reckless. But what would have happened if Halsey had refused battle and four Japanese battleships had pounded Henderson

Field back into the mud? Mahan would have responded, "It's the *carriers.*" A correct strategy may sound simple but exact cruel discipline in execution. Had American carriers been swept from the South Pacific, the marines, instead of being pounded, would have become isolated and, possibly, doomed. Halsey should never have placed his fleet in such a precarious position. He should have accepted battle only when the Japanese were within Guadalcanal's range.

Embarrassed at its lack of success, the Japanese army finally signaled it had taken Henderson Field. Nothing even remotely like that happened. Based on that false claim, Yamamoto began his operation.

The Americans knew the Japanese fleet was in the neighborhood. During 25 October, Admiral Kinkaid worked hard to get a crippling first strike in before his own forces were detected. He launched an extensive search pattern to locate Kondo's carriers. Late in the afternoon, *Enterprise* readied a major strike before nightfall on any contact that might develop. Unfortunately, the scouts didn't flush any targets. *Hornet*'s pilots were night landing qualified. All through the night, Kinkaid held them in readiness to hit any contacts made by PBY "black cats." Sometime after midnight, two of those night stalkers nearly hit *Zuikaku* but the information did not reach Kinkaid in time to influence the battle.

At eleven minutes after midnight on the 26th a PBY radioed an enemy sighting report. Three hours later a second PBY reported an enemy carrier and six escorts on the same course as the first report 200 miles from Kinkaid. Upon receiving the PBY contact report during the early hours of the morning, Halsey radioed to Kinkaid, "STRIKE—REPEAT—STRIKE!"

Thanks to poor communications, Kinkaid didn't receive word of the PBY sightings until 0512. He didn't think the information fresh enough to launch a major strike. Instead, Kinkaid launched a spread of scout planes just before first light. Although he toyed with the idea of sending a strike group of bombers to follow them, he held the bombers back until the scouts found Japanese carriers. Later Halsey, and many other aviation-rated officers, criticized Kinkaid for this hesitation.

First the Americans located the battleships and cruisers of Kondo's Advance Group steaming ahead of Nagumo's carriers. Strike now? Kinkaid continued to hold back his bombers. (Ship tracks for 26 October are displayed on Map 5c.)

Twenty minutes later his scouts spotted the carriers. Search aircraft carried 500-pound bombs. Incredibly, diving scouts blew two holes in *Zuiho*'s flight deck, making it impossible for the light carrier to recover planes. Its aircraft flew off toward Rabaul, and *Zuiho* turned toward Truk. Once again luck had reduced the odds against the Americans. During the battle, the Americans never located *Junyo.*

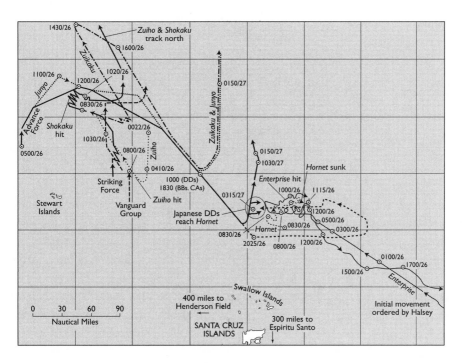

Map 5c. Battle of Santa Cruz. Map by Bill Nelson.

However, the Japanese had already launched their Kates and Vals. Kinkaid's staff had been estimating the Japanese carrier plot based on the PBY sighting and were readying a strike. The admiral demurred, wanting another hard observation. When the radio crackled, he launched everything available toward the reported carrier contact. Incredibly, both strike groups passed their enemy counterpart en route. Now both sides knew trouble was in the air. Each admiral had done his job competently. Neither Kondo nor Kinkaid could do much more except sweat. Pilots and ship captains, gunners and damage control men would now decide the fates of both fleets.

Japanese attackers arrived over *Hornet* before its defending fighters had reached altitude. (Kinkaid would be criticized for this lapse.) Five bombs and a brace of torpedoes left *Hornet* brightly ablaze and unusable. A wounded Val slammed into her stack. A Kate flew into her forward gun gallery and took out the forward elevator. Only dumb luck saved *Enterprise*. She ducked under a rain squall at the last moment.

American dive-bombers from *Hornet*'s first strike badly damaged *Shokaku*. She appeared to have been hit four times and would be out of action nine months for repairs. As her report back to duty postdated a whole slew of new American carriers forming "the Big Blue Fleet," it was almost as good as sinking her. She would not be available during the remainder of Nimitz's rapidly closing period of vulnerability. Kinkaid's other raiders either got lost or, because they were low on fuel, struck the Advance Group instead of the carriers farther back. Cruiser *Chikuma* was severely damaged by four 1,000-pound bomb hits. Battleship *Kirishima* received several 500-pound bombs that did little except rattle topside equipment. Returning American aviators were peeved that poor radios prevented them from receiving location sightings of the other Japanese carriers.

Like *Enterprise, Zuikaku* was shrouded by clouds. Later she recovered aircraft that had flown off the stricken *Shokaku. Zuikaku's* second strike was already plowing toward the recently repaired Big E. That carrier's cloud cover ran out. Dive-bombers screamed down, hitting the American carrier three times. Planes spotted on deck were bounced into the sea by the explosions. Kinkaid was thrown to the deck of the flag bridge. Fourteen torpedo bombers made for Big E. Nine slipped their deadly torpedoes into the waves. But the carrier's captain handled his 20,000-ton ship nimbly. He evaded every torpedo and his gunners brought most of the Kates down. Japanese carrier planes continued to hit the blazing *Hornet,* which the cruiser *Northampton* had taken in tow. An immobile cruiser alongside a flaming hulk is too easy a target. During the last attack a torpedo narrowly missed *Northampton* and slammed into the helpless *Hornet.* Salvage operations had to be discontinued. Despite severe damage to her forward elevator and flight deck, *Enterprise* continued to recover returning aircraft. Soon her flight and hangar decks were crowded by planes from *Hornet* as well as her own squadrons. Kinkaid ordered retirement to the southeast. He knew at least one, maybe two, undamaged Japanese carriers lay to his northwest. They had a lot of daylight in which to generate more air strikes. After all, he was aboard the last American carrier in the Pacific and it contained three smoking bomb holes.

Kondo's Advance Force with *Junyo* had been steaming due south toward Guadalcanal while Nagumo's carriers sailed to the southeast looking for the American fleet. Now this task force changed course first northeast and then southeast to close with the American carriers. *Junyo's* planes were redirected to search out and destroy the badly damaged *Enterprise.* Instead they hit *South Dakota* and punched a hole through the anti-aircraft light cruiser *San Juan. Junyo's* pilots, being less well trained than their counterparts from other carriers, made shallower diving attacks. This made them far more vulnerable to American anti-aircraft gunners.

Hornet had been devastated and *Enterprise* had begun to retire by 1400. There was plenty of daylight for another Japanese carrier strike. The Japanese navy was poised to deliver a coup de grâce. With no operational flight decks and out of range of Guadalcanal, Kinkaid's ships were vulnerable to being slowed by additional carrier strikes and then smashed by battleship fire. Yamamoto's gun power far exceeded what the Americans could muster. After Midway, this was the point of greatest Japanese matériel ascendancy over the Americans. Mahan would have recommended the Japanese attack be pressed through the night and into the next day. Annihilate the Americans and dominate the waters south and east of Guadalcanal. Cut it off and watch Cactus wither. With the Americans cut off, the Japanese could ultimately prevail.

Nevertheless, Yamamoto decided to withdraw to the north that evening. He cited his aircraft losses, which exceeded 100, as reason for withdrawal.[57] Overall oil consumption was on the mind of every Japanese admiral. The fleet's stocks had declined dangerously: this was another consideration.

Better than most, Yamamoto knew time was on the side of American industry. Right here, right now, there was nothing to stop the Japanese fleet. Badly damaged *Enterprise* and her consorts fled toward Espiritu Santo, about 300 miles south of the Santa Cruz Islands. There was nothing there to protect it. At Espiritu Santo, Halsey had not a single naval attack plane or army medium bomber to hit back with. The base contained a squadron of Wildcats, some recon PBYs and Hudsons, and 39 B-17s that almost never hit anything. It was early afternoon. "Pursue a beaten enemy with ardor," Mahan had counseled. Mahan would have insisted Yamamoto sail the emperor's fast battleships, covered by carriers, into Halsey's rear supply base. Rip up the unprotected warehouses and docks. How would Guadalcanal then be resupplied? Then the Japanese could pull back into the 600 miles of ocean between Guadalcanal and Noumea. There would be nothing the United States could do to counter the move. Not a single carrier would remain. There were no single-engine attack planes capable of interfering. Not a single American surface ship would dare make for Guadalcanal for months. Yamamato could have doomed Vandergrift and his heroes that afternoon just by sailing south.

Risky? Yes. But not as risky as Halsey's move north of Santa Cruz. The strategic positions of the adversaries were completely asymmetric. This was Japan's last chance to inflict a serious enough blow to stagger the American behemoth. In nine months, the U.S. fleet would have the carrier power to continuously press the Japanese backward. It was Yamamoto's last chance to secure a positive war result.

Nagumo had failed to follow through at Pearl Harbor; Yamamoto did likewise south of the Santa Cruz Islands. Japan would never have such a chance to shape the war's outcome again. Mahan would have hardly needed to post the failing grade. The West Point Military History Series states: "Admiral Yamamoto probably lost the war for Japan in 1942 when he failed to use his overwhelming air and naval superiority to destroy the American carrier fleet."[58] Here was *the* opportunity.

The emperor himself expressed his distress at the outcome of the efforts to date to capture Guadalcanal. On 29 October, His Majesty damned the navy with faint praise in an imperial rescript: "We are deeply pleased at this time in the South Pacific the Combined Fleet has inflicted great damage on the enemy fleet. However we believe the war situation is critical. Officers and men, exert yourselves to even greater efforts."[59] Ugaki recorded that the fleet's leadership got the message: "We are dismayed by the concern our failures on Guadalcanal have caused the Emperor. Only the quickest possible achievement of our goals can excuse us before His Majesty."[60]

Halsey really had no business in accepting so much risk in pushing his carriers in a badly exposed position against so much available Japanese power. He was lucky that more aggressive Japanese admiralship hadn't crushed Kinkaid's fleet. After the battle he remarked that he would never again permit Yamamoto to "suck" his carriers into waters north of San Cristobal.[61] No one had a right to be that lucky twice.

During the American retreat, the damaged battleship *South Dakota* collided with a destroyer named *Mahan,* sending the smaller ship to the dockyard.

Between the fight at Savo Island in August and the naval battle of Guadalcanal in November, a whole string of night battles were fought in the waters off the north and east coasts of Guadalcanal. Both sides repeatedly demonstrated raw courage and unbending will. At first, superior Japanese training and torpedoes dominated. But American blue jackets continued to learn. The sinking of the destroyers *Murasame* and *Minegumo* off Kolombangara marked the ascendancy of American radar over Japanese night optics. Technical change heavily impacts naval tactics.

After Santa Cruz the United States had no carrier airpower. Japanese troops on Guadalcanal, reinforced by many deliveries by the Tokyo Express, finally outnumbered the Americans. Yamamoto had yet another opportunity to deliver the coup de grâce. He assembled a force of two carriers, four battleships, five heavy cruisers, and twelve destroyers. But the raging Bull wasn't finished yet. He ordered Terrible Turner to forward a massive resupply convoy that included 6,000 combat troops. This convoy, under the tactical command of Rear Admiral Daniel Callaghan, approached Guadalcanal on the evening of 11 November. Halsey ordered the repairmen of the tender *Vulcan* to surpass what their counterparts at Pearl Harbor had achieved before the battle of Midway. In a single day they were to get *Enterprise* seaworthy—to complete repairs that would ordinarily require eleven days. However, even Halsey realized the last U.S. carrier in the Pacific was too important to risk in another knife fight off Guadalcanal. He would hold *Enterprise* well south of the island and out of range of Japanese air. She set sail from Noumea accompanied by a pair of battleships and an escort of lesser warships.

Only carrier *Junyo* accompanied the Japanese fleet south for another attack on Guadalcanal. *Shokaku, Zuikaku,* and *Zuiho* were on their way back to Japan for badly needed repairs. *Hiyo*'s engines were acting up again and she didn't make the trip.

Both U.S. signals intelligence and aircraft spotting reports identified a huge Japanese fleet making for Guadalcanal. As no transports had been reported, Admiral Turner, in tactical command of the American resupply task force, surmised the Japanese intended either to interfere with the American transports or to bombard Henderson Field. American troops and supplies landed just before the upcoming fight. Japanese aircraft did make an attack on them. Everyone knew this was prologue.

American ships were scattered all over the place in penny packets. Not a very good tactical situation. Turner merged Callaghan's ships with Scott's. Surface escorts in the *Enterprise* group were too far away to join in the upcoming night fight. Mahan would not have been happy with the dispersal but he would have applauded Turner's corrective action. While they had a way to go, the American admirals were improving at their profession.

Although Scott was far more experienced, Callaghan assumed command because he was senior. Even in the most desperate of circumstances, some sacred cows cannot be sacrificed for the Cause. Callaghan made a number of serious tactical mistakes. Because he didn't understand the critical advantage radar gives in a night fight, his best radar ships were poorly positioned. Instead of giving his destroyer flotillas free rein to bring their torpedoes to bear on the Japanese, he tied them closely to his battle line. The formation he selected was more appropriate to the age of sail. It appears Callaghan had an opportunity to cross the T of the approaching Japanese ships but didn't take advantage of it.

But there was nothing wrong with the iron constitution of the American sailors that night. Rear Admiral Hiroaki Abe was leading battleships *Hiei* and *Kirishima*, along with their escorts into Iron Bottom Sound to smash Guadalcanal into the mud. The battleships could fire 1,400-pound shells into the thickest American cruiser armor—about 6 inches. In return the heaviest American shell, at 250 pounds, had no chance to penetrate 12-inch armor of the battleships. Nevertheless the American ships relentlessly bore down on the approaching Japanese that appeared on their radar scopes. Not having radar, Abe was unaware of American dispositions. Yet he was ready for a fight that he knew would be quick, violent, and at very close quarters. Action began just after midnight on Friday the 13th.

Admiral Scott was killed on his bridge by one of the opening Japanese salvos. Opposing ships literally sailed right by each other. One of Admiral Callaghan's last orders read: "Odd ships fire to starboard, even to port." Any semblance of order disappeared in the tangle of ships. Friend became interlaced with foe. Some of the light American shells managed to knock out the fire control instruments of *Hiei*. Then one opened the battleship's steering gear room to the sea. The behemoth became uncontrollable. She flailed back with her heavy armament, smashing a pair of American destroyers. Japanese torpedo explosions lifted already damaged *Atlanta* out of the water. Neither she nor her sister ship, *Juneau,* survived the action.

Battleship *Kirishima* was undamaged. She tore heavy cruiser *San Francisco* into shredded metal, killing Admiral Callaghan in the process. A torpedo hit *Portland,* blasting her plates into an unintentional, immovable rudder. Although helplessly turning in a predictable (and targetable) circle, she fired gallantly. Smashed by Japanese high explosives, two American light cruisers and four destroyers were lost. So was a pair of Japanese destroyers. Abe had seen enough. He ordered withdrawal. The entire fight lasted less than twenty minutes. Yamamoto was very disappointed with Abe's decision to turn tail. He saw that Abe never commanded at sea again. Abe resigned his commission in 1943.

Heroic American sailors, many of them now dead, prevented the marines from getting another pounding. In recognition of their heroism, Callaghan posthumously received the Medal of Honor. That medal recognized the lives of nearly 1,000 blue jackets lost that night. The senior surviving American officer afloat, Captain Hoover, was wrongly blamed for leaving the scene even though there still were American sailors in the dark, shark-invested waters. Had he remained, the loss of American life would have been greater. He was relieved of command, a promising career ruined. Later even Halsey admitted Captain Hoover made the right decision and was wrongly treated.[62] The next day U.S. Marine and Navy aircraft caught up with damaged *Hiei* and bashed at her until she turned turtle and sank.

Scott and Callaghan brought Abe to a standstill the night of the 13th. Despite the sinking of *Hiei,* the Japanese were determined to press even deeper the very next night. The advancing Japanese warships screened the movement of a large squadron of Tanaka's transports, eleven *maru*s, and eleven destroyers. They successfully discharged their cargoes at Cape Esperance. Several escorting cruisers entered Iron Bottom Sound and shelled the marines. There was little to stop them. Eighteen aircraft had been destroyed and another thirty-two damaged in the bombardment. President Roosevelt wondered if the island would have to be evacuated.[63]

But the airfield remained operational. On the morning of the 14th American planes caught a heavy and a light cruiser. Both were heavily damaged. The heavy cruiser sank. However, this action allowed a convoy of eleven *marus* escorted by eleven destroyers under the command of the tenacious Admiral Tanaka to steam south. When these were finally sighted, marine and navy aircraft from Henderson took turns pummeling the slow transports. Seven of them sank. The destroyers picked up survivors and Tanaka continued to push south.

That night battleships *Haruna* and *Kirishima*, accompanied by smaller escorts, steamed toward Iron Bottom Sound. Yamamoto was determined to coat Henderson Field with hot metal. Kondo picked up "clear air" spot reports of his passing from American subs. He knew the Americans would want to greet him.

While holding *Enterprise* to the south, Halsey dispatched Vice Admiral Willis A. "Ching" Lee and his battleships *South Dakota* and *Washington,* armor-piercing shells loaded in their gun tubes, to sally into those dark, deadly waters. Many officers in Nimitz's headquarters doubted the wisdom of putting the battleships into such restricted waters at night. But Halsey was determined to stop the Japanese. Halsey once called Lee "expert at every gun from a forty-five to a 16 incher." (Ching had taken home five gold medals for marksmanship from the 1920 Olympics.) He was also considered one of the most knowledgeable officers in the navy about radar. Halsey granted him complete freedom of action.

Four destroyers from Kinkaid's forces were transferred to Lee. As they weren't even from the same destroyer squadron, they were as unfamiliar with each other as with the battlewagons. In the opening moments of the engagement, they maneuvered erratically. Soon several were burning. *South Dakota* embarrassed herself by losing all electrical power, leaving her almost blind. Japanese searchlights illuminated her and soon heavy rounds began smashing her into a smoking hulk. Through good use of radar *Washington* caught *Kirishima* at close range: 16-inch rounds slammed into the Japanese ship, smashing her to bits. Both sides began to withdraw. *South Dakota* also got some licks in against Japanese cruisers. The prayers of the marines on shore had been answered. All these high explosives and screaming hot metal weren't landing on them. Rather than let *Kirishima* linger like *Hiei,* Kondo ordered the crew taken off and the ship scuttled. Lee had triumphed.

But Tanaka was not deterred. While the heavies bludgeoned each other, he had beached his *marus* at Cape Esperance and relieved his destroyers of their cargo. Two thousand shaken soldiers, 260 cases of ammunition, and about

15,000 bags of rice were landed. Compared to what Turner had delivered a couple of days prior, it was a pittance. From 15 November forward, an overall American victory had become inevitable.

Japan's Army Focuses on New Guinea

However vexing the differences between the U.S. Army and Navy, they seemed minor when compared to the almost complete lack of coordination between the Imperial Japanese Army and Navy. The Japanese army carried on a war in New Guinea while almost completely ignoring what the navy was attempting on Guadalcanal. That is why the initial reinforcements for Guadalcanal were Special Naval Landing Force units. An August landing on the island by a Japanese army division supported by the full weight of the navy might have sealed the fate of the Old Breed.

Prior to the American invasion of Guadalcanal, the Imperial General Headquarters viewed further advance in the Solomons with little interest. Port Moresby on the southern shore of New Guinea was the Imperial Army's objective. (Map 7b on p. 253 depicts eastern New Guinea.) A strong air base there would cut off shipping coming into Australia. When the battle of the Coral Sea eliminated realistic possibilities for sailing around the tip of New Guinea, the Japanese generals concluded that a land attack over the rugged, jungle-covered Owen Stanley Range had to be made. On 12 June 1942, the army ordered plans to take the "Kokoda Trail" over the mountains.[64] To gain a base for this effort, Japanese army units landed on the northeast coast near Buna in mid-July and began the trek up the faintest indication of a trace over the overgrown slopes. Maps of the area were nonexistent. So was the "trail." Two reduced-strength divisions began to slog and slip up the jagged rocks. Swamps near the coast and the jungle-covered mountains were even more unhealthy than Guadalcanal.

MacArthur's staff also wanted to land at Buna in July. The Japanese beat them to it. U.S. forces in the southwest Pacific would not get this far until the end of the year. However, this wasn't the general's fault. The entire Pacific Fleet would have needed to race down from Midway to New Guinea and then make big waves toward Guadalcanal by 3 August. This was more than even Nimitz could achieve.

During July, fighting in New Guinea diverted Japanese resources from the Solomons. Well into August, the Imperial General Staff thought New Guinea was much more important than Guadalcanal. To the extent that this decision diverted reinforcements from Guadalcanal, MacArthur's New Guinea operations had some strategic value. At the beginning of September, the desert veterans of the Australian 7th Division crushed an attempted Japanese landing at Milne Bay.

By late November the American 32nd Division was stalled in front of Buna. By then, Australian 7th Division had their hands full at Sanananda.

By this time the risk to Australia's sea lanes, the original objective for both sides, had long since been eliminated. The pivotal battles on and around Guadalcanal had been decided in America's favor. The right question for a strategist to ask became: "Is the battle for bloody Buna necessary?"

In New Guinea both sides were fighting in soggy, disease-ridden jungle. During most of the war American forces were far more lavishly equipped than their adversaries. However, their equipment on hand in New Guinea was a fraction of what was desired. Coastal ships bringing supplies up from Milne Bay were sunk by Japanese aircraft. Despite urgent requests, the U.S. 32nd Division received no tanks and only a single 105mm howitzer. The Allies had no way around stout coconut-log Japanese bunkers. Unsupported American infantry had to charge into the fire of bunkered machine guns.

This was the first major deployment of American combat troops in New Guinea under MacArthur's direct command. Fighting was so hard that some American units broke. Marines and soldiers on Guadalcanal had their situation well in hand while the push on Buna had stalled badly. In the words of the official U.S. Army historian, this was "a bitter pill . . . to swallow."[65] Furious at lack of success, but not in touch with the shortcomings that produced it, MacArthur sent Lieutenant General Robert Eichelberger into New Guinea with orders to "take Buna or don't come back alive."[66] By the time Papua (eastern New Guinea) was secured, MacArthur's forces had suffered 3,100 dead and 5,400 wounded, with many more permanently disabled from various illnesses. Japanese dead probably numbered 13,000.

Allied dead in Papua exceeded American losses on Guadalcanal. Battles over that hellish island resulted in a major strategic decision. Papua added little to the balance.

As combat in and around Guadalcanal intensified, the Japanese army began to get sucked in. After the naval battle of Guadalcanal, the Japanese navy lost interest in adding to the carnage strewn across Iron Bottom Sound. Now the positions within the Japanese military reversed. In late November, Admiral Ugaki, Yamamoto's chief of staff, wrote: "The Army is sticking to Guadalcanal alone, but we should have foresight not to be dragged into the bottomless mire by the army and lose everything in the end . . . if any more useless attritions are added up after repeated desperate struggles, some break will surely take place elsewhere in our national defense."[67] Ugaki earned another A in Mahan's grade book. The Japanese navy was ready to withdraw from Guadalcanal. If the Japanese fleet could not win a decisive victory against the American fleet in the southern Solomons, it was time to pick a location where the correlation of forces was kinder to the Japanese.

The difficulty of shipping and fuel oil pressured Japan's navy back toward reality. There wasn't enough available transportation to continue to reinforce Guadalcanal and supply the home islands with raw materials. During the middle of December, the navy staff concluded that the struggle for Guadalcanal had to be suspended. The army staff, with their prestige now committed to that island, howled. Nevertheless, Yamamoto gave the order to begin withdrawal on 3 January.

Not until long after any hope for meaningful victory had evaporated did the army agree to a withdrawal. However, the January 1943 document authorizing the evacuation of Guadalcanal also called for continued offensive in New Guinea.[68] Reality had not yet cured members of the general staff of "Victory Disease."

Tojo felt a new drive to knock China out of the war would remove the reason why the paths of Japan and the United States had crossed. With that impediment gone, he was certain peace could be negotiated with the British and the Americans. Japan could easily afford to give up the Solomons and the Bismarck Archipelago. Many senior officers subscribed to the belief "Conquer China and the war will go away." It was repeated so often, it became an article of faith.[69]

The loss of Guadalcanal and Buna caused the Japanese Imperial General Staff to re-evaluate their strategy. Barely eight months ago, they had swept their Caucasian enemies from the Pacific and Indian oceans. Now they couldn't hold an island in the face of concentrated American airpower. It was quite a shock. In the hazy vision that had been brought on by Victory Disease, most officers had lost sight of Yamamoto's pre–Pearl Harbor admonition about what would happen in six months or a year.

However, all was not lost. The Imperial General Staff felt Guadalcanal was outside Japan's defensive perimeter. At the beginning of 1943, the Japanese armed forces in the southwest Pacific were ready to furiously resist further Allied advances up the New Guinea coast and the Solomon chain. Japan wanted to make every island, every point on the New Guinea coast a bloody battleground. Unusually good cooperation of the army and navy commanders on Rabaul significantly eased the problems of command and theater strategy.

Strategists at Imperial General Headquarters began looking at America's next moves. They did not think a strike in the central Pacific was likely. The Americans weren't strong enough yet to follow this path. An unlikely alternative might be an advance from western Australia via the Dutch East Indies to the Philippines. The most probable course of American action was an advance up the Solomons toward Rabaul. This would be paralleled by a second thrust up the New Guinea coast toward the same objective. From Rabaul, the attacks would continue toward the Philippines. It was as if the Japanese were reading MacArthur's thoughts. They hoped for a plan similar to what MacArthur was about to propose. A step-by-step advance up the Solomons and along the New Guinea coast that led to the systematic reduction of the Bismarck Archipelago and its fortress at Rabaul would maximize Japan's opportunity to delay and inflict maximum casualties on the squeamish, impatient Americans.

The Japanese Army–Navy Central Agreement dated 4 January 1943 sanctioned withdrawals from Guadalcanal and Buna. However, the document still called for offensive action over the Owen Stanley Range toward Port Moresby. Air strength throughout the South Pacific was to be expanded to "enforce air supremacy over Eastern New Guinea and annihilate enemy air power."[70] A defensive perimeter that started in the East Indies extended through Wewak, Lae, and Salamaua in New Guinea; to New Britain, Rabaul, and the upper Solomons, and on to the Gilberts, Wake Island, and the Aleutians.

In November Yamamoto and Lieutenant General Hitoshi Imamura had a frank talk in Truk. Imamura was the new Rabaul area army commander. Yamamoto was in the dumps. In the past six months the navy had lost 893 planes and 2,362 airmen. Yet there had been no increase in the number of graduating pilots.[71] Previously the army had seen China as the main effort. Now the army was willing to delay China to win in the South Pacific. Imperial General Headquarters was ready to commit the entire fleet and four new divisions from Korea and China to ensure that victory.

Southwest Pacific Strategy Re-examined

Before the war, both navies identified the central Pacific as the decisive theater of the impending Pacific war. Initially, both sides anticipated that the Japanese would ambush the Americans advancing from Hawaii to the Philippines by attacking somewhere in the Marshalls or perhaps the Marianas. Initial Japanese success made an immediate American counterattack impossible. Yamamoto advanced in the central Pacific looking to move the decisive battle to Midway. But he lost one of the most incredible battles in world history.

Almost by himself, King launched the Guadalcanal campaign. It was a brilliant stroke. If Japan risked her entire fleet down in the Solomons, it would become dangerously weak in the central Pacific. So the probability was that Japan would commit subelements of naval strength in sufficiently small packets that the American navy could swallow. In fact, that is what happened.

It was obvious that the U.S. Navy would not have enough strength to execute Plan Orange until a new flock of fleet carriers joined the fleet in mid-1943. Could the American navy remain unutilized for a year? Mahan wouldn't have thought so. Neither did King. He concocted a much less threatening and much slower advance up the Solomons. He sought to whittle down the Japanese fleet while improving the training and experience level of his own. America could easily afford to trade ship for ship. Japan could not.

Had Yamamoto been able to bring Mahanian concentration to bear on *the* critical task, he should have won the Guadalcanal campaign. Guadalcanal was an afterthought extension of initial Japanese strategy. It was part of an effort to cut the sea lanes between the United States and Australia. One option was simply to ignore the American effort. But Yamamoto couldn't afford this. Better than anyone else, he understood that time would bring forth an irresistible American war machine that would crush Japan. Already the odds favored the Americans. Japan's only hope was to inflict a victory so costly in American blood that U.S. resolve melted. If Yamamoto could destroy American carrier strength in being, the Americans would be unable to take any offensive action for a year. Hawaii would again be exposed, although to nowhere near the extent it had been on 6 December 1941. Perhaps the Americans could be induced to negotiate a peace that would ensure Japanese access to critical resources.

Yamamoto had to pick up any gauntlet King threw down. While Guadalcanal was a very long way from Tokyo, American resources were very limited. Basing his primary fleet at Truk gave Yamamoto a central position that prevented a smaller American fleet from getting too frisky. Yamamoto's problem was to strike south to Guadalcanal at the proper time with enough sea power to catch and crush the Americans. One immediately sees the critical nature of intelligence and recognizes that the Americans had a tremendous advantage in what we now call information technology.

The easiest victory could have been achieved the night of 7 August. Mikawa failed to continue beyond the smashed Allied cruisers and shoot up Turner's seventeen vulnerable transports because his objective had not been forcefully underlined. Underlining orders was Yamamoto's job. The loss of a couple of cruisers was immaterial if a major strategic victory could be achieved in the process. Midway demonstrated that carrier aircraft had to work hard to sink heavily armored ships that were protected by dense anti-aircraft fire. Vandergrift might have been isolated on Guadalcanal, requiring a "must-win" rescue effort by American carriers. With the large air base at Rabaul and a fleet of long-range Japanese land-based aircraft, the larger Japanese carrier fleet should have been able to underline the victory with destruction of American carriers as well.

In August, Japanese leadership was slow to recognize what the Americans were up to. For several weeks after Savo Island, the Japanese believed the marines on Guadalcanal were no more than a raiding force. Now Yamamoto's problem was to generate overwhelming force in the waters around that island to suck in and destroy the American carriers. Yamamoto didn't begin to generate enough power at the battle of the Eastern Solomons. Had Fletcher not pushed *Hornet* south to refuel, the Japanese would have been in an inferior position, an incompetent result for Yamamoto. During the campaign he also immobilized the battleship *Yamato,* a major asset. He should have either moved ashore and released *Yamato* or ridden along with his attack fleet. Yamamoto held back several carriers and battleships in reserve. Nimitz bet all—and won where the odds said he should have lost.

Halsey's overaggressiveness at Santa Cruz gave the Japanese an incredible opportunity. Had Japanese carrier power been better concentrated and, as Mahan always advocated, had the Americans been more vigorously pursued, Yamamoto could have achieved a campaign-winning victory. Establishing a blockade south of Guadalcanal would have doomed the marines on that wretched island. Invasion of Noumea rather than constant grinding on Guadalcanal might have yielded better results.

A Japanese victory at Guadalcanal would not have changed the war's outcome. As American carrier strength increased through 1943, the trans-Pacific offensive would still have gained steam. The war might have been longer and taken more American casualties. Perhaps the drive up the Solomons never would have been pursued—which would have been no strategic loss to the Americans. But victory at Guadalcanal in the fall of 1942 was Japan's last hope.

6

CENTRAL VERSUS SOUTH PACIFIC

As the vein-popping tests of strength in and around Guadalcanal faded toward the end of 1942, American worldwide grand strategy had become firmly set. Germany was the greater threat. The first priority was, in concert with our British and Soviet allies, to defeat Hitler. The invasion of North Africa was the first step along that long path. The brilliant success at Midway ended any real fear of a Japanese attack on America. Anyone who doubted the determination and ferocity of America need only look at the blood stains along Bloody Ridge, where the marines had stopped a Japanese attempt to retake Henderson Field, or the skeletons among the wreckage on Iron Bottom Sound. Still, King fretted about the relative inactivity of the fleet.

Often a strategist's most difficult assignment is to pare away all the competing subsidiary agendas that drain resources from the critical concentration on the strategy's number one objective. By early 1943, there was no shortage of such competing agendas. All of the interested parties in Pacific strategy had their own ideas about what should come next. All of them threw as much political weight as they could muster to further their agenda. The strategist has to resist all of this and remain true to his strategy—without being relieved of duty.

Even before Guadalcanal, American planners envisioned a two-pronged advance across the Pacific. Map 6a roughly depicts its two parts. MacArthur would lead one via Rabaul. The navy would advance the other across the central Pacific via the Caroline and the Marshall islands. Both would converge in the Philippines at some future date. MacArthur was anxious to move on to Tasks Two and Three as originally set out by Marshall. According to the agreement among the Washington chiefs of staff, MacArthur was to command these efforts. His staff busily drew up the plans and lengthy troop lists needed to carry them out and to move their boss to his meeting with destiny in the Philippines: "I shall return."

Each theater competed for scarce aircraft, service forces, supplies, and the shipping with which to move them. However, the fleet carriers, battleships, and cruisers produced by the massive American naval building program had limited relevance to the war for Europe. Eventually, these ships would be employed to roll the Japanese back. Even the British admitted that the Allies should not stay completely idle against the Japanese. They needed to be kept off balance lest they so deeply entrench themselves along a static defensive line that only an ocean of blood could remove them.

In 1933, while at the Naval War College, Ernest King had commanded the Blue Fleet in a rendition of War Plan Orange. (Bull Halsey was on the same team as King.) In his memoirs, King recalled it in detail. "There were three possible routes from Hawaii to the Philippines. The first, which King favored, involved a flanking movement north of the Japanese mandated islands (the Marshalls and Carolines) and through the Marianas Islands (Guam, Saipan); the second called for going straight through the Mandates and the third going south of them . . . The third or southern route seemed to King the worst, for it would be subject to flank attacks from Orange [Japan] throughout, and in the end there was a dangerous bottleneck between northwest New Guinea, Morotai and Mindanao."[1] That bottleneck was made by the Bismarck Archipelago, on which Rabaul stood.

For instructional purposes, the War College president ordered King to execute the "wrong solution," the southern advance. After losing a strong appeal to use the northern route, King complied. He moved far to the south, carefully protecting his supply ships. "Real world" duties called King away and another student took over command of the Blue Fleet, which "came to the bad end which was anticipated by everyone but the War College President in the bottleneck be-

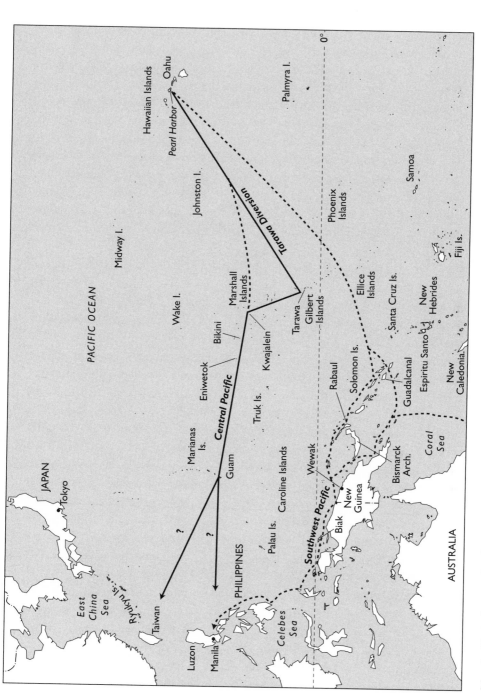

Map 6a. Central versus Southwest Pacific Routes. Map by Bill Nelson.

tween New Guinea and the Philippines."[2] This southern route was Marshall's Task Two and Task Three.

King had never lost sight of War Plan Orange and its central Pacific drive. When he and Nimitz met in San Francisco at the end of June 1942—the meeting that identified Guadalcanal as the next target—King confided to Nimitz that he ultimately expected forward movement via Truk, Saipan, and Guam.[3] This line of thinking was ahead of anything the Joint Chiefs of Staff (JCS) had studied.

A triumphant drive across the central Pacific would suck the Japanese fleet into a decisive fleet engagement and crush it. With its navy sunk, Japan would be helpless to resist a blockade and naval bombardment and could be strangled into submission. There would be no need for a major invasion of the Home Islands. Mahan would have nodded approval. It's the enemy fleet, not geography, that counts.

As naval action wound down during the latter part of the Guadalcanal campaign, King became increasingly impatient. He pushed Halsey and Nimitz for follow-on plans. He knew that the first submissions would mirror the army's methodical progression up the Solomons and the New Guinea coast to Rabaul. King suggested a quick strike north and east of Rabaul to cut off Japanese forces in the southwest theater. They could either evacuate the southern and southwestern Pacific or watch their forces become isolated. However, the CNO's proposal met almost universal resistance. Many could not imagine pulling away from the support infrastructure already emplaced. As Marshall had warned at the beginning of the Guadalcanal operation, the initial steps taken in the South Pacific had developed their own momentum.

King was flinty enough to take on the whole navy and win. However, he ran into an obstacle more difficult to move than even the Japanese. It was the Allied Brits. Before the Americans among themselves could revise Pacific strategy after Guadalcanal, the Joint Chiefs had to leave for North Africa. Churchill, Roosevelt, and the Combined Chiefs of Staff (CCS)—the British and the American service chiefs—met there to work out Allied strategy for the remainder of the war. The meeting took place in Casablanca, Morocco, on 14–23 January 1943.

The British feared that American attention would wander from the most dangerous adversary—Hitler. The Allies had yet to kick the Nazis out of North Africa, let alone invade western Europe. Roosevelt and Marshall were not about to let the Pacific theater eclipse the effort to defeat Hitler. America remained firmly committed to "Germany first." Most of the conference was taken up by the conflict between Britain's desire for a Mediterranean campaign and Marshall's insistence that a direct attack across the English Channel was the fastest way to defeat the Germans.

There is a fundamental difference between a meeting among one country's military leaders and a meeting among the military leaders of more than one allied nation. The military leaders of one nation are *supposed* to have a common objective—that set by the national leadership (the president in the U.S.). Peacetime interservice rivalries are supposed to be left behind for the good of the country.

Meetings among sovereign nations are a different matter. Sovereign nations may have legitimately different priorities. Often it's difficult for individual officers to adapt to the difference. Formal United States policy had one objective: unconditional surrender of all Axis nations. British objectives were a little more complex. Her empire in Southeast Asia, including Singapore and Malaya, had been overrun. America wasn't likely going to actively support re-establishment of British imperial rule. The Americans might even actively oppose it after the war. Britain's grasp on India had slipped and was openly under challenge. In addition to defeating the Axis, Britain wanted to protect its postwar interests in Asia.

British strength east of Aden, such as it was at the end of 1942, was concentrated in the Indian Ocean. British planners had to balance potential deployments in the Indian Ocean and Southeast Asia and their possible repercussions for the British Empire against support for operations in the Pacific directed against Japan. The British military chiefs tended to support efforts designed to support their American ally. While seeking defeat of the common enemy, Churchill carefully weighed the impact of alternative strategies on imperial issues and acted accordingly. While Mahan clearly supported imperial ambitions, his points didn't relate to competition among friends. That dimension of war making is beyond the scope of this work.

The British wanted the smallest allocation of forces to the Pacific. Admiral Sir Dudley Pound, First Sea Lord, suggested that the Japanese be allowed to disperse and dig in their forces. An attack against the Philippines could not be scheduled until after the defeat of Germany.[4] U.S. leaders were not about to postpone it that long. A lot of American blood had been shed to wrest the initiative from the Japanese. King and Marshall, who had been squabbling over command arrangements in the South Pacific, closed ranks against British attempts to freeze the Pacific.

On the afternoon of 14 January King took the floor.[5] King felt that the "geographical position and the manpower of China" would be key in the ultimate defeat of Japan, arguing "that the Japanese could not be beaten by the destruction of their fleet alone; that their ultimate defeat must be brought about by operations from the China coast."[6] (Mahan would have bitten hard on his lip to suppress a cry of "Heresy!") An approach through the Dutch East Indies and the Philippines would be "extremely slow." An advance from the South Seas would then, with Chinese assistance, retake Hong Kong to establish a base area from which to ultimately attack the Japanese Home Islands. What the CNO did want to do was to deflect thinking away from the Dutch East Indies.[7] (President Roosevelt himself was concerned at the slow pace of the island-to-island movement toward Japan.) Instead of a frontal assault on the heavy Japanese defenses in the Dutch East Indies, King pointed out that capture of the Philippines would cut off the movement of raw materials from the South Seas to Japan.

Mahan would have reached a far different conclusion. Take a look at Map 6b. The Indian Ocean coast of Burma is 8,000 miles from Tokyo. An offensive that started there, intending to approach Japan via China, would have to advance around the coast of Southeast Asia, where it would face a huge Japanese army defending on rough and sometimes jungle terrain. On the way, nothing would be done to bring the Japanese fleet into decisive battle. The logistical resources required to reach the Chinese in force would severely limit the Pacific campaigns to first destroy the Japanese battle fleet and then allow unfettered access to the enemy's homeland. This is almost the antithesis of Mahan's approach to war. His objections to the "China card" would have been strong. An analysis according to Clausewitz comes to a similar conclusion. The center of gravity of the Japanese empire wasn't in China. It was in the Home Islands. A solid dose of Mahan at this juncture would have prevented a very long and ultimately unprofitable diversion from the main strategic effort.

King told the assembled chiefs that a war against Japan had been studied at the Naval War College for the last thirty years. Many of the ideas he presented were widely held by America's best naval thinkers. In January 1943 the Philippines were a distant objective. The U.S. chief of naval operations pointed out that a strong naval air base there could be used to cut off Japan from the South Seas. He then outlined three approaches to the Philippines from the Pacific. One could work down the Aleutian chain across the North Pacific to Japan. After a brief analysis of the atrocious weather and logistical handicaps, he ruled out this option. The second route led from Guadalcanal, up the Solomons to Rabaul, and thence to the Philippines. This would take a long time. Furthermore, it would not necessarily force the Japanese navy to come out to fight. King underscored that destruction of the Japanese navy was the critical military-strategic objective. A faster way to get to the Philippines would be via the central Pacific on a line from the Marshalls to Truk (Carolines) to the Marianas. It was the first time at a combined meeting of the conference that the Marianas had been mentioned.[8] King's American and British counterparts were surprised. The Marianas had not been referred to in the pre-conference background papers. That's because their

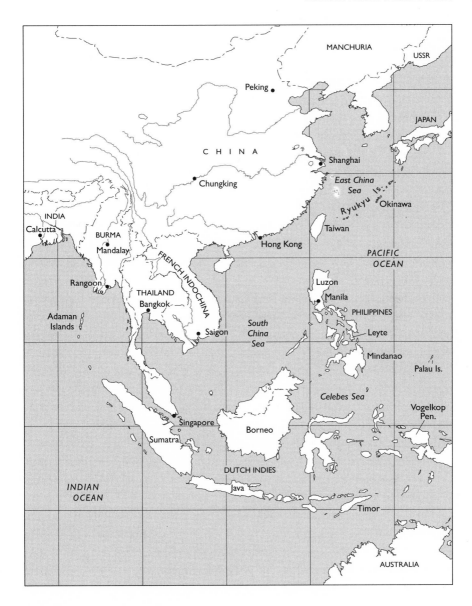

Map 6b. Asia. Map by Bill Nelson.

author, Captain Charles J. Moore, by the time of the Marianas campaign Spruance's chief of staff, didn't think they were necessary to capture the Philippines. King did not explicitly advocate a central Pacific route over continued advance from the southwest Pacific, but his remarks leaned in that direction.

It was War Plan Orange.

For King, the enemy fleet, not geography, was paramount. Invasion of the Marianas would bring the Japanese fleet out to its destruction. King was convinced the Japanese navy would commit its strength to defend them.

Deciding on a final approach to defeating Japan was not part of the agenda. Nevertheless, King recited the benefits of concentrating on a central Pacific drive. With American forces ensconced there, Japanese units in the southwest Pacific could do little except starve. American power based in the Marianas would strangle Japan's sea line of communications. This, he argued, would flush the Imperial Navy out to fight on the open sea.

Mahan would have skipped over the written plan but given the CNO high marks on his oral presentation. After fumbling on the China issue, King, from the podium, got back on the bearing Mahan would have steered. The old naval professor couldn't have said it better himself. Not only had King read the lesson, he had absorbed it.

Previously, General Marshall and General Arnold had not been receptive to King's central Pacific proposal. Both consistently turned down King's request for additional southwest Pacific island garrisons. Both appeared surprised when the British indicated that they considered some minimum level of Pacific activity a good thing.[9] Now they began to see King's logic.[10] Mahan, and all the contributors to War Plan Orange, would have smiled. While Marshall acknowledged the benefits of the central Pacific approach, he expected an advance via Burma into China would ultimately prove more profitable.[11] In his view a central Pacific advance would have to wait until Task Three, capture of Rabaul, was completed.

Initially, General Arnold had focused on China as the best site for his bombers. Now he began to muse about B-29 bases in the Marianas. The concept of defeating Japan with island-based bombers began to jell.

The Casablanca attendees considered it a near certainty that Rabaul would be captured by the late spring of 1943. To minimize the resources committed to the Pacific, the British wanted to restrict operations to their attack to regain Burma and an American attack on Rabaul. They discouraged a central Pacific drive as just another resource drain. King angrily retorted that, while the overall allocation between the Atlantic and the Pacific was an Allied matter, the U.S. Chiefs would determine Pacific strategy. When King agreed that no invasion of the Philippines would begin until after Germany was conquered, the British became quiet on the subject of Pacific strategy. As a result of King's advocacy, the Casablanca Conference authorized the beginnings of a central Pacific offensive into the Marshalls, Carolines, and Marianas as far as a line from Truk to Guam "if time and resources allow."[12] This approval was predicated on the condition that the resources required not impede the war against Germany or Britain's reconquest of Burma.[13]

The admiral had lifted the generals' gaze above the immediate prospect of a step-by-step drive through the southwest Pacific. In time, this view was to prevail. If only the Joint Chiefs could have ordered a return to War Plan Orange without regard to MacArthur's rantings at the beginning of 1943. Marshall warmed to the central Pacific drive—after Rabaul was taken.[14]

The final document produced at Casablanca identified Rabaul as the next Pacific target. Plans to take this objective were set in concrete, precluding for the first half of 1943 any further discussion of the correct strategy to defeat the Imperial Japanese Fleet. After Rabaul, operations would be directed against the Marshalls and the Carolines in the central Pacific. The British chiefs left it to the American chiefs to modify the pace of Pacific operations to reflect changes in the Pacific situation.

Both Roosevelt and Marshall knew MacArthur would take the news from Casablanca hard. Undoubtedly he would perceive "Germany first" as a slight. Major General Albert Wedemeyer, a member of Marshall's staff, was detailed to give the southwest Pacific commander an in-depth face-to-face briefing. At that meeting MacArthur opined that if the resources earmarked for the Mediterranean, especially the amphibious resources, were committed to the Pacific, the Japanese could be overwhelmed in 1943. Note how MacArthur again overlooked the balance of power between the opposing carrier fleets and the huge impact new American building would have toward the end of the year. Except for the short-legged *Ranger,* no American fleet carriers remained in the Atlantic. As Marshall's biographer, Forrest Pogue, comments: "MacArthur's argument is hard to substantiate."[15]

Amphibious shipping would be the most critical swing asset between all the theaters worldwide. Admiral King woefully underestimated the need for "gators." In the end, operations in the southwest Pacific would have to work around central Pacific requirements. To some extent, this would also be true of preparations for the Normandy invasion.

A Sea Change in the Correlation of Forces

During 1943, the American shipyards launched twice as much carrier power as the Japanese had lost at Midway. With the *Essex* class, the Americans gained the edge in carrier capability. By mid-1943, Nimitz could create significantly better than a 1.5:1 advantage in carrier airpower at any one point of his choosing.

Table 6.1: Changes in Japanese and American Carrier Strength

	Japanese navy		American navy	
	CV	CVL	CV	CVL
On hand Jan. 1943	4	2–3	3	1
Added by March 31			+1	+2
June 30			+2	+2
Sept. 30			+1	+2
Dec. 31	+1	+1		+2
		(conversion)		

The January 1943 line overstates available Japanese carrier power. In November 1942, *Shokaku, Zuikaku,* and *Zuiho* left for the repair yards in Japan. *Zuikaku* would be out of service until midsummer. *Hiyo* continued to have engine trouble. The only fully fit fleet carrier was *Junyo. Essex* arrived in Pearl Harbor on 8 June, *Intrepid* in June, *Yorktown* on 11 July, and *Lexington* on 9 August 1943. *Bunker Hill* also arrived in August. Light carriers *Independence* and *Princeton* arrived in July. *Belleau Wood* moored in Pearl Harbor on 9 August and *Cowpens* on 19 September.

American technology added to the disparity. The Wildcat fighter was clearly outclassed by the Zero. By mid-1943, Hellcats had replaced the earlier Grumman fighter on fleet carrier decks, eliminating this disparity and in some characteristics reversing it. American radar and fighter direction techniques substantially improved the defenses of the Big Blue Fleet. So did the vastly increased number of anti-aircraft weapons per ship and improvements in radar-directed gunnery. American dive- and torpedo bombers now clearly outperformed their Japanese counterparts.

A comparison of carrier strengths identifies the relative shift in power between the antagonists. However, the American navy added strength in all categories. Between 7 December 1941 and 31 December 1944, the Pacific Fleet added the following:

8 battleships	7 fleet carriers
4 heavy cruisers	9 light carriers
15 light cruisers	29 escort carriers
207 destroyers	88 submarines
199 destroyer escorts	

Later the fleet would change designation (Third or Fifth) depending on its commander. That didn't matter to the blue jackets. Regardless of who was driving, they dubbed it the "Big Blue Fleet." It got bigger almost every week.

More critically, Japan had not corrected her shortage of trained pilots while American aviators became both very plentiful and very competent. As the Guadalcanal campaign staggered to its conclusion, Japan's pilot and plane losses were even more severe than its carrier losses. Over 900 naval aircraft, including 300 from carriers, had been lost. By the end of February, only 200 army and 100 navy aircraft of modern design remained in the South Pacific.

The Americans could replace their losses. Japan could not. This change moved the correlation of forces 180 degrees from that in the spring of 1942, when Tasks One, Two, and Three were written. Would any American move south of Rabaul now bring forth Japanese carriers? Probably not. Were there any critical land resources (such as Borneo's oil) that justified enduring heavy casualties? Forget the campaign up the Solomons. For that matter, forget King's first idea of breaking the link between Rabaul and Truk. Why not break the link between Truk and Tokyo?

These increases in American carrier air strength created a fundamentally new capability. In 1942, neither navy dared bring its carriers within range of a fully functional land-based air force. By the summer of 1943, the American navy could move within range of Japanese land-based aviation and slug it out. The raid on the Marshalls was the first practical demonstration of this. Now American strategists were freed of the "250-mile rule," which tied advances to supporting distance of already established land-based aviation. The Big Blue Fleet could sail to an area of its choosing and *establish air superiority from its own carrier decks*. This was especially useful in the vast distances of the central Pacific where small atolls meant airfields of limited capacity. This limited the number of defending Japanese land-based aircraft that could be concentrated and the ability to reinforce them from other bases. American carriers could withstand a challenge by the Imperial Navy anywhere in the mid-Pacific. Such was the "*Essex* effect."

Increased American naval air strength invalidated the tactics that had been correct for the U.S. in 1942 and opened vistas to a far more aggressive strategy for 1943. The change promised to save the lives of many Americans wearing green uniforms.

Fleets derive their enormous power from their ability to maneuver. Tie them to a specific piece of geography and they behave more like island airfields. They may generate air superiority in their local area. But they might not be in the right position to influence the theater-wide strategic outcome. Recall the distinction between the operational and strategic levels of war. Tying up the carriers might help one operation's plan but only at the detriment of overall fleet strategy for the Pacific.

Guadalcanal had been a unique pivot point between two fleets of roughly equal striking power. A misstep by either side as they attempted to clench with each other in the surrounding waters could result in a disaster that could change the course of the war. Having land-based airpower at the pivot point helped America enormously. With fleets and logistical support becoming increasingly unequal, there was no other point in the southwest Pacific that was likely to become such a pivot. No other airfield in either New Guinea or the Solomons was likely to generate a similar scenario. By comparison, a 250-mile hop on the 8,000-mile cruise to Tokyo counted for little.

King's first thought was to scrap Tasks Two and Three altogether. Instead, Nimitz could maneuver from the northeast to capture the Admiralties, which lay north of Rabaul.[16] This would cut off most Japanese forces in the Solomons, the Bismarck Archipelago, and most of New Guinea and make a step-by-step advance moot. An American fleet steaming from Honolulu to the Admiralties would cross the sea lanes between Rabaul and Truk. What better way to force the Japanese fleet into another major battle far from home waters?

Mahan would have smiled at this forbidding crust of an old salt. "Exactly right, Admiral King! Concentrate the fleet in waters threatening to the enemy and challenge his fleet to a fight." Mahan's most senior American student was grasping the basic message with far more understanding than the commander of the Japanese fleet.

King's subordinate commanders were nowhere nearly as perceptive. Neither Nimitz nor Halsey wanted any part of such an aggressive operation.[17] Despite pending aircraft and carrier deliveries, Nimitz and Halsey showed no enthusiasm for another huge leap. Midway had been a fantastic bet narrowly won. They had finally prevailed at Guadalcanal by the smallest of margins. How many times could the Americans win the roll of the dice? Of course Guadalcanal had been King's child. Maybe he really did shave with a blowtorch.

Nimitz believed that Japanese air strength was still too much for the Americans to handle. He thought that additional battles of aerial attrition in the Solomons would be required before America could turn toward the central Pacific. In a less than perceptive comment, Nimitz said an approach toward Rabaul via the Admiralties would be exposed to a "flanking attack" from unsuppressed Japanese bases in the Solomons. Again, had it been a land campaign, many generals would have concurred with Nimitz. But the admiral was not taking a broad enough view of the question. There was no need to advance further into single-engine-aircraft range of any of them. With their supply lines cut, no major Japanese naval units could survive in the Solomons. Airpower is fragile. Without gas, bombs, and repair parts, Japanese airpower in the south would rapidly deteriorate. The ideal solution would bring out the Japanese fleet into open combat more than 250 miles away from either Rabaul or Truk, which had the largest concentrations of airfields.

Nimitz saw Japanese air bases in New Britain and New Ireland as interlocking and mutually supporting. Capture of Rabaul would not remove all the blocking forces in the Solomons. Nimitz concluded that there would have to be a step-by-step advance through the chain.[18] Mahan would have frowned at the commander of the Pacific Fleet. The divergent views of Nimitz and King sharply point up the contrast between their respective visions. Mahan would have pointed out that there was no reason to traverse the Solomons. They were part of the Great Pacific Empty. Japan would never again risk its fleet in the South Pacific. Japanese garrisons could keep control of the Solomons for all they mattered. The direct route from Honolulu to Tokyo, and the destruction of the Japanese fleet, were the objectives. Admiral Nimitz needed to pull his head out of the operational-level problems and regain his strategic view. In addition, he had to factor in the "*Essex* effect." Mahan would have thanked the stars in the American flag that King sat on a higher perch than the steady man from the plains of Texas.

Nimitz, who had brilliantly created the swing from Coral Sea to Midway, saw little difference between a slog up the Solomons and what King proposed. He was more concerned that Halsey command whatever effort was made toward Rabaul, rather than with which way it was routed. Nimitz did not yet recognize that Rabaul would not have to be taken. Having to handle all the day-to-day emergencies, Nimitz wanted more resources before plunging into the central Pacific. Until the U.S. had marked naval and air superiority, he thought a central Pacific offensive was inadvisable. Coming from the man who took the audacious calculated risk at Midway, this point of view should not be ignored.

Nimitz pointed out that movement either up the Solomons or along the New Guinea coast would not require the bulk of the fleet. However, if the majority of his ships were in the south, the bulk of the Japanese fleet could easily concentrate in the central Pacific and strike the Americans hard.[19] Nimitz wanted to concentrate most of the fleet's heavy surface forces in Task Force 50 under Spruance and hold it centrally in order to maintain balance. Mahan would have understood Nimitz's desire—and felt a little better about this magnificent commander who had so much vision about Midway at a time when King had been so pessimistic.

Nimitz performed superbly during the battles of 1942. However, the strain had severely depressed him. The enormous responsibility and the close calls undoubtedly had their impact. He was far less optimistic than the CNO. King and Nimitz had met in San Francisco in February 1943 prior to the upcoming full-blown meeting in Washington between representatives from both Pacific theaters and the joint staffs to iron out their differences. The Pacific Fleet commander's entreaties forced King to rein in his enthusiasm for bypassing the Solomons.

Halsey entered the southwest Pacific when the American hold on Guadalcanal was in doubt. He was always ready to grapple with his enemy as rapidly as possible.[20] But he didn't like King's approach to the Admiralties. The fleet would not be within range of American land-based air. Like Nimitz, he wasn't ready to acknowledge the sea change of the "*Essex* effect." At least not yet. And this came from the man who had accepted such a heavy gamble at Santa Cruz.

King's suggestion was too aggressive for the correlation of forces on January 1, 1943. For an August 1943 operation, he might have been too conservative. That is how great the "*Essex* effect" was. Without the ability of the carriers of the Big Blue Fleet to establish air superiority without the aid of land-based air, the Americans were as tied to the "250-mile rule" as the Japanese. MacArthur never freed himself from the notion. With the "250-mile rule" as the standard, a return to War Plan Orange and the central Pacific drive would have been extremely difficult. The combination of Tasks Two and Three, the advance to and capture of Rabaul, the breaking of the Bismarck Archipelago, and a methodical advance toward the Philippines was the "250-mile" step-by-step conservative play. With the fleet freed from the need of land-based air support, that slow alternative became the high-cost (in American lives) approach.

Given all Nimitz and Halsey had endured, their conservatism was understandable. However, they were less prescient than the CNO in understanding the massive sea change in relative naval power the new carrier force would make possible. King alone was the visionary who, perhaps because he never stopped looking for it, first grasped the enormous change in strategic opportunity. King's leadership at this juncture was critical.

The MacArthur Factor

General MacArthur, who upon orders from the President had left the Philippines in early 1942, had a burning determination to return to those islands as soon as possible. He favored the Mindanao axis of advance to the Philippines. Almost as soon as he assumed his new command in the Southwest Pacific Area he began thinking about moving back to the Philippines by a series of amphibious operations along the north coast of New Guinea.[21]

If MacArthur had been a relative unknown outside of the War Department, his opinions might have been controllable, but he was "a political soldier," a phenomenon comparatively rare in twentieth-century American experience. From an early age, he had taken a close interest in partisan politics. He was prepared to use his prestige as a soldier to influence policy decisions in order to override the diplomatic or political objectives of his civilian superiors. MacArthur's influence was irrepressible.[22] If Pacific strategic questions were not answered in a manner acceptable to him, the president of the United States had to expect political reverberations.

General MacArthur was simultaneously one of the most gifted American military leaders of the twentieth century—and one of the most flawed. As a cadet, he performed brilliantly at West Point. Upon graduation, he was posted as an aide to his father, Major General Arthur MacArthur—Civil War recipient of the Medal of Honor, commander of the Army Department of the Philippines, and well-known eccentric outspoken critic of presidents and their policies.

After several lackluster years in the Orient, young Douglas managed to join the expedition chasing Pancho Villa in Mexico and then whined when he wasn't awarded a Medal of Honor for a minor accomplishment during that campaign. Posted to France in 1917, his rise through the 42nd "Rainbow" Division was meteoric. Demonstrating both physical courage and military competence, he attained star rank first as a brigade commander and then briefly as division commander in the closing days of World War I. At the end of the Great War most officers, including gifted ones like Marshall, Eisenhower, and Patton, had to give up their temporary wartime ranks and step down several grades. However, MacArthur was appointed West Point superintendent. That allowed him to retain stars on his shoulders. His mother never stopped pulling strings to enhance her son's advancement. Later MacArthur, as a two-star major general, maneuvered himself into position to be appointed by President Herbert Hoover to be the new Army Chief of Staff in November 1930, far outdistancing Lieutenant Colonel Marshall and Major Eisenhower.

From the beginning of Roosevelt's administration, the president and the general he inherited did not get along. Before he was inaugurated in 1932, FDR had identified what he considered the two most dangerous men in America: Huey Long, the infamous governor of Louisiana, and Douglas MacArthur.[23] During the Depression FDR had ordered the army budget halved. MacArthur, as chief of staff, met with the president to make the army's case. The discussion got very heated. MacArthur, ever reaching for the most purple of prose, recounted his words: "When we lose the next war, and an American boy, lying in the mud with an enemy bayonet through his belly and an enemy foot on his dying throat, spat out his last curse, I wanted the name not to be MacArthur but Roosevelt."[24] Roosevelt replied he couldn't speak to the president that way. After he regained his composure, MacArthur offered his resignation. FDR batted it aside.

Roosevelt once told MacArthur, "You are our best general and our worst politician." By 1939, Republican kingmakers were mentioning the general's name as a presidential candidate.

Marshall had been General John J. "Black Jack" Pershing's brilliant operations officer. He engineered First Army's offensive during World War I. Marshall and Pershing began a close bond that lasted until the end of Black Jack's life. Throughout the dark days of World War II, the overworked Marshall would always find time to visit Pershing at Walter Reed Hospital. Until Pershing passed on, Marshall refused to don a fifth star, lest he outrank his old commander.

The officers surrounding Pershing's headquarters, the "Chaumont gang," saw the youthful General MacArthur as too colorful. MacArthur viewed their "interference" as the work of a cabal trying to hold him back. His opinion had some basis in fact. Pershing had once dressed down General MacArthur for what he thought was poor discipline and slovenly appearance in the 42nd Division. At the end of his tour as superintendent of West Point in 1922, General Pershing rated MacArthur 38th among 46 general officers and damned him with the faint praise as above average.

Between the world wars, Pershing retained tremendous power. Pershing and MacArthur came to a row over a woman. MacArthur was courting a socialite who had been seen in the company of the widowed Pershing. Black Jack reportedly told the woman that if she married Douglas, the MacArthurs would be posted to some place she would not like. Shortly after the wedding the MacArthurs were on their way back to the Philippines. Douglas was pleased but his wife shuddered at the social exile. They eventually divorced.

After that episode, Pershing's support of MacArthur was grudging. MacArthur returned the favor by slighting Marshall. While MacArthur was chief of staff, Pershing asked him to promote Colonel Marshall to one-star rank. Instead MacArthur pulled him from an important headquarters assignment and posted him as an adviser to the Illinois National Guard. Marshall left no record of disappointment over the move to Chicago. However, his wife said she had never seen him more ashen-faced.

To some degree, the World War II problem with MacArthur was of Roosevelt's own making. Roosevelt allowed MacArthur, upon retirement as chief of staff in 1935, to accept President Quezon's appointment as field marshal and commander of the Philippine army. At the time, the president might have felt a perch in Manila was the best place for "one of the two most dangerous men in America." For his part, MacArthur "detested" the president.[25]

During the summer of 1941, MacArthur approached several people, including Marshall (by letter), suggesting he be recalled as the U.S. Army commander for the Far East.[26] The internal War Department review of this proposal wasn't positive, suggesting that he might come back as Filipino department commander of the Philippine army, essentially a colonial organization. Roosevelt personally made the decision to recall MacArthur back to U.S. Army active duty as commander in chief of America's Far East forces, commanding both American and Filipino troops. In doing so, he did not even consult General Marshall or Secretary of War Stimson. Effectively, this created a direct pipeline from MacArthur to Roosevelt.[27] It wasn't for Marshall to interfere with the wishes of his commander in chief and patron. Roosevelt felt it important to have the politically prominent and publicly respected MacArthur on his team in a very exposed area.

MacArthur was very familiar with War Plan Orange both as chief of staff in the 1930s and later as commander of the Philippine armed forces and U.S. Armed Forces, Philippines. Now he found the central Pacific approach to be irrelevant if not dangerous. During the upcoming strategic debate, he would write to Marshall, "The factors upon which the old Orange plan were based have been greatly altered by the hostile conquest of Malaya and the Netherlands East Indies and by the availability of Australia as a base."[28] How do Japanese forces in the South Seas do anything but *increase* Japan's vulnerability to a central Pacific drive that might isolate major military units from the Home Islands? How does a more distant base (Australia) invalidate a strategy predicated on holding a closer base (Hawaii)?

MacArthur reasoned that oil in the South Seas was the key to Japan's warmaking potential. Philippines-based airpower could interdict it. An advance up New Guinea was not safe until Rabaul was neutralized.[29] MacArthur envisioned this campaign generating steady advance of the southwest Pacific's land-based bomber line northwestward to the Philippines by the successive seizure of air base sites along the north coast of New Guinea.[30] MacArthur also recognized that Japanese land-based airpower in the Carolines and Marshalls was too distant to interfere with his New Guinea–Mindanao advance. He saw no reason to enter the central Pacific. Palau was the northernmost base that bothered him.

In an offhand remark to his air chief, General George C. Kenney, MacArthur succinctly stated his grand strategic objectives: "The first mission I want to carry out is to liberate the Philippines and fulfill America's pledge to that people. Then I want to defeat Japan."[31] Admiral King commented sarcastically that MacArthur seemed more interested in accomplishing his personal goal of returning to the Philippines than in winning the war.[32]

A brilliant man, MacArthur had a gift for focusing on the critical decisions he alone needed to make. Oratorical skill was his natural genius. It was MacArthur's undoubted eloquence, the ability on occasion to talk nonsense with confidence, which served not only to delude others but also himself. MacArthur wasn't well schooled in the mechanics of the operational art. In private Dwight D. Eisenhower described some of MacArthur's grand strategies proposed in 1941–42 as more akin to the work of a West Point plebe than a senior commander.[33] MacArthur never attended Command & General Staff School or any of the war colleges. Neither did he systematically study operational mechanics on his own. Instead, he left planning to his staff and seldom commented on details.

Richard K. Sutherland, MacArthur's chief of staff, was an extremely intelligent if very prickly man who had been through the service school system and was a very efficient administrator. As chief of staff, he ran day-to-day operations and attended all but one U.S. strategy conference as the southwest Pacific representative. Many thought he was the de facto southwest Pacific commander while MacArthur paced in a corner, pontificating generalities. Under MacArthur, Sutherland rose from captain to lieutenant general. MacArthur did acquire an airpower ace, General Kenney. General Walter Krueger and his staff, first called Alamo Force and then Sixth Army, were competent if cautious tacticians. He was one of the few senior commanders to survive Marshall's scrutiny during the Louisiana maneuvers. Krueger and his people translated MacArthur's broad directives into actionable operations orders. Without them, MacArthur would have been lost. Vice Admiral Daniel E. "Uncle Dan" Barbey, able commander of the Seventh Fleet Amphibious Force and a loyal supporter of MacArthur, provided the expertise on ship-to-shore operations.

In addition to leaving details to his staff, MacArthur often—in a manner similar to Roosevelt's—pitted one staff member against another while individually charming both. The general's leadership inspired many of his subordinates and he got a lot of work out of them. No one can deny MacArthur's physical courage, tremendous intellect, resilient self-confidence—or his complete inability to discern the difference between his own opinions and absolute fact.

MacArthur and his staff were convinced that FDR, Marshall, and Ike were leaders of a clique that was maliciously conniving to undermine his career.[34] Admiral Barbey recalled MacArthur's words toward the end of a planning conference: "There are some people in Washington who would rather see MacArthur lose a battle than America win a War."[35]

Marshall understood political calculus. But he didn't employ it for his own personal advancement. When Brigadier General Marshall went for his interview with Roosevelt to become chief of staff, the president went off on a long sophomoric harangue about airpower. Marshall said nothing. The president prodded, "What do you think, General Marshall?" His reply: "I don't agree with a word you said, Mr. President." Most of his friends thought his career was over. Roosevelt, displaying his great ability to choose among men, made perhaps his most outstanding personnel selection in World War II.

General Marshall did understand that he had to hold the entire organization together. Being on the wrong side of a fight over MacArthur could jeopardize more than unity of command in the South Pacific. King observed that Marshall "would do anything rather than disagree with MacArthur.[36] It was Marshall who originated the citation for MacArthur's Medal of Honor as a salve for having to leave his troops behind in the Philippines.

General Marshall's strong belief in unity of command had caused him to attempt another solution to Pacific command. When Admiral William Leahy returned from his assignment as ambassador to France, Marshall suggested that he accept command of the entire Pacific. Leahy responded he was too old for the rigors of that command. Marshall could never be accused of placing the parochial interests of the army ahead of those of his country.

Marshall and MacArthur met only once during the war. After the Sextant Conference in Cairo, Marshall traveled to Australia. "The two four star generals finally lunched, like adversaries negotiating a truce, on Goodenough Island."[37] Marshall, who bristled the only time the president addressed him as George, greeted his host and former boss as Douglas. Rear Admiral Charles M. "Savvy" Cooke Jr., Admiral King's principal deputy, who was traveling with General Marshall, unabashedly laid out the navy's proposal for a central Pacific offensive. Speaking for the southwest Pacific group, General Kenney stated a move on that axis was too far away from the forces already moving in from MacArthur's offensive. He felt that navy bases in the Admiralties and on Palau would be able to protect this thrust. Obviously Mahan would have rolled his eyes after hearing the airman's remarks. The two four-star generals remained silent on the issue.

A Divided Command

As we have seen, the establishment of MacArthur in Australia created a major crisis in command. Roosevelt and the Joint Chiefs recognized that MacArthur couldn't be dealt out of the war. The president did not relish the idea of the hero of the Philippines becoming a Republican presidential candidate in 1944. MacArthur had outranked Marshall for many years. His publicity machine generated quite a following both in Congress and with the American people. Nor did MacArthur shrink from cultivating independent political channels to try to bypass his commander in chief. At the height of the controversy over central Pacific vs. South Pacific strategies for the defeat of Japan, Senator Albert Chandler of

Kentucky and four co-sponsors introduced a bill that would have mandated Mac-Arthur become commander of all forces in the Pacific. Several influential papers, including the *Washington Times-Herald* and the *New York Herald Tribune*, picked up the refrain. His displeasure with the decisions made at the Quadrant meeting in Quebec, which we will discuss below, made it into their pages. In September of 1943, MacArthur warmly entertained five senators at his headquarters in Port Moresby. Global politics and the presidency were "openly discussed."[38] Later that month, MacArthur would not allow Mrs. Roosevelt, on a support-the-troops tour, to visit Port Moresby. Roosevelt had to handle MacArthur personally.

The Joint Chiefs would have preferred a single theater commander for the Pacific. No senior leader was more committed to the need for unity of command than Marshall: "A man with good judgement and unity of command has a distinct advantage over a man with brilliant judgement who must rely on cooperation."[39] MacArthur concurred: "Of all the faulty decisions of war perhaps the most unexplainable one was the failure to unify the command in the Pacific."[40] But no one was going to give MacArthur the post. He wouldn't tolerate Nimitz, whose naval background was more attuned to the required campaign, and no one could order MacArthur to accept becoming subordinate given the general's political clout.

Navy feelings about MacArthur ran even deeper. King especially didn't like him. From time to time, Marshall had to admonish the CNO not to exhibit animosity to the South West Pacific Area commander. One would not expect Nimitz, ever the gentleman, to articulate adverse opinions. However, Spruance's biographer, Thomas Buell, stated: "Nimitz had no intention of being subordinate to MacArthur." The Nimitz staff, including Spruance, deeply distrusted the general. Spruance felt that MacArthur was motivated by presidential ambitions, that he sought personal glory, and that he would not cooperate with the Navy in defeating Japan.[41]

Not everyone in a blue uniform disliked the general. In his memoir, Admiral William D. Leahy wrote of MacArthur: "I had always entertained an extremely high opinion of his ability."[42] Leahy and MacArthur had socialized as junior officers in San Francisco as back as 1905 and had maintained a friendship. On more than one occasion, Admiral Leahy would intercede in high-level meetings to maintain a balanced view of the needs of MacArthur's theater.

After the war MacArthur wrote in his memoirs:

> The presence of carriers, with their inherent moveability, would have immeasurably increased the scope and speed of our [New Guinea] operations. I know of no other area in the Theater where they could have been used to such advantage.

> With the fall of Papua . . . the key points around this new [Japanese] perimeter were northern New Guinea, New Britain and the northern Solomons. Northern New Guinea in particular assumed special significance. Not only was it a strategic anchor on the right flank of this new defense line, but its loss would provide the Allies with an ideal springboard for a thrust into the heart of the inner zones of operations.[43]

This is typical MacArthur myopia: allocating carriers to support predictable moves along the New Guinea coast while the Japanese carrier fleet, heavily reinforced by land-based aviation, lay waiting to ambush the American carriers. Unable to maneuver in the confined waters, the American carriers would have been in grave danger. The carriers needed to be deployed to defeat the Japanese navy, not offered up as sacrifices for MacArthur's campaign. Nimitz went on record against carrier deployment in the Solomons for exactly these reasons.[44] Land campaigns needed to support naval operations, not the other way around. In 1943, that wasn't going to be accomplished along the New Guinea coast. Defeat the Japanese navy and Japan would have no ability to hold New Guinea.

Marshall and King showed the British a solid front at Casablanca in January 1943, but upon their return to Washington the army and navy resumed their debate on who was to command in the South Pacific, MacArthur or Nimitz. Often the disagreement was couched in strategic terms that further obfuscated real strategic debate. Almost everyone concerned felt that Rabaul would fall in May of 1943. The Chiefs authorized action in Alaska to eject the Japanese, the continuation of operations in New Guinea and the Solomons, and the beginnings of a drive in the central Pacific. "The Joint Chiefs had clearly intimated that the Philippines were to be approached through the Central Pacific."[45] But they did not enunciate a priority between the central and the southwest Pacific theaters. What would Mahan have said about this? Wouldn't it have been similar to Clausewitz's admonition about the enemy's center of gravity?

In December 1942, MacArthur had drafted a plan for review by the Joint Chiefs. He was very careful not to stray from their July 1942 directive. The descriptions of Tasks One, Two, and Three were verbatim quotes from the earlier JCS directive. To assuage the navy, his plan left the fleet under tactical control of the admirals. Per the earlier document, MacArthur would "direct" operations to achieve Tasks Two and Three. The JCS could redirect the fleet in case of an emergency. Otherwise MacArthur would select fleet taskings.[46] His Plan didn't provide a timetable or a list of forces not in the theater that would be required.

King delayed response for several weeks. MacArthur had been directed to provide detailed plans to execute Tasks Two and Three. What he provided was more a concept than a battle plan. Marshall directed him again to submit a detailed plan.

King did not want to create a major break with Marshall. He could see that the general was adamant. Instead, the admiral stated that matters at issue could not be resolved until MacArthur's detailed plans for Tasks Two and Three were available for review. Several iterations followed that precipitated the need for a major conference in early March.

Marshall was not about to let King's revisionism slow the pace of the agreed-on offensive. On 1 December 1942 he sent King a draft order to execute Tasks Two and Three as previously planned.[47] This methodical, determined man did not want to lose any time. However, he was beginning to understand the navy's need to be free to concentrate the fleet. Marshall's draft stated that the Joint Chiefs reserved the right at any time to recall naval units from their assignments to meet an emergency, presumably a sortie by Japan's Combined Fleet. Marshall focused on preventing loss of momentum and did not react at all to the shift created by the "*Essex* effect."

Coalition warfare immensely complicates military strategy. Wars are fought to attain national objectives. There is no separate U.S. Army or U.S. Navy war objective. The only valid objective is that of the United States of America. A good commander in chief sees that suboptimal objectives on behalf of part of some parochial element are stamped out. When it finally arrived, MacArthur's detailed plan was dubbed Elkton. His staff estimated that 74,000–94,000 Japanese, supported by 383 land-based aircraft, held the area bounded by New Guinea, the Solomons, and the Bismarck Archipelago. To achieve Tasks Two and Three, two separate advances, one along the New Guinea coast and the other through the Solomons, would be required. Each was arranged in methodical jumps each within range of land-based aviation from the previous one. However, it still had a landlubber's cast: "Purpose: To deny the area to JAPAN."[48]

Elkton outlined five specific operations:

I. Seize airdromes on Huon Peninsula of New Guinea to provide air cover for operations against the island of New Britain where Rabaul was located.

II. Seize the airfields on New Georgia, the next island up the Solomons with a Japanese airfield.

III. Seize airdromes on New Britain and Bougainville to provide air cover for operations against Rabaul and Kavieng on New Ireland.

IV. Capture Kavieng and thereby complete the isolation of Rabaul.

V. Capture Rabaul.

The outline contained no time line for execution. Its stated objective repeated the JCS directive—"seizure of the New Britain, New Ireland and New Guinea area." Rabaul is on New Britain. New Ireland lies just to its north.

Army Air Forces planners had complained, "In their prior planning, Army and Navy planners had devoted scant attention to the problems of moving land based aircraft across Pacific atolls or islands or of defending the bases which made such movement possible."[49] This cannot be said of Elkton. Reduced to basics, the plan made a series of 200-mile jumps and stopped to build an airfield each time to cover the next jump.

MacArthur continued to narrow his gaze rather than broaden it. He feared the two axes within Elkton, the New Guinea coast and the Solomons, would result in divergent action. Allied forces would be spread too thin. MacArthur insisted that New Guinea, the farthest point away from Japan and the least likely to bring out the Japanese fleet, must receive priority. One must at least admire MacArthur's consistency.

Back in 1942, advancing beyond the range of land-based friendly fighters was extremely dangerous. However, in the interim the Japanese had lost hundreds of aircraft and almost as many experienced pilots. By the summer of 1943, a plan that achieved initial surprise did not have to adhere to this range limitation. Southwest Pacific planners did not appreciate the change wrought by the swing in relative air power, the *Essex* effect.

MacArthur's was a plodding, methodical plan that gave the Japanese opportunity to delay the Americans at every major island. It was exactly what the Imperial General Headquarters wanted to do. In fairness, buried in the verbiage of the paragraph on "Scheme of Maneuver," the plan stated: "The fleet seeks decisive combat with hostile naval forces." But there was nothing in the plan that would force a decisive engagement at sea as the invasion of Guadalcanal had done.

To execute Elkton, MacArthur asked for an incredible array of forces: 22 divisions, an airborne regiment, an Australian armored brigade, and 45 air groups, "four squadrons each, at maximum strength." Amphibious shipping sufficient to land up to three assault divisions would be required.

The entire plan required five more divisions than the Allies had in the Pacific. Forty-five air groups would contain twice the 1,850 operational aircraft then on hand. An even bigger problem was amphibious shipping. An allocation the size MacArthur requested would prohibit any other action from Burma to Honolulu. All this to accomplish something proper employment of the fleet would make unnecessary. Could Mahan have invented a clearer example of the value of a good strategy and the crippling effect of a poor one?

Unbeknownst to the JCS planners, MacArthur had already drawn up a de-tailed plan for the invasion of the Philippines that grew from Elkton. His longer-range plan was dubbed Reno. To invade or bypass the Philippines was an issue that supposedly the JCS were to debate. Had they been aware of MacArthur's machinations, "they would have been even more aghast."[50]

While appalled at MacArthur's bill, and by no means ready to accede to it, the Joint Chiefs approved continuation of the drive toward Rabaul. On 28 March 1943 they directed that the first three tasks outlined in Elkton be executed. In essence these tasks encompassed the old directive's Task Two, concerning the Solomons and New Guinea, but for lack of resources Task Three, the seizure of Rabaul, was omitted. The July 1942 instructions, which explicitly called for the capture of Rabaul, were canceled. Instead the new directive called for the "ulti-mate seizure of the Bismarck Archipelago."[51]

Both MacArthur's handling of the defense of the Philippines and his first of-fensive across eastern New Guinea (Papua) have been roundly criticized. The mark of great generalship is to take decisive action before the enemy can carry out his plan. Had MacArthur moved more quickly he might have seized New Guinea before the Japanese invaded in July. Instead it took six months of bitter fighting to achieve the same result. Australian and American infantry were com-mitted to attack without proper logistical or fire support. When commanders on the scene reported the need for more firepower, MacArthur, sitting back in Bris-bane, relieved them. He charged their replacements "Take Buna or don't come back alive." MacArthur's "insistence on pressing forward with repeated frontal at-tacks by poorly supported infantry against a heavily dug in enemy was reminis-cent of the worst generalship of the First World War. It might have ended in the same futile slaughter had not the Japanese finally collapsed due to starvation."[52]

Later MacArthur would become a good operational commander; his cam-paigns of 1943–45 show great skill at the operational level of war. He demon-strated finesse in selecting objectives for amphibious attack and allowed the staff assembled under General Walter Krueger to execute them without a lot of inter-ference from above. But he refused to look at overall Pacific strategy from any-thing other than his own perspective: waiting in Australia with a burning desire to get to the Philippines.

If MacArthur could have ever stomached advice, Mahan might have gently edged him to the side of the room. MacArthur, and most generals, would con-tinue to attempt to solve the strategic problem by achieving geographical gains, but the Solomons and Rabaul had nothing of value. What mattered was naval as-cendancy. Yamamoto could still muster four fleet carriers. Rabaul's airfields would add a tremendous amount of airpower. Exposing two American carriers to that striking power would risk their loss. They would be tethered to whatever geography the landing force clung to. The result would most likely negate the enormous victory at Midway. MacArthur's suggestion was naval lunacy. One can see why King and Nimitz were so adamant that the fast carriers never operate under command of an army general. A summer 1943 operation against Rabaul was an inferior strategy to an advance into the central Pacific. Japanese airpower in the Marshalls would be nowhere near as ferocious, Pearl would be closer, and the line of advance would be far closer to Japan.

King pointed out that operations in the South Pacific no longer pinned down the Imperial Fleet. Again he suggested the American fleet be redeployed to the central Pacific in order to engage it.[53] Unfortunately, King's conclusion became lost in the wrangling over command arrangements. It was the Marshall and MacArthur versus King and Nimitz squabble over who would command all over again. Instead of a debate over strategy, everyone's energy was absorbed in hammering out a compromise about the arrangement of personalities within the command structure.

General Marshall continued to focus on the operational problems in the southwest Pacific rather than the overall strategic level that King was thinking on. King recognized MacArthur's operational-level need to secure the New Guinea coast, New Britain, and New Ireland to ensure an orderly advance toward Rabaul.[54] Instead, King was looking for a way to outflank Rabaul altogether and bring the Imperial Navy to battle. With the correct strategy, New Guinea et al. would be unnecessary operations.

In explaining his position backing MacArthur's overall command of the advance on Rabaul, Marshall compared the approach to the Japanese bastion to an inverted "V." The Japanese held the apex. Strong U.S. forces were poised at the bottom of each leg—one commanded by MacArthur, the other by Halsey. Unity of command required that both be commanded by a single officer to most efficiently attack the apex. At the operational level, Marshall was correct. But the strategic level trumped the operational.

King's reply concentrated more on the Nimitz-MacArthur controversy than on his earlier thoughts to skip the remainder of the Solomons altogether. He too advocated a single overall commander—but for the entire Pacific. Of course that was Nimitz, as he could balance Japanese threats in other areas against actions in the southwest Pacific.

King alone saw the right answer. Unfortunately he was not able to move Marshall. Marshall had difficulty conceptualizing King's remarks as anything but a leverage-seeking gambit in the war between the army and the navy, instead of what they were: an attempt to shift fundamental strategy in the Pacific.

March Pacific Conference

To break the impasse on the direction of Pacific strategy, a major conference in Washington convened on 12 March 1943. King presided. Sutherland and Kenney represented MacArthur, Spruance and Forrest Sherman represented Nimitz, and Captain Miles Browning, Halsey's chief of staff, represented his boss. Then Brigadier General Albert Wedemeyer, chief of the army's War Plans Division, and Rear Admiral Charles M. "Savvy" Cooke, King's chief planner, were active participants. Some people said Savvy Cooke was "meaner than King" in supporting Pacific strategy. He definitely knew both King's mind and Mahan's principles.

General Sutherland presented Plan Elkton. In the words of the historian Colonel Spector: "Sutherland, never one to take pains to win friends and influence people, presented these demands in a take it or leave it manner which astounded and infuriated many of the Washington planners."[55] Army planners said they could scrape up less than half the additional forces Elkton called for. Even when eight partially trained Australian divisions were counted, they would be short more than five divisions and twenty-four air groups.

No one seemed to question why the conversation concentrated on divisions and army aircraft rather than fleet units. Nor did Elkton present a detailed analysis of Japanese capabilities to support MacArthur's proposed troop list. Because the Elkton troop list could not be met, the participants from the Pacific theater offered the opinion that only Task Two, now the first three points of Elkton, could be accomplished.

Through Sutherland, MacArthur denounced the entire concept of a central Pacific offensive. In MacArthur's view, all the limited resources allocated at Casablanca to the Pacific should be committed to the South West Pacific Area to facilitate Rabaul's capture.[56] As Sutherland later confided to Manuel Quezon, exiled president of the Philippines, during this visit in Washington, the real but unspoken agenda was taking the Philippines from the southwest Pacific versus taking Formosa via the central Pacific.[57]

King spoke up. Neither a full offensive all the way to Rabaul nor a more truncated version to accomplish only the old Task Two would profitably employ the navy's growing carrier power. Again he tried to get the conference to look beyond the operational problems of capturing Rabaul and to focus on the best overall strategy to defeat Japan.

One of the real surprises was the position taken by Admiral Spruance. His intellect and orderly approach to problems was respected by virtually everyone. In the name of conservatism and minimization of friendly casualties, he began to favor a strategy that resulted in plans that were less likely to meet the objective and more likely to increase casualties from too many subsidiary operations.

Spruance didn't think a central Pacific advance through the Gilberts and Marshalls was a sufficiently important objective.[58] The admiral felt a much larger buildup would be required before a push farther north or west could be made. Captain Browning opined that the South Pacific would be the decisive theater and American naval forces should be massed there. This irascible officer who showed brilliant tactical insight at Midway seemed to be strategically blind. However, in the face of this much resistance, King curbed his advocacy of the central Pacific.

Had Mahan been there, he would have stridently walked to the podium. He might have reluctantly understood the shortsightedness of the general. But he definitely would have taken the two senior Pacific theater naval officers to task. Again the precept was simple: "Gentlemen, create the conditions that bring your superior fleet power into a position that allows you to destroy Japan's fleet. Didn't you learn anything from the War Game Orange at the Naval War College that we worked so hard to create for you?" Admiral King had.

How many times had so many officers, Japanese and American alike, seemed to lose sight of the most elemental, but the most critical, precepts of naval strategy by getting lost among the details of current deployments, logistical problems, and command relationships? The most difficult task of a *strategist* is to separate the essential from the nice-to-have and to starve the nice-to-have in order to beef up the essential. The most difficult task of a *leader* is to remain resolutely focused on the critical objective despite the enormous pressure to address seemingly more urgent, but less decisive calls for action. King was both a great strategist and a great leader. At the March conference, Admiral King could have used a lot of help from Captain Mahan.

Admiral Leahy, the president's personal chief of staff and the one admiral not beholden to King, pointed out that troops in the South Pacific "must be adequately protected. If those troops are neglected, the Joint Chiefs of Staff could not face the people of the United States." Was there anyone in the room who didn't understand where this sentiment came from? Marshall, in order to maintain priority for the Atlantic, wasn't about to release the aircraft MacArthur demanded. Through Leahy, Roosevelt broke the impasse. Remember what Marshall had observed about inertia and the buildup in the South Pacific? Perhaps every strategist should beware of concentration on anything less than the decisive intermediate objective lest it become such a political symbol that further decisions about it become national strategy rather than the domain of military planners.

After rechecking their documents, Washington planners agreed that more shipping could be freed up by October of 1943. Southwest Pacific planners showed a willingness to back away from the extensive troop and aircraft lists they had been demanding. Still, there were not enough resources to support MacArthur's drive all the way to Rabaul.

The Joint Chiefs went into closed session to draft a final directive. At first all the old command differences were rehashed. During deliberations on the final day, King made no further mention of command relationships. He concentrated on keeping the ability to pull the fleet back under Nimitz's command to retain its oceanwide mobility when needed.

Admiral Leahy continued to weigh into the debate. He felt that MacArthur should be given control of all forces moving up from the south toward Rabaul and should be held solely responsible for producing results. Leahy understood King and Nimitz's wanting to retain fleet flexibility and mobility. All ships not directly assigned to MacArthur's efforts would remain under the Pacific Ocean Fleet commander. However, once assigned to MacArthur, a ship wouldn't be withdrawn from him until the mission was completed. Marshall, recognizing the sound command principles being expressed, became noticeably more agreeable. He accepted navy compromise language for the final directive.

The final directive, issued on 28 March 1943, recognized that Rabaul was not feasible in the short run. After an initial operation to seize Woodlark and Kiriwina islands off the tip of New Georgia, there would be a two-pronged offensive up the coast of New Guinea and onto New Britain, on which Rabaul was located. Admiral Halsey would advance through the Solomons to Bougainville, which was within air range of Rabaul.

Again, it was a landlubber's plan. Rather than defeating the Japanese fleet and its ability to operate in the Pacific, its purpose was "to prepare for ultimate seizure of Bismarck Archipelago."[59] Mahan would have protested loudly. American efforts for the remainder of 1943 would yield little of strategic value. As a fortunate side effect of the southwest offensive, Japanese airpower, especially her dwindling number of experienced aircrews, was ground down. But so much more could have been done to engage the central *air and sea* power of the Japanese fleet and to destroy it.

Battle of the Bismarck Sea

In early March, B-25s caught a large Japanese convoy in what became known as the Battle of the Bismarck Sea. Conventional intelligence, confirmed by Ultra, revealed a convoy containing a major portion of the Japanese 51st Division was headed for New Guinea. General Kenney, MacArthur's brilliant air commander, had eschewed doctrinaire high-level bombing for attacks at mast height. Low-level attacks against radar-directed German anti-aircraft defenses were suicide. But anti-aircraft guns were nowhere nearly as dense in the Pacific as they were in Europe. Defying the experts back in Washington, he filled the noses of B-25s with eight machine guns and taught their crews to skip bombs into enemy ships by dropping them only a few dozen feet above the waves. By challenging a strongly held assumption underlined by Hap Arnold himself, Kenney had solved the precision-strike problem and made land-based bombers ship killers.

Even though the Japanese convoy had fighters overhead and a strong de-stroyer escort, the transports were doomed. After initial attacks by four-engine bombers, two separate raids by low-flying Australian and American twin-engine aircraft decimated the ships. Each strike lasted perhaps fifteen minutes over the ships. When the fighting was over, all eight transports and four destroyers had been sunk. Allied commanders designated Japanese in the water as legitimate targets of war. Stories about Japanese atrocities had circulated widely. Some air-crews relished the opportunity to kill more soldiers. Others, sickened by the order, had their stomachs turned as the water around lifeboats churned dark with human blood. War is a grisly business. Over 3,300 Japanese corpses floated on the ocean. Allied losses were a handful of aviators.

Kenney's change of attack method brought to realization what airpower en-thusiasts had hoped for all along: an aerial weapon that could control the seas. One squadron claimed 17 hits out of 37 bombs dropped on the New Guinea–bound convoy.[60] By comparison, from August to November 1943, high-flying B-17s dropped 828 bombs against sixty Japanese ships but had sunk only four.[61]

Mahan always told us that able leaders are often *the* decisive advantage. Yet history defies most nice either-or distinctions. The first two strikes on the Bis-marck Sea convoy were made by handfuls of B-17s. The Fortresses left two ships sinking. Low-level attacks sank the remaining six transports and four of the es-corting destroyers. This nautical massacre shocked the Imperial General Staff.[62] Resupplying the army was becoming a more difficult undertaking than previ-ously understood. The emperor's soldiers were in very poor shape. The Japanese army records that 40 percent of all troops in New Guinea at the time suffered from either disease or malnutrition.[63]

Kenney's victory eliminated any Japanese capability to substantially reinforce their strong points in eastern New Guinea. Previously Japanese planners had considered this island to be a strategic springboard from which to attack the Al-lies. It had been far more important than Guadalcanal. Now it became a liability, soaking up resources that should have been husbanded for a more decisive operation. Continued Japanese operations in New Guinea demonstrated their lack of strategic focus. Mahan would have cut the whole area free and left forces that could not be evacuated to a delaying role. Then he would have pursued Admiral Ugaki's solution.

Yamamoto's Last Fizzle

A major priority for the Japanese navy had been transport of army reinforcements and supplies to New Guinea. After the Battle of the Bismarck Sea, how was the Japanese navy to prepare for decisive battle with the American fleet if it was tied down fighting Kenney for control of waters far to the south? That contest pitted dwindling Japanese naval air assets against growing American army airpower. This Japanese strategy pitted weakness against enemy strength rather than the other way around. Mahan never would have tolerated such a fundamental error. If necessary, he would have demanded a meeting before the emperor to correct it.

A Japanese navy study and war game conducted at the time predicted an inexorable American offensive up the Solomons culminating in landings in the southern Philippines in October 1944. This wasn't far from what ultimately transpired. However, no one on the Imperial Naval General Staff wanted to hear this kind of conclusion. The study was ignored.[64]

A schism between the Imperial Army and the Imperial Navy reappeared. The army wanted to commit divisions to continued land fighting on New Guinea, making only passing references to the defense of the Philippines and the Dutch East Indies. For the Japanese, the oil of the Dutch Indies was the strategic prize that had started the whole war. The Japanese navy was far more concerned about an Allied approach up the Solomons to Rabaul and ultimately the naval anchorage at Truk. Truk was the central base from which the fleet could sally forth to defend the Pacific extremities of the empire. Mahan would have pointed to the Battle of the Bismarck Sea. What significance would army victories on New Guinea have if the navy lost control of the sea lanes to that island?

Despite the merits of this argument, the greater influence of the army prevailed in Tokyo. The Army-Navy Central Agreement of 15 March 1943 gave New Guinea operations priority. However, its tone was defensive in nature: "The objective of the Southeast Area operations lies in securing or occupying the strategic areas in the theater and thus establishing a superior and impregnable strategic position."[65] This would gain time to build up strength for some ill-defined counteroffensive at some unspecified place and time, perhaps in the central Pacific in the summer of 1944.

Japanese intelligence expected the American Pacific Fleet to have ten fast carriers and ten battleships by year end 1943.[66] The intelligence estimate overstated future American strength by only a small amount. Imperial planners could not ignore the pending inferiority of their fleet. Perceptive naval planners on both sides now began to understand the impending "Essex effect." Retaining a fleet in being would become critical for the Japanese. If the Americans were foolish enough to split their carriers in a manner that allowed the Combined Fleet to achieve local superiority, then the Japanese would pounce from a central base like Truk. Otherwise the objective would be to restrict American freedom of action by preserving a credible fleet in being, to make the Americans aware that they must always take into account the possibility of an IJN sortie wrecking overly ambitious plans.

Limited fuel supplies constrained what the Imperial Navy could do. Fleet planning officers constantly fretted lest they have insufficient fuel to maneuver. American submarines had further reduced already insufficient shipping capacity. Unlike the well-stocked American bases, Rabaul had a couple of prewar machine shops employing about 250. Ugaki felt they "looked like junk yards." Lack of logistical support this far down in the Pacific indicated that the lower Solomons should be treated as a delay area while conditions for decisive battle were created to the north or west.

Yamamoto recognized that the balance of naval power would continue to swing against Japan. The Imperial Fleet must strike immediately or be immobilized by growing American might and dwindling fuel supplies. In the beginning of 1943, Yamamoto still wanted to induce the decisive sea battle.[67] But as we have seen he created no plan to bring it about.

While the Americans debated their next move, the pace of the war in the South Pacific slackened. To commit the Combined Fleet to an area reachable by large numbers of land-based American aircraft would be to lose it. However, there were some possibilities. Yamamoto might have created a plan to draw American carriers within range and then, by combining army air and navy carrier strikes, to destroy them. During 1943, Halsey displayed his propensity for taking large risks. Or Yamamoto could have set a similar, if smaller, trap in the central Pacific east of Truk. Instead Japanese officers began talking about a hundred years' war. Superior Japanese fighting spirit and tenacity would outlast the decadent Americans. It was tacit admission the Japanese could no longer win the war; they could only avoid losing it.

Mahan always advocated aggressive action. He would have harshly criticized the Combined Fleet's inaction and inability to force a major sea battle in early 1943. This was Japan's last real chance. By not electrifying the general staff into action, by doing nothing, Yamamoto threw it away. He committed another strategic blunder of the first magnitude.

Instead he created an unrealistic plan, I-GO, to take a minor slap at his main source of frustration, American land-based airpower. Yamamoto concluded he must attack the enemy's strongest arm directly. Smash as many Allied land-based aircraft as possible by attacking their airfields in the South Pacific. Back in Tokyo the general staff continued to debate the merits of the threat from Papua and Guadalcanal. Again, the army prevailed. New Guinea airfields remained the primary target. By the spring of 1943, Japan did not have the strength to successfully strike at them.

Japan's four carriers based at Truk would not dare sail anywhere near Papua or Guadalcanal. Instead, the carriers sent 96 fighters, 86 dive-bombers, and a few torpedo planes to join 86 fighters, 27 dive-bombers, and 72 twin-engine bombers already in Rabaul.

Upon reading the initial plan for I-GO one can imagine Captain Mahan addressing the senior officer of Yamamoto's staff most sincerely: "As you all know, I have always advocated concentrating our battle fleet for decisive combat that cripples the fleet of our opponent. Those of you who have read more closely also recognize the importance of well-trained crews. They are more important than the latest in ship design. Remember, 'quantity will disappear before quality.' Our pilots have the best fighting spirit. Today they no longer enjoy the best training. We must carefully husband our carrier groups and expand their numbers and training at every possible opportunity. *We must not grind our carrier-based aviation against land targets.* This is the role of the brave aviators of the Imperial Army Air Services. We must continue to train our naval aviators while we create the conditions for an engagement to destroy the American fleet. We must go one step farther. We must enlist the help of the Army Air Force in that decisive battle."

The advice sounds simple, but again Japanese naval leadership failed to establish proper strategic priorities.

On 7 April, 224 aircraft, the largest Japanese strike since Pearl Harbor, made for Guadalcanal. Half of the aircraft were fighters. The Americans were prepared. Ultra, radar, and coast watchers combined to give a clear picture of Japanese intentions. In dogfights over the Russell Islands, about 80 miles from Henderson Field, the Japanese lost 18 fighters against 6 downed American aircraft.

Instead of targeting the airfield, the Japanese dive-bombers chased a cruiser force that intelligence indicated was in Iron Bottom Sound. Forewarned, the cruisers escaped. A couple of tankers and cargo ships were sunk. Most crewmen were rescued. The Americans lost 7 fighters and some small vessels. Japanese records show 21 Japanese aircraft lost. These were hardly decisive results. A supposedly maximum effort became little more than an exciting nuisance raid.

Large raids hit Oro Bay near Buna, New Guinea, on the 11th. Again Japanese naval aircraft targeted Allied shipping instead of airfields. They sank one merchant steamer, forced another to beach, and damaged an Australian minesweeper. A high-altitude attack on Port Moresby on the 12th damaged a few American aircraft on the ground. Milne Bay was hit on the 14th. Australian-manned P-40s took on the raiders. Japanese bombers divided their attention between the airfield and shipping in the harbor. A few ships were sunk. A small fuel dump at the airstrip was set ablaze. Irreplaceable Japanese naval aviation committed to the operation was badly shot up. The American timetable continued without interruption.

Returning Japanese raiders claimed unbelievable results: a cruiser, 2 destroyers, 25 transports, and 175 aircraft. Actual losses were one destroyer, a corvette, a tanker, 2 small freighters, and 25 aircraft. Why did the Japanese risk such a fragile asset on such a relatively inconsequential target list? Yamamoto intended this to be a major air offensive designed to emasculate American efforts.[68] During the last half of 1942, the Japanese air corps had repeatedly hit Henderson Field with little result. Targeting four American airfields, each with a single strike, made little sense.

To understand this point, let's look at some numbers on weapons effectiveness. Remember the bombardment of Guadalcanal of 14 October 1942? The airfield was hit with nine hundred 14-inch shells fired from steady gunnery platforms and aimed by experienced fire control officers with good charts and with enough time to correct the fall of their shot. Japanese battleships destroyed about half the installations at Henderson Field. A 14-inch bombardment shell weighs about 1,400 pounds. That is roughly the total bomb load a Betty, a Japanese twin-engine bomber, could carry. In 1942, no high-level bomber could begin to strike with the accuracy of naval guns. It is reasonable to expect that at least 900 bomber sorties over a number of days would have been required to reduce Guadalcanal's capability by half. Yamamoto allocated only 80 bomber sorties in a single strike. How could any staff officer, any commander, believe such a light punch would create serious damage? The tool wasn't up to the task. Using it this way was poor strategy in anyone's book.

Operation I-GO was more injurious to the Japanese than to the Americans. By 1943, well-trained Japanese carrier pilots, rather than the carriers themselves, had become the critical center of gravity. Placing this most critical resource in harm's way with little hope of a decisive result compounded Yamamoto's blunder.

General Kenney summed up the point: "The [Japanese airman] just did not know how to handle air power. Just because he knocked us off on the ground at the beginning of the war, when we were asleep at Pearl Harbor and the Philippines, he got a reputation for being smart, but the way he had failed to take advantage of his superiority in numbers and position since the first couple of months of the war, was a disgrace to the airman's profession."[69] Mahan would have realized that good airmen thought like good seamen.

The I-GO operation was Yamamoto's last. Ultra picked up Yamamoto's travel plans for an upcoming inspection trip. Army P-38s splashed both Bettys carrying the admiral and his immediate staff. Yamamoto died in the crash on Bougainville on 18 April 1943.

Much of Japan's air strength in New Guinea was concentrated in the airfields at Wewak. General Kenney demonstrated Clausewitz's principle of concentration of effort against the enemy's center of gravity. A series of low-level sweeps over Japanese air bases there tore up the source of Japanese airpower in New Guinea. Several times Kenney's treetop raiders caught lines of Japanese aircraft warming up for takeoff. In one huge surprise raid, a large number of aircraft along with their pilots and associated ground crews were incinerated. The Japanese Army Air Service thereafter referred to August 17, 1943 as the "Black Day." By the time the operation had finished burning airmen, aircraft, supplies, and gas, "it was doubtful if the Nipponese could have put over half a dozen aircraft in the air from all four airdromes combined."[70] This was the kind of decisive attack that Yamamoto had wanted to achieve against the U.S. But he didn't come close to a plan that would have accomplished it.

The recently promoted ace carrier captain, Admiral Marc Mitscher, became commander of land-based aviation in the Solomons (COMAIRSOLS) under Halsey. It was an unusual post for an admiral. This self-effacing man understood airmen, bonded with them, and, in turn received their unquestioned respect. "As a leader of pilots, he was second to none," affirmed his biographer.[71] Under his command American aviators of all services continued to improve their skills by downing Japanese airmen, like the ones foolishly committed by Yamamoto. By July, Mitscher's airmen had shot down 500 Japanese aircraft, dropped 2,000 tons of bombs, and ended the air threat in the Solomons.

The victory by Allied airmen complemented the sea change being wrought by the new carriers arriving at Pearl. Once the Americans achieved air superiority in the Solomons and naval superiority in the Pacific, there was no need to conquer Rabaul. Control of the small islands sprinkled across the great Pacific waste east of the Marianas no longer had meaning.

New Georgia

Admiral Bull Halsey thought little of the jockeying for position within the American camp masquerading as highfalutin strategic theory. He once said that all American fighting men should be taken out of their uniforms and put into dungarees with "U.S. Combat Forces" stenciled across their seats. Halsey was in the Pacific to kill Japanese. Now that they had been whipped at Guadalcanal, they should be given no time to regain their feet. He conducted an unopposed landing in the Russells just west of Guadalcanal.

MacArthur envisioned a single jump from Guadalcanal to Bougainville, a distance of 375 miles. Halsey briefly considered that option. However, he recognized that carriers would be required to support such a distant operation. He was hesitant to commit them in the restricted waters among the Solomons, where they would be subject to large land-based air strikes. Halsey strongly felt he needed intermediate airfields so that he would have solid air cover over the entire distance. Air combat over Guadalcanal had been intense. Halsey's campaign plan envisioned a set of five amphibious assaults up the Solomon chain. If the Japanese had carrier air parity, this might have been prudent. Given the actual correlation of naval forces, Halsey's proposal was unimaginative at best. All concerned understood that the final assault on Rabaul would consume a lot of time and American blood. "Of the five landings in the Central Solomons, only Rendova [a small island across channel from Munda] really paid off."[72]

The next bunch of Japanese up the Slot occupied the island of New Georgia. While Port Moresby, Honolulu, and Washington conferred about grand issues, Halsey set about taking it. Like MacArthur he was ready to go step-by-step, cleaning out every Japanese soldier as he went. Nimitz was the first to identify an opportunity to island-hop. He suggested that perhaps New Georgia could be leapfrogged. This intelligent suggestion wasn't taken. After rescuing the survivors of Guadalcanal, the Japanese had increased the fortification of New Georgia. Obviously, it was to be the next battleground. American delay allowed time for the Japanese to reinforce Munda to make its airfield fully operational.

Japanese reaction to landings on New Georgia was similar to their early operations to reinforce Guadalcanal. They could mount neither a major fleet effort nor a successful infiltration of reinforcements. Given its failure at Guadalcanal, only an uninspired quarterback would call the same play.

American operations on New Georgia did not go smoothly. Like many new units, the U.S. Army's 43rd Infantry Division had a lot of problems. Tactical reconnaissance was particularly poor. An attacker must learn exactly where the enemy is and how his defense is organized, otherwise the attack stumbles into it and pays an awful price. A defender must know the enemy's movements, otherwise he curls up in little ball in the dark and waits to die. The 43rd committed errors on both offense and defense. Green troops became enmeshed among interlocking Japanese pill boxes. It took a change of commander and a reinforcing division to sort things out. The capable Major General Oscar Griswold unsnarled the mess and then put the advance toward Munda back on its rails. Even so, major American reinforcements had to be landed. The plan called on 15,000 U.S. troops to displace 9,100 Japanese. The campaign took 45,000 troops and more than three months. Winning the war this way would take forever.

Munda airfield was taken 6 August, but resistance on the island continued until 20 September. Munda airfield "became the best and most used airfield in the Solomons."[73] However, it was too small a gain for the tremendous expenditure of time and resources, not to mention 1,100 lives.

Halsey was climbing the Solomons rung by rung. The alternative—island hopping—was so obvious that many officers independently reached this conclusion. Perhaps the first practical application was by Halsey at Kolombangara. That was the next in the Solomon chain above New Georgia, and it appeared to be heavily garrisoned. At Nimitz's suggestion, Halsey pointed to Vella Lavella, 35 miles closer to Rabaul. It had a good airstrip and was garrisoned by only 250 Japanese.

Halsey sent Vice Admiral Aubrey Fitch to Brisbane to secure General MacArthur's concurrence to bypassing Kolombangara. He departed with a group of staff officers so all aspects of the revised plan could be resolved. When they were ushered into the general's office, Admiral Fitch opened with a simple statement of the proposed switch. MacArthur responded with a dissertation on the war's grand strategy. As he warmed to the topic, he began his familiar pacing. For fifteen minutes he continued, not about the Pacific but about strategy in Europe. Then he stopped, smiled, and thanked the naval officers for coming, without addressing the matter at hand.

Fitch was aghast. What was he to do? After extended pleading, he was granted an individual audience with MacArthur. Again he made a brief statement of the proposal. MacArthur's answer was also brief. "Work it out with General Sutherland. I agree with anything you and Halsey want to do."[74]

In what was dubbed Operation Goodtime, 25th Infantry Division invaded Vella Lavella on 15 August, about a year after the landing on Guadalcanal. The operation lived up to its handle. The only Japanese on the island were a handful of shipwrecked sailors.

The two navies fought four night surface engagements among the Solomon Islands between July and October of 1943: Kula Gulf, Kolombangara, Vella Gulf, and Vella Lavella. Losses were about even. However, American radar and crew performance continued to improve.

On 13 August, Ultra decoded an Japanese order canceling further reinforcements to garrisons in the Solomons.[75] The Tokyo Express would run down the Slot no more. That signal told the Allies there was no further reason to fight in the South Pacific theater.

But progress up the Solomons remained maddeningly slow. Hap Arnold remembered a late 1942 meeting with Roosevelt: "The President once said at one of our Joint Chiefs of Staff meetings with him, that were we to continue our present method of crossing the Pacific, it would require us about 2000 years to reach the mainland of Japan."[76] There had to be a better way than conducting a major island fight every 250 miles across the Pacific.

Trident and a Role for China

Hardly had the 28 March Pacific directive been circulated than the Combined Chiefs met again. The Trident Conference was held in Washington in May 1943. Most of the inter-Allied argument centered on the invasion of France versus further Mediterranean operations. This was the main point of contention between Britain and the United States. The war against Japan was discussed. However, the talks carried an air of unreality about them. Allied thinking about the shape of the offensive against Japan was far different than the final outcome. The Americans, especially Roosevelt, continued to think China could make a large contribution to the final effort against Japan. Both the president and the prime minister had visions of engaging the enormous manpower of the Nationalist Chinese Army against the Japanese. Great Britain maintained it could sustain a major offensive via Southeast Asia.

Most participants at the Trident Conference envisioned an approach to Japan from the south. After capturing Rabaul, MacArthur would continue up the coast of New Guinea and on to the island of Celebes in the southern Philippines. Meanwhile the British would reconquer Burma. From Burma and the Celebes, Allied forces would attack up the Strait of Malacca and recapture Singapore. A direct attack on the Dutch East Indies would be a frontal attack on the strength of the Japanese army. Instead the British proposed moving across the South China Sea from Singapore toward Hong Kong. The Americans would continue to advance through the Philippine archipelago. This would encircle the Dutch Indies, and cut off the flow of oil from the South Seas to Japan. It would also restore prewar British colonial supremacy.

The British said the only way to capture Burma was an amphibious assault on Rangoon. This concerned Roosevelt. He wanted to know what impact this would have on the planned amphibious invasion of Europe.

In the drive on the British Crown Colony of Hong Kong, Chinese troops were to be reinforced by Americans. The British colony would become the primary base for the invasion of Japan.[77] While labeled "a vast undertaking," the invasion of Japan was declared feasible. An advance from Southeast Asia through China would make a campaign across the central Pacific unnecessary. British planning was land-based in nature and didn't focus directly on gaining naval supremacy in the Pacific.

Instead of invasion, the American Chiefs leaned toward defeating Japan by a combination of bombing and blockade. They focused on possible long-range bomber bases. The Joint Chiefs' "Strategic Plan for the Defeat of Japan" dated 19 May 1943 (JCS 287/1), which lists all of these points, went on to state that an "air offense of the required scale can only be conducted from bases in CHINA." It left open the possibility that air bombardment and sea blockade alone might bring about Japan's surrender. While Marshall acknowledged benefits of the central Pacific approach, he expected that an advance via Burma into China would ultimately prove more profitable.

Army planners were far from sure that long-distance bombing by itself would defeat Japan.[78] Some thought this might be accomplished by 1948. Hap Arnold saw China as home for his B-29 campaign against Japan. He noted that ten groups of 28 planes each would be available by October 1944.[79] Arnold, too, deplored the lack of unity of command in the Pacific.[80] He didn't think army and navy planners were sufficiently sensitive to the need of identifying and then capturing bases for his heavy bombers. He was right. No Rabaul-based B-29 would have the range to hit anything of value. If Nimitz and MacArthur planned operations separately, each might order heavy bomber strikes on distant targets that interfered with the other. Arnold's solution was to maintain direct control of the B-29 force.

Army Air Force strategy was contained in AWPD-42. In it the Army Air Force argued that there were insufficient air units to simultaneously attack Germany and Japan. Therefore it was paramount that all available airpower be incorporated into the bombing of Germany through mid-1944. More than any other American group, Army Air Force planners believed in concentration of force.

American strategists badly needed a reality check. Roosevelt clung to a romantic notion of Chinese capabilities under Chiang Kai-shek's leadership. He envisioned hordes of motivated Nationalist soldiers going on the attack against the

Japanese once they had been armed and trained by the Americans. No one who read General Joseph Stilwell's diary could have thought the Chinese army was capable of offensive action. (Stilwell was the senior American officer in China and, nominally, Chiang Kai-shek's chief of staff.) When B-29 airbases were made operational in 1944, small-scale Japanese offensives easily shut them down.

The British had virtually no capability of supporting the major amphibious campaign that they described to retake Southeast Asia. Neither could they take on the Japanese navy in a battle for control of the South China Sea. A large American fleet and a huge American amphibious contingent would be needed. These forces would operate with logistical support coming over the most lengthy supply line on the planet—from America, across the Atlantic, through India, and into Southeast Asia. The Japanese fleet would operate in close proximity to its fuel source in Borneo. It was an absurd idea.

By this time, the American navy, and Admiral King in particular, thought little of proposed British efforts to traverse Southeast Asia. Like his president, King did not want to see a restoration of the British colonial empire. Even the closest of allies frequently have differences in their objectives.

Combat in Burma, New Guinea, and the Solomons indicated how slow and costly an advance against the Japanese army defending in rough, jungle-covered terrain was. At Trident, King reiterated that "decisive action against the Japanese fleet and the seizure of the Marianas Islands were of primary importance."[81] At this stage, Admiral King spoke about taking the Philippines at the culmination of a central Pacific drive.[82]

The final directive from Trident listed five priorities for the Pacific. First, the Americans still held to the notion that Japan would be attacked by air from China. Second, the Japanese must be purged from the Aleutians. Third, submarine attacks on Japanese shipping would continue. Fourth, completion of the old Tasks Two and Three would continue from New Guinea to the Bismarck Archipelago and Rabaul. Fifth, another offensive line through the Carolines and Marshalls would begin. The rivalry between these alternatives became firmly set. At the time, the Combined Chiefs of Staff gave the capture of Burma equal priority with the capture of Rabaul. However, planners wanted to be certain a central Pacific offensive did not slow down operations in Burma.

Admiral Thomas Kinkaid led the advance to clear the Aleutians. Weather proved a far greater adversary than the Japanese. Most of them evacuated before American invaders reached Kiska and Attu. Bougainville and western New Britain (Gloucester Bay) were to be captured by December 1943. However the Allies were not expected to be through the Bismarck Archipelago until April 1944, almost a year away.

The second prong was the British via Burma. However, the British continued to resist any notion of reinforcing the Pacific before the defeat of the Nazis. Should anyone have been surprised when the British reported they would be unable to take Southeast Asia in 1943? In 1944? At the Quadrant Conference in Quebec in August 1943, the British informed their allies that there would be no push in Burma until 1944. Delays in the planned British offensive caused Chiang Kai-shek to renege on his planned offensive into Burma and to attempt to extort an additional $800 million in construction costs from the U.S. for air bases. He did this by insisting on an exchange rate between the dollar and the yuan that was ten times the market rate. Resulting construction costs in China, the land of "coolie labor," were far more than ten times comparable costs in the United States. These actions shocked a lot of pro-Chinese American decision makers and began the decline of the China theater to that of an afterthought.

In the face of these unrealistic plans, King pushed the central Pacific offensive. He continued to identify the Marianas as key.[83] An American advance there would force the Japanese fleet out to fight in open waters that maximized American naval airpower's advantages. He advocated attack from the Marianas, not an approach from the southwest Pacific, as the correct move to flank the Philippines. Given that the British had backed off on Pacific theater strategy once they heard that a return to the Philippines would come after the defeat of Germany, King clawed out a little wiggle room. "On the basis of the agreements reached at the Trident Conference, the Americans could proceed confidently with their plans to open an offensive in the Central Pacific."[84]

War Plan Orange Resurrected

At the end of May, Admirals Nimitz, King, and Cooke met in San Francisco for six days. Nimitz pointed out that the Japanese only had four fleet carriers left. The other carriers weren't good for much besides ferry duty. The Japanese probably would not commit them at the periphery of the empire. Admiral Cooke held that advance through the central Pacific was the best way to induce the Japanese fleet to offer decisive combat. Marshall's admonition that a central Pacific drive had to await the fall of Rabaul had become the standard assumption. Admiral Cooke asked, Why wait? He wanted to avoid a slow, methodical advance through the Gilberts and Marshalls. This opened further possibilities. Mahan would have known why they called King's deputy "Savvy."

Nimitz and King appeared to agree that the Marshall Islands held the most promise as an intermediate base for the advance on the Home Islands. The admirals also discussed the Gilberts. By the spring of 1943, Nimitz had become confident that the JCS would approve some kind of central Pacific operation, probably in the Marshalls.[85]

Nimitz wanted to ensure that the Imperial Japanese Navy (IJN) was pinned down and unable to cause further trouble. He didn't think current American operations and central Pacific planning would do accomplish this.[86] The Pacific Ocean commander had always been concerned that a Japanese fleet raid might damage Honolulu while the majority of the fleet was engaged in South Pacific operations. It is one reason why he kept the old battleships at Pearl.

Savvy Cooke suggested that the Joint Planning Staff formulate a central Pacific plan. Their work product outlined an attack into the Marshalls in November 1943 followed up with an operation to take Eniwetok.[87] This recommendation dovetailed nicely with the "sea change" in carrier strength already alluded to.

King was about to pick up a major ally in his endeavor to focus Pacific strategy.

While the Joint Planners wrestled with command issues disguised as strategy, the Joint Strategic Survey Committee (JSSC), the successor of the Joint Board, reported its conclusions on Pacific strategy.[88] As members of this joint group were serving in their last billet, they were far less susceptible to undue career or service influence. Their opinions were generally respected. These "gray beard" flag officers dropped a fireball into an already heated debate. They concluded that the drive for Rabaul made sense when relative American power was weak and the antagonists were fighting over the initiative. Now that that issue was settled, absolute priority should be moved to the central Pacific. This was the fastest way to advance on Japan and promised the best use of the fleet. A major offensive into the Marshalls and the Carolines was the best way to defend Australia and shorten the sea lanes to her. The JCCS pointed out that only in the central Pacific was there a chance to use the fleet to its best advantage. The "inch by inch" advance against Rabaul had "small promise of reasonable success in the near future." Mahan would have beamed at these elder, and wiser, strategists. Someone was seeing the issue clearly through the smoke emanating from the command squabble in the South Pacific. Finally Mahan could smile. He might have noted that two of the three members of the JSSC were generals. Not all generals were unversed in strategy after all!

Admiral King continued to point out that operations in the Solomons advanced inch by inch. The best way to unbalance the Japanese was by taking Luzon from the flank. The best approach to Luzon wasn't from Australia via New Guinea and the Admiralties as championed by MacArthur. It was from Hawaii via the Marshalls and Marianas. In this manner, the Americans wouldn't have to fight up the length of the Philippine archipelago. Finally the full JCS staff agreed with this position. The best way to Luzon was via the Marianas. Marshall was also coming around. He pointed to the relative inactivity in 1943 of the carrier fleets and wanted to get them into the fight. However JCS planners still endorsed continued pressure against Rabaul. Two offensives would continue.

Away from the heated argument about overall command of operations aimed at Rabaul, the overall logic of an advance on Japan began to emerge. The shortest route between San Francisco and Tokyo goes nowhere near Honolulu. Instead, it lies just to the south of the Aleutians and crosses the international date line at 48 degrees north. Honolulu is 22 degrees north, a significant dogleg. The shortest distance from Honolulu to Tokyo crosses the date line at 28 degrees north. Kwajalein at 9 degrees north is quite a dogleg between Honolulu and Tokyo. But this is nothing compared to Rabaul, which is 5 degrees south latitude. A dogleg into the southern hemisphere when the shortest distance is up near the Aleutians is quite a detour indeed. Honolulu–Tokyo via the Marianas is 5,300 miles. Honolulu–Tokyo via Rabaul is 6,700 miles.

The latest prewar analysis of Orange indicated that about two intermediate operations between Honolulu and the Philippines would be required. King envisioned a landing in the Marshalls and then the Marianas. MacArthur's planned advance on Rabaul envisioned eleven separate operations spread over eight months. The admiral pointed out that most of the atolls of the central Pacific provided very small landmass. Unlike New Guinea or New Britain, on which Rabaul was located, there wasn't sufficient room on these atolls to deploy large Japanese troop formations. Many weren't large enough to support an airfield that could hold more aircraft than a large fleet carrier. Because of the distance between most atolls, only a few could be used to stage strikes against an invasion fleet attacking any one of them. By comparison, Rabaul alone had at least eight airstrips.

A fleet based in the Marianas blocked the sea lanes between Tokyo and either Rabaul or Truk. Nothing to the south would be tenable. Instead of fighting through all of the Japanese defenders in the South Pacific, they could either be left in the "Great Pacific Empty" to wither or to be withdrawn on limited Japanese shipping through the gauntlet of Allied aircraft and submarines.

Ultimately Japan's Home Islands would either be invaded or blockaded. Neither could be accomplished while the Imperial Fleet was intact. The best place to kill it was in the open ocean. Far better to fight the navy away from a large landmass from which large formations of the Japanese Army Air Service could reinforce the navy.

An invasion fleet poised in the Marianas directly threatened the Home Islands. The Japanese had always considered the Marianas as part of their inner defensive perimeter. As the army air force was coming to understand, B-29s based there could carpet bomb Tokyo. The Imperial Fleet would have to respond to a threat to the Marianas. In that light, both Rabaul and Truk were expendable.

If the road to Rabaul had been over land, army strategists could have been forgiven for the journeyman land strategy contained in the three-task Elkton plan, ultimately renamed "Cartwheel," for the conquest of Rabaul. Rabaul was the next major concentration of enemy strength in the southwest Pacific. Advance on it and the Americans would precipitate a major opportunity to engage and destroy the Japanese army. On land such a dominant fort would bar the road and prevent further advance toward the enemy's vitals.

When Truk itself became vulnerable, there was no longer a need to advance on Rabaul. If the link between Truk and Rabaul was broken, all of the Solomons would no longer be viable for the Japanese. This was King's reasoning when he suggested assaulting the Admiralties. It was highly probable the Imperial Japanese Fleet would come out to prevent such a move.

At the operational level, Rabaul continued to appear enticing to army planners. It was the linchpin that held Japanese defenses in the South Pacific together. On the strategic level, it was an empty. Nimitz's fleet of *Essex* carriers attacking to the north of Rabaul would make that base, the Solomons, and most of New Guinea irrelevant to the final defeat of Japan.

Unfortunately, army planners in Washington, Honolulu, and Brisbane didn't have the vision to see the enormous change in conditions at the strategic level. In land warfare, every river between you and the enemy capital has to be crossed, even if you use paratroopers once in a while. In the ocean, virtually every intermediate objective can be bypassed, if your fleet is powerful enough and its sea legs long enough.

MacArthur's success to date in New Guinea caused Japanese reinforcements, principally from what is now Indonesia (the South Seas area), to move east to harden forward defensive positions. This redeployment was of little benefit to the Allies seeking Japan's destruction. About 140,000 Japanese troops lay isolated in Kavieng, Rabaul, and Bougainville. Nevertheless, throughout 1943, MacArthur continued to argue in support of his cherished drive up from Australia. In MacArthur's words, "From a broad strategic viewpoint," the best method of defeating Japan would be to move from Australia through New Guinea to Mindanao.

Of course MacArthur objected to any suggestion of a central Pacific advance. His primary stated objections were that jumps in the central Pacific could not be supported by land-based air the way they could be on the southern axis. Land-based aircraft were "utterly essential." "Moreover," he concluded, "no vital strategic objective is reached until the series of amphibious frontal attacks succeed in reaching Mindanao."[89]

In his words, a central Pacific campaign "involves a succession of independent sea borne attacks, supported by carrier based aviation supported by land based air. Each successive operation contributes little to the next, and the loss of each successive point does not materially weaken the enemy . . . the offensive can never achieve momentum. Taking these outposts of the enemy defense will not cut his lines of communication and curtail his potential. This course of action does not employ in effective combination the three essentials of modern combat: land, sea and air power."[90]

MacArthur wasn't content with raising objections through channels. Right after the Quebec Conference he made statements to reporters that became grist for stories printed back in the States. In the September 22, 1943, editions of both the *New York Herald Tribune* and the *Washington Times-Herald* stories appeared recounting MacArthur's feeling that his efforts had been subordinated to Nimitz's drive across the central Pacific and Mountbatten's through Southeast Asia. Both of these were held to be inferior to MacArthur's southwest Pacific strategy.

The JCS did not find MacArthur's arguments compelling enough to dissuade them from beginning a central Pacific advance. At this point they didn't believe the remainder of New Guinea could be bypassed via an advance through the central Pacific to Mindanao.[91] Both the Joint Planners and the Joint Chiefs thought both operations could be brought forward.

During the summer of 1943, JCS planners came around to the superiority of the central Pacific route. By the end of Trident meetings in May 1943, army planners acceded to pressure from the navy for a central Pacific campaign, as long as ongoing efforts to capture Rabaul were not adversely affected.[92] By mid-June the JCS had tentatively approved commencement of a major central Pacific operation with an assault to establish a base in the Marshall Islands in November. If this proved too ambitious, the fallback would be a scaled-back operation in the Gilberts. The army's Washington staffers had some understanding of the importance of a major fleet engagement. But they doubted a central Pacific advance would precipitate one. Perhaps the Imperial Fleet would show itself to defend against a deep incursion into the Carolines or Marshalls.[93]

The navy maintained it was far better to neutralize Rabaul from the Marshalls. Army planners agreed that the elimination of the need to seize western New Britain would eliminate the need for the 1st Marine Division in the South Pacific theater. If Rabaul could be neutralized by air bombardment instead of direct invasion, the 2nd Marine Division could also be released to the central Pacific. Needless to say, MacArthur's staff would have been doing cartwheels if they had heard these proceedings.

The Joint War Plans Committee therefore recommended that MacArthur and Halsey be ordered to conduct a holding action along the line from the Russell Islands to Woodlark to Kiriwina to Buna until the Marshalls operation was concluded.[94] This recommendation met with little approval from the Army Operations Division (OPD) or from MacArthur. He stated that halting Cartwheel would have political repercussions "both in Australia-New Zealand and this country." There was risk to a central Pacific–only strategy. A defeat in the Marshalls would also bring the entire Pacific war to a halt if southwest Pacific operations were capped.

Army planners still worried that shipping problems would negatively impact Cartwheel. They wanted a 1 January 1944 target for a central Pacific offensive contingent on availability of shipping. General Marshall was determined that Cartwheel not be sacrificed for central Pacific operations.[95] Marshall also thought the proposed central Pacific operations weren't efficiently using shipping. A reworking of this plan demonstrated that enough shipping could be found to support both drives.

The president's chief of staff, Admiral William Leahy, had been a major supporter of MacArthur and his southwest Pacific strategy. This split America's two most senior admirals. Leahy remained opposed to a shift in priority in mid-1943. He wrote in his autobiography that switching emphasis to the central Pacific would be a "complete reversal" of existing strategy.[96] The JSSC report helped tip the balance in the direction Captain Mahan would have advocated most arduously. The JCS communicated their approval of the beginnings of a central Pacific campaign to MacArthur on 15 June. The South West Pacific Area commander's reply was predictable.[97]

Increasingly, the British Chiefs left Pacific theater strategy to King. The British continued to back away from a general offensive from Burma through Southeast Asia. Chinese performance continued to underwhelm the Combined Chiefs. At Quadrant, Churchill suggested that the central Pacific offensive should result in bringing the Japanese fleet to battle. The old First Sea Dog had not forgotten his Mahan. King responded that this was one of the major purposes of the campaign, but this probably wouldn't come about until the American fleet entered the Mariana Islands.[98]

At Quebec, Field Marshal Sir Alan Brooke, the chief of the British Imperial General Staff questioned whether the advance up New Guinea needed to be prosecuted if the Americans advanced through the central Pacific. King argued they were complementary. Marshall said forces were already in theater and reallocating them to Europe would not save transportation. Brooke was no idiot.

Earlier notions about engaging the Japanese with Chinese manpower faded as Chiang's material demands mounted and the combat performance of his troops failed to materialize. General Arnold became disenchanted with China as a base for his B-29s. By the end of the Quebec Conference, the army air force had shifted to the notion of Marianas bases for their best bomber. King had another convert.

In November, en route to Sextant on board the battleship *Iowa,* the JCS briefly considered operations for 1944. When the Pacific came up, Admiral Leahy asked if JCS plans "tied in" with MacArthur's. General Arnold asked if conflicts between the southwest and central Pacific had been resolved. King replied that "dividends would be greater" in the central Pacific and that "nothing should interfere" with operations there.[99] The dance continued. More staff work was assigned and the meeting reconvened on the 17th. Since October, JCS planners had been won over by arguments favoring the most rapid approach to the Marianas.[100] Now that the army air forces saw these islands as the primary B-29 base, they strongly supported King any time he suggested bypassing any intermediate islands in order to speed up the occupation of their future bomber base. On the 17th General Marshall expressed doubts about the wisdom of assaulting Truk and Ponape. Savvy Cooke reminded everyone that the plan document was for guidance only and that they would remain flexible and take advantage of opportunities as they presented themselves. The final 1943 meeting of the Combined Chiefs was held in Cairo in November. As *Iowa* steamed eastward, it was clear which way Pacific strategy was heading.

While the Chiefs met in Cairo, their planners agreed on three assumptions:

1. Invasion of Japan not inevitable.

2. Germany might be defeated as early as spring 1944.

3. Soviets might declare war on Japan when Germany was invaded.

At Cairo Roosevelt and Churchill agreed that Guam and the Marianas landings should be accomplished tentatively by 1 October 1944 to dovetail with B-29 availability. Unrealistic plans about a British offensive in upper Burma were dropped. This essentially eliminated any serious thought of a Nationalist Chinese offensive. Finally reality had set in.

General Sutherland arrived in Cairo and presented MacArthur's plans to attack from the southwest Pacific. He continued to rail against a central Pacific offensive. Repeating the by now familiar arguments, Sutherland had spoken for MacArthur before JCS planners around 8 November, just before the Chiefs departed for Cairo. The only worthy objective in the western Pacific was the Philippines; the only worthy approach was from the South Pacific. The southwest Pacific generals had been listening, however. Sutherland asserted that the invasion of Mindanao might force a decisive fleet engagement. The central Pacific, "in Sutherland's view, would involve the Allies in a frontal assault and a war of attrition without promise of great strategic results." "To attempt a major effort along each axis," Sutherland declared, "would result in weakness everywhere in violation of cardinal principles of war and . . . in failure to reach the vital strategic objective at the earliest date, thus prolonging the war."[101]

However, his presentation made little impression on the Combined Chiefs. An "Overall Plan for the Defeat of Japan" was approved. It sanctioned a two-pronged offensive through both the southwest Pacific up the length of New Guinea and a central Pacific offensive to reach the Marianas. This was to "to obtain objectives from which we can conduct intensive air bombardment and establish a sea and air blockade against Japan and from which to invade Japan proper if this should prove necessary."[102] Target date for the first B-29 sorties was 31 December.

Japan's "New Operational Policy"

By the fall of 1943, the Japanese understood they had lost the initiative. While the defeats at Guadalcanal and Papua (eastern New Guinea) were not by themselves decisive, Japan was now on the defensive. Small losses in the Aleutians had opened another remote but feasible approach to the Home Islands. Allied submarines had sunk 450 vessels and Japan was feeling the lack of shipping. Pilot losses meant the loss of Japan's tactical advantage in the air. Japanese leadership began to fear an American central Pacific offensive.

The Imperial General Staff knew the current line, New Guinea–northern Solomons–Marshalls and Gilberts, would crumble. An "Absolute National Defense Sphere" had to be established and held at all costs. The remainder of the Solomons became a delaying zone to be given up grudgingly in order to gain time. In selecting this boundary American amphibious capabilities had to be taken into account. The new line ran from the Kuriles and Bonins to the Marianas and Carolines, through western New Guinea, and on to the Sunda Islands and the East Indies.[103] It included Saipan and Truk. It did not include Rabaul. The objective of so much Allied strategy had now become part of the sacrificial delaying area. It also excluded the Marshalls and the Gilberts, areas that Allied officers were intensively arguing over.

The new defense area was almost congruent with the Greater East Asia Co-prosperity Sphere. Planners wanted to build one hundred airfields in depth within the area. However, there was insufficient shipping or construction equipment to accomplish this task as enunciated.

Thus, by September 1943, Tojo's view had altered 180 degrees. Now the prime minister, the war minister, and senior generals wanted to abandon the Solomons and the Bismarcks and to retreat to a Wewak-Truk-Marianas perimeter.[104] They felt the next Allied offensive would emanate from Australia. Tojo was now ready to write off the Gilberts, Marshalls, and Solomons as if they had always been delay zones of little intrinsic value.

Because of continued weakness in American carrier strength and the number of new carriers that would hit the water in 1944, Japanese intelligence officers didn't expect a central Pacific offensive in 1943. Neither did they anticipate Soviet intervention.[105] Instead, they expected a methodical advance on Rabaul followed by invasion of the Philippines.

Despite the poor matériel condition of the Japanese armed forces, imperial planners assumed Japan would make a major counterattack. Three army divisions remained on New Guinea. They could tie down a lot of American combat power. The 8th Area Army would hold Bougainville and the Bismarcks as long as possible. General Imamura thought MacArthur would try to directly assault Rabaul, as indeed MacArthur wished to do.[106] Imamura would also hold Cape Gloucester as long as possible. Another division was en route from Shanghai to New Britain to shore up defenses. The equivalent of two divisions remained in the Solomons.

In the new plan, the central Pacific islands were allocated about 40 infantry battalions. However, many of these battalions were lost at sea. The army thought reinforcing the Carolines should take priority, assuming, in the words of the U.S. Army's official historian, that "any threat from the east would presumably be met by the Combined Fleet at Truk. . . . From November on, the Central Pacific was regarded as the more critical area."[107]

All of these arrangements were embodied in Japan's Army-Navy Central Agreement of 30 September, which was roughly equivalent to a JCS directive. Paragraph IIA read: "Defenses of the strategic sectors in the Bougainville-Bismarck Archipelago Area [which includes Rabaul] will be strengthened and efforts will be made to hold them as long as possible." It was rare for the Japanese to admit that they expected less than total victory. This passage also underscores the limited value of the area that Marshall had designated Task Two and Task Three and that had led to plans Elkton and Cartwheel. By the fall of 1943, the southwest Pacific had ceased to matter.

After Yamamoto's Betty crashed into the jungle, Mineichi Koga, a protégé of Yamamato, took command of the fleet. The scowl on his weathered face gave him the look of a fighting admiral. A cruiser/battleship man, he had commanded the China Area Fleet that had taken Hong Kong. Previously, he had been naval attaché to Paris and had served as chief of naval intelligence. "A much more cautious man than his predecessor, Admiral Koga believed in the decisive naval sea battle."[108] But the Solomons were not the place. He recognized the delay value of the Bismarck Archipelago. Japan needed time to improve its interior defenses.

Koga wanted to plant his flag on Saipan. But Japan didn't possess enough tankers to base the fleet that far north. Its major units had to stay near their source of oil in Tawi-Tawi, Borneo. Only the flagship and a few escorts could be sustained at Palau.

There was no shortage of ground forces to reinforce island garrisons. However, there wasn't enough shipping to move them and their barricade materials and to sustain them. Instead of building up positions in the Marianas, Koga focused on battalion-size reinforcements for many islands in the Marshalls and Carolines. Truk received the rump of the 52nd Division shipped directly from Japan. Five divisions under General Anami's 2nd Area Army, including three from China, defended against MacArthur's upcoming southwest Pacific thrust.

During the opening days of the war, Admiral Ugaki had identified the lack of a good replacement pilot system as a major weakness. Over two thousand air crewmen and 2,500 aircraft had been lost in the failed campaign to defend Guadalcanal. The aircraft loss equaled more than five months' production. So many naval aircraft had been sucked from carriers at Truk down via Rabaul that First Air Fleet no longer had its punch. Most of First Carrier Division's pilots had been dispatched to Rabaul where they had been decimated in the air battles in the central Solomons. Later most experienced Second Division pilots would be lost defending the Marshalls. Three-fourths of Third Division pilots were essentially students with just three months of flying experience instead of the usual twelve. Available replacement pilots were nowhere near as experienced as their fallen brethren. Rear Admiral Sakamaki, chief of staff of the 11th Air Fleet, estimated that the replacement pilots had one-third the skill of those who had been lost.[109]

Recognizing their tremendous loss in pilots, the Imperial Navy endowed the First Air Fleet with 1,600 planes and the mandate to produce aviators. Each was to receive at least a year's training in one of two subordinate commands, the 61st and 62nd Air Flotillas. Barely had these units been pulled together than the Big Blue Fleet upset their plans.

Japan's Army Air Force, anticipating a requirement to replace 25 percent of its pilots per month, planned to build its training establishment to produce 105,000 pilots a year in 1944. Early in January 1945 it cut back training to an annual rate of 60,000. Shortly thereafter training classes were halved again to a 30,000 rate.[110] Despite identifying a critical problem, Japan kept eating its seed corn. Meanwhile American pilots were gaining experience while their numbers swelled. In 1942, the United States built 49,455 planes. Japan built 8,861.

7

TWO PRONGS
DIVIDE
THE FLEET

Finally the signal flags had been set to gather the American fleet into the central Pacific. Much has been made of the educational value of the invasion of Tarawa. In 1942 Nimitz made desperate moves to confront the Japanese fleet at Coral Sea and Midway. By mid-1943, the correct solution was to force the Japanese fleet to deal with the U.S. Navy. Just as Nimitz was about to take a giant leap into what would become the decisive theater, one of America's best admirals, "the admiral's admiral," decided to pull back.

Evaluating Central Pacific Targets

War Plan Orange studies of the 1930s well equipped planners for what they would face in the early '40s. Not only did these studies describe the amphibious and mobile fleet basing that would be needed, they noted how paramount was the need for "bypassing superfluous intermediate points and keeping the enemy off balance by momentum."[1]

The Carolines, Marshalls, and Gilberts are strings of small coral atolls. Atolls are created when reefs formed by coral emerge from the sea because of uplifting geological forces. Often the coral has grown in the shape of a large ring with many open gaps, leaving a lagoon of sheltered ocean that ships can enter and exit. The lagoon's sheltered waters give protection like that of a harbor and allow ship servicing and cargo discharge uninterrupted by open-ocean swells.

Beginning in the 1920s, many of the Micronesian islands had been studied by the planners of Orange.[2] They had identified the most likely location of a major naval battle to be the eastern Marshalls or perhaps the Carolines.[3] The target most often identified was Truk,[4] where the innermost Japanese defense line intersected the outermost American aerial recon. The Marshalls are about two thousand miles away from Pearl Harbor. At about this distance, the navy would need a good intermediate base where ships could be repaired and resupplied. After the fleet sailed off, the remaining facilities would have to support enough land airpower to ward off a major Japanese strike.

During the interwar period the Marine Corps embraced the mission of attacking a defended island that would be converted into a fleet base. This was quite a departure from their previous role as seagoing security forces for the fleet. Pioneers, like Majors Earl Ellis and Don Williams, worked out the tactics and equipment that would make possible the most difficult of all military operations, an opposed amphibious invasion. Their Japanese counterparts never mastered the techniques. The first six months of the Pacific war might have had quite a different outcome if the defenders had more vigorously defended the invasion beaches against poorly prepared Japanese invaders.

In the Marshalls, the islands that best fit the air-sea basing requirements were Kwajalein, Wotje, and Eniwetok. Each had large protected lagoons and enough landmass for an airfield. By the mid-thirties Wotje had been identified as the best potential fleet base,[5] though in fact it was less desirable than Truk in the Carolines.

Any good general avoids frontal attacks on fortifications unless there is no other alternative. Planners understood that an attack on a defended atoll would be tantamount to a dangerous amphibious frontal assault on a fortified position. From a land force perspective, minimizing the number of opposed amphibious landings to those necessary to secure the minimum required number of air and naval bases was an absolute imperative. The drafters of Plan Orange wanted to move deeply and swiftly. A 1940 Naval War College study recommended by-

MANCHURIA

JAPAN
Tokyo

PACIFIC
OCEAN

Shanghai
East China
CHINA   Sea
Ryukyu Is.
Okinawa

*Typical single
engine A/C range*

Iwo Jima

Wake I.

Taiwan

Luzon
Saipan   Marianas
Tinian   Is.
Manila   PHILIPPINES
Guam
Bikini
Eniwetok   Wotje
Leyte   Ulithia   Kwajalein   Marshall
Islands
Mindanao   Truk Is.   Maloelap
Palau Is.
Caroline Islands
Celebes   Tarawa
Sea   Morotai   Gilbert
Is.   0°

Admiralty Is.
Bismarck   New   Arch.   Rabaul
Guinea
Solomon Is.
Buna
Timor   Port Morsby   Guadalcanal   Santa Cruz Is.

Map 7a. Central Pacific. Circles denote single-engine aircraft radius of operations.
Map by Bill Nelson.

passing the Marshalls altogether and hitting Truk directly.[6] Early on, Rear Admiral Theodore S. "Ping" Wilkinson latched on to the idea of striking deep and avoiding the most heavily defended islands.

Given that these would be attacks on defended atolls, planners on Nimitz's staff recognized that seasoned amphibious troops would be needed. Calculation indicated two divisions. However, the only two available were the First Marine Division in MacArthur's area and the Second Marine Division with Halsey. The army's 7th Division might fill in at a later date, but it was up in Alaska chasing Japanese out of the Aleutians. Available amphibious shipping could only lift a two-division force.

In the spring of 1943 Nimitz recommended to King that the next step be the Marshalls. That was exactly what the CNO wanted to hear. Planners began drafting an operation to take Wojte, Kwajalein, and Maloelap in the Marshalls.[7] These islands contained about 65 percent of the airfield facilities as well as the best potential naval base in the island group.[8] Kwajalein's central location would facilitate broad coverage by land-based air. Maloelap is adjacent to Wojte. All were out of air range of the large Japanese airfields on Truk.

In August of 1943, Nimitz asked the JCS for a directive to attack the Marshalls. He believed the necessary strength was finally available. He had shied away from earlier invasion dates for lack of resources. A well-established American base in the Marshalls would split enemy sea lanes north and south, and become the springboard for further advances that would close them off altogether. Invasion of the Marshalls was likely to precipitate a major fleet action on terms favorable to the Big Blue Fleet.[9] Mahan would have sat back in his chair and smiled. Nothing more need be said.

Admiral Nimitz's strategic thinking had undergone a very important, if subtle, change. Instead of taking on all of the islands, he had decided to focus on three that had the facilities he needed. Soon thereafter he elected to bypass Maloelap and Yap and to invade only Kwajalein. His entire staff, except Admiral Charles H. "Soc" (for Socrates) McMorris and Forrest Sherman, objected to this bypass. After the Guadalcanal campaign Nimitz didn't want to make a lot of intermediate invasions.

Kwajalein was the center of Japanese administration for the area. It was more rear area than front line. Unlike Tarawa, it wasn't heavily fortified. From Kwajalein, a second round of invasions could take the Americans 375 miles closer to Japan by successfully capturing Eniwetok, whose lagoon Nimitz wanted for an intermediate fleet base. In the final phase, residual forces would clear or neutralize the entire Wake-Gilberts-Marshalls area.[10] While Nimitz had pared down the list of invasions, the last phase of getting approval from Washington was overly laborious. By the first of September, he had secured the approval of the Joint Chiefs.

A major American base in the Marshalls supported by fleet superiority would make Truk untenable for the Japanese. Rabaul was way down the line and already doomed. Nimitz understood the power of carrier air. He dispatched it to neutralize other Japanese airfields in the Marshalls. (Earlier attacks against the airfields had been ineffective.) Little opposition appeared over Maloelap. Quite a few defenders rose over Kwajalein, but the American pilots, ever optimistic, reported them all destroyed. The small gaggle of aircraft based on Wotje hightailed it to nearby Roi-Namur.

In early 1943, the Japanese did not anticipate that deep incursion into the central Pacific would happen until the spring of 1944. The army ceded overall command of this area to the Combined Fleet. The Marshalls weren't reinforced until September 1943, when the Japanese general staff finally realized their offensive phase of the war was over. The last major units arrived in the Marshalls in December. By January, a hundred operational aircraft were based in this island group.[11] Of course, the best time to assault them would have been in the fall of 1943, before defensive preparations had begun.

There was enough carrier power in Pearl Harbor to support a deep incursion. Japan had few aircraft stationed in the central Pacific. The Marshalls had been written off as indefensible from the long-range point of view.[12] By summer, Japanese garrison strengths were as follows:

	Troops	Aircraft
Wake	2,050	
Eniwetok	2,586	15
Kusaie	3,931	
Mille	2,530	(one of heaviest defended)
Kwajalein	933	10
Jaluit	620	
Maloelap	404	50
Wotje	620	9
Roi-Namur	35	
Tarawa	4,500[13]	

In May 1943, the 6th Air Division had 77 bombers, 114 fighters, and 26 recon aircraft. The navy's 11th Air fleet had about 200 operational planes. The 3rd Fleet at Truk also had 200 aircraft.[14]

Japanese planners expected an attack on Rabaul followed by an invasion of the Philippines. They did not expect a central Pacific attack, especially not in 1943, because of U.S. weakness in carriers. On the other hand, shipping losses seriously curtailed the Japanese ability to move forces and reinforce the islands. Intelligence officers had no reason to expect a Soviet attack but worried that Soviet-based U.S. aviation might complicate the war.[15] Japanese estimates of American naval strength were in the ballpark: 5 big carriers, 15 battleships, and 15 heavy cruisers. Nimitz's count was 6 fleet and 5 light carriers, 5 new and 7 old battleships, but only 8 heavy cruisers.

Admiral Koga's principal reaction plan, Operation RO, was designed to cut Allied lines of communication as soon as they became extended. This would delay their advance and buy time for the buildup of the Japanese inner perimeter.[16] In a departure from previous Japanese planning, the American carrier raid at Wake convinced Koga that the Americans were going to strike very deep on the central Pacific axis. Koga wanted the army's air force to center itself in the Marianas. Seeking decisive fleet action, he moved the Combined Fleet from Truk to Eniwetok. Tojo agreed that the Americans must be stopped in the Marianas.[17]

Given the emphasis intended for the central Pacific drive, the selection of the American commander was a major decision. Nimitz recommended Admiral Raymond Spruance. King heartily approved, calling him "the best flag officer in the Navy."[18] He was immediately elevated to three-star rank, surprising Spruance himself.

However, Spruance was aghast at what the planners had cooked up for the Marshalls. From his point of view, they had completely underestimated the difficulty of such an expedition. The Marshalls could not be reached from existing bases by four-engine recon aircraft. Photo intelligence of the current status of these islands was almost nonexistent. He wanted to make an intermediate step to the Gilberts in order to take Tarawa.

Spruance was haunted by the vision of a garrison stranded in the Marshalls without the Big Blue Fleet to protect it. Vandergrift's experience at Guadalcanal was not to be repeated. Spruance did not want to invade the Marshalls as long as the Japanese could continually reinforce them, a capability that had almost cost the Americans victory at Guadalcanal.[19] The admiral knew the fleet was scheduled to swing into the South Pacific to support MacArthur's next jump to Kavieng. While two axes did complicate Japanese defensive plans, they also pulled American strength in opposing directions. While the Big Blue Fleet sailed south, Japanese raiders would be able to prey on supply convoys winding through the atoll-dotted Marshalls. The small Japanese air contingents on Maloelap, Wotje, and Jaluit could score little against the air strength of concentrated American carrier task forces. However, the battle of the Bismarck Sea had demonstrated what aircraft could do to transports lacking air cover.

Spruance's solution was to move 390 miles back from the Marshalls and attack the Gilberts, with Tarawa as his target. Land-based recon aircraft could overfly it. Although its airstrip was small, recon aircraft based there could then complete photographing the Marshalls. At first Spruance was almost alone in recommending a less ambitious plan. "Spruance initially received little backing for his proposal, and he was a voice crying in the wilderness of CinCPOA headquarters," writes his biographer, Thomas Buell.[20] But Nimitz began to listen.

Spruance was afraid that American sailors and soldiers weren't sufficiently seasoned to enter combat in the Marshalls. He was concerned about exposure to repeated attacks by Japanese aircraft based on nearby atolls. Tarawa would provide valuable experience.[21] While it is much farther north, Tarawa sits east of Guadalcanal. There were no Japanese bases nearby. If the Japanese fleet emerged, Spruance envisioned classic battle line with CVs behind providing air support.[22] Initially most of Nimitz's staff thought Spruance's assessment was off the mark.[23] The risks he depicted wore on Nimitz's mind. But at this late date Nimitz and Spruance were reluctant to tell the JCS that Kwajalein was too far to go.[24]

Mentally move the Big Blue Fleet from Hawaii and place it successively on Tarawa in the Gilberts, Bougainville in the Solomons, and Kwajalein in the Marshall Islands. Draw two concentric rings around each. The inner one is 250 miles in radius (operational fighter range) and the outer 500 miles (medium bomber range). Now compare each of these pairs of rings in relation to the red dots on Rabaul and Truk. From this exercise, it's clear that a fleet in the Marshalls dominated both Japanese bases. Bougainville only moves one step up the ladder. Tarawa impacts neither. Nothing of any real value was threatened by Americans taking Tarawa.

Spruance wasn't the only American thinking about Tarawa. Back in Washington, JCS planners wanted to go to the Marshalls but envisioned an intermediate landing either at Wake or in the Gilberts. They too were not sensitive to the potential resistance to these intermediate operations or to the Big Blue Fleet's new ability to penetrate deep into Japanese airspace.

Early in 1943, the Japanese had thought of using the Imperial Fleet to counter an American thrust into the Gilberts. As the American naval fleet accreted, the likelihood of such a thrust diminished. By late 1943, the chances that the Imperial Fleet would sail this far east were almost nil.

In a 1959 interview Spruance recollected that in late 1943 "the Japanese fleet at Truk was about equal to our own in strength."[25] This really wasn't the case. American naval strength was clearly superior to that of the Japanese. Carriers *Zuikaku, Junyo, Hiyo,* and *Zuiho* were at Truk. In January 1943, this would have been a formidable naval force. By late 1943, American carrier-based air could outgun this entire group by more than 2 to 1, not counting clear American technological superiority. It was a fight the Americans should have relished.

Because of the losses around Rabaul, Japanese naval air strength was even less than might have been apparent. When interrogated after the war, Vice Admiral Shigeru Fukudome related, "Consequently, the fleet air strength was almost completely lost, and although the Gilberts fight appeared to be the last chance for a decisive fight, the fact that the fleet's air strength had been so badly depleted enabled us to send only very small air support to Tarawa and Makin. The almost complete loss of carrier planes was a mortal blow to the fleet since it would require six months for replacement. . . . In the interim, any fighting with carrier force was rendered impossible."[26]

In anticipation of an American assault, the Japanese had already begun extensive fortification of the Gilberts. Although additional troops entered the Marshalls, preparations were nowhere near as advanced there. A major advantage of a powerful fleet is its ability to simply sail past forward island positions to strike deeply. If the enemy cannot match your fleet or air strength, there is little he can do. Spruance's concerns were primarily about logistics and reconnaissance, very important considerations to be sure. However, Spruance improperly weighed the most important consideration of all: the comparative strength of the Japanese defenses in the Marshalls and at Tarawa. The incredible strength of Tarawa's defenses led Marine commanders to predict high casualties. Julian Smith, the respected 2nd Marine Division commander, requested that his orders direct him to make a direct frontal assault on Tarawa, so that he bore no responsibility for that aspect of the plan.[27] That was clear warning before the fact from a staff expert on fighting ashore.

Mahan might have torn a page from a Marine manual on amphibious warfare for the well-educated Spruance to study. Land commanders often face a line of interlocking enemy defensive strongholds. The worst thing to do is to charge into all of them in bloody frontal attack. If a flank can't be found, a good general will concentrate overwhelming force on a very narrow front to penetrate the line and then move as deeply as possible into the enemy's rear. Other enemy frontline defenses will first lose strength as their support dries up and then finally fall of their own weight without the need for a bloody assault.

One could see Mahan marking one of a few Cs that Spruance would earn. His inability to weigh the enormous risks the marines ashore would face on Tarawa against the naval risks of striking more deeply at a less well defended target was the most serious mistake he made during the Pacific war. He repeated it at Iwo Jima. As a naval officer, Spruance's lack of perspective on assaulting hardened fortresses on land led to unnecessary risks and casualties on land that were not offset by a sufficient reduction of risks and casualties at sea.

Back in Washington, the Joint Planning Committee wasn't impressed with the plan for the Gilberts campaign. "The committee still considered this approach to be inferior to a direct invasion of the Marshalls, but recommended that it be undertaken if enough forces could not be mustered for the Marshalls."[28] However, both the Army War Plans section and MacArthur preferred the Gilberts over the

Marshalls. Undoubtedly, MacArthur viewed a baby step to Tarawa as less threatening than a thrust into the Marshalls. The official Marine Corps history notes that none of the War Plan Orange alternatives identified any of the Gilberts as a possible intermediate target.[29] By this time the amphibious commander, Admiral Turner, and the marine commander, General Holland Smith, agreed that Spruance's reservations were of concern.[30] Given that Nimitz and King had just concurred on Spruance's appointment as overall commander, they could hardly overrule him on such a momentous decision.

Tarawa's 4,500 defenders hunkered down behind some of the best-constructed fortifications in the Pacific. They were many times more dangerous than the 933 defenders of Kwajalein who had just begun to dig in. There was little in the Marshalls to threaten the Big Blue Fleet. Threats in the Gilberts were nonexistent—except for the omnipresent prowling submarines.

When informed of the plan to take Tarawa, King wanted Nauru, famous for its guano mines, invaded as well to "broaden" the approach. Mahan might have cleared his throat and reminded King to remember to keep the fleet concentrated. Nauru was 380 miles from Tarawa. Mahan would have relaxed when the admirals in Honolulu thought this distance too far from Tarawa to allow for mutual support. After much consternation, they recommended Makin and Betio islands in Tarawa's atoll ring as the final targets. King concurred.

The Tragedy of Tarawa

Tarawa lies 450 miles southeast of Kwajalein and 1,265 miles east of the Japanese anchorage at Truk. Both were out of range of single-engine fighters. The Japanese 4th Fleet based in Truk commanded defenses in the central Pacific. Until the ill-advised raid by 2nd Marine Raider Battalion on Makin in August 1942, the Gilberts had had only a small garrison. Now the 7th Special Naval Landing Force, which had come up from Rabaul, was deeply dug in. It was the organizational counterpart of 6th Special Landing Force in the Marshalls, which also reported to 4th Fleet at Truk. The Japanese viewed the Gilberts as forward defense for the Marshalls.[31] Plan Z, initiated in May 1943, emphasized destruction of American invaders on the beach. Then again, the islets of Tarawa were little more than beach.

Betio, the largest islet, was only 2,000 yards long and 500 across at its widest point. The American 2nd Marine Division would land here. This small area was defended by four 8-inch, four 140mm, four 127mm, six 80mm, ten 75mm, fourteen 70mm, and sixteen 37mm guns interspersed among 82 prepared defensive positions. The island's commander boasted that it could withstand an assault by a million men for a hundred years.[32] Elements of the U.S. Army's 27th Infantry Division would land on even smaller Makin atoll, about 100 miles due north of Tarawa. Butaritari islet's defenders, 500–900 strong, manned four seacoast defense guns, an anti-aircraft gun battery and two light anti-aircraft batteries with 20 heavy anti-aircraft machine guns.[33] There wasn't much of a defending air force. Only 46 aircraft remained in the Gilberts after 12 bombers departed on 12 November.[34]

Carriers hit the Gilberts in mid-September. Nothing flyable remained on Betio's wrecked airfield. Only four recon planes remained at Makin. Tarawa was extensively photographed on 18 and 19 September and again on 20 October. Photo recon revealed the Gilberts' heavy defenses.[35] Intelligence estimated the Japanese to have 2,500–3,100 on Tarawa, a figure arrived at in part by a careful count of latrines.[36] The actual count proved to be 2,600 combat troops plus 1,200 laborers.

At Tarawa, a major concern for the American invasion force was the level of the tides over reef. In mid-September submarine *Nautilus* gathered extensive hydrographic data. The standard landing craft (LCVP—sometimes called a Higgins boat) needed a minimum 3.5 feet of water. Data indicated that less than this would be available at neap tide. Nevertheless, landing was scheduled at neap tide. The landing force was told they would have a 50-50 chance of floating their craft over the coral. In fact a quirk in the tides not understood until the 1990s made the chance that morning zero. LCVPs were hung up in bunches. Tarawa would see extensive use of tracked amphibians (LVTs) that could crawl over the reefs and up off the beaches after a path had been blown through anti-landing obstacles.

The Big Blue Fleet was now a sight to behold. Its 9 fast carriers (six CVs and three CVLs) and 12 battleships outclassed anything Japan could assemble anywhere in the Pacific. They were escorted by 15 cruisers and 65 destroyers. Seven "jeep" carriers (CVEs) carried additional aircraft designed to remain in close support of the invasion should the fast carriers be needed elsewhere. Ten submarines provided supporting patrols. Amphibious forces moved in 29 LSTs and 33 large transports. A service squadron of 22 ships provided the fleet's logistical support. Over 500 navy and 200 marine aircraft were present. Ninety army and 66 navy land-based bombers flew in support.

The invasion achieved operational surprise. The Japanese were not aware of the fleet's objective until the night before the landings. The preparatory shelling of the island impressed the marines and dogfaces waiting to go ashore. On D-day, 20 November 1943, Betio was hit with 3,000 tons of shells. However, individual targets were not plotted; naval gunnery lacked precision targeting. Instead area fire was used.[37] The damage the bombardment inflicted was slight. Most of the Japanese sheltered in pillboxes and stoutly constructed bunkers that only a direct hit could crush. Air strikes caused the Japanese to expend a lot of ammunition but did little else. Few land-based bombers were used. So much for the 250-mile rule. One of the benefits of a pre-attack bombardment is to pin down the defenders so they can't shoot while the assault waves swim in the last few hundred deadly yards. But an overly long pause between the last big naval gun shells and the first touchdown by Marine laden LVTs allowed the Japanese to clear their heads and open up with their weapons.

The invasion force consisted of two regiments of the superbly trained 2nd Marine Division, "probably the best military formation in the U.S. armed forces at that time."[38] (The 1st Marine Division had suffered more at Guadalcanal, and its first rest area there was disease-infested.) On the tiny battlefield of Betio, the Marines had only a 2:1 advantage in infantry. Against a fortified enemy, at least 6:1 superiority at the point of assault is recommended. An advantage of 10:1 is a more realistic estimate of what is needed to ensure success.

The outer beaches were mined, so the marines drove their LVTs into the lagoon and assaulted the inner beaches. A pair of destroyers accompanied them into the lagoon. Brave tin can sailors provided pinpoint gunfire that many a leatherneck testified saved lives. From the moment of touchdown, the beaches were an incredible mess. Burning amphibious tractors and smashed equipment were entangled with bloodied body parts of intrepid men whose lives were cut short. From the beach the senior officers afloat heard a radio call from Colonel Shoup on the beach that stopped hearts: "Situation ashore uncertain." The marine regiment that had been held in reserve was poured into the cauldron.

Three days later it was all over. A total of 3,700 Japanese soldiers and Korean laborers lay dead. A third of the marines in the first assault waves had been killed or wounded. Most units hit that hard cease to operate as military organizations. But 2nd Marine Division persevered, despite suffering 3,100 casualties in three days. All on a 500-by-2,000-yard island which rose no more than ten feet above the sea.

Compared to Betio, Makin was a walkover. A heavily reinforced regiment from 27th Infantry Division took three days to secure the island; 6,500 soldiers attacked 800 Japanese. Compared to Tarawa, casualties were light: 64 dead, 150 wounded.

The Japanese could send little to support the defenders of the Gilberts. The air battles over the Solomons had depleted Koga's carrier groups. Without air cover, his battle line of five battleships in Truk harbor couldn't oppose the Americans at Tarawa. This squandering of Japan's most precious asset, her carrier-trained pilots, created a payoff for the American two-pronged strategy.

Nine Japanese submarines came hunting the Tarawa invasion fleet. From radio intercepts, American intelligence officers created very accurate plots of the approaching subs.[39] Six were sunk. The three surviving subs stalked transports around Tarawa on 22 November. On the 24th, the day after the army had secured operations, one torpedoed and sank the escort carrier *Lipscome Bay*; 641 sailors died, a horribly high toll for a ship of that size. Only 272 were pulled from the waters alive. Many navy officers were bitter that the army had not moved faster to secure Makin so this terrible loss might have been avoided. As Samuel Eliot Morison wrote in his history of the Pacific war, "Makin was a pushover for the ground troops but cost the Navy heavily."[40] However, it does not follow that Japanese submariners might have been less successful if the army had moved a day faster. A different roll of the die might have resulted in losses around Tarawa even if the landing force had been able to complete operations more rapidly. The seeds of bitter interservice rivalry sowed in the Gilberts would bear ugly fruit in the Marianas. On the other hand, had the marines been given more time to reduce Betio, they would have landed on smaller unoccupied islets, emplaced artillery, and systematically reduced Japanese fortified positions before the assault regiments took to their craft. Many lives might have been saved. Perhaps the admirals should have allowed the marines to do this. After all, the Japanese navy, except for its submarines, was not coming.

"Tarawa aroused so much controversy," Morison comments.[41] "Japan reacted weakly and uncertainly to the Gilberts and Marshalls operation."[42] The senior marine at Tarawa, General Holland "Howlin' Mad" Smith, was more direct in his criticism: "From the very beginning the decision of the Joint Chiefs to seize Tarawa was a mistake," he wrote. "Tarawa had no particular strategic importance. . . . Tarawa should have [been] bypassed. Its capture . . . was a terrible waste of life and effort. . . . We should have kept it neutralized from our bases on Baker Ellice and Phoenix Islands."[43] Smith was almost alone among high officers to express this opinion. The flinty old curmudgeon was probably the most honest and correct of his brethren. He was also the most unabashed.

In the semi-official naval history, Admiral Morison counters: "if we had invaded Kwajalein in November without taking the Gilberts, we would have made exactly the same mistake as at Tarawa and encountered infinitely greater opposition."[44] Admirals Spruance, Turner, and Hill also went on record disagreeing with Smith. However, a listing of the defenses on Kwajalein belies Morison's claim. The principal change to the Kwajalein landing plan after Tarawa was the use of a much more intensive naval bombardment. But that island's beaches were nowhere near as fortified as those on Betio Island. As we will see, Kwajalein was to be a low-casualty operation, even though most of the fighting would take place inland where the initial bombardment made little difference.

Tarawa has been called a "dress rehearsal" and cited for the many lessons learned there. Why "rehearse" on one of the most fortified locations per square yard in the central Pacific? Japanese laborers began heavy construction in July 1943 and never stopped. The enemy can fortify only a few areas with the amount of weaponry, concrete, and steel that Tarawa contained. Howlin' Mad commented, "I don't see how they ever took Tarawa. It is the most completely defended island I've ever seen."[45] A good land commander never assaults a fortified position unless there is no alternative. There was no critical need to take Makin on Tarawa. Neither was well-positioned to facilitate attack on another key target. Betio Island was less than 300 acres, the size of a moderate housing development. That's 300 lots with no houses but the ground plowed up by ten tons of detonated explosives—on each lot. Every lot has a dozen corpses on it, lot after lot. One of every four is an American. Not exactly a dress rehearsal. Nothing in the Marshalls had Tarawa's dense fortifications.

A couple of short-range P-39 and P-40 squadrons would be based on Tarawa but they would do little but provide local defense. The sandy ground at Makin proved too soft to build a runway capable of handling bombers. B-24s did stage through Tarawa occasionally, but that hardly justified 4,000 casualties. Carrier planes could (and did) provide required photo coverage of the Marshalls. Admiral Spruance, in his attempt to be cautious, committed a major blunder. He did so by not looking at the ground pounder's perspective of that heavily fortified atoll. As "Howlin' Mad" said: "Tarawa was a mistake."[46]

Correct Deployment of the Big Blue Fleet

Halsey had worked hard at setting up the battle of Santa Cruz Islands to engage the Japanese carrier fleet in late 1942 even though he faced a tactical disadvantage in doing so. The faster the imperial carrier threat could be eliminated, the more freedom of movement the American fleet would have, the greater its ability to sail where it pleased, the fewer the intermediate assaults in the central Pacific American forces would have to undertake. Fewer assaults meant fewer American casualties.

The first *Essex* carrier arrived in Pearl on the first day of May 1943. By the fall Fifth Fleet had 6 full-size fleet carriers, 5 light carriers capable of running with them, and 12 battleships. Spruance could generate 1.5:1 quantitative superiority with little difficulty anywhere in the Pacific. America had opened a wide qualitative advantage over the Japanese. Even if the Americans could do no better than trade losses, they could replace them (and more) while Japan could not. The faster Japan lost carriers and pilots, the greater American superiority would be.

Yamamoto's abortive I-GO operation demonstrated that the Japanese were no longer capable of strategic offensive operation. Pilot for pilot, American aircraft were now far more deadly. Night surface actions in the central Solomons demonstrated that radar-equipped American sailors had at least pulled even with well-drilled Japanese torpedomen and their magnificent Long Lance torpedoes. American fighter direction procedures, anti-aircraft fire control procedures, and the secret proximity fuse with its own mini radar in each shell made American defenses far more deadly than those of either the Japanese or the 1942 version of the U.S. Navy.

In Mahan's view, drawing the six carriers of the Imperial Fleet out to give battle would have been the critical task. The carriers were the nucleus of Japan's open ocean combat power. With the exception of a 250-mile radius around Truk and Rabaul, Japanese land-based aviation was not concentrated enough to influence the balance of power. The Big Blue Fleet could send 600 aircraft aloft. In September 1943, Japan had only eighteen float and recon aircraft at Tarawa. After Japan's withdrawal from Guadalcanal, it was clear that Japan would no longer risk her carriers along the periphery. For Mahan the critical intelligence task was to determine the outermost point that the Imperial Fleet would commit to defend. Could the Americans invade that point? If so, concentrate all effort in a single operation aimed there. Never, NEVER divide the fleet.

While Spruance was Nimitz's chief of staff, the commander of the Pacific Fleet spent a great deal of time with his subordinate. Often they would take long walks together. Many observers have commented that Nimitz carefully ensured that he and Spruance thought in a similar manner and that when Spruance took command at sea he would approach problems the same way as his boss.

Less has been said of King, Nimitz, and Admiral John H. Towers, one of the navy's premier aviation leaders. Admiral King was an aviator. Admiral Nimitz, who oversaw the employment of all carriers in the biggest war in which they ever would participate, was not. Towers's Naval War College thesis was titled "The Influence of Aircraft on Naval History." Like King, he was an innovator of carrier tactics. Although Towers didn't understand it at the time, King saved him from medical retirement several times. The CNO personally saw that Towers was assigned first as Nimitz's naval air "type" commander (an administrative/logistical position at which he excelled) and subsequently as his chief of staff. Unfortunately, Nimitz didn't like him. Nimitz's flag secretary recalled, "I felt that he just didn't like Towers's methods."[47] Before the war, Towers, then chief of aeronautics, unsuccessfully attempted to wrest promotion of aviation officers away from the Bureau of Navigation, the navy's personnel bureau, which was headed by Nimitz at the time. Bureaucratic swords clashed loudly. Towers could be very overbearing and was never accused of being tactful. He had roundly, and unjustly, criticized non-aviator Admiral Kinkaid for his handling of the *Enterprise* at the battle of Santa Cruz. Afterward, King handed Kinkaid the important assignment to command the offensive to regain the Aleutians. Later Kinkaid would be assigned to command the Seventh Fleet, which ran the invasion of the Philippines.

Towers fought bitterly with Spruance over carrier deployment and over Towers's desire to relieve Admiral Pownell, a carrier group commander, after the Gilbert Islands campaign. Over one hundred navy planes had been lost during the carrier raids. A torpedo bomber put a torpedo into the new *Lexington.* One noted biographer described Towers and Spruance as "enemies."[48]

Spruance maintained that his objective wasn't to knock out Japanese central Pacific airpower or the Japanese fleet but to capture Tarawa.[49] "Spruance believed that the Japanese would be defeated primarily through amphibious warfare."[50] Aviators looked for a fleet engagement to destroy the enemy fleet and win the war. "This doctrine deeply disturbed Spruance."[51] Nimitz always indicated that the Japanese fleet might appear. Spruance instructed his admirals that if it did, the defeat of the Imperial Fleet would then become the primary objective. But he planned to do this with 16-inch guns.[52] Spruance had Admiral Willis Lee, commander of the battleships, practice pulling the big gunships out of their assignments escorting the several carrier task groups and forming the battle line.

This approach drove aviation-minded officers, especially Admiral Towers, wild. The "Airedales" held that the carrier was the modern ship of the line and the carriers should roam far and wide to destroy the enemy fleet. The primary attribute of the carrier fleet was its strategic mobility. Fighter aviation placed a defensive bubble over the fleet that protected it from enemy attack. Strike aircraft could decimate the enemy's fleet. Carrier admirals like John "Slew" McCain wanted the Big Blue Fleet to sail far enough west to precipitate a major fleet engagement. This was a critical debate. The carrier admirals favored rapid and deep penetration of the Marshalls to force the Japanese carriers into decisive combat and to avoid needless amphibious operations. Spruance, and many others, favored methodical, well-prepared, sequential advance to avoid unwarranted risk, citing the inability to provide logistical support and the danger from enemy aircraft.[53] Spruance, and the amphibious-minded officers—the "gators," like Turner—wanted to keep the carriers close in to protect the real winners of wars, amphibious operations.

Admiral Spruance was the least Mahanian of the senior American admirals. Throughout the Pacific war, much of his thinking revolved around the geometry of the contemplated movements, much like many generals approach land battles. Spruance gave priority to the complex amphibious and logistical details of the advance across the Pacific expanse toward Japan rather than to drawing the Japanese fleet into battle. Despite his magnificent achievement at Midway, Spruance remained much more battleship-oriented than most other senior leaders. Without a doubt, Captain Mahan would have had difficulty with Spruance's approach. In the controversy between Spruance and the carrier men, Mahan undoubtedly would have sided with the Airedales.

While the Airedales understood the proper tool and the task of destroying the enemy fleet, their geographical focus could go askew. Towers envisioned a set of campaigns that would sweep through the Marianas, on to the Philippines, and then down into Malaya.[54] One can imagine the exasperated look on Mahan's face when Admiral Towers went off on this tangent. While much more Mahanian at the operational level, Towers lost his bearings at the strategic level. Destroy the Japanese fleet and there was no reason not to proceed directly to Japan. After the Japanese fleet was destroyed, why divert to Malaya? With no fleet protection, convoys carrying raw materials couldn't possibly cross the choke points on the seaward approaches to Japan with the Big Blue Fleet in the area. While Captain Mahan would want an extended period to reeducate the very intelligent Admiral Spruance on naval strategy, he would also find Towers in need of some remedial work. When compared with these two very capable men, Admiral King stands as a naval strategist of great vision.

As is almost always the case, interpersonal conflict obscured the critical strategic issue. Towers made it clear he wanted Spruance's job as commander of the Big Blue Fleet. He argued that Spruance, a gun club admiral, and Pownell, his principal carrier commander, did not employ the carrier fleet aggressively enough. The interpersonal heat generated by this argument was so great that the normally unflappable Nimitz invited Towers to leave his staff and become commander of land-based air down in the South Pacific. Instead he was retained in Honolulu in more of a support and aviation logistics role. That in itself was a huge job that Towers handled well.

About the time Spruance gained command of Fifth Fleet, the very gifted Forrest Sherman became Nimitz's operations officer. Sherman came over from Towers's shop, where he was viewed as one of the best minds among the Airedales. Much of the strategic thinking in Honolulu began coming from his office. Increasingly he viewed the central Pacific route via the Marianas as the best approach to defeating Japan. In a roundabout way, with the reassignment of Sherman, King induced the effect he was looking for.

By the summer of 1943, the Big Blue Fleet had become strong enough to challenge simultaneously both the Imperial Fleet and a major complex of onshore airfields. Carrier raids both at Rabaul and in the Marshalls demonstrated the point. (During November 1943, the Japanese lost 73 planes in the Marshalls, mostly to carrier strikes.) This was a major increase in capability brought about by the intense battles around Guadalcanal, large American shipyards and aircraft factories, and the ever-improving skill level of American pilots over their overstretched Japanese counterparts.

It might have happened. During the summer of 1943, Nimitz faced a fleet and an admiral that were ready to give battle. Admiral Koga believed in the decisive fleet engagement. Koga was considered an efficient officer governed by logic. Some thought his plodding style made him a little too predictable. He recognized that Japan's relative strength was waning. The earlier the battle, the better his odds. Koga expected an American central Pacific thrust and planned to give battle there. American carrier raids in January in the Marshalls caused Koga to suspect they were next.[55] The Combined Fleet had concentrated at Truk. First Fleet contained two battlewagons and their escorts. Second and Third Fleets comprised three carriers, two battleships, eleven heavy and three light cruisers, and many destroyers. Japan's "New Operational Policy" of September 1943 called on the Combined Fleet to sail to defense of the Marshalls.

Twice Koga sortied his fleet in an attempt to intercept the Americans. During 17–18 September, Pownell led the fast carriers on a raid against Tarawa. Expecting a deeper thrust, Koga dispatched three carriers, two battleships, seven cruisers, and supporting escorts to Eniwetok. They arrived on the 20th. Had the two fleets collided, Pownell would have had better than 2:1 air superiority. Had Pownell met the Japanese in a major fleet engagement, he might have sunk two or three Japanese carriers and crippled heavy surface units with carrier air. He had several fast battleships that could have finished off the cripples—or stood against the Japanese battle line. Early dispatch of these forces would have greatly reduced the naval threat to planned operations in the Gilberts and Marshalls. The number of landings could have been both reduced and advanced on the calendar. With a major fleet victory, Tarawa could have been canceled.

In mid-October, Japanese radio intelligence indicated U.S. preparations for a raid on Wake. This time the Imperial Fleet sailed with three carriers, six battleships, eight cruisers, and escort vessels. They moved north to Wake via Eniwetok but missed Pownell by several days. With nothing in sight, Koga's ships returned to Truk. A week later the invasion of Bougainville began. Within a month marines ground their way over Tarawa.

After the war, interrogation of Japanese officers revealed Koga's efforts were "not a plan of any positive action to draw the American fleet into a decisive action, but rather to wait until the American Fleet came up; and he felt sure they were bound to come up if he only waited."[56]

As late as 8 March 1944, Koga attempted to trap the U.S. fleet by using a network of island bases instead of aircraft carriers. He planned to use naval air flying from island bases as bait. Dubbed Plan Zebra, Koga intended to kill ships with land-based aviation. In light of American carrier air strength at this late date, Plan Zebra wasn't very realistic. Marc Mitscher proved this on 30 March when he led his carriers to Palau. Americans sank 36 ships totaling 130,000 tons. But Koga had again withdrawn his large warships.

Near Disaster at Bougainville

Lack of firm strategic priorities from the Joint Chiefs caused the Americans to splinter their efforts in late 1943. This is exactly what Mahan (and Clausewitz) would have most feared. Several nonessential and bloody operations resulted, which didn't pose a significant enough threat to engage the Imperial Fleet. Instead the Japanese naval air arm gained time to train more pilots. Because they had divided their forces the Americans gave Admiral Koga an opportunity to inflict a costly naval defeat on two American task groups—a defeat that was only narrowly averted.

As we have seen, by the summer of 1943, the JCS staff had concluded that the primary axis of advance should be via the central Pacific, not via New Guinea. The central Pacific required fewer troops and would cut off Japan from its overseas empire. That threat promised the greatest probability of bringing out the Japanese fleet and creating an opportunity to destroy it in the open ocean.[57] Mahan would have nodded his approval. A central Pacific offensive would outflank New Guinea and make further offensive action there superfluous. If continued, a southwest Pacific drive would traverse larger islands and bring larger Japanese army units into battle. Cutting them off and isolating them would be far preferable to more close-in bloody jungle combat. However, MacArthur refused to consider any alternative to his New Guinea–Mindanao drive.[58] He denigrated anyone who did so.

Unfortunately, the JCS did not state that the central Pacific had absolute priority, as a designated main effort should. Instead, the JCS communiqué underscored the need for a "two pronged offensive." While Nimitz carried the attack through the central Pacific, MacArthur would continue his Cartwheel toward Rabaul. The sole reason the Joint Chiefs authorized an attack on Bougainville was to establish fighter bases to suppress the cluster of airfields there.

"At the end of September Imperial General Headquarters adopted an operational policy for the Rabaul area consisting merely of a whittling down campaign against the enemy which relied upon the momentary use of the crucial [air and naval] battle forces when conditions were favorable."[59] In October 1943, Koga thought something was afoot. Only a four-cruiser squadron remained operational in Rabaul harbor. He moved the entire aircraft strength from his carriers to Rabaul and initiated Operation RO. For the Japanese, this was a major mistake. Trained naval airmen were Japan's most fragile asset. Committing them to heavy combat in what amounted to a delaying zone was the height of folly. For the Americans, wearing down of the best of Japanese naval air was the most important strategic outcome of the battles in the southwest Pacific. Sometimes you win in spite of yourself.

If Japanese army-navy cooperation had been better, Koga might have turned to Japanese army air. The army had a pipeline of squadrons back up through the Philippines and into China. Unfortunately, they were not trained at ship busting and did not display the adaptability to change their methods of operation as Kenney's airmen had done at the battle of the Bismarck Sea.

MacArthur's forces were executing their own two-pronged operation. Southwest Pacific forces continued to work their way up the New Guinea coast. Halsey, commanding South Pacific forces, now reported directly to MacArthur. Surprising as it was to many, the general and the admiral got along well. Halsey's force would attack via the Solomons to threaten Rabaul. The general gave the admiral a free hand and seldom inserted himself into operational details. The admiral kept his commanding general well informed and ran his major decisions by him as recommendations for approval.

With MacArthur's concurrence, Halsey decided to bypass the Shortlands and to land on Bougainville, a 130-by-30-mile volcanic island covered by jungle that was very difficult to traverse. Forty thousand Japanese occupied the island. Most of them were at one of the two ends, where crude airfields were under construction. The center section was only lightly outposted.

MacArthur's initial orders were to land at the south end of the island near two airstrips that were heavily garrisoned.[60] Halsey was determined not to repeat a direct assault into Japanese strength as at Munda.[61] U.S. doctrine stated unopposed landings were always to be preferred. The admiral recommended a landing in lightly garrisoned Empress Augusta Bay, 210 miles from Rabaul—within fighter range. MacArthur approved the modification. Halsey's staff estimated it would take the Japanese four months to bring up sufficient force through the jungle to attack the Americans in strength. That estimate proved to be very close to what transpired. After the initial landing and establishment of airfield perimeters, the Americans would be on the tactical defense. Let the Japanese run into bunkered machine guns for a change! Mahan would have appreciated that. Clausewitz recognized a strategic offensive that allows a tactical defense is a masterful combination.

About the only place in the middle of the island suitable for an airstrip was Cape Torokina, near Empress Augusta Bay. There was a Japanese garrison of perhaps a thousand. American engineers worried that the ground was swampy and the drainage poor. No one knew for sure. The best intelligence came from missionaries and traders who had been on the island before the war.[62] However, the volcanic sand of Bougainville absorbed water far better than that of New Georgia. There was hope. Recon landed by submarine took soil samples from an area near Torokina and it tested OK. Halsey ordered Torokina to be the objective. Again he proved to be lucky. MacArthur would have no such luck at Leyte.

The New Zealanders made a preliminary landing on the Treasury Islands on 27 October without difficulty. The 3rd Marine Division landed on Bougainville on 1 November, 18 days before Tarawa. Compared to Tarawa, the invasion squadron was modest. Only twelve transports, eight APAs and four AKAs, brought the marines in. This many transports were available only because King had six transferred in from Italy for the operation. Because of the risk of Japanese air strikes, use of LSTs (dubbed "large slow targets" by their crews) was prohibited. Operational staffs, referring to the paucity of resources, dubbed it "Shoe String #2." (Guadalcanal had been the first Shoe String operation.) The commander of all ships in the Pacific Ocean area was accused of giving Bougainville only the leavings from Tarawa. "Nimitz, however, estimated that Koga would not risk the heaviest ships of his Combined Fleet in the Solomons. He thought Halsey could do with what he had. If he lent more to the effort in the south, Nimitz feared these ships wouldn't get back in time for the Gilberts invasion."[63] Nimitz did send a second carrier group, which was scheduled to arrive 7 November.

During October, the Americans had flown over 3,200 sorties in support of the upcoming Bougainville invasion. That kept the airfields at Rabaul and Kavieng suppressed. General Nathan Twining, one of America's best air commanders, commanded 14th Air Force, which flew the bulk of the missions. His approach was to do something every day to disrupt the Japanese.

Because of the lack of any harbor, the Japanese commander had ruled out an American invasion at Empress Augusta Bay. The Americans achieved complete surprise. Only a handful of defenders resisted the invasion. A Japanese 75mm gun sank several landing craft. Marines quickly silenced hidden machine guns that survived the preparatory bombardment. Even after the landings, Japanese land commanders considered the landings at Torokina to be a diversion. They remained braced for a main landing in the south. Eight Seabee battalions and a New Zealand brigade began construction of airfields. Several months later the Japanese army would finally drag their weapons to the Torokina perimeter.

Their attack would accomplish nothing other than ending the lives of 5,000 Japanese.

Seeing all the signs of invasion down in the Solomons, Admiral Koga activated Operation RO even before the marines splashed ashore. Japanese aircraft from Rabaul hit the beachhead on the first day. Koga assembled a surface strike force of seven heavy and one light cruiser plus four destroyers at Truk and sent them off to Rabaul. He anticipated forcing another "Savo Island" on the American squadron of light cruisers defending the marines ashore. This time Koga anticipated that Japanese warships would break through to the transports and defeat the Americans. However, the surface ships did not arrive until 5 November, and there were no plans to send carriers south from Truk. Koga realized he would need additional airpower to ward off all the aircraft the Americans were putting into the air. On 24 October he dispatched the carrier air groups from *Zuikaku, Shokaku,* and *Zuiho,* 173 aircraft in all, to Rabaul. They reinforced the 200 aircraft already there that had been under attack for the previous two weeks.[64]

Without their aircraft, the carriers couldn't respond to a major American incursion into the Marshalls that might have been a more serious threat. Koga was taking a big risk. But he was confident it was manageable. Despite the American naval buildup in the central Pacific, Admiral Koga was certain the Americans would not be this bold so early.

Halsey anticipated a strong Japanese reaction to the landings. However, he was not ready for what Ultra communication intercepts revealed. Koga had dispatched seven heavy surface ships from 2nd Fleet toward Rabaul. It also confirmed two Japanese heavy cruisers supported by two light cruisers would sortie against the amphibious shipping in Empress Augusta Bay.[65] The American navy had no heavy cruisers in the area. After earlier operations, most of the American heavy naval strength was preparing for Tarawa. Four American light cruisers under the command of Rear Admiral Aaron S. "Tip" Merrill, along with some destroyers, were supporting the Treasury Island and Bougainville invasions. The Japanese 8th Fleet (two heavy cruisers, two light cruisers, and two destroyers) swept toward the Treasuries on 1 November, but American ships had already departed. Fortunately for the Americans, the Japanese sortie missed Merrill. A planned counterinvasion couldn't get organized in time.

Light cruisers are badly outclassed by heavy ones in both armament and armor. When confronted by heavies, they are supposed to get out of the way—unless there are a bunch of marine-laden transports that can't depart fast enough. On the night of 2 November, Merrill moved to intercept what Ultra told him was coming—the same ships from 8th Fleet. The ensuing battle of Empress

Augusta Bay occurred about 35 miles north of where the transports were. That's about an hour's steaming time for a Japanese cruiser intent on spilling American blood into the ocean.

Thousands of shells were expended as cruiser attempted to bludgeon cruiser. Torpedo salvos from both sides porpoised through brine churned to froth by wildly maneuvering ships. At Savo Island, simple turns had caused American formations to fall apart. Now Tip led his squadron through many complex maneuvers in order to maintain firing position while avoiding becoming victim to Long Lances. Training had matured American sailors. Technology had eliminated the Japanese night advantage and then some.

When it was over, both sides had three ships damaged. A Japanese light cruiser and a destroyer succumbed to the ocean on the way home. Despite heavy Japanese air action after daylight, Merrill's courageous sailors brought all of theirs back to port. One came in under tow. Beating off the Japanese planes with no American air support was described as "phenomenal."[66] As at Savo Island, the Japanese commander was relieved of command for not getting to the transports.

Tip Merrill had brought Bull Halsey incredible good luck. But his small force, its magazines depleted, couldn't hope to even delay the seven heavy cruisers that were now assembling at Truk. "Everyone expected another Savo Island."[67] Halsey himself stated that the Japanese cruiser threat at Bougainville created "the most desperate emergency that confronted me in my entire term as COMSOPAC."[68]

A two-carrier task force under Admiral Frederick Sherman had been detached from the Big Blue Fleet and assigned to Halsey to hit enemy airfields at Buka. They had completed their assignment and were refueling to the south. Halsey's staff calculated that Sherman's task force—fleet carrier *Saratoga* and light carrier *Princeton*—could hit the Japanese cruisers before they refueled and left Rabaul, but only if they maintained a constant speed of 27 knots all night long. No carriers had ever neared that bastion. Naval policy at that time prohibited the use of fleet carriers against heavily protected land air bases.[69] But Halsey was desperate. He committed them to hit Rabaul. "I sincerely expected both air groups to be cut to pieces and both carriers to be stricken. if not lost," he said later.[70] Halsey's chief of staff, Robert Carney, remembered, "Every one of us knew what was going through the Admiral's mind. It showed on his face, which suddenly looked 150 years old."[71] American intelligence estimated the Japanese to have 150 operational aircraft at Rabaul. With the reinforcements the number was over 270. That would give the Japanese a 2:1 advantage. And their base was unsinkable. No admiral would willingly take on these odds. But Halsey had to spike the surface raider threat.

This was the first time carriers had entered the South Pacific since the battles around Guadalcanal. Staff worked though the night on the attack plan. No one knew where in Rabaul harbor the Japanese cruisers would be stationed. Would they be under way? Sherman's task force made the launch point at exactly 0900. The carriers hit Rabaul harbor with 22 SBDs (dive-bombers), 23 TBFs (torpedo bombers), and 52 Hellcats in tight formation. This cloud of blue aircraft apparently intimidated the defending Japanese fighters. They held back from hitting the large formation. Down below, the cruisers weren't maneuvering. One was refueling. They threw up intense anti-aircraft fire, including rounds from the main guns of one of the heavies. While none were sunk, three heavy cruisers, two light cruisers, and two destroyers were seriously damaged. The carrier groups lost ten planes. Discouraged by this incredible show of naval airpower, Vice Admiral Takeo Kurita canceled the sortie against Empress Augusta Bay. No Imperial Japanese cruiser ever sailed off the coast of Bougainville again.

Rabaul's airfields mounted a small counterstrike that caught up with the Americans about dusk. Instead of the carriers they had found several PT boats escorting some large landing craft. However, the paucity of targets didn't prevent Tokyo Rose from claiming that a large carrier, a medium carrier, three cruisers, and a destroyer had been sunk. Halsey's good luck had let him completely sweep the table. Kenney followed up with a series of moderate-size bomber strikes on Rabaul.

Halsey had asked Admiral Nimitz for two carrier groups to carry out the Bougainville operation. Instead he was allocated two carriers. Nimitz correctly didn't want to divide his fleet. At the last minute he relented. A three-carrier task group under Rear Admiral Alfred Montgomery had been dispatched before the emergency. It pulled into Espiritu Santo at the opposite end of the Solomons the night *Saratoga* and *Princeton* made their risky run north. On the 11th they made another strike on Rabaul. Opposition was heavy. Nevertheless, the strikers sank a Japanese destroyer.

Over 100 Japanese naval aircraft lifted from Rabaul's airfields and headed toward Montgomery's task group. They began vicious attacks at noon. All three carriers were hammered by sea surge from near misses. A little different luck and flattops might have had their hulls opened to the sea. A 40mm round from *Independence* actually detonated a bomb falling through the air.

Admiral Koga must have been discouraged by the 11 November strike. Ultra told the Americans that Koga withdrew naval aircrews from Rabaul the next day.[72] Ground crews loaded onto two transports, which American aircraft sank. The remaining garrison was to hold to the last man without hope of reinforcement. During Operation RO, 173 planes and 192 pilots came down from Truk.

By the 11th, 121 of those planes were wrecked and 86 pilots had lost their lives. "The failure of the RO operation also marked the end of Rabaul's importance as the base for Japanese operations against any Allied advance in the Solomons and New Guinea."[73]

Japanese officers felt the plane and pilot losses at Rabaul "had put the carrier air force in a position where further combat would rob it of even a skeleton force around which to rebuild."[74] Losses of surface escorts and planes immobilized the Combined Fleet.

The Japanese troops and landing ships that were supposed to move down toward Bougainville on 1 December finally made shore near Torokina on the 7th. The Japanese had spunk but little tactical finesse. A marine counterattack almost completely wiped out the counterlanding force.

The land behind the beachhead turned out to be a miserable place to build airfields. A lot of swamp was interspersed with dammed-up silt that had poor bearing strength. Forty days after the landing, the first fighter strip at Torokina opened up. A bomber strip became operational on Christmas Day. But their target, Rabaul, had lost its importance. By 1 November, all Japanese airfields on Bougainville had been bombed out of commission. They stayed that way for the remainder of the war. American ground commanders had no intent to take much of the island. All they wanted was enough room to keep Japanese artillery away from the runways. The American perimeter was only 16,000 yards in circumference.

Japanese on the island continued to move toward and attack the American perimeter. A huge banzai attack was mounted in March. More than 5,700 Japanese lost their lives in this blunder and the three weeks of fighting that followed. American dead numbered 263.

By rights the naval crisis off Bougainville should have been an American disaster. Several times, with the odds stacked against them, hard-pressed American sailors prevailed. No admiral, no matter how skilled, can afford to cut it that close.

The fault lay at the strategic level. The United States should not have been trying to undertake two major actions simultaneously. It didn't need to. The intermediate objective of the southern thrust was Rabaul. However, aggressive advance on the central Pacific axis into the Marshalls would have made Truk untenable. If Truk was neutralized, there was no reason for either side to worry about Rabaul.

Events in the waters around Bougainville showed the incredible danger of the two-axis strategy. Change only a few rolls of the dice—have the Americans fight like ordinary men instead of demons, have Japanese admirals a little more aggressive—and American casualties might have been huge. What if 8th Fleet had evaded or overwhelmed Tip Merrill's light cruisers? What if Koga had not lost his nerve after only two of his eight available heavy cruisers were damaged? What if he had followed up by moving a battleship division in behind those lead units? He still retained a potent battle line at Truk that included *Yamato, Mutu, Nagato, Fuso, Kongo,* and *Haruna,* plus supporting cruisers and destroyers. Bougainville could have become another Guadalcanal. Transports lying in Empress Augusta Bay could have been slaughtered. What if the full potential of Truk's aviation had hit Sherman's two carriers? As Halsey feared, both probably would have been lost. A two-carrier task group cannot put up the same type of protective bubble that the entire Big Blue Fleet with many times the fighters can. Weakness in American strategy allowed an unnecessary and highly faulted operation to proceed. A major American defeat was averted only by the grace of some very competent and heroic American sailors. The situation had changed since Midway and Guadalcanal. There was no reason to take on these risks in late 1943. The United States enjoyed immense naval superiority, if deployed properly.

Tactically, attacks on two axes are mutually supporting if fire from forces on one axis can have an impact on defenders on the other. At the operational level in World War II naval combat, a similar rule of thumb might be the 250-mile effective range of naval air strikes. Bougainville is 1,200 miles from Tarawa. The three carriers of Admiral Montgomery's task group, dispatched before Japan's threat to the marines on Bougainville was identified, arrived *after* the critical battle had been fought and won by *Saratoga* and *Princeton.* The distance between the South Pacific and the central Pacific was a cruise longer than the duration of the average battle. The two fleets were out of mutually supporting range. (Reinforcement from Pearl Harbor was out of the question: a normal cruise from Pearl to Tarawa took ten days.) Worse, a Japanese fleet at Truk might have been within range of one of the American fleets while the other was too far away to offer support. This condition is sometimes referred to as the advantage of interior lines—an advantage poor American strategy ceded to the Japanese.

MacArthur's insistence on the importance of the operations under his command was the root cause. Mahan's grade book could only record an F. Poor grades must be handed to MacArthur's superior as well, who let this situation continue to exist. As the historian John Costello states: "But at the same time it was politically impossible to abandon MacArthur's drive up through the southwest Pacific toward the Philippines."[75]

One can be quick to cite the destruction of Japan's naval air groups as a victory for the two-pronged approach. But had Bougainville and Operation RO not

occurred, and had Koga sortied against Tarawa, he wouldn't have had the benefit of air cover from Rabaul and instead he would have attacked into the teeth of
the Big Blue Fleet. Japanese defeat would have been more likely, not less. As it
was, the smashed Zeros around Rabaul were a testimony to the fighting qualities
of American seamen and aviators, not to the strategic acumen of American admirals. Admirals are supposed to cause battle at a time and place of their choosing. They didn't accomplish this. By dividing the fleet between Bougainville and
Tarawa they created a horrible vulnerability that could have led to disaster for
Admiral Sherman's two-carrier task force. American fighting men won anyway.
Sometimes you take what you can get.

Most discussions of American strategy treat the two-pronged advance across
the Pacific by Nimitz and MacArthur as a sensible compromise solution to the
problem of bringing about the speedy defeat of Japan. The events of November
1943 demonstrate how faulty this analysis is. We will see at least two additional
examples of this specious reasoning—at Biak and Peleiu. "The two advances
were also intended to be mutually supporting, yet they might well have led to
disaster had the Japanese taken greater advantage of their opportunities—as they
almost did during the Bougainville–Empress Augusta Bay operation in 1943 and
the Biak operation in 1944."[76]

Full Steam through the Marshalls

The Marshall Islands consist of two parallel chains that run from northwest to
southeast. Recall that initial campaign planning focused on Kwajalein in the
western chain and Wotje and Maloelap in the eastern one. Admiral Spruance
worried that if Japanese airfields in the eastern chain were not taken, reinforcing
convoys steaming to the westward islands would be subject to attack. Both Admiral Turner and General Smith agreed with Spruance. Admiral Towers, having
more faith in the power of carrier-based air, favored a straight shot at Kwajalein.

After Tarawa, Nimitz recognized the requirement to minimize assaults on
fortified atolls. The eastern atolls of the Marshalls held only a handful of planes.
With a major American presence on Kwajalein, the Japanese were unlikely to
waste aircraft in an attempt to reinforce them. If they did, the aircraft would
make easy pickings for American fighters.

Ultra reported that Koga had little intention of defending the Marshalls or
even Truk.[77] The Japanese expected the Americans to make sequential attacks
from east to west. To counter this, Koga reinforced Jaluit, Wotje, Maloelap, and
Mille at the expense of Kwajalein. Otherwise Kwajalein might have had more defenders than did Tarawa.

Despite the intelligence reports, "Spruance was certain that the Japanese air would blast his forces" attempting a landing at Kwajalein from other bases in the Marshalls. He wanted those struck prior to invasion.[78] Initially, he favored taking Wotje and planting an air base there before assaulting Kwajalein. Admiral Sherman, Nimitz's operations head, assured his boss that carrier aviation was strong enough to beat down Japanese air opposition around Kwajalein. However, Spruance wasn't impressed with Sherman's assurance. He thought the ground forces would not have sufficient anti-aircraft strength to hold Kwajalein once the fleet withdrew.[79] At a staff meeting Nimitz polled his senior officers. To a man they recommended that several outer islands in the Marshalls be seized. Nimitz then announced his decision—Kwajalein. Despite repeated objections from his subordinates, Nimitz canceled Wotje and Maloelap to concentrate everything on Kwajalein. Mahan would have smiled. Keep the fleet concentrated and move as quickly as possible to force the enemy into decisive combat. Don't be distracted by some local commerce raiders. This is another major strategic decision that Nimitz alone got right despite the fears of his subordinates. Good intelligence work supported his decision. He wasn't being brash by any measure and his more aggressive style saved lives of many a dogface and jughead among the landing force. The mark of true professional competence is consistency. Perhaps Admiral Nimitz might be called the professional's admiral.

Nimitz's decision broke the methodical, step-by-step pattern the Japanese had become accustomed to. The Combined Fleet staff was divided on whether the Americans would first land at Jaluit or Mille: "Some thought you would land at Wotje but few thought you would go right to the heart of the Marshalls and take Kwajalein."[80] A defender can't turn every possible point of assault into a fortress like Tarawa. Read the recon. Avoid Japanese forward defenses because the Big Blue Fleet can penetrate deeper without fear of Japanese airpower. This is how to avoid another Tarawa.

Spruance still wanted a fleet anchorage. Majuro in the eastern chain had potential. Recon aircraft indicated it was unoccupied. Nimitz relented and allowed a battalion to land there. Kwajalein would receive two divisions. A single Japanese soldier occupied Majuro. It became a major fleet service base. The Americans learned one of the most important lessons: There was no reason to assault an occupied atoll when an unoccupied one could substitute. Japanese ground troops on isolated islands didn't matter and any airfield that was bypassed could now be dominated by American air.

In order to maintain momentum, the staffs in Washington wanted to invade around the first of January. A totally different ground component, one built around the untried 4th Marine Division and 7th Infantry Division, veterans of the Aleutian landings of mid-1943, could be ready. The carriers and battleships could also make ready. But the gators, battered by losses at Tarawa, needed an additional thirty days. The small number of landing craft and transports involved at Bougainville didn't affect the calculations.

The Gilberts had been a "sobering experience."[81] Lessons from Tarawa were absorbed. Most important was a tripling of the pre-invasion bombardment. Additional close-in fire support from destroyers and gun-laden landing craft would lay direct fire in visibly identified targets as troops sloshed ashore. More LTVs were made available. Better pre-invasion photo recon was made.

Kwajalein lagoon is 388 miles long, one of the largest in the Pacific, yet the total land area on the islands to be invaded was only about two square miles. Planners and commanders alike worried about another Tarawa. But there was a critical difference. Kwajalein was the hub of Japanese activity. Since August 1941, it had been the headquarters of the Japanese 6th Base Force, which controlled operations in the Marshalls, the Gilberts, and Mauru and Ocean islands. The islands of Roi-Namur were the center for air. Roi-Namur is 2,300 yards long and 500 yards wide. There were 3,300 Japanese in this small area. At first it sounds like the armed camp at Betio in the Tarawa atoll. However, most of the Japanese on Roi-Namur were either laborers or aviation mechanics. No more than 600 were combat troops.[82] Had Nimitz not taken heed of Spruance's fears, had he skipped the dress rehearsal at Tarawa, he would have invaded an atoll occupied principally by administrative troops. The preliminary bombardment would not have been important. All of the casualties suffered at Tarawa and many of the casualties of the Kwajalein invasion would have been avoided.

Japanese doctrine was to stop the invader at water's edge with little defense in depth. The fortifications that existed looked seaward. The marines landed on the lagoon side. Enemy dispositions on Kwajalein Island were similar. Kwajalein Island is about 2.5 miles long and 800–1800 yards wide. The Gilberts–Marshalls campaign is a case study in the benefits of speed of attack. Go before the defender gets set, even if you haven't completely finished your own preparations. It is a theme repeated many times in military history.

Ultra revealed that the Japanese suspended surface resupply of the Marshalls as of March 1944.[83] Several days before the Kwajalein landings, the fast carriers hop-scotched through the Marshalls hitting principal air bases. The carriers, under the command of Marc Mitscher, one of the best carrier admirals, stripped away the 100-plane contingent based on Roi-Namur. The last Japanese airplane was seen over Kwajalein two days before the first ground troops landed. By 29 January, 1944, Wojte, one of the islands that had been a main source of pre-invasion worry, had no operational aircraft remaining. Admiral Koga was no longer in position to intercede with his fleet. Most of his carriers, now with empty flight decks, had departed for Japan. His cruisers had been bruised down on Rabaul. His battleship line was intact. But sending it forward without air cover against a fleet with twelve fast carriers was suicide. There was no land base for aviation like Rabaul anywhere in the vicinity.

Again the invasion fleet was huge—297 ships and 54,000 invasion troops headed for the Marshalls, compared to 28,000 troops for the Gilberts. The 4th Marine Division landed at the island of Roi-Namur on the north side of Kwajalein atoll. The 7th Infantry Division attacked Kwajalein Island on the south side of the lagoon. A reserve force was composed of a regiment each from 4th Marine Division and 27th Infantry Division. Again Nimitz showed his strategic judgment. He assigned the reserve the immediate follow-on mission of landing 300 miles east at Eniwetok Atoll if they were not needed at Kwajalein. Recall that at Tarawa, the most recent experience, the floating reserve had to be landed when the marine commander ashore radioed that the issue was in doubt. By designating a subsequent objective for the reserve force, Nimitz initiated a very visionary move. Again, his principal subordinate commanders did not agree with Nimitz.

Preliminary operations before both major landings emplaced several battalions of artillery on small islets. This tactic was first employed at New Georgia and would have been repeated at Tarawa if the admirals had given the generals another day to meet their objectives. This time naval gunfire support was very heavy and accurate. At Roi, several battleships came within 6,000 yards of shore and were in plain sight taking on targets with direct fire. The leathernecks dubbed their admiral "Close-In Connolly." Seven thousand 14-inch, 8-inch, and 5-inch shells hit Kwajalein Island. "The entire island looked as if it had been picked up to 20,000 feet and dropped."[84]

Some called the landing at Roi-Namur "the perfect one." Both divisions executed textbook landings. The two connected islands were captured in less than four days. Some navy officers grumbled that the army moved a little slower than the "gyrenes," but it was hard to argue with success. No navy ship took more than a glancing hit. Overall casualties were light compared to Tarawa. A total of 372 American servicemen lost their lives; another 1,385 were wounded. Of the 8,600 defenders on the atoll, 7,900 were dead. Most of the survivors were Korean laborers. To quote the official army history:

> In comparison to Tarawa, the operation was both easy and cheap in terms of lives expended. The reasons for this are not hard to discover. The enemy garrison in northern Kwajalein was fewer in number than that on Tarawa by about a thousand. The Japanese had not been expecting such a deep penetration into the Central Pa-

cific and were generally caught off balance. Their fortifications were not particularly strong nor were they well enough emplaced to resist an invasion from the lagoon shore. Hydrographic conditions were favorable for a landing and the 4th Marine Division were much better supplied with the necessary amphibious equipment to effect such a landing than had been the 2nd Marine Division at Betio. Finally, and most significant, was the tremendous quantity of shells and bombs thrown into and dropped on the target before the main landings took place. Admiral Connolly's Northern Attack Force conclusively demonstrated that in small island amphibious operations a prolonged preliminary bombardment could preclude a high casualty list.[85]

General Holland Smith wrote, "Very few recommendations can be made to improve upon the basic techniques previously recommended and utilized in the Marshalls."[86] He continued: "The quick victories in the Marshalls confirmed the original judgment of the Joint Chiefs and strengthened their resolution to continue the main pressure along the Central Pacific axis."[87]

The successful capture of Kwajalein caused Koga to order that Truk be abandoned. During a trip to Tokyo, he told members of the Imperial General Staff that the Combined Fleet no longer existed. The Americans had destroyed it. He lamented his lack of pilots and the poor training of the few replacements the fleet did receive.[88]

Eniwetok was familiar to many American naval officers. Frequently it had been an intermediate target during Plan Orange war games. Its large lagoon was less constricted by reefs and thought to be a better fleet anchorage than Kwajalein. Nimitz coveted it as a base. It was 326 miles closer to the Marianas than Roi. Saipan was only 1,000 miles away and Truk 669. King viewed it as the anchorage from which the fleet could sally forth and neutralize Truk.

Before the Marshalls operation began, Spruance suggested to Nimitz that they might be able to take Eniwetok on the heels of Kwajalein. Attack speed always paid dividends. As Morison observed, "the closer that one offensive steps on another's heels, the greater will be the enemy's loss and confusion and the less one's own."[89] Mahan would have heartily endorsed this observation. January photos of Eniwetok indicated it was not fortified and was only lightly defended. The Japanese used it as a refueling stop for aircraft ferrying south and little else. They made no attempt to defend Eniwetok until the Gilberts fell. Again, what would Nimitz have found had he struck deep into the Marshalls in November 1943? The principal Japanese defenders, 1st Amphibious Brigade, Japanese army, had just arrived from Manchuria on 5 January. The 2,500 Japanese troops who were supposed to defend the unfortified atoll came ashore with insufficient construction materials and equipment only six weeks before the American invasion.

However, the fast carriers were first scheduled to cruise down into the southwest Pacific to support MacArthur's invasion near Kavieng in the Bismarcks. The original plan called for a ninety-day delay until the fleet returned. The 27th Infantry Division had been alerted on 13 January 1944 for an Eniwetok operation, probably on 1 May 1944. How many improvements would those reinforcements emplace in the three-month interval?

Communication circuits from Spruance to Nimitz to the JCS buzzed. Approval came quickly, a credit both to the signalers and the decision makers at the highest uniformed levels. Eniwetok was an excellent exercise in agility. The JCS approved the operation on 3 February 1944 while fighting on Kwajalein still raged. King commended Spruance's flexibility in planning and execution. King recounted, "The enemy was greatly surprised by the rapidity of our westward advance." As Admiral Morison observed, "Admiral Nimitz chose an opportune moment to order the assault, even a week later would have been much more costly."[90]

On 3 February, the "reserve" landing force was told to begin Eniwetok planning. D-day came on the 17th. Again, a series of islands measured in hundreds of yards and totaling often less than 200 acres, the size of a very small farm, were invaded separately. Each received the attention of a couple of battalions or, at most, a regiment. As at Kwajalein, artillery was emplaced on islets before the main attacks. Battleships pulled within 850 yards of the shore to deliver their one-ton shells. The last of the larger islands was secured on the 21st. A total of 195 Americans were killed in the assault and 521 wounded. Almost 2,700 Japanese military and Okinawan laborers died. Eniwetok became the principal base for navy and marine air assigned to hit Truk.

One reason the Americans moved rapidly through the Marshalls was the lack of dense land-based Japanese aviation that could challenge the Big Blue Fleet. Koga intended to honeycomb the remainder of his perimeter with airfields. Again, lack of transport to move construction materials prevented the execution of a competent plan. Koga expected 500 new pilot graduates to join his forces by about 1 April. To strengthen his most critical defenses, he planned to amass 500 carrier aircraft supplemented by 400–500 land-based planes in the Marianas and Palaus.[91] In addition to pilot losses, Japan was losing many of its trained aviation mechanics, mission planners, and ground crew. They remained behind on islands cut off by American advances. These losses markedly reduced the effectiveness of the planes that remained, as combat during the remainder of 1944 would painfully demonstrate.

By early 1944 the Japanese navy had lost its numerical advantage in vessels and embarked naval aircraft to the Americans. Naval air strength favored the

Table 7.1: Comparative Naval Strength

	CV	CVL	BB	CA	CL	DD	NAVAL FIGHTERS	NAVAL STRIKE A/C
Japan	5	4	5	11	2	28	222	208
U.S.	7	8	7	8	13	69	475	416

U.S. by a wide 2:1 margin. However, the Imperial Navy retained strong surface forces manned by well-trained crews. Japan had used her surface strength well down in the Solomons. Increasingly, Japanese admirals needed to produce campaign plans that would bring this resource to bear decisively on the Americans. This was no small task.

Rear Admiral Richard Connolly said, "The Marshalls really cracked the Japanese shell. It broke the crust of their defenses on a scale that could be exploited at once. It gave them no time to adequately fortify their inner defensive line that ran through the Marianas." And it advanced the American timetable four months.[92] Even the dour King was impressed. He radioed, "To all hands concerned with the Marshalls operation: Well and smartly done. Carry on."

First Carrier Strike on Truk

On 4 November, recon photos of Truk had revealed two carriers, a battleship, five heavy cruisers and four light cruisers, and a plethora of smaller ships at anchorage. The photo recon Liberator tipped Admiral Koga that such a strike was probably imminent. He decided to evacuate the fleet to Palau while he took battleship *Mushasi* back to Japan. American subs would put a torpedo into battleship *Yamato* on the way out. They also sank a light cruiser.

The American carrier admirals had been lobbying Nimitz's staff that they shouldn't be wasting their mobile striking power in close support of the Marshall invasions. Enemy counterair was nil and the amphibs had the situation well in hand. Instead, the fast carriers should be striking deeper targets, ones that might counterstrike the Americans. Towers advocated that Truk be blitzed from the air and bypassed.[93]

As if to punctuate this argument, six four-engine Japanese seaplane bombers flying from Saipan hit the main supply dump on Roi-Namur during the dark hours of the morning of 12 February. Eighty percent of the island's supplies blew sky high. "Even the battleship men were convinced that the airmen had a point."[94] The Eniwetok invasion commander, Admiral Harry Hill, insisted that the carriers do something about the threat.

Nimitz thought hard about Truk before he endorsed Towers's recommendation and sent it on to King for final approval. Ultra indicated the Japanese were abandoning the lagoon.

It was decided that the Big Blue Fleet was ready to take on a target this lucrative. While one carrier task group supported the Eniwetok invasion, Admiral Spruance took most of the rest of 5th Fleet to hit Truk. Mitscher with six fleet and four light carriers, using his knowledge of Japanese search patterns, approached Truk undetected on the night of 16 February 1944.

Although all of the heavy units had evacuated, Spruance's aviators found no shortage of shipping to strike. The first fighter sweep knocked down Japanese defenders. Mitscher's strike claimed 250 of the 365 aircraft at Truk. Then an aerial conveyor belt continuously dropped bombs and torpedoes on shipping in Truk harbor. Americans sank 30 ships totaling 200,000 tons. Compare this to the total kill of American submarines in the year that had just closed: 1.5 million tons. Not bad for two days' work—on the heels of supporting a major amphibious operation. *Intrepid* took one torpedo from a night attacker. American carriers booked a return engagement for April.

To add insult to injury Spruance circumnavigated Truk with several of his surface combatants. American cruisers sank a light cruiser. Battleships *Iowa* and *New Jersey* bagged an escaping destroyer.

During 1943, there had been no carrier versus carrier actions. Since then both American carrier strength and pilot skill had blossomed. The strike on Truk demonstrated the American navy had clear superiority over most of the Pacific. "Carrier warfare had now come of age."[95] As long as the Big Blue Fleet sailed en masse, it could go anywhere it wanted. Its guns and aircraft could defeat any combination of island- or carrier-based Japanese air without the assistance of ground-based American aviation. The Big Blue Fleet was free of the 250-mile rule.

The crisis-induced November raid on Rabaul had given preview of the new capability of American naval aviators. They shot down half of the fighters and most of the strikers that swarmed from Japanese airfields to attack the raiding carriers. Clearly the United States had attained a technological and skill advantage over Japan. The 1.5:1 rule of thumb assumed rough parity between opposing naval air forces. Now Nimitz and his admirals could rely on added advantage.

A debate on whether or not to invade Truk raged in both Washington and Honolulu. The initial decision was to invade. In January 1944 Admiral Nimitz earmarked five divisions for the operation: the 2nd, 3rd, and 4th Marine divisions and the 27th and 77th Infantry divisions. The two-day carrier raid on the vaunted "fortress," now abandoned by the Imperial Fleet, demonstrated how weak and unimportant Truk had become. The Carolines could be bypassed and their defenders left to rot. The five divisions were all reassigned to operations in the Marianas, whose invasion dates were advanced.

King underscored the importance of the successful fleet air strike on Truk. "The strike was of significance in the evolution of carrier warfare," he wrote, "for it showed that such an enemy base might be neutralized by fast carrier forces alone, without either the assistance of land-based planes or seizure by amphibious forces."[96] The earlier argument had now been settled by the boss. The war plan now wasn't about amphibious operations or gaining additional air bases closer to Japan. The Big Blue Fleet could sail where it wanted and smash what it pleased. Bring 'em on!

MacArthur Continues to Cartwheel

The Elkton Plan had matured into a series operations code-named Cartwheel. The operational plan projected an advance on two axes, one through the Solomons, the other up the coast of New Guinea, with the island of New Britain as their common objective. New Britain is a 300-mile-long crescent that lies at the northern edge of the Coral Sea. Its western end almost touches New Guinea's Huon Peninsula and its eastern tip stretches to New Ireland, north of Bougainville. In this manner New Britain blocks further advance north and west.

At the beginning of 1943 the Japanese had attempted another offensive over the spiny back of New Guinea toward Port Moresby. In heavy fighting, Australian forces commanded by their countryman, General Thomas Blamey, who was ground force commander under MacArthur, beat them back and then advanced toward the east coast. All summer the Australians fought through razorback ridges and tough jungle. In early September, the 6th Australian Division landed near Lae at the base of the Huon Peninsula. This offensive was supported by air-landing Australian troops farther up the Markham Valley in Papua. By the end of the month, General Blamey took Finschhafen near the tip of New Britain.

As we have seen, Bougainville, on the other axis, was invaded at the beginning of November. No attempt was made to clear the 40,000 Japanese from that large and jungle-covered island. The jungle itself prevented large movements of troops overland against the enemy. Airfields were built within the defensive perimeter now held by two army divisions. They became operational in early December. Usually only a dozen fighters were stationed at Bougainville, but all fighters escorting strikes on Rabaul fueled there.

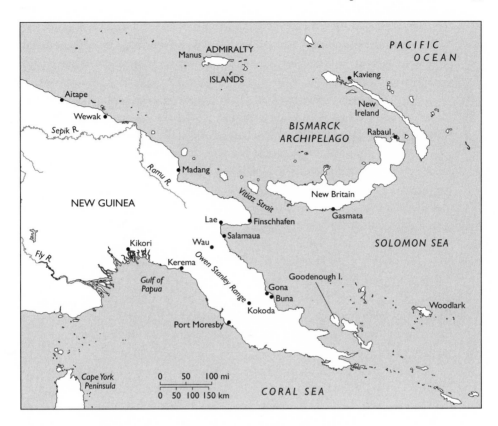

Map 7b. New Guinea and Bismarck Archipelago. Map by Bill Nelson.

In mid-December, MacArthur's forces invaded western New Britain. First an army regiment invaded the southern coast at Arawe against virtually no resistance. Then the 1st Marine Division assaulted the northwestern tip of New Britain at Cape Gloucester. They landed with little opposition but engaged in heavy fighting along Suicide Creek in order to get to the airfield, which was second-rate at best. Rabaul was at the far end of the island, 180 miles away on the other side of the active volcano Mount Talawe. As Morison said, "The capture of Cape Gloucester was an even greater waste of time and effort than Arawe."[97] The area wasn't suitable for airfield construction—or even installation of a PT-boat base. The place was even more miserable. As one member of the Old Breed remarked, "Nothing was ever too bad for the 1st Marine Division." The Japanese defenders infiltrated back to Rabaul, where they remained for the rest of the war. The big argument that MacArthur won over the assignment of the 1st Marine

Division, which had influenced the decision to invade Tarawa before the Marshalls, turned out to be a total bust. What was even worse, General Kenney had objected to the invasion of Cape Gloucester because it was no longer needed as a base to hit Rabaul.[98]

In early January 1944, American soldiers continued MacArthur's advance up the New Guinea coast by landing at Saidor. The Japanese began a difficult retreat back toward Madang that may have cost 10,000 souls, mostly to disease and the elements. New Guinea is a very hostile environment for humans.

Halsey recommended that Rabaul be bypassed.[99] The encirclement of Rabaul began on 15 February when the New Zealanders of the 3rd Division made an almost unopposed landing on Green Island, a speck of land north of Bougainville and almost due east of Rabaul. Recall that Spruance made his massive air attack on Truk the 16th and 17th.

As early as July 1943 the JCS staff had suggested that a move to the Admiralty Islands north of Rabaul might suppress that fortress and obviate the need for a direct assault. They suggested the Admiralties be taken by 1 January. "If the decision had been made to leapfrog Cape Gloucester, that target date might have been met."[100] MacArthur felt the pressure form Nimitz's Kwajalein invasion on 31 January. He needed a dramatic advance lest he be left behind.

On 22 February MacArthur decided to land a reconnaissance in force on Los Negros, a small island in the Admiralties. The 1st Cavalry Division admirably handled the assignment, landing six days later. Despite the risk, the division suffered only 159 killed (if "only" can ever be used to describe death). At the operational level the risk at Los Negros paid high dividends. Both that operation and the jump to Hollandia were brilliant operational maneuvers for which General MacArthur deserves credit. But those positives were nonetheless progress in the wrong direction. The theater strategy was wrong and the operation added nothing at the strategic level. Japanese withdrawal from Truk and the American pummeling of what remained had stripped Rabaul of any strategic value.

MacArthur's next target was Kavieng on the north end of New Ireland, about 150 miles north of Rabaul. The Japanese had heavily reinforced it during December 1943. Its invasion would be quite a fight. The base also contained an extensive air base complex similar to Rabaul's. As late as mid-February, MacArthur continued to plan a major invasion. The carrier groups of the Big Blue Fleet were earmarked for the operation. Admiral Halsey collected the invasion force.

By now it was clear that reducing Rabaul was no longer a major objective. Diverting the fleet southward would cause unnecessary delay of preparations to attack the Marianas. Admiral Nimitz appealed to the Joint Chiefs, who canceled the Kavieng invasion.[101] A regiment of the Kavieng invasion force went ashore on unoccupied Emiru Island, north of Kavieng, on 20 March. This completed Cartwheel. It hardly mattered. The Japanese had begun withdrawing the ground echelon of their air force from Rabaul in early February. The last time Americans saw more than an occasional Japanese plane over the base was on 19 February.

By the end of March 1944, the Japanese defenders of the Admiralties were so short of ammunition and food that they no longer posed any threat to MacArthur's troops. In a little over a year MacArthur had advanced over 1,300 miles and cut off 136,000 troops.

8

DECISIVE COMBAT IN THE MARIANAS

To the Marianas?

To Admiral King, the Marianas had long seemed the way to the western Pacific. Their significance could not be impressed upon General Marshall, but after more than a year of discussion Hap Arnold eventually came to see that his B-29 bombers would find roosts in the Marianas to be far more utilitarian than the previously proposed bases in China.

With the rapid capture of Kwajalein and Eniwetok, one might have assumed the Marianas were next, but there was a surprising lack of consensus among senior American leaders. Of course MacArthur would object. He had had recent success of his own at Los Negros in the Admiralties, which was virtually undefended. The general quickly reinforced his success by landing troops on the island. Now he was in the Admiralties. The Bismarck barrier had been broken. Rabaul no longer was a place of bogeymen.

King had encountered more serious resistance. Until late in 1943, Truk remained on the list of proposed invasions. Nimitz still was leery of advancing directly to the Marianas.[1] His initial plan was to enter the western Marshalls in May and to assault Truk in August. If Truk was bypassed because the Big Blue Fleet could neutralize it, Nimitz wanted to go next to Palau. It was as if American planners could leave no fortified Japanese island undisturbed. In late February the Joint Chiefs had not issued definitive instruction as to what came next.

A delegation from the southwest Pacific led by General Sutherland and including General Kenney met with Nimitz and most of his senior staff in Pearl Harbor on the morning of 25 January 1944. Before the meeting, Kenney had bunked with Lieutenant General Robert C. Richardson, the senior army officer in the Pacific Ocean Areas. Richardson felt the Pacific war wasn't progressing rapidly enough. He favored pooling all resources behind one of the two prongs that the Americans had been thrusting across the Pacific. Kenney had always favored this approach. Soon the evening's discussion centered on the southern advance via New Guinea, the Philippines, Formosa, and Japan. Towers and Kenney had been good friends before the war. The day before the formal meeting, the three got together. Towers had always preferred the southern route to an advance across the central Pacific. He told the others that Admirals Sherman and Carney shared their beliefs. All three senior officers agreed that virtually the entire remainder of the proposed central Pacific campaign should be eliminated except for the invasion of Palau, which would protect MacArthur's northern flank.[2]

The formal meeting, including Admiral Nimitz and Admiral "Soc" McMorris, began the next morning. Much of the discussion centered on logistical requirements. Vice Admiral W. L. Calhoun, commander of the support group, said a single attack from the south would be the easiest to support. He worried about the infrastructure that would have to be created on the small atolls of the central Pacific. Forrest Sherman concurred. Many participants thought the Marianas could be bypassed altogether. Admiral Kinkaid stated that "any talk of the Marianas for a base leaves me entirely cold."[3] Soc McMorris doubted long-range bombers from the Marianas could induce Japan to capitulate. However, he remained an advocate of a central Pacific advance per Plan Orange. Forrest Sherman pointed out the limited capacity of central Pacific harbors. Nimitz favored an advance via the Philippines but held that bases on the Chinese mainland would have to be taken and the Home Islands bombed before Japan would give in. "The consensus at Pearl Harbor seemed to lean toward a sequence of operations which would place the emphasis of the drive to the Philippines in the

Southwest Pacific area."[4] Sutherland and Kenney thought they had won one for MacArthur. That night Sutherland wired MacArthur that Nimitz had been won over to the southwest Pacific approach. However, Nimitz prudently declared that the meeting had been called only to exchange views and it was now over without a formal conclusion being recommended.

When King read the minutes of this meeting, he was furious. Sutherland had effectively shut down the central Pacific drive. Nimitz was seen to agree with him. This opened a chasm between Nimitz and King that caused the CNO to reduce his trust in the Pacific Ocean Areas commander. King wanted to deemphasize the southern offensive and advance via the Marianas to either Formosa or the China coast. His subordinates had not kept the faith. "It was obvious that no one at Pearl Harbor shared King's enthusiasm for the Marianas."[5] Unlike the central Pacific atolls, the Marianas were volcanic islands without large lagoons. The best harbor was Agana on Guam, but it couldn't begin to service the entire fleet. Many naval officers at the Pearl Harbor meeting saw the Marianas as an Army Air Forces B-29 base and little else.

Not surprisingly MacArthur opined that B-29 raids from the Marianas against Japan would achieve negligible results. His air commander, General Kenney, called bombing Japan from Marianas "just a stunt." Instead, Kenney wanted to use the bombers against the oilfield installations on Borneo. MacArthur also held that B-29s would be more difficult to support in the central Pacific than in the southwest Pacific. This defies both distance and any understandable logic.

General Holland Smith, the senior marine, detected a subtle change in the Pacific Fleet commander. "After Tarawa, I could never understand the constant apprehension the Admiral displayed regarding the Pacific situation. Never an exuberant man, he could work up, in his quiet way, an extremely pessimistic mood. Nimitz had no reason to be alarmed. He was a lucky man." Smith went on to itemize the incredible talents of his subordinate commanders and unmatched capabilities of his forces.[6] The enormous burdens and the long casualty lists had understandably begun to take their toll. When Nimitz visited Tarawa right after the invasion, before the huge number of corpses had been buried, he remarked, "It's the first time I smelled death."

But King remained resolute. In a letter to Nimitz dated February 8, 1944, King expressed "indignant dismay" with his subordinates and went on to enumerate his reasons for wanting the Marianas and ultimately a base on the China coast from which to attack Japan.[7] He took Admiral Towers to task for saying the primary reason for taking the Marianas was to provide basing for B-29s. This really raised the CNO's ire. Seizure of the Marianas would uncouple Japan from everything to the south. Anticipating the next round of JCS discussions King went on to say that emphasis on the southern route to the detriment of central Pacific operations "is, to me, absurd."

King shared his displeasure with Towers and Nimitz for not countering the arguments of others. This disagreement between King and Nimitz is all the more surprising since the two had just met in San Francisco in early January. At that meeting, Nimitz had shown some reluctance about a Marianas operation, but King had thought the Marianas issue had been settled. Turner had prepared an outline that indicated he would first take Saipan, then Tinian, then Guam.

At times General MacArthur viewed the decisions on strategy in terms of impugning his own personal honor. He appealed to Secretary Stimson that President Roosevelt was a navy man and that he favored the navy. Neither Marshall nor Stimson was impressed by MacArthur's approach to the question. Marshall tried to assure MacArthur that his honor was not in question.[8] MacArthur's constant conflation of questions of national strategy with his personal agenda was a major and continuous roadblock on the path to the best way to prosecute the war.

What would Mahan have counseled? He would have asked the disputing parties, What was the single overriding objective? In Clausewitz's terms, what was the Japanese center of gravity? The fleet! Japanese carriers hadn't seen combat in a year. True, several of their air groups had been shot up at Rabaul. Mitscher's aviators should be more than a match for them. Where would be the best point for the United States to engage the Japanese fleet? As far away as possible from the large land-based air strength among the very large islands—the Philippines, Formosa, Japan.

Where were the Japanese carriers likely to offer battle? Not south of the Philippines. There was nothing in the South Pacific that was remotely likely to bring the Japanese fleet to battle. By 1944, both Japan and America recognized the distinct inferiority of the Japanese fleet. Japan could risk her capital ships only to defend a critical segment of her final defense line, not some written-off outpost. King argued that the Marianas were an integral part of Japan's inner defense circle and would be defended by the fleet. This was in fact the way the Japanese saw it. Invasion of the Marianas threatened the inner sanctum.

Mahan would have admonished his naval brethren not to dismiss the B-29 out of hand—even if the army manned the machine. Here was a major technological advance to execute a time-honored strategy: blockade of the enemy homeland. More than most countries, Japan depended on coastal shipping as well as imports to keep her economy running. Restricted sea lanes close to the Home Islands were ideal for mining. Ultimately the choice to defeat this tenacious enemy would be either blockade or invasion. Marianas-based B-29s would advance the blockade by a good six months. Bomb cities or mine? That tactical question would best be settled by a dispassionate analysis calculated by the weapons effects specialists. The alternative (or combination of the two) that promised the quickest, least costly (in friendly lives) victory was the best way to go. By spring of 1944 Nimitz and King were convinced blockade would bring down Japan. Certainly bombing Borneo had nowhere near the equivalent potential.

Mahan also might have noted that Japan seemed to be bifurcating her fleet. The most potent section, the carrier task force, was held close to the homeland and was busy training pilots. The battleship divisions hung around Brunei to be close to their source of fuel oil. In open ocean combat, the puny range of their guns often left them impotent. However, give them quick and covered passage to the plethora of amphibious shipping off an invasion beach, not to mention the piles of unprotected and unmovable supplies, and large-caliber guns become a fearsome menace. Halsey had had a narrow escape off Bougainville. As the southern prong shortened the distance to Borneo, home waters for the Japanese battleship line, the danger they posed was something to watch.

How to protect the amphibious operations? One solution might be to detach "Ching" Lee and his fast battleships from the Big Blue Fleet to cover them. Mahan would not have liked this solution. Even though this ploy didn't diminish the main battery of carrier-based aviation, it still detracted from the fleet. American ordnance men assured the seagoing salts that the high velocity of the long 16-inch guns on the *Iowas* would penetrate more armor than the 18-inch batteries of Japan's two largest monsters. Risking thousands of sailors to put their calculations to the test appealed to no one with responsibility for sailors' lives. And the simple fact was *Yamato* and *Musashi* had more armor than the *Iowas* (although the *Iowas*' tremendous speed allowed them to escort the carriers, a most useful characteristic the *Yamatos* never achieved). Remember, Mahan admonished naval commanders to avoid melee combat in which roughly equal opponents just slug it out. This advice is especially pertinent when you have access to an asymmetric alternative.

The big ship killer most feared by the battleship warriors was the torpedo. Early on Mahan saw the potential of this weapon. Almost all lowly escort carriers carried a complement of torpedo bombers, TBFs. Land-based marine aviation boasted many TBF squadrons. The torpedo skills of these naval officers needed to be honed and attention paid to fill the torpedo magazines of the airfields and CVEs these aviators used. Naval intelligence, including submarine pickets, had to maintain real-time information about the location of the small number of deadly behemoths that might stalk American lives.

Another series of plenary meetings was held in Washington in February. Given the speed of events on the Pacific battlefields, the Joint Chiefs were tardy in resolving the strategic logjam that had piled up. Everyone in Washington was thoroughly disillusioned with Chiang Kai-shek's China as well as any serious offensive emanating from the British in Southeast Asia. The only real strategic contenders were King's central Pacific campaign and MacArthur's designs on the Philippines.

Almost everyone agreed that the next phase of the Pacific war was to establish a major base area in what was termed the Luzon–Formosa–China coast triangle. That terminology avoided the even larger argument that would later occupy everyone's attention, including the president's: what alternative approach to which target? General Sutherland, again representing MacArthur, argued that "the concentration of all forces in the Pacific along the New Guinea axis of advance, bypassing both Truk and the Marianas, was the only sensible course of action." However, the JCS planners had better vision than they had had even six months earlier. Many had become impressed with the striking power of the fleet's carriers. In light of the successful carrier raids on Truk, they saw little merit in an assault on that fortress. King's estimate that operations in the Marianas would precipitate a major fleet action carried weight.[9] So did Arnold's desire to commence strategic bombing of Japan from those islands. JCS planners recommended the central Pacific route for the advance westward, either to the Philippines or Formosa.*

General Marshall was a little surprised by the conflicting advice from MacArthur and those in Washington favoring the central Pacific. With both King and Arnold in agreement, the logjam was broken. Some historians wonder what might have transpired had MacArthur made his own arguments in person.[10]

King agreed with Marshall that they should submit the competing proposals to the Joint Strategic Survey Committee (JSSC). Its report was unequivocal. The committee recommended that all resources should be placed behind the central Pacific drive, which should capture the Marianas and then advance directly either to Luzon or Formosa. Further, the committee castigated other planners for not stopping one offensive in favor of the other at an earlier date. Any further operations in the southwest theater should be evaluated solely on their ability to

---

*The Joint Strategic Survey Committee (JSSC), formerly the Joint Board, was composed of three senior flag officers nearing retirement who were tasked with giving the Joint Chiefs an independent assessment of strategic matters. The Joint Staff, or Joint Planners, was an amalgamation of the War Plans Divisions of King (navy) and Marshall (army). The Joint Staff was not a separate entity.

support the success of the central Pacific drive.[11] General Marshall was taken aback at the committee's conclusions. Their recommendation would have diminished MacArthur's role below a level that the current political environment could tolerate.

In March, another meeting was held in Washington to finalize Pacific strategy. Nimitz and MacArthur were invited to attend. MacArthur demurred and sent his chief of staff, Sutherland, in his stead. Sutherland repeated familiar arguments that now had little impact. Admiral Nimitz informed the JCS that his forces would be ready to invade either Truk or the Marianas in mid-June. He agreed Truk could be bypassed. This was a reversal of his position at the beginning of February and reflected the obvious impact of Admiral King. Nimitz insisted on taking Ulithi lagoon in the Palaus. Once this unoccupied atoll was taken, Ulithi would become the major fleet anchorage for the rest of the war. To defend Ulithi, Nimitz concluded Palau had to be at least neutralized. Nimitz reasoned that possession of the rest of the Palaus would be necessary to ensure neutralization of the Carolines and prepare for an advance on the Philippines.[12] MacArthur also wanted these islands secured to protect his right flank as he approached the Philippines. JCS planners who favored going directly to Formosa also thought the Palaus would be useful in neutralizing an unconquered Philippines. So the seeds of one of the great mistakes of the war were carefully planted and nurtured.

Based on the ongoing Washington discussions, Sutherland informed MacArthur that the Marianas invasion was inevitable. Upon closer inspection of timetables and troop lists, MacArthur concluded the proposed Marianas operations would not interfere with his prosecution of the war in New Guinea. Was MacArthur's map upside down?

MacArthur also advanced his initial time line. Now he wanted to land two divisions at Hollandia on April 15, supported by the fleet. He was making a big jump compared to earlier plans to move up New Guinea step-by-step. Quick success at Los Negros had given him an air base in the Admiralties. He repeated his call for "bypassing" the Marianas. Next he recommended that central Pacific forces take the Palaus by 15 July. His forces would invade Mindanao, the southernmost large island of the Philippines, by 15 November 1944.[13]

JCS planners rejected any notion of halting the central Pacific advance in favor of New Guinea. The consensus was that the central Pacific offered the best opportunity. However, in the directive they drafted there was no mention of giving the central Pacific drive absolute priority. To summarize the JCS directive of 12 March 1944:

1. Cancel Kavieng and Woleai.

2. Early invasion of Admiralties.

3. Capture Hollandia. Target 15 April. (Nimitz will provide necessary carrier support.)

4. Neutralize, not capture Truk.

5. Occupy Saipan, Tinian, and Guam. Target 15 June.

6. Palaus. Target 15 September.

7. Occupy Mindanao. Target 15 November.

8. Approach Formosa either directly or via Luzon.[14]

The issue of Formosa versus Luzon was not resolved. However, the directive clearly anticipated that Formosa, not Luzon, should be the final intermediate objective from which the attack on Japan would commence. Target date for either Luzon or Formosa was 15 February 1945. MacArthur must have taken solace in a firm instruction to invade Mindanao. The return to the Philippines was etched in operational directive. King must have been very pleased that the attack on the Marianas had been salvaged after being nearly sunk with the connivance of many of his own admirals. His ultimate vision of attack from Formosa was down in black and white even though the issue of Luzon had not been resolved.

Mahan would not have approved the continuation of a strategy that did not concentrate all power against the primary objective. But he would have been pleased that the fleet wasn't divided. While it would be diverted from its paramount mission for the Hollandia operation, it would remain intact under the overall direction of Admiral Nimitz. Mahan would have found the most essential element, the concentration of the fleet to precipitate a major naval showdown in the Marianas, intact.

In his Naval War College thesis, Admiral Towers had remarked, "Only a great commander can both envision and then persevere in realizing a grand strategic design."[15] Admiral King had accomplished this task.

Japanese Defensive Strategies: Z to A-GO

Around 10 February 1944 successful American operations at Kwajalein and the Admiralties convinced the Imperial General Staff that Truk was no longer tenable.[16] This determination predated Spruance's strike on that atoll. The Imperial Navy had no plans to use the Palaus as more than an advance base until facilities in the Philippines had been readied. American carrier strikes at the end of March led the Japanese to believe the Palaus were about to be invaded. This island group, which was so prominently mentioned in so much preliminary planning, had lost its strategic value.

Admiral Koga retained his faith in the "New Operational Policy." That plan designated all the area the Allies took at the beginning of 1944 as delaying areas. Japan would use the time to reinvigorate her fleet for the decisive battle in defense of the inner ring—the Marianas, Palau, western New Guinea (Vogelkop Peninsula, the "turkey head" of the island). The Americans must not penetrate beyond the Marianas. Mitscher's carriers were to be crushed between the hammer of Ozawa's ships and anvil of land-based air. After a decisive defeat at sea, the Americans would be forced to the negotiating table. So went the fantasy.

After the carrier strike on Truk in February, the Japanese feared that invasion of the Marianas was imminent. They "reached a state of near panic." The Imperial Navy recognized that air strength in the Marianas and Carolines was inadequate to support the fleet.[17] The press of the central Pacific campaign forced the naval general staff to move the 61st Air Flotilla along with 1st Air Fleet HQ to the Marianas and Palaus. Between February and May, 500 aircraft were flown into the Marianas. So much for the training plan. The 62nd Flotilla stayed in Japan because its training was so incomplete.

The Japanese army also decided to expedite reinforcement of the Marianas, previously treated as an administrative area. In early March, 31st Army set up in Guam. Two divisions, 29th and 43rd, were dispatched to shore up the defenses of the Marianas. The convoy from China carrying the 29th to Saipan was devastated by American subs. The Palaus held mostly service troops. Some infantry reinforcements arrived in March. The 14th Infantry Division, initially slated for New Guinea, diverted to the Palaus, arrived on 24 April.

Koga had wanted to move his headquarters to Saipan. But there wasn't enough fuel to base heavy units that far north. Tanker sinkings, largely by American subs, induced a fuel shortage in the Combined Fleet.[18] Battleship *Musashi*, Koga's flagship, remained at Palau. Oil starvation now heavily influenced almost every Japanese tactical decision.

America's two-pronged offensive did confuse the Japanese. Initially they anticipated that MacArthur would thrust up from New Guinea to Mindanao.[19] That was MacArthur's initial plan. Defense plan KON anticipated that the "decisive battle" would be held in these waters. For a little while in May, Koga had based the carriers at Tawi-Tawi along with his battleships. They prepared to sortie either to the Marianas, to Palau, or to New Guinea as needed. Fuel was so short that the flattops could not take to sea to train airmen, as had been done earlier in the year near Japan.

Both Tojo and the navy were convinced the Marianas had to be held at all costs. There were some dissenting views in the army. Fighting in the Marshalls demonstrated that the navy was no longer able to challenge a major movement of the Big Blue Fleet, went the argument. Now it was up to the army and its air force to fight the decisive battle. Some feared the Marianas would become a naval battlefield where American supremacy at sea would prevail. Lieutenant General Y. Sato, commander on Saipan, pointed out to Tojo that there were only seven decent airfields in the Marianas. The American fleet could easily blanket them, thereby nullifying the army air force. Why not pull back into the Philippines, where hundreds of airfields were available? Here the army could make its full weight felt. Mahan would have listened carefully. But Tojo rejected the advice because so much had already been made of the necessity to defend the Marianas. Besides, Tojo was about to force the resignation of the army chief of staff, Sugiyama, and consolidate the power of that office with the others he held.

Even in the navy, there were a few rays of reason in the white heat of emotion surrounding the war. Rear Admiral Sokichi Takagi had been tasked with conducting a scientific examination of aircraft and shipping losses on both sides. Any serious analysis of the data could only lead to one conclusion: there was no way the Japanese could win. Takagi knew that if either his boss Admiral Shimada or Tojo viewed the results, his life would be in danger.[20] With several staff officers, he toyed with the notion of assassinating Tojo. Nothing came of it. No one wanted to be influenced by the facts.

In March, Koga had modified his basic plan. He concentrated Japanese naval and air strength to a degree Yamamoto never achieved. He looked to commit everything available once a major American formation penetrated the Philippine Sea, regardless of the direction from which it advanced. Plan Z counted 500 aircraft on First Mobile Fleet carriers and another 500 in the islands to tackle the Big Blue Fleet. Both numbers would prove to be optimistic.

As intelligence indicators changed, Admiral Kurita shuffled his planes around the western Pacific. First he flew them from the Philippines to New Guinea to oppose hopscotching invasions along the coast. Then they redeployed to defend against and attack against Biak and then on to Palau. After that, the survivors moved from Halmahera to Tinian or Saipan. Up to 80 percent of aircraft were lost before they could be committed to combat, from either ferry/operational losses or interdiction by U.S. action.[21] Admiral Koga himself was killed in a plane crash as he attempted to bring his HQ ashore and base it at Davao on Mindanao, the large southern island of the Philippines.

The same storm that cost Koga his life also caused his chief of staff's plane to go down. A copy of the operations order for Plan Z was retrieved from the flotsam and forwarded to American intelligence. It outlined the major fleet engagement the Japanese intended to precipitate and the plan to target American landing forces as they arrived.[22]

On Koga's death, Admiral Soemu Toyoda took over as commander, Mobile Fleet. This command included 90 percent of naval combat vessels and was essentially the navy minus the convoy defense command. Many viewed Toyoda as brilliant and as a very meticulous planner. Yet he had a sarcastic streak and a caustic manner that made him very hard to work for. Toyoda drove more than a few staffers right to the edge. Even more than Koga, he believed in Mahanian decisive battle. During his lengthy career, he had served in a variety of command and staff assignments, including commander, Fourth Fleet; chief, Intelligence Group, Naval General Staff; and chief of staff of the Combined Fleet in the 1930s. He was promoted to full admiral in 1941 and made a member of the Supreme War Council in November 1942. Admiral Toyoda was known to be extremely aggressive and favored a major naval battle with the American on terms favorable to Japan at the earliest possible occasion.

Toyoda modified Koga's Plan Z, now designated A-GO. Generally it moved Japanese focus away from the southwest Pacific. Toyoda narrowed the intended battle area to the Carolines or Palaus, the eastern approaches to the Philippine Sea, and designated the Palaus as the preferred area for decisive combat. The waters near the big air bases at Yap and Woleai were indicated. If the American fleet entered the Marianas, it was to be engaged by airpower only, then lured south closer to where the First Mobile Fleet lay in waiting.[23] There just wasn't the fuel to do much else.

The Mobile Fleet contained two numbered fleets. Second Fleet contained the battleships and routinely operated in the South Seas while the carriers now stayed farther north. Third Fleet contained three carrier divisions. Division 1 contained three first-rate fleet carriers, the brand new *Taiho* and two Pearl Harbor veterans, *Zuikaku* and *Shokaku*. Division 2 contained the far less capable *Junyo, Hiyo,* and *Ryujo*. The newly formed Carrier Division 3 had a pair of carriers that hardly warranted the label of light fleet carrier: *Zuiho* and *Chitose*.

Admiral Jisaburo Ozawa, who commanded the Mobile Fleet during the battle of the Marianas, was known as an able seaman and a brilliant innovator. Prior to 1939, he had served ably in the surface fleet. Although he was not an aviator (like Spruance and Nimitz), he was promoted to commander, 1st Naval Air Group. Prior to his arrival, Japanese carriers were used only for scouting. Ozawa forged them into offensive weapons, the primary punch of the fleet. At the beginning of the war, he commanded the Southern Expeditionary Fleet that captured the Dutch Indies. He had been promoted to command the carriers when Nagumo was removed after the battle of the Eastern Solomons. An able and respected commander, he was known as a strategic thinker. Admiral Morison described him as "one of the ablest admirals in the Japanese Navy" and "a worthy antagonist to Mitscher."[24] His performance in the Marianas demonstrated why he was regarded as Japan's premier naval tactician.

In May, the navy staff made the difficult decision to allow unrefined crude from Tawi-Tawi to be burned in ship's boilers. While this allowed the battlewagons to sortie as far northeast as the Marianas, burning crude badly damaged burners and piping and created a fire hazard. The practice did, however, increase the immediate fuel supply and freed enough tankers to support the carriers. Without this accommodation, the First Mobile Fleet could not have sailed for the Sulu Sea. Carrier Division 1 had operated from Linga Roads south of Singapore. The remaining carriers had been in home waters training aviators. With this new capability, Toyoda modified his planning to cover that area of greatest concern. He expected the next major sea fight to occur in the Marianas.

Mahan would certainly have admired the concentration of force. However, an inferior fleet should avoid battle with a superior enemy. Were the Marianas the place to have a showdown with the Big Blue Fleet? Clearly, Spruance could amass a 2:1 superiority. Should the Japanese fleet continue to withdraw toward the homeland and remain "a fleet in being" while the American fleet was slowly reduced by land-based aviation from the Philippines or Formosa? Captain Mahan's writings repeated the importance of the fleet in being. As long as it remained a credible threat, it restricted the enemy's freedom of action, which might delay an enemy victory but could not prevent it. One can imagine Captain Mahan glumly choosing this alternative in the hope something better might show up. It would have been hard for a dispassionate analyst to see much opportunity in the Japanese position as the summer solstice approached.

Carrier Raids

After Truk, Mitscher ran his carriers into the Marianas. This sortie took the fleet deep into territory the Japanese had not thought was in play. Again land-based Japanese aviation was heavily punished. Mitscher also brought back good recon photography that was vital for planning the upcoming invasions.

The Palaus were next on Mitscher's list. Hitting these islands was potentially more dangerous than attacking Truk's defenses. Truk remained the great bugaboo. At Palau, 36 ships totaling 130,000 tons were destroyed or badly damaged. Senior American naval officers were increasingly confident they could dominate Japanese naval forces wherever they appeared. Intelligence indicated three battleships and four to six heavy cruisers had been based at Palau. Nimitz was sure they would withdraw rather than face the firepower of massed American carriers.[25] Later Mitscher moved south to support MacArthur's deep amphibious thrust at Hollandia on the New Guinea coast. On the way back to Pearl, Mitscher hit Truk again.

The carrier attack on the Marianas confused most Japanese leaders. They thought Mitscher's raid on Palau portended that the principal Allied axis would be Hollandia–Mindanao.[26] Thus they were predisposed to counterattack the upcoming assault on Biak.

American carrier tactics had changed. Now the fast carriers would slug it out toe-to-toe with land-based Japanese air. As Mitscher said, "There are just so many Jap planes on any island. We'll go in and take it on the chin. We'll swap punches with them. I know I'll have losses but I'm stronger than they are. If it takes two task forces, we'll get two task forces. I don't give a damn now if they do spot me. I can go anywhere and nobody can stop me. If I go in and destroy all their aircraft, their damned islands are no good to them anyhow."[27]

Mahan would find two very important facts in Mitscher's statement. By early 1944, the American navy no longer had to fear the Japanese navy. The American battle fleet could sail where it pleased. While it had not achieved naval supremacy (the ability for *all* friendly ships to sail as they pleased), it had achieved naval superiority and could dominate any one area as it pleased. In early 1942, it took a miracle for the Americans to stop the Japanese navy. From mid-1942 to mid-1943, the American navy had to be careful lest it lose its narrow edge in a clash at sea similar to what had happened to the Japanese at Midway. With the *Essex*-class fleet carriers coming down the ways, reinforced by new light carriers, the Americans now had the undisputed ability to take the initiative.

The second fact that would have caught Mahan's attention is that Japanese-held intermediate islands in the Great Pacific Empty no longer mattered. They could be bypassed at will. The Big Blue Fleet was capable of taking them on without the support of land-based aviation. Now Mahan would push hard for a massive speedup of the war. Forget all the preparatory assaults of fortified islands that cost so much in dogface blood. Instead go straight for the Japanese jugular. Mitscher understood this. So did Halsey and King. Nimitz recognized the change but, as Howlin' Mad Smith pointed out, he had become more conservative. The brilliant but very methodical Spruance had some difficulty switching gears. MacArthur never recognized the huge changes in relative air combat power between U.S. carrier air and Japanese land-based aviation.

Near Disaster at Biak

Biak is a small island 45 miles long and about 20 miles wide off the northern coast of New Guinea just above its "neck" (see Map 7a). Biak is 45 miles long and about 20 miles wide. Three good Japanese airstrips were sited there. At first glance, there appears to be nothing in its location of great strategic importance. However a major sea fight among surface ships almost ignited there in June 1944.

The Japanese saw Biak as key to holding the area and a fulcrum from which a decisive battle against the American fleet might be leveraged. The Americans had planned to develop large bomber airfields at Hollandia, but MacArthur's engineers found the soils wouldn't support the required loads. Biak became the alternative.

At first the Japanese high command decided no more air or naval reinforcements would be sent into the New Guinea area. Land-based air strength in the Marianas plus carrier-based air would be insufficient to handle the Big Blue Fleet. Then Japanese planners feared American airstrips on Biak might threaten the transiting battleships and even the southern flank of the intended ambush in the Philippine Sea. Admiral Toyoda was prepared to commit the bulk of his naval land-based aircraft to defend Biak.[28] Naval air reinforcements, probably from the 62nd Air Flotilla (the training unit in Japan), were ferried into the area. They and heavy naval units would escort an additional army brigade into Biak. So was born Operation KON. Reinforcements were supposed to arrive 3 June.

By spring 1944, it was apparent the Japanese navy had no chance of taking on the Big Blue Fleet without tremendous army air support. After American successes in the Marshalls, the Marianas were the obvious next step. The best location for a major sea confrontation for the Japanese would be near a large landmass with many Japanese airfields but as far away from Tokyo as possible. If the battle could be fought close to Borneo's oil fields, where the battle fleet lay for lack of fuel, so much the better. Wishful Japanese thinking pointed to Biak. The fact that Biak stood astride MacArthur's path of advance from New Guinea to the southern Philippines (Mindanao) gave some hope that something could be arranged. Even more optimistic wishers thought the American fleet might split itself in order to simultaneously take Biak and Palau. This would make it easier for the Japanese to achieve victory at Biak. Despite this optimism, both Toyoda and Ozawa were concerned that Tawi-Tawi was becoming too exposed to remain the battleship anchorage for long. American submarines had sunk several oilers and destroyers nearby.

When evidence came in that Kinkaid's Seventh Fleet was assembling to bring MacArthur to Biak, Ozawa radioed Toyoda that Japan could not afford the loss of New Guinea and its airfields. Reinforcements might draw in the American fleet so that it could be ambushed. Toyoda was about to commit to KON 3—the subplan that defended against invasion of the Philippines—when long-range recon planes spotted elements of Spruance's Fifth Fleet forming up in Majuro on

3 June. What were American intentions? Palau? Marianas? Most of his staff thought the Americans couldn't simultaneously sortie Seventh and Fifth fleets on major operations. They didn't know they were different designations for the single Big Blue Fleet.

Admiral Toyoda was surprised by the suddenness of MacArthur's landing at Biak. Virtually his entire staff thought this was the main American effort. Only his intelligence officer maintained his view that the real blow would come in the Marianas. Toyoda decided to pick up the gauntlet he believed had been cast before his feet. Maybe wishful thinking had brought Japan good luck. He ordered Operation KON activated. Mighty battleships *Yamato* and *Musashi* under the able leadership of Admiral Ugaki sailed from Tawi-Tawi to smash the American invasion fleet and cripple the landings. About 100 aircraft from the Philippines and the Marianas plus another 75 from the Carolines were moved into position.

Instead of the expected easy operation, the American 41st Division ran into hot opposition when it landed on 27 May 1944. A thousand Japanese reinforcements came to Biak by barge at night from Manokwari. The invasion commander requested an additional reinforcing regiment. Bomber bases to be built on Biak would not be ready in time to support the American invasion of Leyte.

It could have been a lot worse. At time of Ugaki's sailing the Japanese hadn't spotted Spruance's Fifth Fleet headed toward the Marianas. Only a pair of heavy cruisers, three light cruisers, and 21 destroyers supported the American Biak invasion force. Ugaki's battleships would have crushed them. Most of the army's logistical installations were near the beach and vulnerable to seaward bombardment. Biak might have become a first-class American disaster.

But the incoming attack in the Marianas was a mortal threat to the empire. Toyoda had no choice but to cancel KON 3 and vector Ugaki's battleships to the northeast. Had the Marianas invasion been scheduled a week later, a lot of American shipping might have been sitting on ocean bottom around Biak, holed by 18.1-inch projectiles.

Spruance Plans for the Marianas

The Marianas campaign was a big win for the United States. However, the naval portion of the fight, called the battle of the Philippines Sea—or the Great Marianas Turkey Shoot—has been surrounded in controversy. Should this victory have been even greater?

Initially, Admiral Nimitz forecast that the Imperial Fleet would not be committed to the defense of the Marianas. Admiral King was hoping for a decisive fleet engagement, but worried that the Japanese fleet, which had had a year to heal itself, would be a tough opponent.[29] King was concerned that neither Spruance nor Mitscher had a plan to counter a fleet-opposed invasion. Rapid expansion of the American fleet meant many seaman and officers had only limited training. American admirals underestimated the quality of their crews while overestimating the recovery of the Japanese. Throughout history, American commanders have had a tendency to do this.

King and Nimitz met again in San Francisco in May. Nimitz told King he thought a fleet engagement unlikely. King vacillated. Maybe the Japanese would wait until an American move on Formosa before committing their Mobile Fleet. After the meeting, Nimitz's lack of concern worried King greatly. Would sufficient training and preparation be made for a fleet engagement?

Nimitz announced that the Saipan landing was scheduled for 15 June 1944. By mid-May, intelligence plotted Japanese movement of heavy fleet units into the Philippines. This was consistent with preparation for a major fleet engagement. Communication intercepts picked up Toyoda's preparation for A-GO. However Admiral Spruance did not believe "the Japanese fleet would come out to attack us, primarily because I thought the enemy would want shore based air support, and I knew that the first thing we would do in the Marianas would be to take out all of the enemy aircraft and thereafter keep them out."[30] Spruance logically concluded that the Japanese fleet wouldn't appear unless it had the advantage. When it did have the potential for advantage at Biak, it didn't sortie.[31] Spruance didn't think the Imperial Fleet would sortie into the Marianas. This line of reasoning probably left U.S. commanders flat-footed.

As the Marianas operation came together, King presumed there were plans to pull all the fast battleships from the four carrier task groups into a single battle line to oppose the Japanese battleships if they appeared. The *Iowa*s were significantly faster than the other American fast battleships. King worried that lack of practice would cause ships with different propulsive capabilities to maneuver out of synchronization, causing major problems for American tactical maneuvers. A very concerned King began reading Spruance's plans. He didn't like what he found. Neither Spruance nor Mitscher had planned for a sea fight.[32]

Nimitz sought to ease King's mind. He cabled the CNO, "Destruction of the enemy fleet is always the prime objective of our naval forces. Attempts by enemy fleet units to interfere with amphibious operations are both hoped for and provided against."[33] This is not exactly what Nimitz ordered Spruance to do. Nimitz's orders made protection of the invasion fleet primary. Along with many others, he didn't think the Japanese fleet would be seen in force until the Home Islands were threatened. The difference between these two alternative missions captures the essence of the argument—and leaves some egg on Nimitz's face. It also underscores how closely often terse military orders are read and how critical choice of phrase truly is.

Reports of the Normandy landings reached the fleet as it made preparations for the Marianas. Everyone was buoyed by the news. The sight of hundreds of ships gathering in the lagoons of the Marshalls brought with it a sense of invincibility.

As Spruance readied to depart from Majuro, a document marked "Combined Fleet Ultra Secret Operation Order No. 73," outlining Japanese Z plans, was given to him. It related the intelligence gleanings from the copy of Plan Z recovered from the wreckage of Koga's aircraft. Spruance noted the following passage: "In some situations, the landing forces will be attacked and destroyed first. . . . Every effort should be made to destroy the major element of the enemy landing forces."[34] These words influenced Spruance to remain on guard during the Philippine Sea fight. His orders were to invade and secure the Marianas, not to chase the Mobile Fleet. Here was evidence that the Japanese might go for the transports first.

Still, Spruance didn't expect the Japanese to interfere with the landings. As his battleship commander, Admiral "Ching" Lee, stated, "Boy, the Jap fleet ain't intended to come out during this operation!"[35] Spruance's instructions to Mitscher were to strike enemy airfields three days prior to the arrival of Turner's gators, provide air defense over the invasion, and support the troops ashore. Spruance said nothing about a possible fleet action. Mitscher made some plans of his own in case the Japanese fleet did appear. But he didn't alert his task force.

Ozawa's Master Stroke

On 11 June, Mitscher's fighters swarmed all over the Marianas, destroying almost a hundred aircraft. Air strikes continued for a second day. Then Lee's fast battleships blasted away at the islands. A day later the older battleships, the real shore bombardment experts, began hitting Saipan. That meant both the fast carriers and the amphibious fleets were swinging into the Marianas.

It dawned on the Japanese leadership: the focus wasn't Biak. Toyoda signaled Ugaki to break off his battleship attack on the shipping off that island and to head north. Toyoda communicated to Ozawa that the branch of A-GO countering an invasion of the Marianas was now operational.

Admiral Ozawa knew his adversaries. Captured American documents identified the able Marc Mitscher as commander of America's fast carriers and Raymond Spruance as overall commander. The Japanese admiral knew the American fleet commander was the very competent sailor who had held steady at Midway and had ripped through the Marshalls. But he knew his adversary was a cautious man who would remain on the defensive. Ozawa counted on Spruance to protect the invasion fleet by not venturing more than 100 miles west of Saipan.[36]

Ozawa commanded the largest carrier force Japan had ever assembled. His task groups were built around five fleet and four light carriers. The spanking new *Taiho,* his flagship, bulked larger than any carrier afloat save the torpedo-scarred *Saratoga.* His flattops sported 222 fighters and 218 strikers, a larger complement than was mustered at Pearl Harbor. Should it be necessary to use them, his battle line counted five battleships, including the monster *Yamato* and her fearsome sister *Musashi.* His ships were given all the fuel they could carry. This was the Imperial Navy's last hope of crippling the Big Blue Fleet and setting it back a year or two.

Ozawa had a pretty good picture of Spruance's order of battle. He knew Mitscher's squadrons badly outnumbered his own. American carrier decks held 475 fighters to his 222, a 2.1:1 advantage. The American edge in dive- and torpedo bombers was 416 to 208—2:1. If these odds summarized the pending fight, it was better for Japan to refuse battle. This was the outer layer of the inner defense perimeter, not the Home Islands themselves. But Toyoda and Ozawa both counted on massive help from land-based aircraft. Five hundred were supposed to support the fleet. Plan A-GO tasked these land-based aircraft to sink or disable a third of the advancing American carriers before the fleets clashed. Once Ozawa defeated Spruance, the army could retake any islands initially lost to the Americans.

The War Ministry promised Ozawa 2,000 land-based planes in addition to 450 embarked on his carriers. Actually there were only 172 aircraft in the Marianas before Mitscher started to whittle them down. The ministry had shuffled more that were farther down the line, including the 134 in the Palaus and 67 on Truk. This move was consistent with the conclusion in A-GO that the Americans would strike from the general direction of MacArthur's forces. Japanese admirals maintained this mindset even though recon aircraft had sighted the Big Blue Fleet in Kwajalein lagoon.

Japanese aircraft, while generally inferior to their 1944 American counterparts, retained a range advantage. This allowed a very skilled Japanese admiral the opportunity to attempt an extremely difficult tactical trick. Sneak up on the enemy and then launch a major strike just inside your range but outside the range of your enemy. Then veer away from him and outrun his counterstrike. Then come in only as close as necessary to recover your own strike. In this manner you hammer your enemy and remain unscathed. Six minutes of luck, such as

Spruance had enjoyed at Midway, and the Japanese fleet could gain superiority against what remained of the Big Blue Fleet.

An alternative tactic was to "shuttle bomb" the Americans. To defend the amphibious shipping, the American carriers would have to stand between the Japanese fleet and the Japanese airfields in the Marianas Islands. If the American carriers sailed only 100 miles from those airfields, the Japanese carriers could stand well out of round-trip range, launch from the carriers, and recover on the airfields after a short hop. The opposing fleet would have no opportunity to respond. Spruance and Mitscher worried a lot about this possibility.

Ozawa's fleet was not a kamikaze. It had a rational plan for victory. Granted the odds were long, but so had been Nimitz's at Midway. The Japanese knew the stakes. The emperor's rescript underscored the significance of the hour: "This operation has immense bearing on the fate of the Empire. It is hoped that the forces will exert their utmost and achieve as magnificent results as in the Battle of Tsushima."

Although Ultra was not particularly productive during this interval, more traditional intelligence sources gave Spruance a good picture of Ozawa's dispositions. Submarine *Redfin* observed First Mobile Fleet as it sailed from Tawi-Tawi on the 13th. CincPac Intelligence correctly concluded the Japanese understood what was going on in the Marianas and predicted Ozawa's course up through the Philippines.[37] American intelligence identified the recall of Ugaki's battleships from their sortie on Biak. They correctly predicted Ozawa's time and approach to Saipan and confirmed the authenticity of plans that had previously been recovered from a Japanese wreck. On the 13th submarines confirmed six carriers, four battleships, eight cruisers, and accompanying destroyers passing through Philippine waters at the predicted time and on the predicted path. That evening two additional battleships, *Yamato* and *Musashi,* were sighted separately coming directly up the Philippine Sea. On the 15th submarine *Flying Fish* confirmed Ozawa's main force emerging from San Bernardino Strait. *Seahorse* spotted Ugaki's force leaving Surigao Strait. Unfortunately, these initial sightings weren't updated during the battle to form a consistent track.

Upon receipt of the sighting reports from the submarines, Spruance began calculating. Major enemy fleet units might oppose the American invasion after all. But they couldn't appear off Saipan until D+2 at the earliest. Spruance allowed preparations to continue so that the primary objective would be assaulted on time. As a precaution, he ordered radar-equipped PBMs, the most modern patrol bombers in the fleet, dispatched to Saipan to reinforce his reconnaissance capability. Admiral Spruance's orderly mind seldom missed a detail.

However, Admiral Spruance's very professional demeanor would have made Captain Mahan very uneasy. The admiral was thinking defensively. Yet he had clear naval superiority. What was the primary objective of all naval action? *Destroy the enemy's battle fleet.* Those weren't Nimitz's literal orders. The Marianas must be taken. Spruance absolutely had to prevent the destruction of the amphibious fleet. However the correlation of forces demonstrated Japanese weakness. Wrecking the Japanese fleet was always high priority. Were the two objectives in opposition? No one said it: if the Japanese fleet was destroyed, the American gators would be protected. But, it was a logical conclusion.

Mahan admonished admirals never to divide the fleet. From the above sightings, Spruance calculated the principal Japanese forces wouldn't come within range before the 17th. So he dispatched two carrier task groups to hit the airfields at Iwo Jima and Chichi Jima on the 15th and 16th. Mahan would have admired Spruance's ability to calculate and manage time, distance, and movement in the manner of Napoleon. Spruance moved offensively to take out a serious threat without exposing the subelements of his fleet to a superior force. In no way did such moves violate the admonition against dividing the fleet, as the enemy could never take advantage by massing against one of the unsupported subelements. Spruance could achieve his subobjective and reassemble the fleet before it faced a greater threat.

It is important to understand what Spruance was proposing and to contrast this strategy with what happened around Bougainville. Spruance knew the land-based threat was serious. These strikes would eliminate the principal island stepping-stones from the homeland into the Marianas and empty the Japanese supply pipeline. Strike analysis identified that 122 enemy aircraft had been shot up in the Jimas. Based on calculation Spruance moved proactively to eliminate a threat. At Bougainville, Halsey had raced against the odds to react against the threat—and got lucky.

Sunrise of 15 June 1944 ushered in a beautiful sky and the promise of a comfortably warm day. But the morning light revealed a sea off the western shore of Saipan swarming with Terrible Turner's amphibians. At 0542 Turner signaled, "Land the landing force." The assault regiments of the 2nd and 4th Marine divisions scrambled into their LVTs. Lines of these tracked beasts headed toward the towers of dust and smoke that the old battlewagons were raising from the shore. Spruance and Turner were pleased with the day's progress. The senior admiral approved his amphibious subordinate's recommendation to proceed with landings on Guam on the 18th as planned.[38]

At 0400, 16 June, Spruance received the submarine sighting reports. Now Ozawa's fleet was in play. Revised calculations indicated the two task groups headed to bomb the airfields on the Bonins had time to make an abbreviated strike and return to the fleet before Ozawa could steam into range. Ever the unflappable decision maker, Spruance ordered them to do so. There was insufficient time to complete the Guam invasion so he postponed it. On the morning of the 16th, Spruance conferred with Admiral Turner and some other subordinates on the amphibious command ship *Rocky Mount*. Plans were made to deal with the threat of a Japanese surface attack. Some cruisers and destroyers were transferred from invasion support to Mitscher's carrier groups to thicken their escort.

Transport unloading at Saipan was to cease at dusk on the 17th. LSTs could make barely 10 knots and would be easy prey. They and most other transports were to move off to the east so they wouldn't be caught in a fixed location. Admiral Jesse Oldendorf moved his seven older fire support battleships, along with their escorts, about 25 miles west of Saipan to form a battle line to prevent Japanese battleships from reaching the marines ashore. Turner was satisfied that these ships, plus the aircraft on seven supporting escort carriers, could handle the threat. All were worried that armor-piercing ammunition on these amphibious support vessels and torpedoes on the jeep carriers were in short supply.

Admiral Ozawa hadn't waited for green-clad American youths to come on deck of their dull gray transports. He sailed from Tawi-Tawi on the same day that Ching Lee's fast battleships opened fire. Ozawa aimed to accomplish what Yamamoto had repeatedly tried to do and failed. He sought to engage the American navy in a showdown battle with all the fleet's carrier aircraft and defeat U.S. carrier power decisively. Toyoda ordered Ugaki and the two super battleships, which had been destined to break up MacArthur's landings on Biak, to join up with Ozawa on the 12th, the day after American air strikes on the Marianas commenced. At 0855 of the 15th Admiral Toyoda signaled that the Americans were landing on Saipan and to "activate A-GO Operation for decisive battle."[39]

Ozawa formed his fleet into three task groups, each centered on one of his carrier divisions. Similar to the battle plan at Santa Cruz, he placed the light carriers of Carrier Division 3 (Cardiv3) in van to act as bait. To defend them he attached Ugaki's battleships. The idea was for American scouts to find the small carriers and draw in Mitscher's strikers, leaving Japan's larger carriers unseen. Ozawa planned to carefully approach the Americans and stay within the "golden band" that put his planes within range but kept the American bombers just out of range. He felt confident that Spruance would never strike first.[40] Hopefully Japanese aircraft sitting on runways in the Marianas would hit the American fleet. Ozawa had no control over them.

Toyoda signaled the fleet a repeat of Togo's admonition at Tsushima: "The fate of the Empire rests on this one battle. Every man is expected to do his utmost."

But A-GO already had gone horribly wrong. The promised 500-aircraft reinforcement had never reached the Marianas. In fact, only 200 were there. According to A-GO plans, one-third of the Big Blue Fleet's aircraft were to be smashed
by land-based air by this time. Instead Spruance had shot up a lot of Japanese
aircraft with few losses to himself. We will return to this juncture.

Spruance was known throughout the fleet for his intellect, hard work, and
honesty in debate. King called him the smartest flag officer in the navy. Captain
(later Rear Admiral) Charles J. Moore, his chief of staff, remembered, "He was
thinking all the time and when the time came for something to be done, he usually anticipated me. He was ready to act on it before I was ready to present him
with my proposals."[41] Spruance was aloof, cautious, brilliant and methodical.

Spruance began to worry. The enemy fleet was now capable of coming within
striking distance of the amphibious fleet. He ordered Mitscher to concentrate his
far-flung carrier task groups so they could defend Turner. Spruance retained the
demeanor of cold steel that characterizes the great admirals in times of crisis.
Frequently during the battle Spruance personally drafted orders to his principal
subordinates in simple, clear language so they would understand his intentions.

As additional information came in, Spruance became convinced the Japanese
intended to attack not Mitscher's carriers but Turner's amphibians. He estimated
Ozawa would use his carriers to lure the American carriers westward and then
slip Japanese battleships in to hit the amphibs.[42] At first Spruance thought they
sought to bring their battle line to bear. Later he changed his mind and thought
they meant to use carrier strikes to hit his transports.

Spruance had an outline plan ready. Initially Mitscher's airmen would concentrate on crippling the carriers. Shut down their carrier decks so they couldn't
conduct air operations. Rather than finishing off the carriers, the strikers would
then shift to the accompanying battleships. The airmen's second priority was to
damage the battleships by whatever means. Rip up their relatively fragile fire
control systems. Slow them down so they couldn't escape or countermaneuver.
Lee felt his two *Iowa*-class battleships could take on the *Yamato*s and that his
battle line would decimate that of his opponents.

The Naval War College always taught officers to plan based on the enemy's
capabilities, not on your guess of his intentions. Spruance ignored that admonition. Even though he didn't know the identity of the admiral opposing him, he
felt he understood how the "Japanese mind" worked. His unshakable conviction
that the Japanese objective was to destroy the invasion fleet constrained his
thinking. Spruance felt his first task was to defend those transports. That is how
Nimitz's order read. The intelligence documents described Japanese tactics to
feint in the center and then seek to outflank the enemy's fleet. Spruance was de-

termined not to let that happen. Maybe Spruance thought a little too hard on one paradigm and convinced himself a little too thoroughly of one course of action. This cast a defensive hue on his thinking. A less rigid line of reasoning would have taken into account the tremendous advantage in absolute numbers, training, and technology that Spruance had at his command. Radar-equipped night sea planes, both carrier-based TBFs and big PBMs operating from the coastal waters of Saipan, eliminated long nights of uncertainty as to the whereabouts of the enemy's ships. Technology had much diminished the risk of an enemy steaming long distances into proximity with the American fleet.

This was not 1942. A more aggressive, offensive plan could have sought out the enemy and destroyed his capability to damage the Americans long before either ships or aircraft emblazoned with the rising sun got within range.

Mitscher was "jubilant" at the receipt of the submarine sighting reports. He went over the plotting boards time and time again. Now it looked like the fleet would have the opportunity to do something it had lusted for since Midway: finish off the Japanese carriers. Mitscher understood that the stated objective was to defend the amphibians. But he and the rest of the carrier admirals stoutly maintained the best defense was an aggressive offense. Moving as a concentrated mass, the carrier groups could steam west and catch Ozawa from the south or southwest before the Japanese were anywhere close to Turner's brood. Massive American air superiority could devastate Ozawa. Should some Japanese sneak past Task Force 58, the old bombardment battleships, covered by the jeep carriers, could hold them while the fast carriers caught up and hammered them against Oldendorf's anvil. When Mitscher took off for Saipan and the 16 June conference aboard Turner's flagship, his staff quipped:

A strike against targets of opportunity on Saipan
Strike leader: Vice Admiral Marc A. Mitscher
Arming: one 10,000 pound operations plan[43]

Captain Mahan would have echoed encouragement. Notice the huge difference in outlook between how supremely competent American admirals as they processed the same information. Mahan's seemingly simplistic admonition that "it's the enemy fleet" makes all the difference. When measured against the opportunity of destroying the main Japanese fleet, the air admirals were willing to accept the small risk of a blow against the well-protected amphibians. The other admirals judged the low risk to be greater than the potential gain from a more aggressive posture. Given Nimitz's orders, it was a choice within a competent band of judgment. But a strict Mahanian analysis would unmistakably have taken the opposite position of what was adopted.

Rear Admiral J. J. "Jocko" Clark (later vice admiral), one of Mitscher's task group commanders, was even more aggressive. He wanted the two task groups returning from the Bonins to swoop down *behind* Ozawa. That would box him in between the task groups of TF 58. Because Clark couldn't raise Mitscher, he decided not to strike out on his own. After the war Mitscher told Jocko such an attempt should have been made.[44] Almost certainly it would have resulted in many exchanges between the opposing carriers.

At the meeting on *Rocky Mount*, Turner's flagship, Admiral Spruance was thinking more about defending the assets needed to complete the primary mission than about killing Japanese carriers. Howlin' Mad Smith asked him if he thought the Imperial Navy would run. The admiral replied, "No, not now. They are after big game. If they had wanted an easy victory, they could have disposed of the relatively small force covering MacArthur's operation at Biak." But the attack on the Marianas was too great a challenge for the Japanese navy to ignore. Smith described Spruance as "a highly competent but cautious sailor" who hoped to cripple the Japanese fleet so it could no longer interfere with American operations. Smith debarked to be with his marines on the island: "When I went ashore I had not the slightest apprehension."[45]

Almost all of the attendees, Spruance included, were certain the Japanese were setting up a strike on the transports. After questioning Turner on his self-defense capability, Spruance said, "Well get everything that you don't absolutely need out of here to the eastward, and I will join up with Mitscher and Task Force 58 and try to keep the Japs off your neck."[46] Spruance's cool demeanor steadied many in the room. The bombardment battleships and their escorts would form a defensive arc 25 miles west of the beachhead. They would be covered by aircraft from three escort carrier divisions. The 10,000-pound aggressive operations plan of the Airedales wasn't adopted. Captain Mahan would have been bitterly disappointed.

On shore, marine commanders continued to plot their advance across the island like the professional warriors they were. Watching the transports leave was a little disconcerting. But this was no Guadalcanal. In a few days they would be back. To show his resolve, Rear Admiral Harry Hill, commander of the landing ships, stayed alongside Saipan in his amphibious flagship, USS *Cambria*. The Japanese defenders must have cheered as hundreds of Yankee ships disappeared over the horizon at sunset. Much of the army's 27th Infantry Division, which hadn't been ordered ashore, left with the transports.

Showing confidence in his subordinate, Spruance left Mitscher in tactical command. To reduce the probability of a night end run by the Japanese, Admiral Spruance planned to steam west during the day, east at night. He wanted TF 58 to remain within supporting distance "until information of enemy requires other action." Mitscher steamed with three carrier groups on line with a battle line of seven battleships, four cruisers, and fourteen destroyers. A fourth carrier group sailed twelve miles north of the battle line to provide air support.

Despite all the technological advances made between 1942 and 1944, the Americans had not improved their inadequate aerial search patterns and procedures. American search aircraft, including radar-equipped PBMs from Saipan, did not find the Japanese on 17 June. For all their carping, the aviation admirals have something to answer for here.

Late the same day, Spruance received another sub report, fifteen ships. He knew Ozawa had at least forty. Was this smaller group a decoy to cover an Ozawa maneuver outflanking him beyond search range to get to the amphibians?

Mitscher read the report differently. Though only fifteen ships had been sighted, this was where the enemy's main body must lie. He asked Ching Lee if he wanted to form up his battleships from the carrier groups and seek a night engagement. His airmen could pounce on whatever was still burning at first light.

Thinking of what can happen in a night engagement when there is little information, Lee demurred: "Do not believe we should seek night engagement. Possible advantages of radar more than offset by difficulties of communications and lack of training in fleet tactics at night. Would press pursuit of damaged or fleeing enemy, however, at any time."[47] Chasing down cripples, accepted doctrine, is one thing. Voluntarily entering a pitch-black room and giving up all your advantages is not an opportunity to be embraced. If a meeting engagement had developed, Lee's seven fast battleships most likely would have bumped into the four battleships escorting the light carriers, *Yamato, Musashi, Haruna,* and *Kongo.* Maybe Lee would have won a glorious victory. Maybe monster 18-inch shells would have sent thousands of American battleship sailors to their deaths in the deep.

Mahan would have liked Mitscher's take-the-offensive spirit but concurred with Lee's assessment. A night gunnery/torpedo duel was one area where the Japanese could still meet the Americans measure for measure. Mahan admonished admirals to avoid melee combat. While Mahan supported aggressive action, he would have wanted an advantage before tackling the enemy fleet.

American air search on 18 June missed Ozawa by 60 miles. However, American officers grew increasingly anxious as Japanese aircraft came within sight of the U.S. carriers. Ozawa's searchers found their quarry at 1514. Some of his staffers wanted to launch a late afternoon raid. Ozawa wanted to hit the Americans with a hammer. This couldn't be done in the remaining light. He canceled a subordinates-planned launch and coolly calculated the navigating required to hit Mitscher full force in the morning.

About 2200 on the 18th, Spruance received RFDF (radio frequency direction finding) of Ozawa's position. In reality, the direction finding was accurate within forty miles, but "the fog of war" began to shroud this truth. Honolulu couldn't read a report from a sub and asked for retransmission. Spruance's radio operators reported this to their admiral. Spruance speculated that Japanese jamming might be responsible. If the sub had sighted the main body, its known position would place the enemy east-southeast of the direction-finding fix. Advancing to a launch site against the fix might place his TF 58 east of the enemy's true location. At 0115 a PBM scanned a 40-ship radar contact almost on top of the "Huff Duff" (high-frequency direction finder) location. That would have confirmed Ozawa's location, but Spruance didn't get this contact report for seven and a half hours.

Mitscher and his staff had been plotting Ozawa's progress all along. Each sighting and intercept clarified their notion of where Ozawa was heading. The Huff Duff intercept only reinforced their conclusion. The Airedales, especially their leader, smelled red meat. Mitscher and his staff understood the calculation of the "golden band" inside of which Ozawa was attempting to remain. Mitscher wanted to push west, set up for a dawn strike, and hammer the Japanese carriers into the Pacific. Confiding in his chief of staff, Arleigh Burke, Mitscher remarked, "It might be a hell of a battle for a while, but I think we can win it."[48] Captain Mahan's endorsement of the course of action would have been most enthusiastic.

Admiral Spruance's flagship, *Indianapolis,* was close by. Just before midnight, Mitscher instructed Burke to get on the TBS (talk between ships). Mitscher advised Spruance to turn west at 0130. This would place American carriers in ideal range of Ozawa's projected position at first daylight. Mitscher felt that the risk of being outflanked was small and that there was sufficient battleship and jeep-carrier-borne firepower with the invasion fleet for it to protect itself. He ordered a night search pattern to launch at 0200. (See Map 8.)

Spruance mulled over Mitscher's advice for an hour. Then he decided to remain on his eastward course. He radioed Mitscher, "[Submarine] *Stingray* more accurate than that determined by direction finder. . . . End run by other carrier groups must not be overlooked."[49] In a postwar explanation of this decision to Morison, Spruance wrote: "We were at the start of a very large and important amphibious operation and we could not gamble and place it in jeopardy."[50]

Mitscher, ever the loyal subordinate, quietly accepted Spruance's decision and retired to his sea cabin. But he couldn't get a wink of sleep. One of his staff re-

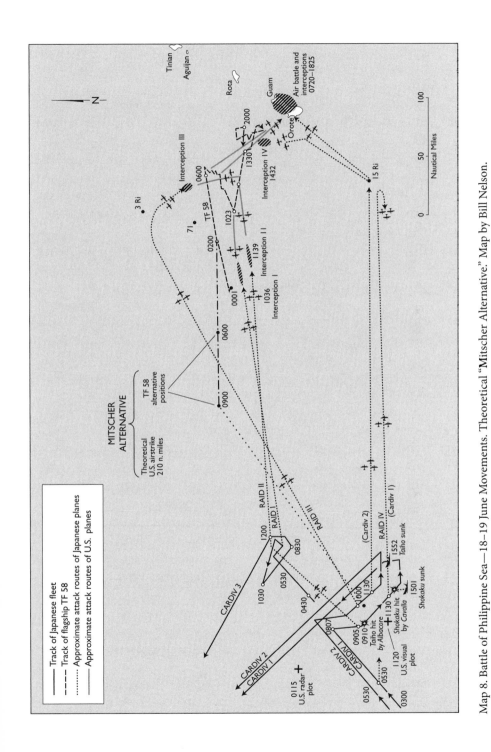

Map 8. Battle of Philippine Sea—18–19 June Movements. Theoretical "Mitscher Alternative." Map by Bill Nelson.

marked, "Every one of the pilots felt depressed when we heard we couldn't go."[51] The staff knew they would get hit in the morning by Ozawa but would be too far away for a counterstrike.

On Map 8 refer to the dashed track marked "Mitscher's alternative." If Mitscher had turned due west at 0130 and made 20 knots, this would have been his course. Mentally plot Ozawa's possible alternative tracks in the general direction east. There is no possible way of evading Mitscher. If Ozawa had followed his historical track (on Map 8), all American carriers would have been in position to deliver massive strikes on the Japanese fleet starting in the early morning. The carnage would have obviated most of the threat that appeared among the Philippine Islands in next two chapters.

During the night of the 18th–19th, Ozawa intended to stay in the golden band and launch his search aircraft before dawn. The huge size of Mitscher's task force made it easy to find. Ozawa never had any intention of maneuvering around Spruance and going for the transports.[52] June 19 was to be the day of decisive battle. By 0415 Ozawa was in position with 300 aircraft on six carrier decks. His first attack, 53 strikers and 16 Zeke escorts, lifted off at 0830. A larger attack launched from his big fleet carriers at 0900. It contained 80 bombers escorted by 48 fighters. His airmen lacked the skill to launch and form up into a single large strike. Unexpectedly a torpedo from the U.S. submarine *Albacore* hit *Taiho* during the launch. *Junyo* and *Hiyo* added a third strike of 22 bombers and 15 escorts at 1000. Yet another strike of 52 bombers and 30 escorts left the fleet carriers at 1100. While not overwhelming, the numbers were impressive.

The Americans didn't know the position of the Japanese fleet. All of the carrier group commanders, as well as Mitscher, were spoiling to take on the enemy fleet. Spruance suggested sending two task groups on a morning strike on Guam. Mitscher politely guided his boss's gaze back to the real object at hand. To assuage him, Mitscher ordered a fighter sweep over Guam to suppress any attack from that direction. Mahan would have smiled. Mitscher had delicately executed the most difficult task of a subordinate: correcting his boss.

At 0200 *Enterprise* had sent out 15 radar-equipped TBFs. Another search, launched at 0530, didn't find Ozawa. They came up 75 miles short. Had TF 58 turned west at 0130, Mitscher's carriers would have been at least 100 miles closer to Ozawa.

During the night, Japanese aircraft had moved up from Truk to Tinian and Guam. On the 19th, they began lifting off from Guam. Mitscher's fighters, investigating the Japanese activity, precipitated a fight over Guam, but did not prevent the Japanese from dispatching strikers against the American carriers.

During the morning and afternoon of the 19th, not a single American strike aircraft appeared over Ozawa's groups. The admiral had achieved something even better than crossing the enemy's T. He had launched multiple strikes without being hit in return. Had the year been 1942, either at Midway or the Eastern Solomons, Ozawa might have expected his airmen to inflict major damage and put a number of American carriers out of action if not actually sinking them. Even if the Americans did finally locate the Japanese, their counterstrike would be much reduced.

But this was 1944. Japanese airmen from Guam showed a little skill and were first to find the American fleet. Then Ozawa's strikes appeared. Instead of boring in, they stood off and circled to regain formation. Their lack of flying experience was obvious. American radio intercept officers picked up the plain Japanese-language transmission of the strike commander who orbited the area and issued detailed attack instructions to his apparently inexperienced charges. Circling gave American fighter directors added time to marshal their interceptors. Hellcats swarmed all over the incoming raiders. The first Japanese strike made only a minor hit on battleship *South Dakota*. Subsequent strikes inflicted a little damage on carrier *Bunker Hill* and cruiser *Indianapolis*, Spruance's flagship. By the end of day, 23 American planes had been shot down. Six were operational losses. But of 373 carrier aircraft committed, the Japanese lost 243. Another 50 from Guam never made it home.

The single torpedo launched from an American submarine that hit *Taiho* during her aircraft launch shouldn't have been a serious problem. *Tahio* was a well-built and heavily armored ship. But an inexperienced damage control officer, in an attempt to flush the ship of fuel fumes, opened all the ventilating shafts. Aviation gas fumes were sucked into the shafts, mixed with air, and sent the equivalent of fuel-air explosive all over the ship. She went up with a mighty blast that buckled both her bottom plates and her armored deck. A total of 1,650 crewmembers went down with the wreck. A little earlier *Shokaku*, one of the two surviving carriers that wore the Indian head decal of a Pearl Harbor veteran, had taken three torpedoes from yet another submarine. Gas fires started and spread to a bomb magazine. The resulting explosion tore the large ship apart.

Admiral Ozawa transferred his flag from *Taiho* to *Zuikaku*. Upon arriving on deck, he learned only 200 aircraft remained operational. His fleet wandered around its assembly area in a state of confusion. Captains were too afraid to refuel lest American raiders appear overhead. Ozawa wasn't completely sure of the extent of his aircraft losses. Perhaps some pilots had continued on to Guam. The Japanese admiral wanted to recover, refuel, and rearm on the 20th and resume strikes on the 21st. Returning flyers claimed four American carriers sunk (Japanese propagandists raised this fairy tale to eleven). But Ozawa was disconsolate. The offensive capability of Japanese naval air was at an end.

For most of the 19th, Mitscher's ships headed east to have wind over their flight decks for air operations. His gigantic task force sailed within sight of Rota and Guam. One carrier task group left to fuel and pound islands. The other three turned west under Spruance's orders. Mitscher failed to send out another search pattern, which might have caught Ozawa's force in its confused, disorganized state.[53]

Ever aggressive, Mitscher launched his strikers very late in the day even though Ozawa's location was not known. American officers guessed the bearing of Ozawa's fleet from his returning air strikes. Crews scurried across flight decks to get their brood off before the radar blips turned into flame-spitting meatballs. Ozawa had turned west two hours earlier to open the range and maintain the "golden band." Actual range between enemy fleets was about 325 miles.

Despite the fading light, American airmen found Ozawa's carriers and struck with over 200 aircraft. *Hiyo* sank. *Ryujo* escaped with minor damage. *Junyo* was damaged, as were some surface combatants. *Zuikaku* absorbed so many hits that Ozawa thought she would have to be abandoned.

Late launch meant the strikers would have to return at night. A night landing on board a pitching carrier is about the most difficult feat any airman has to master. As they prepared the launch, everyone had known there would be trouble when the strikers returned.

Recovering aircraft took two hours. Disregarding the submarine threat, Mitscher used deck lights to aid night landing. His pilots loved him for the concern for their safety he always showed. Despite this effort, more American aircraft were lost during the night landings than during the day's combat. Fortunately, many of their aircrew were fished up from the dark but warm waters. Eighty aircraft splashed but only 16 pilots and 33 crewmen were lost. When the final count was made, Ozawa's mobile fleet lost about 475 planes and about 445 aviators. The U.S. lost 76 aviators, including 49 from the late strike of 20 June. Good air-sea rescue had saved many American lives.

Spruance started to give Ozawa chase but it became apparent he wasn't going to catch him. At first, the Japanese admiral called on his battle fleet to prepare for surface engagement. Soon he thought better of the idea. Ozawa retired to Okinawa with 50 planes. Nagumo, the Japanese admiral who had been in tactical command at Midway and Eastern Solomons, had been demoted to island commander on Saipan. Later in the campaign, he would shoot himself in a cave.

Ozawa had clearly "out-admiraled" Spruance. He maneuvered his weapon well. Unfortunately it had no cutting edge. The skills of the 1944 U.S. Navy and the technical superiority of its equipment made the result *almost* inevitable. No amount of admiralship could overcome these overwhelming advantages. Had he had Yamamoto's weapon, Ozawa would have severely wounded the American force. Mahan gave great weight to able leaders. He also gave great weight to well-trained crews. Missing one of the two repeatedly proved to be a losing combination for the emperor.

The Turkey Shoot Reconsidered

Before the battle of the Philippine Sea, neither side could admit to itself how poorly prepared Japanese naval aviators were. The "bean count" of airplanes between the opposing sides depicted a fighting chance for the Japanese. But history is replete with battles where well-trained, experienced troops slaughter many times their numbers of untrained enemy. Mahan underlined the importance of well-trained crew. Many of Ozawa's aviators had but two months' flying experience. Mitscher's boys had two years.[54] It was almost the reverse of early 1942. Ozawa had 222 fighters and 200 attack planes. Mitscher's ships carried 500 fighters and 400 strikers. Admiral Kakuji Kakuta, who commanded land-based planes, misled Ozawa about the extent of his losses.[55]

As he did at Tarawa, Spruance chose what appeared to be the most conservative, the most prudent option. By ordering Mitscher to turn east, Spruance virtually eliminated any chance that the Japanese task group could penetrate to the transports. What if the Japanese carriers had remained in the "golden band" of ranges? No one had seen Japanese carriers in action in a year. Perhaps experienced pilot reserves made them a potent force. If so, they might inflict severe damage to some American carriers. Spruance might have been faced with the choice of sacrificing them or continuing to maneuver to defend the beachhead. But a bold move west would have brought the Japanese carrier group within range where superior American numbers were likely to prevail. More aggressive maneuvering of the American carriers could have brought more safety, not less.

There is a reason why wartime admirals have such furrowed faces.

Most of the air admirals were critical of Spruance's performance. As might be expected, Towers was particularly vociferous. The air admirals would argue that even if the battleships had gotten east of Spruance, the striking range of aircraft would have been sufficient to sink them before they entered the formations of amphibians. But that depended on where the battleships were. Had air search located the Japanese task groups on the 18th, navigator's geometry could have calculated the best location for Spruance's various forces. That failing comes home to roost with the Airedales.

Had he been on Spruance's flagship, there is no question that Mahan would have counseled more aggressive action. Even if carrier pilot quality was equal for the opponents, which was unlikely, Spruance had a 2:1 edge in raw numbers. Mahan always counseled decisive engagement of the enemy fleet when you had the advantage. In addition to numerical advantage, American technical advantage was apparent to everyone by June 1944. Spruance could properly point to his orders from Nimitz to protect the invasion force rather than destroy the enemy fleet. Nimitz must be roundly criticized for not instructing Spruance to destroy the Imperial Fleet should it appear. After all, he had told King this instruction had been issued.

Clausewitz wrote that one must accept great risks in order to decisively defeat one's enemy. Admiral Spruance didn't appear ready to accept even a small risk. One of Mahan's basic tenets was that the fleet that sought to dominate must take the offensive. Naval warfare contains a lot of risk. We have seen what can happen in six minutes. The risks facing Spruance were comparatively small. He had overwhelming air strength at sea that no rational observer could deny. The risk to Turner's transports was minimal. Japanese capital ships would have had to steam another 450 miles to get within gun range. The transports were under way and would have to be located. A line of Oldendorf's sturdy old battleships stood in the way. Over 150 aircraft from the jeep carriers, half of them fighters, backed them up. The best thing that could have happened is that the Japanese would get caught between the two American forces. Their total annihilation would have been almost a certainty. American battleships would have cleaned up a lot of cripples that had no path of escape. There would have been no Japanese ships to create what would go down as the largest naval fight in history, just off the Philippines during the subsequent invasion of those islands.

There is a major asymmetry between Spruance's situation and either Ozawa's or Nimitz's at Midway. Spruance could win without taking a major risk. The other two faced a desperate situation. It is difficult to capture the enormous weight of the risk in words. One should not discount its impact.

The Big Blue Fleet could take care of itself very well. A long series of carrier operations before 15 June 1944 had established that for anyone willing to take an unbiased view. During the fight for the Marianas, a series of unanswered major strikes hit Mitscher's carriers at the beginning of the battle. The strikers lost heavily for a couple of inconsequential lucky hits. Air-to-air combat over the American fleet was a disaster for the Japanese. Had Spruance followed Mitscher's advice on the evening of the 18th and generated a major air strike on Ozawa on the morning of the 19th, so much the better. But Spruance concluded he must remain within air-striking distance of Saipan to provide Turner's fleet proper security.

Eight years later, Spruance wrote to Morison: "I think that going out after the Japanese and knocking their carriers out would have been much better and more satisfactory than waiting for them to attack us; but we were at the start of a very important and large amphibious operation and we could not afford to gamble and place it in jeopardy."[56] Right after the battle, Commodore Arleigh Burke prepared a report critical of Spruance's performance at the Philippine Sea. Mitscher read it and agreed it was true. However, the wizened admiral thought it didn't make any difference and told Burke to tone it down.

Towers demanded that Nimitz fire Spruance for his inappropriate handling of the carriers. Nimitz thought Spruance did well. Arriving in Saipan in July 1944, he told Spruance, "You did a damn fine job there." Turner also approved of Spruance's decisions. In a 1949 presentation before the General Line School, he stated, "To capture Saipan, we needed the transports afloat and not sunk. Suppose at 0800 of June 19th Admiral Mitscher had been 600 miles away with all his planes in the air! Admiral Spruance's decision to adhere strictly to a course of action that would ensure the accomplishment of the major objective of that great military adventure was sound and wise."[57]

Saipan, Guam, and Tinian Taken

The Marshalls, Carolines, and Gilberts are hard coral that has been thrust only a few meters above sea level. The Marianas are volcanic and are characterized by rugged mountains rising as much as 1,500 feet. Unlike the atolls, there are no large lagoons. Harbors among the islands are small and not suitable for sheltering immense fleets. However, there is a lot of room to build logistic complexes and sufficient space for wharfs for the cargo ships. There is plenty of fairly level ground on which to construct airfields and crushed coral is good runway building material.

The tiny central Pacific atolls have dry land measured in a few acres. The main islands of the Marianas all are substantial in size. They had been Japanese possessions since World War I. Saipan and Tinian were Japan's sugar islands. Smaller Tinian, 50 square miles, was the center of the trade as 90 percent of its relatively flat plateau was tillable. The island measures about 12 miles long but only 5 miles at its widest. The 1,554-foot Mount Tapotchau at its center dominates the irregular shape of mountainous Saipan's 72 square miles. The southern tip of Saipan is but 6 miles from the northern tip of Tinian. In 1944, virtually all of Tinian's 18,000 inhabitants were Japanese settlers. Native Chamorros had been displaced to smaller islands not involved with sugar. Most Japanese viewed these islands as part of Japan, the way Americans viewed Hawaiian territory as part of their country. After all, the distance between Tinian and Tokyo was half that from Honolulu to Los Angeles. That is also why American control of the Marianas was so directly threatening.

Guam, by far the largest of the islands, covers 225 square miles. It is about 30 miles long southwest to northeast and varies between 4 and 8 miles wide. America acquired Guam as a result of the war with Spain in 1898. Various naval treaties prohibited its fortification, and before the war the island had generally been treated with benign neglect. The small naval garrison got along well with the local population of about 21,000. The southern end of the island is cut by a number of small, fertile valleys that sheltered most of the local agriculture at the time. The island's north end is made up of a jungle-covered plateau. Apia harbor is the best in the Marianas. Because Guam was unfortified, the Japanese took it quickly in December 1941.

When Japanese air corps planners began looking for an alternative to basing B-29s in China, they needed enough land to base 1,000 of the mammoth aircraft. The Marianas fit this requirement.

American intelligence badly underestimated Japanese strength on Saipan. Due to the presence of many shipwrecked servicemen, about 31,600 Japanese military were on the island, double the U.S. estimate. The defenders included a 26-tank regiment. Everyone understood that the Marianas were part of the final defense line for the Home Islands. These weren't remote unknown outposts someplace down in the South Pacific. Instructions from Tokyo told the defenders of the Marianas: "The Mariana Islands are Japan's final defensive line. Loss of these islands signifies Japan's surrender."[58]

Until late in the war Japan never thought it would have to defend the Marianas against direct invasion. Few fortifications were laid down before the beginning of 1944. Coastal defense guns had not yet been sited. Few trenches and blockhouses had been constructed. American attacks on Saipan-bound shipping deprived the garrison of needed construction materials. Two engineer regiments assigned to fortify the island arrived only two months before the invasion. At the last minute, the Japanese tried to reinforce Saipan. However, the Truk commander said he lacked shipping. Two infantry companies and a few field pieces left Guam on barges, but wound up on the small island of Rota to the south. They remained there for the duration.

The Japanese contemplated a strong defense at the shoreline combined with a mobile defense in the area behind the better landing beaches.[59] Saipan's defenders included two army divisions: the 29th, which had moved from Manchuria to Saipan in February, and the 43rd, which had arrived from Japan in May. Over 1,400 troops of the 29th Division had been lost when Americans sank one of their transports. The navy had 55th and 65th Naval Guard Forces in place. Nine thousand Japanese, including ground elements of seven air squadrons, were available to defend the island. Most of the defenses were situated in the south and west to cover the large beaches. Again one can estimate the lesser resistance a faster-moving American offensive might have encountered. A U.S. Marine Corps engineer study estimated that an October 1944 landing would have been three times as costly and difficult as the actual one in June.[60]

Turner's amphibious plan for Saipan was straightforward and unimaginative. The horrible burden Admiral Turner had carried since the beginning of the war had taken its toll on the man. He constantly complained about being exhausted. His heavy drinking became more noticeable. Ever the gentleman, Raymond Spruance covered for his subordinate—as long as Turner's condition didn't affect his work.

Four assault regiments from two marine divisions would land on the best beaches on the southwestern part of the island. They would work their way across the island, then turn north toward the large central mountain to finish clearing resistance.

Saipan's Japanese commander didn't think the preliminary bombardment was prelude to the invasion. Nevertheless the marines had a tough time at the waterline. They came ashore at the point most heavily defended. Japanese artillery exacted a heavy toll of Americans compacted along the narrow beachhead. At least sixteen 105mm and thirty 75mm field pieces were behind the first reverse slope near the invasion beaches, which shielded them from the low-trajectory bombardment from the ships' guns. Two 150mm batteries of four guns each were also within range. Wave after wave of LVTs intermixed and added to the wreckage along the beach. Field-grade marine commanders took charge and sorted it out. But not before a heavy price was paid. Holland Smith's operations officer remarked that "the most critical stage of the battle for Saipan was the fight for the beaches, for the security of the landing beaches, for sufficient area into which troops and heavy equipment could be brought."[61]

While marine units showed a great deal of aggressiveness, their tactical handling was not without room for improvement. Even Howlin' Mad commented that marine units had failed to call for massed artillery fires and failed to follow up artillery preparations with quick assault. "Infantry will closely follow artillery concentrations and attack ruthlessly when the artillery lifts. Absence of tanks is no excuse for failure of infantry to press home the attack."[62]

Based on the fighting for the beaches, the army's 27th Infantry Division (27ID), the floating reserve, was hurried ashore. It was inserted between the marine divisions for a sweep across the island. Much of the fighting for Saipan was characterized by "bang ahead" frontal assault. Both the 2nd Marine and 4th Marine divisions showed greater stomach for this kind of combat than did 27ID. The New York National Guardsmen confronted a heavily defended depression dubbed "Death Valley." It ran between Mount Tapotchau in the northwest and "Purple Heart Ridge" to the southeast. The army made little progress into the valley while marine divisions to either side advanced. Soon each had an open interior flank exposed because 27ID hadn't advanced. Leadership of the 27th had not failed for lack of trying. A regimental commander, three battalion commanders, and twenty-two company commanders of the 106th and 165th regiments became casualties on Saipan. Only 18 rifle companies were committed.

Dogfaces felt they faced tougher defense and terrain than the marines on their flanks. Attacking straight up a valley when the enemy is dug deeply into both ridges that form it is not conducive to living a long life. In a tactically correct solution, Major General Ralph Smith, commanding 27ID, planned to move a regiment southeast of the ridge. Its mission was to attack farther down the ridge away from its most heavily defended area and then to work back along it, thereby freeing the remainder of the division to advance.

Dissatisfied with the slow pace of 27ID, Howlin' Mad Smith didn't wait to see if the maneuver would solve the problem. After conferring with Turner and Spruance, he relieved 27ID's commander. His successor executed the attack that Ralph Smith planned.

In fairness to Howlin' Mad, 27ID was not exactly a pack of raging tigers. The American infantry frequently became disorganized when it met any significant resistance. Time after time, local commanders ordered, or allowed, forward companies to fall back to the line of departure instead of defending whatever gain they had made.

Some historians have pointed out that the fight for Saipan was as costly, on a proportional basis, as Tarawa. Four thousand soldiers and marines died on Saipan (2,518 marines, 1,465 army). There were 14,100 casualties, about 20 percent of the landing force of 71,000. The casualty list was twice as long as the one at Guadalcanal. Japanese dead topped 30,000. At Tarawa, 2nd Marine Division also lost about 25 percent, 3,300 casualties out of a landing force of 12,000. This simple comparison, which doesn't reflect significant tactical differences, misses a far more important point. Saipan was an important strategic objective, and it forced the Japanese fleet into battle on unfavorable terms. Tarawa was not, and did not.

Initially Admiral Turner wanted to mirror-image the invasion of Saipan on Tinian. He wanted to land the marines on the best beaches in the south near Tinian Town. Of course, this was the best-defended terrain on the island.

Both Howlin' Mad Smith and General Harry Schmidt, who had commanded 4th Marine Division since it was formed, objected to attacking into the teeth of the Japanese defenses. Instead, Schmidt wanted to land on very small but less defended beaches to the north. These would be within range of extensive American artillery firing across the five-mile-wide channel between it and Saipan. Turner balked. The northern beaches were only 200–400 yards wide and blocked by 4- to 6-foot cliffs and low sea walls.

Neither Admiral Hill, Turner's subordinate who would command the immediate assault force, nor Howlin' Mad Smith liked the Tinian Town plan. Turner was adamant and ordered them to plan a frontal assault at Tinian Town. Smith became just as adamant that they would land on the small beaches in the north and that the landing force commander, not the delivering admiral, would have the last word. The argument went on for hours "and generated considerable unprintable language."[63] The general finally extracted a promise from the admiral that no final decision would be made until the results of beach recon were analyzed. Navy frogmen supported by marine recon landed at night. As the navy men took their measurements, they could hear Japanese construction parties using explosives to dig in bunkers. By attacking the north shore, landing craft could debark straight from Saipan and take advantage of massed artillery sited there. However, any screwup in the landing of supplies could hopelessly tie up these tiny beaches.

Admiral Hill took the impasse to Spruance, who convened a conference. After everyone endorsed the north beaches, Turner announced he was in favor of them as well.

A very successful feint at Tinian Town evoked tremendous Japanese response. For example, the battleship *Colorado* was hit 22 times by 6-inch coastal guns. She, and a destroyer that took six hits, suffered 62 killed and 245 wounded.

While 2nd Division marines made a demonstration of boarding landing craft opposite Tinian Town, 4th Division marines approached the north beaches in columns of companies because of the narrowness of the target beaches. A sharp but short firefight cleared the beach entrances of the small number of defenders. Attacking columns proceeded inland. Each regiment took about three hours to land. Ramps were preconstructed and emplaced to speed vehicles off the beach. The first day's casualties were 15 Marines killed and 225 wounded versus a Japanese body count of 438. Compared to Saipan, the price in American blood was small. The 2nd Marine Division landed behind 4th Marine Division the next day.

A smooth, tank-assisted sweep of the island ground up the defenders. The last desperate banzai charge at end left 600–800 dead but never penetrated marine positions. Compared to almost 4,000 American dead on Saipan, the marines lost only 328 killed on Tinian. Japanese dead were pegged at 8,000. In eight days marines controlled the island.

Howlin' Mad said it best: "We completely outfoxed them at Tinian and vindicated the soundness of the most unorthodox plan of assault ever attempted in the Pacific. We sneaked in the back door, uninvited and unexpected while the Japanese waited for us at the front door. Surprise, fatal to Japanese mentality, threw them completely of balance."[64] Had this spirit been imbued in the senior admirals at the strategic level, the war and the army and marine casualty lists would have been shorter.

Everyone involved had good words for the leadership displayed at Tinian. Admiral Spruance stated, "The Tinian operation was probably the most brilliantly conceived amphibious operation conceived in World War II."[65] Smith wrote, "Tinian was the perfect amphibious operation in the Pacific war."[66]

The contrast between Saipan and Tinian underscores the need for each branch to be free to use its expertise to employ its forces. Allowing naval officers to properly deploy their carriers and generals to employ their troops and then resolving any conflicts *after* expert consideration of each set of problems is the way to minimize casualties and achieve success. Left to his devices MacArthur could have misused carriers as badly as admirals misunderstood the employment of troops at Tarawa and Saipan. As we shall see, the lesson that was not learned resulted in the carnage that would be Iwo Jima.

Guam

Documents captured on Saipan provided an accurate picture of Guam's defenses. The Japanese concentrated on protecting Apia harbor on the west coast and the airfields situated near it. "Close-In" Connolly led the pre-invasion bombardment, which lasted 13 days. The pattern of the bombardment and actions of UDT (underwater demolition team) men performing their recon gave the Japanese a good idea of where the Americans would land. Marines under Major General Roy Geiger landed on Guam on the 21st of July. His III Marine Amphibious Force included 3rd Marine Division, 1st Provisional Marine Brigade, and an "Army of the United States" (read "draftees") division, the 77th, initially raised from New Yorkers. After many disparaging remarks about "doggie" outfits, many marines found the 77th just as aggressive as their compatriots in marine green.

Until the winter of 1944, Guam was poorly defended. At the end of February 1944, the Japanese 29th Division in Manchuria was notified it would travel to Pusan and then depart for Guam. By the time of the invasion about 18,500 troops defended Guam. From January to June, 45,000 troops were dispatched to the Marianas. Of these, 3,600 were lost at sea. Maybe 5,000 of the remainder were unequipped stragglers whose weapons had gone down with their transports. Both Admirals Toyoda and Koga before him wanted great aerial strength transferred into the Marianas. Under construction were fourteen airfields and two seaplane bases that could accommodate the 600 aircraft that were expected.

The fight for the beach at Guam was a tough one. Marines suffered many casualties until they took a strong enemy position that could fire on the invasion beaches. Veteran units braced for the usual first-night counterattacks. Instead, the tank-led Japanese counterassault came the next morning. Shermans dismantled Japanese armor at close range. Heavy Japanese casualties left gaps that the Americans exploited in their advance. Several other fierce counterattacks punctuated the following days. In one, a marine battalion suffered 50 percent casualties—but held. In another, Japanese charged directly into concentrated American artillery. The final push up the island toward the last Japanese bastion at Santa Rosa placed 3rd Marine Division on the left and 77th Infantry Division on the right. Using an entire tank battalion as a single concentrated maneuver unit, the army made the final assault. The human toll was high. When it was all over 8,780 Americans had become casualties, including 2,124 dead. Of the Japanese garrison, 11,000 lay dead. Almost another 10,000 scattered into the jungle on the north side of the island. They provided combat training for American troops until the end of the war. (A few holdouts continued to run through the boonies until 1960!) The ground pounders also uncovered the primary Japanese liquor store for the Marianas. At least they had a little consolation.

"The effect of our seizure of the Marianas Islands upon informed opinion in Japan was very striking, and it was recognized almost immediately that Saipan was the decisive battle of the war, and that its loss removed hope for a Japanese victory."[67] General Smith stated, "I have always considered Saipan the decisive battle of the Pacific campaign."[68] Tojo announced to country "a great national crisis of unprecedented proportions." Many millions of Japanese realized the war was lost.

One person, the only person who really mattered, wasn't willing to admit this—Emperor Hirohito. The emperor understood that Tokyo would shortly be within range of hundreds of B-29s. Someone had to go. Hirohito had become increasingly disenchanted with Tojo's leadership. Tojo had only recently, on February 17, increased his grip on Japan by sacking the army chief of staff and assuming his duties. Criticism around him had increased. Prince Chichibu, referring to his increasing attempt to control everything, called him "Emperor Tojo."[69] In an offhand rebuke of his intellectual powers, some army officers referred to Tojo as Jotohei ("superior private"). But he didn't have to worry about the stability of his position as long as he had the emperor's support.

With the loss of the Marianas, the emperor withdrew his support from Tojo. Tojo attempted to retain some form of diminished power by relinquishing some of his offices and negotiating with his Japanese enemies. They would have none of it. Alone among former prime ministers, he was refused a seat on the Council of Elder Statesmen.

Tojo blamed his lackey, Navy Minister Admiral Shigetaro Shimada, for the fall of Saipan. This drove an even greater wedge between army and navy, making interservice coordination even more difficult. The new government attempted to heal this rift with efforts promulgated under the banner "harmony between Army and Navy."

Had American leadership understood these machinations, they might have realized that in Hirohito they were dealing with a dictator the likes of Hitler. When one person has that much power, the ultimate war objective is to convince *him* that he has been beaten. Those American leaders who feared only a grinding invasion and subjugation of Honshu had a concrete reason for their concern in the mindset of the emperor. Would Mahan have realized this? At the level of naval strategy, it didn't matter. Whether the end state was blockade or invasion, the facilitating precondition was the destruction of Japan's carrier airpower, by eliminating the carriers or the pilots.

MacArthur's Advance

As of April 1944, after the Marshalls had fallen and while Spruance prepared to advance into the Marianas, the Japanese still had an enormous number of troops in the southwest Pacific. Some 60,000 in the 18th Army remained in eastern New Guinea. Another 50,000 occupied western New Guinea, and 80,000 remained in the Solomons and Bismarcks. Behind them were 50,000 in the Dutch East Indies and 100,000 in the Philippines, including about 45,000 ground troops. Compare this to the 31st Army defending the central Pacific, which controlled about 60,000 troops.

Imperial Headquarters recognized in March that the forces in New Guinea were lost. Japan simply didn't have the transport to evacuate them. On 14 March those formations were ordered to hold the best they could.[70] That also meant there was little reason to conduct additional ground combat against them. General Kenney's airmen were strong enough to destroy what little offensive air-power remained and to maintain the blockade.

MacArthur's campaign in western New Guinea was an operational master-piece. The jump to Hollandia was breathtaking. But the campaign amounted to a strategic null. MacArthur's 1,400-mile drive from Madang to Morotai did not generate a long casualty list. That is, as long as you were not one of the loved ones of the 1,630 men who lost their lives in combat during this operation. Over 26,000 Japanese also lost their lives. Central Pacific operations in the Marianas and Palau cost 7,000 Americans their lives along with 46,000 Japanese. (Of those Americans, 3,400 died during the taking of Saipan.) Some, including MacArthur, have argued that the length of these two American casualty lists demonstrate something important. They do not. The central Pacific drive attained important strategic objectives. After an 18-month hiatus, the Japanese carrier fleet was drawn into battle and its aviation destroyed in the Great Marianas Turkey Shoot. Bases capable of sustaining the B-29 offensive against Japan were secured. The inner defense line of Japan itself was shattered, which precipitated the fall of the Tojo government. Ulithi, the most important naval base west of Honolulu, was secured for a song.

By 1944, the American navy had learned much about sustaining fleets that ranged a long way from home port. Despite a shortage of refrigerated replenishment ships, naval supply officers could provide fresh provisions over 80 percent of the time. Ships could stay at sea as long as "sixty days before the sailors began serious grumbling about their food."[1]

Refueling at sea had long since been mastered. The Big Blue Fleet had eight refueling units, each with three fleet oilers. Escort carriers sailed with the refueling groups to provide fleet carriers with replacement aircraft.

Repair ships carried 5,000 line items of repair parts and could fabricate major items in their machine shops. Floating drydocks could lift many vessels from the sea to effect major repairs. Ammunition ships transferred prodigious tonnages of bombs and shells. Augmenting thirty-four fleet oilers, tankers moved millions of barrels of black oil, aviation gas, and motor gas for troops ashore. But transfer of such heavy cargo and most repairs still could not be performed in the swells of the open ocean. The fleet needed protected anchorage to complete these tasks.

Even before the Marianas campaign, it was clear the fast carriers could operate anywhere they pleased. One of the places that pleased was Ulithi, an atoll in the Palaus with a beautiful lagoon. Only five Japanese weathermen were found there. Service Squadron 10 moved in and created the greatest and westernmost of the navy's operating bases in World War II. The fleet needed no more stepping-stones before taking on the final objective: Japan.

Ulithi was the prime example of the fact that many unoccupied locations could provide good sites for American bases. Japanese-occupied islands needed to be tackled only when they supported forces capable of projecting combat power over long distances. Fighters and attack aircraft ranging only several hundred miles from island bases had little impact on the American fleet's ability to transit the vast Pacific. This underscored the fundamental point that Mahan constantly repeated. Concentrate on the enemy fleet. Destroy it and then you are free to go where you please.

With the complete freedom of maneuver brought about by the destruction of the enemy's battle line—its carrier groups—the critical point, the Clausewitzian center of gravity, became the Japanese national government located in the Home Islands. All else could be ignored once the Americans were ready to deal with them. How to take them on was still an open question. Would an invasion be required? If not, a very good blockade would be needed. It might be possible to defeat Japan solely by aerial bombardment. Brigadier General Lawrence Kuter, one of General Arnold's air planners, confided to General Kenney that many on the air staff thought B-29 bombardment just might force Japan out of the war even before an invasion of the Philippines or Formosa was completed.[2] But no one who did not wear a U.S. Army Air Forces uniform believed this would work.

Initially B-29s from the Marianas could only lift 30 percent of a full bomb load if they carried sufficient fuel for very high altitude approach. By changing tactics and equipment loads, General LeMay would substantially improve on this. But in the spring of 1944 it was apparent to everyone that the American armed forces would need one more base closer than the Marianas to take the final objective. It had to be close enough to allow medium-range aircraft to strike the Home Islands and had to have enough land mass to support an invasion army group. Luzon was not close enough to meet the first criterion. Formosa was better but still not ideal.

Which Way to Tokyo?

The army and the navy always had diverging views on the proper course to steer through the western Pacific. "In the Navy view," wrote King afterward, "all operations were aimed at a drive through the Pacific, probably via Formosa, to China thus by-passing the Philippines."[3] As we have seen earlier, for MacArthur there was no route but the route to the Philippines.

In Washington, the navy displayed a solid front. No one dared defy the man who shaved with a blowtorch. Out in the Pacific, King's commanders were nowhere near as sanguine. As Howlin' Mad Smith astutely observed, Nimitz was not as optimistic or aggressive after Tarawa as he had been at Midway and Guadalcanal. After the Marianas, Nimitz wanted to use carriers to raid the Philippines in order to precipitate another major fleet action.[4] Nimitz wanted to get a base in the southern Philippines first. Halsey was ready to invade the Philippines but not "Formosa which I considered more redoubtable and more useless than the Palaus."[5]

Upon his return to Washington from his Goodenough Island meeting with MacArthur in December 1943, Marshall did what he could to expedite additional aircraft to the southwest Pacific. Heartened by evidence of sincere support from Marshall, MacArthur began to worry that talk of his presidential candidacy might spike his efforts to return to the Philippines.[6] Might Roosevelt curtail support for his effort and favor the navy's central Pacific drive? Less southwest Pacific publicity might yield a less formidable opponent for the incumbent in the fall 1944 presidential elections. MacArthur dispatched General Sutherland to Washington to buttress his case for assault on the Philippines from the southwest Pacific. Nimitz sent Forrest Sherman back to Washington at the same time. Marshall assured Sutherland that events were turning in favor of MacArthur's views. Meanwhile Sherman had to do little to reinforce the central Pacific strategy to King. When the two chiefs met, King proposed retaining the two-pronged drive but designating the central Pacific as the main effort. Marshall responded that the Joint Planners should study the matter and come up with a recommendation.

Earlier, Brigadier General Osborn of the War Department staff had returned from meetings with MacArthur with a personal communiqué from the Commander of the Southwest Pacific to the Secretary of War.[7] MacArthur wrote that Roosevelt might be slanted in the wrong direction, but Secretary Stimson might prove to be the proper counterweight to return the ship of state to its proper course in the Pacific. A lifelong Republican, Stimson had also been governor general of the Philippines.

In his missive, MacArthur recounted his leapfrogging tactics that had advanced American air bases against the enemy at low cost in American lives. He compared this to the "frontal attacks by the Navy, as at Tarawa, are tragic and unnecessary massacres of American Lives. . . . The Navy fails to understand the strategy of the Pacific, fails to recognize that the first phase is an Army phase to establish land-based air protection so the Navy can move in." These words are antithetical to both the teachings of Mahan and the strategy promulgated by the carrier-minded admirals of the navy.

MacArthur made an impassioned appeal: "Mr. Roosevelt is Navy minded. Mr. Stimson must speak to him, must persuade him. Give me central direction of the war in the Pacific, and I will be in the Philippines in ten months."

King and Nimitz met in San Francisco on 5–6 May 1944 to discuss what came after the Marianas. Nimitz and Halsey had previously pointed out the repercussions of bypassing Mindanao. Savvy Cooke pointed out that operations in mainland China would face far more Japanese army resistance than an invasion of Formosa. He recommended invading Formosa in November 1944. If the Formosa operation could be advanced, the island could be taken with fewer than the twelve divisions Nimitz had been estimating. In June 1944 intelligence revealed Japan was reinforcing island garrisons, including Formosa. That meant the earlier the invasion, the better. King mused that seven divisions might be sufficient. Whether with seven or twelve divisions, conquering Formosa would be a job for the army.

Nimitz still saw landings in mainland China and supplying the Nationalist Chinese Army as important objectives. Attacking the Home Islands via Korea was also identified as an option. Nimitz and Cooke agreed that an operation against Korea would be amphibious, not overland from China. Cooke believed a firm anchor on the Chinese coast would secure the final blockade of the Home Islands. An invasion might still be required.

After the Marianas, the Imperial General Staff expected a Philippine invasion next. Ultra was filling in the picture for the Allies. Twenty thousand reinforcements were routed to the Philippines to upgrade four brigades to divisions. The first large East Indies island east of New Guinea, initially MacArthur's next objective, was fortified heavily and reinforce with 350 aircraft. Two air divisions from Manchuria and two additional air regiments from Burma were transferred into the Philippines, more than doubling Japanese air strength in these islands. An army division came down from Korea and occupied the southern Philippine island of Mindanao. MacArthur could see that Japan was turning his beloved Philippines into a major defensive bulwark.

General Marshall warned MacArthur about the increasing strength being deployed against his advance into the Philippines.[8] Marshall clearly anticipated the

Pacific drive would require entry into China. He wrote that "culmination of the war against Japan undoubtedly will involve the use of a portion of the China coast." General Marshall leaned toward an invasion of Formosa on 1 November, which would "come, therefore, more or less as a complete surprise." Instead of hitting the hard outer crust being formed in the Philippines, General Marshall wanted to follow the time-honored strategy of "hitting them where they ain't," a phrase Americans have been inculcated to associate with MacArthur. Marshall wanted to use the carrier fleet to hit Kyushu, the southernmost of the Japanese Home Islands, which would shut down sea and air communications between Japan and its possessions to the south. "There would be lift for six divisions, with a follow up of three divisions" to Formosa by 1 November. "There is little doubt, however, that after a crushing blow is delivered against the Japanese fleet then we should go as close to Japan as quickly as possible in order to shorten the war."

General Marshall cautioned MacArthur "not to allow our personal feelings and Philippine personal consideration to override our great objective, which is the early conclusion of the war with Japan." His cable was blunt: "In my view, 'bypassing' is in no way synonymous with 'abandonment.'" Marshall and King were in agreement: Formosa.

General MacArthur replied: "The proposal to bypass the Philippines and launch an attack across the Pacific directly against Formosa is unsound . . . The occupation of Luzon is essential in order to establish Air Forces and bases prior to the move on Formosa. . . . I do not believe a direct assault without air support can possibly succeed."[9] MacArthur still did not, did not *want*, to get it. He did not recognize the air superiority the Big Blue Fleet could establish wherever it conducted operations.

Marshall increasingly did not want America to fight its way through the ground strength Japan was accumulating in the Philippines. Staff studies were under way to determine whether early invasion of Formosa or Kyushu would hit the Japanese before their defenses were prepared. The chief of staff had learned something since Tasks One through Three down in the Solomons.

Mahan would have had a great deal to add to this debate. What was the objective of the war? Defeat of Japan. The ability of the Imperial Fleet to disrupt and destroy American operations to directly attack the homeland was the principal obstacle to achieving that objective. While the Japanese fleet hadn't been totally crushed, the Great Marianas Turkey Shoot demonstrated that it had been emasculated. Neither it nor land-based aviation could constrain the Big Blue Fleet from going wherever it wanted. Attack only those landmasses required for the final solution to Japan, be that blockade, bombardment, or invasion. That wasn't the Philippines. It might not even be Formosa.

Lieutenant General Joseph T. McNarney, deputy chief of staff and a man on whom Marshall relied, wanted to bypass the Philippines entirely. So did General Arnold. True to form, General Marshall wanted to proceed directly to Kyushu.[10] Mahan would have been far more comfortable in the company of these generals. A direct attack on Kyushu would have to plan to deal with a sortie of the Japanese battleship line. By hiding in coastal waters and approaching at night, they might reach the assault transports and kill a lot of American servicemen if they weren't sunk beforehand. After the initial beachhead was taken, the carriers would make little difference as there was plenty of space ashore at existing airfields. The principal naval threat would be battleships and kamikaze boats seeking to intermix with American amphibians.

To sort out the competing arguments, we need to review earlier positions on China, its potential role in the Great Pacific War, and alternative paths to Japan. The prewar Plan Orange had been predicated on a central Pacific offensive of the fewest possible hops culminating in the recapture of the Philippines. Early versions circled Mindanao as the site of the fleet base as it was farther from Japan and *unlikely to be occupied*. Later versions envisioned American battleships escorting oilers into Manila harbor.

Until 1943, planners had no formal guidance about ending the war except "unconditional surrender." Even that declaration wasn't made until January of that year. In the Joint Chiefs memorandum for the defeat of Japan, dated 19 May 1943, the Philippines were explicitly listed as a major objective for American forces. From there the Americans were to join British and Chinese forces in the recapture of Hong Kong. The final conquest of Japan was to be marshaled from bases in China. During early 1943, the emphasis on engaging the Japanese with the Chinese army underscored the need to drive to the Chinese coast. Now that the Americans had a more realistic opinion of the viability of that strategy, there was little need to invade the mainland to supply the Chinese. Chinese forces would do little to end the war. By late 1943, the JCS staff had shifted the primary attack from New Guinea and into the central Pacific. The JCS directive of 12 March 1944 instructed Nimitz to seize the Marianas. Nevertheless, MacArthur was to continue his advance up the New Guinea coast to Hollandia and to neutralize Kavieng, Rabaul, Truk, and Palau. MacArthur took great umbrage at a JCS suggestion to bypass the southern Philippines for the alternative of a Luzon-Formosa-China triangle.

Instead of Formosa, Admiral Spruance advocated seizure of air and naval bases just south of Shanghai.[11] Halsey didn't want to attack the China coast. He thought it would lead to endless peripheral operations that war-weary Americans couldn't sustain.

By mid-1944, events in China did not favor the Allies. For the longest time, Roosevelt depended on a Chinese offensive. He funded an extensive aid program to this end. After lugging their own gas and bombs over the "Hump" of the Himalayas from India, the first B-29 raid from China hit Bangkok on 5 June. On the 18th the steelworks at Yawata, Japan, marked the first B-29 raid on the Home Islands. The effects on the Japanese economy were negligible. Outraged, the Japanese army immediately launched an offensive to shut down the B-29 bases. The Chinese army was powerless to even slow them down. Any hope of basing B-29s in China vanished as the Japanese moved at will against the Chinese. Chiang Kai-shek lost what little remained of his credibility in western capitals.

Many Allied planners hoped for a Chinese offensive to retake Hong Kong. Instead it was the Japanese army that attacked. They drove down the railroad line from Hankow to Hanoi, ultimately cutting Chiang's forces off from the entire southern coast. By August, they captured Hengyang, the rail junction to Canton. In order to conserve fuel, the Imperial Navy moved its battleship line from the Sea of Japan to Singapore. This naval move, along with the offensive in China, led the British to believe another attack might be mounted toward India. Effectively they told the Combined Chiefs of Staff that any thought of a British offensive to take Singapore and Hong Kong was out of the question.

This militated against an American operation against Formosa. From there, mainland China was within the reach of short-range fighters. Japanese forces in China were powerful formations that did not have to be tangled with. Why invade an island when there was an insuppressible source of aircraft with which the Japanese could pummel your operation?

By mid-1944, successful capture of the Marianas had proved the wisdom in weighting the central Pacific drive. B-29s were about to begin their operations from Saipan and Tinian. Japanese civilians anxiously awaited the arrival of "B-san" in the skies over the Home Islands. The battle of the Philippine Sea effectively eliminated the Imperial Navy's carrier-based airpower. Three carriers and most of the experienced aviators had been lost. All that was left was Japan's battleship line, which could not possibly take to the open ocean in the face of American airpower.

A quick victory in the Marianas reinforced the opinion of the U.S. Joint Chiefs of Staff that the main drive against Japan should be made in the central Pacific.[12] Army planners in Washington were very aware of the tremendous heat the Philippines versus Formosa argument would generate.

MacArthur was not idle. While combat swirled through the Marianas, he moved 1,000 miles up the New Guinea coast. Leapfrogging operations at Wakde, Biak, Noemfoor, and Sansapor carried the general's forces into the Vogelkop

Peninsula, the western "head" of the New Guinea turkey. At the operational level, MacArthur had performed brilliantly. Gone were the frontal attacks of Papua. However, this New Guinea axis led nowhere. The Marianas fighting had destroyed the bulk of Japanese carrier strength, captured bases from which Japan could be bombed, and led more directly to both the Philippines and Japan. There was even less reason for MacArthur's 1944 New Guinea campaign than there had been for Cartwheel. If there had been no semi-autonomous (and politically dangerous) uniformed power center in the southwest Pacific, would any of this been undertaken?

With American naval power ascendant, all Japanese forces south and east of the Marianas became irrelevant. If left alone, Japanese forces in the Philippines could contribute little to the defense of Japan. Why tackle massive Japanese occupation forces stationed there? Why not bypass them?

The Philippines offered no strategic advantages, such as Okinawa's airfields, which are within B-17 range of Japan and of Borneo's oil. As Morison wrote, "There can be no question that the Philippines campaign was a thorn in the side of those eager to get on with the Pacific War as rapidly as possible."[13]

MacArthur had a four-part plan to retake the Philippines. First an air base would be seized on a southern Philippine island, probably Mindanao. This would require two divisions. Second, a five-division force would seize Leyte. With Leyte in hand, Luzon, the economic, political, and cultural heart of the Philippines, would be taken. With Manila in hand, American forces would again turn south and clear the rest of the island commonwealth.[14] Admiral Kinkaid, commander, Seventh Fleet, and MacArthur's naval commander, was concerned about Japanese airpower in the Visayans, in the central portion of the Philippine archipelago. He advocated a slow island-by-island advance to establish land-based air before going to Mindoro or Lingayen Gulf on Luzon.[15]

Surprisingly, at the Honolulu meeting MacArthur told the president the next steps from the Philippines should be south, not north. In *Reminiscences* he wrote that "once I held the Philippines, I would begin the re-conquest of the Dutch East Indies."[16]

A series of carrier raids convinced Halsey that little Japanese presence remained on either Mindanao or Leyte. Although not known to be a "big picture" strategic thinker, he certainly capitalized quickly on any opportunity left unguarded by the enemy. Halsey's impression proved half right. Mindanao was scratched for the Leyte invasion. Leyte would be a big fight.

As early as mid-1943, the JSSC and many Washington planners were glimpsing a faster alternative. They found favor with King. He was all set to land on Formosa, north and west of the Philippines. He wanted all sea lanes between Japan and the South Seas blocked. Capturing Formosa would "put the cork in the bottle." In King's words, "Battering through the Philippines would be a long and costly process."[17] General Marshall, reluctant to commit the army to a bloody ground campaign that could be avoided, could see King's logic. A quicker end to the war might just redeem the Philippines without the need for the blood, civilian and military, which extensive land combat would spill. The army estimated the capture of Formosa would take nine divisions.[18]

Some army planners stated that logistical problems would make it impossible to mount an assault against Formosa under any circumstances before February 1945. On closer inspection, this estimate assumed the Philippine campaign would be fought in late 1944. Admiral William Leahy thought Formosa would shorten the war but increase the loss of U.S. life. He worried that untouched Japanese air bases on Luzon would threaten interdiction of the sea lanes to Formosa. However, only long-range aircraft could do so.

"Studying plans for Allied entry into the strategic triangle, the Joint Chiefs and their subordinate advisory committees concluded that Formosa constituted the most important single objective in the target area."[19] In a delicately phrased communication JCS asked Nimitz and MacArthur if bypassing "presently selected objective prior to operations against Formosa," or "bypassing presently selected objectives and choosing new ones including the home islands" was appropriate.[20] (In this radiogram, one hears Marshall's suggestion to bypass all intermediate objectives and assault Japan directly.)

In his response, MacArthur said it would be unsound to bypass the Philippines and go directly to Formosa. Such a jump would not have the benefit of land-based air cover that was "based in Hawaii, 5,100 miles away." It is hard to understand why MacArthur made that reference as he had earlier acknowledged that the Marianas air bases were about to become operational and that ones in the Marshalls already were. "In my opinion purely military reasons demand the reoccupation of the Philippines in order to cut the enemy's communications to the south and to secure a base for our further advance."[21] The central Pacific campaign dramatically disproved the notion that the Big Blue Fleet needed to be constrained to the range of supporting land-based air. MacArthur's "military reasons" were specious.

Even if purely military reasons were not sufficient, MacArthur thought bypassing the Philippines would be a major mistake. In his words, "Philippines is U.S. Territory . . . practically all the 17,000,000 Filipinos remain loyal to the United States and are undergoing the greatest deprivation . . . We have a great national obligation to discharge."[22] Many Americans would have subscribed to these sentiments during the war.

MacArthur continued, "Moreover if the United States should deliberately by-pass the Philippines leaving our prisoners, nationals, and loyal Filipinos in en-emy hands without an effort to retrieve them at earliest moment, we would incur the gravest psychological reaction. We would admit the truth of Japanese propa-ganda to the effect that we had abandoned the Filipinos and would not shed American blood to redeem them; we would undoubtedly incur the open hostil-ity of that people[,] we should probably suffer such loss of prestige among all the peoples of the Far East that it would adversely affect the United States for many years."

Most Americans might have found these words harsh. Realists recognized that the victor in the Pacific would command both overwhelming power and prestige regardless of what happened in the Philippines. Many, Roosevelt in-cluded, were determined not to use American arms to support or reestablish Eu-ropean colonial control. America had promised Filipinos independence. It would keep its promise. By 1944, most of the prisoners were American. What of the Fil-ipino casualties involved in wholesale fighting?

The army chief of staff got it about right. Dismissing MacArthur's objections to a Formosa operation, Marshall said, "Neither operation in my opinion is un-sound in the measure you indicate." As we have seen, Marshall's view was that bypassing did not equal abandonment. The defeat of Japan was the quickest way to clear the Philippines of Japanese. He might also have added that it would defi-nitely be less costly in Filipino blood.

Seemingly undaunted, MacArthur directed his staff to produce Reno V, the invasion plans for the Philippines. Mindanao would be invaded on 15 November and Leyte on 20 December. MacArthur wanted intermediate objectives in order to create air bases to support the coup de grâce—invasion of Luzon. After some preliminaries, the main Leyte landing was scheduled for 1 April 1945.

Admiral Mitscher stated in his assessment of MacArthur's plan for the Philip-pines that the consensus in the fleet was that the Imperial Navy would not fight. Nimitz thought the Japanese might not even come out to defend Formosa. King was the one who predicted a major fleet engagement.[23] Nimitz found the taking of Leyte advisable. Nimitz worried about the accelerated time schedule, espe-cially Leyte by 15 November. He didn't want to address the question on bypass-ing until further developments unfolded.

Halsey was all for bypassing as many intermediate objectives as possible. How-ever, he felt an incursion into the Philippines would be to attack "the soft under-belly of the Imperial Dragon." Halsey's chief of staff was even more revealing. When King asked Rear Admiral Robert Carney if he wanted to turn Manila into another London, he replied, "No, Sir, I want to turn Luzon into another Britain."[24]

The farsighted Spruance raised the ante on King. Essentially he advocated skipping all but the last step to invasion in favor of heading directly to Okinawa, 400 miles closer to Tokyo. Okinawa had enough landmass to provide bases for the final assault on Japan and was within long-range fighter range of Kyushu, the southernmost home island. Okinawa offered many firm, level, well-drained sites for airfields.

Unquestionably, Mahan would have picked up on Spruance's recommendation. If there was any objective short of the Home Islands that would draw out forces scheduled to defend Japan from final invasion, Okinawa was it. Any attempt by the remaining Japanese battle line to intervene would be smashed by American airpower in open ocean. The distance from Japan placed Japanese air raiders flying from the Home Islands at a disadvantage. Those that did would transit a long over-ocean approach subject to American interception. Okinawa was the ideal base to cut off Japan from both China and the South Seas.

The radiograms of July clearly were trial balloons to see if there had been similar changes of opinion among senior American officers in the Pacific. MacArthur's response and its potential for setting off political turmoil undoubtedly were expected. Hence the trial balloon rather than directives from the chief of staff.

By September 1944 "King alone among the high level planners seems to have retained a strong conviction along these lines [Formosa]."[25] Marshall had taken a backseat. Navy planners worried about Formosa's lack of good ports and the undesirability of invading mainland China to take a port. An impasse developed between MacArthur and King concerning the Philippines versus Formosa. While he didn't want to oppose MacArthur, Marshall favored the faster Formosa route if he couldn't enlist anyone in a direct attack on Japan.

MacArthur let it be known he wanted to travel to Washington to personally plead his case if the Philippines were to be bypassed. That could have been political dynamite. FDR had picked MacArthur to lead American forces in the Far East back in 1941. How would it look if he overruled the general on such an important matter without even hearing him out? With a chasm between King and MacArthur, FDR must have instinctively known that only specific direction from the commander in chief would resolve the issue. The president was concerned about the political damage he might suffer by appearing to abandon the Filipinos.[26] MacArthur had become the lightning rod for anti-Roosevelt sentiment. The prospect of a MacArthur resignation over the Philippines was a less than palatable prospect for Roosevelt.

At the direction of the White House, Marshall summoned MacArthur to Honolulu to confer with Nimitz on future war plans. The meeting was scheduled for 26 July 1944. Both Marshall and King were in the Pacific at the time. The president invited neither of them. Both had been proponents of bypassing the Philippines. Nimitz had supported invasion of the islands—the objective, one might add, of the old War Plan Orange. Having assumed that Marshall would be in attendance, MacArthur was a little surprised to see Roosevelt without his chiefs. FDR was going to deal with his problem directly.

Ostensibly, Roosevelt arrived to listen to the army's views as promulgated by MacArthur and the navy's case for going directly to Formosa, as presented by Nimitz. According to some observers, Nimitz did not agree with King and might not have been the most convincing advocate for bypassing the Philippines. It should be noted that, back in April, MacArthur had publicly stated he wouldn't run for president. However, Roosevelt felt a MacArthur resignation could upset the fall 1944 elections and "he wasn't too happy about the prospect." Given war weariness among the electorate and the constant tugging of the isolationists, Roosevelt felt he "must take care about MacArthur."[27]

Everyone involved understood the gravity of the dispute. Throughout the war, each theater commander clamored for more resources, arguing that if his demands weren't met he would be unable to reach his assigned objectives. Now Admiral Leahy commented that both theaters believed they could achieve the objective with forces assigned. Obviously neither side wanted to handicap itself by presenting a bill before the menu selection had been made.

Had the Japanese carrier fleet been stronger at the end of the Marianas campaign, Mahan would have held that its destruction trumped any other competing alternative. The need to focus everything on its destruction would have been overwhelming. To embrace a secondary objective in light of a major Japanese naval threat would have been incompetent strategy. Entering the restrictive waters of the Philippines, which increased the likelihood of ships approaching to within gunnery range of each other, would not have been a good idea. But the Imperial high seas fleet could no longer impede movement of the American fleet. Granted, the bight of Japanese battleships was something to reckon with. But the Americans would have to maneuver in a manner that allowed the Japanese ships to come within gunnery distance.

There is no indisputable evidence as to why FDR, on this single occasion among all of the meetings during the war, chose to exclude Marshall and King from a major conference on strategy. However Marshall's 24 June radiogram to MacArthur provides the strongest possible circumstantial evidence. Both of the president's chiefs strongly favored Formosa. Mahan would have concurred with the chiefs if he couldn't convince them to jump even farther to Okinawa. Formosa-based air and sea power would have permanently sealed the final sea lanes from the South Seas to Japan. B-17s and B-24s could reach the Home Islands as well as B-29s. Formosa provided sufficient land space on which to organize the final assault on Japan. It held the promise of improved communications with the Chinese Nationalists. Remaining Japanese forces in the Philippines, as well as the battleships based in the South Seas, would be cut off from Japan. So would the oil. A single stroke, as opposed to a step-by-step campaign through the Philippines, would leave American forces far closer to defeating Japan. One can argue a Formosan campaign would have led to a shorter war and therefore an earlier final liberation of the Philippines. Certainly there would have been fewer Filipino casualties, especially given the bloodbath that developed in Manila.

By the summer of 1944, the Allies were so far ahead that a secondary war aim other than the defeat of Japan could be seriously entertained. A change of this magnitude would require a change in national strategy. The only person who could order that change was Roosevelt himself.

According to some accounts MacArthur gave Roosevelt some very sharp words in a few private minutes during the Honolulu trip. If the president decided to bypass the Philippines, he said, "I dare to say that the American people would be so aroused that they would register most complete resentment against you at the polls this fall."[28] Was that a political threat? Wouldn't the president have understood the threat even if MacArthur had never actually uttered these words? Just a few days before the Pearl Harbor meeting on Pacific strategy, FDR had been renominated to run for a fourth term by the Democratic convention in Chicago. In the words of one of MacArthur's staffers: "During the twenty-four months preceding the convention of 1944, MacArthur was involved in Presidential politics. The facts of the involvement are incontrovertible and obvious."[29]

FDR had words of his own to consider. In the dark days of late 1941, he had broadcast to the people of the Philippines: "News of your gallant struggle against the Japanese aggressor has elicited the profound admiration of every American. As President of the United States, I know that I speak for all of our people on this solemn occasion . . . I give to the people of the Philippines my solemn pledge that their freedom will be redeemed and their independence established and protected."[30]

Many historians believe Roosevelt had made up his mind before he left Washington. On the evening of the first day of the meeting Roosevelt is reported to have picked up a pointer, placed it over the Philippines on the wall map, and said, "Well, Douglas, where do we go from here?" MacArthur responded, "Leyte, Mr. President, and then Luzon."[31] MacArthur relayed a similar story to his staff, but said the president pointed to Mindanao. The distinction was probably more important to MacArthur as it held implications for the immediate futures of the central Pacific versus South Pacific campaigns. One of MacArthur's most distinguished biographers suggests a deal was made. The president would support Luzon. MacArthur would indirectly help FDR's campaign by spinning how well the war was going in his press releases.[32]

Later, when MacArthur and Nimitz made their formal presentations to Roosevelt, Nimitz made a tepid pitch for Formosa instead of Luzon. Just prior to the president's trip, King had been in Honolulu. He impressed on Nimitz the importance of Formosa over Luzon. Later, King would say, "Nimitz let me down."[33] MacArthur took the floor. The tone of the meeting was surprisingly cordial. The general complimented Admiral Nimitz on his emphasis on the Pacific, even if there were a few questions of strategy that remained unresolved. Without notes, MacArthur made an eloquent presentation of his case. In the course of his presentation he lectured the president: "You cannot abandon 17 million Filipino Christians to the Japanese in favor of first liberating Formosa and returning it to China. American public opinion will condemn you, Mr. President. And it would be justified."[34] Resolution of the issue wasn't announced in Honolulu. But Nimitz surmised from the conversation between MacArthur and the president during their motor tour of bases on Oahu that the two were in agreement. On his return to Australia, MacArthur told his staff, the president had accepted his recommendations and approved the Philippines plan.[35] Admiral Leahy's recollection of the meeting was that MacArthur, Nimitz, and the president all had informally agreed on the Philippines by the time the meeting broke up.[36] Subsequent events in Washington seem to favor Leahy's recollection.

Smiling appearances aside, the president didn't enjoy MacArthur's lecture. He demanded of an aide: "Give me an aspirin. In fact give me another aspirin to take in the morning. In all my life, nobody has ever talked to me the way MacArthur did."[37]

Back in Washington, the JCS continued to heatedly debate the issues. To make a long story short, FDR decided in favor of MacArthur. In classic FDR style, he never communicated this formally to the Joint Chiefs. Admiral Leahy carried the president's water. Roosevelt expected the JCS to return a recommendation consistent with his wishes. Marshall got the message. King, obstinate as ever, dismissed MacArthur's plea as so much histrionics and remained adamant on Formosa. Then he began to fish for a "Leyte for Formosa" deal. Mahan would have been tapping the desk pretty hard at that one. This was a decided step backwards. Invading both Leyte and Formosa would be a much slower approach to Japan than a Leyte-only strategy. In the end the Joint Chiefs issued orders to invade through Leyte. Supposedly the issue of Luzon versus Formosa remained open. Right. In a nationwide radio address broadcast from the Bremerton Navy

Yard on 12 August, the president referred to "my old friend General Mac-Arthur" and intimated that the two were in accord with respect to future operations.[38]

Creating the Philippines as an objective unto itself takes us out of the realm of military strategy and into that of national strategy. It was a decision for an elected official, not a uniformed officer. If the naval balance had been as precarious as it was at Guadalcanal in the fall of 1942, the top military officers would have been derelict if they hadn't pointed out that any subsidiary requirement would jeopardize the primary objective. By the summer of 1944, this was not the case. America had an overwhelming advantage in the Pacific.[39]

America would liberate the Philippines. Did the president decide on this course of action because of the burning issues surrounding the "political general"? The fact that this question is even asked overshadows whatever else Mac-Arthur contributed in World War II.

Upon the conclusion of the conference, Nimitz communicated to King that a cordial discussion had resulted in a decision for MacArthur to invade the central Philippines. This probably didn't disappoint the Pacific Fleet commander. Leahy observed that MacArthur and Nimitz treated each other well and were likely to work well together. After the war Admiral Nimitz told Morison, "From hindsight, I think the decision [to invade Luzon] was correct."[40]

Marshall now supported operations through the Philippines. Talk of national honor had made its impact. The army was not an independent entity unto itself. It was to achieve the objectives set out by national strategy. He sided with both MacArthur and the president.

MacArthur's assertion that occupation of the Philippines would have important geopolitical ramifications deserves closer analysis. At the beginning of the twenty-first century, an observer can fairly summarize the benefit. The end of the impact of the liberation of the Philippines can be marked by America's withdrawal from Subic Bay naval base in 1991, in response to pressure from the Philippine government. Unlike the economies of Korea, Japan, or Indonesia, the impact of the Philippine economy on world trade was small. During the Cold War, Subic Bay became the largest overseas American naval base with major repair and supply installations. It employed many Filipinos. Clarke Field proved to be an excellent transit and training field. However, alternative sites existed, for instance in Guam (the twenty-first-century choice), Okinawa, and Japan proper. After the war, the Philippine government faced strong opposition from communist-oriented HUK guerrillas. Had the American invasion not occurred, the guerrillas' hand might have been strengthened. A leftist-neutral Philippines could have created problems for the Americans in the ideological struggles of the 1960s. However, the Vietnam War could have been prosecuted without installations in the Philippines.

A major result of Japan's invasion of the South Seas was the dissipation of the myth of the white man's invincibility. Prior to 1941, the French owned Indochina, the British Malaya, and the Dutch most of what is now Indonesia. American presence in the Philippines was distinguished from that of the European powers in the area only by the promise of independence in 1945 (a date picked before the war). Roosevelt was determined not to aid the European countries' postwar reassertion of their colonial interests. On this issue, Roosevelt reflected the majority of American opinion.

Initially, many Filipinos received the Japanese as liberators. Japanese arrogance was even worse than American condescension. American submarines had devastated Japanese shipping by the summer of 1944. A food shortage had developed in the Philippine islands. The Japanese regularly shorted the rations of their Filipino subjects to fill their own bellies. This approach to the problem was not lost on the general population.

Little of Indonesia was liberated before war's end. Mostly in reaction to European colonialism, Indonesia did go through a period of Soviet-leaning leftist neutrality. Soviet-supplied Indonesian aircraft occasionally shadowed transiting American forces. During the early 1960s some conservative American commentators viewed the country as "lost to communism." However, none of this restricted western access to critical Indonesian oil. Over time, the United States established cordial relations with Indonesia as well as Malaysia.

In retrospect, it is difficult to imagine that the Philippines would have generated major problems for the U.S. if there had been no American liberation of the islands. To the end "Admiral King still opposed liberating Luzon, predicting it would slow up the war for mere sentimental purposes."[41]

While the Americans debated their next move, Admiral Toyoda created a plan to concentrate his forces no matter where the Americans appeared. The Japanese SHO plan was a gigantic mobile defense. Land-based aircraft would race back and forth from Japan to Okinawa, Formosa, or the Philippines like football linebackers to concentrate forces against any attempt to break the Japanese line. While air elements raced to the threatened area, the army would act as the defensive front line, holding off the initial thrust. This would give airmen time to gather. Under the cover of all available airpower, the remnants of the navy would seek to close into the invasion area and destroy as much of the amphibious shipping as possible. Placing Japanese battleships among troop-laden transports would be the fastest way to kill Americans. The navy understood that lack of airpower would limit any attempt to seek a decisive sea battle. While air-

craft production was pushed up to 1,700 per month in March 1944, pilot training programs withered.

While it might seem a little far-fetched, Toyoda sought to win a final decisive
battle to thwart the Americans. Given the Japanese position in the summer of
1944, concentrating his forces against the American offensive when and where it
appeared was the best strategy. One can see some similarity to the earlier Z and
A-GO plans. However, the role of the Imperial Navy, especially its carriers, was
much reduced. There wasn't a great deal of combat power left in the mobile fleet
after the Great Marianas Turkey Shoot. Most of the battleships were based just
south of Singapore because of chronic fuel shortages. In Japanese planning, an
important shift in the perceived American center of gravity had taken place. No
longer was the primary objective the destruction of Mitscher's fast carriers. The
identified American weak spot was all the transports and their densely packed
cargos of young American fighting men. Don't go for the American airpower as
you can't beat it anyway. Kill as many Americans as possible.

Toyoda knew his situation was desperate. "If the worst should happen there
was a chance that we could lose the entire fleet; but I felt that chance had to be
taken. . . . Should we lose in the Philippines operations, even though the fleet
should be left, the shipping lane to the south would be completely cut off so that
the fleet, if it should come back to Japanese waters, could not obtain its fuel supply. . . . There would be no sense in saving the fleet at the expense of the loss of
the Philippines."[42]

SHO 1 was designed to counter a thrust into the Philippines. SHO 2 defended
Formosa and the Ryukyus, which includes Okinawa. SHO 3 defended the southern home islands. In the unlikely event the Americans came from the north,
SHO 4 defended Hokkaido. The best the Japanese could hope for was an American strategy that allowed the Japanese to sequentially execute SHO 1, SHO 2,
and SHO 3. This would maximize Japan's opportunity to inflict casualties and
delay. That might force the Americans to offer softer terms at the peace table.
Most Japanese strategists expected the Americans to strike the Philippines first.
Leyte was the most popular bet. Additional army and air units were shipped
there to prepare for SHO 1.

The "Tiger of Malaya," General Tomoyuki Yamashita, was resurrected from
the obscurity of command of First Area Army in China and took command of
the Philippines. A jealous Tojo had banished him to China for being such a star
in the capture of Singapore. Now Tojo was gone. Yamashita was the best the
Japanese had and good on anyone's scale of commanders. Nine divisions, including one armored, plus four separate brigades were assembled under him. The
general knew what he was up against. He confided in his chief of staff that he

feared the Philippines was "going to be another Battle of Minatogawa"—the historical conflict where the commander knew he was doomed before the opening engagement.[43]

On the other hand, the air commander, Lieutenant General Tominaga Kyoji, was known as "a petty bureaucrat playing soldier" with "no combat experience." Even the emperor was taken aback by Tominaga's appointment. He had done Tojo's dirty work from his previous position as director of the Personnel Affairs Bureau. During his entire career, he had served but three years in the field. Japanese land-based air strength in the Philippines was built up to 545 army and 426 naval aircraft. This compared to the Big Blue Fleet's count of 800 carrier-based aircraft when all four task groups were on line.

A Fighting Admiral Precipitates Practical Change

After lengthy discussion in Washington, the following timetable was promulgated:

Mindanao	15 November 1944
Leyte	20 December 1944
Luzon	20 February 1945

In late August Halsey set sail from Eniwetok at the head of the Third Fleet edition of the Big Blue Fleet. His mission was to suck Japanese airpower out of the Palaus and Mindanao as a precursor to MacArthur's invasion of the latter. On the way, he was to sideswipe the Bonins, which include Iwo Jima.

Mitscher hit Iwo Jima first. Then he sailed south. Japanese aerial opposition over the Palaus and Mindanao was almost nil. Naval airmen could see that Kenney's airmen had been busy prior to their arrival. Halsey's pilots ranged over the southern Philippines at will. An occasional Japanese plane was caught in the air and quickly dispatched. Navy aircraft destroyed 200 planes, mostly on the ground. American attacks were so ferocious Toyoda signaled that SHO was to be implemented. U.S. carriers moved into the central Philippine islands. Again opposition was nil. During the entire operation Halsey lost only eight planes in combat.

Halsey was astounded. He signaled his carriers, "Because of the brilliant performance my group of stars has just given, I am booking you to appear before the best audience in the Asiatic Theater."[44] He set course for launch points to hit Manila. Halsey smelled weakness. What he didn't know was that the Japanese had purposely held back their aircraft for the upcoming "decisive air battle."

Halsey consulted his staff. Of course he had Ultra warnings of the air buildup in the Philippines. After careful deliberation, he radioed a recommendation to cancel everything preliminary to the invasion of Leyte. He radioed Nimitz, King, and MacArthur that the "enemy's non aggressive attitude unbelievable and fantastic" and that "the area is wide open."[45] Halsey wanted to cancel invasions of Morotai, Peleliu, Yap, and Mindanao. Invasion forces for Morotai and Peleliu were already assembling. Halsey recommended they move directly to Leyte. At the time the Joint Chiefs and the president were meeting with their British counterparts at the Octagon Conference in Montreal. Marshall had MacArthur consulted by telex.

When Marshall's radiogram arrived at Southwest Pacific GHQ, MacArthur was under radio silence at sea on the way to the invasion to Morotai. Answering the chief's question fell to Sutherland. He gathered other senior staff members, including Kenney and Brigadier General Stephen J. Chamberlin, MacArthur's G3 operations officer. What happened next was incredible.

> They knew from Ultra that there was at least twenty-one thousand Japanese on Leyte and that Japanese air power, though bruised by Halsey's recent forays, was far from broken. They also knew that no matter what Ultra augured, Sutherland could not tell Marshall that a direct assault against Leyte was not feasible because to do so would immediately endorse the option to invade Formosa.[46]

But General Kenney was convinced that Japanese airpower was finished. Ever since his airmen had clobbered Japanese aerodromes around Hollandia his fighter pilots complained that opportunities for air-to-air victories had become scarce. And he knew that "MacArthur believed in moving fast when he was winning."[47] Mahan would have heartily endorsed that point of view.

"MacArthur's"—Sutherland's—affirmative reply came within two days. As General Marshall wrote, "Having the utmost confidence in General MacArthur, Admiral Nimitz, and Admiral Halsey, it was not a difficult decision to make. Within 90 minutes after the signal came into Montreal, General MacArthur and Admiral Nimitz had instructions to execute the Leyte operation on 20 October."[48] After all the acrimonious debate earlier in the year, the Chiefs acted with admirable flexibility and dispatch. Mindanao was to be bypassed and the schedule moved up two months.

While returning from the Morotai landing on board *Nashville* and after hearing about the communications with the Chiefs accelerating Leyte, MacArthur contemplated simultaneous landings at both Leyte and Lingayen Gulf on Luzon. Two divisions would land on the former and four on the latter. Upon MacArthur's return, his senior staff unanimously declined the idea.[49] Sutherland politely pointed out there would be no land-based air support anywhere. Kenney and Kinkaid immediately agreed. Scattering American soldiers over two islands would leave them unsupported and weak everywhere. The Big Blue Fleet couldn't cover both simultaneously without seriously dividing itself.

Admiral Nimitz objected to cancellation of the Peleliu invasion as preparations were already far advanced. Unfortunately his recommendation to go forward was approved.

Objectives and Command Relationships

As we have seen, during the year prior to invasion of the Philippines, the United States executed a two-pronged offensive across the Pacific. General MacArthur commanded efforts to advance up the coast of New Guinea and into the Philippines from the south. Admiral Nimitz commanded the march across the central Pacific and into the Philippines from the east. Now that these previously separable efforts had converged, who was going to command?

Unity of command is a hallowed principle of war. As Napoleon once quipped, "Give me one poor general over two brilliant ones." General Marshall believed in unity of command above all. However, the offensive in the South Pacific almost ground to a halt over this intractable issue. Invasion of the Philippines promised to be principally a land campaign. One might expect MacArthur to command, supported by the fleet under the command of Nimitz. Alternatively the southwest Pacific theater could be extended to cover the Philippines. All naval forces, including the entire Big Blue Fleet, could be grouped under Admiral Halsey and he subordinated to MacArthur. After all, these two leaders had worked well together in the past. This would retain Nimitz's independence and create a precedent for him to be the supreme commander for a subsequent operation like Okinawa with the Big Blue Fleet swinging back. As the Japanese fleet no longer had the ability to take independent open-ocean initiative, there was little reason to worry about other contingencies.

Merging the ground forces proved an easy task. Marine divisions would not enter the Philippines. Without prodding, Nimitz offered up his principal army force. MacArthur graciously accepted XXIV Corps, which had been previously slated for Yap. It was integrated into Krueger's Sixth Army and became one of two assault corps at Leyte. But there was no way King was about to let the fast carriers come under the command of anything but an all-navy chain of command.

MacArthur's naval arm would remain the Seventh Fleet under the command of Admiral Kinkaid. The general had taken a liking to his fleet commander.[50] Seventh Fleet had grown to impressive size. It had all the amphibious paraphernalia to carry the entire Sixth Army across an ocean. Most of the amphibious assets of the Big Blue Fleet, as well as the old battleships and the escort carrier groups, had been moved into Seventh Fleet for the Philippines operations. The gators were under the tactical command of a pair of great amphibious commanders, Vice Admiral T. S. "Ping" Wilkinson and Rear Admiral D. E. "Uncle Dan the Amphibious Man" Barbey. Six old battleships and several heavy cruisers under Rear Admiral Jesse Oldendorf spearheaded the fire support unit. Rear Admiral Thomas L. Sprague commanded an impressive air support task force that could launch 240 fighters and 186 torpedo bombers configured for close air support from the decks of sixteen escort carriers.

During the largest naval battle in history, Admiral Halsey commanded the Big Blue Fleet, now designated the Third Fleet. Admiral Mitscher was in command of Halsey's carrier task forces. Halsey reported to Admiral Nimitz, commander, Pacific Ocean Areas. So, two large American forces under separate commanders approached the Philippines: an invasion army and associated amphibious fleet under MacArthur and a huge "blue water" fleet under Nimitz with Halsey in tactical command.

MacArthur forbade Kinkaid from communicating directly with Halsey.[51] Despite the pleasantries there was a great deal of professional jealousy in the air.

Careful description, or lack thereof, of the fleet's mission had proved to be critical in the Marianas. Given the dispute that arose over this issue, one might expect the wording of Nimitz's directive to Halsey would be given careful consideration.

Virtually everyone agreed division of command was something to be avoided. However, what was the proper mission for the Third Fleet? The autonomic reaction is "Destroy the enemy fleet. The carriers are the center of the Japanese fleet. Destroy the carriers." However, this response is a simplistic application of Mahan's principles.

After the Philippines, what would be the remaining missions? Invade one or more intermediate objectives (Formosa? Okinawa?) and then at least isolate, if not invade, Japan. Mahan's underlying objective in attacking the enemy fleet is to gain complete freedom of maneuver on the seas. In this case, what would impede movement of the fleet?

To analyze this problem in a Mahanian framework, one must go a little deeper into the meaning of his writings. Distilled, Mahan's number one priority is to maintain the ability to sail the oceans while denying that freedom to the enemy. Usually that means the destruction of the enemy main battle line. However, the Japanese carrier fleet no longer had a credible aviation component. It was as if the enemy's main battle line had no guns aboard. No longer was it the number one threat. Increasingly, the American navy would have to dominate littoral waters near the Philippines, Formosa, the Ryukyus, and the Japanese islands themselves. The threat had been reduced to coastal defense forces. Yet these remained formidable. The Mahanian approach is to eliminate the greatest threat to fleet mobility.

If not intercepted, Japanese airpower could move back and forth from the Philippines to the Home Islands and all points in between. Japanese strategy depended on it. By the summer of 1944, land-based airpower was the most deadly threat to the fleet. By 1944 land-based air had some of the characteristics of nineteenth-century coastal artillery. Normally a fleet wouldn't mess with coastal batteries. That would be Mahan's recommendation. But American naval aviation had shown it was up to the task. This was a technological change that altered basic strategy. The fleet could take on Japanese army air when it had to—and win. Nevertheless, the Japanese army was best left to its U.S. counterpart when they were within range. That preserved navy air to suppress the Japanese before and during amphibious assaults. And the biggest task of all, invasion of the Japanese Home Islands, was looming so that suppressing land-based air was essential.

Usually Japanese battleships were perceived as a lower-level threat. As we have seen, the American fleet repeatedly avoided disastrous incursions by the narrowest of margins. If a battleship could get within range of Allied shipping, its tremendous firepower could create a first-rate disaster. As the Allies approached the Home Islands, the probability of an encounter increased. Eventually, the battleships would have to be destroyed or they would sit right on top of the vulnerable beaches of the Home Islands, a threat to any invasion force. Battleships are very hard targets and very difficult to sink. The last place the American navy wanted to take on the battleships was right under the largest possible cloud of Japanese land-based aircraft. By basing their battle fleet down near first Borneo, then Singapore in order to preserve fuel oil, the Japanese gave the Americans an opportunity to defeat these units divorced from the Japanese air force. By the same token, the geography of the Philippine archipelago gave the Japanese battle fleet, sailing from the south, added opportunity to approach the American amphibious fleet. After land-based air, the proximity of the battle fleet was the second gravest threat to the American fleet. When the Japanese battle line approached within one night's sailing of an amphibious fleet that could not maneuver out of the way, it became the number one menace.

The big advantage of carrier-based aviation is its ability to maneuver concentrated airpower to a point where the enemy cannot respond. For the most part, this is on the open ocean. Out there, there are no landing fields except on carrier decks. In the final approach to Japan, surviving aircraft could fly from the airfields of whatever landmass—Leyte, Taiwan, or Japan itself—the Americans were about to attack. Carriers per se, as opposed to their air complements, would not be very important for the Japanese. Carriers were now the third-priority threat to the American fleet, behind battleships and land-based air.

Usually the fleet commander has responsibility for the amphibious task force. In the Philippines, this was not the case. Explicit instructions were needed to prioritize amphibious protection and close support rather than chasing whatever enemy fleet units might appear. As the only headquarters superior to both MacArthur and Halsey was the Joint Chiefs, they must accept full blame for lack of unity of command and most of the blame for any lack of clarity in the instructions. Nimitz still held responsibility for all naval units both in MacArthur's area and in his own. He must share some blame as he directly issued Halsey his instructions.

As already recounted, tremendous controversy had arisen from Nimitz's lack of instruction to Spruance with regard to the destruction of the Japanese fleet in the Marianas. Admiral Nimitz was careful not to repeat this oversight. Halsey's order, which Nimitz approved, states in Section 3x: "In case opportunity for destruction of major portion of the enemy fleet is offered, such destruction becomes the primary task."[52]

That statement reversed the priority of missions that Spruance had assumed in the Marianas. There he sought first to protect the amphibians and then to attack the enemy fleet if possible. This time, destruction of the enemy fleet came first. It is hard to envision Mahan objecting to Nimitz's wording.

Otherwise this was the fleet's mission:

To cover and support the Leyte Operation by:
   A. Striking Okinawa, Formosa, and Northern Leyte on 10–13 October;
   B. Striking Bicol peninsula, Leyte, Cebu, and Negros, and supporting the landings on Leyte, on 16–20 October;
   C. Operating in "strategic support" of the Leyte Operation, by destroying enemy naval and air forces threatening the Philippines area, on and after 21 October.[53]

MacArthur's instructions to Kinkaid were as follows:

   1. To transport and establish landing forces ashore in the Leyte Gulf–Surigao Strait area, as arranged with the Commanding General, Sixth U.S. Army
   2. To support the operation by:
      a. Providing air protection for convoys and direct air support for the landing and subsequent operations, including anti-submarine patrol of the gulf and combat air patrol over the amphibious ships and craft, from his escort carriers;

   b. Lifting reinforcements and supplies to Leyte in naval assault shipping;
   c. Preventing Japanese reinforcement by sea of his Leyte garrison;
   d. Opening Surigao Strait for Allied use, and sending naval forces into Vis-
      ayan waters to support current and future operations;
   e. Providing submarine reconnaissance, lifeguard service, and escort of
      convoy.[54]

Halsey expressed his understanding of the mission in no uncertain terms. He
was out to kill what remained of the Japanese carrier fleet. He would pursue it in
priority to all other missions. For most of the war Mahan would have agreed.
Now the lesson was more subtle. He would have advised caution about such a
mission statement.

Kinkaid's instructions clearly gave him responsibility for Surigao Strait. (See
Map 10a.) By implication, he also had responsibility for the small strait between
Samar and Leyte that emptied into Leyte Gulf. San Bernardino Strait lay 125
miles to the north between Samar and Luzon. Should Kinkaid cover this as well?
He didn't have a free running force to do so. His old battleships and escort carriers would presumably be in close proximity to the Leyte landing beaches providing close support to the invasion. Halsey's instructions said nothing about San
Bernardino Strait, but he had the mission of "destroying enemy naval and air
forces threatening the Philippines area" from the level of "strategic support." He
had the fast battleships and fleet carriers to undertake such missions. But
Kinkaid's orders prohibited communication with Halsey to straighten out the
issue of who was to cover San Bernardino Strait.

The instructions were not specific. More important, there was no single admiral in overall command to resolve such oversights.

For his part Kinkaid addressed the potential threat from San Bernardino
Strait. In his operations order, he stated, "Any major enemy naval force approaching from the north will be intercepted and attacked by Third Fleet covering
force."[55] Admiral Nimitz and his staff were aware of Kinkaid's operations order.

Peleliu Blood Sump

From early in the war, U.S. planners identified the Palau Islands as a threat to an
invasion force headed toward the Philippines. An enemy fleet base there would
be a problem. This had been underscored in some prewar permutations of War
Plan Orange. Palau is 800 miles from Leyte. Only four-engine aircraft were able
to make a round-trip. Early in the Marshalls campaign, Admiral Koga decided
the islands were too vulnerable as a fleet base. The Imperial Fleet withdrew toward Borneo. By the time the Americans captured the Marianas, little remained

of Japanese aviation. While the garrison had been reinforced, the Imperial General Staff had decided nothing more was to be sent. The garrison was on its own.

Still MacArthur perceived Japanese possession of these islands as representing a threat to his flank. Nimitz had always been interested in them. They were the object of many of his beloved map inspections. Peleliu Island received most of his attention. At the January 1944 strategy meeting at Pearl Harbor, all participants thought it was necessary to invade the Palaus,[56] especially the participants from the southwest Pacific theater who took a jaundiced view of the Marianas. The southwest Pacific planners also had their eye on Morotai.

With no real Japanese offensive threat in the Palaus, only one of the two islands made any sense as a base for American long-range aviation. Morotai was far less defended and offered good airfields. It was also 125 miles closer to Leyte. Yet both Morotai and an invasion of Peleliu remained in the master plan. The Allies knew the ground defenses of the Palaus had been heavily reinforced. Ultra warned the Americans that the island was being turned into a fortress.

Carrier raids in March 1944 convinced Imperial General Headquarters that a Palau invasion was imminent. Initially the garrison was one under-strength regimental combat team (RCT) of 35th Division. To reinforce it, 14th Division from north China, initially destined for New Guinea, was rerouted to reinforce it. Since few aircraft remained based in the Palaus, large airfields in Mindanao could conceivably be used to reinforce. After July 1944 only the barest trickle of supplies arrived in the Palaus. By September, the Japanese would not risk even as much as a supply barge. "All the Palau Sector Group could look forward to was death or surrender."[57] About 11,000 Japanese resided there, outnumbering the natives.

Halsey had little stomach for an invasion of these islands. At the May 1944 meeting in San Francisco with Nimitz and King, he expressed his feeling that "they would have to be bought at a prohibitive price" similar to the one paid for Tarawa.[58] Despite warnings of this nature Nimitz insisted that the Peleliu operation not be canceled when, on Halsey's recommendation, the entire Philippines operation was advanced.

Given Ultra, Nimitz should have seen the wisdom of Halsey's recommendation. Tarawa should have been a sufficient lesson. The only other officer who could have intervened was King. Although it would have been wonderful had he done so, it's hard to envision the CNO taking action from Washington to overrule his commander on the spot.

Before the invasion, the Americans didn't quite understand the tremendous difficulty Peleliu's terrain would pose for an attacker. The island had razor-sharp coral ridges that shot several hundred feet almost straight up. They were covered with caves. Tunnels from the phosphate mining on the island added to the labyrinth. The Japanese had reinforced these available redoubts with concrete to narrow the openings, making them harder to hit and destroy.

Major General W. H. Rupertus, commander of First Marine Division, which would assault the island, "was very, very optimistic" about the ability of his troops to quickly secure the island.[59] He thought it could be taken in four days. In fairness to Nimitz, Rupertus's forecast promised a short casualty list. Instead Peleliu turned into one of the bloodiest, most gruesome battles of the war.

The Peleliu operation suffered from a series of tactical mistakes. Reconnaissance was extremely poor. As a result, the Americans had little idea of Japanese strength and dispositions. The scheduled bombardment was inadequate to neutralize actual Japanese fortifications. Further, the bombardment force didn't have intelligence on many specific targets and had to rely on area fire. Japanese defenders displayed great discipline in not exposing their positions until American landing craft were in their final assault run.

When the situation is vague, most land commanders will lead with a small force and hold most of their combat power in reserve until the enemy's dispositions and intent are developed. The commander doesn't want to stumble into more than he can handle. He needs to retain sufficient troop strength to decisively attack whatever enemy subelement that must be defeated to ensure a path to success.

Despite the lack of information, General Rupertus landed all three of his regiments abreast, retaining only one battalion in reserve. In effect this committed First Marine Division to a frontal assault against the entire Japanese garrison. Japanese defensive tactics had changed. Instead of defending at the water line and then engaging in bloody banzai counterattacks, the Japanese had prepared a defense in depth. With most of the marines committed during the initial landing, there was precious little combat power available to concentrate to attack in depth in response. General Rupertus rejected the notion of using troops from the army's 81st Division as a reserve and attack force.

Because of the caves and the concrete, artillery and air strikes proved ineffective. Mudfaces had to hump up to each opening in the coral and attack with flamethrowers and satchel charges. Temperatures on the island hit 115 degrees and water was severely rationed. II Amphibious Corps had 49,500 troops assigned for the operation. Some 1,800 were killed and 8,000 were wounded. That amounted to a casualty rate of almost 20 percent.

Despite the high cost of capturing Palau, the fleet made little use of it. Its airfields weren't ready to accept bombers until a day after the landings on Leyte. "From the vantage point of hindsight, it would appear that Halsey was right and that it may not have been absolutely necessary to take the Palaus."[60]

Two army regiments invaded the lightly defended island of Angaur in the Palaus. They made short work of the 1,600 occupation troops. By 17 October, two air strips were operational. As discussed in the previous chapter, the real prize was Ulithi atoll with its large, protected lagoon. Elements of the 81st Infantry Division landed there unopposed.

Because Ultra identified the large buildup on Halmahera, MacArthur wisely substituted Morotai. A reinforced army division invaded on 15 September. Only 500 Japanese occupied the island. The army rolled over them with little difficulty. In short order engineers created a fighter and two bomber airstrips. "The Morotai operation ranks as one of the most economical and worthwhile undertakings of the Southwest Pacific war."[61] However, only a handful of sorties from Morotai flew over Leyte.

Muddy Leyte

MacArthur's plan had always been Mindanao, then Leyte, and finally Luzon. To understand why Leyte, one must examine Luzon. (See Map 10b.) Leyte is very mountainous. The best beaches for large-scale amphibious operations rim Lingayen Gulf on the western side of Luzon. A broad plain extends from Lingayen Gulf to Manila. Given that Manila Bay was closed by heavy coast artillery and fortifications, Lingayen was the obvious choice for a field-army-size invasion. The Japanese used the identical corridor when they invaded in 1941.

In the summer of 1944, the west side of Luzon bordered waters that were still Japanese dominated. Both the South China Sea and the Sulu Sea were considered Japanese lakes. Threading an invasion fleet through the narrow interisland passages, such as San Bernardino Strait, would subject ships to heavy air attack while giving them no room to maneuver. Coming up through the Sulu Sea exposed the attacker in the narrow waters of the Sulu archipelago to air and surface attacks from Borneo and the southern Philippines. The best approach might be to the north between Luzon and Formosa. But that stretch of open ocean is only 200 miles wide. Japanese aircraft based in Formosa could fiercely contest this passage. A move of that nature would almost beg for a Formosa invasion *before* Luzon was invaded. But that would not suit MacArthur's needs.

For MacArthur, the obvious solution was to create a huge air base at Leyte. This would ease transit through the interisland straits. He planned a very aggressive air buildup that bedded down five air groups in Leyte by the fifth day of the invasion (A+5). More specifically, he anticipated the following accretion of airpower on Leyte:

	A+5*	A+30	A+45	A+60
Fighter groups	2.33	+.33	+1	
Bomber groups	1.33	+2	+2 heavy	
Transport groups				2
Patrol squadrons	3		+1	+1
Recon squadrons	2	+1		+2

*Attack (landing) day +5.[62]

(A group normally contained 3 flying squadrons of about 25 aircraft.)

Leyte is a good-sized island running about 115 miles north to south with a width measuring 15–40 miles. It is very mountainous with sharp volcanic ridges running north to south. The steepness of these ridges prevents most east-west movement except on the coast. Two large valleys, Ormoc in the west and Leyte Valley near the east coast, also run north-south. Heavy rainfall feeds dense vegetation. In 1944 there was little development on the island.

Advancing up the New Guinea coast, MacArthur's airmen and engineers learned the critical importance of proper soil composition and drainage in picking airfield sites. General Kenney observed, "Where there was plenty of coral, the engineers could give us a field in a matter of a few days. In the case of ordinary sand-clay soils, the period would be a month or two."[63] Kenney rejected initial plans to land in the Maffin Bay area due to poor soil conditions at potential airfields. He strongly favored the Biak operation because it offered airfield sites that "were fairly free of tree growth, flat, well drained and solid coral."[64]

MacArthur and his chief advisers hoped Leyte Valley could be developed as a major logistical and air base complex. Even a cursory reading of the data showed this area was not well suited for this purpose. The best existing "roads" had only a light bituminous surface and were incapable of supporting two-way military traffic.[65] The biggest problem was drainage. Heavy rains turned the soil into soup with little bearing strength. There were only two operational Japanese air strips of any size. Together they had but 65 hardstands, insufficient to support only a single fighter group and no heavier twin-engine aircraft.

The Allied Geographical Section performed at least 110 detailed terrain studies. It completed Terrain Study 84, Leyte Province on 17 August 1944. A three-volume War Department Survey of the Philippines dated 15 February 1943 also existed. Engineers recognized heavy rains, poor drainage, and soil with poor load-bearing characteristics would be a major problem.[66] On 10 August, Sixth Army Engineers formally protested selection of Leyte in typhoon season as an amphibious target and potential logistical base. They cited the soil as "most unstable." Runway and apron construction would be extremely difficult. The available harbor was shallow and blocked by coral. The engineers concluded, "The construction mission cannot be satisfactorily accomplished with the engineer troops available, particularly in the first ninety days." They recommended selection of some area other than Leyte.[67]

The report was forwarded to MacArthur's chief engineer. GHQ decided to go ahead anyway. A postwar National Security Agency report cites MacArthur's proclivity to disregard intelligence reports that didn't conform to his preconceived notions: "During the Second World War [MacArthur] had disregarded Comint (Communications Intelligence) that contradicted his plans."[68]

MacArthur knew Leyte from firsthand experience. As a young officer and aide to his father, who was then military commander in the Philippines, he had traveled extensively on the island. The general's stenographer recalls typing a letter signed by MacArthur about the difficulty in constructing airfields in Leyte.[69] MacArthur realized airfield construction and logistical buildup would be a big problem. For the first time, he created a Service Command under his two-star engineer officer to oversee base development on Leyte.

Communications intercepts gave the Americans a good picture of Japanese air strength. Over 400 aircraft were available but only half were operational.[70] This poor availability rate underscores the fragility of airpower and the critical importance of maintenance capability. In previous Pacific campaigns, Japanese air capability was limited. In the central Pacific, the Japanese had only a few fields on which to base aircraft to oppose the American invaders. This was also true for most of MacArthur's New Guinea campaign after 1942. By comparison, 70 air strips were sited on Luzon; islands in the southern Philippines contained another 50. Last year's mega-stronghold, Rabaul, had 50. Luzon's airfields lay in areas that had far better flying weather than rain-soaked Leyte. As a result, the Japanese could generate more sorties per available aircraft. As Colonel Thomas E. Griffith, author of Kenney's biography, points out, "There was also little recognition among any of the commanders that the air battle for the Philippines would be fundamentally different from any other invasion."[71] Airfields in the Philippines could be easily reinforced all the way from Japan via Formosa and Okinawa. If many airfields remained operational, the full weight of Japanese airpower could be shifted against Leyte, where the Americans would have great difficulty. "None of the air commanders, Kenney included, seemed to anticipate this difference or believe that it would have any impact."[72] Later Kenney would admit that he "didn't like the looks of the prospective airdrome situation in Leyte."[73]

Failure to recognize the air-basing problem on Leyte must be placed at MacArthur's feet. He suppressed the implications of the tremendous engineering problems that would prevent the Americans from achieving immediate air superiority. Such disclosure would have forced giving consideration to invading Lingayen Gulf directly, as Leyte was a useless intermediate step. The most likely was a naval approach from the north between Taiwan and Luzon. The implication would have been obvious. Invade Formosa instead. Whether motivated by his desire to return to the Philippines or a result of ignoring information that was contrary to his preconceived notions, it is a major failing of his generalship. The navy depended on Leyte airfields in order to move the fleet away in a timely manner. Without sufficient army aircraft based on Leyte, the carriers had to stay in harm's way in order to protect the beachhead from Japanese bombers and kamikazes. MacArthur's actions suppressed the disclosure of a preventable risk.

In the spring of 1944, the Japanese had only minor units available to set up an organized defense of Philippines, but by the time of the Leyte invasion 432,000 Japanese had gathered in the Philippines, including construction and air force personnel.[74]

In the final days before the landing, Halsey's airmen pounded Japanese aviation in the central Philippines. Japanese airpower remained but its commanders held back, waiting for the decisive moment under SHO 1 to counterattack. Kinkaid's Seventh Fleet contained eighteen escort or "jeep" carriers (CVEs) in Task Group 77.4, under command of Rear Admiral Thomas Sprague, to provide close air support for the invasion while the Third Fleet under Halsey roamed farther afield. Aircraft from the jeep carriers dominated the air above the beaches on A-day.

Four assault divisions landed on the eastern shore of Leyte on 20 October. Some tactical surprise was obtained by landing in the far north of the bay where it appeared that an invasion fleet would be too vulnerable. The Imperial Army had learned it was impossible to contest beaches in face of overwhelming American gunfire. Initial U.S. preparation fire hit little of importance. Despite this the Americans easily came ashore. At first Japanese resistance wasn't heavy and American infantry moved inland rapidly. However, they ran into stiff resistance in the heavy overgrowth, usually after moving less than 1,000 yards inland. The Japanese were fighting a delaying action back into the central mountain range. This gave Admiral Toyoda time to initiate SHO. Admiral Ozawa sailed south from Japanese waters with what was left of the Mobile Fleet. The battleships and cruisers that had anchored near Singapore, now designated 1st Attack Force under Admiral Kurita, set sail for Leyte. A much smaller 2nd Attack Force came from the north, also headed for Leyte. Toyoda was about to spring his carefully set trap.

Americans secured the largest air strip, Tacloban, in the first few days. General Kenney and the engineers understood how important it was to quickly establish airfields. The sooner the army could take over air defense, the sooner the fleet could be pulled from harm's way. However, there was little hardstand near the beach on which to land supplies. GIs took to the expedient of piling them on the runways of Tacloban airfield. Kenney threatened to bulldoze them back into the sea if they weren't moved.

"Scarcely had the assault troops landed when the gloomy predictions of Colonel Ely [staff engineer] that conditions of soil and weather on the island would make it unfit for the establishment of major bases began to be realized."[75] Leyte Valley, adjacent to the eastern landing zones, was interlaced with streams and covered with rice paddies. It rained 35 inches in 45 days. In the latter part of November all construction work on the three fields around Burauen stopped and they were abandoned. A minimum 8-inch gravel base was required before even steel matting could be laid. No gravel was available. Only Tacloban airfield (45 hardstands) was usable during the rainy season. It was described as "a thin slice of metal laid on a jelly mold."[76] Two fighter squadrons attempted to use it. On 25 October, 25 of 100 aircraft that tried to land crashed. One of the crashes set the fuel dump on fire.

Initially General Yamashita wanted to leave Leyte lightly defended so he could concentrate most of his combat power for the upcoming battle for Luzon. Imperial General Headquarters wanted greater effort expended on Leyte. After observing American difficulties on Leyte, Yamashita saw added value in reinforcing that garrison to further delay and attrit the Americans. He decided the best way to defend Luzon was to create a large land battle on Leyte. Exaggerated Japanese claims of kills on both land and sea encouraged Japanese leaders into thinking they were winning. Before he was done Yamashita would send nine coastal convoys carrying 45,000 troops and 10,000 tons of supplies to Leyte. Many landed at Ormoc on the opposite side of Leyte.

From the beginning, clouds of Japanese aircraft, principally from Luzon, contested Leyte airspace. After the initial surprise on A-day, there were more aircraft than Kinkaid's jeep carriers could handle. At times the Japanese even achieved temporary air superiority over the island. Army and navy anti-aircraft gunners heated their gun tubes red-hot fighting off the "meatballs." The few American aircraft that flew into Tacloban airfield were heavily bombed. A number of them were left burning. Kenney remarked, "The bombing was the worst I had ever seen the Jap do. . . . The Nipponese kept us busy all day getting in and out of slit trenches again."[77]

Poor pilot training hampered the Japanese. Had their aim and operational co-ordination been better, the Americans might have been handed a serious set-back. Instead the pilots of the 30 or so P-38s that Tacloban could support repeat-edly tore up Japanese attacks of several times their size. Semi-trained Japanese pilots simply couldn't compete. "The Japanese flyer of October 1944 was an ex-ceedingly inferior successor to the aggressive, skillful, reckless fighter that had preceded him in 1942 and 1943."[78]

Although U.S. Army aviators were knocking down Zeros, they were too few to interdict Japanese reinforcements from landing on Leyte. On 1 November the Japanese 1st Division landed virtually unscathed. It advanced toward the Amer-icans, who had lost their familiar close air support. Torrential rains had all but cut American supply lines. Additional fighting along Leyte's steep ridges engaged previously undiscovered Japanese. Krueger had his hands full. Japanese attacks threatened to split his force. With Halsey's exhausted fleet withdrawing to Ulithi (see chapter 10 for a description of the sea battle), he had to worry about Japan-ese landings in his rear as well. Who would have thought Americans would find themselves in such a difficult situation in the Pacific this late in the war?

American airpower finally began to make itself felt among the Japanese trans-ports seeking to disgorge their cargoes on Leyte. It was a little like the Solomons all over again. American airpower ultimately sank 46 *marus*. The delay of oper-ations against Mindoro and Luzon gave Krueger a break. He swung the 77th Di-vision around by sea and landed at Ormoc on the third anniversary of Pearl Har-bor.

In a different context, General Kenney summed up the Leyte campaign: "We cannot take another chance like Leyte."[79]

10
THE NAVAL CAMPAIGN FOR THE PHILIPPINES

Previously it was not considered feasible to send carriers into areas defended in depth by land-based air. However, Nimitz was ready to do this in the Philippines. "He hoped the attacks on the Philippines might precipitate another fleet action" and destroy enough Japanese airpower, thereby "creating an opportunity for the Allies to secure control over the approaches to the Luzon-Formosa-China coast."[1]

After all the hoopla over Luzon versus Formosa, the naval battle for the Philippines actually began with a series of air strikes on Formosa. For three days Halsey's planes challenged anything on Formosa that could fly. Admiral Toyoda thought these attacks heralded the American main effort and executed SHO 3, defense of Formosa. Japanese airpower went after Halsey's carriers with all the strength they had. Toyoda committed over 500 aircraft to the swirling fur balls over Formosa. It was a supreme test of carrier versus land-based air. But the Americans cheated. They had trained their pilots.

Americans bored in. What little air strength the Japanese carrier fleet had been able to assemble was over Formosa in response to the all-out effort required by SHO 3. It was shot to pieces. The Japanese lost about a third of their fighters intercepting the first strike. Most of the rest succumbed while opposing the second. After that, U.S. aircraft came and went as they pleased. A total of 396 Japanese aircraft and 14 *marus* were lost in exchange for about 90 of Halsey's planes. American fliers decimated the new crop of Japanese aviators. By late 1944, there was no question that American carriers could dominate the best the Japanese could assemble on the fifty airfields of Formosa. Admiral Fukudome had been transferred from his staff position to command all naval forces on Okinawa. "Fukudome's confidence evaporated rapidly as he watched his planes fall in flames after futile attacks on the American raiders."[2]

Many Japanese pilots pressed home their attacks with great determination. Halsey's fleet did not come away unscathed. A pair of light cruisers and the carrier *Hancock* suffered hits. In addition, a pair of American heavy cruisers were badly damaged by aerial torpedoes. They were formed into "Crip Div 1" and steamed away from the scene. During their trek away from Formosa, American sailors referred to them as "Bait Div 1." Several Japanese cruisers and destroyers sallied forth to hit the cripples. When their scout planes saw the number of American carriers in the area, the Japanese hunters quickly broke off.

Third Fleet's raids virtually on the doorstep of Japan didn't bring forth the Combined Fleet. Halsey and Mitscher concluded that loss of aviators and planes had paralyzed the Japanese. Many staff officers back in Honolulu concurred. The Japanese fleet would not fight for the Philippines. So the Americans thought.

Japanese aviators returning to Formosa made fantastic claims. According to aircrew reports, eleven American aircraft carriers, two battleships, and three cruisers had gone to the bottom. Even deflated by half, this would have been an incredible victory. Ultra intercepts demonstrated that the Japanese high command really believed these wild claims and thought the American fleet had been badly gored. Heartened by these "facts," Toyoda and the Imperial Naval Staff were encouraged to continue on with their SHO counterattacks. If the claims were true, there was a genuine chance for the Imperial Fleet to build on their success. In the eyes of the Japanese admirals, the upcoming battles were not suicidal. They really could hand the Americans a serious tactical defeat in Leyte Gulf.

Toyoda was convinced the Americans were about to invade Formosa. Then the Americans invaded Leyte. Their plan was now unmistakable to the Japanese.

While the defenders of Leyte fell back toward the central mountains, Japanese air and sea power had to be redirected southward.

Battle in the Marianas proved for anyone who cared to observe that the Japanese navy could no longer successfully counter the Big Blue Fleet. As he sallied from home waters to the sea east of Luzon, Admiral Ozawa had a fleet carrier (*Zuikaku*), three light carriers, and two bastardized old battleships fitted with an aft deck that could launch, but not land, aircraft. By any standard, this fleet was far less potent than any one of Halsey's four carrier task groups.

The Japanese battle line remained intact. Two 18.1-inch superdreadnoughts, a 16-inch gun battleship, and four 14-inch battleships could still wreck a lot of shipping if only Japanese admirals could figure a way to get them within range of MacArthur's invasion transports. That became the basis of Toyoda's plan.

As a part of SHO 1, defense of the Home Islands against invasion, Admiral Toyoda created a very original plan to bring his battleships to bear on the American invasion fleet. The principal striking power was the 1st Attack Force commanded by Admiral Kurita, which consisted of battleships and cruisers that had sailed from near Singapore. The 1st Attack Force would curl around Mindoro, transit the Sulu Sea, slip through San Bernardino Strait, and descend on the American Leyte invasion fleet from the north. A smaller force consisting of a pair of battleships, a cruiser, and four destroyers under Admiral Nishimura, and three cruisers plus seven destroyers of 2nd Striking Force under Admiral Shima would rendezvous off the southern tip of Negros, transit the Mindanao Sea, and enter Leyte Gulf through the Surigao Strait, between Leyte and Mindanao. Shima's force came down from the north.

Land-based aviation might partially shield the battleship-cruiser forces as they crossed the inland seas of the Philippines. But the larger threat they faced was a massed strike from the concentrated carriers of the Third Fleet. There was no way Toyoda could beat this. The once-proud carrier aviation of First Mobile Fleet was now only a small squadron of nearly empty flight decks holding only 114 aircraft and a handful of carrier-qualified pilots. Instead of integrating the carriers into a striking force, Toyoda employed them as decoys. First Mobile Force would sortie from the north and show itself considerably east of Luzon. In this manner, Ozawa might draw off the American fast carriers. The Japanese knew the aggressive Halsey was in command. If Ozawa could pull the bulk of American naval air off to the northeast, it would ease the task of Japanese land-based air to protect the gunship forces advancing from the west. Interviewed a year later Admiral Ozawa stated, "I expected complete destruction of my fleet but if Kurita's mission was carried out, that was all I wished."[3]

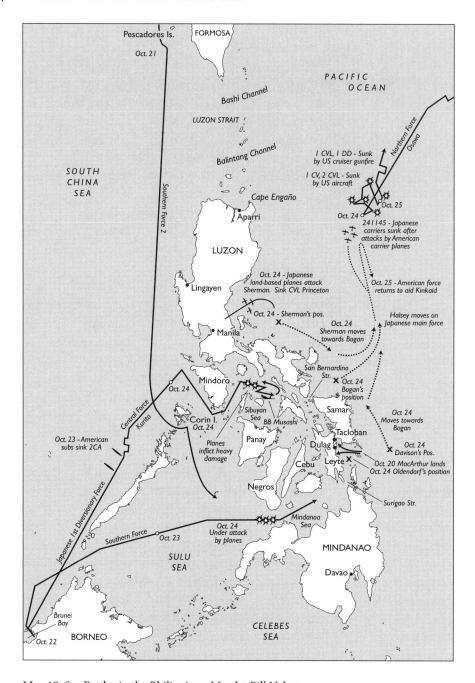

Map 10. Sea Battles in the Philippines. Map by Bill Nelson.

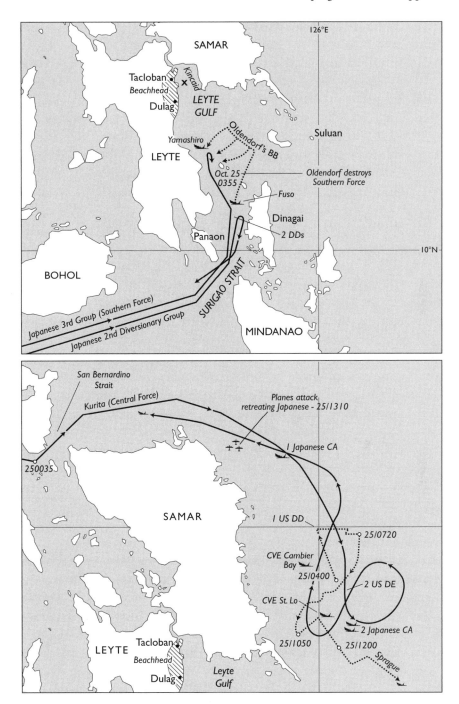

Map 10 continued. Sea Battles in the Philippines. Map by Bill Nelson.

For the Americans, Ultra provided little inkling of Kurita's moves. A better picture of the Imperial Fleet's locations and intentions came from American sub and aircraft sightings than from Ultra. "Although the possibility existed that the Japanese Fleet, which was based in waters near the home islands, might move to the Philippines, most American intelligence analysts considered it doubtful."[4]

Map 10 displays the Philippines. The map on p. 334 depicts how the overall moves fit into the whole and the carrier battle east of Cape Engaño (Luzon). The map at the top of p. 335 shows the battleship duel in Surigao Strait. The bottom one does the same for the incursion through San Bernardino Strait, the fight between battleships and "jeep" carriers off Samar, and its proximity to the anchorages off the Leyte landing beaches.

On 23 November American submarines discovered 1st Attack Force coming up from Linga Roads near Singapore. Kinkaid received the submarine reports that five battleships, ten heavy cruisers, two light cruisers, and sixteen destroyers were steaming up from the south. This was Admiral Kurita's force. Submarines sank two of the Japanese cruisers and so damaged a third that it had to return to port. One of the sunken cruisers was *Atago*, Kurita's flagship. The admiral had to be fished from the sea by a responding destroyer. The main force plowed on.

Both Halsey and Kinkaid were aware of this large force from the subs' sighting reports. The large advancing surface force did not surprise Seventh Fleet. The enhanced intelligence unit set up by Kinkaid had been tracking Japanese surface units for some time. Fleet intelligence now estimated the large surface force would transit San Bernardino Strait. But no one knew where the Japanese carriers were. American subs around the Home Islands sighted several heavy units moving into the Inland Sea but didn't detect Ozawa's force sailing south through the Bungo Strait. Kinkaid moved Oldendorf's battleships to cover Surigao Strait. Obviously he thought San Bernardino Strait was Halsey's responsibility.

Three of Halsey's carrier task groups were spread out in a line 50–100 miles east of the Philippines. Task Group (TG) 39.4 was due east of Leyte Gulf, TG 38.2 was northeast of San Bernardino Strait, and TG 38.3 was due east of Manila. TG 39.4 and TG 38.3 were almost 400 miles apart and not really within mutual supporting distance. TG 38.1 was on its way to Ulithi to replenish. Halsey and Mitscher really had not concentrated their fleet. Instead they had spread it out to facilitate strikes on Japanese airfields that were similarly dispersed. Just before dawn, they moved closer to shore to achieve the best launch site for searches.

At about 0812, Halsey's scouts sighted Kurita's battleships rounding the southern tip of Mindoro. Halsey ordered a major air strike. TG 38.1 was recalled and arrangements made to fuel it at sea.

Halsey wasn't the only commander launching air strikes. Three waves of Japanese land-based aircraft hit TG 38.3. A single Japanese bomber got lucky and left the light carrier *Princeton* burning. A string of torpedoes on torpedo bombers (TBMs) parked on the hangar deck were set off. A mushroom-shaped cloud rose from the stricken ship. Despite a heroic effort, she couldn't be saved.

Halsey's raiders arrived in a series of strikes. In all, 259 sorties were flown against Kurita's ships. No Japanese air cover was available. Vice Admiral Fuku-dome, commanding land-based aviation (Sixth Base Air Force and Second Air Fleet), thought it better to send his fighters to escort his maximum effort against TG 38.3. Super-battleship *Musashi* received a lot of attention. She fought back with massive barrages, including several salvos of anti-aircraft shells from her 18-inch main battery. Nineteen torpedoes and seventeen bombs hit the seagoing monster. It was more than she could bear. Over a thousand souls entered Davy Jones's locker. Another cruiser with damaged propeller shafts turned back to-ward Brunei. But three battleships, six heavy cruisers, and perhaps eleven de-stroyers were still battleworthy as the last of the American strikers turned toward the east. Two of the battleships had taken bombs. The pyrotechnics of those ex-plosions impressed the airmen but the ships were undamaged. The departing airmen reported that Kurita's force had turned to 290 degrees by late afternoon. In fact Kurita did call a temporary retreat. Initially, all the advancing surface forces, whether traveling by the San Bernardino or the Surigao Strait, were to pass through those narrow channels during the night and arrive among the American amphibious shipping at dawn.

Despite Ozawa's attempt to bring attention to himself by launching a strike at Halsey's northernmost task group, he was not sighted by the Americans until midafternoon. It was too late to generate a major strike against the Japanese car-riers. Halsey was itching to sink flattops. Before initial plans to separate out the battleships under Vice Admiral "Ching" Lee, Halsey's battleship commander, were made operational, Ozawa's carriers were sighted. Halsey received solid con-firmation of Ozawa's location at 1515. At 1700 Kurita's ships were observed milling about and retreating. Halsey was influenced by reports from returning American aviators of far more extensive damage than Kurita's force had actually sustained. Any careful analyst of this operation must keep in mind that the fog of war was wafting over a key issue: the extent of Kurita's battle damage.

Carrier *Independence* was dedicated to night flight operations. One of her scouts sighted Kurita's force heading 120 degrees, back toward San Bernardino Strait. This sighting was made at 1935. At 2030 another *Independence* scout spot-ted Kurita's eastward movement. Halsey's flagship noted the report. Another sighting was made at 2120. American aviators also noted that navigation lights in the strait, normally completely off, were brightly lit.

Halsey believed he had three options.[5] First, he could remain off San Bernardino Strait with his entire fleet. He rejected this because Ozawa's entire carrier fleet would get away. Second, he could leave Lee's battle line as a cork for the strait. Lee was certain that Kurita was coming through the strait. Several times he signaled Halsey's flagship that it would be wise to pull the battleships from the carrier groups and form the battle line to block the strait. Initially Lee thought his battleships, backed up by a carrier task group, would be assigned the job.[6] Lee was ready to take on this task even without air support. Halsey did not respond except to acknowledge the message.

In light of recent air attacks from Luzon, it was clear that enemy air might inflict major losses on Lee's task group. After all, TG 38.3, fighting essentially independently, had just lost *Princeton*. If Halsey split his fleet in this manner, he realized that Japanese air and surface naval power "might inflict far more damage on my half fleets separately than they could inflict on the fleet intact."[7] In principle, Mahan could not have argued with that. A competent observer could admire Lee's aggressiveness and Halsey's prudence. Halsey selected what he perceived to be his third alternative: chase Ozawa with his entire fleet. Halsey's motivation was not to bring the battleships along to finish damaged carriers but to *not* leave his battleships in a position where they would not have air cover.

That was enough. Halsey concentrated the carrier task groups of his Task Force 38 and headed north toward an early morning launch at Ozawa's carriers. He dispatched sixteen carriers, seven battleships, and a cloud of escorting cruisers and destroyers toward them. Admiral Sherman commented, "The carrier forces to our north were our meat, they were close enough they could not get away."[8]

Over the years, Halsey's decision to leave San Bernardino Strait and send the entire Third Fleet tearing after Ozawa's pitiful carrier group has been roundly criticized. Who was responsible for guarding San Bernardino Strait? Orders were vague on this point and, of course, there was MacArthur's order to Kinkaid not to talk directly with Halsey. Many have concluded that, in his haste to get at Ozawa, Halsey did not take care to secure the strait. Supposedly Halsey wanted to execute what doctrine called for, damaging enemy ships with airpower and finishing them with gunfire, and ignored other responsibilities. Many opine he should have left Lee's battle line behind to defend San Bernardino Strait.

Should Halsey have positioned Lee's battle line to seal off Kurita? Not as his first choice. Recall that Mahan admonished admirals to avoid melee combat with the enemy. An undamaged *Yamato* was likely to extract a fearsome toll even when confronted by several *Iowa*-class battleships. Precipitating a battleship versus battleship fight with *Yamato* and her lesser consorts was not a good idea. With armor heavier than that of the *Iowas, Yamato* and her 18-inch guns would likely have extracted a high price in blood even though the higher velocity 16-inch guns of the *Iowas* had better penetrating power. A gunnery slugfest was sure to generate two long casualty lists. A conveyor belt of air strikes would eventually sink all the Japanese heavy ships with the least exposure of American life. Unlike in the Marianas, there wasn't a conflict between protecting the amphibians and attacking the most important element of the Japanese fleet. They were one and the same.

Had Lee's offer been accepted, an interesting alternative fight might have developed. Certainly Lee would not have advanced into San Bernardino Strait. Nimitz expressly forbade such a maneuver in his written instructions to Halsey. The strait was probably mined. If Lee had been committed to engage Kurita, he should have employed the deftest of tactics to avoid a head-on fight with 18-inch guns. With warning, Sprague could have moved his jeep carriers out of harm's way and pummeled Kurita from a distance. The most prudent plan would have had Ching Lee waiting in the wings to pounce on Kurita's cripples. Lee had a speed advantage. His battleships could outpace the slower Japanese battleships. And he had 100 miles of sea, the length of Samar Island, to play with. Perhaps his best bet would have been to deploy a screen of destroyers to pick up his adversary and then retreat his own battle line while American carriers concentrated on damaging Japanese battleships. If they could be separated due to battle damage, Lee could reverse course and picked off damaged Japanese battlewagons one by one. This was doctrine accepted by both antagonists. Of course he might have been drawn into a battle line versus battle line fight to prevent Kurita from breaking through, but only as a last resort.

A battle of this length would have extended into daylight hours. Sprague's old-style Wildcat fighters wouldn't have been the best defense against the Japanese airpower that had smothered TF 38.3 the day before. Recall that the American army on Leyte didn't have enough aircraft to defend the beachhead. As Halsey had pointed out, there was significant risk.

Rear Admiral Gerald F. Bogan, commander of TG 38.2, which included *Independence,* also counseled Halsey to leave a strong force to cover San Bernardino Strait. He suggested the battle line, which was designated Task Force 34 when formed, supported by the carriers of TG 38.2, be assigned to cover San Bernardino Strait. In retrospect this might have been about right. Not even Mahan would have thought the remaining carrier groups an insufficient fleet to tackle

Ozawa's depleted force. A single carrier group with 200 planes actually had a 2:1 advantage over the weakened air groups on Ozawa's decks. Bogan realized that the question was whether one carrier task force was sufficient to hit both the greatest threat *and* the greatest target of opportunity—the battleships. A solution of this type is the informal favorite among most naval historians. However, it might be too much "Monday morning quarterbacking" by people who weren't there to feel the heat of the game on Sunday afternoon. One must commend Admiral Bogan for his perceptiveness at the time. It is interesting that Fleet Admiral Halsey did not list Bogan's suggestion as a fourth alternative when he wrote his memoirs.

Based on the limited information that was reviewed, Halsey decided to concentrate his force against what he thought was the greater threat—the carriers.

The critical information was available to Halsey and his staff but they hadn't assembled it properly. Mahan might have gone a step further: three battleships (after *Musashi* sank) and seven heavy cruisers were a more important future threat than Ozawa's empty carriers. He might have advised Halsey to concentrate all of his airpower against the advancing surface forces. Never again would they be so vulnerable. Better sink them all now in the open ocean while they had limited air support than have them bear down on an invasion fleet in Japanese home waters. Armored ships can take a lot of punishment before they go down. If they can get within range, their heavy guns can wreck an invasion fleet. Their existence in the face of a conventional invasion of Japan would seriously complicate that operation. The carriers would not. More careful analysis, taking in the well-known results of the battle of the Philippine Sea and the geography ahead of the fleet, would have identified the battleships as the number one target.

Mahan always counseled to keep the fleet together. He wanted to hit the main enemy formation with the maximum advantage possible. But this principle did not envisage the overwhelming advantage Halsey possessed. As Admiral Morison observed, "Halsey had enough gun and air power to handle both Kurita and Ozawa."[9]

It was very clear that Halsey was aching to go north first to hit Japanese carriers with carrier air and then to annihilate Ozawa's surviving ships with a sweep of his magnificent battleships—just as doctrine recommended. Most of Halsey's staff, including his most trusted air and operations officers, was in full agreement. Halsey told his chief of staff, Rear Admiral Robert B. Carney, "Here is where we're going, Mick," pointing north on the chart, "carriers, battleships and all." Admiral Carney understood. He was a big believer in not dividing the fleet. After reviewing the sightings from *Independence*'s scouts, one of the intelligence officers on duty remembers, "[i]t seemed clear enough to us at the intelligence desk the two enemy forces were advancing via the two straits to strike at the Leyte beachhead in a combined assault." Carney had a reputation for being a creative thinker and an independent voice. Years later, he remarked, "I might have had other ideas."[10] The intelligence plot showed Nishimura's Force C heading for Surigao Strait and Kurita's Force A heading for San Bernardino Strait in a pincer movement with the Leyte transport in between the pincers. The potential for trouble was obvious but Carney held his counsel. Halsey estimated that even if the Japanese center force made it through San Bernardino Strait, it couldn't inflict crippling damage. All officers present at Halsey's staff meeting concurred: leave San Bernardino Strait unguarded and move north to annihilate Ozawa's carriers.[11]

Since the beginning of the fight, Halsey had acted as officer in tactical command in addition to fleet commander. He routinely bypassed Admiral Mitscher and issued instructions directly to the carrier task groups. Mitscher's chief of staff, Commodore Burke, had noted Ozawa's air strike did not return to their carriers. Instead, they continued on to air bases on Leyte. Burke realized that the carriers must be a decoy meant to pull Halsey north. Mitscher also thought so but wouldn't communicate this to Halsey unless asked to do so. Mitscher said, "I don't think we ought to bother Admiral Halsey. He is busy enough."[12]

Later that night, Burke brought to Mitscher's attention the *Independence* sightings of Kurita's ships again steaming east. Burke strongly felt Task Force 34 should be formed and sent to deal with Kurita. TF 34 would contain only four battleships plus supporting cruisers and destroyers. Mitscher, who had counseled Spruance at the Marianas in an almost opposite situation, responded, "Does Admiral Halsey have that report." Yes was the answer. Mitscher continued, "If he wants my advice, he'll ask for it."[13] Then he returned to his bunk.

Captain Mike Cheek was newly installed as Third Fleet intelligence officer on board Halsey's flagship. Previously he had won the Navy Cross for his intelligence work and was one of the last evacuees from the Philippines in 1942. But he was not an aviator and had not yet become one of the boys. One of Cheek's subordinates, Lieutenant Harris Cox, had been studying a translated copy of the Z plan, which had been recovered from the wreckage of Koga's plane. It clearly stated that land-based aviation would be massed to stop future invasions and that the fleet's new primary target wasn't American carriers but rather transports. Surface forces would make for the transports while Japanese carriers could strike from the flank and move out of effective American air range. That was exactly what was happening.

Cox easily convinced Cheek of the correctness of this analysis. Captain Cheek took his case to the assistant officer of the watch, Douglas Moulton. Moulton was

Halsey's air officer and a trusted member of Halsey's staff. After the sightings by the night fliers from *Independence,* a "furious argument" had broken out in the staff compartment between Cheek, who wanted to do something about Kurita, and Moulton, who did not want to be diverted from what they considered to be the more important target, the carriers.[14] Afterwards, Cheek went to Carney to ask permission to see Halsey. The chief of staff said the admiral had already turned in and was not to be disturbed. Third Fleet continued its run north toward Ozawa and his decoys.

Back in Honolulu, Nimitz's headquarters monitored communications from both fleets. When Halsey's order to move north was posted, Admiral Spruance placed his hand on the chart just east of where San Bernardino Strait debouched into the Philippine Sea and said softly, almost to himself, "If I were there, I would keep my force right there."[15] Here was a fellow commander making his point before the fact: he would have selected Halsey's first option. At the time, CinCPOA staff assumed TF 34 had been formed and was guarding San Bernardino Strait.

Meanwhile, Admiral Kinkaid was methodically planning a reception for the Japanese surface raiders that intended to reach the American amphibians via Surigao Strait. These Japanese were the combination of Force C from the South Seas and 2nd Striking Force that had come in from the north.

Navy sea planes observed the advance of the two smaller Japanese surface squadrons toward Surigao Strait about 0940. They were not spotted by aircraft for the remainder of the day. No aircraft were available to strike the advancing Japanese. All of Task Force 38 was hitting Kurita's force. Kinkaid's escort carriers were busy supporting the army on Leyte.

After some navigational calculations, Kinkaid's staff estimated the Japanese battleships would enter Surigao Strait about 0200. A night action would be needed to stop them. That meant one thing: Oldendorf's old battleships, resurrected from the mud of Pearl Harbor, would have to form a battle line and take on the Japanese in an old-fashioned gunfight. Six old American battleships, three cruisers, a brace of light ones, and twenty-six destroyers would engage in a manner the fast battleships' crews could only dream of. They would oppose two Japanese battleships, three heavy and one light cruiser, and eleven destroyers. Mahan would have liked those odds.

By midafternoon all empty transports were formed into a convoy and moved from Leyte Gulf. Three amphibious command ships plus 28 Liberty ships were herded into the north end of Leyte Gulf and provided with a small destroyer screen. Sprague's jeep carrier groups were brought within mutual supporting distance and placed 50 miles to the east where they wouldn't become gun targets.

Later their aircraft might be used to finish off Japanese surface ships. Kinkaid then radioed Halsey that he had covered Surigao Strait and expected Third Fleet to take care of the force headed toward San Bernardino Strait.[16]

The Americans set up a gauntlet within Surigao Strait. The Japanese would enter from the southwest. First they would have to pass a cloud of 45 PT boats looking to develop the situation. Then destroyers deployed along the west side of the strait would salvo torpedoes into the passing enemy ships. Then destroyers would move up on the opposite side and add to the warheads plowing through the water. Oldendorf's battle line of six old battleships cruised east–west at the north end of the strait, corking it. They would cross the T of any column emerging from the gauntlet of small ships. Cruisers placed ahead and to each flank of the battleships, along with additional destroyers, would add more hot steel to the torrent aimed at the hapless Japanese ships. Quoting W. C. Fields, Admiral Oldendorf quipped, "Never give a sucker an even chance."

The two Japanese squadrons never rendezvoused. Instead they entered the strait independently. First came Nishimura's force, charging ahead with four destroyers in the lead followed by two battleships and a heavy cruiser in line one kilometer apart. Initial contact with the PT boats was made at about 2300. Most of the boats launched torpedoes. Japanese return gunfire hit several of them. A destroyer took an American torpedo. However the PT boat action did little to slow the Japanese.

U.S. destroyers picked up the fight about 0200. The Americans intended to engage with torpedoes only. Gun flashes would only reveal their location. Five-inch shells would do little against battleship armor. Left and right flank attacks fired 47 torpedoes and maneuvered out of the way. A pair of torpedoes tore into battleship *Fuso,* splitting her into two flaming chunks. Three Japanese destroyers were hit. One blew up and sank with a hiss that emanated from hell. Japanese return gunfire was heavy but scored nothing at all.

A second and then a third wave of destroyers attacked the advancing Japanese. The cruiser and the second battleship, *Yamashiro,* took torpedoes. Another Japanese destroyer exploded. Again the American destroyers executed their turns without being hit a single time. American torpedo men had come a long way from Savo Island.

The exchange of main gunfire was almost anti-climatic. Only one of the Japanese battleships, the cruiser, and one destroyer made it to the gunfight. Within thirty minutes of the opening American rounds, *Yamashiro* had sunk. The American ships had concentrated on her. Cruiser *Mogami* and the destroyer turned away. Many cruiser and destroyer hits set the Japanese cruiser afire. Pursuing American cruisers sank her later that morning. Only a single Japanese destroyer escaped. Several American destroyers absorbed hits; some of them came from friendly guns.

The second Japanese squadron—two heavy cruisers, a light cruiser, and four destroyers—entered the strait not far behind the first. As they did, radio messages revealed the first squadron was under PT boat attack. The PT boats made runs at this new set of targets. The light cruiser took a torpedo and fell out of formation. Later that morning army bombers would finish her off. The remaining Japanese ships turned tail and made their escape. Oldendorf, in his flagship *Louisville*, led the left flank cruisers in pursuit. They finished off several of the crippled Japanese warships. "In no battle of the entire war did the United States Navy make so nearly a complete sweep as in that of Surigao Strait."[17] Halsey said it more pithily: "He [Oldendorf] not only 'crossed the T,' which is every naval officer's dearest ambition; he dotted several thousand slant eyes."[18] While that statement makes twenty-first-century readers squirm in their chairs, it reflects the prevailing attitude of the time.

Rock Hard Saltwater Taffy

Kurita's battle force passed through San Bernardino Strait without further molestation under dim moonlight from a cloudy sky. At 0400, while Surigao Strait was alight with burning Japanese warships, Kurita sailed south along Samar Island. He expected to reach Leyte Gulf around 1100. His officers looked forward to "the decisive battle." Kurita radioed Toyoda, "By Heaven sent opportunity, we are dashing to attack enemy carriers. Our first Objective is to destroy the flight decks, then the task force."[19]

It was the rainy season and weather along the east coast of Samar was frequently foul. The morning was dark with squalls, limiting visibility. Unexpectedly lookouts on *Yamato* sighted masts at 0644. A carrier! No—three carriers, three cruisers, and two destroyers. At least this is what *Yamato*'s lookouts sang out.

The lookouts on the ships of Taffy 3, the northernmost group of Admiral Thomas Sprague's jeep carriers, were equally shocked. Jeep carriers were supposed to provide close air support or maybe chase submarines. But engage battleships?! At 0658 there could be no question. Eighteen-inch shells began falling among the startled Americans.

When the Americans were sighted, the Japanese squadron was in the process of adopting a circular formation to ward off American aircraft. Kurita bungled the orders for attack formation. Fortunately for the tiny American ships, this limited the ability of the Japanese to bring their big guns to bear. There were no

American cruisers. Taffy 3 was screened by three destroyers and four even smaller destroyer escorts which were armed with only 3-inch guns. Rear Admiral Clifton "Ziggy" Sprague commanded Taffy 3, which was part of TG 77.4, headed by Admiral Tommy Sprague, an escort carrier group that also contained the similarly organized Taffy 1 and Taffy 2.

By 0700 Japanese spotters had seen all six escort carriers of Taffy 3. Escort carriers could make barely 18 knots, one of the reasons they could never run with the fast carriers of the Big Blue Fleet. Neither could they even begin to pull away from Kurita's 27-knot battleships, which continued to close range although they had yet to score hits. Japanese radio operators could hear pleas for help broadcast from Taffy 3 "in the clear." A return message promised help within two hours. This news unsettled Japanese commanders. What other heavy American ships were in the vicinity that might ambush them?

Conflicting orders caused the Japanese ships to veer first south-southwest and then south-southeast. Many lost sight of their American quarry. Some of the jeep carriers' aircraft began buzzing about. Many of the aircraft had little to shoot with; only six torpedoes had been allocated to each jeep carrier. Some were very thankful they had loaded more. One strike disabled the rudder of cruiser *Chokai*. She fell behind.

American destroyer men showed incredible bravery. Ziggy Sprague ordered the destroyers to open fire while the carriers maneuvered in the sight of the Japanese battleships in order to launch their aircraft. They charged their gigantic attackers, launching torpedoes into the gray-green water. Destroyer *Johnston* smacked a 5-inch shell into cruiser *Kumano,* followed by a torpedo that tore off her bow. This cruiser fell out of formation as well. For her heroics, *Johnston* received three battleship shells from *Kongo*. A third cruiser was hit by a bomb and fell back. Sprague ordered: "Small Boys [destroyers and destroyer escorts] on my starboard quarter interpose with smoke between Men [jeep carriers] and enemy cruisers." Shortly thereafter he followed up: "Small Boys form for second attack."

Despite the numbing surprise of facing huge dinosaurs while armed only with peashooters, American officers lost neither their composure nor their courage. Destroyer *Hoel* fired two spreads of torpedoes at battleship *Kongo* and a heavy cruiser before it was shattered by 1,400-pound battleship rounds. Destroyer escort *Samuel B. Roberts* hurled 608 shells at the Japanese before being shredded into a sinking mass of twisted metal.

But American luck began to wear thin. Jeep carrier *Gambier Bay* was hit by gunfire and began to sink. Gallant *Johnston* was now fighting off five Japanese destroyers. The odds overwhelmed her and she began to go down. The Japanese destroyer commander was so taken by *Johnston*'s gallantry that he saluted her as she went beneath the swells. Carrier *Kalinin Bay* took 14 large-caliber hits. Incredibly, she remained afloat.

Taffy flyers hit a fourth Japanese cruiser and it began to sink. Several destroyers were also damaged. At 1148 *Yamato*'s top lookout sang out again: "Masts of Pennsylvania type battleship bearing 0 degrees."[20] Of course there were no American heavy ships in the area. But Kurita had more to worry about. A float plane was sent off to confirm what the Americans had to the north. The scout could not confirm the sighting. At 1310 a 70-aircraft strike came from the north (it was from TG 38.1, which was steaming up from its refueling and had been on its way north to catch up with the rest of Task Force 38). Damage was negligible.

Japanese signal interceptors aboard Kurita's ships picked up American messages that reinforcing U.S. ships were making for Leyte Gulf. The Japanese commander and his staff had slept little in the last seventy-two hours and they were exhausted. Kurita reasoned that if he entered Leyte Gulf, American airpower could ambush him in that cramped space and cripple his unprotected ships. His staff concurred. At 1313, Kurita ordered his ships to break off their engagement with Taffy 3 and sail due north to engage with the unseen enemy that was supposedly coming to the rescue.[21] On deck, the change in course was greeted with "Banzai" from the sailors. They were off to another "decisive engagement."

Admiral Ugaki commanded Battleship Division One (*Yamato* and the now-sunk *Mushashi*) during this fight. An intelligent and courageous officer, he wrote in his diary, "The enemy task force seemed to have prepared for our attack into the Leyte anchorage by taking a mobile disposition. As the enemy situation at Leyte was unknown, our attack into Leyte could only make us easy prey for the enemy. Instead, better to turn about and attack an enemy task force located at 113 miles bearing 5 degrees off Suluan Light at 0945, when it least expected us to come."[22] There was no such force. The Japanese left behind three heavy cruisers sinking or sunk, while the Americans lost two destroyers, a destroyer escort, and a jeep carrier. A second jeep carrier would fall victim to one of the first kamikaze attacks that afternoon.

Later Kurita told a Japanese interviewer, "As I consider it now, my judgement does not seem to have been sound. Then the decision seemed right, but my mind was extremely fatigued."[23] His chief of staff, Admiral Koyanagi, later stated, "I think now we should have gone into Leyte Gulf. So does Admiral Kurita." However, these comments beg the question, Why not use float planes to find out where the enemy was? Japanese cruisers carried them. Over and over again, we see poor tactical reconnaissance (remember Midway) result in poor decisions.

Twenty-eight Liberty ships and twenty-three LSTs were still in the gulf. Although the carnage would have been terrible, the invasion of Leyte would have continued and have succeeded even if all of this shipping had been lost. Kurita has been roundly criticized for not pushing onto them from only 50 nautical miles away. Had he done so and had Oldendorf made flank speed, the two battle lines would have clashed before Kurita could have possibly finished the transports off. But Kurita's battle line was the last fleet in being the Japanese possessed. He knew this. On 25 October 1944, was it clear that the last grouping of Japanese major units should be sacrificed? Even if mighty *Yamato* took an old American battleship or two along with it? Then again, Kurita didn't know what set of targets he might find in Leyte Gulf. Could enough shipping be destroyed to change the course of this battle? There is no way to replicate the crushing weight of these uncertainties on Kurita and his staff.

Viewing this battle from a Japanese perspective underscores the enormous pressure, the intense risk, the overwhelming uncertainty, and constant possibility of near-instantaneous disaster that officers in all of the war's naval battles had to withstand. As Mahan continually emphasized, the most important element in naval warfare is the trained and hardened officers that can continue to function with immediacy in an environment that would paralyze lesser men. In an information-rich hindsight, it is easy to criticize decisions that had to be made with the only information available. Reflecting on the enormity of the task one must marvel at great men like Halsey—and Kinkaid, the Spragues, and a legion of others—who could make crisp, unequivocal decisions on the spot. They were rare and valuable leaders.

Sprague's call for help reached Kinkaid about 0700. Kinkaid confronted the dilemma: defend the beachhead or rescue the jeep carriers? Kurita's cruisers were greyhounds. Even his lumbering battleships could easily catch the escort carriers. Only Taffy 3 was at immediate risk. But good use of air recon would reveal additional plump targets within Kurita's reach. Kinkaid urgently requested Halsey's help. He ordered that all available naval airpower supporting the beachhead be redirected at Kurita. Before it was over Kurita would be hit by at least 253 fighters and 143 torpedo planes. That was no small strike.

At 0800, Admiral Oldendorf's battle line was a good 65 miles from the engagement between Kurita's heavies and Sprague's intrepid Small Boys. It would have taken more than three hours for his old 20-knot ships to join the fight. Oldendorf's chief of staff, Captain Bates, reminded his admiral that the best strategy was to deploy the battle line where it could "T" Kurita's force as it entered Leyte Gulf. Ugaki's speculation about a potential trap wasn't all wrong. *Yamato* clearly outclassed the old American ships but they were more evenly matched against the other three. The American force would remain close enough to return to Surigao Strait should a surprise develop from that quarter. This disposition was a well-balanced one for discharging Oldendorf's primary mission, defense of the Leyte beachhead.

At 0850, Oldendorf received a radio message from Kinkaid ordering him to move to the vicinity of Hibuson Island. Kinkaid's first impulse was to affirm "Olie's" dispositions. But his chief of staff, Commodore Valentine H. Schaeffer, vehemently objected. Leaving Oldendorf in a static position meant that at least Taffy 3 was to be sacrificed. Kinkaid discussed the pluses and minuses with his chief of staff before reluctantly agreeing. At 0957 a second message from Kinkaid ordered Oldendorf to split his force, sending half to assist Sprague and holding the other half to defend Leyte Gulf. One can understand Kinkaid's desire to help, but Mahan would have repeated Captain Bates's advice: All or none. Don't divide your fleet. Avoid melee combat. Shape the fight to your own advantage. Soon thereafter Kurita broke away from Taffy and headed north, and Kinkaid canceled his order.

Dawn of the 25th found Halsey's sleek gray ships slicing through the waters off Cape Engano headed toward Ozawa's underarmed fleet. After the previous day's strike Ozawa had but 29 aircraft left among his brood, fleet carrier *Zuikaku*, three light carriers, and two semi-converted battleships. His pitiful screen consisted of nine destroyers and three light cruisers.

Fifteen defending Zeros splashed when hit by the first wave of attacking Hellcats at about 0800. All day long aircraft from three of Halsey's carrier groups savaged Ozawa's almost defenseless carriers. TG 38.1 never made it to the fight. Four waves of strikers hurled bombs and torpedoes at what was left of the mobile fleet. Like rotten timber hit by a massive sledgehammer, Ozawa's pathetic force splintered. A smaller tool would have done just as good a job. That night several of Halsey's cruisers caught up with a few cripples and finished them with gunfire just as doctrine envisaged. *Zuikaku*, the last surviving carrier with the Indian head emblem worn by those who raided Pearl Harbor, had gone to the bottom along with three light carriers, a light cruiser, and four destroyers.

"Where Is Task Force 34?"

At 1512 on the 24th, prior to the night action in Surigao Strait, Kurita's move for the eastern exit of the San Bernardino Strait, and the sighting of Ozawa's carriers, Halsey's operations officer, Captain Rollo Smith, had issued a preliminary order stating Task Force 34, Admiral Lee's battle line, was to be formed. While Lee would be in command, Halsey would be aboard one of Lee's subordinate battleships (*New Jersey*) and in tactical command of Third Fleet *including TF 34*.[24] Kinkaid's radiomen monitored Third Fleet transmissions. They picked up the warning order to form Task Force 34 and apparently thought the order had been executed. Remember MacArthur had forbidden Kinkaid to communicate directly with Halsey, so a request for confirmation would have been difficult under all but the direst of circumstances. Nevertheless at 0648 on the 25th, Halsey did receive a signal from Kinkaid: "Am now engaging enemy surface forces Surigao Strait X Question is TF 34 guarding San Bernardino Strait." In Halsey's words: "To this I replied in some bewilderment 'negative X It is with our carriers now.'"[25] Lack of a single commander at sea had generated potentially deadly confusion at the highest level of battle commanders. Blame for letting intraservice command squabbles destroy unity of command must be laid unceremoniously at the feet of King and Marshall.

Back in Honolulu, Nimitz was becoming increasingly concerned that no one was covering San Bernardino Strait. He asked his assistant chief of staff, Captain Bernard Austin, to gather any available information on the situation. Staffers recall Admiral Nimitz sounded a good many buzzers that morning in his search for information and opinions. About the third time he summoned Austin, the captain responded, "Admiral, couldn't you just ask Admiral Halsey the simple question: Where is Task Force 34?"[26]

The now famous message from Nimitz to Halsey was sent. An inexperienced communications officer failed to strip away the padding—additional words that were not part of the real message but were transmitted to confuse Japanese eavesdroppers—with the result that the message that reached Halsey said "Where is Task Force 34? The World Wonders."

It is hard to imagine Nimitz ever addressing anyone in such a rude manner. Understandably, upon receiving this message, Halsey turned red, threw the communications tape on the deck, and stamped on it.[27] The battleships were almost within gun range of Ozawa. Nevertheless, Halsey ordered Lee to turn away and head toward San Bernardino Strait. Anyone with dividers in Flag Plot could calculate that the battleships wouldn't arrive until the next day, long after the crisis would have been resolved. The carriers of TG 38.2 followed in their wake.

Interestingly, Kinkaid didn't believe the split command had been an insurmountable problem. Speaking out in 1960, he said, "I had a mission and Halsey had a mission. In spite of the fact that we did not have a common superior, I have frequently said that if both Halsey and I had carried out our respective missions correctly there would have been no confusion. . . . One commander would not have been better than two where each of us had his mission . . . very clearly stated."[28] Kinkaid felt that Halsey's mission of "strategic support" included covering San Bernardino Strait. By inference, one must conclude that Kinkaid wished that part of the mission had been more clearly stated.

Better staff work would have calculated that TG 38.1 wasn't likely to make it to the fight with Ozawa and that it should have been diverted to cover San Bernardino. While it wouldn't have arrived before first light, it still would have been a savior for Sprague and his jeep carriers, and air cover for Lee if he was in the vicinity, without putting Kinkaid and Oldendorf in a dilemma.

Rear Admiral "Jocko" Clark was back in Washington during the battle for Leyte Gulf. He happened to be in King's office just after the pleas from the Taffies had been received. Clark recalled, "Like a tiger he [King] was pacing up and down in a towering rage." Complaining about Halsey, King growled, "He has left the strait open for the Japanese to strike the transports at Leyte."[29]

After hearing from Kinkaid and Halsey, King concluded that Kinkaid should have provided proper recon for San Bernardino Strait. Later King blamed Kinkaid, not Halsey, for leaving the strait unguarded.

Thomas Buell, King's definitive biographer, thinks King had some culpability in Halsey's going north. He probably directed Nimitz to make Halsey's prime objective destruction of the enemy fleet.[30] Note Kinkaid ordered Tommy Sprague to search San Bernardino Strait at first light. That search was late getting off. Sprague bears some responsibility for his own predicament, but Kinkaid never criticized him for it.

Admiral King remarked, "The Battle for Leyte Gulf presents a curious antithesis to the Battle of the Philippine Sea."[31] There Spruance refused to be pulled too far away from the invasion fleet and missed an opportunity to destroy Ozawa's carriers. Halsey allowed himself to be pulled away by Ozawa's fleet, which was but a shadow of its former self, and almost precipitated a disaster by allowing Kurita's battleships free passage to the invasion fleet. America should be grateful that Halsey was so lucky. Of course Halsey defended his decision. But in a telling moment in 1953, he said, "I wish that Spruance had been with Mitscher at Leyte Gulf and I had been with Mitscher in the Battle of the Philippine Sea."[32]

Retrospective

The well-studied dilemmas faced by Spruance and Halsey and the less famous one faced by Kinkaid at Leyte underscore a common and very difficult problem. In both land and sea warfare, great emphasis is placed on concentrating overwhelming combat power on the single most important enemy center of gravity. In Mahanian terms, this is inevitably the enemy's fleet or, more precisely, his main battle line. When faced with the real threat of the enemy concentrating and smashing your own greatest vulnerability while you attempt to do the same to him at a different time and place out of supporting range of your own attack force, what do you do? When faced with real risk to a great many men's lives, the choice is nowhere nearly as easy as it is in the pages of a primer on strategy. Nevertheless, Mahan does provide guidance: "The nation that would rule the sea must always attack." In relation to seas, fleets are small. The side that is on the offensive has the initiative and dictates where the course of combat is going to go. The attacker acts; the defender must react. Despite the risk of falling into an enemy trap, if you begin to assume a defensive posture you cede to the enemy the opportunity to dictate the time and place of combat. The tide of battle will swing toward your vulnerabilities and away from those of your enemy.

In these three battles, do we see a gap developing in Mahan's thought? In land warfare, a general is schooled to balance the principles of concentration and offensive with the need for providing security for his force. Contemporary emphasis on information warfare aids us by providing some terms for ideas that are far older than Mahan. Concentrate enough power to overwhelm the enemy's center of gravity you have chosen to attack. However, you must provide sufficient light forces to warn of enemy movement or action in time for you to do something about it. This calculation of time and space is critical. Warning with insufficient time to react is little more than a premonition of disaster. But do not assign a single ship of the line to such duty. Mahan simply could not bear that. The analogous advice to a general on the ground would be, Screen your flanks with outposts but do not allocate stronger forces with the mission to guard or to put up significant resistance to an enemy incursion.

In the age of sail, navies had squadrons of fast frigates to ferret out the enemy so the battle line could maneuver in sufficient time to crush him. In the age of steam, fast cruisers of the scouting force provided the same mission for the battle force. As communications and aviation advanced, this need became even more important. However, Mahan did not sufficiently develop the notion of force security from the several hundred years of naval history that he used as his database.

Still, Mahan provides additional valuable guidance. It's the balance of power between the opposing navies at the end of the battle that matters. If confronted with seemingly equal opportunities (or threats), select the course of action that results in greatest damage to the enemy fleet with least risk to the continuing existence of one's own. Ozawa's single large fleet carrier and a couple of light ones hardly could have opposed even one of Mitscher's carrier groups in the open ocean. A functional battleship division, covered by land-based air, could seriously jeopardize an amphibious operation, especially when several dispersed landings are made, as would be likely in upcoming operations among the Home Islands.

Comparing the three naval battles around the Philippines with the problem Spruance faced in the Marianas, Spruance had the most difficult task. His opponent had the vast open ocean on which to slip his small fleet by. However, the range of Spruance's aircraft allowed him to recover from the initial stages of a penetration before Japanese battleships got within gunnery range. And Terrible Turner had arranged Oldendorf's old battleships to provide final protection while the amphibious ships weighed anchor and became far more difficult targets to hit. In retrospect, one must side with Mitscher's desire to maneuver offensively after Spruance had done such a marvelous job in arranging Turner's forces to minimize their exposure. Spruance had radar-equipped flying boats and carrier-based Avengers, also with radar, to search out the night. A little better management of these assets would have given him better information on the crucial night of 18 June 1944.

Halsey had an easier problem. His combat power was so overwhelming that he could split his forces and still mass overwhelming combat power against two enemy fleets out of range of mutual support. His night fliers already had identified Kurita resuming his advance toward San Bernardino Strait. By detaching a few destroyers he could have gained continuous contact with his maneuvering enemy the way a general uses his cavalry (horse, mechanized, or helicopter, depending on the era). That "naval cavalry" could have provided sufficient warning to keep Taffy out of harm's way while the jeep carriers rained a large amount of punishment down on Kurita.

Halsey made a more fundamental mistake. He misidentified the center of gravity of the Japanese fleet. Up to the Marianas, it had been the carriers. Now it was Kurita's battleships. At the time there was sufficient evidence to indicate that Ozawa had few aircraft available. Simple inspection of the charts from the Philippines to Tokyo demonstrated the two fleets would never again clash in open ocean away from large Japanese land air bases. Formosa, Okinawa, and the Home Islands themselves were the likely scenes of battle. Japan wouldn't need floating air strips. Halsey should have allocated sufficient combat power to destroy Kurita's force and then calculated whether he had sufficient combat power remaining to chase Ozawa's empty carrier decks.

No matter how brilliant the senior commander, it is impossible to write instructions that cover every possible eventuality. No one is that clairvoyant. Over and over again down through history, unity of command has proved critical. A single commander on the spot is the best way to exploit unforeseen opportunities and parry enemy threats. The best way to deal with Kurita might have been to rearrange forces from both Third and Seventh fleets. Sprague's carriers had sufficient speed to deal with an advancing Kurita as long as they had sufficient warning never to get within 100 miles of him. Combine Ching Lee's TF 34 with the Taffies plus TF 38.1 and one could have a very powerful force with which to destroy Kurita. Then Halsey's remaining carrier strength could dispatch the Japanese carriers. But that would have required a single admiral on the spot to reshuffle assets. Hopefully that admiral could react with the aplomb of those brave sailors that manned Sprague's "Small Boys."

Oldendorf's dispositions in Leyte Gulf after the battle of Surigao Strait made sense. But Kinkaid's final solution was the correct one. Much Japanese combat power had already been sunk or had been spotted at locations that posed no threat to Leyte Gulf. Oldendorf had long-range flying boats to maintain a distant search and a swarm of PT boats in Surigao Strait to provide constant monitoring of any attempt by the Japanese to retrace their steps. Kinkaid had sufficient security to allow him to move *all* of Oldendorf's heavy ships north to protect Sprague and pummel Kurita. If he only could have reached that (correct) conclusion a little earlier. Then again he didn't have the advantage of reading sixty years of debate in an easy chair.

By the end of the battle for Leyte, the Big Blue Fleet has sunk what was left of the once proud First Mobile Fleet. For all intents and purposes the navy versus navy war had been won. There remained a single final objective: the surrender of Japan. Would she succumb to blockade and aerial bombardment? Or would an invasion be needed? The final steps should involve only those operations necessary to execute the final strategy for the defeat of Japan.

Luzon and Afterward

After Leyte Gulf, the Formosa versus Luzon debate was resurrected. However, there was little practical alternative. A field army would be needed to invade Formosa. MacArthur had two—the Sixth and Eighth—and the troops to fill them both out. But he was not about to let go of either. In Washington, the army told the navy there were insufficient troops to assault Formosa until after Luzon was taken. Ahem.

MacArthur would invade Luzon via Lingayen Gulf northwest of Manila Bay. The planned route for amphibious forces left Leyte Gulf via Surigao Strait and then wound northwest through the Sibuyan Sea and the South China Sea to Lingayen Gulf. (See Map 10.) These restricted waters were ringed with Japanese airfields. This path was fraught with restricted choke points that would keep invasion ships from maneuvering in the face of huge enemy air strikes. The sea lanes into Leyte needed to be secured. Kurita's battleships and cruisers had limped back into the South Seas. They remained a distant and improbable threat. However,

Japanese airpower in the northern Philippines had demonstrated its teeth. There was more to come.

Protecting the Luzon invasion fleet should have been the job of army fighters based on Leyte. As much as the engineers tried, they could not increase airfield capacity in the mud and torrential downpours. There wasn't sufficient army airpower to defend army installations, let alone a slow-moving amphibious fleet while it transited several hundred miles of ocean. Leyte never became an important base for air operations.

The poor choice of Leyte as a site for airfields immediately created problems. Originally, MacArthur stated he would have his own air support in place by the 27th. When that day arrived, he requested two carrier task groups from Halsey for suppression of Japanese air. Fewer than 60 army fighters were ashore, and they had to deal with several hundred Japanese aircraft based on Luzon. It was unimaginable that an American force could lose air superiority on any battlefield in late 1944. But that is exactly what happened at Leyte.

Sprague's jeep carriers had been doing great work but they needed to pull away to refuel. Besides, they carried Wildcat fighters that were nowhere nearly as potent in dealing with Zeros as Hellcats, which only the fast carriers possessed. Halsey and Nimitz chafed at using their prize strike force for such mundane tasks as convoy air defense. Despite TF 38's need to return to Ulithi for some rest and repair, they agreed to leave a single task group behind to support the invasion.

The Japanese air strikes were taking their toll on Kinkaid's ships supporting the invasion from Leyte Gulf. On 1 November Kinkaid lost one destroyer and had four others damaged by raiding Japanese aircraft. Losses were getting serious. Kinkaid told MacArthur that Seventh Fleet would not be strong enough to protect the voyage to Luzon. He suggested MacArthur request that Nimitz order the Big Blue Fleet to return and take out Japanese airfields on Luzon and those westward islands that could interfere with upcoming operations. MacArthur did so and also requested that TG 38.3 remain in close support of the troops that were grinding their way across Leyte.[33]

A large number of surface ships were scheduled to leave Philippine waters for overhaul before the next large amphibious operation. At the end of 1944 Kinkaid asked to retain all the battleships, a large contingent of destroyers, plus some cruisers. He needed them to protect against a sortie by elements of the Japanese battle line coming either up from the South Seas or the waters around the Home Islands. Nimitz correctly saw the error of this request: Kurita's surviving ships were even less seaworthy. The incident demonstrates the psychological power of a fleet in being and also the need to retain the initiative with offensive action.

When Vice Admiral Onishi assumed command of First Air Fleet in the Philippines in mid-October, he was appalled to find only about 100 of his aircraft operational. In conventional use, they would accomplish little. Onishi had studied the disaster of the Great Marianas Turkey Shoot. He concluded that the major problem wasn't aircraft but trained pilots. A pilot needed at least 18 months of training with 800 hours in the air before he could be posted to a carrier. There was no way that pilots would get this level of training before being committed to combat.

The so-called "special attack units"—kamikazes—had been discussed for some time. Onishi may have been the first Japanese to begin thinking systematically about suicide attackers. Kamikaze pilots would need little training. With a paucity of resources, Onishi gave the go-ahead. Thus was born the precision-guided munition, human guided. The notion was immediately embraced by a number of the pilots. Twenty-four volunteers were combined into the first special attack unit. From this dubious beginning sprang a revolution in weaponry that was to have as much impact on warfare as the nuclear weapon. But it would take forty-five years until it achieved technological sophistication far from the Pacific Ocean in the sands of Iraq.

Three kamikazes participated in the first attack on ships off Leyte. Two were shot down. The third hit the foremast of HMAS *Australia*, killing twenty men, including her captain. On 5 November one slipped through American defenses and crashed into carrier *Lexington*. The kamikaze threat provoked concern. As Halsey said, "We first dismissed the Special Attack Corps as a flash in the pan. Now it seemed less a flash than a blast."[34]

The land-based air situation on Leyte wasn't getting any better. From 5 November to 15 December, 35 inches of rain fell on the poor engineers who were trying to establish a surface firm enough for an aircraft to land on. It was a losing proposition. Attempts to construct airfields at Bayug, Bui, Dulag, and San Pablo had to be abandoned. In a night raid, Japanese destroyed 27 P-38s on Leyte's only serviceable airfield. The Japanese navy began nightly runs into Ormoc on Leyte. Some 45,000 troops and thousands of tons of supplies and equipment made it ashore. During the operations, either army or carrier planes caught and sank a number of Japanese transports as well as four destroyers, in engagements reminiscent of those with the Tokyo Express back in 1942 at Guadalcanal. Because of the incessant rain, American army ground attacks made little headway against the mud and the increasing number of Japanese defenders.

The fast carriers returned to Philippine waters on 12 November. Initially their target was shipping being used to reinforce the Japanese on Leyte rather than the still very potent land-based air threat. They scored well. A light cruiser, another four destroyers, and seven transports went to the bottom. Halsey felt it was far more productive to hit enemy airfields than to simply provide air defense for Leyte. Between 5 and 25 November he hit Japanese airfields six times. Mahan would definitely have approved. Take the offensive against the most potent threat at every opportunity.

After refueling, Halsey's carriers returned to Luzon on 25 November. Japanese air was waiting for them. Aircraft reinforcements had continued to arrive via Formosa, and large numbers of planes rose to intercept the attacking Americans. More seriously, the fast carriers began to be peppered by small kamikaze strikes. Four of nine carriers were hit, although only one carrier was damaged seriously enough to suspend flight operations. Halsey was losing his taste for dueling with land-based special attack forces. Because three carriers had to be withdrawn for repairs, TF 38 consolidated four groups into three. This reduction was a far larger impact on the deployment of American forces than the Japanese navy induced during the battle of the Philippine Sea and Leyte Gulf combined. The expectation of constant air attacks wore down all aboard ship. Flight surgeons began grounding pilots because of stress and exhaustion. The Big Blue Fleet needed a rest.

Halsey suspected that leaks in American communications had tipped the Japanese to the location of TF 38. Several possible codes were examined. Then someone tried an experiment. Several ships were sent out and emulated the radio signature of a carrier task group readying a strike. Japanese reaction was immediate. While the Japanese were not breaking codes the way the Americans were, they had become expert in the use of radio traffic analysis. The always-talkative Americans were very vulnerable to this kind of signal intelligence. For the remainder of the war, the American fleet adopted better deceptive and manipulative radio patterns.

The quagmire on Leyte affected the situation in the air. The remainder of the Philippine campaign was now in jeopardy. How was the fleet going to get to Lingayen Gulf without air superiority? Halsey refused to bring back his carriers in time to meet MacArthur's deadline. His crews were simply too worn out.

General Kenney was determined not to enter Luzon without air superiority guaranteed by land-based aviation. He wanted a minimum of four fighter and nine bomber groups—a force of as many as 700 aircraft. Plans were drafted to seize the island of Mindoro (Map 10) and construct airfields to cover the Lingayen landings. While everyone pinned their hopes on the better engineering geology found on Mindoro, the planes would still require landing fields on Leyte. Those needed a lot more work, which meant more time. Kenney also wanted a delay. He described his meeting with Sutherland and MacArthur on the subject as a "real brawl."[35] MacArthur would not hear of a delay.

Despite the rain and the lack of air superiority, MacArthur was determined to maintain his Luzon schedule. On the day TF 38 departed for Ulithi, he convened a meeting to finalize preparation for the invasion of Mindoro, which was only 10 days away. Despite having only a fraction of the planned air force in place on Leyte, General Kenney expressed optimism. Kinkaid's chief of staff, Commodore Schaeffer, estimated that 2 percent of the ships in the invasion fleet might sustain damage. General Krueger, commander, Sixth Army, stated he couldn't sustain such losses and retain sufficient combat power to land in Lingayen Gulf on 5 January 1945. MacArthur threw the ball back to Kinkaid. Could his escort carriers provide cover? Kinkaid said yes, but it wasn't a good solution. Escort carriers were not designed to take the punishment Japanese airpower could dish out.

The more Kinkaid and his staff thought about this solution, the less they liked it. Several of his subordinate commanders went on record opposing the Lingayen landings altogether as too risky. On 30 November, six days before the operation was to begin, Kinkaid had a heated meeting with MacArthur. The admiral could not move the general. Reluctantly Kinkaid drafted an urgent cable to King stating the planned operation could be disastrous. Kinkaid was to meet with MacArthur again for dinner that evening. He fully expected to be relieved of command by MacArthur.

Admiral Nimitz had been monitoring Kinkaid's predicament. Nimitz's chief of staff, Forrest Sherman, had been in Tacloban and had been apprised of Kinkaid's arguments and MacArthur's unbending response. Just before dinner, a cable from Nimitz to MacArthur arrived in the Philippines.[36] Nimitz also believed that the fast carrier crews needed a rest. However, if given a short break they could be back on station. Details from Halsey were to follow. Around dessert time, the contents of Halsey's cable to Nimitz arrived. If the movement to Mindoro was delayed ten days, Halsey could cover it. After seeing this MacArthur agreed to a ten-day delay for Mindoro and a twenty-day delay for Lingayen Gulf. Kinkaid had stood up for what was right. Fortunately the ever capable Nimitz found a solution before the dispute had to go all the way back to Washington.

Krueger also put the delay to good use. He staged two short "end around" amphibious operations onto the west coast of Leyte to secure the island. These effectively eliminated any further Japanese reinforcement of the island and were also tactically effective. During these operations, three destroyers and a Liberty ship were sunk by Japanese aircraft. Six destroyers were heavily damaged.

A day before the Mindoro landings, Halsey's carriers returned to pound Japanese airfields. American aircraft continued attacking for three days. Halsey's fliers claimed over 400 enemy aircraft destroyed. Six Seventh Fleet escort carriers provided close-in combat air patrol over the invasion fleet. They claimed another 66 Japanese aircraft. After all the worry, the invasion fleet's passage to Mindoro was uneventful. Though challenged by Japanese aircraft, the Americans retained control of the sky. Only about 1,000 Japanese were on the island. Apparently Yamashita hadn't recognized Mindoro's potential as an air base. Some 27,000 Americans came ashore and made short work of the defenders. Engineers completed an air strip the day after the 15 December landing. Mountains on the island deflected the worst of the rainstorms. By the end of a week, the field supported 105 aircraft—including 13 B-25s, 44 P-38s, 28 P-47s, and 20 P-40s. At about the same time, 290 aircraft based on Leyte remained operational. By the time of the Luzon invasion, five fighter and two bomber groups were operating from Mindoro.

Japanese raiders continued to hit resupply convoys through the end of 1944. Four supply ships were sunk and another six were heavily damaged. On the day after Christmas a Japanese heavy cruiser, one light cruiser, and six destroyers raided Mindoro. They fired a few rounds into the port and airfield with little effect. An American cruiser-destroyer force attempted to intercept them but didn't arrive in time. One Japanese destroyer was sunk by a torpedo from a PT boat. Aircraft from Mindoro bombed the Japanese ships, damaging several but not sinking another.

Of all things, 39 Japanese transport aircraft dropped paratroopers on two of the operational Leyte airfields, Buri and Bayang, on the night of the 6 January 1945. Paratroopers took complete control of the Buri airstrip. Air force service personnel had withdrawn without much of a fight. The immediate reaction force at San Pablo air strip consisted of engineers and artillerymen of the U.S. 11th Airborne Division. Paratroopers fought paratroopers. Machine guns peppered the headquarters of Fifth Air Force, narrowly missing its commander, Major General Ennis Whitehead. Some of the raiders held out for five days. A handful of American aircraft were destroyed.

Seventh Fleet assembled a huge amphibious force to land four divisions at Lingayen. Again Kinkaid would take the southern approach, similar to the Mindoro operation. Halsey's Third Fleet, or more specifically the fast carriers of TF 38, would provide "strategic support." This time there was no conflict between supporting the amphibious operation and chasing the Japanese fleet. Japan no longer had a fleet. Instead, several disjointed squadrons were all that remained. The four remaining conventional battleships had retreated to the waters of the

Home Islands. The two hermaphrodite battleships with truncated flight decks had gone south to hide.

Kinkaid and especially Oldendorf did worry about surface attack. Admiral Morison observed, "Allied naval authorities had more respect for the striking power of Admiral Toyoda's Combined Fleet than it deserved."[37] The real threat was kamikaze and everyone knew it. Oldendorf was even more worried about them and had been very vociferous about the subject with Kinkaid. Halsey started out by hitting the airfields on Okinawa. Then he moved on to Formosa.

Oldendorf's bombardment group, augmented by several escort carriers, moved ahead of the main body by a day. His TG 77.2 became a lightning rod for kamikazes. Japanese special attack aircraft sank an escort carrier, damaged two more, badly hit two of six battleships, three cruisers, and a host of smaller vessels. On top of this, Oldendorf received warning that Japanese heavy ships were sortieing from just west of Kyushu. If all four Japanese battleships came south, Oldendorf would have his hands more than full.

Those losses electrified Halsey back into action. On 5 January he sent three task groups to pummel Japanese airfields. For two days Americans pounded these aerodromes. Carrier pilots claimed 439 enemy aircraft destroyed, although, like most claims, this was almost certainly an overestimate. Japanese aircraft continued to hit shipping waiting to unload in Leyte Gulf.

The invasion of Luzon was scheduled for the 9th. Two minesweepers were sunk by kamikazes on the 7th. On the 8th they hit two escort carriers, a previously damaged cruiser, and three smaller vessels. Fortunately for the Americans, the combination of losses suffered while attacking Oldendorf and the impact of the air strikes from Halsey's fast carriers had largely obliterated the Special Attack Corps. By the beginning of the invasion, fewer than 150 Japanese aircraft remained on Luzon.

King worried that the fast carriers would be tied up off Luzon for six weeks. MacArthur assured the admiral this wouldn't happen. In order to free up both Halsey's fleet carriers and Kinkaid's jeep carriers, a steel mat airfield was constructed at an already level spot at Lingayen. The air strip became operational seven days after the invasion. C-47 cargo planes and twin-engine P-61 fighters came in the first day. A few fighters landed on D+4. A second strip received fighters in five days and bombers in eleven. The Mindoro air strips, the jeep carriers, and newly constructed airfields on Luzon would support the invasion.

Halsey went on to sweep the South China Sea looking for the hermaphrodite battleships *Ise* and *Hyuga*. He didn't find them. They had escaped north to join *Yamato, Nagato,* and *Haruna* in the Inland Sea. (Battleship *Kongo* had been torpedoed by submarine *Sea Lion* on 21 November 1944.) But Halsey's ships and aircraft sank 41 ships caught at various locations south of Luzon.

Yamashita knew better than to attempt to defend a beach against American firepower. On the first day, 65,000 Americans landed at Lingayen. Krueger attained some tactical surprise by landing on the less favorable south beaches of Lingayen Bay instead of the eastern beaches where the Japanese had landed in 1941. But the Tiger of Malaya put up a terrific battle inland. It took almost a month for Krueger to fight his way down the central valley to Manila. MacArthur prodded him all the way to increase speed.

In 1942 MacArthur had declared Manila an open city. Despite the efforts of Yamashita to abandon the metropolis, the Japanese in the city were not about to give up without a major fight. Street-by-street combat lasted another month. The Pearl of the Orient was ground to fine powder and drenched in blood. Over 100,000 Filipinos died from the artillery, Japanese debauchery, and house-to-house fighting. That was more people than would die at Hiroshima. Manila had absolutely no military value to the Japanese. Did they give any value to the Filipino souls their crimes murdered for no gain? For the people of the Philippines was this toll preferable to being bypassed and liberated after the general surrender six months later?

By the time the carnage was over, MacArthur had landed 400,000 soldiers against an estimated enemy combat force of 150,000. Luzon had become a major land campaign. The Japanese lost over 205,000 men on Luzon, including aviation support personnel. American casualties were 8,310 dead and 29,860 wounded. That was more than the Americans had lost during the entire advance across the central Pacific.

MacArthur had no authorization for additional operations in the Philippines after the fall of Luzon. But he proceeded to continue his campaign by turning south and liberating most of the remaining islands of the Philippines. Eighth Army did most of the yeoman work. By making 52 separate landings from February to July, this endeavor tied up a great deal of strength in manpower, matériel, and shipping.

General "Vinegar" Joe Stilwell wrote in his dairy about May 10, "Doug obviously out of control W.D. (War Department) afraid of him."[38] The official army history states, "JCS simply permitted MacArthur to do as he pleased up to a point."[39] It goes on: "If during the height of the Luzon versus Formosa debate in 1944, the Joint Chiefs had foreseen that MacArthur would send his forces to reconquer all of the Philippines south of Luzon and then move on to Borneo, they would have undoubtedly endorsed the King-Nimitz plan to attack Formosa instead."[40]

Liberation of the southern Philippines opened approaches to Borneo. Both the Japanese navy and air force had been largely destroyed. In his last operation, MacArthur employed Australian I Corps to invade that island. The Australians were none too enthusiastic about this endeavor. By that late date there were no Japanese merchantmen left to carry oil back to Japan. Iwo Jima had been captured and the fight for Okinawa was well in hand. MacArthur continued his advance south—in the wrong direction.

Yamashita and his 50,000 remaining troops made an orderly retreat into the rugged mountains of northern Luzon. Sixth Army pursued them and fought until the end of the war. Yamashita didn't surrender until 15 September. Although he had nothing to do with the horrible treatment of prisoners during the Bataan death march and he had attempted to limit civilian loss of life by declaring Manila an open city, MacArthur saw to it that Yamashita was tried as a war criminal. He was hanged February 1946.

11

MAHAN
AND THE
SUBMARINERS

In the age of sail frigates could be assigned to one of two alternative missions. Either they could scout for and support the battle fleet or they could be assigned to commerce raiding.

Through a good part of the eighteenth and nineteenth centuries, the British had the dominant fleet. The French, not being able to compete on the gun line, emphasized commerce raiding as a way to win the naval aspect of a war. About commerce raiding, Mahan said: "It is doubtless a most important secondary operation of naval war, and is not likely to be abandoned till war itself shall cease; but regarded as a primary and fundamental measure, sufficient in itself to crush an enemy, it is probably a delusion."[1] Commerce raiding promised victory on the cheap. The navy that concentrated on winning the battle among fleets would prevail.

Like frigates, conventional submarines of the mid–twentieth century could be assigned two broad missions. Either they could be sent out to prey on the enemy's merchant shipping or they could be used as supports and scouts for the battle fleet. Unlike frigates, however, they were much slower than the battle fleet. That was a major limitation on their deployment. At first both Pacific powers concentrated on this difference. Try as they might, neither Japanese nor American naval architects could come up with a submersible that could keep pace with a fleet advancing across the vast Pacific. This caused many thinkers to dismiss submarines from any major role in strategic planning. On the plus side, their ability to escape underwater when attacked made them far more difficult to counter, especially in an anti-merchant role. This characteristic, a seminal change in naval technology, altered one of Mahan's basic precepts of naval strategy.

Most histories of submarine warfare recount Germany's World War I success in sinking merchantmen crossing the Atlantic. Less often cited are the twenty-eight large warships that fell victim to U-boats. Many American as well as Japanese officers argued submarines made a valuable addition to the battle fleet's combat power. The Naval Limitation Treaties almost assured the Japanese would face an American battle line that would be larger than their own. In order to even the odds, they planned to attack the advancing American fleet with light forces in order to whittle it down. The Japanese weapon of choice was the torpedo. No other navy expended as many resources on torpedoes and their delivery tactics than the Japanese, who also employed destroyers to attack capital ships at night with torpedoes.[2]

The Imperial Japanese Navy's "General Instructions for Submarine Warfare and the Decisive Battle" succinctly defined the mission in its first sentence: "Submarines are deployed effectively for the purpose of achieving their main goal: surprise attack on the enemy's force."[3] Mahan's pen couldn't have done better. Japanese planners assumed the Americans wouldn't begin their trek toward *the* decisive engagement until they had transferred their Atlantic-based capital ships to the Pacific. Japan needed submarines to provide information about American ship movements. More importantly, the Japanese needed weapons that could attack the American fleet as it steamed west and whittle it down. The "General Instructions" stated that "most submarines constitute an advance expeditionary force. These advance submarines launch early attacks on the enemy main body."[4] They gave little, if any, thought to employing submarines as commerce raiders. The "General Instructions" make no mention of commerce raiding. To be effective, commerce raiding must be prosecuted over an extended period. Japanese decision makers were determined to achieve their goals in a short, violent war.

Captain Mahan would have thoroughly approved of the Japanese approach. He repeatedly eschewed the siren song of commerce raiding. It sounded good but often diverted resources from the all-important decisive battle.

Japanese I-class boats were first-rate and manned with good, trained crews. The separate Sixth Fleet under command of a vice admiral controlled most of them. Doctrine called on submarines to set up ahead of the surface fleet a screen called the Advance Expeditionary Force. Many officers on the Naval General Staff expected submarines to be instrumental in sinking American carriers and battleships that sortied against the Japanese fleet.[5] Japanese submarines were not equipped with radar until very late in the war. Information sharing with Japan's excellent long-range flying boats was rare. Without continuous exploitation of the best intelligence available, their prospects in the hunt were poor. Despite the advice of their Nazi allies, Japanese submariners remained fixated on the American fleet to the exclusion of merchant traffic.

Looking back from war's end, the Japanese decision appears to have been in error. The tremendous success of the American submarine campaign in interdicting Japanese merchant shipping is credited by both Americans and Japanese as one of the major reasons why the Japanese lost. The analysis is a little complicated. Remember what Japan needed to accomplish in order to reach a favorable war result: a rapid victory and a negotiated settlement before 1943 was very old. In that period a campaign of merchantman attrition would have added little to the outcome. It must be grudgingly admitted that Mahan's position has some merit.

A war-opening strike that cut down the American carrier fleet and suppressed Pearl Harbor would have changed the dynamics of the analysis. There would be no need to attrit an advancing battle fleet (as it wouldn't be advancing), but there would now be a clear need for submarines to stalk the U.S. West Coast and intercept transports trying to bring reinforcements to what remained of the American position in the Hawaiian Islands. Perhaps we would be allowed an observation that does not come from Mahan but has repeatedly been observed in history. Weapons frequently have been employed for tasks not originally envisioned for them. Flexibility and a cant toward general purpose use have paid handsome dividends for many a weapon design.

During 1942, Japanese submarines contributed a major effort to deciding the balance between the carrier strength of the opposing battle fleets. Subs took *Saratoga* out of the war for many months and sank *Yorktown* at Midway after she was damaged by air strikes. During the Guadalcanal campaign, Japanese submariners almost delivered the coup de grâce to the American carrier fleet. Japanese subs seriously damaged *Saratoga* again, sidelining her for most of the year. They sank *Wasp*, reducing the American fleet to a single damaged carrier. Subs crippled the only American fast battleship in the Pacific, the *North Carolina*. For several months Japanese battleships could roam Iron Bottom Sound at night without worrying about being engaged by enemy battleships. Frankly Japan could have taken better advantage of this opportunity. Submariners gave Japan an opportunity for decisive victory in the Solomons. Had Yamamoto capitalized on this opportunity, Japan's choice (and Mahan's preference) would have looked pretty good.

While American shipping was stretched very thin by the battle of the Atlantic, it is doubtful that a Japanese anti-merchant submarine campaign in 1942 would have achieved much. Japan didn't have the naval intelligence capability that would prove so decisive for the Americans. Neither did it have the forward basing structure that would allow it to do much hunting in the South Pacific or between Hawaii and the mainland. For Japan, Mahan's advice would have fit the circumstances created by the centrifugal campaign strategy.

After the sea battles around Guadalcanal, the Japanese might have switched to a counter-shipping campaign. However, the United States had no critical import vulnerability that the Japanese could reach. Cutting the sea lanes to Australia was a possible objective.

Initially, the American shipbuilding program included a huge number of destroyer escorts. These, linked with escort carriers and long-range patrol bombers, would have been the proper counter against free-ranging submarine attacks against shipping. Successfully diverting these assets would have done little to hinder the Big Blue Fleet's crushing advance across the Pacific. In the end, the production of destroyer escorts was traded for a large number of *Baltimore*-class cruisers that King intended for the postwar fleet. Reverting to the original building plan would not have been much of a problem.

Laying in wait along lonely sea lanes and whacking transports wasn't very appealing to those submariners filled with the samurai spirit. Navies of both countries tended to ignore assignments that were not in line with what they perceived as their primary tasks. A more fruitful mission would have been to attack the massive amphibious convoys to which American invasion forces became addicted. Disruption of amphibious logistics might have slowed the American juggernaut and almost certainly would have increased its human cost. Linking a submarine assault with a barrage of kamikazes was Japan's best long-shot bet. The best employment of Japanese submarines remained Mahanian.

Instead the Imperial Fleet frittered its subs away by diverting them to a lot of strategically unimportant assignments. Japan assigned subs to surface bombardment, communications relay, patrol plane refueling, and the like. As the war progressed, many were diverted to resupplying isolated bases and islands.

Japan lost forty submarines in 1942–43. During the first half of 1944, they lost another forty. Many of the survivors were concentrated to support fleet operations to prevent further American incursion westward. The battle for the Marianas was the subs' last hurrah. American hunter killer groups stalked and destroyed much of Ozawa's submarine recon line that stretched from New Guinea to Truk. Forward-firing "hedgehogs" (clustered mortars that fired a pattern of anti-sub rounds some distance from the ship) increased the deadliness of American tin cans. Getting credit for a single kill earned boasting rights. Destroyer escort *England* bagged six, winning special praise from King himself.

Japan's meager shipyard capacity was stretched even to repair damaged hulls. New submarine construction waned and then disappeared altogether. From about the fall of 1944, the only submersibles coming out of the yards were miniature kamikaze boats.

America's Inauspicious Beginnings

After World War II, everyone recognized the incredible contribution the American submarines had made toward winning the war. Sixty percent of all Japanese merchantmen lost succumbed to American submarines. Admiral King rightfully observed "through their efforts the Japanese were much nearer the end in the late spring of 1945 than was generally realized."[6]

It didn't start out that way. During World War I American submarines didn't sink a thing. After the war, the American navy viewed submarines as harbor defense forces. They could lie in wait in the approaches to a port and ambush the invaders. Short range and slow speed kept them from operating with the fleet.

Lieutenant Chester Nimitz was one of the first to see that the "steady development of the torpedo together with the gradual improvement in the size, motive power and speed of submarine craft of the near future will result in a most dangerous offensive weapon and one which will have a large part in deciding fleet actions."[7] But the young Nimitz in his 1912 writings foretold no anti-merchant campaign. As Mahan would have instructed, he focused strictly on attacking warships opposing the fleet. In fact, Article 22 of the London Naval Treaty of 1930 forbade subs from attacking merchantmen unless the latter's crews were first taken to a place of safety. That was an indirect effort to outlaw attacks on merchantmen by making such action all but impractical. American submarine doctrine of 1939 directed American sub skippers to concentrate on enemy capital ships.[8]

Plan Orange envisioned boats with sufficient range and surface cruise speed to accompany the fleet as it headed west. Like the Japanese, American war planners viewed fleet support as the sub's proper role. This requirement heavily influenced the design of American submarines. In order to accompany the fleet across the Pacific at the planned 17 knots, American boats had to be large, fast, and possess good sea-keeping qualities. These same attributes served American sub commanders well as they embarked on long-range commerce raiding missions, a role that was not envisioned for them when the subs were laid down.

On the surface a World War II–era fleet boat could make 20 knots on a calm sea. While they might sprint at 9 knots for a very limited time underwater, battery life restricted them to 2.5 knots for 48 hours. Conventional subs don't chase their quarry. They must anticipate the enemy's course, surreptitiously move ahead of the enemy's track, and patiently lie in wait for him to arrive. A normal patrol lasted about 60 days. Typically submarines left dock with 24 torpedoes.

At the beginning of the war, the U.S. had about 55 submarines in the Pacific, split between Pearl and Manila. Even with heroic efforts submarines still couldn't keep up with the fleet. Doctrine didn't allow them to work in close proximity to the fleet. Instead they were assigned duty as long-range scouts. Some were supposed to take station off the Japanese Home Islands.

Despite heavy training schedules that had filled most of 1940 and 1941, most Pacific-based boats weren't ready to go on patrol on 7 December. On that day only three of fourteen fleet boats based at Pearl were ready for sea. By New Year's only seven were on patrol.[9]

During the Centrifugal Offensive, American subs tried vainly to impede the Japanese naval advance. American subs attempted, with dismal results, to attack Japanese warships. They did little to halt the advance into the South Seas or the subjugation of the Philippines. No one thought to attack ships returning to Japan with the raw materials to sustain the war.

After some bumbling around, the Americans committed the bulk of their subs to attacking merchantmen. Mahan wouldn't have agreed. He would have counseled that the fleet boats retain their orientation toward providing recon for the fleet and attacking Japanese warships in the combat zone. Based on World War II's record, he would have been wrong.

After the Japanese advance, what was left of the large Philippine squadron finally retreated to Fremantle, Australia. They might have been pulled back to Pearl. The ever-aggressive King ordered them to remain in place and attack whatever Japanese they could find in the South Seas. British subs from the Indian Ocean reinforced this effort. This was the beginning of what would become the most successful submarine offensive in history. King directed submarines to target capital ships as first priority; merchantmen and tankers took second place.[10] During the second half of 1942, Nimitz tasked some of his Pearl-based boats to snoop around, see what they could learn, and sink anything that went by. That's how the American submarine anti-merchant campaign began. Slowly this effort would grow into a blockade that strangled Japan's sea lanes. Other boats patrolled around Saipan and the Home Islands. Those patrols that entered the backwaters of the East China Sea were the most productive.

Close-support fighter pilots will tell you it is easier to shoot up the tanker trucks that fuel the tanks than the tanks themselves. A paucity of fleet oilers hampered the deployment of both the Japanese and the American navies. Oilers plod along at much slower speeds than do warships, making them far easier targets. It is a little surprising that neither navy embarked on an early campaign to cripple their opponent's fleet by systematically attacking such soft and critical assets.

American submarines were also dissipated on a number of tasks during 1942. Special operations such as landing raiders, supporting guerrillas, and delivering spies amounted to little. During the first six months of the war American sub attacks against Japanese merchantmen were less than impressive. No more than thirty-five *marus* were taken. Poor American torpedoes, poor tactics, less-than-aggressive behavior on the part of some American skippers, and easy-to-counter close blockade tactics were the root cause of the poor performance. Inexperienced crews also made poor use of the radio intelligence that was available.

During the battle of Midway, 19 of the 26 boats available out of Hawaii were assigned to fleet support.[11] Most of the others moved away from their assigned patrol areas in a vain attempt to intercept Japanese men-o-war retreating from Midway. Even when guided by Ultra, stalking Japanese warships bore little fruit. Chasing after Japanese warships instead of lying in wait for *marus* was not a useful assignment for a battery-powered submarine. Only a third of the 1942 effort was directed at Japanese merchant shipping. Many subs were sent "port watching" or, in Mahanian terms, close blockade. They achieved little. The Japanese merchant marine began the year with about 5.775 million tons. Corrected by Japanese records, American subs sank about 725,000 tons. The entire merchant fleet decreased by only 89,000 tons, net of new building, due to American submarines.[12] This 1.5 percent reduction had no measurable impact on Japanese imports or the ability to move its military forces. Tanker tonnage actually increased from 575,000 to 686,000 tons. This inauspicious start may have lulled the Japanese into thinking American submariners were not much of a strategic threat.

Although Japan did organize the First Convoy Escort Fleet to meet the minuscule threat, that command became a dumping ground for creaking old destroyers and motorboats and an alternative to retirement for overage officers. It took a year for American subs to account for about what the U-boats put under the waves in a good month.

Continuing problems with torpedo exploders and depth controls were particularly exasperating. Just prior to the war, the United States developed what was then a high-tech magnetic influence exploder. A torpedo properly equipped with one of these devices did not have to strike a ship in order to sink it. The magnetic detection device, sensing the proximity of the hull, would detonate. More important, torpedoes could be aimed underneath an enemy ship. By exploding under the hull, the torpedo was likely to break the target's keel, ensuring a kill.

The torpedoes were never tested against a real target at sea; despite reports that the Germans were having trouble with a similar device, the Bureau of Ordnance didn't want to incur the expense of expending a high-cost torpedo and sinking a decommissioned target ship. Talk about pound wise but tonnage foolish. Sub commanders on combat patrol soon discovered the devices didn't work right, refusing to explode in proximity to a target—or sometimes at all. The depth controls weren't properly calibrated, causing the "fish" to run too deep to do any good. Japanese ships came into port with unexploded torpedoes sticking out of their hulls. Some Japanese sailors quipped that "a tanker cannot sink if it is torpedoed."[13] American submariners swore as they risked their lives slamming dud ordnance against juicy targets. Sub commanders complained, but the Bureau of Ordnance refused to listen. The problems weren't completely solved until September 1943.

Based on the 1942 evidence, one might have argued that fleet support made more sense than commerce raiding. Clay Blair, who wrote the definitive history on Pacific undersea warfare in World War II, blames the ineffective American record on senior leadership's failure "to set up a broad, unified strategy for Pacific submarines aimed at a single specific goal: interdicting Japanese shipping services."[14] After all, German U-boats had turned in quite an impressive record for 1942.

Bringing in newly promoted Rear Admiral Charles A. Lockwood to command the submarines in Fremantle went a long way toward improving performance. Among his first observations was the lack of aggressiveness and technical competence of many of the sub skippers. A surface ship commander can always make his maneuvers and actions conform to what everyone else in the squadron is doing. He isn't likely to find an excuse to bolt in face of battle. A submarine skippered by a poorly trained or overly cautious commander can easily move completely out of position and become ineffective.

Poor performers were easy to spot. Junior officers compared notes at the bar in port. One needed only to look at the transfer requests for those seeking competent leaders to take them into battle. Lockwood had the initiative to ruthlessly replace skippers who couldn't measure up. A third of them changed jobs. As a result crew morale soared. Lockwood secured hotels so that crews who had been crammed into a small hull for extended periods and placed under intense stress could unwind when in port.

He also tackled the torpedo problem head-on. Defying the Bureau of Ordnance, he ran his own test. Virtually all of his skippers volunteered to participate. By June of 1942, over 800 torpedoes had been fired in combat. Not one had been expended in a measured test. A torpedo was set to run at ten feet and fired into a net. It passed through the net at a depth of 25 feet. Admiral King "lit a blow torch under the Bureau of Ordnance."[15] Odds of a torpedo sinking a ship up to late 1943 were about 20 percent. With corrective action, the probability of a sinking rose to 50 percent.[16]

Later King would reach "Down Under" and pull Lockwood into Pearl Harbor as the three-star commander of the submarines under Nimitz. Place good men in positions of leadership. That's what Mahan underscored above all else.

Japan started the war with about 5.4 million tons of merchant shipping, excluding tankers. Until late in the war there was no central office with power to assign shipping or prioritize cargoes. The army had its own transports and jealously guarded their use. Of course the navy had its own. Because of the ships assigned exclusively to the armed services, there were insufficient bottoms to move the war materials needed to keep up defense production in the Home Islands. Further, shipping had to make a long transit from the South Seas to Japan. Local naval units or aircraft could not provide cover for much of the distance. Little thought was given to forming defensive convoys. As a result, Japanese merchant shipping offered a very brittle, vulnerable target to American submariners. Solid attacks would precipitate an immediate economic problem for the Japanese.

No major strategic pronouncement directed American submarines to switch from chasing warships to stalking *marus*. American submarine commanders simply began plotting patrol courses where targets were plentiful. As Admiral Morison colorfully relates, "Ships in waters of the main Japanese islands were as thick as Geisha girls in Tokyo, and as easy."[17] Introduction of radar increased the probability that submariners would find their quarry.

In the spring of 1943, Australian-based boats began to interdict the convoy route between Palau and Rabaul. A lot of shipping transited the area on its way to the South Pacific battlefields. Unlike the transports bringing oil and raw materials up from the South Seas, these convoys were heavily guarded. Little wonder results were meager. Overall operations were hampered by lack of submarines and reliable torpedoes. Officially the primary targets remained capital ships, but more skippers began departing for the East China Sea and waters off Japan. Lockwood recognized that these patrols sank far more tonnage than patrols off Truk.[18] Intelligence supplied more and better fixes on potential targets. The role of good intelligence can't be overemphasized. Information on *maru* movements proved very valuable. Data on capital ship movements was sometimes counter-productive as boats were assigned to intercept targets that were difficult to take down because of their speed and maneuverability.

Losses in the East China Sea finally began to sting. The Japanese naval staff increased convoy usage and requested that 360 escort vessels be added to convoy protection. They were given 40. American submarines began to penetrate the Sea of Japan, the body of ocean that lies east of Korea between Japan and Russia.

During the summer of 1943 a conscious effort was made to target tankers off the oil-producing ports of Borneo. In the Atlantic the Kriegsmarine had honed their wolf packs into vicious hunting organizations. American sub skippers eschewed similar tactics because of the risk of boat-to-boat communications revealing their position. However, the concentration of boats in an area had a positive effect. Some boats began informally cooperating with each other. While U-boat losses escalated, Japan developed little of the Allies' mounting anti-submarine expertise and technology.

These conditions and the growing size of Japanese convoys finally convinced Admiral Lockwood to formally organize wolf packs. A few departed for hostile waters in 1943. Concentrated firepower was needed to break into and wreck bigger convoys. The Bashi and Balingtang channels of the Luzon Strait—the narrow neck of water between the northernmost major island of the Philippines and Formosa—looked like the ideal hunting ground. Narrows that must be traversed markedly improve the odds for submarines that must lie in wait to strike at their quarry. Belatedly Lockwood focused effort on the abundant targets flowing through the strait. Years after the British and Americans had almost succumbed in the battle of the Atlantic, American submarine efforts were evolving into an anti-commerce campaign.

Submarines were grouped into packs of three, each with a commander in addition to the three skippers. Radio transmissions were held to a minimum. Subs attempted to form a gauntlet through which the targeted convoy would have to pass. Each boat attacked in turn to avoid fratricide. Torpedo runs came first from port then starboard in order to drive targets toward the next submarine as they sought to escape. One sub could draw off escorts that were pounding another of her sisters. It worked well. Sinkings increased. One of the first Pearl-based packs damaged the small carrier *Unyo*.

In 1943 American subs conducted about 350 patrols, the same level as in 1942, but much greater emphasis was placed on the anti-merchant-shipping role. Fifty percent of sorties from Pearl Harbor were assigned this mission. They sank 1.5 million tons, about double the 1942 figure. Net Japanese merchant shipping tonnage declined about 1.1 million tons to only 4.1 million tons. That made a significant impact. Lack of oil crimped movements of the Imperial Navy. Lack of aviation gas curtailed all-important pilot training.

By the end of 1943, Japanese planners were acutely aware of their shipping crisis and the tremendous damage American and British subs were inflicting. Japanese planners projected submariners would sink 100,000 tons per month.[19]

Japan "overlooked the most critical lesson of World War I, the absolute importance of an island empire's maintaining its sea communications at all costs," observes Walter J. Boyne.[20] By the time Japan realized the threat, it had fewer than fifty anti-sub ships. In November 1943 the navy ministry established the Grand Escort Command under Admiral Koshiro Oikawa to control convoy escorts. Troop convoys remained heavily escorted. Occasionally an escort carrier was employed. But escort duty remained the province of second (or third) line officers and ships. Japanese skippers were very hesitant to press their attacks and often didn't properly solve the geometry problem of where to drop their depth charges. The depth charges themselves were too small and suffered problems with their depth settings. Often Japanese escorts would break off an attack at the faintest sign that it might have been successful. This allowed many a threatened American boat to escape.

Throughout the war Japanese anti-submarine efforts remained low priority and ineffective. During the war they sank only 44 American subs. By comparison, the Allies sank 781 U-boats. The Japanese lost 128 subs of their own despite a far less aggressive plan of deployment.

In 1943, Japanese subs sank an escort carrier, a destroyer, and an American submarine. Compared to 1942, this was a paltry score. Most Japanese subs were withdrawn from offensive operation and employed resupplying isolated garrisons.

Nineteen forty-four was the year of the U.S. submarine. Admiral Lockwood had culled the second-stringers from his list of star sub commanders. Poor engines had been replaced and many other mechanical problems solved. Now armed with the good Mark 18 torpedo and equipped with radar, the 75 fleet boats were the most lethal undersea killers the world had seen in combat. Ultra intelligence became timely, plentiful, and well exploited by the crews. American submariners were poised to skewer their quarry.

However, there still was no overarching strategic plan to give the hunters direction. No one isolated tankers or oilers as the key weakness and said, "Apply pressure here." Instead, sub commanders followed their noses to where the game seemed to be running. Officially, capital ships remained the number one target. Because the American navy found itself constantly short of the utilitarian destroyer, Admiral King reasoned the Japanese fleet must be even more strapped. In April 1944 he moved enemy destroyers to number two target, ahead of transports. This demonstrates how unfocused on commerce raiding America's formal submarine strategy was.

By the first quarter of 1944, the impact of the commerce raiding American subs had accomplished was unmistakable. Japanese aircraft production was scheduled to rise to 4,000 per month. Due in good part to problems with shipping and raw materials it was half that amount.[21] Losses of both tankers and troop ships were especially worrisome. During the first two months of 1944, Japan lost 21 tankers, as many as in all of 1943.

Early in the year, the coast of Borneo became particularly appealing. Tankers moved to and fro fetching the ever more scarce black liquid to fuel the war machine. To stay close to their source of fuel, much of the Imperial Fleet remained in these waters. Troop and cargo transports moved from Asia to forward areas bringing reinforcements. The combination created an especially target-rich environment. It also placed submarines in position to provide excellent movement reports in June when the battleships first sortied for Biak and then made for the Marianas. The recon line also scored against Japanese aircraft carriers during the battle of the Philippine Sea.

Wolf packs continued to show their effectiveness in the Luzon Strait. After the Marianas, submarines increasingly entered the East and South China seas look for more prey. This was the route the remaining merchantmen transited carrying what they could back to the Home Islands. By default, American submariners began to concentrate more on an anti-commerce strategy. However, patrols near the Home Islands saw a declining number of kills as *marus* began hugging the coast, seeking safety in shallow waters that submarines avoided.

After the fall of the Marianas, serous debate over the end game with Japan took hold. This debate started with the Philippines versus Formosa knife fight between MacArthur and King. Another dimension of the problem was invasion versus blockade. Would the Home Islands have to be taken by amphibious assault, or would a naval blockade starve the Japanese into a condition where they would be unable to continue organized resistance despite their unbending will?

As we have seen, most admirals favored blockade. This was a task ready-made for submariners. Mahan spent a lot of time discussing blockade and the merits of "close versus distant" blockade. He would have heartily endorsed plans in this direction and would have had quite a bit to say.

Mahan concentrated on *first* destroying the enemy fleet. Once that task is accomplished, the fleet is free to do what it *wills*. In classic naval warfare, the second—and final—step is to blockade the enemy's homeland.[22] The Great Marianas Turkey Shoot showed that the Japanese navy was finished. The battles around the Philippines that summer finished what was left. At this junction, Mahan would have undoubtedly turned attention to building the blockade of the Home Islands. His analysis both of British actions against the French from 1715 until the demise of Napoleon and of the Union against the Confederacy during the American Civil War demonstrated that the distant blockade—that is, fleet action to interdict opposing enemy action, as opposed to close blockade, posting sentinel ships at the mouth of every enemy port—was more effective. Mahan would have supported the evolution of American submarine strategy in 1944. After Leyte, he would have insisted on it. Better to get to the party late than to never arrive.

Regardless of the merits of a Formosa strategy, MacArthur was adamant that he would return to the Philippines. The general didn't think much of a blockade strategy either. Troops under his command would have to march on Tokyo. In this debate, MacArthur's views were squarely in the mainstream of most army thinking. Marshall wanted to end the war without a bloody invasion, but even he didn't think it was possible.

Submarines hunting in the waters southwest and northwest of the Philippines were in great position to simultaneously sink Japanese freighters and support MacArthur's invasion of the islands. However, their assigned mission was to interdict reinforcements attempting to make landfall in the Philippines.[23] Submariners provided good sighting reports of Japanese warships as they maneuvered toward the Philippines. They sank a pair of heavy cruisers while damaging another pair. Ozawa's retreating decoy carrier group had to negotiate its way through a gauntlet of American submarines.

During the naval battle of the Philippines eight of the good Japanese I-boats entered Philippine waters. While they damaged an escort carrier and a destroyer escort, six of them were sunk by the Americans. Another group of I-class subs fitted with human-guided torpedoes attempted to attack the fleet anchorage at Ulithi. A *kaiten*, as the kamikaze torpedoes were called, sank a fully loaded fleet tanker in a spectacular fireworks show. Most of the rest of the *kaiten* proved defective. Two of the I-boats fell prey to sub hunters. By 1944, fleet attack by Japanese submarines proved to be of little value.

American intelligence knew the location and composition of Japanese defensive minefields. Japanese anti-submarine efforts were technically backward and not very well organized. American subs could enter the Sea of Japan. Although submariners were loath to admit it, American minefields had shut down a good deal of Japan's few remaining sea lanes making the submarines' targeting problem that much easier. Some optimists projected that Japan would burn through her last oil reserves in as little as three months.[24]

At the beginning of 1944, American squadrons numbered almost 100 boats. Patrols increased almost 50 percent to 520. In 1944, U.S. submarines sank 548 *marus* totaling 2,541,914 tons. This was more than the combined total for 1941, 1942, and 1943. Such a huge kill taken down by a comparatively small den of wolves must be heavily attributed to Ultra. At times every boat on patrol was engaged in developing a contact from Ultra. Admiral Lockwood attributed 50 percent of all sinkings from 1943 onward to leads from Ultra.[25] One Japanese POW stated, "You could walk from Singapore to Tokyo on American periscopes."[26] Imagine what the U-boat commanders could have done had they had such a detailed and reliable source of intelligence.

Mission planners employed Ultra to select the best areas for subs to patrol. Ultra intercepts often gave near-real-time reports of the location, size, and headings of Japanese convoys. Having precise information about enemy convoys allowed American sub skippers to plot a point of intercept and move there without conducting inefficient searches for their quarry.

Total Japanese merchant tonnage afloat dropped from 4.9 million tons to 2.9 million. Imports fell disastrously. Commodity imports dropped from 16.4 million tons the previous year to 10 million tons. This decline seriously crimped war production. Fuel oil was so short the Japanese navy based its battleships down in the South Seas in order to keep them in fuel.

After the invasion of Mindoro, the cork was lodged in the Luzon Strait. Imports of oil from the South Seas virtually stopped. As in the Atlantic in 1942, submarines were choking an island nation to death. Ultra was spewing out intelligence at an incredible rate. One wonders if a more coherent anti-commerce, anti-oil strategy might have been even more decisive before invasions such as Tarawa were scheduled.

For the most part, the submarine war against Japanese shipping had ended by December 1944. There weren't enough targets left on the open ocean. What remained were a few steamers sneaking across the Yellow Sea or the Sea of Japan, hugging the coast and pulling into harbor before sunset.

American submarines also scored heavily against men-of-war by sinking a battleship, three fleet aircraft carriers, four light carriers, two heavy cruisers, seven light cruisers, thirty destroyers, and seven Japanese submarines. Many of the heavy units were sunk during battles in the Marianas and in Philippine waters. In contrast, by mid-1944 Japanese submarine attacks were almost completely ineffective.

At the beginning of 1945, Halsey took the Big Blue Fleet into the South China Sea. American submarines had been very active in the area. In reaction the Japanese shipping that was left hugging the Malay-Indochina-China coast. American submarine skippers went right in after them. Halsey was looking for the battleship-carrier conversions *Ise* and *Hyuga* that had eluded him during the battle off Samar. The Japanese hermaphrodites weren't spotted. But 47 ships were sunk east of Indochina, paralyzing what was left of the Japanese merchant fleet. That was the end of any oil and raw materials from the South Seas—the reason Japan had started the war in the first place. The American submarine squadron that had been chased down to Fremantle returned to the Philippines.

Japan imported 22 million tons in 1940. By 1945 imports had tumbled to 2.7 million. Ninety percent of the emperor's merchant shipping was lost; 2,259 merchant ships totaling 8.1 million tons had entered Davy Jones's locker. Another 275 merchant ships (775,000 tons) had been laid up for repairs. U.S. subs counted for almost 60 percent of these losses.

Mahan emphasized that technological change could revolutionize naval tactics in short order. But technology's impact on strategy was far less pronounced. Carriers and aircraft with the capacity to haul ship-killing weapons revolutionized naval tactics but left Mahanian precepts of naval strategy largely untouched. Not so the submarine. Its capabilities changed the fundamental balance between fleet combat and commerce raiding, and allowed a thinking admiral to contemplate a strategic reversal in emphasis. The sub created a more fundamental change in strategic thinking than did the conventionally armed airplane.

The Atlantic analog to War Plan Orange was War Plan Black (black for Germany). It received far less attention than Orange. In Black, the American Atlantic Fleet held itself in readiness to defeat the German battle line in the western Atlantic. That plan assumed that England had already been defeated.

One can see Black's Mahanian roots. Based on Black, American admirals responsible for the Atlantic refused to release destroyers for the anti-submarine war. It was Marshall who finally brought King to realize that such parsimony could lose the war. If Mahan had run the Atlantic war and kept the destroyers with the fleet instead of assigning them to anti-commerce raider duty, we might have had a disaster.

Tojo himself stated that submarines were one of three main reasons why Japan lost (leapfrogging and the capability of the fast carriers were the other two). The United States Strategic Bombing Survey was even more succinct: "The war against shipping was perhaps the most decisive single factor in the collapse of the Japanese economy and logistic support of Japanese military and naval power." On the other side, Admiral Fukudome said at the end of the war, "The Japanese expected much from its submarines. . . . But when it came to the test of actual warfare, the results were deplorable."[27]

American undersea success did not come without great cost. Twenty-two percent of American submariners died at sea. Submariners from Germany, Japan, and the United States alike did not lack for valor.

12

DULLING
THE MIGHTY
BLADE

After the great sea battles around the Philippines, the Japanese surface navy ceased to exist as a threat to massed American sea power. Japanese submarines posed little threat. They had no capability to conduct a commerce raiding campaign against the Americans. On the other hand, the American submarine campaign was strangling the Land of the Rising Sun. Oil and rice imports from the South Seas were virtually nil. Coke imports from China had dropped 60 percent. The American navy had won the navy versus navy war.

Now it was time to enter the war's end stage. In the Mahanian tradition, King and Nimitz agreed that Japan would be defeated by blockade and bombing.[1]

Hap Arnold and his airmen retained their faith that strategic bombing could end the war. But high-level precision bombing was proving to be a failure. They were worried. Marshall and most other army leaders would have been overjoyed to see a blockade bring down Japan but feared an invasion was inevitable.

Ever since the fall of the Marianas, the only rational strategy for the Japanese was to negotiate the best possible peace with the Americans. Given the intensity with which Americans fought in the Solomons and at Tarawa and the ease with which they now swept away Japanese military resistance, imposition of American will upon the Japanese warlords was inevitable. The only question to be answered was how many humans were going to die before the Japanese leadership would admit to reality.

But the Japanese leadership showed no signs of surrender. It was the duty of the emperor's subjects to endure the ravages of war. Japanese strategists defined a final decisive battle in Japan proper. Formosa, the Bonins, a little piece of China, and Korea became the final "outer defense sphere." Japan's newly unveiled weapon, the kamikaze, could make the final assaults so costly in American blood that the United States still might negotiate. Perhaps the kamikaze could bleed the American navy white.

Kamikaze

The American navy's final tasks were to blockade Japan, take on enemy land-based air, and, if necessary, transport troops to their final destination. In an earlier age, fleets avoided dueling with shore batteries. Land-based guns, which didn't have to compensate for the roll of the ocean or to sink if hit, retained significant advantages.

At the beginning of the war, most naval strategists felt land-based air had similar advantages over its carrier-based counterpart. Out of desperation, Halsey tested that proposition at the end of 1943 at Rabaul to defend his forces off Bougainville. To his pleasant surprise, U.S. naval aviation proved more than a match for the fighters based on Rabaul's air strips. American carrier admirals became bolder. By conscious design, American carrier-based planes repeatedly went up against land-based aviation at Truk and during the Marianas campaign and completely dominated their adversary. A little later Halsey splintered every airplane the Japanese could muster over Formosa.

Then, flying from Luzon, the kamikaze appeared. For accuracy, they relied on a suicidal human instead of circuits printed on silicon. (In September 1943, a single German radio-controlled Felix glide bomb sank the Italian battleship *Roma.*) The kamikaze strikes unnerved American sailors. At first, they discounted the magnitude of the threat. After a lot of damaged ships, many intense anti-aircraft battles, and enough frazzled nerves to rattle an entire fleet, Halsey had had enough. He shied away from the kamikazes.

Destroyer *Mahan* was badly hit by a kamikaze on 7 December 1944 and had to be sunk by American torpedoes. It was a bad omen. Everyone in the fleet dreaded what was coming.

Admiral Ugaki, who became the commander of the Special Attack Corps, came to see kamikazes as a "feature of the decisive battle."[2] They were a tool with which to forge another attempt at Mahanian Armageddon. In March 1945, 6,000 aircraft were assigned to defend Japan; 4,000 of them were kamikazes.

Even in the insanity of war, there is something ghoulish about another human so determined to kill you that he forfeits his own life. American propaganda made kamikazes out to be automatons who had trained since childhood to die for the emperor. Actually, most kamikaze pilots were university students who tended to be from the middle class. Few had deep religious convictions or had been steeped in the tradition of Bushido the way many army privates had. Some saw kamikaze as a way to make their inevitable death meaningful. In Japanese society peer pressure is enormous. Many young pilots simply succumbed to what appeared to be the collective will. Nevertheless, some lost their nerve and refused to enter the cockpit for their final journey. A few avoided crashing into ships and ditched their aircraft instead. Most of these average Japanese middle class students performed the duty they volunteered for.

Although its effect on most strategic principles was minimal, Mahan held that technology caused naval tactics to change constantly. Off Luzon, Halsey and his people began adapting to the human-guided munition. They began thinking in terms of layering defenses, a tactic that gained in popularity for the remainder of the twentieth century. Long-range 24-hour CAPs (combat air patrols) were placed near originating Japanese airfields. Kamikaze pilots were not very experienced flyers. Daylight CAPs shot down many as they took off and attempted to form up. American night fighters discouraged any activity during darkness. At medium range the Americans developed three tactics to counter specific Japanese modes of attacks. Radar picket destroyers were placed a distance from the fleet in order to give warning. To nullify the usefulness of American IFF ("Identification, Friend or Foe" radar transponders), Japanese attackers would try to follow American aircraft home. Now returning aircraft were instructed to circle picket destroyers in a characteristic manner so interlopers could be scrubbed off their tails. Attackers would attempt to bore in from high altitudes at nulls (holes) they detected in American radar coverage. Higher and more distant CAPs countered this. Low-level attackers would penetrate under radar coverage. The fleet posted low-level "Jack patrols" to counter these.

Little could be done initially to improve short-range defenses except to give crews more practice. On larger ships, many of the small-caliber automatic weapons were operated by cooks and the like as an added duty. For the first time, the American navy routinely allowed African Americans to man guns. Despite the dramatic movie footage automatic weapons created, guns of 40mm and below didn't have the accuracy or hitting power to down kamikazes consistently. After the war they were replaced by radar-controlled three-inch mounts.

Getting firepower to hit vulnerable targets instead of creating flashy pyrotechnic displays that did little to damage the enemy was a problem even in Mahan's day. Naval officers were aghast when they learned how few of the rounds that Dewey's ships fired in Manila Bay in 1898 actually hit anything. By the end of the twentieth century, defense publications were full of references to command and control. Improving fire direction techniques was the beginning of efforts to apply modern technology to that old problem.

Fighters were generally viewed as defensive. Dive- and torpedo bombers delivered the main punch. This late in the war, one would expect fighters to be off-loaded to make more room on board carriers for more bombers. But the reverse happened. Indirectly this was a measure of the effectiveness of the kamikaze program. It is only partially attenuated by the fact that Hellcats sometimes assumed strike missions with 500-pound bombs.

Kamikazes were deadly. When they struck a ship, it sank 2.9 percent of the time.[3] Off the Philippines Japan expended 378 kamikazes, along with 102 escort planes that were shot down, in order to sink two escort carriers, three destroyers, and eleven smaller vessels. Another 87 ships were damaged, including seven fleet and two light carriers.[4] While enormously painful, this was hardly a crippling blow. But compare it to the 430 Japanese planes lost in the Great Marianas Turkey Shoot against no American ship losses.

(The Japanese navy had another "kamikaze," a destroyer by that unhappy name. It seemed every ship [including cruisers *Haguro* and *Ashigara*] *Kamikaze* escorted wound up on the bottom. Superstitious Japanese mariners saw her as a cursed "Jonah ship." She survived the war, the only one of her class to do so, but ran aground off the coast of Honshu in June 1946 while conducting repatriation duties and was lost.)

Formosa?

Almost to the eve of the invasion fleet's leaving for Leyte, King continued to argue for Formosa instead of Luzon as the next objective. Mahan would have agreed entirely. Formosa had many pluses and a few minuses, such as its proximity to the large Japanese army on the mainland. But the argument was moot. After the transfer of XXIV Corps to MacArthur, the only ground troops Nimitz retained were the marines. They did not have the strength to secure an island as large and heavily defended as Formosa. There was no way MacArthur would release army forces without taking Luzon. And there was no one in Washington who was about to fire him if he didn't.

For a while King tried to cut a deal with Marshall. The navy would drop its objections to Luzon if the army would subsequently provide resources to invade Formosa. Mahan would have tapped the tabletop vigorously. Obviously King had lost sight of the strategy and was simply trying to win *something*. Marshall was far too good a strategist to give this notion any serious consideration. He advocated a direct assault on Japan. King retorted he would not support such a move unless the army was ready to invade Honshu, take control of its central plain, and capture Tokyo.

In mid-July King and Nimitz flew out to Saipan to see firsthand what was happening in the Marianas. Afterward they retired to Spruance's flagship, *Indianapolis*. King struck up a conversation about future strategy. Of course he led off with an argument in favor of Formosa, which had been dubbed Operation Causeway. Spruance was not in favor of Formosa to the exclusion of obtaining bases someplace in the Philippines. When King asked where they should go next, Spruance unflinchingly responded, "Okinawa." King took note. He had a lot of respect for Spruance's intellect.

Spruance's response would have been echoed by Mahan. The Japanese navy had dissolved into the brine during the Great Marianas Turkey Shoot and could no longer seriously interfere with the movement of American invasion fleets. This was the desired end state of the navy versus navy war. Now that the Americans had freedom of maneuver, the best strategy would be the one that most quickly finished off the enemy and resulted in the smallest loss of life. An invasion of Okinawa promised to draw out the kamikazes to a range where they would be at a disadvantage. Okinawa would allow the U.S. Army's huge tactical air forces to bear on the Home Islands. It should also be noted that Lieutenant General Robert C. Richardson, senior army commander in the Pacific Ocean Area, favored Okinawa after Leyte.

Another in the series of San Francisco strategy meetings was held on 29 September 1944, twenty-four days before MacArthur's troops splashed ashore from Leyte Gulf. Nimitz brought along Lieutenant General Simon B. Buckner, recently appointed commander of Tenth Army, who would command army forces under Nimitz, and Lieutenant General Millard F. Harmon, commander, Army Air Forces in the Central Pacific, as well as Rear Admiral Charles H. McMorris,

Nimitz's chief of staff. Buckner estimated Formosa would cost 50,000 casualties and require nine divisions. With his people in support, Nimitz finally persuaded King to drop Formosa.

One assumption did not change. The Joint Chiefs planners remained convinced that an invasion of Japan would still be necessary. While blockade and bombardment might work, the military had to stay on schedule for invasion.

Although American land-based airpower had become overwhelming, only B-29s could make the trip from the Marianas to Japan. A site closer to Japan for airfields and invasion logistics installations was an absolute requirement. Clark Field on Luzon was 1,300 miles from Kagoshima on southern Kyushu. Formosa to southern Kyushu was 725 miles. Okinawa to Kyushu was only 325 miles, well within the reach of long-range fighters in 1945. Ulithi–Okinawa was about 1,400 miles, as was Okinawa–Guam. Despite Spruance's protestations about the current inability to transfer heavy shells and bombs from ship to ship on the open ocean, the fleet didn't need another intermediate base. In fact, it wouldn't establish another one during the war. Halsey's pummeling of the large Japanese air force over Formosa demonstrated that carriers could dominate the air over Okinawa.

Okinawa had several very good airfields, some flat land on which to pile supplies, and some moderately useful anchorages. It was a good forward base to support either invasion or blockade of Japan. Spruance didn't want to invade Japan. For him Okinawa was the ideal position from which to conduct the blockade.

At the September 29 strategy meeting in San Francisco, King again asked Spruance his thoughts about future operations. Spruance modified his initial position. He now wanted to take Iwo Jima first, then Okinawa.

Why Iwo Jima? Spruance considered himself an excellent strategist. His approach to strategic problems was very methodical. For him, geography and lines of communication were the essence of strategy.[5] He liked a clean, unencumbered approach to his current strategic target from secure bases. Having available land-based air support was more important to him than to many of the more carrier-minded admirals. Spruance's approach to the Marshalls and Gilberts is very instructive. At the end of 1943, almost every supporter of a central Pacific drive wanted to strike deep into the Marshalls. Enough fast carriers had been delivered to support this. It was Spruance who talked Nimitz into the more modest attack on Tarawa in the Gilberts. He advocated this shallow maneuver even though the Japanese fleet was incapable of offering serious resistance that far to the east, and surrounding island air bases were too small to offer much of a threat. After Tarawa, Spruance wanted to take many more intermediate islands before Kwajalein. It was Nimitz who waved all objections aside and sent the Big Blue Fleet directly into that excellent lagoon.

Even before the invasion of the Philippines was finalized, Spruance was looking ahead. He spent a lot of time studying the charts for the Bonins and Ryukyus. Spruance favored an attack on Okinawa. However he felt an intermediate jump to Iwo Jima would be needed to support Okinawa, which was 1,400 miles from Saipan. He told Nimitz and King so when they visited Saipan in mid-July.[6] Spruance wanted "an American air base on Iwo Jima to augment the big carriers. *Iwo Jima's value to the Air Force B-29 campaign was not Spruance's initial rationale for seizing that island.*"[7] He wanted to use Iwo Jima as both a fleet and an air base.[8]

The CinCPOA planners liked Spruance's suggestion of taking Iwo Jima and Okinawa. Admiral Towers recognized the value of Iwo to enhance B-29 operations emanating from Tinian. But Iwo Jima had little to offer the seagoing navy. It possessed nothing that remotely resembled a harbor. Little more than a PT boat could tie up there. Volcanic islands, the Jimas had no lagoons to shelter fleet logistic ships. Japanese reinforcements coming only 600 miles from Tokyo went first to Chichi Jima and then were barged to Iwo.

Upon his return to Pearl from fleet command during the fights in the Marianas, Nimitz informed Spruance his next assignment would be invasion of Formosa.

"I don't like Formosa," said Spruance.
"What would you rather do?" asked Nimitz.
"I would prefer taking Iwo Jima and Okinawa."
"Well," said Nimitz, "It's going to be Formosa."[9]

The JCS staff presented two thick volumes to Spruance detailing the rationale and plans for Formosa. He waved them aside and said he wouldn't waste time planning for Formosa. Then he went off on leave without reviewing them.

Mahan would have stood aghast. Hadn't anyone learned anything from Tarawa and Peleliu? Assaulting small heavily fortified islands was one of the most costly of undertakings, to be avoided if at all possible. There was nothing essential about Iwo Jima. Mahan would have been far more comfortable when King growled he wanted "nothing to do with that sinkhole," referring to Iwo Jima.[10]

When Spruance first proposed Iwo Jima, Nimitz didn't anticipate major problems. Then General "Howlin' Mad" Smith, after studying photographs of the volcanic island, predicted 20,000 casualties. "This is our toughest yet."[11] Smith's prognostication shook Spruance but did not change his mind.

From the beginning, the B-29 project had been Hap Arnold's personal baby. Twentieth Air Force, which controlled all Superfortress operations, bypassed the regional supreme commanders and reported directly to him. Army air forces planners independently identified the importance of an intermediate landing field between Tinian and Tokyo. On 14 July he made a formal request to the Joint Planners for an airfield in the Bonins.[12] Chichi Jima, a larger island than Iwo, was briefly examined. However, its topography was less suited to airfield construction and it was even more heavily fortified. On 3 October 1944, the Joint Chiefs gave Admiral Nimitz the go-ahead to invade Iwo Jima in early 1945 provided that it didn't interfere with the timing of other Pacific operations. It was much later, after the island had been taken, that General Curtis LeMay, commander of B-29 combat operations over Japan, said, "Without Iwo Jima, I couldn't bomb Japan effectively."

Tragedy of Iwo Jima

Iwo Jima (the name means "sulfur island") is a volcanic cinder of barely eight square miles, about one-third the size of Manhattan. Mount Suribachi, at the extreme southern end, rises 550 feet. This dead volcano dominates deep black sand and cinder that covers the island. Walking on this light, constantly shifting ash is difficult. Running is out of the question. A wheeled vehicle doesn't have a chance. Boiling sulfur pits, some with steam jetting out of them, adds to the impression of hell. Located roughly halfway on a straight line between Tinian and Tokyo, it was a spot on the ocean where B-29 crews returning from Japan would definitely like to find a friendly airfield. Administratively, the island was under the jurisdiction of the city of Tokyo, about 635 miles away.

Neither Formosa nor Iwo received much fortification until the Marshalls were invaded. Seven thousand men and a dozen coast defense guns, the first defensive preparations at Iwo, were landed in May 1944, while the Americans prepared to invade the Marianas. Japanese strategists recognized the likelihood that Iwo Jima would be attacked and began turning the island into an impregnable fortress. Lieutenant General Tadamichi Kuribayashi was more than up to the job. When the marines invaded Saipan, Japanese reinforcements en route to that island diverted to Iwo Jima. Some 1,500 reinforcements were lost on *maru*s that fell victim to subs.

Even with their empire shrinking, the Japanese didn't lack for cement and steel. Plenty of each was stored on the island, left over from shipments never made to islands now fallen. Coastal guns were emplaced in concrete casements and sited to fire down the invasion beaches. While the naval personnel on the island wanted to defend the beaches, Kuribayashi placed his main defenses inland. Defensive positions were positioned in the many natural caves, connected with tunnels and heavily camouflaged. Successive defensive lines across the island were established. Eventually the entire island itself was covered with hard-to-destroy redoubts. Elaborate range cards were prepared so the defenders could hit any potential target without having to find the range. The number of fortified positions was incredible. The U.S. 5th Marine Division destroyed 5,000 pillboxes and caves in their area of operation alone.[13]

Major General Harry Schmidt, commander, V Amphibious Corps, and the marine in tactical command, expected a tough ten-day fight for the island. Tough it was, but it was to last a month. Howlin' Mad Smith wanted ten days of naval bombardment. There wasn't enough ammunition to do more than the scheduled three. Given the number and stoutness of Japanese positions, seven more days of bombardment probably wouldn't have made much of a difference. Up until touchdown of the first wave, the operation "went off like a parade."[14] Almost immediately the LVTs bogged down in the volcanic ash. A twelve- to fifteen-foot terrace blocked the way inland. As marines jumped over the sides, they were hit hard with gunfire. The bleeding wouldn't stop for thirty days. The beach immediately began to resemble "Bloody Omaha" of D-day infamy.

When the bombardment began, only a pair of serviceable fighters remained on the island. Both Zeros took off, but neither made it past Mount Suribachi before being shot down. Despite twenty-one days of air strikes and three days of intense naval bombardment, Japanese bunkers and fortifications were barely scratched. Now warships moved in, delivering gunfire directly into Japanese fortifications. Battleship *Nevada,* which had been beached at Pearl Harbor, became the "Marine Corps sweetheart." Despite receiving hits from Japanese coastal batteries, she came in close and used her 14-inch guns like sniper rifles. Direct hits from 1,500-pound armor-piercing shells ripped apart blockhouses and cave entrances.

A total of 30,000 marines came ashore that morning. By midnight 2,400 were casualties.

Any regular infantry outfit might have been stopped at the beach by the horrible fire and casualties. But the heroic marines pressed inland, fighting their way through knee-deep volcanic ash. Marine assault parties using flamethrowers and fearless engineers with their hand-emplaced explosives began blowing holes in the defensive matrix. Searing close-in combat continued even while marines raised the Star-Spangled Banner atop Mount Suribachi. Just as the large flag was being raised, the secretary of the navy, James Forrestal, touched down on the beach after being ferried on from the command ship *Eldorado*. Seeing the large flag snapping in the breeze, he said, "This insures there will be a Marine Corps for the next five hundred years."

The intensity of fighting was unbelievable. Counting both Japanese and Americans, there were 10,000 combatants for every square mile. This rivals the battlefield densities of the American Civil War and World War I but with incredible fixed defenses and even more massive firepower. Given what had happened at Tarawa and Peleliu, it did not take a military genius to forecast a horrible bill to be paid in blood.

Nevertheless, the cost was hard to fathom. One out of every three marines who landed was hit by Japanese fire: 22,558 of them were seared by fire and hot metal. Of that number 5,521 would never see home again. Three of the only six marine divisions were shot to pieces. Sixty percent of the men in 3rd Marine Division's infantry regiments bled into the sand of Iwo Jima. The regiments of 4th and 5th divisions suffered 75 percent casualties. These divisions would not see further combat in World War II. It was a lot of combat power to sacrifice for an eight-square-mile volcanic heap that had no harbor.

Often one reads apologies for Iwo Jima that cite the number of B-29 crewmen aboard aircraft that landed at Iwo Jima and a statement to the effect that "costly as the conquest of Iwo Jima was, it therefore saved more American lives than it took."[15] This argument is specious. Although marines scaled Mount Suribachi on 23 February, Iwo Jima wasn't declared secured until 26 March 1945. Okinawa was invaded on 1 April and good airfields were secured in the first few days. While Okinawa was a dogleg for a damaged or gas-starved Tokyo–Guam bomber, it was about the same distance from Tokyo as Iwo. One of the nuclear bomber missions recovered on Okinawa. There were only a handful of days that Iwo Jima received B-29s (some landed while combat still raged on the island) when Okinawa was not available.

Between March and August of 1945, B-29s made 2,400 landings on Iwo; 82 percent of the landings were for fuel. Had Iwo Jima not been available, Okinawa would have been. By this time in the war the typical B-29 carried seven men. Air-sea rescue saved just under half of all B-29 crews that either bailed out or ditched at sea.[16] The percentage saved of those who ditched at sea was somewhat higher. Only a small number of aircraft that made emergency landings on Iwo could not have reached an Okinawan field.

It wasn't the possession of Iwo Jima that benefited the B-29 missions to the Japanese mainland. Instead it was the decision to move the B-29s to lower operating altitudes, which allowed General LeMay to pull belly gas tanks out of the planes; remove most of the defensive machine guns, gunners, fire control, ammunition, and all their associated weight; fill the bomb bays with ordnance; and still make the flight from Guam. The ability to base fighter escort on Okinawa and Iwo added little to the B-29 campaign.

Nothing can detract from the valor American fighting men displayed at Iwo Jima. But from the gruesome calculus of lives lost, the island proved to be a poor investment.

Kamikazes appeared off Iwo Jima. Often they would attack singly, hiding behind returning American aircraft at sunset. Escort carrier *Bismarck Sea* went to the bottom. Tough old hard luck "Sister Sara" took two bombs and four kamikaze hits. Under her own power she pointed her bow toward Pearl Harbor with the dignity of a lady.

Tarawa, Peleliu, and Iwo Jima were three bloody battles that had very weak strategic rationales. Initially Nimitz wanted to strike into the Marshalls but the more conservative Spruance convinced him Tarawa was a safer bet. In early plans many officers pointed to Peleliu as a flank guard for any invasion fleet headed into the Philippines. After the Great Marianas Turkey Shoot and Halsey's pounding of the concentrated airfields of Formosa, a flank guard was no longer required. Spruance had identified Iwo Jima as an intermediate air and naval base, but in 1945 no more were needed. Later, support for B-29 operations was added to the justification almost as an afterthought. General Rupertus was far too optimistic about his task on Peleliu. Marine commanders at Tarawa and Iwo Jima gave fair warning of the impending cost in blood, saluted when they were overruled, and heroically took their assigned objectives despite the carnage inflicted on their beloved men.

The strategic requirements for taking the Marshalls and Marianas were undeniable. Sometimes a commander has no choice but to frontally assault a position he simply has to have. The Marshalls demonstrate the lives that can be saved when rapid maneuver hits the enemy before his defensive preparations are completed. It is a lesson drawn repeatedly throughout history. Audacity is often the less risky course of action.

Tarawa, Peleliu, and Iwo Jima are three costly errors that must be charged to two great admirals. The navy rightfully held that generals didn't understand enough to control the Big Blue Fleet. Here we see that admirals might have avoided many American casualties if they had understood the mechanics of ground combat a little better. If anyone needs justification for emphasis on joint education, training, and planning, he need look no farther than the Great Pacific War.

Okinawa

The next move was obvious to everyone. The long axis of Okinawa runs north-east-southwest. The island is 60 miles long, 2 to 8 miles wide, and totals 485 square miles. That's sixty times the size of Iwo Jima. While not world-class anchorages, two bays on its eastern side would make acceptable naval bases. Several excellent cargo harbors were available.

After finishing their survey, army engineers concluded Okinawa could hold eighteen airfields and nearby Ie Shima another four. They could handle B-29s and all the aircraft redeploying from Europe. Plans called for the island to become a giant air base servicing over 5,000 aircraft. Tactical airpower comprising 5th, 7th, and 13th Air Forces would be consolidated under General Kenney. The 8th Air Force would redeploy from Europe and re-equip with B-29s. Britain planned to add 600 Lancaster bombers. This air armada would smash defenses in the Home Islands before the dogfaces made the final landings.

Okinawa was centrally located—about 350 miles to Taiwan, the China coast, and Kyushu. It was 830 miles to Tokyo, within range of B-17s, B-24s, and long-range fighters. While Okinawa was sovereign Japanese territory at the beginning of 1945, most Japanese tended to look down on Okinawans as "rustics" with little culture.[17] The Japanese in control did nothing to raise the low standard of living of the native population, which numbered about 463,000. At the start of hostilities, there were only 259 cars and 88 buses on the entire island. Many derided the Okinawans for their passiveness and lack of understanding of Bushido. Nevertheless, most Okinawans considered themselves loyal subjects of the emperor. The militia would fight willingly and hard. The southern portion of the island was densely settled, with some areas containing over 2,700 people per square mile. Many lived in thatched huts. The northern half of the island was rugged and covered by pines and dense undergrowth. The south is more rolling. Much of the land there was under cultivation.

Americans dubbed the invasion "ICEBERG." Planners assumed that all remaining Japanese airpower would be concentrated on Formosa, the Ryukyus, and the Home Islands. To successfully invade Okinawa, Japanese airpower in both Formosa and Kyushu had to be neutralized.[18] This proved to be no small task. The 65 airfields on Formosa and 55 on Kyushu were more than the Big Blue Fleet could suppress.

Okinawa wasn't heavily garrisoned until April 1944. Fortunately for the Americans, the Japanese 9th Division had transferred from Okinawa to Formosa. Lieutenant General Mitsuru Ushijima, a consummate defensive tactician, commanded 67,000 regular troops, 33,000 reservists 9,000 sailors, and 20,000 members of the Okinawan Home Guard.

U.S. Tenth Army, Lieutenant General Simon Bolivar Buckner commanding, totaled 172,000 troops by the time the landings were completed. Another 115,000 service troops also came ashore. XXIV Corps contained four infantry divisions, while III MAF had the three marine divisions that hadn't been decimated on Iwo Jima. Essentially, Tenth Army comprised the forces that had fought through much of the central Pacific reinforced by one of MacArthur's divisions and a freshly minted marine division, all concentrated in one place.

Ushijima understood it was futile to challenge American firepower at the water line. Actually he was willing to cede most of the island and fortify the hills and ravines in the south. At first the warlords in Tokyo insisted on defending all of the island. As plans developed, only a 3,500-man naval special landing force was left to defend the north. The Japanese "Outline of Army and Navy Operations, January, 1945" designated Okinawa as a fortified delaying zone. Ushijima's mission was to inflict maximum casualties on the Americans and "seriously delay the final assault on Japan." The final decisive battle would be fought in the Home Islands. Until American troops debarked, Japanese airpower would be withheld to conserve strength.

For the Japanese the strategic objective was to hold the American fleet in close as long as possible so it could be hammered with kamikazes. Japan could not prevent the Americans from establishing airfields on Okinawa. However, if the Big Blue Fleet could be crippled, then the homeland might yet be spared invasion. The longer the Japanese army could hold out on Okinawa, the greater the possible carnage among the American ships at sea. To the Japanese leadership this objective was worth the death of all those Japanese troops. There should be no heroic but useless banzai charges. Make the Americans pay for every last drop of Japanese blood—in kind. The Okinawans themselves simply didn't matter. There was a cruel logic in Japan's strategy that could not be denied.

The United States Navy had amphibious operations well in hand. At Okinawa the best amphibious practitioner of all, Terrible Turner, would create another masterpiece. The challenge for the U.S. navy was to maintain station in the face of hordes of kamikazes. Operations orders for Okinawa emphasized the kamikaze threat. Mahan held that changes in naval weaponry and technology impacted strategy to a minor extent. But kamikaze aircraft were beyond his experience. They were beyond everyone's experience. As Nimitz said, they were the great surprise of the war.

Admiral Mitscher's first move was to hit the kamikaze fields on Kyushu. In two days of low-level attacks 45 fields were hit and perhaps 400 Japanese aircraft destroyed. In return, kamikazes scored on *Yorktown* and *Enterprise*. From 23 March to April Fools' Day Mitscher's carriers concentrated on softening up Okinawa and the adjacent islands. Because of the sweeps over Kyushu, air opposition was light. But the Japanese were gathering their strength.

Six days before the Okinawa invasion, 77th Infantry Division landed against light resistance on the islets of Kerama Retto, which lie 15–20 miles due west of Okinawa. They became an excellent anchorage for 10th Service Squadron and refuge for many a kamikaze-damaged vessel. Two hundred fifty kamikaze speedboats were captured there. Supposedly unoccupied Ie Shima had 3,000 defenders that had to be defeated.

U.S. planners selected invasion beaches on Okinawa near two principal Japanese airfields on the southwest coast. As Morison summarized: "At Okinawa, it was the essence of victory that airfields be secured promptly, so that land based planes could help the carrier planes to ward off enemy air attacks and eventually relieve them."[19]

Dogfaces also went ashore on April Fools' Day from an invasion fleet of over 300 ships. They landed on a four-division front. (Only three American divisions landed by sea in Normandy on 6 June 1944.) The Japanese had long since stopped opposing the Americans on beaches where U.S. naval gunnery could annihilate defending positions. Admiral Turner conducted a nearly perfect operation. By nightfall 50,000 troops were ashore. The two airfields were quickly taken. Near the beaches the invaders advanced over ground that was suitable for additional airstrips. During the first week, as the Americans swept north, it appeared as if the Japanese had given up. Virtually no resistance was encountered. This was the last time Americans would receive only light resistance on Okinawa, and it yielded the critical terrain needed to support further attacks on the Home Islands. Engineers got busy. Afterward, General MacArthur commented, "In three or four days after the landing the American forces had all the area that they needed, which was the area they wanted for their airplane bases. They should have had the troops go into a defensive position and just let the Japanese come to them and kill them from a defensive position, which would have been much easier to do and would have cost less men."[20] One wonders what MacArthur's brilliance could have accomplished if he hadn't been obsessed with returning to the Philippines.

When Buckner's troops moved south, resistance became intense. Americans ran into fortifications and obstacles of the Shuri line, which was the main Japanese line of resistance inland. Buckner attempted to maneuver to the right to avoid the hardest position in the center of the line. That move brought little relief. Each enemy-encrusted hole had to be taken with satchel charges and flamethrowers. Japanese fought ferociously to the end. American commanders shuddered at their tenacity. Was this what warfare on the Home Islands was going to be like? In a hideous way Japanese strategy achieved its objective of preventing an invasion of the Home Islands. It strengthened American resolve to bomb Japan into oblivion rather than to invade.

Fighting to gain Okinawa was one bloody battle. Defending against the kamikazes was another. From radio intercepts Americans knew it would take about four days for the Japanese to react. L+4 (landing day plus four days) would be the critical day.[21] The first kamikaze raid came on L+6. Six hundred sixty aircraft, 355 of them carried by the "divine wind," concentrated on the radar picket destroyers. They sank three destroyer types, an LST, and a pair of ammunition ships. Loss of all that ammunition crimped Tenth Army's artillery operations. Another nine destroyer types and a minesweeper were damaged. Tin can sailors began to feel the targets the divine wind had pasted to their backs. *Essex*-class carrier *Hancock* was heavily damaged and had to withdraw.

On the same day battleship *Yamato* and an escort of a cruiser and eight destroyers left port headed on a one-way mission to Okinawa. Without waiting for instructions from Spruance, Mitscher lit out after them. That evening Spruance ordered Mitscher to leave *Yamato* to the old battleships of TF 51 and to concentrate on countering the kamikaze threat. Mitscher was not to be deterred. Spruance hadn't prohibited Mitscher from striking the *Yamato*. However, the Fifth Fleet commander issued instructions for the two battleship divisions of TF 51 to form their battle line. About noon the next day Hell Divers and TBFs hit the supership. Torpedoes are the real killers of heavily armored vessels. *Yamato*'s hull was hit with at least ten of them. She turned turtle, blew up, and sank. A light cruiser followed her down. The cruiser and four destroyers made it home. Mitscher lost only four pilots and eight crewmen. What would the casualties have been on the American battleships? Mahan: Don't engage in melee combat.

Ultra warned that the next kamikaze attack would arrive on 12 or 13 April. On those dates, attacks totaling 185 aircraft bore in. Perhaps 60 percent of them were splashed. The attacks kept coming. Over a period of two and a half months, ten large kamikaze attacks and many smaller ones were made. The Japanese mounted 6,300 sorties against the Allied fleet; 3,000 of them were kamikazes. Seven percent of the kamikazes hit something.[22] Three large raids were launched in close succession between 12 and 15 April. Both *Enterprise* and *Intrepid* had to leave the area to lick their wounds. While it was launching aircraft, a 500-pound bomb hit the *Essex*-class carrier *Franklin*. Six explosions followed as ordnance on her aircraft went off. *Wasp* and a destroyer took less serious hits. Although carrier *Franklin* managed to limp back to the United States, it was written off and never repaired. The kamikazes achieved something the Japanese carrier navy never had: because of the losses Task Group 58.2 was disbanded. There was a lot of hurt among the fleet.

Mitscher believed he could destroy more kamikazes by staying in close proximity to Okinawa.[23] He simply didn't have the resources to suppress all the airfields in range. The fleet operated in a 60-square-mile area 350 miles from Kyushu until it was released on 18 May.

The final kamikaze toll included 17 named ships sunk, mostly destroyers and transports; 198 ships including 12 carriers and 10 battleships were damaged; 43 were damaged so heavily that they didn't return to service during World War II; 4,300 brave American sailors died in the kamikaze onslaught. Another 5,400 were injured. These losses surpassed the blood toll paid in the waters around Guadalcanal when the opposing navies were far more equal. Eighteen hundred nine kamikaze sorties were counted. At least 930 of those aircraft were lost, presumably with as many Japanese.

By the end of the fighting on the island, 135,000 Japanese military and Okinawan Home Guard lay dead. Some 75,000 Okinawans, out of a prewar population of 500,000, also perished. (Because many Okinawans had been transported to Japan, the percentage of those actually on the island who were killed was actually higher than 15 percent.) On land, United States forces suffered almost 7,400 dead and almost 32,000 wounded. Lieutenant General Buckner was one of two three-star American officers to die in combat during World War II. He was killed by Japanese artillery fire as he observed operations. (The other was Lesley McNair, who was killed by bombs from American planes that fell short of their targets during the breakout from Normandy.)

Okinawa was declared secure on 21 June. The Japanese commander, Ushijima, committed seppuku that evening.

Leyte, Luzon, Iwo Jima, Formosa, Okinawa Reconsidered

Now that we have recounted what actually happened, it is time to reconsider the strategic question: where should the Americans have gone after the Marianas?

Spruance in the Marianas and Halsey in his successful raids on Formosa established, beyond doubt, that the Big Blue Fleet could seize air superiority at will in its area of operations. In both cases, maximum Japanese efforts from both land and naval air were unable to contest what Mitscher's airmen could achieve. There was no absolute need to move only within the protective umbrella of land-based aviation. The revolutionary Japanese weapon, the kamikaze, increased the cost of U.S. operations but did not change their result. The Big Blue Fleet could establish air superiority anywhere it chose. Ulithi was the last major intermediate naval base the fleet needed. Therefore there was no naval requirement for another operation between the Marianas and the Home Islands.

When tackling strategic problems, it is best to firmly establish what end state is required. From that end state, one can work backwards to identify the critical intermediate conditions or objectives that are absolutely necessary. War Plan Orange architects' debate between the "through ticket" and the need for an intermediate base is just such an analysis. Frequently an intermediate battle is required to draw out enemy forces at a place of your time and choosing to engage them under conditions more favorable to you. Guadalcanal can be seen as an excellent example. King created conditions that induced the Japanese to commit their fleet piecemeal in an important but peripheral set of battles. The packets of warships Yamamoto sent down were (just) small enough for the American navy to handle. Japan couldn't replace the losses. America could replace the ships and airplanes. And her warriors got better. This was the critical result that Mahan would have most heartily endorsed.

The jump to Kwajalein and its low-cost extension, Bikini Atoll, were necessary intermediate stops. Again Mahan would have approved. The Marianas met three criteria: it was a required intermediate base, it was a base from which a serious aerial bombardment of Japan could begin, and it was important enough to force an increasingly recalcitrant Japanese fleet to offer decisive battle.

While it wasn't as clean a victory as many would have liked, the open ocean capability of the Japanese fleet was destroyed in the Philippine Sea just west of the Marianas. The critical condition Mahan always advocated had been achieved. The U.S. fleet could now sail where it pleased. With that freedom came the freedom to strike wherever American strategy dictated.

Everything the United States had seen in the Pacific screamed the warning to avoid land combat with the Japanese army unless it was absolutely necessary. Regardless of the enormous cost in Japanese blood, it resulted in a great many American casualties. Leave the Japanese alone on an island while the United States had air and sea superiority, as it had after the Marianas, and they became ineffective for the duration. Again the desired end state had to be examined. General Marshall and many others within the army were certain an invasion of Japan would be required. Why not skip further preliminaries and just do it? That is what the supremely logical Marshall advocated. Given the required end state Mahan would not have quibbled with the general's reasoning.

But King and Nimitz expected to win in a far less bloody manner. They wanted to blockade Japan and starve her into submission. Mahan undoubtedly would have advocated blockade rather than invasion as an end state. He wrote extensively about blockade.

To complete a blockade, the passage up from the South China Sea to Japan needed to be corked. The circle from Clark Field to the China coast is 500 miles in radius. Two-engine medium bombers would be required to close the sea passage. Bases on Formosa would provide the 250-mile radius necessary to close the passage. Virtually any single-engine fighter or marine attack plane could do the trick. A 350-mile radius from Okinawa could do the same thing with long-range fighters (P-38s and P-51s) to perform the duty.

While not required, it is nice to have land-based aviation to support landings. Note the distances below:

	Okinawa	Kyushu	Tokyo
Okinawa		375	825
Formosa	350	575	1175
Clark Field, Luzon	750	1200	1575

Long-range fighters and medium bombers from Clark barely make it to Formosa. From Formosa the same machines cover the China coast and Okinawa. B-24s can hit Kyushu, reinforcing the B-29 effort from the Marianas. All the above-mentioned aircraft can hit Kyushu from Okinawa. Okinawa–Nagoya is about the same mileage as Okinawa–Tokyo, so Okinawa-based P-51s can perform similar escort duty. A diversion from Tokyo to Okinawa is about 200 miles longer than one to Iwo Jima. That's a small premium given the bill that had to be paid in blood for the small volcanic island.

If blockade of Japan causes her to surrender, then blockade is the least costly way, in human blood, to end the war. Okinawa or Formosa would be required to set up an effective blockade. One of the two would also be needed to base tactical aviation if an invasion was required. From this, it is clear that an invasion from the Marianas to Okinawa was the least-cost option. A more conservative approach would have been the invasion of Formosa, which corks the flow of raw materials to Japan, followed by Okinawa. Heavy land-based air support of an Okinawan operation from Formosa would have eliminated the need for the fleet to stand off the Ryukyus for an extended period. This would have significantly lessed the carnage wrought by kamikazes off Okinawa. Two-thirds of the 4,000 navy deaths occurred in the final twenty days of the campaign.

In the actual campaign, the fleet conducted two invasions without land-based air support in the presence of mass Japanese land-based aviation. These were Leyte and Okinawa. Taken together, Mindoro and Luzon (Lingayen Gulf) constitute a third. In the alternative above, only one such landing (either Formosa or Okinawa) needs to be made. The actual campaign had four very bloody land campaigns: Leyte, Luzon, Iwo Jima, Okinawa. The alternative could have been one or, at most, two. Further the alternative would have achieved the desired end state several months before the actual one did. The drain on the fleet, and the blood of its sailors, would have been far less.

In the actual campaign, the Japanese pumped all the aircraft Luzon could employ via Formosa. Given that some aircraft would have been retained to defend the Philippines, the total air resistance on Formosa or Okinawa might have been less. Japanese leaders expected the invasion of the Philippines. An early invasion of either Formosa or Okinawa would have taken the Japanese by surprise. The bill for the Marshalls was far less because the United States took those islands by surprise.

A Formosa–Luzon campaign would have been far superior to a Leyte–Luzon approach. Formosa would have started the blockade of Japan earlier and provided air for the Lingayen Gulf operation. Operations in Philippine waters would have been far less harrowing. Eliminating Iwo Jima would have undoubtedly lowered the overall bloodletting even if a Formosa-supported invasion of Okinawa had been retained.

Liberation of the Philippines is often justified by some vague geopolitical considerations. Sitting in Washington in late 1944, it was clear to any informed observer that the struggle for China was going to be a far higher stakes game than returning the Philippines to its prewar path toward independence. If required, sending the Eighth Army to Luzon after Formosa had been taken, supported by the Fifth Air Force on Formosa, would have been far more useful than the inconsequential operations it engaged in south of Luzon during the actual campaign.

When viewed from this perspective, Leyte must be rated one of the larger strategic blunders of the war. While it never threatened to be fatal, it gained nothing. Leyte contributed almost zero to the invasion of Luzon. If there had been no Philippines campaign, there would have been no need for Peleliu, another of the great and bloody blunders.

From an unbiased strategic analysis of American interests in mid-1944, it is hard not to conclude that King had a far superior solution than did MacArthur. Spruance's initial conclusion, Okinawa, beat both of them. But King was right when he said he'd have nothing to do with Spruance's modification—Iwo Jima.

Iwo Jima was not necessary. Therefore it was a mistake. Mahan would have strongly objected to Spruance's thought process and analysis of the problem. Spruance viewed Iwo Jima as the focus of an arc that ran from Tokyo through

Kyushu to the Ryukyus.[24] This was similar to the position the Marianas held as the focus of an arc than ran from Tokyo through Kyushu, the Ryukyus, Formosa, and the Philippines to New Guinea. Spruance wanted to defend from within these arcs against forces attacking from the arcs. In this manner, he would have the advantage in maneuvering his forces on the interior of the arc while his enemy had to transit the longer distances along the arc. This advantage is the well recognized one referred to as the advantage of interior lines of communications.

Spruance's reasoning centered on geography. Its specifics were different but the basic approach is similar to the one Marshall used to break the advance on Rabaul into three discrete tasks. The single most important element in Mahan's reasoning began with a focus on the enemy rather than geography.

Had Spruance's ample intellect been more focused through the lens of Mahan, he might not have been sidetracked by places like Tarawa and Iwo Jima and several others that Nimitz correctly edited out. Spruance might have also reached the same conclusion Mitscher did on the evening of 16 March in the Marianas, sailed west, and crushed Ozawa's carriers.

When all is said and done, King more closely paralleled the thinking of Mahan than any other admiral on either side of the Great Pacific War. Above all, he was King Strategist.

In early 1942, the then brigadier general Eisenhower was head of Marshall's War Plans Division and the main keeper of Orange's successor, Rainbow 5. He had served under MacArthur for many years. Upon MacArthur's extrication from Corregidor in March 1942, Ike wrote in his diary: "I am doubtful that he'd do so well in complicated situations. . . . I cannot help believing that we are disturbed by editorials and reacting to public opinion rather than military logic. . . . If brought out [of the Philippines], public opinion will force him into a position where his love of the lime light may ruin him."[25]

Ike concluded that MacArthur shouldn't be given a theater-level command upon his return to Australia. Had his superiors been willing—or able—to control MacArthur, the war in the Pacific might have been a year shorter and far less costly in human blood. Perhaps the real lesson is never to let a serving uniformed officer create an independent political power base.

13

B-SAN

The first ones looked to some Japanese like small silver sailing toys hanging way up in the air. Somehow they were beautiful as they crawled across the sky 30,000 feet above the ground. Another of America's scientific achievements; a technological marvel. Many Japanese used the honorific and referred to them as "B-san"—like Papa-san.

Then the bombs began exploding.

In 1932, Billy Mitchell predicted the final campaign that was to end World War II. In an article published for *Liberty Magazine*, "Are We Ready for War with Japan," he speculated that Japan's end would come in a strategic bombing campaign prosecuted by bombers with the then fantastic range of 5,000 miles. From bases in either Alaska or Midway, they would pummel the Japanese into submission without the need for invasion.[1]

Since the first writings of Douhet, the first prophet of aerial bombardment, airpower advocates have extolled the virtues of replacing costly surface battles against the enemy's most hardened target, his military forces deployed for battle in the field or at sea. Airpower would directly attack the strategic sources of enemy power, and the will of their populations and leaders to continue the fight.

The notion of defeating the enemy's will to resist is as old as organized warfare. General William Tecumseh Sherman practiced it in his March to the Sea through Georgia. "I will make war such a Hell that southerners will wage it no more."

Following World War I, a collection of captains teaching at the Air Corps Tactical School at Maxwell Air Force Base kept the theory of strategic bombing alive. It was elevated to the most central belief of the U.S. Army Air Corps. When asked to write a plan to win the war, the air corps produced AWPD1 as a blueprint. First, American airpower would sweep its enemy from the skies. With a path to the enemy's homeland clear, high-altitude bombers would hit selected "bottleneck" target systems (such as oil and electrical power generation). Without these key industries, the entire economy would break down. The enemy would no longer have the means to carry on modern war. Both FDR and General Marshall were very impressed with this argument.

To produce this result, the plan outlined a program of airplane construction, pilot training, and putting into place the infrastructure for the upcoming campaigns. Little attention was given to tactical support of armies or navies. In 1942 many air planners envisioned an air campaign that would defeat Hitler without an invasion of the European continent.

The idea of precision air bombardment is intriguing. The questions before America's ranking admirals and generals were, Did the airmen have the technological ability to execute their ideas? What if the machines couldn't execute the strategy? Then America's military leaders would have to face the ominous decisions to invade Europe and Japan.

Aviation's technical ability to deliver destruction where it could have decisive impact could not meet the requirements of a strategy of precision air bombardment. In 1943 individual bombs created fearful devastation at their point of impact. Unfortunately, they could not be delivered via high-flying multiple-engine bombers with anywhere near the accuracy to strike the critical aim points a strategic campaign against bottlenecks required. The technical solutions were either to vastly increase the destructive power carried in a single sortie or to dramatically increase the accuracy of warhead delivery. The Americans followed the first route with increasingly lethal B-29 armament, first wide-area fire-bombing, and then with the atom. The Japanese followed the second route by fielding the first precision-guided munitions in the form of human-guided kamikazes.

Anti-air defenses proved far tougher than expected. Radar was a major surprise. Interwar theorists thought bomber raids would seldom be detected in time to launch an effective interceptor force. In fact virtually all raids were detected in time.

The lesson is to expect the unknown countermeasure. The most senior commanders have to retain a "gut it out" alternative in the event the wonder weapon isn't so wonderful. The American Joint Chiefs of Staff did this by retaining a credible plan for invasion. They were right in doing so. No one can fault them for comparing the cost in American blood of alternatives to that nightmare.

Surface commanders readily embraced the uses of tactical airpower. Fighters in close support of mobile tank columns can tear huge holes in defensive lines and spread panic throughout the enemy's support area. Naval dive-bombers can extend the fleet's ability to deliver large armor-piercing projectiles from 20,000 yards (via gun) to 200 miles.

With twenty-twenty hindsight, we scoff at the "gun club" admirals who clung to their battleships in the face of the new carriers. However, we saw that 1930-era carrier aircraft couldn't deliver ship-killing ordinance with sufficient speed and in sufficient quantity to be effective. If 1935 had been the final year of World War II, battleships most likely would have been the final arbitrators of the Great Pacific War.

Similarly, 1931 bombers couldn't have leveled Japan. However, it didn't take the 1941 B-29 to do the job. No doubt this magnificent flying machine itself was a major advance over the 1935 B-17. That unpressurized bomber, employing firebombs delivered over a wide area the way the RAF did over Germany, could have vanquished Japan, albeit six months later, from the more forward base of Okinawa. More important for our inquiry, improperly deployed B-29s—that is, B-29s operated according to the precision bombing strategy for which they were designed—would not have brought about the end of the war.

The B-29 was thought of as a huge engineering problem. More than any other officer, Hap Arnold was the plane's primary advocate.[2] Initial work on a 5,000-mile bomber, a bomber that could strike Japan, began at the major air corps R&D facility at Wright Field in July 1933. Cryptically it was dubbed "Project A." To disguise its offensive intention from the rest of the American military bureaucracy, it was described as a plane that could defend Hawaii or the Panama Canal from the continental United States.

Detailed engineering drawings reached the air corps in May 1940. While the marines were struggling to retain Guadalcanal in late September 1942, the first

B-29 prototype took to the air. Arnold envisioned B-29 operations that would lead to Japan's surrender.[3] He bet big chips on the untried bomber. Before the prototype flew, 1,664 production copies had been ordered. B-17s and B-24s would wreck Germany before the Superfortress would be ready for combat. The B-29 program focused strictly on Japan.

To power these machines, aircraft engine technology had been pushed to the limit. B-29s continued to be plagued by power-plant problems. For example, the rearmost cylinders routinely overheated to the point of meltdown during ground holds in hot weather. Field mechanics jury-rigged crossover tubes to bring additional cooling oil into the overheating parts.

Initial planning called for B-29s to strike Japan from four directions. Twentieth Air Force, the B-29 air force, originally contained four bomber commands. China, the Marianas, either the Philippines or Formosa, and the Aleutians each were to base one of the commands. Unlike other air forces, the Twentieth would be commanded directly by the Joint Chiefs with Hap Arnold as Twentieth Air Force Commander and executive agent for the Joint Chiefs. The B-29 was an instrument of global warfare.

China was the first to receive B-29s. Each B-29 mission from China had to be supported by seven sorties flying over the "Hump" of the Himalayas from India to haul in supplies. The logistical burden was impossible. Technical teething trouble kept many B-29s from completing missions on which they were dispatched.

After a disappointing warm-up mission to bomb the Bangkok rail yards, the first B-29 raid on Japan, 68 planes strong, left China on the evening of 15 June 1944. That was the evening of the invasion of Saipan. Only 47 B-29s ever found the primary target. Each was to engage in high-level precision bombing per doctrine. Intelligence analysts could only find 28 percent of the impact points, the bombs had scattered so badly. Some fell 20 miles away. The closest hit 3,700 feet from the aim point. Precision bombing! The targeted factory was undamaged.

From June 1944 to January 1945, B-29s struck the Japanese island of Kyushu only nine times. The critical bottleneck industry of the Japanese economy had been identified as aircraft engine production. That was supposed to be the critical vulnerability. Five of the nine missions targeted the engine plant at Omura. Only 75 of the 573 tons of bombs dropped fell within 100 feet of the factory. Not much to show for the incredible logistical effort required to launch the mission.

General Curtis LeMay had some colorful words to describe the B-29's initial period of operation. "B-29s had as many bugs as the entomological department of the Smithsonian Institution. Fast as they got the bugs licked, new ones crawled out from under the cowling. . . . The B-29 was not ready for combat by any means. . . . There are something like 55,000 different parts in a B-29; and frequently it seemed that maybe 50,000 of them were all going wrong at once. . . . The scheme of operations had been dreamed up like something from the Wizard of Oz. . . . I've never been able to shake off the idea that General Arnold himself never believed that this [China-based B-29 operations] would work. It didn't work. No one could have made it work. It was founded on an utterly absurd logistic basis."[4]

Results for the resources expended on the China raids made little sense. The Quadrant Conference at Quebec in August 1943 identified the Marianas as the best basing alternative for the Superfortresses. Prior to that conference, invasion of the Marianas looked like a 1946 issue. Instead, the American air staff, led by the B-29's father, Hap Arnold, recommended capture of the Marianas to coincide with availability of the B-29 in the summer of 1944.[5] This timing was confirmed at the Cairo meeting of the Combined Chiefs in November 1943. Limited China-based operations were continued until January 1945, more to boost Chinese morale than anything else.

The first B-29 bomb wing did not arrive in the Marianas until early November. Airfields and facilities were not ready to receive them. The B-29 was a complex machine pushing the state of the art. Maintaining them with little ground equipment and few spare parts on hot, dusty aprons with little cover almost stymied operations.

In conformity with the doctrine of precision bombing key bottleneck industries, the first raid attacked the Musashino aircraft engine factory. The climb to high altitude was hard on B-san's engines. Clouds kept most of the aircraft away from the primary target. The Americans little understood the jet stream, which is particularly strong over Japan, High winds scattered the bombs that were dropped. Only 1 percent of the buildings and 2 percent of the machine tools at the plant were hit.[6] Ten more high-altitude daylight precision-bombing missions against engine factories were made in the following two months. Five were against the same Musashino plant, four against the Mitsubishi plants in Nagoya, and one against Kawasaki at Akashi. Mechanical problems prevented about half the B-29s from gaining high altitude to strike their primary targets. Clouds continuously obscured targets. Radar bombing wasn't accurate enough to hit point targets. High winds and mistakes made by inexperienced crews scattered bombs all over the countryside. Damage was done, but it wasn't enough to justify the cost of the operations. The B-29s were failing. The mantra of high-altitude precision bombing was not working.

What if the long-range bomber campaign had never been fixed? Men like Nimitz, MacArthur, and King had to plan for that eventuality. One cannot bet a world war on an untried weapon that is having teething trouble. In January 1945

it was not at all evident that the bombing campaign was going to make a significant contribution. Senior leaders had to ready plans for a massive blockade—or
invasion of Japan.

When the American daylight bombing campaign in Europe was in big trouble, a taciturn and demanding general, Curtis LeMay, swept aside what didn't
work along with the supposed "experts" who had promulgated doctrinaire solutions. He substituted what practice had proven to be successful. When he arrived
in Europe in 1943, most bomber pilots believed a straight and level bomb run in
the presence of flak was suicide. LeMay pulled out a pencil and an ROTC artillery manual and calculated the probability of a hit. The numbers said it was
small. LeMay forced pilots to straighten out their bomb runs. Bombing results
improved dramatically but casualties didn't increase.

German fighters were decimating American bombers. LeMay worked out the
tight "combat box" formation that maximized the coverage from bomber machine guns and lessened losses. Losing airmen was a personal matter to LeMay.
He had commanded the infamous Regensburg raid. Losses over Schweinfurt-
Regensburg were so enormous that air commanders seriously considered sus-
pension of daylight raids over Germany

LeMay was the fastest rising star in Europe; Arnold tapped him to straighten
out the B-29 problems in China. LeMay gained valuable B-29 operational experience. Initially LeMay continued the policy of high-altitude precision bombing.
He lowered bombing altitudes and improved crew training, which led to incremental improvements. But that wasn't enough.

Hap Arnold replaced the B-29 commander in the Marianas with "Old Iron
Ass" LeMay. As General Lauris Norstad, Hap Arnold's handpicked deputy commander of B-29s in the Pacific, said to LeMay: "You go ahead and get results
with the B-29. If you don't get results, you'll be fired. If you don't get results, also,
there will never be any strategic air forces of the Pacific—after the battle is finally
won in Europe, and those ETO forces can be deployed here. If you don't get results it will mean eventually a mass amphibious invasion of Japan, to cost probably half a million more American lives."[7]

Even before LeMay arrived, planners in the Marianas began to analyze whether shifting to nighttime area firebomb raids on Japan's highly inflammable cities
might not be a better tactic.[8] Officers pointed out the dispersed nature of Japanese
industry, the light wood construction and crowded conditions of Japanese cities,
and the poor results of conventional high-altitude precision bombing to date.

The first experiments with high-altitude incendiary bombing were less than a
smashing success. Incendiaries scattered too badly on the way down to start
large, all-consuming fires. LeMay's review of the data led to a single conclusion.

High-altitude operations, which were designed to minimize the threat from Japanese flak and fighters, would not bring success. LeMay ordered the bombers to lower altitude. This reduced the impact of cloud cover and winds on operations. Engines could be operated at much-reduced power settings, reducing failures and improving gas consumption.

An analysis of Japanese fighter attacks against B-29s showed that few were effective. In order to increase bomb tonnage and fuel carried, LeMay ordered all but rear gunners and most machine gun ammunition to be left on the ground. Many pilots felt flak would tear them up at low levels. LeMay compared Japanese anti-aircraft practices to those of the Germans and concluded they were far less a threat. Most Japanese anti-aircraft artillery couldn't hit anything at 8,000–10,000 feet. That was the altitude he would order the bombers to fly at. To minimize the enemy threat, they would go in at night and blanket the target with incendiaries. Japanese radar direction was very crude and her night fighter capabilities almost nonexistent. "We looked at the photos and we didn't see any light AA. But you never know for sure. I had to order them in. Somebody has to be the commander."[9]

Crews met with despair the news that they would be carrying out low-level night incendiary bombing without the benefit of much defensive armament. As some recalled, "A sort of cold fear gripped the crews."[10] Some thought LeMay must be mad. Much of the staff was against his decision.

The first firebomb raid hit Tokyo on the night of 9 March. Each B-29 was stuffed with seven tons of M69 napalm bombs. Each was actually a cluster weapon containing 38 submunitions filled with jellied gasoline to be dropped from altitudes of 5,000–8,000 feet.

Pathfinders marked a large area of Tokyo with firebombs. Three hundred B-29s followed; 1,665 tons of firebombs hit the Japanese capital. Many small fires broke out in the city. Rapidly they expanded and merged into one huge conflagration. Crewmembers recall the stench of burning wood and flesh that rose from the city. Those poor souls that might have survived the flames had the oxygen sucked out of their lungs by the drafts roaring into the blaze. Eighty-three thousand Japanese died in Tokyo that night; 267,000 buildings, one-quarter of those in the city, were destroyed, and 16.4 square miles of Tokyo obliterated by all-consuming fire. Millions were dazed, without food, shelter, or much ability to do anything coherent as they shivered in winter weather among the ashes. Fourteen B-29s that departed that night did not come back.

Instantly the B-29 was transformed from temperamental underperformer to decisive weapon. The key to their use was to use them to create a massive conflagration. When the density of firebombs per acre was reduced, the required result was not achieved. There was a right way to firebomb and a lot of wrong ways. B-29s carrying heavier bomb loads due to the elimination of defensive armament and the need to climb to high altitude were instrumental.

Within a week four additional massive firebomb raids were executed. Nagoya received a 313-bomber raid on 11 March. Osaka was blitzed by 301 B-29s on the 13th; 8.1 square miles burned to a pile of carbon cinders. Kobe's turn was on the 16th. Twenty-one percent of Kobe was reduced to ash. On the 19th Nagoya suffered the attention of 290 Superfortresses. Several square miles of Nagoya were consumed by flames. LeMay had to pause after five raids. He had run out of firebombs.

Leaflets had been dropped warning civilians to move away from the cities. The cities and their war plants, not the populations, were the targets. LeMay, pointing to earlier Japanese atrocities, wasn't happy about the deaths but felt he could justify them.[11] Wars fought to unconditional surrender are not fought according to Marquess of Queensberry rules. A lot of people had already died horrible deaths. As in any war, your own countrymen are everything. The lives of your enemies weigh little in the balance.

Initially few Japanese responded to the leaflets dropped on the first three missions. After news of the horrific firestorms, many Japanese began moving out of the cities. Fortunately, the number of civilian casualties dropped.

New supplies of bombs did not arrive until mid-April. Often the B-29s dropped 3,000 tons of them a night. (The two atom bombs had yields of between 12,000 and 20,000 tons.) Usage was so high that ordnance was sent directly from shipside to planeside. There was not enough supply to bother with a bomb storage dump.

By mid-May a sustained firebomb campaign began that continued until the end of the war. Most weeks would see several large raids. Tokyo was hit repeatedly. One raid burned a third of Yokohama. In all sixty-five major cities were incinerated.

All in all, 178 square miles of urban Japan were immolated. That amounted to 40 percent of the urban area of Japan's 66 largest cities. As many as 900,000 civilians died, compared to 780,000 uniformed Japanese who died during the war.[12]

On 7 April, Iwo Jima–based P-51s escorted B-29s to Japan for the first time. P-51s did not routinely provide escort until end of May. Japanese night fighters did not down a single B-29, and B-29s probably shot down more Japanese fighters than did P-51s. "After about the first of June 1945 it was almost safer to fly a B-29 combat mission over Japan than it had been a year or so earlier to fly a B-29 training mission in the United States, because the casualty rate was lower."[13]

Mine Laying—the Blockade of Japan

Mines had been effectively used in the American Civil War. ("Damn the torpedoes—full speed ahead!") During World War I, mines had closed in the German High Seas Fleet and had sunk three Allied battleships during the Dardanelles campaign. Mining from aircraft was devised at CinCPOA headquarters and strongly supported by Nimitz.[14] Mahan would have instantly recognized the new technology as enhancing the old strategy—distant blockade, i.e., closing shipping lanes instead of ports. Furthermore, this task could be done by auxiliary vessels—without dispersing the fleet. Few wouldn't have jumped at the opportunity. One recognized airpower authority described the mining operations as "one of the least known B-29 operations and yet arguably the most effective."[15]

While B-29 mine laying had been anticipated before XXI Bomber Command arrived in the Marianas, the army air forces resisted the mission. The B-29 was a strategic *bombing* weapon. Generals from Arnold's staff to B-29 unit commanders in the Marianas fought this "diversion" from the B-29's hallowed mission. It took Nimitz's intercession with Arnold to get the program started. Even then Nimitz had to negotiate a reduced campaign to satisfy the air commanders. In the end Arnold may have compromised because he didn't want to give the navy a reason to pursue long-range aviation of its own. LeMay was a little more receptive to the mining mission than many other army air force generals.

The first mines were laid down on March 27. Eventually 8,814 tons of mines were planted. When the mining campaign began, Japan was receiving about 520,000 tons of shipping a month. By war's end, this had dropped to a paltry 8,000 tons a month. Japanese imports were cut to 10 percent of pre-mining levels. By April 1945 Japan was forced to allocate almost all of its shipping to food importation to fend off starvation.[16] Japanese in Korea packed rice in wooden barrels and set them adrift, hoping they would wash up in Japan.

Submarines and mines created the blockade. During the relatively short campaign forty B-29 mine-laying aircraft sank 1.2 million tons. One cost analyst figured the B-29 mining campaign cost $6 per ton sunk. Subs sank ships for $55 per ton.[17] Mines delivered by other means added another half a million tons. But submarines had already sunk 4.9 million of the total 8.1 million tons the Japanese lost at sea. Sub strangulation caused Japanese production to peak in 1944 before B-san had really introduced himself. In the last stage of the war, carrier aviation concentrated on hitting immobilized warships rather than destroying merchant shipping. Navy surface ships did not concentrate on blockade.

Adapting the Tool to the Job

From 1942 on, Japanese air defenses had shown weakness. General Kenney had extolled the virtues of accurate weapons delivery from low-level attack aviation. Hap Arnold angrily admonished Kenney not to push the concept as "there was no such thing as low level attack aviation in the Army Air Forces." Against integrated German defenders, such tactics were prohibitively expensive. The facts in the Pacific were different.

The World War II record demonstrates the premium one must place on leaders who can coldly assess all the available information and make carefully reasoned judgments despite the prevailing opinions and prejudices. Despite all its faults, the American system excelled at producing this type of leader. In the eyes of Mahan, nothing was more important.

In the end, the B-29 delivered what the airmen promised, but not in the mode that was promised. Japanese fighting spirit was unsurpassed by that of any other nation. The firebombing, the mining, and finally the atomic bombing broke that spirit without the need for a final bloodletting of the 2.5 million men Japan readied for the final defense of their home islands.

What if events had turned out differently? Had the B-29 been a technical failure, the B-17s and B-24s could have carried the firebombs and the mines from Okinawa. Effective use of B-29s did not commence until March 1945. Large-scale four-engine firebomb raids could have begun from Okinawa by September. The B-29 might have shortened the war by four to six months. It had an impressive record, but it was not the decisive weapon. It wasn't the airplane, but the adaptive tactics using the firebomb that ended the story.

By the summer of 1945 only a handful of scientists had any real understanding of the implications of the atom bomb's radioactivity. Senior military men, Japanese and American, saw the bomb as a more efficient way to firebomb a city. A single 20,000-ton detonation concentrated at one point could do about as much damage as 2,000 tons of firebombs delivered in a optimal pattern across an entire city by 300 B-29s.

What if the army air force generals had not been able to tear themselves away from their cherished belief in daylight precision bombing? This would have been a far more worrisome alternative. In all, 2,838 B-29 sorties in 51 raids were carried out on Japanese airframe and aircraft engine factories. Sixteen thousand tons of bombs were dropped in these precision raids. A total of twenty-six targets were hit although three factories made 75 percent of the airframes and just two made two-thirds of the engines. The Musashino engine plant was hit nine times. Seventy percent of the roof area was destroyed. However, most of the machinery remained intact and the factory lost only 0.6 months of production. The other major engine plant was hit seven times and lost 8.1 months of production.[18] The Japanese had huge reserves of airframes at the end of the war. B-29s also dropped 10,600 tons of bombs on oil refineries, although most of these facilities had stopped production because submarines and mining had already deprived them of crude. Conventional explosives delivered by B-29 were not inflicting serious military damage.

Carrier-based dive-bombers, *could* hit precision targets, yet compared to four-engine bombers, the tonnage they could deliver was minuscule. A maximum B-29 effort could deliver 3,000 tons. All of Halsey's carriers together would drop only 300 tons a day. In 1945, carrier groups could not be city killers.

Without the firebombing and the mining, it is fairly clear that precision attacks on engines, airframes, and oil would not have broken the intense war-fighting spirit of the Japanese—or brought them to their senses. The Japanese never did run out of airframes, but engineless and fuelless planes could kill no Americans. The bombing would have helped. But the need for an invasion would have been overwhelming. Tens of thousands of Americans who did live would not have—and not because of a failure in technology but because of a failure of leadership that almost occurred. Practical air generals won out over doctrinaire air generals (and admirals).

The decisions to firebomb and mine were far more important than the invention of the B-29 or even the atomic bomb. A firebomb raid is a horrible weapon. An atom bomb did not add a new capability—only a more efficient way to create hell on earth. After the carnage every combatant people had suffered, there was scant room to be squeamish about civilian targets. A *Time* magazine article that described LeMay's work as "a dream come true . . . properly kindled, Japanese cities will burn like autumn leaves" reflected what many who had witnessed the horrors perpetrated by the Japanese war machine felt at the time.

When Does a Totalitarian State Quit?

In February 1945 a study conducted by Rear Admiral Takeo Takagi concluded that fleet aircraft and merchant shipping losses had been so enormous that it would be impossible to import enough raw materials and that Japan could not possibly win the war. Takagi thought Japan should seek a compromise peace.[19]

All the American military commanders would have understood Admiral Takagi's analysis. Senior American leaders understood that Japan's position after the fall of the Marianas was hopeless. Why wouldn't they quit? Would this supremely disciplined war machine that induced such loyal warriors willingly throw away those lives away rather than surrender?

Would the Japanese leadership ever quit?

In February 1945 Germany's defeat seemed inevitable. Even with hordes of Allied tanks on German soil, Hitler wouldn't capitulate.

Similarly, by February the Imperial Japanese Army could not withdraw further formations from the Asian mainland in order to defend the homeland. The navy was gone. B-29s roamed Japan's sky at will, burning everything in their path. Hirohito consulted seven elder statesmen—six former prime ministers, including Tojo, and a former Lord Keeper of the Privy Seal, an emperor's closest adviser. Despite the seeming hopelessness of their predicament, they expressed an overwhelming consensus to go on with the struggle.[20]

Elder statesman Kantaro Suzuki, who had retired in 1927, had long been identified with the faction that counseled peace. Before the war he had been brought out of retirement and made a member of the Supreme War Council. For most of the war, neither the emperor nor Tojo had been swayed by his advice. When he saw the horrible destruction LeMay wrought, he concluded that "it seemed . . . unavoidable that in the long run Japan would be almost destroyed by air attack so that merely on the basis of the B-29s alone I was convinced that Japan should sue for peace."[21]

Nine days after the first horrific firebombing of Tokyo in March 1945, the emperor and a small entourage, traveling in several chrysanthemum-marked limousines, toured the devastation. Smoke rose from mile after mile of embers that had once been Tokyo. Everything smelled of burnt death. One of Hirohito's aides remembers the empty looks of "exhaustion and bewilderment on the faces of the victims as they poked through the ash."[22] Horror had wiped their minds completely blank. In one version of the story that circulated shortly after the end of the war, the emperor was horrified at the devastation and concluded the war must be brought to an end.

That wasn't his actual reaction. More recent scholarship demonstrates that as late as 5 May Hirohito still hoped for a victory on Okinawa.[23] The suffering of the people by itself wasn't a main concern. It was the fate of the people to be patient and to endure. Instead, the emperor continued to worry about the continuance of the imperial dynasty. Prince Konoe saw even a greater danger than an Allied. Internal communist revolution might tear the social fabric of Japan asunder and destroy the imperial house more thoroughly than any external threat.[24]

It was Hirohito's concern for the continuation, not of himself personally, but of his family's dynasty, that caused additional Japanese to die by the thousands.

The elder statesmen wanted the imperial throne to be preserved and available to control revolutionary forces that were bound to be unleashed. The authoritarians were willing to sacrifice Japanese lives by the hundred thousand as long as a recognizable Japanese authoritarian rule survived. Remember the Japanese political movement of the thirties?

It wasn't until the overwhelming loss of Okinawa and the devastation of sixty Japanese cities that Hirohito seriously started looking for a way to bring peace. Marquis Koichi Kido, an inner member of the emperor's entourage and regarded as a guardian of the emperor's prerogatives, records that the first time emperor was asked to seriously think about peace was June 8. But on June 9 the Japanese Imperial Diet passed measures to prepare a homeland defense based on all types of suicide weapons and attacks.

"The twin psychological shocks of the first atomic bomb and Soviet entry into the war," writes Herbert P. Bix in his study of Hirohito, "coupled with Kido's and the Emperor's concern over growing popular criticism of the throne and its occupant, and their almost paranoiac fear that, sooner or later, the people would react violently against their leaders if they allowed the war to go on much longer—these factors finally caused Hirohito to accept, in principle, the terms of the Potsdam Declaration."[25] Reports from chiefs of police from all over the Home Islands revealed that ordinary Japanese citizens were beginning to speak of "the Emperor as an incompetent leader who was responsible for the worsening war situations."[26]

The emperor told Chief of Staff Yoshijiro Umezu, who was a strong advocate of continued resistance, "If this battle turns out badly, the army and navy will lose the trust of the nation. We have to think about the impact it could have on the future war situation."[27]

In his study of the impact of strategic bombing and its war-ending influence, Robert Pape argues that it is the destruction of military capability, "not threats to civilians," that brings about war termination.[28] Totalitarian states especially are not likely to succumb because their populations are punished. In the case of Japan, Pape argues that "the attitudes of civilian leaders were determined largely by their losing confidence in Japan's ability to execute the Army's Ketsu Go plan" for the final defense of the homeland.[29]

The blockade brought about by mine and submarine tore out the hamstrings of the Japanese military monster. LeMay's bombers burned directly into its remaining functional muscles. But the monster retained the capability to resist. While it teetered, the Allied leaders could not see the hesitation in the monster's heart. But they could envision the endless list of American casualties emanating from the upcoming invasion beaches in the Home Islands.

As a condition of "unconditional surrender," the Allies agreed to retain the emperor, if only as a figurehead. It was a practical and humane concession. Much in Japanese behavior generated deep hatred and anger among Americans. To those who might cast the American leadership as cold and heartless, this act of magnanimity—or common sense despite the rage—is conclusive counterproof that something other than hatred prevailed.

MacArthur ruled after the war as a virtual viceroy with almost plenipotentiary powers. The general had the emperor call on him. There was no question as to who was boss. But Hirohito didn't face the gallows. It was in everyone's interest to subscribe to the myth that Hirohito was a peace-seeking captive of the Japanese militarists who couldn't break out until the atomic bombs fell.

Blockade brings some nations down quickly. Many more hold out a long time against seemingly impossible odds. Look at Great Britain in 1940. The president and most of his senior advisers knew the American people would not stand around and wait forever. They had set a deadline. Defeat Japan no more than twelve months after the fall of Germany. Despite Mahan's doctrine and the belief of all the senior admirals, blockade couldn't be counted on. The horror of invasion never left the minds of the senior generals, the elected leaders—and the loved ones of all the soldiers and marines preparing to land on Japanese soil.

The Decision to Drop the Bomb

For many years, Americans had watched as Japanese butchered their way through China, Southeast Asia, and the Pacific. In the view of many Americans at home and in combat, they seemed to have little regard for human life—even their own. Repeatedly they committed suicide rather than submit to capture. How do you make creatures like these quit fighting? As Admiral Leahy wrote after the war, "The best psychological warfare to use on those barbarians [the Japanese] was bombs, and we used bombs vigorously."[30] In August of 1945, that sentiment was probably among the most polite one would have found among the American servicemen preparing to invade Japan.

The atomic bomb was dramatic. But it wasn't the war's biggest killer—even of Japanese. Firebomb raids hold that horrible distinction.

American bombers devastated huge areas of Japanese cities. But the Allies did the same to·Germany. By 1945 our capability to devastate had increased. Japan never developed the defensive capability that Germany did to impede that destruction. "If you tried going over a German target at five or seven thousand feet with heavy bombers, they would have murdered you."[31]

Estimated Japanese Deaths from Bombing

First Tokyo firebomb raid	80,000
All non-nuclear bombing	530,000*
Hiroshima (12.5 KT weapon)	70,000†
Nagasaki (22 KT weapon)	35,000‡

*Minimum estimate.

†Estimates of those killed by the Hiroshima bomb vary from 54,000 to as high as 130,000.

‡Estimates of those killed by the Nagasaki bomb range from 35,000 to 70,000.

Japan was not the first culture to face total destruction. Ask the Carthaginians. Revisionist historians who impute racial hatred as the primary motivator of American decision makers are far wide of the mark. William Tecumseh Sherman was the first American to wage total war on civilians. He vowed to make war so horrible that Southerners would no longer make it. In 1945, as in 1865, American policy makers desperately sought an end to all the killing—not an end to a people.

Urban devastation by the Allies in World War II is ranked below:

Urban area	Square miles obliterated
Tokyo	56.3
Osaka	16.4
Nagoya	12.4
Berlin	10.0
Hamburg	9.7
Hiroshima	4.7
Nagasaki	1.5[32]

Some claim that America wouldn't have dropped atom bombs on other Caucasians. The nuclear-capable 509th Bomb Group had been organized to operate two simultaneous operations: one in Europe and the other in the Pacific. The operational details are clear. The United States prepared to use the bomb in both primary theaters of the war. How about the Japanese? In 1945, there was no reason for the Japanese to fight for Manila. General Yamishita declared it an open city. Yet Rear Admiral Iwabachi, the local naval commander, and most of the Japanese sailors in the city ignored his order. A hundred thousand Filipinos died in the battle for Manila: "Japanese atrocities accounted for a shockingly high toll."[33] That roughly equals the number of Japanese who died from the two atom bombs. The Filipinos never attacked or embargoed anybody. Preventing the invasion of Japan by ferociously defending Okinawa was a long shot. Yet the Japanese thought little of sacrificing 75,000 Okinawans in this endeavor.

In 1957 General Marshall stated that the A-bombs were dropped to "shock [the Japanese] into action."[34] Nagasaki's bombing was timed so the Japanese would conclude that America could launch a nuclear strike every few days.[35] The Nagasaki bomb was the last atom bomb we had in theater.

"We're at war with Japan. We were attacked by Japan. Do you want to kill Japanese, or would you rather have Americans killed," was Curtis LeMay's assessment.[36]

If there is any one human responsible for the horror of Hiroshima and Nagasaki, his name is Hirohito.

Consider the following horrible statistics:

	OKINAWA	IWO JIMA	JAPAN
Civilian population	450,000		70,000,000
Civilian dead	75,000		?
American troops committed	172,000	65,000	889,000
American dead	7,374	6,800	?
Japanese troops committed	130,000	21,000	2,500,000
Japanese military dead	130,000	20,000	?

Would you want to be responsible for filling in the question marks?

Given the demonstrated tenacity and insensitivity of the Japanese leadership, it is probable that blockade alone would not have met America's objective of full surrender within a year. The only alternative to a bloody invasion was destruction from the air. Precision bombing wouldn't have done the job either. As valuable as the aircraft was in shortening the war, it wasn't the B-29—or the atom bomb—but the decision to firebomb until the Japanese either no longer responded to their government—a fear of the Japanese leadership—or were physically unable to physically carry on that ended the war. The horrible deaths lay not at the feet of the firebombers, but the senior Japanese leadership—the emperor and his advisers—that continued to engage in their grotesque fantasy long after any hope of victory had been eliminated. Had they been anywhere near responsible rulers, they would have spared their long-suffering country perhaps half a million deaths.

At war's end a single Japanese battleship, *Nagato*, remained, crippled but afloat. She would be sunk a year later in an atom bomb test. A pair of heavy cruisers remained in Singapore. A pair of light cruisers remained seaworthy. Forty-two destroyers were afloat but only five were fully operational. For the next year ships that could move were used by their former crews to bring home some of the hundreds of thousands of Japanese servicemen who had been stranded by the war. That is how the Imperial Japanese Navy ended.

NOTES

1. Sink Ten Ships and We Win the War!

1. Ronald Spector, *Eagle against the Sun,* p. 43.

2. William L. Neumann, "Franklin Delano Roosevelt: A Disciple of Mahan," *Proceedings, U.S. Naval Institute* 78 (July 1952): 718.

3. E. B. Potter, *Admiral Arleigh Burke,* p. 73.

4. Alfred Thayer Mahan, *The Influence of Sea Power on History,* p. 133.

5. Ibid., p. 433.

6. Ibid., p. 289.

7. Ibid., p. 290.

8. Ibid., p. 119.

9. Ibid., p. 79.

10. Ibid., p. 184.

11. Ibid., p. 209.

12. Ibid., p. 457.

13. Ibid., p. 436.

14. Ibid., p. 129.

15. Ibid., p. 109.

16. Ibid., p. 110.

17. Ibid., p. 83.

18. Ibid., p. 357.

19. Ibid., p. 391.

20. Ibid., p. 4.

21. Ibid., p. 67.

22. Donald M. Goldstein and Katherine V. Dillion, *Pacific War Papers,* pp. 9–10.

23. George Dyer, *Amphibians Came to Conquer,* vol. 1, p. 40.

24. Richmond Kelly Turner "The Strategic Employment of the Fleet," 28 Oct. 1937, unpublished manuscript, Naval Historical Collection, Naval War College.

25. Mark Stoler, *Allies and Adversaries,* p. 7.

26. Reprinted in Ernest J. King, *Fleet Admiral King,* p. 284.

27. Samuel E. Morison, *History of U.S. Naval Operations in World War II,* vol. 4, *Coral Sea, Midway and Submarine Actions,* p. 76.

28. Kaisen Yoh-Murei quoted by Yokoi Toshiyuki in *Proceedings, U.S. Naval Institute,* 86, October 1960, p. 71.

29. Atsushi Oi, "Why Japan's Anti-submarine Warfare Failed," p. 601.

30. For a good discussion of center of gravity, see Michael J. Handel's *Masters of War,* pp. 53–65.

31. Baron Antoine-Henri de Jomini, "The Art of War," in *Roots of Strategy,* Book 2, ed. James Donald Hittle (Harrisburg, Pa.: Stackpole Books, 1987), p. 461.

32. Clark G. Reynolds, *Admiral John H. Towers,* p. 255.

33. Ibid., p. 247.

34. Minoru Genda, quoted in Donald M. Goldstein and Katherine V. Dillon, *The Pearl Harbor Papers,* p. 7.

35. Ibid., p. 5.

36. Jan Van Tol, "Military Innovation and Carrier Aviation," *Joint Forces Quarterly* (Summer 1997): 77–87.

37. Ibid., p. 80.

38. Spector, *Eagle against the Sun,* p. 24.

39. "The Employment of Aviation in Naval Warfare," Naval War College Pamphlet (14 December 1939).

40. Samuel E. Morison, *History of U.S. Naval Operations in World War II,* vol. 3, *The Rising Sun in the Pacific,* p. 83.

41. David C. Evans and Mark R. Peattie, *Kaigun,* p. 446.

42. Thomas E. Griffith Jr., "Airpower in the Pacific," *Joint Forces Quarterly* (Autumn 2000): 33–34.

43. George C. Kenney, *General Kenney Reports,* p. 66.

44. W. F. Craven, and J. L. Cate, *The Army Air Forces in World War II,* p. 600.

45. Hiroyuke Agawa, *The Reluctant Admiral,* p. 103.

46. Spector, *Eagle against the Sun,* p. 148.

2. Initial Japanese Strategic Choices

1. Hiroshi Fujimoto, *Fifty Years of Light and Dark: The Hirohito Era* (Tokyo: Mainichi, 1975), pp. 215ff.

2. Hoyt, *Japan's War,* p. 29.

3. Morison, *History of U.S. Naval Operations,* vol. 3, p. 10.

4. Herbert P. Bix, *Hirohito and the Making of Modern Japan*, p. 267.

5. Hoyt, *Japan's War*, p. 146.

6. *Asahi Shimbun*, 10 Aug. 1944.

7. Van der Vat, *Pacific Campaign*, p. 44.

8. John H. Bradley, *The Second World War: Asia and the Pacific*, p. 14.

9. Van der Vat, *Pacific Campaign*, p. 87.

10. Hoyt, *Japan's War*, p. 276.

11. Imperial Japanese Army pamphlet, cited in Hoyt, *Japan's War*, p. 198.

12. Samuel E. Morison, *History of U.S. Naval Operations in World War II*, vol. 6, *Breaking the Bismarcks Barrier, 22 July 1942–1 May 1944*, p. 20.

13. Bradley, *Second World War*, p. 11.

14. Stoler, *Allies and Adversaries*, p. 10.

15. Evans and Peattie, *Kaigun*, pp. 528–29.

16. Goldstein and Dillon, *Pacific Papers*, p. 30.

17. John D. Potter, *Yamamoto*, p. 68.

18. Hoyt, *Japan's War*, p. 221.

19. Mitsuo Fuchida and Masatake Okumiya, *Midway: The Battle That Doomed Japan*, p. 31.

20. Gordon W. Prange, *At Dawn We Slept*, pp. 15–16.

21. Agawa, *Reluctant Admiral*, pp. 44–45.

22. Spector, *Eagle against the Sun*, p. 79.

23. Prange, *At Dawn We Slept*, p. 15.

24. Message Canto to Tokyo #95, July 14, 1941, in U.S. Congress, *Investigation of the Pearl Harbor Attack*, part 12, p. 2 (hereafter *Pearl Harbor Investigation*).

25. William D. Leahy, *I Was There*, p. 45.

26. *The U.S. Army in World War II*, War in the Pacific series, *Strategy and Command: The First Two Years*, by Louis Morton, p. 95. Hereafter Morton, *Strategy and Command*.

27. Ibid., p. 94.

28. Morison, *History of U.S. Naval Operations*, vol. 3, p. 58.

29. Stoler, *Allies and Adversaries*, p. 60.

30. Ibid., pp. 54–56; *Pearl Harbor Investigation*, part 14, p. 1361.

31. Morton, *Strategy and Command*, p. 95.

32. Van der Vat, *Pacific Campaign*, p. 44.

33. Morton, *Strategy and Command*, p. 95.

34. Ibid., p. 96.

35. Fuchida and Okumiya, *Midway*, p. 27.

36. Ibid., p. 33.

37. Evans and Peattie, *Kaigun*, p. 482.

38. Ibid., p. 203.

39. Ibid., p. 202.

40. Fuchida and Okumiya, *Midway*, p. 31.

41. Morton, *Strategy and Command*, p. 126.

42. Letter, Stark to Hoover, 5 Aug. 59, in Morton, *Strategy and Command*, p. 143.

43. U.S. Strategic Bombing Survey, *European War, Pacific War,* pp. 51–52.

44. Kenneth S. Davis, *FDR: The War President, 1940–1943* (New York: Random House, 2000), p. 319.

45. Clayton James, *The Years of MacArthur,* vol. 1, p. 590.

46. Fuchida and Osumiya, *Midway,* p. 31.

47. Bix, *Hirohito.* See part 3, especially chapter 11.

48. Ibid., p. 375.

49. Ibid., p. 401.

50. Evans and Peattie, *Kaigun,* p. 455.

51. Ibid., p. 201.

52. Van der Vat, *Pacific Campaign,* p. 75.

53. Bix, *Hirohito,* p. 418.

54. Goldstein and Dillon, *Pacific Papers,* p. 12.

55. Fuchida and Okumiya, *Midway,* p. 29.

56. Hiroyuke Agawa, *The Reluctant Admiral,* p. 346.

57. Fuchida and Okumiya, *Midway,* p. 33.

58. Yamamoto to Onishi, in *Pearl Harbor Investigation,* p. 53.

59. Harry Gailey, *War in the Pacific,* p. 68.

60. Fukudome, "Hawaii Operations," cited in C. Boyd and A. Yoshida, *The Japanese Submarine Force and World War II,* p. 188.

61. Matome Ukagi, *Fading Victory,* p. 41.

62. Paul S. Dull, *A Battle History of the Imperial Japanese Navy, 1941–45,* p. 6.

63. Bradley, *Second World War,* p. 110.

64. Van der Vat, *Pacific Campaign,* p. 121.

65. U.S. Strategic Bombing Survey, *European War, Pacific War,* p. 53.

66. Morton, *Strategy and Command,* p. 110.

67. Morison, *History of U.S. Naval Operations,* vol. 3, p. 82.

68. Morton, *Strategy and Command,* pp. 95–96.

69. Cited in Morton, *Strategy and Command,* p. 125.

3. Pearl Harbor

1. Morison, *History of U.S. Naval Operations,* vol. 3, p. 132.

2. *Pearl Harbor Investigation,* part 26, p. 207.

3. Bradley, *Second World War,* p. 12; Fuchida and Okumiya, *Midway,* p. 28.

4. Prange, *At Dawn We Slept,* p. 184.

5. Spector, *Eagle against the Sun,* p. 79.

6. Ibid., p. 81.

7. Prange, *At Dawn We Slept,* pp. 530–547; Agawa, *Reluctant Admiral,* pp. 150–51, 246, 253, 265–69.

8. Fuchida and Okumiya, *Midway,* p. 25.

9. Matome Ugaki, *Fading Victory,* p. 13.

10. Dull, *Battle History of the Japanese Navy,* p. 10.

11. Fuchida and Okumiya, *Midway,* p. 36.

12. Ibid., p. 36.

13. Bradley, *Second World War,* p. 14.

14. Van der Vat, *Pacific Campaign,* p. 19.

15. Minoru Genda, Analysis No. 1 of the Pearl Harbor Attack, in Goldstein and Dillon, *Pearl Harbor Papers,* pp. 18–19; Morison, *History of U.S. Naval Operations,* vol. 3, p. 84.

16. Genda, in Goldstein and Dillon, *Pearl Harbor Papers,* p. 19.

17. Ibid., p. 10.

18. Morton, *Strategy and Command,* p. 115.

19. Pacific Fleet Confidential Letter 2CL-41, in *Pearl Harbor Investigation,* p. 85.

20. Samuel E. Morison, *History of U.S. Naval Operations in World War II,* vol. 3, p. 83.

21. Goldstein and Dillon, *Pearl Harbor Papers,* pp. 96–99.

22. Compiled from Prange, *At Dawn We Slept,* p. 539, and *Pearl Harbor Investigation.*

23. Fuchida and Okumiya, *Midway,* p. 48.

24. Minoru Genda, "Analysis No. 2 of the Pearl Harbor Attack," in Goldstein and Dillon, *Pearl Harbor Papers,* p. 43.

25. Fuchida and Okumiya, *Midway,* p. 48.

26. Potter, *Yamamoto,* p. 127.

27. Prange, *At Dawn We Slept,* p. 544.

28. Yamamato to Ozawa at Truk in late 1942, Statement by Ozawa, Dec. 22, 1948, in Gordon W. Prange, *Pearl Harbor: Verdict of History* (New York: McGraw-Hill, 1986), p. 501.

29. Ugaki, *Fading Victory,* p. 48.

30. Fuchida and Okumiya, *Midway,* p. 45.

31. Prange, *At Dawn We Slept,* pp. 575–576.

32. Fuchida and Okumiya, *Midway,* p. 37.

33. Ibid., p. 42.

34. Morison, *History of U.S. Naval Operations,* vol. 3, p. 219.

35. Ibid., p. 212.

36. Ugaki, *Fading Victory,* p. 20.

37. Thomas B. Buell, *Master of Sea Power: A Biography of Fleet Admiral Ernest J. King,* p. 158.

38. Potter, *Yamamoto,* p. 79.

39. Morison, *History of U.S. Naval Operations,* vol. 3, p. 133.

40. *Pearl Harbor Investigation,* part 6, p. 2812.

41. Statement given by Minoru Genda, 16 Nov. 1961, in Goldstein and Dillon, *Pearl Harbor Papers,* p. 5.

42. Morison, *History of U.S. Naval Operations,* vol. 3, p. 214.

43. Van der Vat, *Pacific Campaign,* p. 44.

44. Hap Arnold, *Global Mission,* p. 369.

45. Memo, CNO for Cof S, 11 Dec. 41, "The Dangerous Strategic Situation," in Morton, *Strategy and Command,* p. 147; Morison, *History of U.S. Naval Operations,* vol. 3, p. 219; Minutes, Joint Board Meeting, 9 Dec. 41, in Morton, *Strategy and Command,* p. 146.

46. Memo, "The Dangerous Strategic Situation," in Morton, *Strategy and Command,* p. 147.

47. Adapted from Morton, *Strategy and Command,* p. 110.

48. James Dunnigan and A. A. Nofi, *Victory at Sea,* p. 331.

49. John J. Stephan, *Hawaii under the Rising Sun,* chapter 10.

50. Bradley, *Second World War,* p. 66.

51. Jacob Neufeld, "The Japanese Octopus," in *The Pacific War,* ed. Bernard Nalty, p. 57.

52. Bradley, *Second World War,* p. 67.

53. Walter J. Boyne, *Clash of Titans: World War II at Sea,* p. 147.

54. Ibid., p. 147.

55. Ibid., p. 161.

56. Van der Vat, *Pacific Campaign,* p. 122.

57. Clayton James, *The Years of MacArthur,* vol. 2, p. 13.

58. Ibid., p. 15.

59. *The U.S. Army in World War II,* War in the Pacific series, *Fall of the Philippines,* by Louis Morton, pp. 65–69. Hereafter Morton, *Philippines.*

60. Joseph Alsop, *FDR: A Centenary Remembrance* (New York: Viking, 1982), p. 236.

61. James, *Years of MacArthur,* vol. 2, p. 7.

62. Morton, *Philippines,* p. 64.

63. Ibid., p. 28.

64. Ibid., p. 69.

65. Ibid., p. 169.

66. James, *Years of MacArthur,* vol. 2, p. 91.

67. Ibid., p. 92.

68. James, *Years of MacArthur,* vol. 2, pp. 33–34; Ernest B. Miller, *Bataan Uncensored* (Long Prairie, Minn.: Hart Publications, 1949), p. 75.

69. Jack Greene, *The Midway Campaign, December 7, 1941–June 6, 1942,* p. 27.

70. James, *Years of MacArthur,* vol. 2, p. 27.

71. Ibid., p. 28.

72. Ibid., p. 26.

73. Spector, *Eagle against the Sun,* p. 111.

74. Ibid., p. 117.

75. Gailey, *War in the Pacific* p. 119.

76. Robert H. Ferrell, ed., *The Eisenhower Diaries,* Jan. 13, 1942, entry.

77. Davis, *FDR,* p. 540.

78. James, *Years of MacArthur,* vol. 2, pp. 89–90.

79. Spector, *Eagle against the Sun,* p. 138.

80. Stimson's diary, quoted in Forrest C. Pogue, *George C. Marshall: Ordeal and Hope, 1939–1942,* p. 247.

81. Buell, *Master of Sea Power,* p. 46.

82. Ibid., p. 29.

83. Van der Vat, *Pacific Campaign,* p. 145.

84. Leahy, *I Was There,* p. 104.

85. King to Roosevelt, 5 March 1942, in Ernest J. King, *Fleet Admiral King,* p. 384.

86. Buell, *Master of Sea Power,* p. 137.

87. Leahy, *I Was There,* p. 68.

88. Van der Vat, *Pacific Campaign,* p. 150.

89. Dyer, *Amphibians Came to Conquer,* vol. 1, p. 253.

90. Buell, *Master of Sea Power.*

91. Van der Vat, *Pacific Campaign,* p. 154.

92. Morison, *History of U.S. Naval Operations,* vol. 4, p. 4.

93. Ugaki, *Fading Victory,* p. 103.

94. Ibid., p. 87.

95. Buell. *Master of Sea Power,* p. 157.

4. Yamamoto Defies Mahan

1. Potter, *Yamamoto,* p. 142.

2. Gordon W. Prange, *Miracle at Midway,* p. 16.

3. Hoyt, *Japan's War,* p. 261.

4. Ugaki, *Fading Victory,* p. 75.

5. Ibid., p. 79.

6. Van der Vat, *Pacific Campaign,* p. 144.

7. Dyer, *Amphibians Came to Conquer,* vol. 1, p. 254.

8. Agawa, *Reluctant Admiral,* p. 346.

9. Fuchida and Okumiya, *Midway,* p. 57.

10. Ibid., p. 53.

11. Ibid., p. 56.

12. Interview with Captain Yasuji Watanabe, 25 September 1964, cited in Prange, *Miracle at Midway,* p. 21.

13. Agawa, *Reluctant Admiral,* pp. 209 ff.

14. Richard B. Frank, *Guadalcanal: The Definitive Account of the Landmark Battle,* p. 21.

15. Morton, *Philippines,* p. 201.

16. Fuchida and Okumiya, *Midway,* pp. 62–64.

17. Morison, *History of U.S. Naval Operations,* vol. 4, p. 11.

18. Ibid., p. 13.

19. Craven and Cate, *Army Air Forces in World War II,* vol. 1, p. 449.

20. Prange, *At Dawn We Slept,* p. 166.

21. Prange, *Miracle at Midway,* p. 97.

22. Van der Vat, *Pacific Campaign,* p. 123.

23. Fuchida and Okumiya, *Midway,* p. 208.

24. Agawa, *Reluctant Admiral,* pp. 293 ff.

25. Morison, *History of U.S. Naval Operations,* vol. 4, p. 5.

26. Admiral Raymond Spruance, foreword to Fuchida and Okumiya, *Midway,* p. 7.

27. Fuchida and Okumiya, *Midway,* p. 102.

28. Ibid., p. 84.

29. Ibid., p. 93.

30. Prange, *Miracle at Midway,* p. 103.

31. CinCPac Op. Plan 29–42, in Gerald E. Wheeler, *Kinkaid of the Seventh Fleet,* p. 227.

32. Cited in Morison, *History of U.S. Naval Operations,* vol. 4, p. 84.

33. Fuchida and Okumiya, *Midway,* p. 84.

34. Spector, *Eagle against the Sun,* p. 177.

35. Morison, *History of U.S. Naval Operations,* vol. 4, p. 77.

5. Guadalcanal

1. Frank, *Guadalcanal,* p. 44.

2. Ugaki, *Fading Victory,* p. 176.

3. Morton, *Strategy and Command,* p. 290.

4. King to Roosevelt, reprinted in King, *Fleet Admiral King,* pp. 384–85.

5. James, *Years of MacArthur,* vol. 2, p. 185.

6. Chief of Naval Operations, Report to the Secretary of the Navy, *U.S. Navy at War, 1941–45* (Washington, D.C.: Government Printing Office, 1946), p. 49.

7. Ibid., p. 45.

8. Memo, King to Marshall, 2 March 1942, in Morton, *Strategy and Command,* p. 292.

9. Marshall to Dill, May 22, 1942, Secret, in Larry I. Bland and Sharon Ritenour Stevens, eds., *The Papers of George Catlett Marshall,* vol. 3, p. 208.

10. Potter, *Admiral Arleigh Burke,* p. 68.

11. Morison, *History of U.S. Naval Operations,* vol. 4, p. 146.

12. Morton, *Strategy and Command,* p. 295.

13. King, *Fleet Admiral King,* p. 387.

14. Davis, *FDR,* p. 474.

15. Bland and Stevens, *Papers of George Catlett Marshall,* vol. 3, pp. 262–63.

16. Robert E. Sherwood, *Roosevelt and Hopkins,* pp. 783–84.

17. Buell, *Master of Seapower,* p. 117.

18. Memo from R. L. Sherrod to D. W. Hulburd on Marshall's Conference, classified restricted, in Bland and Stevens, *Papers of George Catlett Marshall,* vol. 2.

19. Interview of Rear Admiral Frank Fletcher by Admiral Dyer, 25 May 1963, in Dyer, *Amphibians Came to Conquer,* vol. 1, p. 433.

20. MacArthur and Ghormley to JCS 1012, 8 Jul 42, OPD Exec. Files, in Morton, *Strategy and Command,* p. 306.

21. Morton, *Strategy and Command,* p. 307.

22. Buell, *Master of Sea Power,* p. 203.

23. Ibid., p. 245.

24. Letter, Ghormley to Nimitz, 11 Aug. 1942, in *The U.S. Army in World War II,* War in the Pacific series, *Guadalcanal: The First Offensive,* by John Miller Jr., pp. 82–83.

25. Hoyt, *Japan's War,* p. 309.

26. Awarded the Medal of Honor for his sterling performance at Guadalcanal, General Vandergrift went on to become Marine Corps commandant.

27. Interview of attendee Captain Peyton by Admiral Dyer, in Dyer, *Amphibians Came to Conquer,* vol. 1, p. 433.

28. John Winton, *Ultra in the Pacific,* pp. 67–70.

29. Nimitz to Ghormley 063309 July; radio 022100 July 1942 Nimitz to Ghormley, in Morton, *Strategy and Command,* p. 310.

30. Arnold, *Global Mission,* p. 342.

31. John Toland, *The Rising Sun,* vol. 2, p. 402.

32. Wheeler, *Kinkaid of the Seventh Fleet,* p. 248.

33. Ibid., p. 248.

34. Miller, *Guadalcanal,* p. 205; Spector, *Eagle against the Sun,* p. 192.

35. TF16 War Diary, 8 August; CTF 61 to COMSOPAC 081807W, in Wheeler, *Kinkaid of the Seventh Fleet,* p. 249.

36. Samuel E. Morison, *History of U.S. Naval Operations in World War II,* vol. 5, *The Struggle for Guadalcanal, August 1942–February 1943,* p. 59.

37. Ugaki, *Fading Victory,* p. 183.

38. Japanese Opns in SWPA II, in Morton, *Strategy and Command,* pp. 126–28.

39. Ugaki, *Fading Victory,* p. 183.

40. Hoyt, *Japan's War,* p. 308.

41. Ugaki, *Fading Victory,* p. 193.

42. Ugaki, *Fading Victory,* p. 193.

43. This is at odds with Morison, who did not have the benefit of Ultra when he wrote. Detailed tracking of Japanese carriers is contained in Winton, *Ultra,* pp. 71–79.

44. CinCPac Command Summary, 10 Aug. 1942, in Wheeler, *Kinkaid of the Seventh Fleet,* p. 252.

45. Frank, *Guadalcanal,* p. 164, Dull, *Battle History of the Imperial Japanese Navy,* p. 206.

46. Ugaki, *Fading Victory,* pp. 188–89.

47. Clay Blair Jr., *Silent Victory: The U.S. Submarine War against Japan,* p. 301.

48. Dull, *Battle History of the Imperial Japanese Navy,* p. 214.

49. Frank, *Guadalcanal,* p. 197.

50. *The U.S. Army in World War II,* War in the Pacific series, *The Approach to the Philippines.* by R. R. Smith, p. 86. Hereafter R. R. Smith, *Approach to the Philippines.*

51. Morison, *History of U.S. Naval Operations,* vol. 5, p. 117.

52. Some sources say they were 8 in howitzers. See Dull, *Battle History of the Imperial Japanese Navy,* p. 232.

53. Hoyt, *Japan's War,* pp. 310, 314.

54. Griffith, *MacArthur's Airman,* p. 180.

55. Winton, *Ultra,* p. 78.

56. Frank, *Guadalcanal,* p. 428.

57. Dull, *Battle History of the Imperial Japanese Navy,* p. 241.

58. Bradley, *Second World War,* p. 117.

59. Bix, *Hirohito,* p. 458.

60. Ibid., p. 459, Ugaki, *Fading Victory,* p. 277.

61. Morison, *History of U.S. Naval Operations,* vol. 5, p. 261.

62. Boyne, *Clash of Titans,* p. 270.

63. Morison, *History of U.S. Naval Operations,* vol. 5, p. 263.

64. Bradley, *Second World War,* p. 125.

65. *The U.S. Army in World War II,* War in the Pacific series, *Victory in Papua,* by Samuel Milner, p. 202.

66. Robert L. Eichleberger, *Jungle Road to Tokyo,* p. 150.

67. Ugaki, *Fading Victory,* pp. 286–87.

68. Morton, *Strategy and Command,* Appendix G, "Japanese Army-Navy Central Agreement Concerning South Pacific Area Operations, 4 January1943," paragraph II B.

69. Hoyt, *Japan's War,* p. 328.

70. Morton, *Strategy and Command,* Appendix G.

71. Hoyt, *Japan's War,* p. 314.

6. Central versus South Pacific

1. King, *Fleet Admiral King,* pp. 239–40.

2. Ibid., p. 242.

3. Buell, *Master of Sea Power,* p. 202.

4. *The U.S. Army in World War II.* War Department series. *Strategic Planning for Coalition Warfare, 1943–1944,* by Maurice Matloff, p. 32. Hereafter Matloff, *Strategic Planning.*

5. Minutes of the 56th meeting of the Combined Chiefs of Staff in Casablanca, 14 Jan. 1943, in Morton, *Strategy and Command,* p. 438.

6. King, *Fleet Admiral King,* pp. 420, 432.

7. Morton, *Strategy and Command,* p. 383.

8. Buell, *Master of Sea Power,* p. 317.

9. Dyer, *Amphibians Came to Conquer,* vol. 1, pp. 245–46.

10. Buell, *Master of Sea Power,* p. 317.

11. Matloff, *Strategic Planning,* pp. 33–35.

12. Combined Chiefs of Staff memo 155/1, 19 Jan. 1943, in Morton, *Strategy and Command,* p. 385.

13. Combined Chiefs of Staff memo 153, "Situation to Be Created in the Eastern Theater-Pacific and Burma in 1943," 17 Jan. 1943, in Morton, *Strategy and Command,* p. 383.

14. Matloff, *Strategic Planning,* p. 33.

15. Forrest C. Pogue, *George C. Marshall: Organizer of Victory, 1943–1945,* p. 161.

16. Radiogram, King to Nimitz and Halsey, 30 Nov. 1942, in Morton, *Strategy and Command,* p. 370.

17. E. B. Potter, *Nimitz,* p. 210.

18. Morton, *Strategy and Command,* p. 371.

19. Radiogram, Nimitz to King, 8 April 1943, in Morton, *Strategy and Command,* p. 440.

20. Radiogram, King to Nimitz and Halsey, 30 Nov. 1942, in Morton, *Strategy and Command,* p. 370.

21. R. R. Smith, *Approach to the Philippines,* p. 3.

22. Buell, *Master of Sea Power,* p. 420.

23. Rexford C. Tugwell, *The Democratic Roosevelt,* p. 349.

24. Douglas MacArthur, *Reminiscences,* p. 101.

25. Tugwell, *Democratic Roosevelt,* p. 653.

26. Morton, *Philippines,* p. 15.

27. William Manchester, *American Caesar,* p. 209.

28. MacArthur to Marshall, 20 June 1943, in Morton, *Strategy and Command,* p. 465.

29. GHQ, SWPA, Estimate of Situation and Rough Draft Reno Plan, 25 Feb. 1943, OCMI, in Morton, *Strategy and Command,* p. 443.

30. Letter, Chief of Staff, GHQ, SWPA, to Commanders, Allied Land, Air, and Naval Forces, SWPA, 13 May 1942, in Miller, *Guadalcanal,* p. 34.

31. James, *Years of MacArthur,* vol. 2, p. 425.

32. Daniel Barbey, *MacArthur's Amphibious Navy: Seventh Amphibious Force Operations, 1943–45* (Annapolis, Md.: Naval Institute Press, 1969), p. 183.

33. *Eisenhower Diaries,* pp. 43–47.

34. James, *Years of MacArthur,* vol. 2, p. 86.

35. Letter, Barbey to Chamberlin, 26 Aug. 1960, in James, *Years of MacArthur,* vol. 2, p. 341.

36. Buell, *Master of Sea Power,* p. 200.

37. Manchester, *American Caesar,* p. 406.

38. James, *Years of MacArthur,* vol. 2, p. 361.

39. Craven and Cate, *Army Air Forces in World War II,* vol. 1, p. 367.

40. MacArthur, *Reminiscences,* p. 172.

41. Thomas B. Buell, *The Quiet Warrior: A Biography of Admiral Raymond A. Spruance,* p. 176.

42. Leahy, *I Was There,* p. 65.

43. MacArthur, *Reminiscences,* pp. 167, 169.

44. Potter, *Nimitz,* pp. 185–86.

45. *The U.S. Army in World War II,* War in the Pacific series, *Seizure of the Gilberts and Marshalls,* by P. A. Crowl and E. G. Love, p. 11. Hereafter Crowl and Love, *Gilberts and Marshalls.*

46. Morton, *Strategy and Command,* p. 370.

47. Ibid., p. 370.

48. Elkton Plan, GHQ, SWPA, 28 Feb. 1943, in Morton, *Strategy and Command,* Appendix V.

49. Craven and Cate, *Army Air Forces in World War II,* vol. 3, p. 428.

50. James, *Years of MacArthur,* vol. 2, p. 307.

51. "Joint Directive for Offensive Action in the Southwest Pacific Area," in Morton, *Strategy and Command,* Appendix E.

52. Spector, *Eagle against the Sun,* p. 217.

53. *The U.S. Army in World War II,* War in the Pacific series, *Cartwheel: The Reduction of Rabaul,* by John Miller Jr., p. 16. Hereafter Miller, *Cartwheel.*

54. Pogue, *George C. Marshall: Organizer of Victory,* p. 162.

55. Spector, *Eagle against the Sun,* p. 224.

56. Buell, *Master of Sea Power,* pp. 338–39.

57. Paul Rogers, *The Bitter Years: MacArthur and Sutherland,* pp. 7–8.

58. Morton, *Strategy and Command,* p. 443.

59. Joint Chiefs of Staff Directive, "Offensive Operations in the South and Southwest Pacific Areas during 1943," 28 March 1943, in Morton, *Strategy and Command,* Appendix K.

60. Lex McAulay, *Battle of the Bismarck Sea,* p. 88.

61. Ibid., p. 88; Craven and Cate, *Army Air Forces in World War II,* vol. 4, pp. 62–64.

62. Spector, *Eagle against the Sun,* p. 228.

63. Eighth Area Army Operations, vol. 4, Japanese Monograph No. 18, in Morton, *Strategy and Command,* p. 369.

64. Morison, *History of U.S. Naval Operations,* vol. 6, p. 21.

65. Japanese Army-Navy Central Agreement on Southeast Area Operations, 15 March 1943, in Morton, *Strategy and Command,* Appendix J.

66. Morison, *History of U.S. Naval Operations,* vol. 6, p. 24.

67. Dull, *Battle History of the Imperial Japanese Navy,* p. 277.

68. Winton, *Ultra in the Pacific,* p. 106.

69. Kenney, *General Kenney Reports,* p. 234.

70. Ibid., p. 279.

71. Theodore Taylor, *The Magnificent Mitscher,* p. 272.

72. Morison, *History of U.S. Naval Operations,* vol. 6, p. 153.

73. Miller, *Cartwheel,* p. 167.

74. In *Nimitz and His Admirals,* Edwin P. Hoyt reports this from a September 1969 interview with Admiral Fitch, p. 261.

75. Winton, *Ultra in the Pacific,* p. 121.

76. Arnold, *Global Mission,* p. 372.

77. Morison, *History of U.S. Naval Operations,* vol. 6, pp. 8–9.

78. Matloff, *Strategic Planning,* p. 70.

79. Craven and Cate, *Army Air Forces in World War II,* vol. 5, pp. 17–18.

80. Arnold, *Global Mission,* pp. 347–48.

81. Minutes, 92nd meeting, CGS, 21 May 1943; King, *Fleet Admiral King,* p. 438.

82. Morton, *Strategy and Command,* p. 385.

83. Matloff, *Strategic Planning,* p. 137.

84. Morton, *Strategy and Command,* p. 460.

85. Buell, *Quiet Warrior,* pp. 182–83.

86. Ibid., p. 178.

87. JPS 205, Preliminary Report by JWPC, 10 June 1943, in Crowl and Love, *Gilberts and Marshalls,* p. 20.

88. JCS 386, 28 June 1943, Strategy in the Pacific, in Crowl and Love, *Gilberts and Marshalls,* p. 22. Members were Lieutenant General S. D. Embick, U.S. Army; Vice Admiral Russell Wilson, U.S. Navy; and Major General Muir Fairchild, U.S. Army Air Force.

89. Radiogram, MacArthur to Marshall, GM-1N 13149, 20 June 1943, and GM-1N 13605, 22 June 1943, in *The U.S. Army in World War II,* War in the Pacific series, *Triumph in the Philippines,* by Robert Ross Smith, p. 8. Hereafter R. R. Smith, *Triumph.*

90. Communication, MacArthur to JCS, 31 Oct. 1943, cited in Courtney Whitney, *MacArthur: His Rendezvous with History,* p. 120.

91. Morton, *Strategy and Command,* p. 467.

92. Matloff, *Strategic Planning,* pp. 186–87.

93. OPD Brief, 29 June, Strategy of Pacific, JCS 386, in Crowl and Love, *Gilberts and Marshalls,* p. 22.

94. JPS 205 10 June 43; Operations against Marshall Islands, in Morton, *Strategy and Command,* p. 468.

95. Morton, *Strategy and Command,* p. 525.

96. Leahy, *I Was There,* p. 248.

97. Message, JCS to CINCSWPA 15 June 1943, and message, MacArthur to Marshall, 20 June 1943, in R. R. Smith, *Approach to the Philippines,* p. 8.

98. King, *Fleet Admiral King,* p. 487.

99. Minutes, JCS meeting, 15 Nov. 1943, in Morton, *Strategy and Command,* p. 502.

100. JPS 288, 4 Oct. 1943, in Morton, *Strategy and Command,* p. 603.

101. Morton, *Strategy and Command,* p. 541.

102. CCS 417, 2 Dec. 1943, Overall Plan for Defeat of Japan, in Morton, *Strategy and Command,* Appendix T.

103. Morton, *Strategy and Command,* p. 546.

104. Morison, *History of U.S. Naval Operations,* vol. 6, p. 24.

105. Morton, *Strategy and Command,* p. 544.

106. Ibid., p. 551.

107. Ibid., pp. 552, 555–57.

108. Winton, *Ultra in the Pacific,* p. 159.

109. Frank, *Guadalcanal,* p. 512.

110. Arnold, *Global Mission,* p. 530.

7. Two Prongs Divide the Fleet

1. Morison, *History of U.S. Naval Operations,* vol. 6, p. 423. Miller, *Cartwheel,* p. 186.

2. Edward S. Miller, *War Plan Orange,* p. 194.

3. Ibid., p. 188.

4. Henry I. Shaw, Jr., Bernard C. Nalty, and Edwin T. Turnbladh, *History of U.S. Marine Corps Operations in World War II,* vol. 3, *Central Pacific Drive,* p. 4. Hereafter Shaw et al., *History of USMC Operations.*

5. E. Miller, *War Plan Orange,* p. 191.

6. Morison, *History of U.S. Naval Operations,* vol. 6, p. 126.

7. Crowl and Love, *Gilberts and Marshalls,* p. 19.

8. Ibid., p. 168.

9. CinCPac to Cominch, 20 Aug. 1943, in Morton, *Strategy and Command,* p. 530.

10. Crowl and Love, *Gilberts and Marshalls,* p. 19.

11. Edwin P. Hoyt, *To the Marianas,* p. 22.

12. Crowl and Love, *Gilberts and Marshalls,* p. 210.

13. Japanese records cited in Crowl and Love, *Gilberts and Marshalls,* p. 210; plane count is on p. 211.

14. Southeast Area Opns Pf IV 8th Area Army, p. 25, in Crowl and Love, *Gilberts and Marshalls,* pp. 68–69.

15. Morton, *Strategy and Command,* p. 544.

16. Miller, *Cartwheel,* p. 233.

17. Hoyt, *To the Marianas,* p. 343.

18. Buell, *Master of Sea Power,* p. 337.

19. Buell, *Quiet Warrior,* p. 180.

20. Ibid., p. 182.

21. Ibid., pp. 184–85.

22. Reynolds, *Admiral John H. Towers,* p. 426.

23. Buell, *Quiet Warrior,* p. 181.

24. Ibid., p. 204.

25. Letter, Spruance to Hoover, 17 July 1959, in Morton, *Strategy and Command,* p. 523.

26. Cited in Crowl and Love, *Gilberts and Marshalls,* p. 70.

27. Julian C. Smith, "Tarawa," in *Proceedings, U.S. Naval Institute* (November 1953), p. 1167.

28. JPS 205/2, 18 June 1943, Operations against Marshall Islands, in Morton, *Strategy and Command,* p. 464.

29. Shaw et al., *History of USMC Operations,* p. 23.

30. Letter from Spruance to Isley, 3 July 1949, cited in Crowl and Love, *Gilberts and Marshalls,* pp. 168–69.

31. Crowl and Love, *Gilberts and Marshalls,* p. 60.

32. Samuel E. Morison, *History of U.S. Naval Operations in World War II,* vol. 7, *Aleutians, Gilberts and Marshalls, June 1942–April 1944,* p. 103.

33. Crowl and Love, *Gilberts and Marshalls,* p. 31.

34. Morison, *History of U.S. Naval Operations,* vol. 7, p. 138.

35. Winton, *Ultra,* p. 147.

36. Shaw et al., *History of USMC Operations,* p. 29.

37. Ibid., p. 37.

38. Winton, *Ultra,* p. 149.

39. Blair, *Silent Victory,* p. 508.

40. Morison, *History of U.S. Naval Operations,* vol. 7, p. 121.

41. Ibid., p.vii.

42. Ibid., p. 136.

43. Holland M. Smith, *Coral and Brass*, pp. 111–12.

44. Morison, *History of U.S. Naval Operations*, vol. 7, pp. 183–84, note.

45. Smith, *Coral and Brass*, p. 130.

46. Ibid., p. 134.

47. Captain P. V. Mercer, as recounted in Reynolds, *Admiral John H. Towers*, p. 407.

48. Buell, *Quiet Warrior*, p. 238.

49. Hoyt, *Nimitz and His Admirals*, p. 280.

50. Buell, *Quiet Warrior*, p. 238.

51. Ibid., p. 238.

52. Reynolds, *Admiral John H. Towers*, p. 427.

53. Buell, *Quiet Warrior*, p. 238.

54. Reynolds, *Admiral John H. Towers*, p. 431.

55. Hoyt, *Japan's War*, p. 342.

56. Cited in Crowl and Love, *Gilberts and Marshalls*, p. 68.

57. Miller, *Cartwheel*, p. 223.

58. R. R. Smith, *Approach to the Philippines*, p. 4.

59. After a General Headquarters G2 study & Southeast Area Naval Operations, OCMH, cited in Crowl and Love, *Gilberts and Marshalls*, p. 69.

60. GHQ, SWPAOI 32, 13 June 1943, in GHQ, SWPA, G-3, Jnl 14 June 1943, in Miller, *Cartwheel*, p. 226.

61. William F. Halsey, with J. Bryan III, *Admiral Halsey's Story*, p.173.

62. Ibid., p. 174.

63. Morison, *History of U.S. Naval Operations*, vol. 6, p. 289.

64. Morton, *Strategy and Command*, p. 575.

65. Winton, *Ultra*, p. 126.

66. Morison, *History of U.S. Naval Operations*, vol. 6, p. 320.

67. Ibid., p. 303.

68. Halsey, *Admiral Halsey's Story*, pp. 180–81.

69. Morison, *History of U.S. Naval Operations*, vol. 6, p. 324.

70. Halsey, *Admiral Halsey's Story*, pp. 180–181.

71. Ibid., p. 181.

72. Winton, *Ultra*, p. 127.

73. Morton, *Strategy and Command*, p. 577.

74. Japanese Monograph no. 50 OCMH 25–26, cited in Miller, *Cartwheel*, p. 255.

75. John Costello, *The Pacific War*, p. 445.

76. Spector, *Eagle against the Sun*, p. xiii.

77. Blair, *Silent Victory*, p. 558.

78. Buell, *Quiet Warrior*, p. 237.

79. Potter, *Nimitz*, pp. 264–65.

80. Statement of a Japanese staff officer, U.S. Strategic Bombing Survey, *European War, Pacific War*, p. 193.

81. Buell, *Quiet Warrior,* p. 233.

82. Japanese strengths from Shaw et al., *History of USMC Operations,* vol. 3, pp. 140–41.

83. Winton, *Ultra,* p. 196.

84. CINCPAC-CINCPOA Opns in POA Feb 44, in Dyer, *Amphibians Came to Conquer,* vol. 2, p. 685.

85. Crowl and Love, *Gilberts and Marshalls,* pp. 331–32.

86. VPhib Corps Flintlock Report, cited in Crowl and Love, *Gilberts and Marshalls,* p. 370.

87. Crowl and Love, *Gilberts and Marshalls,* p. 372.

88. Hoyt, *Japan's War,* p. 342.

89. Samuel E. Morison, *History of U.S. Naval Operations in World War II,* vol. 8, *New Guinea and the Marianas, 1944,* p. 341.

90. Morison, *History of U.S. Naval Operations,* vol. 7, p. 185.

91. Documents of 31 Army cited in Morison, *History of U.S. Naval Operations,* vol. 8, p. 12.

92. Morison, *History of U.S. Naval Operations,* vol. 7, p. 332.

93. Reynolds, *Admiral John H. Towers,* pp. 459–60.

94. Hoyt, *Carrier Wars,* p. 127.

95. Morison, *History of U.S. Naval Operations,* vol. 7, p. 315.

96. King, *Fleet Admiral King,* p. 536.

97. Morison, *History of U.S. Naval Operations,* vol. 6, p. 378.

98. Miller, *Cartwheel,* p. 273.

99. Halsey, *Admiral Halsey's Story,* p. 187.

100. Morison, *History of U.S. Naval Operations,* vol. 6, p. 433.

101. Ibid., p. 423.

8. Decisive Combat in the Marianas

1. Potter, *Nimitz,* p. 420.

2. Reynolds, *Admiral John H. Towers,* pp. 461–62.

3. Minutes, Pacific Conference, and memo, Ritchie for Handy, cited in *The U.S. Army in World War II,* War in the Pacific series, *The Campaign in the Marianas,* by Philip A. Crowl, p. 14. Hereafter Crowl, *Campaign in the Marianas.*

4. R. R. Smith, *Approach to the Philippines,* p. 7.

5. Buell, *Master of Sea Power,* p. 418.

6. Smith, *Coral and Brass,* pp. 156–57.

7. Radio COMINCH to CINCPOA, CM-IN, in Buell, *Master of Sea Power,* pp. 418–19.

8. Pogue, *George C. Marshall: Organizer of Victory,* pp. 439–41.

9. R. R. Smith, *Triumph,* p. 11.

10. Buell, *Master of Sea Power,* p. 422.

11. JCS 713, "Strategy in the Pacific," 16 Feb. 1944, in Crowl, *Campaign in the Marianas,* p. 18.

12. R. R. Smith, *Approach to the Philippines,* p. 10.

13. Reno plan draft, 6 March 1944, in Crowl, *Campaign in the Marianas,* p. 18.

14. JCS, 12 March 1944, in R. R. Smith, *Approach to the Philippines,* pp. 11–12.

15. Reynolds, *Admiral John H. Towers,* p. 422.

16. R. R. Smith, *Approach to the Philippines,* p. 90.

17. Ibid., p. 349.

18. Morison, *History of U.S. Naval Operations,* vol. 6, p. 214.

19. Dull, *Battle History of the Imperial Japanese Navy,* p. 314.

20. Toland, *Rising Sun,* vol. 2, pp. 597–98.

21. Hoyt, *To the Marianas,* p. 95.

22. Potter, *Admiral Arleigh Burke,* p. 141.

23. Combined Fleet Order 76, quoted in Morison, *History of U.S. Naval Operations,* vol. 8, p. 215.

24. Morison, *History of U.S. Naval Operations,* vol. 8, p. 217.

25. Taylor, *Magnificent Mitscher,* p. 193.

26. Potter, *Admiral Arleigh Burke,* p. 144.

27. Taylor, *Magnificent Mitscher,* pp. 188–89.

28. James, *Years of MacArthur,* vol. 2, p. 457.

29. Buell, *Quiet Warrior,* pp. 422–23.

30. Letter from Spruance, 16 June 1964, in Buell, *Quiet Warrior,* p. 280.

31. Ibid., p. 280.

32. Buell, *Master of Sea Power,* pp. 423–24.

33. Radiogram, Nimitz to King, 28 May 1944, cited in Buell, *Master of Sea Power,* p. 424.

34. Potter, *Admiral Arleigh Burke,* p. 414.

35. Morison, *History of U.S. Naval Operations,* vol. 8, p. 29.

36. Interview of Ozawa cited in ibid., p. 232.

37. CinCPac Intelligence Bulletin, 14 June 1944, in Winton, *Ultra,* p165.

38. Buell, *Quiet Warrior,* p. 284.

39. Cited in Morison, *History of U.S. Naval Operations,* vol. 8, p. 221.

40. Hoyt, *To the Marianas,* p. 134.

41. Buell, *Quiet Warrior,* pp. 282–83.

42. Potter, *Admiral Arleigh Burke,* p. 146; Buell, *Quiet Warrior,* p. 286.

43. Taylor, *Magnificent Mitscher,* p. 216.

44. Jocko Clark and C. G. Reynolds, *Carrier Admiral,* pp. 166–67.

45. Smith, *Coral and Brass,* pp. 165–67.

46. Buell, *Quiet Warrior,* p. 285.

47. CF Action Report, in Morison, *History of U.S. Naval Operations,* vol. 8, p. 291.

48. Taylor, *Magnificent Mitscher,* pp. 220–21.

49. CinCPac Monthly Analysis, June 1944, in ibid., p. 81.

50. Letter, Spruance to Morison, 20 Jan. 1952, in Morison, *History of U.S. Naval Operations,* vol. 8, p. 315.

51. Taylor, *Magnificent Mitscher*, p. 222.

52. Morison, *History of U.S. Naval Operations*, vol. 8, p. 249.

53. Ibid., p. 289.

54. Ibid., p. 235.

55. Dull, *Battle History of the Imperial Japanese Navy*, pp. 317–19.

56. Letter, Spruance to Morison, 20 Jan. 1952, in Morison, *History of U.S. Naval Operations*, vol. 8, p. 315.

57. R. K. Turner, Presentation at the General Line School, 5 Dec. 1949.

58. Cited in Shaw et al., *History of USMC Operations*, p. 442.

59. TF 56 Rpt Forager, Incld, G-2 Rpt, Annex F, p. 7, cited in Crowl, *Campaign in the Marianas*, p. 93.

60. Morison, *History of U.S. Naval Operations*, vol. 8, p. 169.

61. TF 56 Rpt Forager G-3 Rpt, p. 5, cited in Crowl, *Campaign in the Marianas*, p. 93.

62. NTLF Opn Order 19–44, 1 Jul 1944, cited in Crowl, *Campaign in the Marianas*, p. 220.

63. Smith, *Coral and Brass*, p. 205.

64. Ibid., pp. 203–204.

65. Crowl, *Campaign in the Marianas*, p. 269.

66. Smith, *Coral and Brass*, p. 201.

67. King, *Fleet Admiral King*, p. 560.

68. Smith, *Coral and Brass*, p. 181.

69. Toland, *Rising Sun*, vol. 2, p. 635.

70. R. R. Smith, *Triumph*, p. 91.

9. From Honolulu's Conference Table to Leyte's Mud

1. Morison, *History of U.S. Naval Operations*, vol. 8, p. 344.

2. Kenney, *General Kenney Reports*, p. 378.

3. King, *Fleet Admiral King*, p. 537.

4. R. R. Smith. *Approach to the Philippines*, p. 475.

5. Halsey, *Admiral Halsey's Story*, p. 195.

6. Pogue, *George C. Marshall: Organizer of Victory*, p. 440.

7. Message, MacArthur to Stimson, 21 Jan. 1944, delivered by Osborne.

8. Radio WAR 55718 (Top Secret); Marshall to MacArthur, 24 June 1944, in Bland and Stevens, *Papers of George Catlett Marshall*.

9. MacArthur to Marshall, Radio CX-13891, 20 June 1944, in R. R. Smith, *Approach to the Philippines*, p. 8.

10. R. R. Smith, *Approach to the Philippines*, p. 6.

11. Halsey, *Admiral Halsey's Story*, p. 195.

12. Bradley, *Second World War*, p. 161.

13. Morison, *History of U.S. Naval Operations*, vol. 8, p. 179.

14. R. R. Smith, *Approach to the Philippines*, p. 18.

15. Ibid., p. 23.

16. MacArthur, *Reminiscences,* p. 198.

17. Samuel E. Morison, *History of U.S. Naval Operations in World War II,* vol. 13, *The Liberation of the Philippines—Luzon, Mindanao, the Visayas, 1944–1945,* p. 5.

18. R. R. Smith, *Approach to the Philippines,* p. 11.

19. R. R. Smith, *Triumph,* p. 4. See also JCS713, 16 Feb. 1944, "Strategy in the Pacific"; JCS713/1, 10 March 1944, "Future Opns in the Pacific"; and OPD ABC 384 Pacific 1–17–43, in Wheeler, *Kinkaid of the Seventh Fleet,* p. 360.

20. Radio, JCS to CINCSWPA and CINCPOA CM-OUT 30007, 13 June 1944, in *The U.S. Army in World War II,* War in the Pacific series, *Leyte: The Return to the Philippines,* by M. Hamlin Cannon, p. 3. Hereafter Cannon, *Leyte.*

21. Radio CINCSWPA to CofS, 18 Jun 1944, CM-IN 150580, in Cannon, *Leyte,* p. 3.

22. Ibid.

23. Morison, *History of U.S. Naval Operations,* vol. 8, p. 11.

24. Halsey, *Admiral Halsey's Story,* pp. 194–97.

25. R. R. Smith, *Approach to the Philippines,* p. 13.

26. Costello, *Pacific War,* p. 490.

27. Tugwell, *Democratic Roosevelt,* pp. 654–55.

28. Whitney, *MacArthur,* pp. 27–28.

29. Rogers, *Bitter Years,* p. 22.

30. Cited in Whitney, *MacArthur,* pp. 27–28.

31. Comment by FDR to Morison, quoted in Samuel E. Morison, *History of U.S. Naval Operations in World War II,* vol. 12, *Leyte, June 1944–January 1945,* p. 9.

32. James, *Years of MacArthur,* vol. 2, pp. 533–34.

33. Buell, *Master of Sea Power,* p. 443.

34. Potter, *Nimitz,* p. 318.

35. James, *Years of MacArthur,* vol. 2, p. 534; Rogers, *Bitter Years,* p. 140.

36. Leahy, *I Was There,* p. 251.

37. Manchester, *American Caesar,* p. 369.

38. James, *Years of MacArthur,* vol. 2, p. 535.

39. U.S. Strategic Bombing Survey, *Employment of Forces under the Southwest Pacific Command,* p. 32.

40. Letter, Nimitz to Morison, 10 Feb. 1951, in Morison, *History of U.S. Naval Operations,* vol. 12, p. 10.

41. Morison, *History of U.S. Naval Operations,* vol. 12, p. 11.

42. U.S. Strategic Bombing Survey, *European War, Pacific War,* p. 281.

43. Toland, *Rising Sun,* vol. 2, p. 668.

44. Halsey, *Admiral Halsey's Story,* p. 199.

45. Radio, Com 3rd Flt to CINCPOA, CINCSWPA, and COMINCHINCH, CM-IN 12893, 13 Sept. 1944, in Cannon, *Leyte,* p. 9.

46. Edward J. Drea, *MacArthur's Ultra,* p. 158; italics added.

47. Kenney, *General Kenney Reports,* p. 395.

48. *Biennial Report of the Chief of Staff to the Secretary of War, July 1, 1942, to July 1, 1945* (Washington, D.C.: Government Printing Office, 1945).

49. Rogers, *Bitter Years,* pp. 159–62.

50. James, *Years of MacArthur,* vol. 2, p. 358.

51. Potter, *Admiral Arleigh Burke,* p. 189.

52. Com Third Fleet Operation Order 21-44, 3 Oct. 1944.

53. Ibid.

54. Extract of order from (CTF) Vice Admiral Kinkaid, "Report of Operations for Capture of Leyte," in Wheeler, *Kinkaid of the Seventh Fleet,* p. 386.

55. CTF77 Op. Plan 13-44, Appendix 2, Annex E, in Morison, *History of U.S. Naval Operations,* vol. 12, p. 193.

56. R. R. Smith, *Approach to the Philippines,* p. 7.

57. R. R. Smith, *Triumph,* p. 462.

58. Halsey, *Admiral Halsey's Story,* p. 195.

59. Spector, *Eagle against the Sun,* p. 420.

60. Ibid., p. 421.

61. James, *Years of MacArthur,* vol. 2, p. 488.

62. GHQ Operations Instructions Number 70, 21 Sept. 1944, Para 3.a.

63. Kenney, *General Kenney Reports,* p. 395.

64. Ibid., p. 400.

65. Cannon, *Leyte,* p. 11.

66. Ibid., p. 35.

67. Aug 1944 Memo Col Ely Exec Officer, Sixth Army Engineers, in Cannon, *Leyte,* p. 36.

68. NSA, Comint and the PRC Intervention in the Korean War, in Stanley Weintraub, *MacArthur's War* (New York: Free Press, 2000), p. 21.

69. Rogers, *Bitter Years,* p. 181.

70. Drea, *MacArthur's Ultra,* p. 162–63.

71. Griffith, *MacArthur's Airman,* p. 201.

72. Ibid., p. 202.

73. Kenney, *General Kenney Reports,* p. 452.

74. Cannon, *Leyte,* pp. 49, 93.

75. Ibid., p. 184.

76. Originally in *Reader's Digest,* February 1945, p. 8; recounted in Cannon, *Leyte,* p. 187.

77. Kenney, *General Kenney Reports,* pp. 466, 465.

78. Ibid., p. 469.

79. Griffith, *MacArthur's Airman,* p. 207.

10. The Naval Campaign for the Philippines

1. R. R. Smith, *Approach to the Philippines,* p. 455.

2. Spector, *Eagle against the Sun,* p. 424.

3. Morison, *History of U.S. Naval Operations,* vol. 12, p. 167.

4. Cannon, *Leyte,* p. 22.

5. Halsey, *Admiral Halsey's Story*, pp. 216–17.

6. Carl Solberg, *Decision and Dissent: With Halsey at Leyte Gulf,* p. 118.

7. Halsey, *Admiral Halsey's Story,* p. 216.

8. Potter, *Admiral Arleigh Burke,* p. 204.

9. Potter, *Bull Halsey,* p. 327.

10. Solberg, *Decision and Dissent,* p. 118.

11. Morison, *History of U.S. Naval Operations,* vol. 12, p. 194.

12. Potter, *Admiral Arleigh Burke,* p. 206.

13. Taylor, *Magnificent Mitscher,* pp. 261–62.

14. Solberg, *Decision and Dissent,* pp. 124–25.

15. Potter, *Nimitz,* p. 336.

16. Wheeler, *Kinkaid of the Seventh Fleet,* p. 397.

17. Morison, *History of U.S. Naval Operations,* vol. 12, p. 240.

18. Halsey, *Admiral Halsey's Story,* p. 219.

19. Toland, *Rising Sun,* vol. 2, p. 704.

20. Ugaki, *Fading Victory,* p. 496.

21. Dull, *Battle History of the Imperial Japanese Navy,* p. 339; Ugaki, *Fading Victory,* pp. 496–97.

22. Ugaki, *Fading Victory,* p. 497.

23. Told to Masanori, reported in Toland, p. 710.

24. Solberg, *Decision and Dissent,* p. 114.

25. Halsey, *Admiral Halsey's Story,* p. 218.

26. Potter, *Bull Halsey,* p. 339.

27. Solberg, *Decision and Dissent,* p. 118.

28. John T. Mason Jr., *The Pacific War Remembered* (Annapolis, Md.: Naval Institute Press, 1986), pp. 274–75.

29. Clark and Reynolds, *Carrier Admiral,* p. 201.

30. Buell, *Master of Sea Power,* p. 451.

31. King, *Fleet Admiral King,* p. 579.

32. Taylor, *Magnificent Mitscher,* p. 265.

33. CINCSWPA to CINCPOA, 1 Nov. 1944, in Wheeler, *Kinkaid of the Seventh Fleet,* p. 407.

34. Halsey, *Admiral Halsey's Story,* p. 230.

35. Griffith, *MacArthur's Airman,* p. 208.

36. CINCPAC to CINCSWPA 11/292349Z, in Wheeler, *Kinkaid of the Seventh Fleet,* p. 413.

37. Morison, *History of U.S. Naval Operations,* vol. 13, p. 158.

38. Barbara Tuchman, *Stilwell and the American Experience in China, 1911–1945* (New York: Macmillan, 1970), pp. 518–21.

39. Morton, *Philippines,* p. 214.

40. James, *Years of MacArthur,* vol. 2, p. 716.

11. Mahan and the Submariners

1. Mahan, *Influence of Sea Power,* p. 539.

2. David C. Evans, ed., *The Japanese Navy in World War II: In the Words of Former Japanese Naval Officers,* p. 220.

3. Boyd and Yoshida, *Japanese Submarine Force;* English translation in Appendix 1, p. 191.

4. Ibid., p. 191.

5. Goldstein and Dillon, *Pacific War Papers,* p. 12.

6. King, *Fleet Admiral King,* p. 603.

7. Chester Nimitz, "Future of Submarine Operations," *Proceedings,* U.S Naval Institute (December 1912): 1198.

8. Morison, *History of U.S. Naval Operations,* vol. 4, pp. 190–91.

9. Van der Vat, *Pacific Campaign,* pp. 159–60.

10. Blair, *Silent Victory,* p. 306.

11. Morison, *History of U.S. Naval Operations,* vol. 4, p. 205.

12. Blair, *Silent Victory,* p. 360. These tonnage figures and all subsequent ones not otherwise identified are from Blair.

13. Winton, *Ultra,* p. 139.

14. Blair, *Silent Victory,* p. 362.

15. Ibid., p. 277.

16. Dunnigan and Nofi, *Victory at Sea,* p. 62.

17. Morison, *History of U.S. Naval Operations,* vol. 4, p. 205.

18. Blair, *Silent Victory,* p. 423.

19. Morton, *Strategy and Command,* p. 546.

20. Boyne, *Clash of Titans,* p. 125.

21. Morton, *Strategy and Command,* p. 557.

22. Mahan, *Influence of Sea Power,* pp. 81–87.

23. Blair, *Silent Victory,* p. 767.

24. Ibid., p. 694.

25. Winton, *Ultra,* p. 193.

26. Ibid., p. 193.

27. Mochitsura Hashimoto, *Sunk: The Story of the Japanese Submarine Fleet, 1941–45,* trans. E. H. M. Colgrave (New York: Henry Holt, 1954), p. 245.

12. Dulling the Mighty Blade

1. Buell, *Master of Sea Power,* pp. 326–27.

2. Ugaki, *Fading Victory,* p. 528.

3. U.S. Strategic Bombing Survey, *Japanese Air Power,* p. 76.

4. Dunnigan and Nofi, *Victory at Sea,* p. 195.

5. Buell, *Quiet Warrior,* p. 332.

6. Buell, *Master of Sea Power,* p. 441.

7. Buell, *Quiet Warrior,* pp. 332–33; emphasis in the original.

8. Buell, *Master of Sea Power,* p. 443.

9. Buell, *Quiet Warrior,* p. 330.

10. Morison, *History of U.S. Naval Operations,* vol. 13, p. 5.

11. Potter, *Nimitz,* p. 358.

12. Craven and Cate, *Army Air Forces in World War II,* vol. 5, pp. 586–87.

13. "Engineers on Iwo," *Marine Corps Gazette* (October 1945), cited in Samuel E. Morison, *History of U.S. Naval Operations in World War II,* vol. 14, *Victory in the Pacific,* p. 73.

14. Morison, *History of U.S. Naval Operations,* vol. 14, p. 38.

15. Potter, *Nimitz,* p. 368.

16. Kenneth P. Werrell, *Blankets of Fire: U.S. Bombers over Japan in World War II,* p. 145.

17. *The U.S. Army in World War II,* War in the Pacific series, *Okinawa: The Last Battle,* by Roy E. Appleman, p. 9.

18. Ibid., p. 21.

19. Morison, *History of U.S. Naval Operations,* vol. 14, p. 91.

20. Comments made to Major General James G. Christiansen, related in James, *Years of MacArthur,* vol. 2, p. 733.

21. Winton, *Ultra,* p. 213.

22. Dunnigan and Nofi, *Victory at Sea,* p. 197.

23. Taylor, *Magnificent Mitscher,* pp. 295–96.

24. Buell, *Quiet Warrior,* p. 332.

25. Ferrell, *Eisenhower Diaries,* pp. 48–49.

13. B-San

1. Curtis E. LeMay and Bill Yenne, *Superfortress: The B-29 and American Airpower,* p. 14.

2. Ibid., p. 23.

3. Arnold, *Global Mission,* p. 347.

4. LeMay and Yenne, *Superfortress,* pp. 321–22.

5. Ibid., p. 66.

6. Werrell, *Blankets of Fire,* p. 132.

7. LeMay and Yenne, *Superfortress,* p. 347.

8. AAF Evaluation Board POA, 15 Jan. 1945; COMAF20 TO COMGENBOMBCOM 21, "Incendiary Attack," 12 Feb. 1945.

9. LeMay and Yenne, *Superfortress,* p. 352.

10. *History of 497 Bomb Group,* March 1945, p. 19.

11. LeMay and Yenne, *Superfortress,* p. 125.

12. Craven and Cate, *Army Air Forces in World War II,* vol. 5, pp. 643, 674–75; U.S. Strategic Bombing Survey, *European War, Pacific War,* pp. 17, 20.

13. LeMay and Yenne, *Superfortress,* pp. 141, 376.

14. Potter, *Nimitz,* p. 368.

15. Werrell, *Blankets of Fire,* p. 170.

16. U.S. Strategic Bombing Survey, *European War, Pacific War,* pp. 15, 20.

17. Boyne, *Clash of Titans,* p. 343.

18. Werrell, *Blankets of Fire,* pp. 227–28.

19. Robert J. C. Butow, *Japan's Decision to Surrender* (Stanford, Calif.: Stanford University Press, 1954), pp. 7–26.

20. Bix, *Hirohito,* p. 487.

21. U.S. Strategic Bombing Survey, *Interrogations of Japanese Officials,* n.p.

22. Bix, *Hirohito,* p. 491.

23. Ibid., p. 485.

24. Ibid., p. 489.

25. Ibid., p. 511.

26. Ibid., p. 523.

27. Cited in ibid., p. 484.

28. Robert A. Pape, *Bombing to Win,* p. 10.

29. Ibid., p. 119.

30. Leahy, *I Was There,* p. 72.

31. LeMay and Yenne, *Superfortress,* p. 346.

32. The preceding data are midrange estimates taken from Werrell, *Blankets of Fire,* pp. 217–18. Other estimates vary. No one knows for sure how many people died in these strikes.

33. James, *Years of MacArthur,* vol. 2, p. 642.

34. Forrest C. Pogue, *George C. Marshall: Statesman, 1945–1959* (New York: Viking, 1987), p. 19.

35. LeMay and Yenne, *Superfortress,* p. 154.

36. Ibid., p. 352.

BIBLIOGRAPHY

Agawa, Hiroyuke. *The Reluctant Admiral*. Tokyo: Kodansha, 1981.

Alden, John D. *U.S. Submarine Attacks during World War II*. Annapolis, Md.: Naval Institute Press, 1989.

Alexander, Joseph. *Storm Landings*. Annapolis, Md.: Naval Institute Press, 1997.

———. "What Was Nimitz Thinking?" in *Proceedings, U.S. Naval Institute* 124, no. 11 (November 1998): 42–46.

Arnold, H. H. "Hap." *Global Mission*. New York: Harper & Row, 1949.

Ballendorf, Dirk A., and Merrill L. Bartlett. *Pete Ellis*. Annapolis, Md.: Naval Institute Press, 1997.

Bischof, G., and R. Dupont. *The Pacific War Revisited*. Baton Rouge: Louisiana State University Press, 1997.

Bix, Herbert P. *Hirohito and the Making of Modern Japan*. New York: HarperCollins, 2000.

Blair, Clay, Jr. *Silent Victory: The U.S. Submarine War against Japan*. Annapolis, Md.: Naval Institute Press, 1975.

Bland, Larry I., and Sharon Ritenour Stevens, eds. *The Papers of George Catlett Marshall*, vols. 1–4. Baltimore: Johns Hopkins University Press, 1991.

Boyd, C., and A. Yoshida. *The Japanese Submarine Force and World War II*. Annapolis, Md.: Naval Institute Press, 1995

Boyne, Walter J. *Clash of Titans: World War II at Sea*. New York: Simon & Schuster, 1995.

Bradley, John H. *The Second World War: Asia and the Pacific*. West Point Military History Series, ed. Thomas E. Griess. Wayne, N.J.: Avery Publishing, 1984.

Buell, Thomas B. *Master of Sea Power: A Biography of Fleet Admiral Ernest J. King*. Boston: Little, Brown & Co., 1980.

————. *The Quiet Warrior: A Biography of Admiral Raymond A. Spruance.* 1974. Reprint, Annapolis, Md.: Naval Institute Press, 1987. Citations are from the 1987 edition.

Bywater, Hector C. *The Great Pacific War.* New York: Houghton Miffin, 1925. Reprinted with new foreword, New York: St. Martin's Press, 1991.

Chandler, A., and S. Ambrose, eds. *The Papers of Eisenhower,* vol. 1. Baltimore: Johns Hopkins University Press, 1970.

Clark, "Jocko," and C. G. Reynolds. *Carrier Admiral.* New York: McKay, 1967.

Cole, Bernard D. "Struggle for the Marianas." *Joint Forces Quarterly,* no. 7 (Spring 1995): 86–93.

Costello, John. *The Pacific War.* New York: Rawson, Wade, 1981.

Craven, W. F., and J. L. Cate. *The Army Air Forces in World War II.* 7 vols. Chicago: University of Chicago Press, 1947.

Davidson, Joel R. *The Unsinkable Fleet: Navy Expansion in World War II.* Annapolis, Md.: Naval Institute Press, 1996.

Denfield, D. Colt. *Hold the Marianas.* Shippensburg, Pa.: White Mane Publishing, 1997.

Drea, Edward J. *MacArthur's Ultra.* Lawrence: University of Kansas Press, 1992.

Dull, Paul S. *A Battle History of the Imperial Japanese Navy, 1941–45.* Annapolis, Md.: Naval Institute Press, 1978.

Dunnigan, James F., and A. A. Nofi. *Victory at Sea.* New York: Morrow, 1995.

Dyer, George C. *The Amphibians Came to Conquer: The Story of Admiral Richmond Kelly Turner.* 2 vols. Annapolis, Md.: U.S. Department of the Navy, 1969.

Eichelberger, Robert L. *Jungle Road to Tokyo.* New York: Viking, 1950.

Ellis, John. *World War II Statistical Survey.* New York: Facts on File, 1993.

Esposito, Brigadier General V. J. *The West Point Atlas of American Wars, Vol. 2.* New York: Praeger, 1959.

Evans, David C., ed. *The Japanese Navy in World War II: In the Words of Former Japanese Naval Officers.* Annapolis, Md.: Naval Institute Press, 1969.

Evans, David C., and Mark R. Peattie. *Kaigun: Strategy, Tactics and Technology in the Imperial Japanese Navy, 1887–1941.* Annapolis, Md.: Naval Institute Press, 1997.

Ferrell, Robert H., ed. *The Eisenhower Diaries.* New York: Norton, 1981.

Frank, Richard B. *Guadalcanal: The Definitive Account of the Landmark Battle.* New York: Random House, 1990.

Fuchida, Mitsuo, and Masatake Okumiya. *Midway: The Battle That Doomed Japan.* Annapolis, Md.: Naval Institute Press, 1955; New York: Ballantine, 1955. Citations are from the Ballantine edition.

Gailey, Harry A. *War in the Pacific: From Pearl Harbor to Tokyo Bay.* Novato, Calif.: Presidio Press, 1996.

Goldstein, Donald M., and Katherine V. Dillon, eds. *The Pearl Harbor Papers.* Washington, D.C.: Brassey's, 1993.

————, eds. *The Pacific War Papers.* Dulles, Va.: Potomac Books, 2004.

Greene, Jack. *The Midway Campaign, December 7, 1941–June 6, 1942.* Rev. ed. Conshohocken, Pa.: Combined Press, 1995.

Griffith, Thomas E. *MacArthur's Airman: General George C. Kenney and the War in the Southwest Pacific.* Lawrence: University of Kansas Press, 1998.

Harries, Meirion, and Susie Harries. *Soldiers of the Sun.* New York: Random House, 1991.

Halsey, William F., with J. Bryan III. *Admiral Halsey's Story.* New York: McGraw-Hill, 1947.

Hammel, Eric. *Guadalcanal: The Carrier Battles.* New York: Crown Publishers, 1987.

Handel, Michael J. *Masters of War.* 3rd ed. New York: Frank Cass Publishers, 2001.

Hess, William. *Pacific Sweep.* New York: Kensington Books, 1974.

Hoyt, Edwin P. *The Battle of Leyte Gulf.* New York: Weybright & Talley, 1972.

———. *Carrier Wars: Naval Aviation from World War II to the Persian Gulf.* New York: McGraw-Hill, 1989.

———. *Glory of the Solomons.* New York: Stein & Day, 1983.

———. *Japan's War: The Great Pacific Conflict.* New York: McGraw-Hill, 1986.

———. *Nimitz and His Admirals.* New York: Lyons Press, 2000.

———. *Storm over the Gilberts.* New York: Mason Charter, 1978.

———. *To the Marianas.* New York: Van Nostrand, 1980.

Ienaga, Saburo. *The Pacific War, 1931–45.* New York: Random House, 1978.

James, Clayton. *The Years of MacArthur.* 2 vols. New York: Houghton Mifflin, 1972 and 1975.

Jentschura, Hansgeorg, Dieter Jung, and Peter Mickel. Trans. J. D. Brown. *Warships of the Imperial Japanese Navy, 1869–45.* Annapolis, Md.: Naval Institute Press, 1992.

Kenney, George C. *General Kenney Reports.* New York: Duell, Sloan & Pearce, 1949; reprint, Washington, D.C.: Government Printing Office, 1997. Citations are from the reprint edition.

King, Ernest J., with W. M. Whitehill. *Fleet Admiral King.* New York: Norton, 1952.

Larrabee, Eric. *Commander in Chief.* New York: Harper & Row, 1987.

Leahy, William D. *I Was There.* New York: Whittlesey (McGraw-Hill), 1950.

LeMay, Curtis E., with M. Kantor. *Mission with LeMay.* Garden City, N.Y.: Doubleday, 1965.

LeMay, Curtis E., and Bill Yenne. *Superfortress: The B-29 and American Airpower.* New York: McGraw-Hill, 1988.

Lindley, John M. *Carrier Victory.* Paris and New York: Talisman, 1978.

Lockwood, Charles A. *Sink 'em All.* New York: Bantam, 1951.

Long, Gavin. *MacArthur: His Life and Battles.* London: B. T. Batsford, 1969.

Lorelli, John A. *To Foreign Shores.* Annapolis. Md.: Naval Institute Press, 1995.

MacArthur, Douglas. *Reminiscences.* New York: McGraw-Hill, 1964.

Mahan, Alfred T. *The Influence of Sea Power on History, 1660–1783.* Boston: Little, Brown, 1890.

Manchester, William. *American Caesar: Douglas MacArthur, 1880–1964.* Boston: Little, Brown, 1978; reprint, New York: Dell, 1983. Citations are from Dell paperback edition.

McAulay, Lex. *Battle of the Bismarck Sea.* New York: St. Martin's Press, 1991.

Miller, Edward S. *War Plan Orange.* Annapolis, Md.: Naval Institute Press, 1991.

Monsarrat, John. *Angel on the Yardarm: The Beginnings of Fleet Radar Defense and the Kamikaze Threat.* Newport, R.I.: Naval War College Press, 1985.

Morison, Samuel E. *History of U.S. Naval Operations in World War II.* Vol. 3, *The Rising Sun in the Pacific, 1931–April 1942.* Boston: Little, Brown, 1948.

———. *History of U.S. Naval Operations in World War II.* Vol. 4, *Coral Sea, Midway and Submarine Actions, May–August 1942.* Boston: Little, Brown, 1949.

———. *History of U.S. Naval Operations in World War II.* Vol. 5, *The Struggle for Guadalcanal, August 1942–February 1943.* Boston: Little, Brown, 1949.

———. *History of U.S. Naval Operations in World War II.* Vol. 6, *Breaking the Bismarcks Barrier, 22 July 1942–1 May 1944.* Boston: Little, Brown, 1950.

———. *History of U.S. Naval Operations in World War II.* Vol. 7, *Aleutians, Gilberts and Marshalls, June 1942–April 1944.* Boston: Little, Brown, 1950.

———. *History of U.S. Naval Operations in World War II.* Vol. 8, *New Guinea and the Marianas, 1944.* Boston: Little, Brown, 1953.

———. *History of U.S. Naval Operations in World War II.* Vol. 12, *Leyte, June 1944–January 1945.* Boston: Little, Brown, 1953.

———. *History of U.S. Naval Operations in World War II.* Vol. 13, *The Liberation of the Philippines—Luzon, Mindanao, the Visayas, 1944–1945* (1959). Boston: Little, Brown, 1959.

———. *History of U.S. Naval Operations in World War II.* Vol. 14, *Victory in the Pacific.* Boston: Little, Brown, 1960.

Mullins, Wayman C., ed. *1942: Issue in Doubt.* Austin, Texas: Eakin Press, 1994.

Nalty, Bernard C., ed. *The Pacific War.* London: Salamander, 1999.

Null, Gary. *Weapon of Denial: Air Power and the Battle for New Guinea.* Washington, D.C.: Government Printing Office, 1995.

Oi, Atsushi. "Why Japan's Anti-submarine Warfare Failed." in *Proceedings, U.S. Naval Institute* 78 (June 1952).

Overy, Richard. *Why the Allies Won.* New York: Norton, 1995.

Pape, Robert A. *Bombing to Win.* Ithaca, N.Y.: Cornell University Press, 1996.

Pawlowski, Gareth L. *Flattops and Fledglings.* New York: Castle Books, 1971.

Pogue, Forrest C. *George C. Marshall: Ordeal and Hope, 1939–1942.* New York: Viking, 1965.

———. *George C. Marshall: Organizer of Victory, 1943–1945.* New York: Viking, 1973.

Potter, E. B. *Admiral Arleigh Burke.* New York: Random House, 1990.

———. *Bull Halsey.* Annapolis, Md.: Naval Institute Press, 1985.

———. *Nimitz.* Annapolis, Md.: Naval Institute Press, 1976.

Potter, John D. *Yamamoto.* New York: Viking, 1965.

Prados, John. *Combined Fleet Decoded.* New York: Random House, 1995.

Prange, Gordon W. *At Dawn We Slept.* New York: McGraw-Hill, 1981.

———. *Miracle at Midway.* New York: McGraw-Hill, 1982.

Reynolds, Clark G. *Admiral John H. Towers.* Annapolis, Md.: Naval Institute Press, 1991.

Rogers, Paul. *The Bitter Years: MacArthur and Sutherland.* New York: Praeger, 1991.

Schom, Alan. *The Eagle and the Rising Sun.* New York: Norton, 2004.

Shaw, Henry I., Jr., Bernard C. Nalty, and Edwin T. Turnbladh. *History of U.S. Marine Corps Operations in World War II.* Vol. 3, *Central Pacific Drive.* U.S. Marine Corps, Headquarters, Historical Branch, 1966.

Sherwood, Robert E. *Roosevelt and Hopkins.* New York: Harper & Brothers, 1948.

Smith, Holland M. *Coral and Brass.* New York: Charles Scribner's, 1948.

Smith, S. E., ed. *The United States Navy in World War II.* New York: William Morrow, 1966.

Smith, Stan. *The Navy at Guadalcanal.* New York: Lancer Books, 1963.

Smurthwaite, David. *Pacific War Atlas, 1941–45.* London: HMSO, 1995.

Solberg, Carl. *Decision and Dissent: With Halsey at Leyte Gulf.* Annapolis, Md.: Naval Institute Press, 1995.

Spector, Ronald H. *Eagle against the Sun.* New York: Vintage Books, 1985.

Stafford, Edward P. *The Big E.* New York: Dell, 1962.

Stephan, John J. *Hawaii under the Rising Sun.* Honolulu: University of Hawaii Press, 1984.

Stoler, Mark. *Allies and Adversaries.* Chapel Hill: University of North Carolina Press, 2000.

Sumida, Jon T. *Inventing Grand Strategy and Teaching Command.* Baltimore: Johns Hopkins University Press, 1997.

Symonds, Craig L. *Historical Atlas of the U.S. Navy.* Annapolis, Md.: Naval Institute Press, 1995.

Taylor, Theodore. *The Magnificent Mitscher.* Annapolis, Md.: Naval Institute Press, 1954.

Toland, John. *The Rising Sun.* 2 vols. New York: Random House, 1970.

Tugwell, Rexford C. *The Democratic Roosevelt.* Garden City, N.Y.: Doubleday, 1957; reprint, New York: Penguin, 1969. Citations are from the 1969 paperback edition.

Ugaki, Matome. *Fading Victory: The Diary of Admiral Matome Ugaki, 1941–1945.* Trans. Masataka Chihaya. Ed. Donald M. Goldstein and Katherine V. Dillon. Pittsburgh: University of Pittsburgh Press, 1991.

The U.S. Army in World War II. War Department series. *Strategic Planning for Coalition Warfare, 1943–1944,* by Maurice Matloff. Washington, D.C.: Office of the Chief of Military History, Department of the Army, 1959.

The U.S. Army in World War II. War in the Pacific series. *Okinawa: The Last Battle,* by Roy E. Appleman. Washington, D.C.: Office of the Chief of Military History, Department of the Army, 1947.

———. *Leyte: The Return to the Philippines,* by M. Hamlin Cannon. Washington, D.C.: Office of the Chief of Military History, Department of the Army, 1954.

———. *The Campaign in the Marianas,* by Philip A. Crowl. Washington, D.C.: Office of the Chief of Military History, Department of the Army, 1960.

———. *Seizure of the Gilberts and Marshalls,* by P. A. Crowl and E. G. Love. Washington, D.C.: Office of the Chief of Military History, Department of the Army, 1955.

———. *Cartwheel: The Reduction of Rabaul,* by John Miller Jr. Washington, D.C.: Office of the Chief of Military History, Department of the Army, 1959.

———. *Guadalcanal: The First Offensive,* by John Miller Jr. Washington, D.C.: Office of the Chief of Military History, Department of the Army, 1949.

———. *Victory in Papua,* by Samuel Milner. Washington, D.C.: Office of the Chief of Military History, Department of the Army, 1955.

———. *Fall of the Philippines,* by Louis Morton. Washington, D.C.: Office of the Chief of Military History, Department of the Army, 1953.

———. *Strategy and Command: The First Two Years,* by Louis Morton. Washington, D.C.: Office of the Chief of Military History, Department of the Army, 1962.

———. *The Approach to the Philippines,* by R. R. Smith. Washington, D.C.: Office of the Chief of Military History, Department of the Army, 1952.

———. *Triumph in the Philippines,* by Robert Ross Smith. Washington, D.C.: Office of the Chief of Military History, Department of the Army, 1963.

U.S. Congress. *Investigation of the Pearl Harbor Attack: Report of the Joint Committee on the Investigation of the Pearl Harbor Attack.* 79th Congress. Washington, D.C.: Government Printing Office, 1946.

U.S. Strategic Bombing Survey. *Campaigns of the Pacific War.* Washington, D.C.: Government Printing Office, 1946.

———. *Employment of Forces under Southwest Pacific Command.* Washington, D.C.: Government Printing Office, 1947.

———. *European War, Pacific War.* Maxwell AFB, Ala.: Air University Press, 1987. Reprint of 1946 original.

———. *Interrogations of Japanese Officials.* Washington, D.C.: Government Printing Office, 1947.

———. *Japanese Air Power.* Washington, D.C.: Government Printing Office, 1946.

———. *Pacific (Summary).* Washington, D.C.: Government Printing Office, 1946.

U.S. War Department. *Command and Employment of Air Power,* Field Manual 100-20, 21 July 1943. Washington, D.C.: Government Printing Office, 1944.

———. *Handbook on Japanese Military Forces.* Technical Manual TME 30-480. 1944.

———. *Biennial Report of the Chief of Staff to the Secretary of War 1941, 1943, 1945.* OCMI reprints.

Van der Vat, Dan. *The Pacific Campaign.* New York: Simon & Schuster, 1991.

Werrell, Kenneth P. *Blankets of Fire: U.S. Bombers over Japan in World War II.* Washington, D.C.: Smithsonian, 1996.

Wheeler, Gerald E. *Kinkaid of the Seventh Fleet.* Annapolis, Md.: Naval Institute Press, 1996.

Whitney, Courtney. *MacArthur: His Rendezvous with History.* New York: Alfred A. Knopf, 1955.

Winton, John. *Ultra in the Pacific.* London: Leo Cooper, 1993.

Wohlstetter, Roberta. *Pearl Harbor: Warning and Decision.* Stanford, Calif.: Stanford University Press, 1962.

Y'Blood, William T. *The Little Giants: U.S. Escort Carriers against Japan.* Annapolis, Md.: Naval Institute Press, 1999.

INDEX

Note: Page numbers in *italics* indicate information contained in maps or tables. Country affiliations of military units or operations are indicated by (J) and (U.S.).

JOHN A. ADAMS
is an airline executive and longtime business strategist with an interest in the use of economic principles to analyze history. He has held corporate staff positions at major airlines, written plans for successful startup airlines, and pulled a regional carrier out of bankruptcy. During that time he has extensively researched military strategy and tactics.